CZECH &

SLOVAK

REPUBLICS GUIDE

BE A TRAVELER - NOT A TOURIST!

CRITICAL ACCLAIM FOR
OPEN ROAD TRAVEL GUIDES!

Whether you're going abroad or planning a trip in the United States, take Open Road along on your journey. Our books have been praised by **Travel & Leisure**, **The Los Angeles Times**, **Newsday**, **Booklist**, **US News & World Report**, **Endless Vacation**, **American Bookseller**, **Coast to Coast**, *and many other magazines and newspapers!*

Don't just see the world – experience it with Open Road!

ABOUT THE AUTHOR

Ted Brewer is a professional travel writer who has written and contributed to guides on Utah and the US. Having lived in Prague off and on for a number of years, including during the writing of this book, Ted now makes his home in Salt Lake City, Utah.

BE A TRAVELER, NOT A TOURIST - WITH OPEN ROAD TRAVEL GUIDES!

Open Road Publishing has guide books to exciting, fun destinations on four continents. As veteran travelers, our goal is to bring you the best travel guides available anywhere!

No small task, but here's what we offer:

• *All Open Road travel guides are written by authors with a distinct, opinionated point of view – not some sterile committee or team of writers. Our authors are experts in the areas covered and are polished writers.*

• *Our guides are geared to people who want to make their own travel choices. We'll show you how to discover the real destination – not just see some place from a tour bus window.*

• *We're strong on the basics, but we also provide terrific choices for those looking to get off the beaten path and experience the country or city – not just see it or pass through it.*

• *We give you the best, but we also tell you about the worst and what to avoid. Nobody should waste their time and money on their hard-earned vacation because of bad or inadequate travel advice.*

• *Our guides assume nothing. We tell you everything you need to know to have the trip of a lifetime – presented in a fun, literate, no-nonsense style.*

• *And, above all, we welcome your input, ideas, and suggestions to help us put out the best travel guides possible.*

CZECH &

SLOVAK

REPUBLICS GUIDE

BE A TRAVELER - NOT A TOURIST!

Ted Brewer

OPEN ROAD PUBLISHING

To my brother, Emery, for being there.

2nd Edition

Cover photos by Kim Grant. Maps by Rob Perry.
    The author has made every effort to be as accurate as possible, but neither the author northe publisher assume responsibility for the services provided by any business listed in this guide; for any errors or omissions; or any loss, damage, or disruptions in your travels for any reason.

TABLE OF CONTENTS

1. INTRODUCTION   13

2. OVERVIEW   14

3. SUGGESTED ITINERARIES   23

4. LAND & PEOPLE   29

5. A SHORT HISTORY   41
Czech History   41
Slovak History   57

6. PLANNING YOUR TRIP   63
When to Go   63
What to Pack   64
Making Reservations   64
Study Tours/Language Learning Programs   65
Passports & Visas   65
Customs   66
Getting To The Czech & Slovak republics   67
From Prague Airport to the City   67
Getting Around The Czech & Slovak republics   68
   By Air   68
   By Bicycle   68
   By Bus   69
   By Car   70
   By Train   71
For More Information   72

CONTENTS

7. BASIC INFORMATION   73

8. SPORTS & RECREATION   84

9. TAKING THE KIDS   90

10. ECO-TOURISM & TRAVEL ALTERNATIVES   92

11. FOOD & BEER   94
Food   94
Eating Out   96
Food Glossary   100
Beer   103
Wine & Spirits   107

12. BEST PLACES TO STAY   109
Prague   109
South Bohemia   110
West Bohemia   111
West Slovakia   112
East Slovakia   113

13. PRAGUE   114
Orientation   115
Getting Around Town   117
Where to Stay   122
Where to Eat   137
Seeing the Sights   147
   Inside the Historic Center   149
   Outside the Historic Center   214
Nightlife & Entertainment   224
Sports & Recreation   236
Shopping   239
Day Trips & Excursions Around Central Bohemia   241
   Sázava Monastery   242
   Česky Šternberk   243
   Konopiště   243
   Karlštejn   244
   Křivoklát   246
   Kutná Hora   246
Practical Information   252

CONTENTS

14. SOUTH BOHEMIA   255
Tábor   256
České Budějovice   261
   Excursion: Hluboká Castle   268
Třeboň   269
Český Krumlov   273
   Excursion: Zlatá Koruna   279
   Excursion: Rožmberk nad Vltavou   280
   Excursion: Vyšší Brod   280

15. WEST BOHEMIA   282
Plzeň   283
Mariánské Lázně   293
Karlovy Vary   302
   Excursion: Loket nad Ohří   311
Cheb   312
Františkový Lázně   316

16. NORTH BOHEMIA   318
Terezín   319
Litoměřice   323
Děčín   329
České Švýcarsko   333
Liberec   337
   Excursion: Ještěd   343

17. EAST BOHEMIA   344
Hradec Králové   345
Pardubice   352
Český ráj (Czech Paradise)   356
   Jičín   360
   Prachovské skály   360
   Trosky Castle   361
   Hrubá Skála   361
   Valdštejn Castle   361
   Turnov   362
Krkonoše Mountains   363
   Vrchlabí   367
   Špindlerův Mlyn   367
   Pec pod Sněžkou   368

CONTENTS

18. SOUTH MORAVIA   369

South Moravian Wines   370
Brno   371
   Excursion: Slavkov U Brna   384
   Excursion: Moravian Karst   385
   Excursion: Pernštejn   386
   Excursion: Moravský Krumlov   386
Jihlava   387
   Excursion: Žďar nad Sázavou   390
Telč   391
   Excursion: Slavonice   395
Jaroměřice nad Rokytnou   395
Znojmo   396
   Excursion: Vranov nad Dyjí   400
Mikulov   401
Valtice & Lednice   406
Zlín   412
Kroměříž   418

19. NORTH MORAVIA   423

Olomouc   424
   Excursion: Šternberk   430
   Excursion: Bouzov Castle   431
Rožnov pod Radhoštěm   432

20. WEST SLOVAKIA   437

Bratislava   438
   Orientation   440
   Arrivals & Departures   440
   Getting Around Town   442
   Where to Stay   442
   Where to Eat   445
   Seeing the Sights   447
   Nightlife & Entertainment   455
   Sports & Recreation   456
   Shopping   457
   Day Trips & Excursions   457
      Devín   457
      Rusovce   458
      Modra & Červený Kameň   458
      Trnava   459
   Practical Information   459

CONTENTS

Nitra   460
Piešťany   463
Čachtice Castle   466
Trenčín   467

21. CENTRAL SLOVAKIA   473

Banská Bystrica   473
  Excursion: Zvolen   479
Banská Štiavnica   480
Žilina   485
  Excursion: Čičmany   489
Vrátna dolina in the Malá Fatra Mountains   490
Liptovsky Mikuláš   493
Demänovská dolina in the Low Tatras   497
Poprad   501
The High Tatras   504
  Excursion: Ždiar   516

22. CENTRAL SLOVAKIA   518

Kežmarok   519
Levoča   522
  Excursion: Spiš Castle   527
  Excursion: Spišská Kapitula   528
Košice   529
Prešov   537
Bardejov   542
Medzilaborce   546

INDEX   548

MAPS

Czech & Slovak republics   15
Central Europe   28
Prague Hotels & Restaurants   127
Prague Sights   148
České Budějovice   266
Plzeň   291
Litoměřice   327
Hradec Králové   349
Brno   377
Bratislava   449
Košice   535

CONTENTS

SIDEBARS

Famous Czechs 33
Some Useful Words & Phrases
  in Czech/Slovak 35
Celebrities of Slovak Descent
  38
National Holidays 74
"Don't Get Ripped Off" Price List
  75
Exchange Rate 77
Phone Woes 81
Essential Telephone Numbers
  83
Camping & Hiking Laws 93
Where Food is Served 98
Pub Protocol 105
Prague Walking Tours 117
Prague's Best Hotels 123
Prague's Best Bets for Budget
  Lodging 137
Prague's Classiest Restaurants
  138
Good Cheap Eats in Prague 142
Prague's Illustrious Cafes 145
What is Sgraffito? 159
Classical Concerts 166
Legend of the Astronomical
  Clock 177
Jan Palach Square 185
The Myth of Šárka & Ctirad 212
Irish Pubs in Prague 225
Getting Tickets & Information
  228
Prague Spring Festival 229
Prague Nightlife 233
Beer in South Bohemia 255
South Bohemia Finds &
  Favorites 256
West Bohemia Finds &
  Favorites 283

The Incredible History of the
  Hotel Continental 286
North Bohemia Finds &
  Favorites 319
East Bohemia Finds &
  Favorites 345
South Moravia Finds &
  Favorites 370
Types of South Moravian
  Wines 370
For Brno's Noon Bells,
  Timing is Everything! 379
The Liechtenstein Family
  Holdings 407
Bat'a - Shoemaker & Film
  Producer 417
North Moravia Finds &
  Favorites 423
The Wallachians 432
Exchange Rate in the
  Slovak Republic 437
West Slovakia Finds &
  Favorites 438
Bratislava Cafes 446
Central Slovakia Finds &
  Favorites 474
Andrej Hlinka's
  Controversial Legacy 488
The Slovak Robin Hood 493
Take Precautions When Hiking
  The High Tatras 512
East Slovakia Finds &
  Favorites 519
The Marian Pilgrimage 527
Slovak Ruthenia &
  The Ruthenians 538
Wooden Churches
  Around Bardejov 545

ACKNOWLEDGMENTS

I extend my love and appreciation to Šárka Červená, who greatly enriched my stay in the Czech Republic. Thanks goes out to my sister-in-law Radka, who deserves my utmost gratitude for helping me out during some dire times; to Jirka Velebil, a good friend and inspiring conversationalist in the pub; to Jo, Lieve, Johan, and Barbara, for putting me up and putting up with me in Belgium; and to the rest of my friends in Prague, among them Honza, Daša, Jana, Michal, Tomáš, Petra, Libor, and the Červen family. And, as usual, special thanks to my parents, for their inexhaustible love and support.

1. INTRODUCTION

After more than 40 years of slumbering behind the Iron Curtain, the Czech and Slovak republics have recaptured their rightful places as the gems in the tiara of Central Europe's new democracies. And people are definitely taking notice, especially of the Czech Republic, which is now one of the most popular tourist destinations in the world. Surprising? Not really, when you consider that the Czech Republic has the densest concentration of castles on the European continent, not to mention a capital city boasting a thousand years worth of architecture.

But both the Czech and the Slovak republics offer more than just historic sights and monuments. They both offer landscapes that are too idyllic to be believed. From the undulating hills of the Czech Paradise in northeastern Bohemia to the sublime peaks of the High Tatras in Central Slovakia, the landscape of the two countries conjure a desperately romantic image that most North Americans picture when they dream about going to Europe for the first time.

Most of all, the Czech and Slovak republics cater to those who have crossed the Atlantic with the intention of experiencing Europe at its most authentic. Both republics escaped World War II largely unscathed, which means you have the opportunity to see cities, towns, and villages that have changed hardly a lick in the last hundred years.

Part and parcel of that experience is seeing and tasting for yourself the customs and traditions that have been around for centuries in both republics. Of course, one such tradition you won't be able to get enough of in the two republics is that of drinking some of the best, if not the best, beer in the world. Indeed, there are few sounds as mirthful as the sound of two beer mugs clinking in a toast to good health and happy travels.

Whether you're planning a leisurely trip taking in Prague's many delights, castle-hopping through Moravia or Bohemia, or an adventure-packed romp of hiking, biking, or skiing in Slovakia's gorgeous Tatra Mountatins, this book will show you the way with lots of detail and honest reviews. Have a great trip!

2. OVERVIEW

PRAGUE & BOHEMIA

By now it's no secret: **Prague** is a stunningly beautiful city. For many people, it's the most beautiful city in the world. However you rank it, the capital of the Czech Republic certainly lives up to the storybook fantasy of old Europe, where castles loom above the spire-studded skyline, where cafés and pubs spill out onto the cobblestone lanes that lead to and from glittering squares, and where art is a matter of course in the architecture of the houses, palaces, and churches.

On top of being one of the best possible European destinations you could choose, Prague has an ideal location in the heart of Bohemia, putting it within a few hours' reach of many rewarding destinations. On a day trip from Prague, you could take in two soaring, Gothic castles – the much-hyped **Karlštejn** and the lesser-known but equally majestic **Křivoklát**. Also within easy reach is the town of **Kutná Hora**, the former European center of silver mining featuring the Gothic masterpiece, **St. Barbara's Cathedral**.

Of course, there is more to the Czech Republic than just Prague and its surroundings, something too few visitors here realize. Case in point is the bucolic region of **South Bohemia**, filled with rolling hills and quaint villages, dotted with hundreds of lakes, and adorned with a fair share of the country's castles – among them the archetypically romantic **Hluboká**. Here in South Bohemia you can soak in the sights around the gorgeous main square of **České Budějovice**, get lost in the intriguing lanes and underground cellars of **Tábor**, go on a tour of the 600 year-old Regent brewery in **Třeboň**, or spend some of the finest hours of your Czech travels touring the must-see medieval town of **Český Krumlov** and its breathtaking castle.

In **West Bohemia**, things become a little more sedate, but no less beautiful. Here is where you'll find a cluster of the Czech Republic's notorious spa towns, the queen of which is **Karlovy Vary**. Known as Karlsbad to the German world, Karlovy Vary offers an outrageous

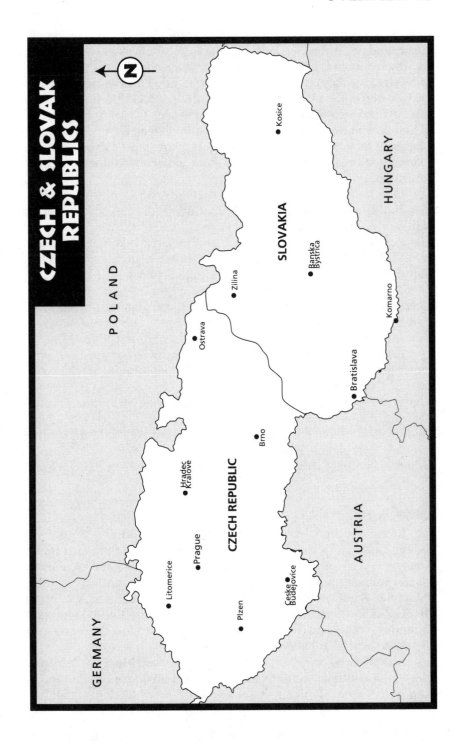

collection of turn-of-the-century architecture along its genteel promenade and up its wooded hillsides. Not so big, but just as ornate, is the
nearby spa town of **Mariánské Lázně** (or Marienbad), cradled in a lush,
pine-strewn valley and sporting a riot of fin-de-siecle mansions. A little
farther north, the intriguing medieval town of **Cheb** features a main
square festooned with colorful, winsome houses. Closer to Prague, the
regional capital and European beer mecca of **Plzeň** offers beer enthusiasts the chance to pursue their delights touring the Pilsner Urquell
brewery and visiting an excellent museum dedicated to the making (and
consumption) of beer.

In spite of its harsh industrialism, **North Bohemia** still offers a
handful of worthwhile destinations, including the graceful hamlet of
Litoměřice and the walled, former Jewish ghetto of **Terezín**, where you
can learn about the unremitting horror Jews faced in this town during
World War II. Further north, along the German border, you'll find the
lofty hills and so-called "rock cities" of **České Švýcarsko** (Czech Switzerland), where you can take off on some beautiful hikes or raft the
precipitous Kamenice River gorge. If you're need of some urbanity, you
can move from there to the surprisingly handsome city of **Liberec**,
featuring the most impressive town square in northern Bohemia.

In **East Bohemia**, there aren't as many worthwhile destinations as in
other parts of the country, but the region is the location for the aptly
named **Český ráj** (Czech Paradise), a wondrous area filled with cone-
shaped hills, majestic castles, and clusters of soaring rock pinnacles. Not
far from there are the **Krkonoše**, the Czech Republic's biggest mountains
and its most popular area for skiing and hiking. To the south are the
region's two biggest cities, **Hradec Králové** and **Pardubice**, both of
which offer attractive historic centers that you can see on a day trip from
Prague.

MORAVIA

Moravia's capital and its most vibrant city is **Brno**, with its own
hilltop castle and a web of intriguing medieval lanes. Here, you could
easily spend two or three days seeing the sights and making excursions
to any number of great places, among them the sinuous caves of the
Moravian Karst; the majestic castle of **Pernštejn** (one of the most impressive Gothic fortresses in the Czech Republic); and the village of **Moravský
Krumlov**, where you can tour a museum dedicated to the famous Art-
Nouveau artist Alfons Mucha.

Around Brno, which lies at the center of **South Moravia**, there are
dozens of additional great destinations all within two or three hours by
car, train, or bus. Perhaps the most-rewarding of these destinations,

located to the west, is the perfectly preserved Renaissance town of **Telč**, featuring a grand chateau and one of the republic's most stirring town squares. The perfect compliment to Telč is another well-preserved Renaissance town called **Slavonice**, located on the Austrian border a scenic hour away by train. A little further to the east is the elegant, cliff-top castle of **Vranov** and the city of **Znojmo**, where you can set your sights on an soaring Gothic tower, examine an extraordinary Romanesque rotunda, or go on a tour of the city's network of underground passages and cellars.

A little way to the east of Znojmo is South Moravia's bountiful and beautiful wine-producing region of **Pálava**, centered around the town of **Mikulov**. A former center of Jewish education in Central Europe, Mikulov hosts a web of alluring lanes huddled around a soaring castle. Enticingly close to Mikulov are the twin chateaux of **Valtice** and **Lednice**, set apart by some stunning landscaped grounds adorned with neo-Classical temples, monuments, and statues.

A big change of pace to South Moravia's provincial appeal is the eastern city of **Zlín**, almost entirely built between the wars to the avantgarde taste of the shoe manufacturer and philanthropic millionaire, **Tomáš Baťa**. Back in line with the Czech Republic's medieval character is the nearby town of **Kroměříž**, featuring one of the country's most grandiose chateaux.

A severely industrial and polluted region, **North Moravia** is probably the Czech Republic's least popular region for tourism. But there is one destination here that should take priority on your Moravian itinerary, and that's **Olomouc**, a bustling university town with a number of gorgeous churches, a magnificent Trinity Column, and a ring of quaint parks. From Olomouc, it's not far to a couple of good castles, including the mighty **Bouzov Castle**. Also, you can't forget the town of **Rožnov pod Radhoštěm**, boasting three excellent open-air museums of folk architecture.

THE SLOVAK REPUBLIC

For most of this century, Slovakia played second fiddle to the Czech Republic, which is perhaps why it gets overlooked by most people planning a trip to the former Czechoslovakia. But little do those tens of thousands of people dashing to Prague know that a much more sedate vacation, fraught with a number of very rewarding destinations, awaits down south in Slovakia.

There is a different sort of appeal to Slovakia; its landscape is as gorgeous and mountainous as any on the European continent (with the possible exception of Switzerland). And, though I hate to compare,

Slovakia has it hands down over the Czechs when it comes to cuisine (most of my Czech friends actually agree with this!)

Food is one good reason (among many) to visit **Bratislava,** the capital of the republic, in **West Slovakia**, offering several great museums and a handsome historic center that reflects the city's brief period as capital of the Hungarian Kingdom. On the outskirts of Bratislava you can see the cliff-top castle ruins of **Devín**. North of Bratislava lies the pleasing, wine-producing village of **Modra** and the hulking **Červeny Kameň** castle, housing a good museum of period furniture. Somewhat off the beaten path is the city of **Nitra**, featuring a hybrid cathedral atop an abandoned-looking castle. Further to the north is **Piešťany**, Slovakia's biggest spa town sedately set along the banks of the **Váh River**. From there, it's not far to the bone-chilling castle ruins of **Čachtice**, where a real-life vampire, Countess Elizabeth Báthori, tortured and murdered hundreds of servant girls by biting into their flesh. Further up the Váh River valley is the attractive town of **Trenčín**, dominated by yet another sensational castle.

Central Slovakia is where the Slovak Republic's physical beauty hits home. In this region, you'll find the sublime, glacial-carved peaks of the **High Tatras**, where you can take a hair-raising gondola ride to the summit of **Lomnicky štít**, carve some turns on any number of challenging ski slopes, or go for an all-day hike using the Tatra National Park's excellent network of trails.

But the High Tatras aren't the only range of mountains in this region. To the south are the **Low Tatras**, which are not so majestic as the High Tatras, but equally good for skiing and hiking, especially in the gorgeous **Demänovská dolina** (valley). Another valley replete with gorgeous ravines and adventurous trails is **Vrátna dolina** in the **Malá Fatra Mountains**, located in the vicinity of the pleasant city of **Žilina** and the painted wooden village of **Čičmany**. And when it's time to get back to civilization, there's always the delightfully small city of **Banská Bystrica**, featuring one of Slovakia's most handsome town squares and an engrossing museum devoted to the Slovak National Uprising. From Banská Bystrica, it takes about hour to reach the enchanting medieval mining town of **Banská Štiavnica**, its Gothic and Renaissance houses marching down the slopes of the **Štiavnica Highlands**.

East Slovakia is probably the republic's least-visited region. Regardless of that, it's still the most fascinating area you could choose to visit in the Slovak Republic. Near the High Tatras in the western part of East Slovakia is the German-colonized **Spiš** region, where you can tour a couple towns that attest to the former wealth that this region generated. One of these towns is **Kežmarok**, featuring a Renaissance castle and a richly detailed wooden church that's characteristic of the region. But the real gem in this area is the walled town of **Levoča**, where you can admire several flamboyant Renaissance buildings and set your sights on the largest wooden altar in the world. Levoča also serves as the perfect base for visiting the stunning white ruins of **Spiš Castle**, the biggest and most indelible castle in Slovakia.

Košice, the region's capital and Slovakia's second biggest city, offers a surprising taste of sophistication in its big, bustling historic center. Just north of Košice, located in the middle of East Slovakia, is **Prešov**, center of the Uniate Church in Slovakia and home to a couple of good museums. To the north, not far at all from the Polish border, is the adorable Renaissance town of **Bardejov**. Finally, in the remote northeastern town of **Medzilaborce**, is perhaps the oddest thing you'll find in Slovakia – a museum dedicated to the Slovak-American Pop artist Andy Warhol.

CASTLES & CHATEAUX

There is no greater concentration of castles and chateaux in Europe than in the Czech and Slovak republics. There are some 2,500 of them sprinkled throughout both countries. Indeed, you could happily spend your vacation in the two republics doing nothing but hopping around from one castle or chateau to another.

Some of the castles, such as **Prague Castle**, date back 1,000 years, over which time their royal and aristocratic owners endowed them with palaces, chapels, towers, theaters, churches, or in the case of Prague Castle, a cathedral. What this means is that in the Czech and Slovak republics, you have the unique opportunity to view a millennium's worth of art, furniture, fixtures, and decorations all in the single setting of one castle.

At times, Czech and Slovak castles strike an impression that couldn't be rendered more dramatically in a storybook. Some of the castles – including **Karlštejn** and **Křivoklát** in Central Bohemia, **Krumlov** in South Bohemia, **Bouzov** in North Moravia, and **Trenčín** in West Slovakia – command the tops of thrusting hills and impose their weight and majesty on the humbled onlookers below. Others are actually quite friendly-looking, and look as though Disney may have had a hand in designing them. A good example of this is **Hluboká** in South Bohemia, a winsome castle designed by its aristocratic owners with a Gothic nostalgia in mind.

You'll be surprised by just how well-preserved some of these castles are, as well they should be, since many of them were occupied by their aristocratic owners right up to the end of World War II. Now, with the laws of restitution in effect, some of these aristocrats have reclaimed the castles and chateaux that have been in their families for centuries, and have turned them into museums, and in some cases, hotels.

Not all castles are in perfect shape. But that doesn't mean they're any less impressive because of it. Case in point is the brooding **Spiš Castle** in East Slovakia, its walls and ruins sprawled across a high hilltop, an awe-inspiring sight. Another good example is **Devín** just outside Bratislava, which appears as a natural extension of the sheer limestone cliff it occupies.

As you'll learn on your travels through the two republics, the line distinguishing a castle from a chateau is often a fuzzy one. Conceived as castles, the defensive fortifications were removed or became ornamentations, as the new owners transformed the place into a nobleman's palatial estate, which now makes these ex-castles chateaux.

Perhaps the best region in which to go chateau-hopping is South Moravia, a good chunk of which was owned by the Liechtenstein family from the 16th century until they were expelled from Czechoslovakia in 1945 for collaborating with the Nazis. The Liechtensteins graced this bucolic region with numerous grand chateaux, not least of which are the twin gems of **Valtice** and **Lednice**.

South Moravia also features the biggest Baroque chateau in Europe – **Jaroměřice**, a hulking pile decked out in all the excesses of the age. The nearby town of **Telč** boasts a Renaissance chateau abounding with exquisite details. And on the opposite end of the region, in the town of **Kroměříž**, you'll find what has to be the most astounding chateau in either republic, the **Archbishop's Chateau**, captured in all its lavish glory in the film, *Amadeus*.

Yes, there is a dizzying number of castles and chateaux in the two republics. But don't feel pressured to tour every one. Some are best left seen from the outside; the rooms are either just too bare or the tours too drawn-out to make it worth your while. (I've recommended when you should and shouldn't go on the tours.)

BEER

Beer drinking is an essential part of your experience in the Czech Republic. Even President Bill Clinton couldn't resist having a glass of beer when he came to Prague in 1994. Who wouldn't be tempted by the golden elixir that's brewed to perfection and so inexpensively available in the Czech Republic?

You certainly don't need to be a connoisseur to have a delightful time sampling beers in the Czech Republic. Czech beer, unlike some of the stodgy or heavy stuff that comes out of Germany and Belgium, is immediately likeable, and certainly doesn't require that you have refined tastebuds in order to enjoy it. After all, beer is the great egalitarian beverage, meant to be enjoyed by presidents and janitors alike.

And what better place to enjoy the great egalitarian beverage than in the great egalitarian establishment – the pub. No doubt, the pub is a fundamental ingredient in Czech culture, a culture that seems to base itself on the belief that all men and women deserve at least one simple pleasure in life – to have a seat in the local pub and throw back a glass or two of fine beer.

Of course, no people practice this belief more so than Praguers do. In Prague, you'll find a pub on virtually every block in the center, making it as convenient as possible to do your beer sampling. You could easily spend the evening hopping from pub to pub and trying out a different beer at each one. (See the section in the *Prague* chapter entitled "Prague Pubs.")

But not all Czech beers are available in Prague, so you'll need to venture out of the capital to experience the wide spectrum of beer making in the Czech Republic. In fact, many beers are available only in the particular region where the beer is produced. What this means for the beer-loving traveler is that almost every destination brings with it another beer to be sampled. No need to worry about not knowing where to find the local brew, because it's almost always available at the local pub. (To make things easier, I gladly sought out the more likeable of these pubs and review them in the section entitled "Entertainment & Nightlife.")

What makes things all the more enticing is that beer is cheap in the Czech Republic – and I mean dirt cheap. How does 75 cents for a half-liter of Pilsner Urquell sound? (If prices got much higher than that, there would probably be mass protests on the streets.) It's easy to see then why many foreigners who travel through the Czech Republic see little else other than the sights located between two pubs.

OVERCOMING THE STIGMA OF EAST EUROPE

Thankfully, there is no longer an Iron Curtain drawing a line between "East" and "West" Europe. The idea of a geographic, historical, and cultural Central Europe is with us again, and the Czech and Slovak republics would have to be counted as the center of Central Europe.

Still, the Czech and Slovak Republics and the rest of the former Eastern bloc countries sometimes evoke bleak images of dour factory towns riddled with smokestacks and behemoth concrete apartment blocks. It's an image that's hard to get over, and may give you doubts about whether there is anything attractive at all about these two countries once united under a hardline Communist government.

But you can put your mind at ease, because few towns in the Czech and Slovak republics are the industrial wastelands you may picture them as. Granted, there are some coal-burning factory towns that you'll want to steer well clear of, especially in North Bohemia and North Moravia (the cities of Ústí nad Labem, Teplice, and Ostrava). And there are those ugly blocks of apartments in just about any town with a sizable population. But the near-sighted planning of the former Communist regime didn't go so far as to spoil the charm that abounds in these two republics.

With little money to spend, the former government had no choice but to refrain from the Western European impulse to build over or otherwise destroy in the name of progress. Consequently, both republics today feature a host of towns and historic city centers where time has seemingly stood still, giving little indication that the industrial or even the Communist revolution ever took place. This isn't to say the former government took good care of their towns, but it did let many of them alone, often to the point of letting them fall into decay, which is now being answered for in the furious restoration occurring all over the two republics.

Just like any country in the world, there are places to avoid and places to cherish. I'm positive you'll find plenty to cherish in both these republics.

3. SUGGESTED ITINERARIES

Here are three suggested itineraries, for seven, ten, and fifteen day vacations in the Czech and Slovak republics. You'll find a description for each city, town, and attraction in the chapters that follow. Bear in mind, these itineraries were made with the presumption that you'll be flying in and out of Prague and that you'll be traveling through the two republics by car. It would be difficult, if not impossible, to squeeze in all the recommended destinations if you're traveling by train or bus, unless you add some days to the itineraries.

Also keep in mind that most museums and castles are closed on Mondays, but check the following listings to make sure. And remember, spare enough time to follow your whims and tastes. The republics are chock-full of intriguing places and sights, and you never know what you may discover on a spontaneous detour from the beaten path.

ITINERARY 1: SEVEN DAYS IN THE CZECH REPUBLIC
Day 1
Arrive in Prague
Go to Wenceslas Square and stroll down to Old Town Square
Have a look around Týn Church and Church of St. Nicholas
Catch Old Town Hall's Astronomical Clock do its thing at the top of the hour
Climb to the top of the Old Town Hall tower
Stop into the U zlatého tygra pub for a beer and maybe something to eat
Walk across the Charles Bridge
Tour the Church of St. Nicholas in Malá Strana
Stroll across Kampa Island
Have dinner at U zlaté hrušky

Day 2
Go back to Malá Strana
Walk up Nerudova ulice (street) to the castle

Take the grand tour of Prague Castle and St. Vitus Cathedral
Stroll through the Royal Gardens
Visit the National Gallery at the Sternberg Palace
Wander aimlessly through Malá Strana
Have dinner at the Opera Grill
Catch a performance at the National Theater

Day 3
Ride the funicular to the top of Petřín Hill
Visit the Strahov Monastery
Have a beer and a bite to eat at U černého vola
Visit the Loreto Church
Check out the collection of František Bílek's art at the Bílkova vila
Walk across Letná park
Spend an hour or two looking at the National Gallery's collection of
    modern art at the Veletržní palác
Dine at Circle Line Brasserie
Attend a performance at the Rudolfinum

Day 4
Tour the Old Jewish Cemetery and the rest of the sights at Josefov,
    Prague's old Jewish ghetto
Tour the St. Agnes Convent
Take a cruise on the Vltava River
Wander aimlessly through the districts of Staré Město and Nové Město
Take the metro to Vyšehrad Castle and watch the sun go down
Have dinner at Ambiente

Day 5
Travel to Kutná Hora in east-central Bohemia
Check in at Hotel U vlašského dvora
Walk around the old town center
Tour the Italian Court
Tour St. Barbara's Cathedral
Visit the "bone church" in nearby Sedlec
Dine at Hotel U vlašského dvora

Day 6
Travel to České Budějovice in South Bohemia
Walk around the town's main square, náměstí Přemysla Otakara II, and
    climb up the Black Tower; have lunch or a beer at Masné Krámy
Travel to Český Krumlov
Take a tour of Krumlov Castle

Spend the rest of the afternoon and early evening walking around town
Stay the night at Hotel Růže and go on the hotel's ghost tour

Day 7
Travel to and tour the castle of Rožmberk nad Vltavou
Tour the monastery in the town of Vššyí Brod
Return to Prague, stopping off at Hluboká Castle along the way
Bid farewell to Prague with dinner at Parnas

ITINERARY 2: TEN DAYS IN THE CZECH & SLOVAK REPUBLICS

The first four days as outlined in Itinerary 1 plus:

Day 5
Travel from Prague to Telč in South Moravia, stopping off at Jihlava
    along the way for a look its main square
Walk around Telč's main square, náměstí Zachariáše z Hradce
Tour the Telč chateau
Spend the night at Hotel Telč, Hotel Celerin, or Hotel na hrázi
Dine at Hotel na hrázi

Day 6
Spend the morning walking around the town of Slavonice
Continue eastward to Vranov nad Dyjí and tour the castle there
Go directly to Mikulov
Check in at the Hotel rohátý krokodýl
Visit the Mikulov castle
Walk around town, and be sure to see the old Jewish Cemetery
Dine at Hotel rohátý krokodýl

Day 7
Tour Valtice and Lednice, two chateaux just east of Mikulov
Drive south to Bratislava, Slovakia
Check in at Hotel No. 16
Stroll around Bratislava's Old Town
Have dinner at Modrá hviezda

Day 8
Visit the museums at Bratislava Castle
Visit the Slovak National Gallery
Go for a cruise on the Danube River
See the Little Blue Church

Eat dinner at Presbourg
Attend a performance at the Slovak National Theater

Day 9
Drive from Bratislava to Brno, the Czech Republic
Check in at the Grand Hotel
Visit the Old Town Hall and climb its tower
Peruse the modern art branch of the Moravian Gallery
Watch the sun go down from Špilberk Castle
Attend a performance at the Janaček Theater or the Mahen Theater

Day 10
Head back to Prague
Along the way, stop at (but don't feel pressured to tour) Konopiště Castle
Splurge on dinner at Parnas in Prague

ITINERARY 3: FIFTEEN DAYS IN THE CZECH & SLOVAK REPUBLICS

The first four days as outlined in Intinerary 1 plus:

Day 5
From Prague, take a day trip to Karlštejn and Křivoklát castles
Back in Prague, dine at Vinárna U Maltézských Rytířů Malta

Day 6
Drive from Prague to Brno, stopping off at Konopiště Castle along the
   way
Check in at the Grand Hotel in Brno
Stroll around the historic center
Walk up to the Cathedral of St. Peter and St. Paul
Dine at La Braseria

Day 7
Peruse one or all three branches of the Moravian Gallery
Visit Brno's Old Town Hall and climb to the top of its tower
See the mummies at the Church of the Holy Cross
Tour the Špilberk Castle
Visit the Church of the Assumption of the Virgin
If there's enough time, visit the Mendelianum museum
Dine at Radniční Sklípek

Day 8
Travel to the South Moravian town of Kroměříž and take a tour of the
    Archbishop's Chateau there
Drive to the North Moravian town of Olomouc
Check in at the Hotel Lafayette or Hotel Gemo
Visit St. Wenceslas Cathedral
Tour the Přemysl Palace
Walk through the Olomouc Museum of Art
Wander aimlessly around the old town and through its ring of parks
Dine at Pietro Trattoria

Day 9
Travel to the town of Rožnov pod Radhoštěm in North Moravia and walk
    around one of the *skansens* (open-air museums of folk architecture)
Drive to Tatranská Lomnica, one of the resorts in the High Tatra Moun-
    tains in Central Slovakia
Check in at the Hotel Tatry
Have dinner at Reštaurácia Júlia

Day 10
Spend the day hiking in the High Tatras
Have dinner at the Hotel Grand in Starý Smokovec

Day 11
Take the gondola to the top of Lomnický štít (the second highest peak in
    the High Tatras)
Drive to the East Slovak walled town of Levoča
Check in at the Hotel Satel
Walk around Levoča's historic center, making sure to take a look inside
    at the Church of St. James
Eat dinner at the Hotel Satel

Day 12
Tour the Spiš Castle
Drive to Košice
Check in at the Hotel Centrum
Visit the Cathedral of St. Elizabeth
Tour the Mikluš Prison museum
See the Košice Gold Treasure at the East Slovak Museum
Have dinner at Reštaurácia Grand
Attend a performance at the State Theater

Day 13
Drive to Banská Bystrica in Central Slovakia
Check in at the Hotel Arcade
Wander around Banská Bystrica's historic center
Look inside the Church of Our Lady
Visit the SNP Museum
Eat dinner at Reštaurácia U Komediantov

Day 14
Spend the morning in Banská Štiavnica
Visit the open-air Mining Museum there
Drive to Trenčín in West Slovakia
Check in at the Hotel Tatra
Tour the Trenčín Castle
Have dinner at the Hotel Tatra

Day 15
Return to Prague
Bid Prague farewell by having dinner at Parnas

4. LAND & PEOPLE

LAND

Czech Republic

Westerners, especially Americans, tend to think of the Czech Republic as an East European country. Well, the Cold War is over (thank god), which means Europe is no longer divided by a wall distinguishing "East" from "West." The idea of a geographical and historical Central Europe is with us again, and the Czech Republic would have to be counted as the most central of the Central European countries, with Austria, Germany, Poland, and Slovakia surrounding it.

At 78,864 square kilometers (30,449 square miles), the Czech Republic is smaller than the state of New York. It consists of two major areas – **Bohemia** to the west and **Moravia** to the east, which together have been considered the "Czech Lands" since the Middle Ages. Bohemia's principal city is of course **Prague**, while Moravia's is **Brno**. The western half of **Silesia** (an historical region divided between Poland and the Czech Republic) is also part of the republic, but has since 1928 been amalgamated with Moravia.

Bohemia is practically encircled by mountains and tree-studded rolling hills. The **Šumava Mountains** in the southwest, the **Bohemian Forest** (Český les) in the west, and the **Ore Mountains** (Krušné hory) to the northwest all together form the border with Germany. The **Giant Mountains** (Krkonoše) of East Bohemia and the **Jeseníky Mountains** of North Moravia, both considered part of the **Sudeten Range**, run along the eastern border with Poland. And along the southeastern border in Moravia rise the **White Carpathians**, beyond which is Slovakia.

There are two major rivers in Bohemia. The longest is the **Vltava River** (called the Moldau in German), springing from the Šumava Mountains in southwestern Bohemia and heading north through Prague before spilling into the **Labe River**, which continues through North Bohemia into Germany (where it becomes known as the Elbe River). The main river in Moravia is appropriately called the **Morava River,** originating in the **Jeseníky** Mountains and flowing south along the Slovakia-Austria border and emptying into the Danube.

Slovak Republic

The Slovak Republic lies at the geographic crossroads of Eastern and Western Europe, bordered by the Czech Republic, Austria, Hungary, Ukraine, and Poland. At 49,036 square kilometers (18,921 square miles), Slovakia is roughly the size of Portugal.

Compared to the Czech Republic, Slovakia holds much greater appeal to those who love the great outdoors. Its greatest feature are the monumental **High Tatra Mountains** (Vysoké Tatry), fronting the Polish border in the north-central region. Not so sublime but pretty in their own right are the **Low Tatras** (Nízké Tatry), paralleling the High Tatras a ways to the south. Running through the north-central part of Slovakia are the duel ranges of the **Malá Fatra** and **Veľka Fatra**.

The western section of the country is a completely different world, characterized by the flat, treeless lowlands that make up the Danubian plain and basin. The exception to the plains are the smallish **White Carpathian Mountains**, fronting the Czech border and extending down to **Bratislava**, the capital of Slovakia.

The country's longest river is the **Váh**, originating in the High Tatras and flowing southwest through the Danubian Basin of West Slovakia, where it and the smaller **Nitra River** dump into the **Danube River** (called the "Dunaj" in Slovak). Forming the border with Austria is the **Morava River**, which empties into the Danube a little bit upstream from Bratislava. A little ways downstream from Bratislava, the Danube runs a short ways along the border with Hungary before flowing south and eventually spilling into the Black Sea.

PEOPLE

The Czechs

Sitting in a pub one night, a Czech man told me, "Czechs are proud of one thing – of not being proud." I raised my mug of beer and pointed at it.

"Yeah," he said, "that too. But that goes without saying."

I would have to agree: the Czechs are humble people (and do make the best beer in the world). But, at the same time, they are extremely self-assured. And they have every right to be, considering they bear a rich cultural legacy that goes back more than a thousand years, a legacy from which a solid cultural identity has taken shape.

To understand that identity, which in itself is an extremely liberal one, it's important to know a little something about Czech history, especially regarding the Hussite movement. The Hussites were follow-ers of Jan Hus, an early-15th century Czech preacher whose progressive, anti-Catholic teachings and consequential martyrdom ushered in the Czech Reformation a good century before Martin Luther nailed his 95 theses to the door.

After battling it out with the Holy Roman Empire shortly after Hus' death, the Czech Hussites ruled the Czech lands in some manner or another for nearly two centuries, even though they were pegged as heretics by the papacy and the rest of Europe. But once the ardent Catholic Austrian Hapsburgs got a leash on the Czechs, the majority of whom were Hussites, the Czech people suffered the full brunt of the Counter-Reformation, in which their culture and language were nearly wiped out. In spite of this history, Catholicism is the most popular religion in the Czech Republic today, accounting for four million of the country's 10.3 million people, as compared with 400,000 Hussites.

So it's easy to understand why Czechs are not particularly religious people these days. That isn't to say they are decadent or even immoral. But they are intensely alert to the sort of religious fanaticism that has compelled men to suppress, persecute, and kill.

It's no wonder then that Czechs have always held greater respect for their artists, writers, composers, musicians, and architects than they have for their generals, politicians, and other leaders. It's also not so surprising that the Czechs would elect an absurdist playwright, Václav Havel, as the president of their country.

You could argue (and the Slovaks do) that Czech liberalism made it easy for the Communists to take over in Czechoslovakia. In the past few years, however, the Czechs have done a pretty thorough job in putting communism behind them, which has been a feat both in political and psychological terms.

During their initial years of freedom, the Czechs underwent what Havel described as a "post-prison psychosis" – a state of mind in which you cannot think or act independently. The Czechs indeed had to re-learn how to stand on their own, without the state telling them what to do and how to think.

Having mostly overcome this "psychosis," the Czechs have adapted well to democracy, evident in the fact that theirs is one of the few remaining nations of the former Eastern bloc that have not given Com-munists a majority of votes since the Cold War ended. They have also taken well to a market economy, as seemingly every young Czech these days aspire to be successful at some business or another.

Yes, money holds an unreasonably great appeal these days in the Czech Republic, and a lot of people are looking to make a fast buck. Taxi drivers, particularly the ones in Prague, are the ones most guilty of this.

Also guilty are hotel proprietors, many of whom exploit their foreign guests by overcharging them, knowing foreigners generally have more money to spend. Restaurant servers often do the same to foreigners by using a tricky system of pricing. But these unethical practices have been on their way out ever since the country began its pursuit to join the European Union, which told the Czech government that it needs to ban such practices before Czech membership will be considered.

Another thing that will hopefully be on its way out soon is the general disregard for ethnic minorities living in the country, especially for the country's 114,000 Gypsies (or *Romanies* as they prefer to be called). Descendants of Indic-speaking nomads who arrived in Europe in the 1100s, Romanies have endured centuries of persecution, culminating when Hitler sent thousands of them to the gas chamber and when the Communists unsuccessfully tried to integrate them into society by forbidding their nomadic customs and banning their language. Though Czech Romanies enjoy constitutional guarantees of freedom today, they still face a general Czech populace that considers them thieves by nature, illegally forbidding them from entering many restaurants, pubs, bars, and even cinemas.

In 1997 a local station broadcast a documentary about a Czech Romany family finding asylum in Canada and living a much higher quality of life than in the Czech Republic. Hundreds of Romanies consequently sold their possessions and flew to Canada, only to be sent back by Canadian officials. To stem the flow of Romany immigration and recover its international reputation (tarnished by so many Romanies fleeing the Czech Republic), the Czech government established the Interministerial Commission for Romany Affairs, which now works to change Czech social attitudes regarding Romanies.

The Language Barrier
Here's a Czech tongue twister that might give you some idea of what you're up against: *Strč prst zkrz krk,* meaning "stick your finger through your neck." Not all Czech words are devoid of vowels like those above, but a lot of them are. Learning Czech pronunciation isn't the hard part, however. The big doozy for native English-speakers is the highly complex grammar, which bears little similarity to the grammar of English, German, or any of the Romance languages.

Getting by in the Czech Republic without any knowledge of the language does take some perseverance. But you are already in a fairly good position because you speak English. And if you know some German, even better.

Before the Velvet Revolution, Czechs had little opportunity to learn English, as Russian was the compulsory second language in schools.

FAMOUS CZECHS

Tomáš Garrigue Masaryk – philosopher, professor, and first president of Czechoslovakia, who incidentally had an American wife.

Jaroslav Seifert – the one and only Czech to win the Nobel Prize for Literature.

Miloš Forman – Academy-award winning director of such films as "One Flew Over the Cuckoo's Nest" and "Amadeus."

Otto Wichterle – inventor of the contact lens.

Tom Stoppard – avant-garde playwright born in Czechoslovakia but raised in England.

Václav Havel – world-renowned absurdist playwright who had a slight change in profession.

Martina Navrátilová – one of the best women tennis players of all time.

Ivan Lendl – another tennis great. He won all the Grand Slam titles, except for Wimbledon.

Ivana Zelníčková – member of the 1972 Czechoslovak Olympic ski team who went on to marry and divorce a guy by the name of Donald Trump.

Jaromír Jágr – member of the NHL's Pittsburgh Penguins and all-around hockey sensation.

These days, students have a choice between English and German, and most are opting for English. There are a couple of obvious reasons for that. First, English is the language of pop culture, something the Czechs have been eating up ever since the Velvet Revolution opened the floodgates to American films, television programs, and music. Second, students are wising up to the idea that if they want to excel in their chosen professions, then they'll be better off speaking English.

As for the adults who never had English in their school curriculum, they are now signing up in droves at the scores of private language schools – staffed mainly by the thousands of Americans who have besieged the country in recent years.

So, where will you find English spoken in the Czech Republic? Almost all hotels and pensions in Prague and other major cities have English speakers working the front desk. And in the nicer restaurants, you're likely to get a menu in English, if not a server who speaks some English. But once you get out of the cities and into the small towns, you'll find nary an English-speaker, as most are accustomed to speaking German as their second language. If you speak some German, then you should have no problem getting by at hotels and restaurants. Otherwise, you'll just have to come up with some good hand signals.

But do make the effort to say something in Czech, most importantly the phrase *dobrý den*, meaning "good day" or "hello." It's customary to say this when you enter a small shop, café, or pub or when you are greeting someone other than a good friend, in which case you would use the more informal *ahoj* or *čau* (ciao). When leaving a small shop, café, or pub, it's polite to say *na shledanou* (pronounced something like "nas-kh-led-ano"). Another key word is of course *děkuji* (said something like "dya-kwee") or *diky* ("deeky"), meaning "thank you" or "thanks." And, in reply, *prosím*, which can mean either "please" or "you're welcome." Whatever else you can blurt out in Czech will be greatly appreciated, and just may compel a Czech or two to go out of his way for you, as I learned once in a Mariánské Lázně restaurant.

Needing a place to stay for the night, I decided to ask my waitress if she knew of any reasonably priced hotels in town. A look of amusement passed over her face as I plodded through the Czech asking my question. She said she didn't know of any off-hand, but would go and find out. I thought she would then go ask the other waitress or someone in the kitchen. But no; instead, she got out the phone book and called every hotel in town to see what their rates were and if they had any vacancies. I'm fairly certain that, after dealing with Germans all day long in *their* tongue, my waitress was so delighted to hear a foreigner speak *her* tongue (even if he sounded like an idiot doing it) she decided to do something nice for him.

A Guide to Pronounciation

The pronounciation of Czech and Slovak characters appear daunting, but they are not as bad as they seem. The only pronounciation that poses a serious problem for English speakers is the ř, a character that appears in Czech only. Two vital things to remember when pronouncing Czech or Slovak words are that the accent *always* falls on the first syllable and that every letter in the word is pronounced.

Here are some Czech and Slovak characters, their pronounciations, and words in which the characters are used:

á   like the "a" in father. For example, *láska* (lah-ske), which means love.

c   like the "ts" in gets. For example, *cena* (tsen-a), which means price.

č   like the "ch" in cheese. For example, *český* (che-skee), which means Czech.

ch   like the "ch" in the Scottish word *loch* or the German word *achtung*. For example, *záchod* (zah-khod), which mean bathroom.

é like the "ai" in aid. For example, *léto* (lay-to), which means summer.

ě like the "ye" in yellow. For example, *děkují* (dye-kwee), which means thank you.

í/ý like the "ea" in meat. For example, *zítra* (zee-tra), which means tomorrow.

j like the "y" in young. For example, *jídlo* (yeed-lo), which means food.

ř sounds like "r" and "ž" combined. For example, the composer *Dvořák* (something like Dvo-rshahk).

š like the "sh" in shirt. For example, *špatný* (shpat-nee), which means bad.

ú like the "oo" in zoo. For example, *útery* (oo-te-ree), which means Tuesday.

ž like the "s" in measure. For example, *žena* (zhe-na), which means woman.

SOME USEFUL WORDS & PHRASES IN CZECH/SLOVAK

Yes	*ano/áno, or hej*
No	*ne/nie*
Hello (formal)	*dobrý den/dobrý deň*
Hello (informal)	*ahoj (ahoy) or čiao (chow)*
Goodbye (formal)	*na shledanou (nas-kh-led-anou) /do videnia*
Good Morning	*dobré ráno*
Good Evening	*dobrý večer*
Good Night	*dobrou noc/dobrú noc*
Thank You	*děkuji/ďakujem*
Please & You're Welcome	*prosím*
Do you speak English?	*Mluvíte anglicky? /Hovoríte anglicky?*
I understand	*rozumím/rozumiem*
I don't understand	*nerozumím/nerozumiem*

Getting Along with the Czechs

Historically, the Czechs have been a very passive people (though prone to hurling important figures out the window at key historical moments, as you'll read about in the next chapter). That passivity is reflected in their easy going, almost acquiescent nature that makes them quite sociable (as you can tell on any given night in a pub).

But Czechs do have a tendency to be surly at times, especially in Prague, where there are a lot of day-to-day headaches that make people surly. Unfortunately, too many experiences with less-than-polite people have been the big downer for many Americans visiting the city. The best advice I can offer in the case of meeting such a person is to forget about it and just get on with your vacation. More than likely you'll meet another Czech who will give you a better opinion of the people.

So what do Czechs think about Americans? For one, Czechs are curious. During the Cold War, Americans were the "other," about which Czechs knew very little, except whatever the Party-controlled media wanted Czechs to think about a corrupt American society. These days the portrayal of America is almost as bad, as Czechs are learning about Americans from shows such as *Beverly Hills 90210*, *Melrose Place*, or *M.A.S.H.* (yes, *M.A.S.H.* has made a comeback in the Czech Republic). But the Czechs are not so stupid as to rely on Hollywood's interpretation of Americans, and therefore are quite interested when the real article comes along.

This interest in Americans, however, isn't as great these days in Prague, where there are so many Americans that Praguers have become almost indifferent to them. But once you get out of the cities and to places where Czechs are used to seeing only German and Austrian tourists, then the attitude changes, and Americans once again hold some novel value.

Whatever opinion Czechs may have of Americans, it won't help that opinion if you don't acknowledge a few of their customs. Here are some you should know about: If you happen to be invited into a Czech household, remember to take off your shoes when you enter. (With all the dog poop on the sidewalks, it's an easy habit to understand.) If you're invited for lunch or dinner, remember to bring some offering of gratitude, such as a bottle of wine, candies, flowers, or some other small token. And when riding on a packed metro, tram, or bus, it's good manners to give your seat to an elderly person or to a pregnant woman.

The Slovaks

First, let's set the record straight. Slovaks are different from Czechs. Their languages, though mutually understandable, are different; their cultures are different; and theirs habits are different. Of course, there are a lot of similarities, but don't make the faux-pas of grouping the two people under the umbrella title of "Czech" (as was common during the existence of Czechoslovakia), especially if you are talking to a Slovak. The Slovaks are a bit touchy when it comes to issues of nationality, and are quick to assert their separate identity.

So, what makes Slovaks different from Czechs? First and foremost is their difference in attitude towards religion. In Slovakia, the Catholic Church is nearly as strong as in Poland, claiming 60 percent of the country's 5.3 million people, while the country's biggest Protestant church, the Evangelical Church of the Augsburg Confession, has some 369,000 members.

But the numbers don't hit home until you see the Slovaks in action. On Sundays, Slovak churches (and I mean all churches) become standing room only. And during the weekdays it's a common sight to see dozens of students, workers, or shoppers stop in to a church on their way home to say a group prayer or attend an afternoon mass. (This is indeed a far cry from the Czech Republic, where mainly tourists, and not just the faithful ones, fill the churches.)

Slovak history has certainly played a big hand in making Slovaks the religious people they are today. Whereas the Czechs had several centuries worth of political and religious independence, the Slovaks endured a millennium under the Magyar (Hungarian) thumb, during which time Slovaks made up the peasantry in a land considered the northern reaches of the Hungarian Kingdom. As a result, the Slovaks had little leeway to dabble in religions other than the one aligned with the kingdom – the Catholic Church.

This is perhaps why it took a group of Slovak Lutheran ministers, whose vision extended beyond Catholic Hungary, to instigate the Slovak National Revival of the 19th century, which finally made Slovaks aware of their cultural identity, an identity deriving from the country's wealth of folk customs.

To this day, these customs color just about anything that's considered truly Slovak, from the country's language and speech to its song and dance to its food and drink. But the customs are most conspicuous when it comes to decorative arts. Each region, albeit each village or town, would seem to have their own signature style in decorating their houses, furniture, ceramics, musical instruments, and, particularly, their folk costumes. Colorfully hand-stitched skirts, shirts, jackets, dresses, vests, pants, shawls, and aprons – worn by dancers going through the steps of traditional dances – make for a brilliant fanfare at the country's numerous religious festivals. Try to catch one of these festivals if you can.

CELEBRITIES OF SLOVAK DESCENT

Paul Newman – *the American movie star*
Steve McQueen – *supposedly had a Slovak father*
Andrej Varchola – *better known as Andy Warhol, whose parents*
  emigrated to American from the Ruthenia region of East Slovakia
Robert Maxwell – *media mogul who also emigrated from Ruthenia*
Eugene Cernan – *the last man to walk on the moon*

The Hungarian Factor

From the 10th century all the way up to World War I, Slovakia was an integral part of the Hungarian Kingdom, with the Magyars often out-populating the Slovaks in certain regions. So when the Czechoslovak-Hungarian border was drawn up in 1918, more than 700,000 Hungarians found themselves north of that line, suddenly making them Czechoslovak citizens. After a millennium of Slovaks playing peasants to the Hungarian lords, the two peoples were not about to have a jolly time together. However, the Czechoslovak government – from President Masaryk to President Havel – was sympathetic to the Hungarian cause, extending them rights that protected their language and culture from Slovak suppression.

So when the Slovak nationalists' dream of an independent Slovakia came to fruition in 1993, the 600,000 Hungarians living in Slovakia justifiably feared they would lose many of those rights. And indeed those fears were well founded, as parliament passed a law making Slovak the official language of the Slovak Republic. This law had two results that were a slap in the face of the Hungarians: it placed heavy restrictions on the use of Hungarian on the airwaves and it banned bilingual signs in towns and on streets. (The law also meant, for a brief time at least, that Czech films and television programs – though completely understood by Slovaks without any need for translation – had to contain Slovak subtitles.)

The Slovak government has since eased their blatant anti-Hungarian policies, because they understand it wouldn't have a chance in hell of joining the European Union if it didn't. But relations between Slovaks and ethnic Hungarians are still far from friendly, as the Hungarians have been demanding ethnic autonomy. The Hungarian government in Budapest has come to their defense, and has made that autonomy a central issue in relations between the two countries. It's a potentially explosive situation, one that will have to be monitored closely.

A situation that has exploded a few times already involves the Romanies (gypsies), who – along with the Hungarians, Poles, and Ruthenians – account for 14 percent of Slovakia's population. Romanies have been the first to lose their jobs when companies needed to make cutbacks, which has rendered the majority of the Romany community destitute. Tension is highest in East Slovakia, where they are said to make up 20 percent of the population. There and in some other regions, Romany families are the targets of violent neo-Nazi attacks, to which the police or local governments rarely ever respond.

The Slovak Language Barrier

Slovak – like Czech, Polish, and Lusatian – belong to the West Slavonic group of Indo-European languages. Slovaks and Czechs have no problems understanding each other, because their languages are so similar. Some of your more chauvinist Czechs even consider Slovak a dialect of the Czech language, based on the fact that Slovaks used Czech as their written language until the turn of the 19th century, when Anton Bernolák published his books on Slovak grammar and spelling.

In Bratislava, a town packed with university students, you'll run into a lot of Slovaks who can speak wonderful English. All the nicer hotels are staffed by English-speakers, and most restaurants offer a menu in English. But when you get out of Bratislava, chances are you'll find nary a soul who can speak a word of English, even at hotels. You will, however, find plenty of people who can speak German.

The best way to break the ice with the Slovaks is of course to say a few things in their language. It's customary at any time of day to say *dobrý deň* (good day) when you greet someone or when you enter a small shop, café, or bar. When you leave, Slovaks like to hear you say *do videnia* (goodbye). Other key words are *ďakujem* (pronounced "dya-ku-yem"), meaning "thank you," and *prosím*, meaning "please."

Getting Along with the Slovaks

With all due respect to my Czech friends, I find Slovaks much easier to get along with than Czechs. Even in the country's biggest and noisiest city of Bratislava, I was continually astounded by how downright friendly and helpful the Slovaks are. For example, in several of the city's wonderful museums, the man or woman supervising a particular room or hall will often tell you a little something extra about the exhibits or about Bratislava, and then ask you something about yourself, such as where you come from, how long you're staying in Slovakia, and so on. Even the restaurant servers, who can be the crustiest of people in the Czech Republic, are amazingly polite in Slovakia.

Without sounding too chauvinistic, it helps to be an American in Slovakia, because Slovaks are genuinely interested in them. Most Slovaks have had very few first or even second-hand experiences with Americans, which makes them greatly curious about the people they see portrayed in the countless films and television programs they import from the States. (An indication of how few Americans ever travel to Slovakia; an estimated 100 Americans visited the country's biggest attraction, the High Tatra Mountains, in 1994.)

Of course, they won't think much of you no matter where you come from if you accidentally offend them. To avoid that, see the last paragraph in "Getting Along with the Czechs." Czech and Slovak customs of politeness are pretty much the same.

5. A SHORT HISTORY

On January 1, 1993, Czechoslovakia officially split into the **Czech** and **Slovak republics**, ending a 74-year marriage as one united country. Despite their loose association under the Great Moravian Empire in the 9th and 10th centuries and their union from 1918 to 1992, the Czechs and Slovaks have very different histories, though both could sit down to a glass of beer and well commiserate over a past in which they were both subjected to Hapsburg rule.

CZECH BEGINNINGS - PREHISTORY TO 700 AD

The first trace of human activity in the Czech lands dates back at least 600,000 years, but the trace is so small that it's hardly worth mentioning. More substantial are the findings of the so-called "mammoth hunters," whose effects from 22,000 years ago have been unearthed in and around South Moravia.

Sometime around 500 BC Celtic tribes began wondering into the Czech lands. One of those tribes, called the **Boii**, gained the attention of Rome, and the area in which they settled received the Latin appellation of Boiohemum, later translated into German as Böhmen and into English as Bohemia. Strangely enough, the Czechs have never used this name when referring to their country or themselves, opting rather for the Slavic name **Čechy**.

In the 5th century, during a period known as the **Migration of Nations**, the first Slavic tribes flowed into the Slovak and Moravian lowlands and into the Bohemian basin, driving out the Germanic tribes who had replaced the Celts. But the Slavs were soon followed by the mighty **Avars**, a tribe of Turko-Tartar origin, who occupied most of present-day Hungary and waged arbitrary assaults against the Slavs. Rather than live under the constant threat of their belligerent neighbors, the Slavs unified, crushing the Avars under the leadership of **Samo**, a Franconian merchant who went on to build the first western Slavic empire, which included Bohemia, Moravia, parts of Slovakia, and a bit of Bavaria. But that empire, which was a loose federation of tribes devoted to one man, died with Samo sometime around 659 A.D.

THE GREAT MORAVIAN EMPIRE - 830-907

The Great Moravian Empire also gelled from a group of Slavic Moravian tribes, taking as their first leader **Mojmír I** (830-846). By the time he and subsequent rulers finished conquering neighboring lands, the empire spanned across a great deal of Central Europe, including Moravia (of course), Bohemia, Silesia, Slovakia, southeastern Poland, northern Hungary, and parts of eastern Germany. The Czechs and Slovaks have argued for years over where the capital of the empire was located, as each says it was in their own respective territory. But most archaeologists believe the political and cultural center was in one of two possible towns – Mikulčice or Staré Město (both located in South Moravia near present-day Uherské Hradiště).

Mojmír's successor, **Rostislav**, first made the initiative to bring Christianity to the empire, requesting from the Byzantine Emperor in Constantinople (and not the pope in Rome) that he dispatch a mission to Moravia. The emperor sent two Greek brothers by the names of **Cyril** and **Methodius**, who arrived in Moravia in 863 bearing a Bible translated into Old Church Slavonic, an artificial language based on a southern Slavic dialect that was readily understood by the disparate Slav tribes in the empire. It was the first time that the Slavs acquired a written language. But **Svatopluk**, Rostislav's nephew, put an end to the Old Church Slavonic liturgy when he ousted his uncle and allied himself with the Latin-based Catholic Church.

Squabbling among the tribes that made up the Great Moravian Empire set it on the road to dissolution. The biggest blow came when the Czechs broke from the empire and swore allegiance to the Eastern Franconia **King Arnulph**. And when the Magyars (Hungarians) invaded in 907 and captured most of Slovakia, the empire crumbled, setting in motion the separate cultural and social development of the Czech and Slovak nations.

THE PREMYSLID DYNASTY - 870-1306

Sometime around the year 870 **Prince Přemysl Bořivoj**, ruler of the Czech tribes, moved his residence from Levý Hradec (where he had established the first church in Bohemia) to a certain hill above the Vltava River, an event that went down in history as the founding of the **Prague Castle**. Though it took a century after the founding of the castle to unite the Czechs, the Přemyslid princes managed to emerge as rulers of Bohemia despite conflict within the family that reached its peak when the pagan **Boleslav the Cruel** had his devout brother, **Prince Václav I** (Wenceslas), assassinated in 929, an event which later made Václav the country's patron saint, not to mention its "eternal ruler."

By the time **Boleslav the Pious** (son of the Cruel) ascended the throne in 967, the Czech lands had come under the jurisdiction of the Holy Roman Empire, which was so loosely organized in those days that the Přemyslids were able to maintain a high degree of autonomy. Under Boleslav, the Czech principality expanded by leaps and bounds, as the rest of Bohemia and all of Moravia became its territory. Not long after the death of Boleslav however, the principality was eaten up piecemeal by the Poles, leaving the Přemyslids with only Bohemia proper. But the Czechs, under **Prince Břetislav I** (1034-1055), rallied back in the 11th century and recovered Moravia, tied from then on to the Czechs and ruled by the youngest son of whomever sat on the throne in Prague.

It was during the 13th century that the Přemyslid dynasty truly came into its own. Taking advantage of an ebb in the Holy Roman Empire's command over Europe, **Otakar I** persuaded the pope to issue Bohemia the **Golden Bull of Sicily** (1212), a formal edict that accorded Otakar I and his heirs the royal title and, in effect, promoted Bohemia from principality to kingdom.

These were indeed happy times for Bohemia. Newly-discovered gold and silver deposits boosted the kingdom's wealth, as did the development of trade-center towns such as Staré Město in Prague, České Budějovice in South Bohemia, and Znojmo in South Moravia. It was also during this time that Germans, Flems, and Jews began to settle in the Czech lands, bringing with them the much-needed legal and financial know-how to help make these towns flourish.

By 1273, the Bohemian Kingdom had come to include Austria and the Alps. Riding this wave of economic and territorial expansion, **King Přemysl Otakar II** set his sights on being elected Holy Roman Emperor. Not only was he denied the crown, but he was ordered to cede Austria and the Alps to the man who became emperor, **Count Rudolf von Hapsburg**, whose family until then held little political sway. Infuriated, Otakar rebelled, declaring an ill-fated war against the newly elected emperor, a war which took Otakar II's life in 1278.

The political situation in Bohemia got messy after Otakar's death, but expansion continued nonetheless under Otakar's successor, **King Václav II**, who managed to become King of Poland. His brilliant statesmanship, used also in obtaining the Hungarian throne for his son **Václav III**, came as too big of a match for the heir, who had to renounce the Hungarian crown soon after his father died and concentrate his efforts on Poland, a country that didn't take well to being ruled by a Czech. In 1306, Václav III was murdered in Olomouc by an unknown assassin. With no male heir left to take the throne, the Přemyslid dynasty came to an abrupt end.

CHARLES IV & THE GOLDEN AGE - 1310-1400

Faced with a kingless kingdom, the Czech nobles elected the first Hapsburg to the Bohemian throne, **Albert I**. But Albert hardly had a chance to settle into Prague Castle before he was murdered by his own nephew. The crown fell to his son **Rudolf I**, but he too died an early death. So once more the Czechs were in the market for a king.

This time the crown fell to **John of Luxembourg**, husband of Václav III's sister and nothing less than Holy Roman Emperor. But John stayed out of Bohemia's internal affairs, and contented himself instead with expanding the Czech lands, adding Silesia and Upper Lusatia. His first-born son and successor, **Charles IV** (Karel), would prove to be the most praised king in Czech history.

Educated in the court of the French king and fluent speaker of five languages (including his mother's native tongue of Czech), Charles IV was, if anything, a brilliant leader and statesman. Needing help in managing his Czech affairs, his father appointed Charles joint ruler of Bohemia, and from the beginning Charles proved himself extraordinarily qualified for the job, kicking off his rule by landing an archbishopric in Prague. By the time John of Luxembourg passed away, which happened next to his son in the Battle of Crécy, Charles had already become a shoe-in to succeed his father as Holy Roman Emperor, which occurred in 1346.

The list of Charles' achievements is too long to detail, but his most formidable accomplishment was turning Prague into a city worthy of its status as capital of the Holy Roman Empire. During his reign, Prague and the rest of the Czech lands experienced its **Golden Age**, in which they became the recipient of a wealth of Gothic architecture. **St. Vitus Cathedral** was erected, the **Charles Bridge** built, Prague's district of **Nové Město** laid out, and **Karlštejn Castle** constructed. To top it off, Prague became the home of Central Europe's first university, appropriately called **Charles University**.

When Charles IV died in 1378, Bohemia unfortunately slipped into a decline heralded by an onslaught of the plague, which claimed up to 15 percent of the Czech population. What Bohemia desperately needed but didn't have was a strong leader. Charles IV's son, **Václav IV**, proved to be incompetent, taking to drink more often than to his responsibilities as King of Bohemia and Holy Roman Emperor. During Václav's decadent reign, in which he was deposed from the Holy Roman throne and twice jailed, Czechs who had enjoyed the flowering of Bohemian life under Charles IV could only assume that God was punishing them. And with one man claiming the papacy in Rome and another doing the same in Avignon, France (in what was to be called the Great Schism), Czechs undertook a serious reevaluation of the religious and political powers of the day.

THE HUSSITE REVOLUTION (1400-1526)

The voice of conscience during these troubled times was none other than **Jan Hus** (sometimes anglicized as John Huss), Rector of Charles University and preacher at Prague's Bethlehem Chapel. Heavily influenced by the teachings of John Wycliffe, a 14th-century English reformer who opposed the authority of the Pope, Hus propagated the idea that Czechs and the Czech language have priority in Bohemia, an idea that earned him the resentment of Prague's large German minority and incurred the wrath of the Catholic clergy, which had serious objections to the priest delivering his sermons in Czech (the language of the masses) rather than in Latin.

When Hus spoke out against the Catholic practice of selling indulgences (pardons given by priests to repentant sinners) in order to finance the Great Schism wars, the church responded by ordering Hus to the Council of Constance in 1415, where he found himself brought up on charges of heresy. Hus refused to renounce his beliefs, and, as a result, was burned at the stake on July 6, 1415, even though **Holy Roman Emperor Sigismund** had promised him safe passage back to Prague.

The martyrdom of Jan Hus sparked a religious and nationalist uprising back in Prague, from where it spread like wild fire throughout the Czech lands. In the eye of the storm was **Jan Želivský**, a fiery preacher whose mad-as-hell sermons triggered Prague's **first defenestration**, in which a mob of **Hussites** (as Hus's followers became known as) hurled several Catholic councilors from a window in Prague's New Town Hall. King Václav IV perhaps saved himself a similar fate when, upon hearing he had a revolution on his hands, suffered a heart attack and died.

By the time Václav passed on, the Hussites had already gathered overwhelming support throughout the Czech lands, which they managed to seize control of in no time. Under Emperor Sigismund (Václav IV's brother and next in line to Bohemia's throne), the Holy Roman Empire mounted an all-out crusade against the Czech nation, which they perceived as a heretical threat to the stability of Catholic Europe.

But before the Hussite Wars got underway, a division within the Hussite movement had already begun to undermine its organization. On one hand were the radical **Taborites**, who wanted to rid the world of Catholicism and so proved it by going around burning churches and killing priests. On the other hand were the conservative **Utraquists**, mostly made up of Czech nobility (the Estates) who found the Taborite call to surrender all earthly possessions rather disturbing. Whatever the conflict might have been, it didn't prevent the Hussites, under the ingenious military command of the one-eyed **Jan Žižka**, from giving the bigger and better-armed Holy Roman forces a series of whippings.

With no hope of beating the superior military of the Hussites, Emperor Sigismund was forced to the bargaining table, held at the **Council of Basel** in 1433. The Utraquists handed over the Bohemian throne to Sigismund in exchange for religious tolerance in the Czech lands. The Taborites, who saw this agreement as a sell-out on the part of the Utraquists, went on wreaking havoc on Catholic institutions across Central Europe, but that came to an end when the Utraquists and Catholics joined forces to crush the Taborites at the **Battle of Lipany** in 1434.

Enjoying a wide degree of religious tolerance in ensuing years, the Czechs readily took up the Hussite faith, so much so that by 1458, 70% of those living in the Czechs lands considered themselves Hussites even though the pope still considered them heretics. In spite of the view from Rome, the Czech Estates put the first Hussite (and last Czech) on the Bohemian throne in 1458. This was truly a remarkable occurrence, considering that **King George (Jiří) of Poděbrady** didn't come from a dynastic family and was regarded as a heretic by the rest of Europe.

Nonetheless, George proved to be a ruler light years ahead of his time. He reached out to the rest of Europe, attempting to form a European council that would solve international conflict by diplomacy rather than by warfare. But George's peaceful intentions were met with hostility from all sides, especially from the pope, who called Catholic countries to renew their fight against the Czech heretics. After George's death in 1471, the Czech Estates capitulated and handed the Bohemian throne to the Polish **Jagiellon dynasty**, who ruled over Bohemia until the dynasty went extinct in 1526.

THE HAPSBURGS TAKE OVER - 1526-1800

In 1526, the Czech lands once more came under the Hapsburg dynasty, as the Czech Estates elected **Archduke Ferdinand I** King of Bohemia on the condition that religious tolerance be maintained. Despite his agreement, Ferdinand made the first steps towards the Counter

Reformation by inviting the most radical of Catholics, the Jesuits, to set up churches and missions in the Czech lands. Ferdinand also stripped Prague of its royal charter, relegating it to a provincial town in the Hapsburg empire. But thanks to **Rudolf II**, who took the throne in 1576, Prague regained its prestige. With the Turks knocking at Vienna's back door, Rudolf transferred the Hapsburg seat of power to Prague, ushering in Prague's second golden age. Rudolf endowed the city with a magnificent collection of art and Renaissance architecture, and invited some of Europe's leading minds, such as **Tycho Brahe** and **Johan Kepler**, to conduct their studies in the royal court. Rudolf also ensured religious freedom in the Czech lands when he signed the **Imperial Charter of 1609**, establishing widespread acceptance of all Protestant faiths.

Unfortunately, Rudolf suffered from bouts of insanity, and was forced to abdicate the throne to his brother **Matthias**, who was not so enlightened. Matthias reneged on the Imperial Charter, and, with the help of his successor **Ferdinand II** began chipping away at the religious rights of Protestants. Infuriated at this turn of events, a group of Czech nobles marched to the Prague Castle on May 23, 1618, and threw two Hapsburg councilors out the window. Known as Prague's **second defenestration**, the event went down in history as the catalyst for the **Thirty Years' War**, a complex war in which scores of dynasties and countries were embroiled.

Following the defenestration, the Czech Estates expelled the Hapsburgs from Bohemia and put **Frederick of the Palatinate**, the so-called "Winter King," on the throne. But the Czechs' shaky independence came to an abrupt halt at the **Battle of the White Mountain** in 1620, in which the Hapsburg forces gave a mostly mercenary Czech army a severe thrashing. To add insult to misery, the Hapsburgs ordered the public execution of 27 Czech nobles in Prague's Old Town Square. The nobles who didn't have their heads lopped off were forced into exile, and their property confiscated and handed over to families from countries loyal to the papacy.

During the Thirty Years' War, the Swedes and Saxons laid waste scores of Czech towns (including a good deal of Prague) in their fight against the Hapsburg forces, breaking Bohemia's economy and reducing the population by one-half. After the war, the Hapsburgs made sure that the Czech populace (what was left of it anyhow) came to bear the full brunt of the **Counter Reformation**, a period in which the Czechs look back on as their dark ages. All Protestant religions were outlawed and education was placed in the hands of the fanatical Jesuits. On top of that, Germans poured into the Czech lands and for the next 200 years controlled all civil institutions, relegating Czechs to the lowly status of peasants and artisans.

By the mid-18th century, Czech culture and its language were on the brink of extinction. But a couple of changes, brought on by the **Age of Enlightenment**, prevented that from happening. After expelling the Jesuits from the Hapsburg Empire, **Empress Maria Theresa** made it possible for all Czechs to pursue an education. On top of that, her son **Joseph II** signed the **Edict of Tolerance** of 1781, legalizing Protestant and Orthodox faiths. He also abolished serfdom when a series of peasant uprisings shook the empire in 1775. Though power was still centered in Vienna and German firmly established as the official language in the Czech lands, these reforms nonetheless planted the seeds for the Czech National Revival.

CZECH NATIONAL REVIVAL - 1800-1900

At the dawn of the 19th century, the lucrative production of glass, iron, and coal in Bohemia and Moravia made the Czech lands the focus of the Industrial Revolution in the Hapsburg Empire. Czechs poured into towns and cities from the countryside and a Czech middle class began to form.

In the first half of the century, the Czech cause was taken up mostly in the realm of academics, as **Josef Jungman** and **Josef Dobrovský** set out to reinvigorate the Czech language, elevating its literary value to a level on par with major European languages. At the same time **František Palacký** set upon reviving Czech history, reviving pivotal Czech figures such as Jan Hus and King George of Poděbrady.

Palacký stood at the forefront of the revolution that was to sweep through Central Europe in 1848, organizing the **Pan-Slav Congress** in Prague, in which representatives of the Hapsburg-controlled Slavic nations drew up a comprehensive list of political demands. The Hapsburg reacted to the congress, and to the mass protests raging on Prague's streets, by declaring martial law, effectively curbing (but not crushing) Czech aspirations for independence.

Embroiled in war against Bismarck's Prussia, the Hapsburgs were forced to capitulate to the Hungarian demand for equality in 1867, granting them independence under a dual Austrian-Hungarian monarchy. This event, which did nothing to change the Czechs second-class status, fueled the movement for Czech independence, which at that time had splintered into two major groups – the **Old Czechs** (led by Palacký) and the **Young Czechs**. The Old Czechs strived for the same agreement reached between Austria and Hungary, which would keep them under the Hapsburg monarchy but would give them equal status as an autonomous state. The Young Czechs, on the other hand, wanted nothing more to do with the Hapsburgs, demanding nothing less than complete independence. The most eloquent voice to emerge from this camp was a Charles University professor by the name of **Tomáš Garrigue Masaryk**, a man who was also throwing around the novel idea that the Czechs and Slovaks should, by virtue of their historical ties, unite.

CZECHOSLOVAKIA & THE WORLD WARS - 1914-1945

As the Czechs were hesitantly fighting alongside their old Austrian and Hungarian enemies during WWI, Masaryk was in the United States drumming up Allied support for an independent Czech and Slovak federation. With the help of **Edvard Beneš** and the Slovak **Milan Štefánik**, Masaryk got the approval of the US, France, and England (who were all banking on winning World War I) for the creation of Czechoslovakia – a nation of two equal republics united under one federal government. The Czechs and Slovaks agreed to their union at two historic conferences, held in Cleveland in 1915 and Pittsburgh in 1918. But the Czechs later reneged on making Slovakia a seperate republic, which would cause all sorts of political havoc in coming years.

With the Austro-Hungarian Empire down at its heels following World War I, **Czechoslovakia** was finally realized, declaring its independence on October 28, 1918, and electing Masaryk as its first president. Having acquired nearly 80 percent of Austro-Hungarian industry, Czechoslovakia walked into an unbelievably fortunate economic situation, one that established the country as one of the ten most industrialized nations in the world.

But there were problems from the onset, most notably in the form of ethnic tension. Not only were the two million Slovaks clamoring for more rights, but so were the country's three million Germans and 700,000 Hungarians. Holding it all together was Masaryk, under whom Czechoslovakia became one of the world's most progressive democracies, granting all citizens the right to vote and instituting bilinguality in any region where there was a strong ethnic minority. But the country began to fall apart at the seams once Masaryk finally stepped down in 1935 and the presidency was put in the hands of the Socialist Edvard Beneš.

At the same time, Konrad Henlein's **Sudeten German Party** was consolidating its power with financial backing from Nazi Germany, gaining the most seats of any party in the 1935 parliamentary elections. By 1938, after a series of meetings with Hitler, Henlein was calling for the secession of the Sudetenland into the German Reich, a demand taken up in September 1938, by Hitler himself.

In what was perhaps the biggest sell-out in modern diplomacy, English Prime Minister Neville Chamberlain and French Prime Minister Daladier accepted Hitler's demands, as outlined under the **Munich Agreement,** without hesitation and without first consulting the Czechoslovak government. Beneš, who knew all too well that the Czechoslovak army was no match for the Germans, capitulated to the agreement, resigned as president, and then took off for England, where he later formed a Czechoslovak-government-in-exile. As planned, the Nazis marched into the Sudetenland in October 1938. It was only a matter of months before they would take the rest of the Czech lands and proclaim Bohemia and Moravia a Reich Protectorate, which happened the day after the **Hlinka Slovak National People's Party,** under **Jozef Tiso,** declared independence for Slovakia.

In charge of the Protectorate of Bohemia and Moravia was **Reinhard Heydrich.** Jewish deportation and mass arrests climaxed under his command, which was cut short when parachutists, given their orders by Beneš' London-based government, assassinated him on the outskirts of Prague in June 1942. The results of the assassination were disastrous. The Germans exacted revenge by decimating the town of Lidice and promptly uncovering and quashing whatever underground activity had previously been established in Bohemia and Moravia.

By the end of 1944, Russian troops had liberated much of the country. On May 5, 1945, the people of Prague finally rose up against the Germans, and managed to rid the city of Nazi troops the day before the Red Army officially liberated the city on May 9. General Patton's Third Army had already taken Plzeň, but stayed put on their side of the demarcation line, much to the chagrin of later Czech generations.

COMMUNISM TAKES HOLD - 1945-1968

With blessings from the Americans, British, French, and Soviets, Beneš reestablished Czechoslovakia with himself as president once World War II came to its conclusion in 1945. First thing on his agenda was to expel the German-speaking population from the country, with approval given for it at the post-war Potsdam Conference. Not only were the 2.5 million Germans booted from the country, but their property confiscated and nationalized in keeping with the new Socialist programs instigated by Beneš.

With Western betrayal (i.e. the Munich Agreement) and the Soviet liberation still fresh on their minds, Czechoslovaks began directing their sympathies towards Russia. Communist Party membership boomed, and in the 1946 elections the Party secured 36 percent of the popular vote, obliging Beneš to appoint Communist leader **Klement Gottwald** prime minister and installing a number of other Party members in key cabinet positions. For the time being, Gottwald and his Party still spoke in favor of parliamentary democracy, but that tune changed after Gottwald returned from talks with Stalin in 1947.

The decisive events which were to seal the fate of Czechoslovakia for the next 41 years came in February 1948. After again securing the majority of seats in parliament, the Communist Party declared a false state of emergency, calling on workers to arm themselves against an impending counter-revolution and go on a general strike. On February 25, Gottwald presented to President Beneš his all-Party nominees for cabinet positions. Considering the mass hysteria stirred up by the Party and the Soviet tanks lined up on the border of Hungary, Beneš had little choice but to accept all of Gottwald's nominees. Without a drop of blood spilt, the Communist had thus staged their coup, prompting some two million people to flee to the West.

The Communists wasted no time in drafting and passing a new constitution, one that established the Party's dominance. Refusing to sign it, Beneš resigned in deference to Gottwald, who thus became Czechoslovakia's first Communist president. The Czechoslovak government promptly began Stalinizing the country, initiating an all-out nationalization of industry and collectivization of farms. Party membership became mandatory in order to hold any position of power, as the bourgeoisie found themselves barred from good jobs and their children prevented from getting a university education. It was only a matter of time before the gulag mines were up and running, and "enemies of the revolution" sent there to do heavy labor.

During the early 1950s, the Communists held on to an economically depressed Czechoslovakia by again generating an environment of fear and intimidation. Rumors of counter-revolution, economic sabotage, and Western espionage were spread in the papers and on the airwaves – creating an appropriate atmosphere of hysteria in which to carry out Stalinist purges and show trials, climaxing when 13 leading members of the party, including Foreign Minister **Vladimír Clementis** and Gottwald's right hand-man **Rudolf Slánský**, were executed.

When Stalin died in 1953, Czechoslovakia experienced none of the cultural and political thaw that Russia did. In fact, it took the neo-Stalinist President and First Secretary, **Antonín Novotný**, ten years after Stalin and Gottwald's deaths to make some very lame reprisals for the purges. He also forestalled any headway toward economic liberalization, despite a recession that was shattering Czechoslovakia's economy. Novotný's half-baked New Economic Model of 1965 did little to appease the mounting intra-Party opposition, which had gathered enough steam by early 1968 to oust Novotný (who, incidentally, was later proven to have been an informer for the Gestapo during WWII).

PRAGUE SPRING & NORMALIZATION - 1968-1989

Taking up the position of First Secretary in January 1968, was a young, mild-mannered Slovak by the name of **Alexander Dubček**. He immediately pushed through a number of reform-minded policies that promised to bring about "socialism with a human face." These policies were outlined in April 1968, when the party released its Action Program, which proposed a separate but federated Slovak republic, a democratic parliament, freedom of assembly, and, most astoundingly, the abolition of censorship. Popularly known as the **Prague Spring**, Dubček's initial months in office brought about a cultural blossoming in Czechoslovakia, a period that many Czechs and Slovaks look back on as a blissful time.

But Soviet interference was imminent, as the Kremlin issued threats to the Czechoslovak Communist Party that it better bring itself back into line or else. When it became clear that Czechoslovaks wouldn't bow, the Kremlin ordered the invasion of Czechoslovakia. On the night of August 20-21, 1968, Warsaw Pact forces rumbled into the country. By the end of the day 58 people had lost their lives, and Dubček and other reformers were arrested and flown to Moscow for talks with Brezhnev, returning home broken men. For months after, people took the streets in non-violent protest, peaking when **Jan Palach** set fire to himself on the steps of Prague's National Museum in January 1969.

Dubček managed to stay on as First Secretary until April 1969, when he was replaced by hardliner **Gustav Husák** and sent into domestic exile as a minor official with the Slovak forestry commission. Husák proceeded to wipe out all of Dubček's reforms (except the one that made Slovakia a separate but federated republic), and he weeded out and expelled from the Party some 500,000 members and functionaries who had been in favor of the liberal reforms. As a result of Husák's efforts to "normalize" the country by reinstating totalitarian oppression, more than 150,000 people fled the country before the Iron Curtain clamped shut and once again barricaded Czechoslovakia from the western world.

Husák's virulent secret police, the infamous **StB** (Statní bezpečnost), kept a watchdog's eye on the country throughout the stagnating 1970s and 1980s, quelling just about any organized opposition before it could get off the ground. But there was one opposition force in the country that held Western attention, and therefore couldn't be so effortlessly weeded out.

In 1976, members of Plastic People of the Universe, a rock band at the center of the country's underground music scene, were accused of spreading subversive ideas and brought to trial. In reality, the puritanical leadership wanted to rid society of people who had long hair, played alternative music, and otherwise led "decadent" lives. An assorted group of 243 artists, writers, intellectuals, and former Party members came to the band's defense, signing a public document demanding civil rights for the band members and for Czechoslovak citizens in general. Those who signed this document went on to form **Charter 77**, an organization that monitored human rights abuses in Czechoslovakia. The most prominent and most outspoken member of Charter 77 was the absurdist playwright, **Václav Havel**. Steadfast in their ideals and vigilant in their resistance, Havel and other Charter dissidents endured a decade of constant surveillance, interrogations, and imprisonments. Though Charter 77 managed to expose the corruption of the Communist regime, it unfortunately failed to rouse mass opposition and demonstrations like Poland's Solidarity movement was able to do.

But history would play itself out to the advantage of Charter 77. By the late 1980s, Czechoslovakia's hardline government found itself shunned by its most important ally – the Kremlin, as Mikhail Gorbachev set perestroika in motion. In 1987, **Miloš Jakeš** replaced Husák as General Secretary, introducing a watered-down version of perestroika that did little to appease the voice of opposition that was getting louder and louder as it became more and more apparent that the Berlin Wall was about to crumble. But by the time that happened on November 9, 1989, Czechoslovakia had yet to set spark the revolution that would bring down their Communist government. It would take an unfortunate event to get the revolutionary ball rolling.

THE VELVET REVOLUTION - 1989

On November 17, the official Communist youth group held a state-approved demonstration on Prague's National Avenue commemorating nine Czech students who had been executed exactly 50 years before by the Nazis. About 5,000 of the 50,000 students who participated in the peaceful demonstration were inexplicably clubbed and beaten by the police. Incensed at this unprovoked police violence, Praguers took to the streets in protest, filling Wenceslas Square to capacity every night in the weeks that followed.

Two days after the beatings, opposition groups such as Charter 77 took the initiative to coalesce into **Civic Forum** (Občanské Forum), with Havel at its forefront. Civic Forum organized the mass demonstrations of November which forced the Communist regime to the bargaining table. In addition to demanding the resignation of Communist hardline leaders, Civic Forum called for an inquiry into the November 17 beatings and an amnesty for all political prisoners. In Bratislava, **People Against Violence** (Verejnosť proti nasiliu or VPN) took up the cause for Slovakia, putting forth the same demands and organizing Slovak protests.

After a nation-wide strike and a demonstration of 750,000 people on Prague's Letná Hill (at which Dubček made his first public appearance since being ousted in 1969), **Prime Minister Adamec** promised, but failed to deliver, cabinet positions to a spectrum of non-Party members. Civic Forum and VPN reacted by calling for more demonstrations and another general strike. Wisely, Adamec threw in the towel, leaving **Marián Čalfa** to save whatever dignity the Communist Party had left. On December 10, the day before the planned nationwide strike, Čalfa announced the **Government of National Understanding**, which officially put an end to 42 years of one-party rule in Czechoslovakia.

But there was still one more goal to be met – the election of Václav Havel as president. Posters demanding "Havel na Hrad" (Havel to the Castle) were plastered on walls across the country. And sure enough, the Federal Assembly elected Havel by a unanimous vote on December 29, the same day on which Alexander Dubček was elected speaker of the National Assembly. Again, the passive Czechs had staged a revolution free of bloodshed and violence – a Velvet Revolution, as it were.

THE BIG DIVORCE

Euphoria would probably best characterize the mood in Czechoslovakia going into the 1990s. But there were, and still are, mammoth problems inherited from the previous regime. First off, the country faced a devastated environment, brought on by a Communist commitment to industrialization at any cost. (To this day, parts of North Bohemia and North Moravia are considered the most polluted areas in Europe.) The industry that the Communists did build, once the envy of the Eastern bloc, was a technological dinosaur. And the economy, its condition no longer hidden behind a subterfuge of propaganda, was in shambles.

The new government, mostly made up of members from Civic Forum and VPN (who had together captured 60 percent of the vote in the June 1990 elections), set about rebuilding the economy by passing a restitution law, making it possible for Czechoslovaks to reclaim property that had been confiscated from them (or relatives) after the February 1948 coup. Privatization was, of course, a priority. But just how quickly it should be done was the big question.

It was this very issue that compelled Civic Forum to split in two parties: the left-of-center **Civic Movement** (Občánské hnuti or OH), led by former dissident and foreign minister **Jiří Dienstbier**; and the right-of-center **Civic Democratic Party** (Občanská demokratická strana or

ODS), led by the Thatcherite finance minister **Václav Klaus**. OH pressed for gradual reforms, but Klaus succeeded in pushing through his radical coupon privatization plan instead, allowing all citizens to become share holders of formerly state-owned businesses. Klaus' plan proved to be (for the most part) successful, as the Czech Republic enjoyed the fastest economic growth of any former Eastern bloc country in the early 1990s. His plan also ensured an ODS victory in the June 1992 elections, which propelled Klaus to the position of prime minister.

Slovaks came out of the Velvet Revolution in a much less advantageous position than the Czechs, who held most of the nation's profit-making industry on their side of the country. With the dissolution of the Eastern bloc and the USSR, Slovakia lost the market for its three big money-makers of steel, agriculture, and armaments. This immediately became apparent in the Slovak unemployment rates, which had shot up to 20 percent by 1992 in some parts of the republic, as compared to three or four percent in the Czech Republic (not to mention an amazing one percent in Prague).

Understandably, Slovak resentment of their better-off cousins in the Czech Republic reached fever pitch in just a few short years after the revolution, and finally found a hard-to-ignore voice in the demagogic figure of **Vladimír Mečiar**, leader of his own **Movement for a Democratic Slovakia** (Hnutí za demokratické Slovensko or HZDS), which called for Slovak independence and a much more gradual approach to economic reform that the one Klaus had in mind.

By the time the 1992 elections rolled around, Mečiar had served as prime minister of Slovakia, but had been ousted by the Slovak National Council following revelations of his involvement with the StB (the pre-revolution secret police). But that didn't stop him and his party, which had promised Slovak independence if elected, from gaining the majority of Slovak votes in the election, once again making Mečiar Prime Minister of Slovakia.

In a series of talks between Klaus and Mečiar, Klaus made it clear that he wouldn't budge from the economic reforms he had set in motion, and that if the federation were to stay together, then Slovakia would have to accept that fact. Klaus, who had previously said he supported the federation, effectively turned the tables on Mečiar, indicating to Mečiar that the Czech Republic would rather not carry the burden of Slovakia. In any case, they and their two respective parties agreed to a declaration of sovereignty, even though – according to one poll held at the time – 85 percent of all Czechoslovaks were against the breakup.

President Havel, a strong supporter of the federation all along, called for a referendum. But it didn't happen, and Havel resigned in protest, refusing to preside over the breakup (though he would later accept his election as first president of the Czech Republic). Alas, on January 1, 1993, two new countries – Česká Republika and Slovenská Republika – came into existence.

AFTER THE SPLIT

From 1993 to 1996, the Czech Republic enjoyed a general boost to its overall quality of life – its economy was on a roll, unemployment held to a bare minimum, and inflation kept to a reasonable level. Helping it along was an overwhelming surge in tourism, indicated when the World Tourism Organization announced that the Czech Republic was the most popular tourist destination in the world for 1994 and 1995. According to its statistics, a staggering 100 million people visited the country each of these years! Not bad for a little country in the middle of Europe.

Of course, Klaus's government vigorously campaigned for Czech membership to the European Union. No one knows for sure just when that will happen, but everyone is banking on the Czech Republic being the first of the Eastern bloc countries to get the invitation. The Czech Republic also lobbied for NATO membership.

And it's paid off. In July 1997, the European Commission, issuing its first comprehensive report cards on the economic and democratic progress of the former Communist countries, placed the Czech Republic as the front runner for joining the EU by the year 2000. This report came a week after the Czech Republic, along with Poland and Hungary, received the invitation to join NATO – something that Havel had been vigorously campaigning for since 1994.

July of 1997 was certainly a month of up's and downs for the republic. As the country received the good news concerning EU and NATO membership, the eastern part of the country was experiencing the worst floods of the century, causing an estimated $2 billion worth of damage and laying to waste some 1,600 homes and damaging some 10,000 homes in more than 500 towns and villages.

In 1997, Klaus' cabinet collapsed, the consequence of a funding scandal involving him and his ODS party. A caretaker cabinet, formed by interim Prime Minister **Josef Tosovky**, led the country from November 1997 to an early election in June 1998, in which the Social Democrats (ČSSD) and its leader **Miloš Zeman** garnered the most votes. ČSSD, however, was unable to form a coalition with other left-of-center parties. In a deal brokered between ČSSD and Klaus' ODS party (which received the second most votes), Zeman became prime minister and Klaus chairman of parliament. The election represented the first shift to the left since the fall of Communism, the consequence of an economy that has declined sharply beginning in 1997, when the currency was floated and unemployment rose to 4.5%. (At the end of 1998, it stood close to 10%.) Despite the shift in ideology, the new government has pledged to maintain efforts to join NATO and the European Union.

All in all, the Czech Republic has firmly entrenched itself in democracy and free market capitalism, having come out of their 41-year freeze well intact.

UNDER THE MAGYARS • 896-1514

Slovakia's early history departs from that of the Czech lands when the Great Moravian Empire ceased to exist in 896. Having lost its Czech allegiance, the empire under **Bratislav** was reduced to present-day Slovakia when Poles attacked from the east and Magyars (Hungarians) from the south, the latter seizing all of Slovakia by 1018. The Magyars wasted little time in comfortably ensconcing themselves as warlords over a Slovak peasantry, sealing the fate of Slovakia for the next millennium as an integral part the Hungarian Kingdom.

The 13th century brought waves of Tatar attacks from the east, leaving Slovakia (and the rest of Hungary) in tatters. But the Magyars, under the **Árpád dynasty**, regrouped, and proceeded to build an economy by inviting German miners and craftsman to found and develop towns in Slovakia such as Banská Bystrica and Levoča.

Uprisings again and again punctuate Slovakia's history under the Magyars, but none were so successful as **Matúš Čák's** rise as self-appointed "King of the Váh and the Tatras" in the early 14th century. A renegade warlord based in the Trenčín Castle in West Slovakia, Čák ruled over a fief that came to include much of present-day Slovakia. Suffering only one military defeat during his lifetime, he held at bay the royal forces of Emperor John of Luxembourg and Hungarian King Charles Robert. But Čák's mini-kingdom died with him in 1321.

Another Slovak attempt to break free of Magyar rule came in 1514, when **Juraj Dáža** and his army of 50,000 peasants rose up against their Hungarian warlords. That, however, proved to be a blood bath, when royal troops moved in and violently quelled the rebellion.

THE HAPSBURGS TAKE OVER - 1526-1800

In 1526, Hungarian **King Ludvík II** lost his life (and most of Hungary) to the Ottoman Turks at the Battle of Mohács. The Hungarian Diet filled the power vacuum by handing the Hungarian crown to the Austrian Hapsburg, **Ferdinand I**, who already had two crowns – that of the Holy Roman Empire and the Kingdom of Bohemia. But Ferdinand had worn the Hungarian crown for ten short years before the Ottoman Turks sacked the Hungarian capital of Buda (of the modern-day Budapest). Capital status fell to Bratislava as a result, giving Slovakia a much-needed cultural and economic boost. But when the Hapsburg and Polish forces expelled the Turks from Buda and drove them out of Central Europe in 1683, Bratislava lost its capital status, as Buda once again became the seat of Hungarian rule.

For the next century, Slovakia remained a bastion of feudalism in the Hungarian Kingdom, with the Slovaks playing the role of serfs to their Magyar lords. But all-out Hungarian exploitation of the Slovaks was held in check by Vienna, to which the Hungarians first had to answer.

The 18th-century Enlightenment did little to further the Slovak cause, other than prompt **Empress Maria Theresa** to grant the Slovak peasantry the right to receive an education. The Enlightenment also brought about a Hungarian national revival, which was largely xenophobic in its outlook and condescending to Slovaks. Condemnation was so harsh that any Slovak who wanted to rise above their peasant origins had to become "Magyarized" in order to do so.

SLOVAK NATIONAL REVIVAL - 1800-1913

For the most part, the Industrial Revolution passed Slovakia by. The country remained largely agrarian, which did more than anything to keep the feudal system in place and prevent any Slovak middle class from forming. Thus, the National Revival was left to a small group of Slovak intellectuals, most of whom were Protestant, virulently anti-Hungarian, and firmly pan-Slavic. At the forefront of the revival was **Ľudovít Štúr**, a pivotal figure in the establishment of the Slovak written language at the turn of the 19th century (until then Slovaks had used Czech as their written language).

The 1848 revolution in Central Europe drove the Hapsburgs from the Hungarian Kingdom, allowing for a brief constitutional government to take over in Budapest. Štúr, who had managed to become the only Slovak in the Hungarian Diet, submitted his "Demands of the Slovak Nation" to the government, only to see it scoffed at by the Diet. Infuriated at the Hungarians, Štúr and his small rebel army threw their support behind the Hapsburgs, who by August 1849 had regained Hungary with the assistance of the Russian Tsar's army. Perhaps as a reward for his support, the Hapsburgs agreed to Štúr's demand that serfdom be abolished in Slovakia. But that was about all that Štúr got out of the Hapsburgs. Despite the abolition of serfdom, the Slovaks remained essentially second-class citizens, something they tried to change when they issued the **Martin Memorandum** in 1861, requesting from the Austrian parliament that they establish a North Hungarian district with Slovak as the official language. Though it was flatly ignored in Vienna, the memorandum did bring about **Matica slovenská**, a cultural and educational institution set up in the town of Martin to promote the Slovak language through education, literature, and the arts. But that lasted only until 1867 – the year Austria had to submit to a dual monarchy and grant Hungary equal status under a newly-formed Austro-Hungarian Empire.

Instead of the heavy Germanization the Slovaks had to undergo after 1848, they now endured an even harsher Magyarization, in which Hungarian alone became the official language in Slovak schools and other institutions. On top of that, crops began to fail and hunger set in, creating a situation that, by 1914, had compelled 20 percent of the Slovak population to emigrate to the United States and Canada.

SLOVAK NATIONALISM - 1918-1993

The **Pittsburgh Agreement of 1918** guaranteed Slovakia status as a separate republic under a Czechoslovak federation. But the Czechs reneged on the agreement once it came around to actually establishing the Czechoslovak state. Thus, from the beginning of the Czech and Slovak marriage, there was resentment on the part of the Slovaks towards their Czech cousins, resentment voiced loudest by **Andrej Hlinka** and his **Slovak People's Party**.

Hlinka, a Catholic priest, already had a reputation for his caustic opposition to Magyar rule. And when it became clear that the Slovaks had gotten the short end of the Czechoslovak stick, Hlinka came out raging, calling for Slovak independence. But the Slovaks were enjoying their first taste of freedom too much to give Hlinka and his party much thought. When the Great Depression set in and Prague centralization became too much to bear, however, support mounted for an independent Slovak state.

On March 14, 1939, the day before the Nazis occupied Bohemia and Moravia, the Slovak dream for independence became a reality. The leader of this state was **Jozef Tiso**, another Catholic priest who had taken over the reigns of the renamed Hlinka Slovak National People's Party. Backed by the German Reich, Tiso's fascist government followed the Nazi lead, banning all opposition parties and silencing any criticism with all-out censorship. Tiso even went as far as to establish his own version of the SS – the **Hlinka Guards**, put in charge of the terrorization and mass deportation of Slovak Jews (which, by the end of the war, amounted to 73,000 people).

This government, of course, was nothing more than a Nazi puppet state, prompting the London-based Czechoslovak government-in-exile to take steps to bring it down. In 1944, it sent orders to **Lieutenant-Colonel Ján Golian** to form an army of resistance, which he did by amassing a group of Slovak army deserters, escaped prisoners, and Soviet partisans in the mountain town of Banská Bystrica. Known as the **Slovak National Uprising** (Slovenské národné povstanie or SNP), the attempted coup brought down Tiso's government, but was suppressed by the German army after two months of heavy fighting, resulting in the loss of 30,000 Slovak lives and horrendous Nazi reprisals – all of which ended when the Soviets liberated the country in April 1945. Despite its ill fate, the Slovak National Uprising is today commemorated virtually everywhere you go in Slovakia, evident in the scores of streets, squares, bridges, and monuments that bear the uprising's name.

After the war, Communism came to Slovakia undesired by most Slovaks, people who have always been devoutly Catholic and thus wary of any ideology that took atheism as its basic tenet. It wasn't surprising then that Gottwald's Communist Party failed to get more than 30 percent of the Slovak vote in the 1946 elections, while the Democrats succeeded in getting the majority. But Slovakia's vote counted for little, as it still hadn't gained autonomy as a separate republic in the Czechoslovak federation. That would change, however, during the Prague Spring of 1968, when First Secretary **Alexander Dubček** authorized Slovakia's federalization, providing Slovakia with more freedom to conduct its own affairs. It was, in fact, the only one of Dubček's reforms to survive Gustav Husák's counter-reforms. But the scales of power still weighed in favor of the Czech Republic, even after the Velvet Revolution broke the country of one-party rule and brought democracy to Slovakia.

SLOVAKIA AFTER THE BIG SPLIT

"Slovakia is yours," proclaimed **Vladimír Mečiar** as the bells chimed in 1993 on Bratislava's SNP Square, where 50,000 people had amassed to celebrate their first moments of Slovak independence.

But the shouts of joy on the square that night were not echoed in the country's southern regions, where 600,000 ethnic Hungarians feared that the nationalist wave Slovakia was currently riding would crash into them. (Their fears later proved to be well founded, as parliament passed laws banning bilingual signs and restricting Hungarian language on radio and television.)

Many ethnic Slovaks also soon grew disenchanted with their newly established independence, owing to Mečiar's policies. First, he immediately slowed privatization to a snail's pace, forestalling any possible economic growth. Second, he began silencing those who criticized him and his policies, which he did by gaining government control over a good chunk of the national media and firing the editorial boards that spoke out against him and his party, Movement for a Democratic Slovakia (**HZDS**). Mečiar's autocratic methods even began to wear on members of the HZDS, to which they responded by joining opposition parties. Within 16 months of the breakup, almost all of Mečiar's ministers and all but one HZDS parliament member changed parties. By March, 1994 the parliament had had enough of Mečiar, and passed a vote of no-confidence, effectively ousting him from office.

Mečiar's former foreign minister, **Jozef Moravčik**, took over as prime minister, and presided over an interim government that would stay in place until the September 1994 elections. The government swiftly voted for a second wave of across-the-board privatization, which went into effect immediately. This did wonders for Slovakia's economy, which suddenly and inexplicably began to outperform the Czech Republic's.

But Mečiar, a former professional boxer, would not be kept out of the ring for long. He rebuilt the HZDS party, and came back to win the September elections with 36 percent of the vote – the first time in European politics that a prime minister has twice been dismissed from office and twice re-elected.

From 1994 to 1998, tension between Mečiar and his opposition (led mainly by President Michal Kováč) was at fever pitch. Mečiar openly discredited the president, and attempted to oust Kováč in revenge for initiating the no-confidence vote passed on Mečiar in March 1994. The tension was so tight that the prime minister and the president refused to speak to one another.

And in the midst of all this tension, something bizarre happened. On August 31, 1995 the president's 34-year-old son, Michal Kováč Jr., was kidnapped near Bratislava and dumped in the Austrian town of Hainburg. There, he was taken into police custody in response to an international warrant for Kováč Jr.'s arrest – issued by German authorities for his alleged role in swindling $2.3 million from a giant import-export business based in Bratislava. Opposition politicians and newspapers blamed Mečiar and his secret service for the kidnapping, calling it and the charges against Kováč Jr. a ploy to discredit the president. Their accusations became hard to ignore when an agent for the secret service later confessed to helping in the kidnapping. Mečiar, of course, denied any involvement, but was facing a majority in polls who thought he had something to do with it.

In the spring of 1998, Kovač's term ended. With the parliament unable to agree on a new president, Mečiar assumed many of the responsibilities of the office, including the power to grant amnesty, which he did for a number of people involved in the kidnapping case. This essentially brought the case to an end, as did the murder of a key witness. But it also increased NATO and the European Community's doubt about Slovakia's democratic status. Both organizations consequently excluded Slovakia from the first round of membership talks.

In October 1998, the Slovak people finally decided enough was enough, giving the opposition a majority of votes and effectively ending Mečiar and his party's stranglehold on the country. The new government, headed by **Mikuláš Dzurinda** of the Christian Democratic Movement, has begun to turn the country around, dismantling the regime that Mečiar built. In what direction the Slovak Republic goes from here has yet to be determined, but it's sure to be more democratic, more European mainstream.

6. PLANNING YOUR TRIP

WHEN TO GO

There are three factors you'll want to take into account as you plan your visit to the Czech and Slovak republics: the weather, climate, and crowds.

The summers can get uncomfortably hot, with temperatures getting up into the mid-80s during the day and seemingly getting no better for days on end. The nights bring some relief, but not a whole lot. And when it isn't hot, it's raining. Hard. But the worst thing about the summers are the crowds, especially in Prague's historic center, which becomes an utter mob scene in July and August. If you don't reserve far enough in advance, you'll be lucky to get a centrally-located room in Prague or in other tourist hotspots during that time.

The winters in the republics are pretty glum. The temperatures regularly drop below freezing (and below zero in the mountains) and the skies are almost always overcast. What makes things even worse is the air, which gets downright disgusting in the cities thanks to the coal smoke and diesel exhaust. It does snow often in the mountains and in the lowlands, which is good news for skiers and for people who like to breath clean air once in a while. The crowds are down to a bare minimum during the winter, as are hotel rates. The big exception to this is the Christmas-New Year's holiday, when the mob scene returns to Prague.

Another exception are the ski resorts, which are pretty busy all winter long, but are a nightmare during the holidays when all Central Europeans seemingly drop in. Also remember that many museums, castles, and other attractions (except for those in Prague, Bratislava, and the other major cities) are closed during the winter.

The spring and autumn are perhaps the most pleasant times of year to travel in the republics. The skies are blue and the temperatures are mild (and even a little nippy at night). It does rain frequently then, but not as bad as in late June or July. Best of all, the crowds are down to a manageable level.

So, the most ideal times to plan your visit to the republics are April, May, early June, September, and early October – in late October you're flirting with the possibility of freezing temperatures.

WHAT TO PACK

This depends on your form of transport through the two republics. If you're going by car, then you can allow yourself more luggage. But if you're going to be using trains and buses, then you should try to follow that age-old adage: get it down to a bare minimum and then cut it in half.

You won't see much of the republics if you're not on your feet walking, so do come with some sturdy, comfortable shoes. The cobblestones in Prague and other towns can wear your shoes out in no time, so make sure yours have got plenty of miles left in them. You'll also probably want to bring one nice suit, dress, or anything else that won't make you feel out of place in a fancy restaurant or at the theater.

Pickpocketing is rampant in Prague and other tourist hotspots, so be sure to bring a money belt of some kind in which to store your cash, travelers' checks, passport, and credit cards. If you lose your passport, a photocopy of it can save you a lot of hassle at the embassy.

MAKING RESERVATIONS

As soon as you know when you're visiting Prague, call and make hotel reservations. Hotels, especially in the center, book up months in advance. Don't wait until you get there to make reservations, or else you'll most likely end up staying somewhere in the boonies. If you have an itinerary in mind, then go ahead and make reservations for hotels at other destinations as well. (For information about calling the two republics from the US or Canada, see "Telephones, Telegraphs, & Faxes" in Chapter 7, *Basic Information*).

Čedok and **Slovak Travel Service** (see below) can book rooms for you, which will save you the hassle of dealing with someone on the phone who doesn't speak English.

Travel Specialists & Agents

Čedok offers a wide range of package tours through the Czech Republic (as well as other Central European countries). Contact them in the US at *10 E. 40th St., Suite #3604, New York, NY 10016 (Tel. 800/800-8891 or 212/689-9720); in Prague at Na příkopě 18, 111 35 Praha 1 (Tel. 420/2/241 971 11)*.

Slovak Travel Service, at *10 E. 40th St., Suite 3601, New York, NY 10016 (Tel. 800/753-0582 or 212/213-3865)*, can arrange individual or group itineraries to Slovakia and other parts of Central Europe.

Fugazy International in New Jersey *(Tel. 800/828-4488)* also has package tours to both republics and East Europe, as does **Paul Laifer Tours** *(Tel. 800/346-6314)*. **Land of the Lakes Tours** in Great Britain offers a small-group, luxury tour of Prague and the Czech Republic. You can contact them by calling *800/441-2558* (toll free from the US and Canada) or by writing to them at *4 Green Moss, Oakthwaite Road, Windermere, Cumbria, LA23 2BB, Great Britain.*

There are a couple of agents offering bicycle tours that go through the two republics. These are: **Romantic Czech Tours**, *266 N.E. 45th St., Seattle, WA 98105 (Tel. 888/547-4376;* and **Backroads**, *1516 5th St., Suite A431, Berkeley, CA 94710 (Tel. 800/GO-ACTIVE or 510/527-1555).*

STUDY TOURS/LANGUAGE LEARNING PROGRAMS

Interhostel (for adults over 50) and **Familyhostel** (for parents, children, and grandparents) offer study tours of the Czech Republic in which you'll learn from local university professors about Czech people, culture, art, history, and philosophy. Write Interhostel at *6 Garrison Ave., Durham, NH 03824 or call 800/733-9753.*

If you have the gumption to learn some Czech while there, look into the intensive Czech courses offered to foreigners by the Charles University in Prague. Write **Fakulta Filosofická Karlova Universita**, *náměstí Jana Palacha 2, Prague 1, Czech Republic.*

PASSPORTS & VISAS

Americans need only show a current passport for entering either republic for a stay of up to 30 days. Canadians need only show a current passport for a stay in either republic for up to 180 days. Americans who would like to stay longer than 30 days and Canadians who would like to stay longer than 180 days should contact a Czech/Slovak embassy or consulate to ask how to apply for a long-stay visa.

In the US:

• **Czech Embassy,** *3900 Spring of Freedom St. NW, Washington, D.C. 20008 (Tel. 202/274-9100)*

• **Slovak Embassy,** *2201 Wisconsin Ave. NW, Washington D.C. 20007 (Tel. 202/965-5164)*

In Canada:

• **Czech Embassy,** *541 Sussex Dr., Ottawa, Ontario K1N 6Z6 (Tel. 613/562-3875)*

• **Slovak Embassy,** *50 Rideau Terrace, Ottawa, Ontario K1M 2A1 (Tel. 613/749-2496)*

CUSTOMS

Arriving

On entering either republic, you are allowed, duty free, up to 3,000 Kč/Sk (about $120/$102) worth of goods, as well as up two liters of wine, a liter of booze, and 250 cigarettes. But most likely you'll sail right through customs, at least at the Prague airport, where they rarely even ask if you have anything to declare. On occasion, Czech and Slovak authorities will check your bag, but only to keep up appearances.

Departing

Before you buy anything real expensive in either republic, find out how much it will cost to take out of the country. This way you won't be surprised if you get levied a huge duty for that set of crystal or glassware you bought. Officially, you're allowed 500 Kč/Sk worth of consumer goods duty-free (about $20/$17 at going exchange rates), after which you supposedly have to pay a 20 percent tax. In practice, this is rarely ever done, unless you're spotted with big boxes labeled "Fragile – Crystal."

Also, it's forbidden to export any antiques that are considered genuine. I can't imagine that many Czech customs officials know genuine from generic. But again, play it safe and find out if the antique you want is exportable. You can do that by contacting a curator at the **National Museum in Prague,** *Tel. 02/242 304 85,* or **National Museum in Bratislava,** *Tel. 07/311 444,* or at the **Museum of Decorative Arts in Prague,** *Tel. 02/248 112 41.*

US Customs Requirements

As a US resident, you are allowed, duty-free, no more than one liter of alcohol (of any kind), and no more than 200 cigarettes or 100 cigars (no Cuban ones at all, however). Baked, canned, and cured goods are allowed, but other fresh food is forbidden. All plants (even cuttings and seeds) must be declared. If you are carrying more than $10,000 in currency of any kind, that too must be declared.

You are allowed a total exemption of $400 worth of items, after which you will be asked to pay a flat ten percent duty on the next $1,000 worth of goods. If the value of your goods total more than $1,400, then you'll have to pay a duty assessed to each particular item. Duty can be paid by cash, check, and, in some locations, credit cards. Travelers' checks can be used if the checks do not total more than $50 over your assessed duty.

For more information, call 703/318-5900 in the Washington, D.C. area or 02/245 108 47 in Prague.

GETTING TO THE CZECH & SLOVAK REPUBLICS

The quickest and easiest way to reach the Czech Republic is to fly to Prague. But the only direct flights to Prague from the US and Canada are offered by ČSA (Czech Airlines), servicing Newark, Montreal, and Toronto; and by **Delta Airlines**, with flights from New York to Prague with a stopover in Stuttgart. The number for ČSA in the US and Canada is *Tel. 800/628-6107*, in Prague *Tel. 02/201 043 10*. The number for Delta in the US and Canada is *Tel. 800/221-1212*, in Prague *Tel. 02/242 810 40*.

Here are some airlines that fly from the US and Canada to Europe and have connecting flights to Prague:

• **Air France**, with direct flights to/from Paris *(Tel. 800/237-2747, Prague 02/242 271 64)*

• **Austrian Airlines**, with direct flights to/from Vienna *(Tel. 800/843-0002, Prague 02/201 141 87)*

• **British Airways**, with direct flights to/from London *(Tel. 800/433-7300, Prague 02/201 135 45)*

• **Lufthansa**, with direct flights to/from Frankfurt *(Tel. 800/645-3880, Prague 02/248 110 07)*

• **Northwest/KLM**, with direct flights to/from Amsterdam *(Tel. 800/225-2525, Prague 02/242 286 78)*

• **Swissair**, with direct flights to/from Zürich and Geneva *(Tel. 800/221-4750, Prague 02/248 121 11)*

At present, there are no airlines with direct services to Bratislava from North America. But the charter airline, Tatra Air, does have flights from Zürich, Switzerland to Bratislava and Košice. For reservations, call **Tatra Air**, *Tel. 07/292 306 in Bratislava*.

If Bratislava is your first destination from the US or Canada, it's easiest then to fly to Vienna's Schwechat Airport, and from there you can take an Austrian Airlines shuttle or regular bus to Bratislava (see "Arrivals & Departures" in the section on Bratislava below). Or you may just want to fly directly from Prague to Bratislava aboard ČSA, which has several direct flights departing daily.

FROM PRAGUE AIRPORT TO THE CITY

Taking a cab from the airport to the center of town used to be a risky venture. Cab drivers charged as much as they figured they could get out of a passenger. The city has apparently cracked down, fixing the price at 250 Kč for the ride – a fair deal at about $8.

Another possibility is to take the **ČSA shuttle** from the airport to the airline office in Old Town (near the Náměstí Republiky metro station). The shuttle, which costs 30 Kč (around $1), runs both ways ever half hour between 7:30 a.m. and 7:30 p.m. and takes about 30 minutes. Cheaper yet is to take **city bus #119** to Dejvická metro station, from where you can take a metro, tram, or cheaper cab to your hotel. It departs about every 30 minutes and takes about 25 minutes to reach Dejvická. Buy your 12 Kč-ticket (40 cents) at one of the airport newsstands.

GETTING AROUND THE
CZECH & SLOVAK REPUBLICS
By Air
ČSA, *Tel. 02/201 043 10 in Prague,* flies from Prague to Brno and to the Slovak cities of Bratislava and Košice. In addition to ČSA, there are a couple of charter air companies with services within and between the two republics. **Tatra Air,** *Tel. 07/292 306 in Bratislava,* services Bratislava, Košice, and the Czech city of Brno. **Air Ostrava,** *Tel. 02/240 327 31 in Prague,* services Prague, Brno, and Ostrava.

By Bicycle
If you are an avid cyclist, then I would highly recommend seeing the two republics by bicycle. It can be a sensational way to go, especially around West and South Bohemia and South Moravia: the spa towns of West Bohemia, the foothills of the Šumava Mountains in southwestern Bohemia, the lake region in and around the town of Třeboň in southeastern Bohemia, and the Pálava and Moravian Slovácko regions in South Moravia. In these areas are plenty of backroads to be explored and strings of quaint villages, chateaux, and castles to be discovered. And in South Moravia are hundreds of vineyards and wine caves where you can stop off to sample the local *víno.*

Mountain bikers will be happy to know that you can actually bike from Prague to Vienna through South Bohemia and South Moravia along a series of trails put together by the Czech Greenways. For more information on the Greenways, see the *Eco-Tourism & Travel Alternatives* chapter.

Another excellent region for cycling is Central and East Slovakia. But you need to be in excellent shape in order to conquer this mountainous landscape. Some of the roads, especially around the High Tatras, can be grueling, but worth the sensational alpine scenery.

You can take your bike on the train. What you need to do is present your train ticket and your bicycle at the train station luggage office. They'll have you fill out a tag with your name and destination, charge you ten percent of the regular fare, and then hand you a slip which you must have in order to later claim your bike. Before you get on the train, wait and see in which freight car they put your bike. And when you get to your destination, go immediately to that car and claim your bike. Simple as that.

By Bus

If you don't have your own wheels, bus is usually the easiest, cheapest, and fastest way to get around the republics. ČAD (Česká autobusová doprava, or Czech Bus Transport) serves just about every town in the Czech Republic, while SAD (Slovenská autobusová doprava) does the same for Slovakia. *For bus information in the Czech Republic, call ČAD in Prague at Tel. 02/242 110 60. In Slovakia, call SAD in Bratislava at Tel. 07/212 222.*

In the Czech Republic, there's also Čebus, a private company servicing Prague and Brno. *Call them in Prague at Tel. 02/248 116 76 for information.*

The biggest problem going by bus (and by train) is deciphering the highly complicated timetables. The timetables used by ČAD and SAD show you the destinations, times of departures and arrivals, and a bunch of symbols designating what day a certain bus does or doesn't run. There's also a key (always in Czech or Slovak) to these symbols, which you must refer to again and again in order to figure out if your bus is running or not. Needless to say, you can go absolutely batty reading these timetables, no matter how good your Czech or Slovak is.

So instead of trying to decipher the hieroglyphics, head to the information counter with the big "I" over it and tell the clerk your destination. Most likely that clerk will not be able to speak English. So you may want to write down the date (day then month) and time (in military style, for example: 20.00 equals 10 pm, 14.00 equals 2 pm) you'd like to leave, and then the clerk will offer you the closest thing.

Easier still would be to just drop into the nearest tourist information office, which almost always has an English speaker and bus schedule on hand.

If you are traveling long distance or between the two republics, you'll need to purchase your ticket ahead of time at the bus station. If you're traveling a short distance within one of the republics, then you can buy your ticket on board from the driver. Just tell him your destination and he'll hand you a little ticket with the price written on it.

The center of the Czech bus network is Prague's **Florenc Station**. All international buses arriving and departing Prague do so here. If you are heading out of Prague to someplace in the Czech Republic or Slovakia, then chances are you'll catch your bus here. Florenc is located on the northeastern edge of the Nové Město district on *Křižíkova Street*, accessed by taking the metro or tram to Florenc metro station.

In addition to Florenc, there are eight obscure bus terminals in Prague, serving particular nearby regions. You'll find them at these metro stations: **Anděl, Hradčanská, Nádraží Holešovice, Palmovka, Roztyly, Smíchovské nádraží**, and **Želivského**. None of these terminals have information offices, so you'll want to call the ČAD number given above or ask at Florenc station for times and places of departure (chances are you'll find someone who speaks English working here).

By Car
If you are only going to Prague, do yourself a favor and drop the idea of having a car. Finding your way around Prague's narrow streets and lanes while trying to avoid trams can be a nightmare. On top of that, parking is a headache, theft is commonplace, and accidents happen all the time.

But a car can be a blessing in other parts of the Czech Republic and in Slovakia. Obviously, you can see a lot more, as many out-of-the-way castles, chateaux, and villages are just not accessible by train or bus, and if they are, they require a number of time-consuming changes. The thick network of backroads in the two republics are fairly good and fairly safe, taking you through many picturesque valleys, forests, mountains, and villages. Czech and Slovak drivers are generally courteous and safe (not at all like the many Germans on the roads, who are used to driving at a demon's pace on their autobahn).

Some rules of the road to remember: Czech and Slovak laws require that drivers have a zero percent blood-alcohol level (which means you can't have a drop to drink if you're driving); children under 12 must sit in the back seat; and all passengers must wear a seatbelt (which means there can only be as many passengers in a car as there are seatbelts).

To rent a car, all you need is a driver's license from your state or province. Rental agencies provide the insurance at an extra charge. There's a big difference in what agencies charge per day. The familiar American ones generally charge a lot more than the Czech and Slovak ones.

If you want to do some comparison shopping, which I highly recommend doing, here are some agencies in Prague you can try:
- **Alamo,** *Prague Airport; Tel. 02/201 135 34*
- **Budget,** *náměstí Curieových 5/43 (Hotel Inter-Continental), Prague 1; Tel. 02/248 899 95*
- **Car Service** (with limousine service), *Výstaviště Exhibition Grounds, Prague 7; Tel. 02/201 036 25*
- **Europcar,** *Pařížská 28, Prague 1; 02/ 248 105 15*
- **Hertz,** *Karlovo náměstí 28, Prague 2; Tel. 02/297 836*
- **Avis,** *Prague Airport; Tel. 02/231 55 15*
- **Czechocar,** *5 května 65, Prague 4; Tel. 02/612 220 79*

By Train

The big train company for the Czech Republic is **ČD** (České drahy or Czech Railways) and its Slovak counterpart is **ŽSR** (Železnica Slovenskej republiky or Railways of the Slovak Republic), and together they form a network considered one of Europe's densest.

Czech and Slovak trains go just about everywhere, stopping in the dinkiest of towns and villages. Traveling by them can be a fun, pretty, and even romantic way to go. But it can be time-consuming and inconvenient, especially when not traveling between major railroad hubs. Going even a short distance often requires one or two changes and a long layover. And compared to West European trains, the ones in the Czech and Slovak republics can be slow, sometimes tediously so. Also, the train interiors tend to get overheated, a little grimy, and overcrowded, especially on weekends (for obvious reasons).

There are some train classifications you should know about in choosing which trains you want to take or avoid. Quickest and most expensive is *expres* or *rychlík* (fast) trains. These are shown in red on the big signs announcing arrivals and departures. "Speeded trains" (*spěšný vlak*) stop more often and cost a little less, while local trains (*osobní vlak*) stop at every dinky station on the line – but tickets for local trains are dirt cheap.

For information about ČD fares and destinations, call Tel. 02/242 176 54 in Prague. For information about ŽSR fares and destinations, call Tel. 07/204 4484 in Bratislava.

Train timetables are a lot like bus timetables (see above), but have twice as many symbols designating the days certain trains do and don't run. Again, save yourself from going cross-eyed and head to the information counter or drop into a tourist information office. Or call ČD or ŽSR.

As the center of the Czech train network, Prague has several stations. Unless you're heading for some obscure part of the country, you're more than likely going to depart from one of the first two stations listed below.

Hlavní nádraží, *three blocks north of Wenceslas Square on Wilsonova street (metro or tram #5 or 9 to Hlavní nádraží station); tel 02/242 176 54.* Prague's main station, where most international and domestic trains arrive and depart. If you're coming from West Europe, this is where you'll probably arrive. Avoid hanging around here at night.

Nádraží Holešovice, *north of the historic center in the district of Holešovice (metro or tram to Nádraží Holešovice station); Tel. 02/246 158 65.* Servicing Budapest, Berlin, Bucharest, and several regions in the Czech Republic.

Smíchovské nádraží, *southwest of the historic center in the district of Smíchov (metro or tram to Smíchovské nádraží station); Tel. 02/246 150 86.* Servicing mostly West Bohemia.

Masarykovo nádraží, *on the northern edge of the historic center in the district of Nové Město (take metro to Náměstí Republiky station or tram to Masarykovo nádraží stop); Tel. 02/242 242 00.* Only domestic trains arrive and depart here, usually to/from East Bohemia.

FOR MORE INFORMATION

There is no official Czech tourist bureau in the US, but the unofficial office is called the **Czech Center,** *1109 Madison Ave., New York, NY 10028 (Tel. 212/288-0830).*

For more information about the Slovak Republic, contact the **Slovak Information Center,** *406 E. 67th St., New York, NY 10021 (Tel. 212/737-3971).*

7. BASIC INFORMATION

BUSINESS HOURS

Don't expect the 24-hour conveniences of America when you travel through the two republics. Business hours, though they vary from cities to smaller towns, generally stick to the nine-to-five regimen. In Prague, however, you can usually get whatever you need at all hours of the night, but not without some effort.

Government offices are open from 8:30 a.m. to 5 p.m., Monday through Friday. Tourist offices have the same hours, but tend to stay open on Saturdays. Museums, castles, chateaux, and other tourist attractions usually close on Mondays, their hours depending on the season. Post offices, except for the 24-hour main post office in Prague, are open 8:30 a.m. to 6 p.m. on weekdays and until noon on Saturdays.

Banks and most shops not selling food or tobacco are open from 9 a.m. to 5 or 6 p.m. on weekdays and sometimes until noon on Saturday. *Potravinys* (grocery stores), *zelininas* (produce shops) *tabacs* (tobacco shops), and *trafikas* (tobacco shops with newsstands) have longer hours, and are generally open from 7 a.m. to 6 p.m. on weekdays and until noon on Saturday.

Restaurants generally open for lunch around 11 a.m. and stay open until 10 or 11 p.m. They are usually open on Sundays. Pubs, on the other hand, are sure to be open every day from around 10 a.m. until 11 p.m., or whenever the beer runs out.

COST OF TRAVEL

In comparison to North America, the cost of travel in the Czech and Slovak republics is affordable, sometimes to the point of being dirt cheap. The big exceptions to this are Prague, the spa towns of West Bohemia, and the ski resorts in the Tatra Mountains – places where you pay Western prices at most hotels and at some of your fancier restaurants.

NATIONAL HOLIDAYS
Czech Republic

Most everything – except for pubs, restaurants, and museums – is closed on these following holidays in the Czech Republic:

January 1

Easter Sunday and Monday

May 1 – the biggest day of the year when Czechoslovakia was Communist, now merely Labor Day.

May 8 – commemoration of Czech liberation of Prague in 1945 (used to be May 9 – the day Soviets marched in).

July 5 – the day on which Cyril and Methodius supposedly introduced Christianity and a written language to the Slavs.

July 6 – the day Jan Hus was burned at the stake.

October 8 – anniversary of the founding and independence of Czechoslovakia.

December 24-26 – Christmas

Slovak Republic

Almost nothing, except for restaurants and museums, is open on these following holidays in the Slovak Republics:

January 1 – New's Year Day and anniversary of the founding of the Slovak Republic in 1993.

January 6 – official end to the Christmas season.

Easter Friday, Sunday, and Monday

May 1 – see sidebar on Czech holidays.

July 5 – see sidebar on Czech holidays.

August 29 – commemorates beginning of the ill-fated Slovak National Uprising in 1944.

September 1 – commemorates founding of Slovak constitution in 1992.

September 15 – St. Mary's Day (I told you the Slovaks were heavily Catholic)

November 1 – All Saints' Day

December 24-26 – Christmas

Public transportation within cities and between towns is a steal in both republics. For example, a one-way train ticket from Prague to Brno (a 196-kilometer or 122-mile trip) costs about 100 Kč, which is roughly the equivalent of $4. And in Prague, one ticket for the metro, tram, or bus costs 12 Kč – roughly the equivalent of 40 cents.

Because of the high inflation rate in Slovakia and the consequent devaluation of its currency, you'll find things a bit cheaper in the Slovak Republic than in the Czech Republic.

As I mentioned before, a lot of Czechs and Slovaks are looking to make a fast buck by overcharging unsuspecting foreigners. Therefore, you should have a rough idea of how much certain items cost so as you don't get ripped off. The sidebar below lists some basic items and their average prices in Czech crowns (Kč) and Slovak crowns (Sk). Low end represents prices found in more obscure areas, while high end represents prices found in tourist hot spots such as the historic centers of Prague and Bratislava, the spa towns of West Bohemia, and ski resorts in the High Tatras.

"DON'T GET RIPPED OFF" PRICE LIST

The Czech crown is roughly 30 Kč to the US dollar, and the Slovak crown is roughly 35 Sk to the dollar.

•Accommodation for one night in a hotel (double occupancy) – from 3,000 Kč/2,000 Sk to 6,000 Kč/5,000 Sk.

•Bottled water (liter-and-a-half from a shop) – 12 Kč/10 Sk most anywhere

•Cup of coffee or espresso – from 10 Kč/8 Sk to 30 Kč/25 Sk

•Glass of wine – from 25 Kč/15 Sk to 50 Kč/40 Sk

•Half-liter of beer in a pub – from 10 Kč/12 Sk to 30 Kč/35 Sk

•Loaf of bread – from 4 Kč/3 Sk to 8 Kč/7 Sk

•Main course in a restaurant – from 70 Kč/60 Sk to 200 Kč/175 Sk

•Museum ticket – 25 Kč/20 Sk to 80 Kč/50 Sk

•Pack of American cigarettes – from 35 Kč/30 Sk to 60 Kč/50 Sk

•Theater ticket – from 200 Kč/175 Sk to 700 Kč/250 Sk

ELECTRICITY

The current in the Czech and Slovak republics runs at 220 volts – twice that of the current used in America and Canada. The plugs are shaped differently as well, so you'll need to buy an adapter (found at any Radio Shack) for your hairdryer, electric razor, or what have you. The guys at Radio Shack say you need to use a menacingly heavy transformer if you plan on being in Europe for a long time, or else the electronic stuff you bought in America or Canada is sure to eventually burn out on the 220 voltage.

Most laptop computers, however, come with a universal AC adaptor, for which you just need to buy the plug adaptor. (But I'd call the helpline of your computer model just to make sure.)

HEALTH CONCERNS

People with respiratory problems should steer clear of North Bohemia and North Moravia during the winter months when sulphur dioxide levels regularly reach three times World Health Organization safety levels. They should also think twice about going to Prague in the winter, where a mixture of diesel exhaust, coal smoke, and weather inversions can make the air dangerously polluted on certain days.

Other than that, I wouldn't worry too much about getting seriously ill in either republic. Public hygiene is well respected, and rarely have I heard of people getting food poisoning at restaurants. But if you plan on spending a lot of time in some out-of-the-way places, then it might be a good idea to protect yourself against hepatitis-A and tetanus.

Thanks to Communist mismanagement and a current lack of funds for modern medical equipment, health care in the Czech and Slovak republics isn't quite up to par with Western standards, though it is rapidly progressing. Doctors and nurses are notoriously overworked and underpaid, which sometimes takes it toll on the quality of patient care. But like anywhere else, there are good doctors and bad doctors, as well as good hospitals and bad hospitals. If your ailment is none too serious, then I would have no worries about walking into any clinic or hospital for treatment.

As a foreigner, you receive emergency care free of charge in both republics. Other than that, you'll have to pay for any medical care you receive, so it's essential that you have some sort of medical coverage during your stay. Canadians are pretty well covered in any country by their provincial health plans, but Americans should check out the details of overseas coverage with their health insurance carriers. Usually, insurance companies will reimburse you for most medical expenses incurred abroad. Just be sure to bring back proof of those expenses.

It's unlikely you'll find any English-speaking doctors, dentists, or pharmacists in the two republics other than in Prague and Bratislava, where there are numerous clinics and hospitals catering to the large number of foreign residents.

In Prague, a hospital with English-speaking doctors and dental services is **Na Homolce**, *Roentgenova 2 in the district of Motol (Tel. 02/529 22146; take bus #167 from Anděl metro station)*. There's also the **Canadian Medical Center**, *Veleslavinská 1 in the district of Dejvice (Tel. 02/316 5519, after hours call 0601 212 320)*. The **24-hour pharmacy** in Prague is just off Wenceslas Square at *Na příkopě 7 (Tel. 02/242 102 29)*.

For other clinics and hospitals in Prague and Bratislava, see *Practical Information* in their respective chapters. The **emergency ambulance phone number** for all of the Czech and Slovak republics is *155.*

Speaking of health concerns, here are some useful Czech/Slovak words to remember: *doktor/lékar* (doctor), *lékarna* (pharmacy), *polyklinika* (clinic), and *nemocnice/nemocnica* (hospital).

MONEY & BANKING

Since the breakup of Czechoslovakia, the Czech and Slovak republics have established their own currencies with their own notes and coins. Hence, the old Czechoslovak crown is now an archaic tender, which means you should never accept a bill or coin with the words *Korun československych* written on it.

The current unit of currency for the Czech Republic is the *Koruna česká* (or Czech crown), abbreviated **Kč**. It comes in coins of 1, 2, 5, 10, 20, and 50 Kč, and in bills of 20, 50, 100, 200, 500, 1,000, and 5,000 Kč. *Haléř*, the Czech equivalent of cents, comes in 10, 20, and 50 haléř. But these are virtually worthless, and you'll most likely end up with a pocket-full of them by the time you head home.

The unit of currency for the Slovak Republic is the *Slovenská koruna* (or Slovak crown), abbreviated **Sk**. It comes in coins of 1, 2, 5, and 10 Sk, and in bills of 20, 50, 100, 500, and 1,000 Sk. *Halierú*, the Slovak equivalent of cents, comes in 10, 20, and 50 halierú. These are as irritating as the Czech haléř.

EXCHANGE RATES

After plummeting in 1997 to 34 Kč to the US dollar, the Czech crown surged back in October 1998 with the fall of the dollar. At press time, the crown was going for around 30 Kč to the dollar. The Slovak crown, not as strong as the Czech crown, has leveled out at around 35 Sk to the dollar. Before you leave, check the Wall Street Journal, New York Times, and other major papers for exchange rates. Once in Europe, see the International Herald Tribune or the European Wall Street Journal for daily exchange rates.

Changing Money

Finding a place to exchange dollars for crowns is as easy pie in the Czech Republic, and is becoming easy in the Slovak Republic too – just look for the signs that say *Směnárna* (Czech), *Zmenáreň* (Slovak), or *Change*. Banks usually offer the full market exchange rate at the lowest commission for travelers' checks – usually at one or two percent, if there is a commission at all. For cash, you'll receive a bit poorer of an exchange rate and a little bigger commission.

The **American Express** office, *Tel. 02/242 277 86* in Prague, the only one in either republic, charges no commission for their travelers' checks and usually gives you a full-market exchange rate. It's at *Václavské náměstí 56 (Wenceslas Square; metro to Muzeum or Můstek station)*. In Bratislava, American Express is represented by **Tatra Tour** at *Františkanské námestie 3, Tel. 07/335 852.*

Hotels, though convenient, charge you as much as a five-percent commission for travelers' checks. Also convenient but expensive are the scores of tiny "Change" outlets that are on virtually every street corner in Prague's historic center. Many of them advertise "no commission." Well, they're lying. Their commissions are built into their exchange rates, which are set well below the full-market value of your currency.

Wherever you exchange money, don't do it on the streets with a shady-looking guy who comes up to you and says, "Change, change." For one, it's illegal. Two, you'll hardly ever get a better exchange rate than what's offered at the banks. And three, chances are you'll end with a pile of worthless Polish zloty or expired Czechoslovak crowns.

Before you leave either republic for the West, make sure you sell back your unused Czech or Slovak crowns for western currency, because banks in North America or West Europe won't accept Czech or Slovak currency. In order to sell back your crowns, you'll need to present your original exchange receipts, so be sure to save them.

All banks in Slovakia will buy your Czech crowns, and most banks in the Czech Republic will buy your Slovak crowns.

Credit Cards & Cash Advances

In the Czech and Slovak republics, it's becoming easier every day to use your American Express card, MasterCard, Visa card, and, to a lesser extent, Diners Club card. Almost all hotels accept two or three of them, as do most upscale restaurants and shops. It makes sense to use these cards because it saves you the hassle of carrying around a lot of cash. It can also save you the cost of conversion fees, because your bank gives you the full market value whenever it exchanges your charge in crowns for its payment in dollars.

A few select banks will give you cash advances on your credit cards at no charge. **Životenská banka** (see "Practical Information" in the Prague chapter) takes MasterCard and Visa, while **Slovenská Sporiteňá** (see "Practical Information" in the Bratislava section) takes only Visa.

It's becoming increasingly easier to find an automatic teller in Prague (especially around Wenceslas Square) and other places where there's a considerable amount of tourists. If your ATM card is hooked into one of the international electronic banking systems, just do as you would at home. Stick in your card, punch in your four-digit pin number, and count your cash when it comes out the slot. Czech and Slovak banks usually do not charge for the transaction, but your bank at home will.

POST OFFICE

First, you need to know a post office when you see it. In both republics, a post office is called *pošta*, and it is perhaps the most infuriating of places in either republic.

Here is the general scenario of a Czech or Slovak post office: You walk in and see a lot of windows for everything under the sun but only one for sending mail, which is where the long line is, of course. So one clerk furiously works away while the others think about how lucky they are they didn't get assigned the mail window. With so many impatient people lined up at his window, the clerk posting letters is understandably not in the best of moods, especially when you step up and say something in pidgin Czech or in English, which is when he looks up at you with murder in his eyes.

The message: avoid sending mail at the post office.

So, if you just need to mail a letter or postcard, go to a *tabac* or *trafika* (tobacconist/newsstand) and ask for *známky*, or stamps. A postcard to America or Canada takes 7 Kč/Sk postage (about 20 cents), while a letter takes between 9 and 20 Kč/Sk postage, depending on the weight. Then go in search of a little orange box sticking to the side of a building (always found outside a post office) and drop the letter or postcard inside.

Now, wasn't that easy?

Of course, you may want to send a package, which makes the post office unavoidable. In the Czech and Slovak republics, you can, in theory, mail up to two kilograms abroad at any regular post office. If it's heavier than that, the clerk may send you to a customs clearance office, called *pošta-celnice* in Czech and *vyclievacie oddelenie* in Slovak. In Prague, the customs clearance office is at *Plzeňská 139 in the district of Smíchov*. In Bratislava, it's at *Gunduličova 3*. Be sure to arrive at this office with your package unsealed, because the customs official will want to see what you're sending.

If you'd like to receive mail while you are in the republics, have it sent to the **poste-restante** at the main post office in whichever town you happen to be. In Prague, that address is: *c/o Poste Restante, Jindřišská 14, 110 00 Praha 1, Czech Republic*. In Bratislava, that address is: *c/o Poste Restante, 35 Námestie SNP, 816 25 Bratislava, Slovak Republic*. You'll need to present your passport in order to receive your mail.

SAFETY & TAKING PRECAUTIONS

The Czech and Slovak republics face none of the violent crime that plagues America's streets. But that doesn't mean you shouldn't take some precautions, at least to avoid pickpockets. Pickpocketing is rampant in the historic center of Prague. As I've mentioned before and as I'll mention again, be sure to carry your passport, credit cards, travelers checks, and cash in a money belt. Pay attention when getting on metros or trams or when walking through a big crowd of people.

Car theft has turned into a major problem in all of the former Eastern bloc countries, including the Czech Republic. Thieves break into cars at all hours of the day and have them across the border in a matter of hours. Swamped by car theft cases, the police are either unable or unwilling to do anything about it. Though there's little you can do to prevent it from happening to you, you can make your car a less tempting target if you don't leave your luggage or any valuables inside.

If you are unfortunate enough to have something stolen from you, report it to the police. Not that they will be of much help, but they will file a report that's essential for collecting insurance from your carrier back home.

The **emergency police number** is *158* for all of the Czech and Slovak republics.

In Prague, the central police station is at *Konviktská 14 in the Staré Město district*. In Bratislava, it's at *Sasinkova 23*.

SHOPPING

What to buy, what to buy? That's the big question. First, there is **glass** and **crystal**, for which Bohemia is acclaimed worldwide. You'll have no problem finding a shop that sells it, because they are located anywhere tourists go. If you're serious about buying some, I would do some comparison shopping first, because prices differ wherever you go. A rule of thumb in Prague: the further you get away from the historic center, the cheaper the prices.

And of course there are **marionettes**, which are fun to look at but are not as fun when you take them home and try to figure out how to use them. Wooden toys are another specialty of both republics. Most are simply ingenious, but may prove to be too low-tech for American and Canadian children jaded on computer gadgets. The **ceramic ware**, especially in South Moravia and Slovakia, is fantastic as well. They usually come with traditional floral designs particular to a region. Also in South Moravia and Slovakia, you'll find some beautiful **folk costumes**, hand stitched and colorfully designed. **Linen** and **lacework** are usually abundant wherever you go as well.

Antique shops are also plentiful in both republics, but you need to be careful about what you buy. In theory, you can't take a work of art produced before 1920 out of the country. Refer to the section on Customs in Chapter 6 for details.

For more details on shopping, see Prague and the other destination chapters later in this guide.

TELEPHONES, TELEGRAMS, & FAXES

Generally, you can make calls or send faxes and telegrams at the main post office of whichever city or large town you happen to be in. Most big post offices have international telephone service. And most hotels have direct dial telephones in their rooms and fax service at their reception desks.

Though there are a few coin-operated public telephones still around, most now take phone cards (*telefon karta*) only. The cards go for 200 Kč/ Sk a pop, and you can purchase them at any tabac, newsstand, or post office. You can use them to call abroad, within the republic, or locally. (One local call costs 2 Kč/Sk.) It's irritating but true: Though you can use the same card in any town of the same republic, you cannot use the same card in both republics.

PHONE WOES

Warning: Because the telephone service of Czechoslovakia was in an appalling state going into the 1990s, both republics are now in the process of revamping their systems, which means that telephone numbers are changing all the time. Unfortunately, that also means numbers listed in this book are subject to change. If you find that the number given here has changed, then call the **information line** *for the Czech and Slovak Republics, which is 121.*

You'll also notice that I list few phone numbers for various sights, because very few sights and attractions (including in Prague) have English-speakers working their phones – when they have anyone at all answering! I've listed the addresses, directions, and hours of operation for all sights in this book, but if you feel the need to call ahead at selected places, have your hotel do it for you.

If you need to call the US or Canada from either republic, dial 00 for an international line, then 1 for the US and Canada, then the area code, then the number you want. If you'd like to reverse the charges or charge the call to your calling card, dial *00 42 00 0101* for an **AT&T operator**; dial *00 42 00 0112* for an **MCI operator**; dial *00 42 00 0151* for a **Canadian operator**.

The **telephone country code** for the Czech Republic is 420. The telephone country code for the Slovak Republic is 421. Each city and town has its own code that starts with 0. All numbers listed in this book begin with that code (designated by the digits left of the slash). You do not need to dial the city code if you're making a local call, only if you're calling from another town within the two republics.

If you're calling from outside the two republics, do not dial the 0 at the beginning of the city code. For instance, if you're calling Prague from the States, you would dial 011 for the international line, 420 for the country code, 2 (not 02) for Prague, and then the number in Prague you want. But if you are calling Prague from Brno for instance, then you would dial 02 for Prague, then the number you want.

TELEVISION

Almost all upscale hotels in the two republics have satellite television in their rooms, so you can always receive CNN. Usually, you can also get the British Sky channel, the European version of TNT (mostly cartoons and old movies), and Eurosport.

On Czech and Slovak stations, you can catch the occasional American or British film in its original version. The ČT 2 channel in the Czech Republic carries the English-language *Euronews*, weekdays from 8:00 a.m. to 8:45 a.m. and weekends from 7:00 a.m. to 8:00 a.m.

TIME

The Czech and Slovak republics are both on **Central European Time** (CET), which is one hour ahead of Greenwich Mean Time (GMT) (two hours ahead during daylight savings) and six hours ahead of Eastern Standard Time (EST). So when it's noon in Prague, it's 11 a.m. in London and 6 a.m. in New York. Clocks are set to daylight-savings time on the last weekend in March and are turned back on the last weekend in September.

Czechs and Slovak don't always give the time in terms of our a.m. and p.m. clocks. Instead, they give it in military (24-hour) time. And when writing out the time, Czechs and Slovaks use a period instead of a colon to separate the hour from minutes. So when it's 12:00 a.m., they'll write or say it as 0.00. Or when it's 9:22 p.m., they'll write or say it as 21.22.

TIPPING

The first thing you should know about tipping in restaurants, cafés, and pubs is: never leave the tip on the table as you're leaving. Protocol is to wait until the server has added up your bill and then tell him how much you want to pay, which should be the bill amount plus tip. A tip of five, ten, or fifteen percent is fine, depending on the service and the type of establishment it is.

In hotels, if a porter brings your bags up to the room, hand him a 5 or 10 Kč/Sk tip, depending on if he had to carry them up the stairs or had the luxury of an elevator.

In taxis, give the driver a tip of five or ten percent. But if you strongly suspect the driver is overcharging you, which is most often the case in Prague, naturally offer him zilch as a tip.

WEIGHTS & MEASURES

Like most everywhere else in the world (with the exclusion of a certain North American country south of Canada), the Czech and Slovak republics use the metric system. For Americans who don't yet know how to think in terms of the metric system, I've included the American system equivalent where possible.

Czechs and Slovaks write out their numbers differently than North Americans. Where we would put a comma to designate the thousandth, millionth, etc. place, they put a period. And where we would put a period to designate a decimal place, they use a comma. For instance, our 23,324.07 would appear as 23.000,07 in the Czech or Slovak Republic. This is crucial when reading prices, which usually appear in the two republics with a dash at the end.

For instance, you may see a price tag with "3.233,- Kč" written on it. You may misinterpret that price as something close to three crowns. No, it's not the bargain you think it is. It is three-thousand, two-hundred, and thirty-three crowns.

ESSENTIAL TELEPHONE NUMBERS

Information: 121
Medical Emergency: 155
Police: 158
Fire: 150
Emergency Road Service: 154
24-Hour Pharmacy in Prague: 02/573 206 63
American Embassy in Prague: 02/245 108 47
Canadian Embassy in Prague: 02/243 111 08
American Embassy in Bratislava: 07/330 861
Canadian Embassy in Bratislava: 07/361 277
American Express (for stolen or lost card): 02/242 199 92
      during business hours only
MasterCard, Visa & Diners Club (for stolen or lost card): 02/
241 253 53 *during business hours only*

8. SPORTS & RECREATION

BICYCLING

Almost anywhere in the two republics, except in the big cities, there are several good opportunities for biking (see "Getting Around the Czech & Slovak Republics" in the *Planning Your Trip* chapter). Some good places to go for a ride are around the towns of Český **Krumlov** and **Třeboň** in South Bohemia, between the towns of **Telč** and **Slavonice** in South Moravia, and between the towns of **Mikulov, Valtice,** and **Lednice** also in South Moravia.

If you haven't brought your own bicycle, you might have some trouble finding one to rent. In Prague, there are a couple of places that rent bikes (see "Getting Around Town" in the Prague chapter). In other places, many upscale hotels loan bicycles to their guests. It's best to check with the local tourist information office, which generally has a list of places that rent bicycles.

CAVING

There are numerous opportunities to go on cave tours in both republics. The most awesome caves are in the **Slovak Karst** (Slovensky kras) region of East Slovakia, which boasts a system of caves, called the **Domicas**, considered one of the longest in the world. More accessible and nearly as impressive are the caves in the **Moravian Karst** (Moravský kras), just northeast of Brno in South Moravia. Not so impressive but less crowded are the **Javořičko Caves** north of Olomouc in North Moravia.

FISHING

You can go fishing in the republics, but you'll need to get yourself a license and respect local laws regarding particular days, weeks, and seasons you can and cannot fish. Check with Čedok or any local tourist information office to see about getting a license. In the **Třeboň region** of South Bohemia are some 6,000 ponds which are excellent for fishing. The tourist office in the town of Třeboň can issue you a license on the spot.

GOLFING

Believe it or not, there are twelve golf courses in the Czech Republic. Hosting the professional Czech Open each summer, **Golf club Marianské lázně** sits just outside the spa town of the same name in West Bohemia. Nearby Marianské Lázně, the spa town of **Karlovy Vary** also features an 18-hole course. At the golf club in **Karlštejn**, the newest club in the Czech Republic, you can play 18 holes of golf while taking in the majestic Karlštejn castle. (One hotel in Prague, Hotel Paříž, offers golf packages at the Karlštejn club – see "Where to Stay" in the *Prague* chapter). And if you are really desperate, you can shoot nine holes in Prague and Brno. Green fees run you between 800 and 1,600 Kč, and golf clubs are usually for rent. For more information about all the courses mentioned above, see "Sports & Recreation" under their respective chapters. Your hotel receptionist or the local tourist information office can usually reserve a tee time for you.

HIKING & WALKING

One of the favorite activities in both republics is what the Czechs and Slovaks call tramping, which means dressing up in Vietnam-era fatigues, hopping on a train, and spending the weekend tromping through the woods, sitting around the campfire, and having sing-alongs.

This activity makes sense when you realize how easy it is get around on foot in both republics. There are some 37,000 kilometers of trails in the Czech Republic alone, criss-crossing mountains, rolling hills, forests, and countryside. (Even within the Prague city limits, there are dozens of trails going through the city's 60-plus protected landscape areas.) Czech and Slovak trails are extremely user-friendly. Color stripes on the trees keep you on the right path and markers every half-mile or so tell you how far the nearest town, village, or train station is.

In fact, you could very well walk your way through the two republics, something **Czech Greenways** has come close to making possible. Encouraging eco-tourism in the republic, this organization has created a system of trails from Prague to Vienna through South Bohemia and South Moravia. (For more information on the Greenways, see the *Eco-Tourism & Travel Alternatives* chapter.)

But if you're into hard-core, high-country hiking, look no further than the **High and Low Tatras** in Central Slovakia, where you'll find a network of well-groomed trails reaching sublime, glacial-carved heights. Not so sublime but good for a day of hiking are the nearby **Malá Fatra Mountains**. In East Slovakia, you can't go wrong in the **Slovak Paradise** (Slovenský raj), filled with deep gorges and soaring cliffs, or in the **Slovak Karst** (Slovenský kras), honeycombed with a network of caves.

The Czech Republic doesn't hold a candle to Slovakia in terms of mountain hiking, but there are numerous ranges and other natural areas that make for worthwhile hikes. In East Bohemia are the **Krkonoše Mountains**, which unfortunately have been badly scarred by acid rain. Better yet in East Bohemia is **Český ráj** (Czech Paradise), a romantic landscape dotted with clusters of rock pinnacles and peppered with castles.

In North Bohemia, there's some good hiking to be done in **Česky Švýcarsko** (Czech Switzerland), a mountainous region with impressive sandstone formations and deep gorges. And in southwestern Bohemia are perhaps the republic's best mountains for long distance hikes – the **Šumava**, a range of densely-forested hills free of the acid rain damage you find in most mountains in the Czech Republic.

HOCKEY

After soccer, ice hockey is the biggest of sports in the two republics. When the Czech hockey team beat the Russians to win the gold medal at the 1998 Winter Olympics, the mood in the Czech Republic was nothing short of euphoria. And many of their players – Jaromír Jágr, Miloš Holraň and Dominik Hašek to name a few – have made it big in the National Hockey League (NHL).

It's easy to catch some national hockey action wherever you go in the two republics. A Canadian friend of mine says the level of play can sometimes be as impressive as in the NHL. In Prague, the team to watch is Sparta Praha, a team that regularly dominates the national league.

Tickets for the matches are always cheap and always available at the rink (rarely do they sell out). The hockey season lasts from late September until early April. For more information about seeing hockey in Prague, see "Sports & Recreation" in the *Prague* chapter.

HUNTING

The number of trophy heads hanging on the walls in any given castle will tell you that hunting has always been a traditional pastime in the two republics. The two republics are indeed rich in game, in particular pheasant, wild duck, wild boar, roe, mouflon, and red deer. But the republics do have strict laws regarding when and where you can hunt. They also charge foreigners a hefty sum for licenses. In the Czech Republic, a license good for one month costs 3,000 Kč – roughly the equivalent of $120.

For all the information you need regarding hunting in the Czech Republic, contact **Pragolov**, *Národní třída 37 in the Nové Město district of Prague, Tel. 02/242 184 19*. They can arrange accommodations near hunting areas, issue you a license, and tell you which animal is or isn't in-season. There are some hotels around the two republics that offer hunting packages as well.

For information about hunting in Slovakia, contact the travel agency **Satur**, *Jesenského 3 in Bratislava, Tel. 07/367 613*, or the **Slovak Travel Service** in New York at *Tel. 800/753-0582 or 212/213-3865.*

SKIING

The Czechs and Slovaks love to ski, and it shows in the number of folks lining up at the lifts. And with the thousands of Germans flowing into both republics to take advantage of the cheap accommodations and lift tickets, those lift lines can get pretty long. To avoid the traffic jams at the lifts and on the mountain roads, plan your skiing vacation anytime other than during the Christmas-New Year's vacation, a time of year when the crowds are simply intolerable. Easter also may not be a good time to go.

If you're used to skiing in the Rocky Mountains, then you probably won't be satisfied with anything less than the **High Tatra** or **Low Tatra** mountains in Central Slovakia. Though the facilities aren't exactly up to par with Aspen, the skiing is some of the best you'll find in Europe outside the Alps. Another good option in Slovakia is the **Vrátna Valley** (*dolina* is Slovak for "valley") in the **Malá Fatras**. But the verticality here isn't so great as in the Tatras, so it may be better suited for cross-country skiing. The **Veľká Fatra Mountains** in Central Slovakia and the **Slovak Paradise** (Slovenský raj) in East Slovakia are two other good options for cross-country skiing.

In the Czech Republic, your best option for downhill skiing would be the **Krkonoše Mountains** in East Bohemia, especially at the resorts around the town of **Špindlerův Mlýn**. The **Šumava Mountains** in southwest Bohemia also have a handful of resorts, good for downhill and cross-country skiing alike. In North Moravia, you can also do both kinds of skiing in the **Beskydy Mountains** above the towns of **Rožnov pod Radhoštěm** and **Frenštát pod Radhoštěm**. You can rent decent equipment easily enough at the resorts.

If you'd like to set up a skiing holiday in either republic, contact Čedok or the Slovak Travel Service in New York at *Tel. 800/753-0582 or 212/213-3865.*

SOCCER

Like most Europeans, Czechs and Slovaks can't seem to get enough of playing or watching *fotbal* (soccer). If there's a professional game on television, Czechs and Slovaks everywhere are sure to be glued to it, especially down at the pub. And if there's a game at the local stadium, there will be the typical chanting and horn-blowing that is now routine at European soccer matches.

In Prague alone, there are several teams that play in the national league. And just about any reasonably sized town has its own national league club. The team to watch in either republic is **Sparta Praha**, which has always been a serious contender in the European leagues (see "Sports & Recreation in the *Prague* chapter).

The soccer season runs from September to December and from March to June, and games are usually held on Saturdays or Sundays. No matter whose playing or how important the game is, tickets are almost always available at the stadium box office. Tickets go for a buck or two.

SPAS

Unfortunately, the Czech and Slovak spas are not like the ones in Budapest where people just pop in after work for a soak in a luxurious pool of steaming water and then go and have a sauna and massage. Rather, they are for patients who go there to take the waters, internally and externally, for such ailments as rheumatism, allergies, stomach disorders, and anything else under the sun. Every spa has a special disorder or two they treat, depending on the sort of mineral waters that spring at the spa.

Though many American and Canadian doctors would consider these spa treatments tantamount to quackery, Czech and Slovak doctors regularly prescribe a week or two at the spa for their patients. It does seem to do the patients some good, for a while at least. But you can never be too sure if it's because of the water or the totally relaxed atmosphere at these spas.

The treatments last anywhere from a week to a month, and they include room and board. Rates run about $55 to $100 a day. They are not the most exciting weeks you could spend abroad, but you are guaranteed to go home completely refreshed. If you suffer from some chronic ailment and would like to give a Czech or Slovak spa a try, I would first consult your doctor at home.

Several spa towns, especially Karlovy Vary and Marianské Lázně in West Bohemia, make for great destinations, but don't go expecting you can just drop in for a treatment. You need to book well in advance, which you can do for Czech spas by contacting **Balnea**, *Pařížská 11, 110 01 Prague 1, Czech Republic; Tel. 02/248 121 01, fax 02/248 116 00.* For Slovak spas, contact **Slovthermae**, *Radlinského 13, Bratislava, Slovak Republic; Tel. 07/ 581 80, fax 07/580 59.* Both these agencies can give you information on particular spas and what illnesses are treated there. Alternatively, you could check with Čedok or the Slovak Travel Service.

TENNIS

Having produced the likes of Martina Navrátilová, Ivan Lendl, and Petr Korda, the Czech Republic would have to be counted as one of the stronger tennis nations in the world. In spite of that, the game isn't wildly popular in the Czech Republic. But there are plenty of courts (usually clay) around the Czech Republic, and to a lesser extent around Slovakia. Your hotel receptionist or the local tourist information office can usually reserve a court for you at the nearest club.

For information on playing tennis in Prague, see "Sports & Recreation" near the end of the *Prague* chapter.

9. TAKING THE KIDS

It's a question you'll have to wrestle with: Should I or shouldn't I bring the little ones? Of course, that all depends on what kind of little ones you've got. It also depends on their ages. It would be real tough with a six or seven-year-old, but would probably be a lot of fun with a boy or girl older than 10 or 11.

These countries aren't exactly Orlando or Las Vegas when it comes to accommodating the whole family. But the two republics can get downright enchanting for kids. For instance, kids may think they've gone to Disneyland when you show them any number of *real* castles – but it might be another story once the castle tour begins and they have to hear all that boring stuff about history, art, and furniture!

It would make things a whole lot easier on you and your kids if you travel by car. Unless you get on a Eurocity train, there won't be any dining cars where you can grab a bite to eat or get something to drink. On the other hand, your child might get a kick out of a short train ride somewhere. Just remember to buy food and drinks beforehand.

Most hotels in the republics are pretty good about arranging lodging for the whole family. Almost all hotels have rooms or apartments that can accommodate three or more people, and if those rooms are already booked, then there's usually no problem in having an extra bed or two sent up.

In Prague, there is one hotel, called **Flathotel Orion**, that rents apartments (or flats) with fully-equipped kitchens, which might make things easier if you've brought the whole family. On the same street as Orion is **Olea Hotel**, which also rents apartments but without kitchens. Other kid-friendly hotels in Prague include **Hotel Sax** in Malá Strana and **Pension Větrník** in Břevnov. (For more information on all the hotels mentioned above, see "Where to Stay" in the *Prague* chapter.)

Your child might die of boredom going around to all the churches and museums in Prague. But there's more to the city than just churches and museums.

Here are some fun things you might want to try doing with your children:
- visit the **Toy Museum** at the **Prague Castle**
- hop on the funicular railway to the top of **Petřín Hill**, visit the Mirror Maze (called Bludiště) there, and then climb the mini-Eiffel Tower
- attend one of the daily performance at the **National Marionette Theater** in Staré Město district (they're in Czech, but easily understood visually)
- go for a **boat ride** on the **Vltava**
- rent a **paddle boat** on **Slav Island**, opposite the National Theater
- feed the ducks and swans on the river bank
- visit the amusement and kiddie parks set up at the **Výstaviště exhibition grounds** in the district of Holešovice (from mid-March to October only)
- visit the **Prague Zoo** in the district of Troja (it's a pathetic zoo, but does have all the regular animals, as well as a kiddie train)
- have a burger at McDonald's, if all else fails

In Bratislava, the number of fun things to do with your children aren't so great. A boat ride on the Danube might be fun, as would a visit to **Bibia** – an international art museum for children, which has weekly art classes and the occasional excursion.

10. ECO-TOURISM & TRAVEL ALTERNATIVES

CZECH GREENWAYS

Walking and biking are two excellent alternatives for traveling in both the republics. Easy-going roads and trails connect scores of small historic towns, quaint villages, majestic castles, and grandiose chateaux.

Modeled after the Hudson River Greenways in New York, **Czech Greenways** promotes "light tourism" in the Czech Republic. The organization has linked hundreds of trails along which you can actually walk or bike the 300 kilometers (180 miles) from Prague to Vienna. Czech Greenways has joined forces with the New York-based World Monuments Fund in creating the system and in drawing world attention to the wealth of historic monuments in the Czech Republic.

Not only does Czech Greenways provide the maps (available in English), they can also help you decide on an itinerary and help you find a bike to rent. They also supply a list of hotels, pensions, and inns found along the trails. Of course, there's no need to go the whole distance from Prague to Vienna.

You could have a delightful vacation completing just one greenway or segment of the system, of which there are several to choose from, including:

- **Lower Vltava River Valley** (including the towns of Bechyně, Tábor, Sedlec, and Prčice)
- **Upper Vltava River Valley** (including Český Krumlov and České Budějovice)
- **Bohemia Lake District** (including Jindřichův Hradec and Třeboň)
- **Towns of the Renaissance** (including Telč, Dačice, and Slavonice)
- **Dyje River Valley** (including Znojmo and Vranov nad Dyjí)
- **Pálava Hills** (including Valtice, Lednice, Mikulov, and Pavlov)

For maps, brochures, and any other information, contact **Zelené stezky** (Greenways), *Lublanská 18, 120 00 Prague, Czech Republic (Tel. 02/ 290 033, Fax 02/296 048).* In the U.S., contact **Friends of Czech Greenways,** *Tel. 718/258-5468 or 800/TRAIL-92, fax 718/258-5632, or by e-mail at friendsgw@aol.com.*

MOUNTAIN CHALETS & CAMPGROUNDS

In virtually every mountain range in the two republics are scores of mountain chalets (called *chata* or *bouda*), found along various trails or at the top of chairlifts or funiculars. Some are similar to ski lodges in the US and Canada, while others are simply just wooden shelters, for which you'll need your own bedding. Rates depend on the type of chalet it is, but usually are dirt cheap (about $5 or $10 a night). The nearest tourist information office can usually make a booking for you, or you can try just showing up (but do so early in the day, or your chances of getting a room won't be very good.)

If you're traveling by car through the two republics, look for signs that say *autokempink*. Here, you can park your RV, pitch a tent, or rent a bungalow for the night. Most have communal showers and toilets, communal kitchens, and a snack bar (if not a pub). Some can be quite nice, and may even be located next to a river or stream where you can take a dip. Others, however, are nothing more than parking lots. Rates will run you anywhere from $5 to $20 a night.

CAMPING & HIKING LAWS IN THE CZECH AND SLOVAK REPUBLICS

Before you decide on roughing it in the two republics, there are some local laws you ought to know about. First, open fires are forbidden everywhere. But you wouldn't know it by all the young Czechs and Slovaks who head for the woods and build campfires. However lax enforcement is, I definitely wouldn't test the law in any of the national parks. There, you'll have to stick to designated camp sites or else stay in one of the mountain chalets (see above).

In addition to national parks, there are thousands of protected land-scape areas, marked by the Czech or Slovak crest. Camping is not permitted in these areas and you must stick to the trails. And as always, pack out what you pack in, wherever you go camping or hiking.

11. FOOD & BEER

In this chapter, food and drink terms are accompanied with their equivalents in Czech and Slovak. If there is no slash separating the two, then the same or nearly the same word is used in both countries.

FOOD

One thing is for sure: The Czech and Slovak republics aren't exactly world-renowned for their cooking. There are a couple of reasons for this. One is that Czech and Slovak cuisines lack originality. There's just not a whole lot that distinguishes their cooking from that of other Central European countries such as Germany, Austria, Poland, or Hungary. Of course, each republic has their own specialties, but usually these are variations on dishes found throughout this part of Europe. Another reason is that neither republic has a wide spectrum of foods harvested domestically. The Czech and Slovak republics, two landlocked countries, have long, cold winters, which means you don't get the variety in fresh produce, not to mention the availability of fresh seafood. As a result, the cuisines of both republics are overwhelmingly meat-based.

However unoriginal the food may be, that doesn't mean you won't get a good meal in the two republics. You will. You just need to know where to find it. And luckily, that's becoming easier these days as compared to a few short years ago, when almost all restaurants dished out the same stodgy fare. You also need to know what to order, or else you may end up with something unidentifiable on your plate, something which could turn out to be the tongue (*jazyk*) or kidneys (*lednivky / obličky*) of some animal. Most upscale restaurants in Prague and other touristy areas will have an English menu. If there isn't, then refer to our trusty food glossary below.

So, what are the Czech and Slovak cuisines like and are there any differences in the two? To answer the latter question first: No, there aren't many differences. But Slovak cooking does tend to be spicier than Czech cooking. Slovak (and South Moravian) cuisine has more of an Hungarian slant, which means sauces, soups, and vegetables are heavily seasoned with paprika. Czech food, on the other hand, is more German-influenced, favoring caraway seeds and marjoram over anything else. In my opinion, Slovak cuisine has it hands down over Czech cuisine. Their sauces are thicker, jazzier, and more flavorful; their soups are more fanciful; and the general diversity in dishes is greater.

Whatever the differences may be, both nations indulge in meat, and lots of it. A typical meal in the Czech or Slovak Republic is centered around a hunk of meat (usually pork) doused with some sauce and served up with a side of potatoes, dumplings, or rice. For your vegetable: almost invariably cabbage or potatoes. A meal you would see on the majority of Czech and Slovak menus is *vepřová s knedlíkem a se zelím*, which means roast pork with dumplings and sauerkraut. It's the quintessential meal of the two republics.

Now, your reaction might be: how incredibly boring. And you're partially right; there is a lack of imagination here. But there's another factor you need to take into account – the sauces, which can be truly outstanding. If good, they are wonderfully thick, almost like gravy. A liberal amount of red or white wine usually goes into them, as does perhaps fruit (like cherries or berries of some kind), freshly-picked mushrooms, or caramelized onions. No matter what is on your plate, the sauce can make your meal. And you'll be glad for those potatoes or those bready dumplings, with which you can soak up every last drop of the luscious stuff.

Unfortunately, the cut of meat (*maso/mäso*) under that scrumptious sauce can be disappointingly fatty or tough, because much of what's butchered in the two republics has been raised in factory farms. Though good cuts of meat are now widely available in the markets, you're still bound to get, at least once during your stay, a slice of something in which you'll need a saw to get through. But restaurants with a good reputation will veer away from these meats, and usually offer something tender.

When in doubt about the quality of the restaurant, stay away from beef (*hovězí/hovädzie*) and pork (*vepřové/bravčové*) and order some kind of poultry, such as chicken (*kuře/kura*) or duck (*kachna/kačica*). In fact, if you can't make up your mind at all, go for the duck. For some odd reason, most restaurants know how to roast a good duck and prepare a good cherry or red wine sauce to go along with it. Or you could bypass meat altogether and order fish (*ryby*), of which there are two or three varieties at most any restaurant. Almost always, those two choices are trout (*pstruh*) and carp (*kapr/kapor*), which are grilled or broiled, doused with a tasty herb-butter sauce, and usually served whole – bones, tail, and all. Unfortunately, the freshness of fish is always suspect in the two republics, so you are taking your chances in ordering it.

For Americans who know carp as that mangy fish that feeds off trash at the bottom of lakes and reservoirs, you can put your mind to rest. The carp harvested in both republics are done so mainly at fish farms, if not at artificial lakes drained clean every year. The traditional Christmas meal in the two republics, carp is definitely not for everybody. I, for one, am not crazy about it. The meat is tough and usually tasteless, and eating it involves poking through an inordinate amount of bones.

Something that isn't so tough are the infamous dumplings, called *knedliky* in Czech and *knedle* in Slovak. By the time you go back home, you probably will have had enough dumplings to last you a lifetime. Rolled into a loaf, boiled in water, and then cut in slices, the Czech and Slovak dumplings resemble spongy pieces of thick bread – not at all like the dumplings made in North America. Restaurants usually serve two kinds of dumplings, *houskové knedliky* (made from actual pieces of white bread) or *bramborové knedliky/zemiakové knedle* (made from grated potatoes). Sometimes you can also get them with bits of bacon or cabbage thrown into the batter.

And for dessert, you may have the good fortune of eating *ovocné knedliky*, round dumplings filled with strawberries, cherries, or peaches and smothered with melted butter, powdered sugar, and cinnamon. It may cause a cardiac arrest on the spot, but you'll die happy.

EATING OUT

If there's been any big change to the two republics in the last few years, it's been in the quantity and quality of their eating establishments. There are hundreds of restaurants that have recently opened their doors, offering food that's a far-cry better than four or five years ago, when you were lucky to get a meal that ranked any higher than just mediocre. With a greater availability of fresh produce, higher quality meats, and better trained chefs, Czech and Slovak restaurants are making eating out an occasion again, and not just a necessity for people who don't have a kitchen.

Your chances of eating well does vary from town to town. Prague is in a different league altogether, presenting a far greater range of restaurants (and not just Czech ones) than any town or city in the two republics. Bratislava is also a good place for people who like to eat. But when you go to more obscure places in the two republics, your chances of eating diversely, or even well for that matter, becomes slim, and may be limited to hotels.

There are several ways of choosing a restaurant. One is, of course, following the recommendations I've listed under *Where to Eat* in each chapter. People working at tourist information offices are often happy to give advice, too. Or, when walking through town, keep an eye out for restaurants that look respectable (which more often than not means the food is respectable as well). Menus are usually posted outside to let you know what's being served.

Menus (*jidelní lístek/jedálny lístok*) can at times be tediously long, and choosing something to eat can become more of a task than a pleasure. Items on the menu – be they drinks, starters, or main courses – are given in terms of weight, so you know exactly the amount of food or drink you're getting. (And, by God, chefs actually do measure it out on scales in the kitchen.)

Usually, the menu will start out with cold appetizers (*studené předkrmy / studené predjedlá*). Here is where you'll find listed the infamous *Pražská šunka*, or Prague ham, in addition to other cold cuts, cheeses, butter, and bread (bread is usually not brought to your table unless you order and pay for it). Warm appetizers (*teplé předkrmy/teplé predjedlá*) follow, which usually includes something made with eggs, such as an omelette (*omeleta*) or scrambled eggs on toast.

Then, there are soups (*polévka/polievka*), something most Czechs and Slovaks order first by instinct. You too should make it a habit when eating out, because soups in the two republics are usually top-notch, and sometimes can be the highlight of a meal. Any soup with mushrooms (*žampiony/šampiňóny* or *houbová/hríbová*) is usually a winner. Another luscious soup to look out for is goulash soup, or *gulášová*, seasoned in Slovakia with lashings of paprika and in the Czech Republic with a dash of marjoram.

Salads (*salát*) have only recently become a popular starter. Lettuce and many other vegetables we take for granted are hard to come by in the two republics, which means most salads are limited to one or two vegetables, usually tomato (*rajský/rajčinový*) and cucumbers (*okurkový/ uhorkový*). A good salad you'll find on many menus is a version of Greek salad called *šopský* or *balkánský*, composed of tomato, cucumber, green bell pepper, and Balkan cheese – something which resembles Greek feta.

Entrées (*hlavní jídla/hlavné jedlá*) are generally sub-headed into two categories: ready-to-serve (*hotová jídla*) and prepared when ordered (*jídla na objednávku*). The portions of dishes from the former category are usually smaller, and probably will suit you better for lunch than for dinner. At most restaurants, the latter category of main dishes is further divided into groups such as beef (*hovězí/hovädzie*), pork (*vepřové/bravčové*), poultry (*drůbež/hydina*), game (*zvěřina/divina*), fish (*ryby*), and meatless (*bezmasá/bezmäsité*).

Usually, but not always, you'll need to a order a side dish (*přílohy*) to go along with your entrée. The choices are normally limited to rice (*ryže/*

ryža), dumplings (*knedlíky/knedle*), or potatoes (*brambory/zemiaky*). Pickled cabbage or tomatoes usually comes as a garnish.

Desserts (*moučnik*) are not the most inspiring affairs at Czech or Slovak restaurants. Usually, *palačinky* is about your only option. It's something akin to a French crepe, with jam, cocoa, ice cream, or whipped cream plopped on top. Sometimes, you can get a regular bowl of ice cream (*zmrzlina*) as well, but it usually is not all that good. For cakes and ice cream, you're better off stopping into a good café or sweet shop.

WHERE FOOD IS SERVED

Bufet - *Though quickly becoming outdated, these are joints where you can order a small meal from a buffet line. Quality of food is always suspect here.*

Cukrárna/Cukráreň - *A sweet shop with a wide variety of cakes, pastries, and ice cream. You can usually get a coffee or espresso here without the cigarette smoke that accompanies all pubs and cafés.*

Hospoda or *Pivnice* - *Pub. Usually you can get an informal bite to eat here, if not a full restaurant meal.*

Kavárna/Kaviáreň - *Café serving tea, espresso, cappucino, and other espresso-based drinks. The fancier ones serve pretty cakes and ice cream sundaes, as well as breakfast items (see "Breakfast," below).*

Koliba - *A homey Slovak restaurant specializing in chicken roasted over an open fire.*

Pekárna or *perkařství/pekáreň* - *Bakery with fresh breads and pastries. You can sometimes grab a coffee here as well.*

Restaurace/Reštaurácia - *Where you'll get a formal meal.*

Vinárna/Vináreň - *A wine bar by name, but usually a full-fledged restaurant with an extensive selection of wines.*

Breakfast - *Snídaně/Raňajky*

Most hotels and pensions include breakfast in the price of their rooms, so you'll rarely ever have to go out in search of something to eat in the mornings. In the Czech or Slovak Republic, that means you'll receive a basket filled with dark wheat and rye breads (*chléb*), plaited buns (*houska/žemla*), and/or white rolls resembling hotdog buns (*rohlíky*).

You'll also get a platter of cold cuts, cheeses, butter, and jams and your choice of tea or coffee. You can usually get juice (*džus*), but you'll be charged extra for it. Some hotels serve yogurt and cereal as well, while only those with a large North American or British clientele serve eggs. (Eggs are considered an appetizer for lunch or dinner in the two republics.)

But if you want to eat on the run, then stop into a bakery for a croissant or *koláče* – a Czech-style pasty with jam, poppy seeds, or cream cheese on top.

Lunch - *Oběd/Obed*

Taken between 11 and 1 o'clock, this is the main meal of the day for most Czechs and Slovaks, so there's little difference, if any at all, between lunch and dinner menus.

But if you are not in the mood for a big lunch, then look for the *hotová jídla* category on the restaurant menu, where you'll see smaller portioned meals served up quickly and with little fuss. Pubs usually have only these sort of meals on their menus and are therefore good places to eat lunch.

Some popular lunchtime items include *guláš* (goulash), *svíčková* (roast beef swimming in a creamy sauce and topped with lemon and lingonberries), and the all-too-common *vepřová s knedlíkem a se zelím* (roast pork with dumplings and cabbage). Some other choices for lunch might be any number of deep-fried foods such as *smažený syr* (fried cheese) or *smážené žampiony* (fried mushrooms).

Of course, you may be on a sight-seeing march through town and be looking for something just to tie you over until dinner. In that case, grab a *párek/párok* (hotdog), *klobása* (spicy sausage), or *hamburgery* (ground pork, not beef, with sauerkraut, mustard, and ketchup in a bun) – all available at street stands everywhere. You may also see stands selling *langoše*, which are greasy fried dough snacks coated with butter, jam, cinnamon, garlic, etc. Pizza has become wildly popular in the two republics in recent years. So keep an eye out for the odd pizza stand or the more common pizzeria, some of which are actually quite good.

And of course, you can always do your own by stopping into a *potraviny* (small food store) for bread, cheese, cold cuts, and whatever else your heart desires.

Dinner - *Večeře/Večera*

As the work day in both republics becomes more hectic, Czechs and Slovaks are finding less and less time for their usual long lunch. Consequently, dinner is becoming a grander affair in the two republics, especially in Prague, where it's not uncommon for certain restaurants to fill up every night of the week.

Most restaurants in the two republics stay open from lunchtime until about 9 or 10 p.m., offering the same menu throughout the day. Therefore, it doesn't matter when you go eat, so long as it's not after the kitchen has closed, which can be as much as an hour before the advertised closing time. But restaurants are generally busiest from 7 to 9 p.m. In tourist hotspots, it's always a good idea to reserve a table. This is especially true in Prague, where a reservation has become almost mandatory at just about every upscale restaurant in town.

Eating dinner at Czech or Slovak restaurants isn't the long, drawn-out affair it is in many European countries, where you're expected to order course after course and spend a good three hours eating away. At the same time, restaurateurs don't expect you to rush through dinner. Make of it what you will, and don't feel pressured to order something from every category on the menu. Czechs and Slovaks rarely ever do.

When ordering from a menu, be prepared to ask questions, because you may be confronted with inexplicable items to the tune of King George's Sword, Mystery of the Chateau, or Moravian Sparrow, which are codes for some special local preparations.

And when choosing a restaurant for dinner or even lunch, don't overlook the several ethnic restaurants around the two republics. Prague is littered with restaurants serving anything from Chinese to Italian to American cuisine, any of which can be a godsend after stuffing yourself on meat, dumplings, and potatoes for days on end. And when in Slovakia, don't forget about Hungarian (Magyar) restaurants, which can hardly be categorized as "ethnic," considering that Hungarians hold a majority of the population in many Slovak towns.

FOOD GLOSSARY (IN CZECH/SLOVAK)
The Basics
chléb/chlieb - bread
chlebíček - open-faced sandwich
cukr/cukor - sugar
džem - jam
hořčice/horčica - mustard
houska/žemla - plaited roll
knedlíky/knedle - dumplings
máslo - butter
maso/mäso - meat
med - honey
mléko/mlieko - milk
ovoce/ovocie - fruit
pepř/čierne korenie - pepper
rohlík - long roll resembling a hotdog bun
ryby - fish
rýže/ryža - rice
smetana/smotana - cream
sůl/soľ - salt
sýr/syr - cheese

vejce/vajcia - eggs
zelenina - vegetables

Fruits & Vegetables
   banán - banana
   broskev/broskyňa - peach
   brambory/zemiaky - potato
   česnek/cesnak - garlic
   chřest/špargľa - asparagus
   cibule/cibuľa - onion
   citron - lemon
   fazole/fazuľa - beans
   hranolky - French fries
   hrách - peas
   hruška - pear
   jahody - strawberries
   květák/karfiol - cauliflower
   jablko - apple
   maliny - raspberries
   mrkev/mrkva - carrots
   okurka/uhorka - cucumber or pickle
   paprika (*červená* or *zelená*) - bell pepper (red or green)
   pomeranč/pomoranč - orange
   rajče/rajčina - tomato
   špenát - spinach
   třešeň/čerešna - cherries
   žampiony/ šampiňóny - mushrooms
   zelí/kapusta - cabbage

Meats, Fish, Poultry, & Game
   bažant - pheasant
   biftek - beef steak
   drštky/drňky - tripe
   hovězí/hovädzie - beef
   husa/hus - goose
   játra/pečeň - liver
   jelení/jelenina - venison
   kachna/kačica - duck
   kanec/divá sviňa - boar
   kapr/kapor - carp
   králík - rabbit
   krůta/moriak - turkey
   kotleta/rebierko - cutlet

kuře/kurča - chicken
makrela - mackerel
pstruh - trout
řízek/rezeň - wiener schnitzel
sardinka - sardine
sekaná - meat loaf
slanina - bacon
šunka - ham
svíčková/sviečkovica - roast beef
telecí/teľacia - veal
vepřové/bravčové - pork
zajíc/zajac - hare

Preparations
čerstvý - fresh
domácí/domáci - homemade
dušený/dusený - stewwed
grilovaný/na rošte - roasted on the spit
kyselý/kyslý- sour
nadívaný - stuffed
nakládaný - pickled
pečený - roasted or baked
roštěná (na ro tu)/ro t nka (na ra ni) - broiled
sladký - sweet
smažený/vypražený - fried
syrový/surový - raw
uzený/údené - smoked
vařený/varený - boiled

Objects At the Table
lžíce/lžica - spoon
nůž/nož - knife
párátko/špáradlo - toothpick
popelník/popolník - ashtray
šálek/šálka - cup
sklenice/pohár - glass
talíř/tanier - plate
ubrousek - napkin
vidlička - fork

Beverage Glossary
Note: Water is never served automatically with meals. Ask for mineral water (see below), carbonated water (*s bublinami* or with bubbles),

or plain water (*bez bublin* or without bubbles). Though Czechs or Slovaks rarely drink it straight, regular tap water is safe to drink, even in Prague.

Becherovka - clear herbal spirit
burčák - sweet, young wine
čaj - tea
destiláty - spirits
džus - juice
  pomerančový - orange
  jablečný - apple
  ananasový - pineapple
Fernet - brown, bitter herbal spirit
preso - espresso
káva - coffee
  překapávaná - filtered coffee
  Turecká - Turkish (boiled water poured over grounds)
  Vídeňská - Viennese coffee
koňak - cognac
láhev/fľaša - bottle
led - ice
limonády - fruit-flavored carbonated drink
minerální voda - mineral water
mléko/mlieko - milk
pivo (světlé, tmavé or *černé)* - beer (light, dark, or black)
slivovice - plum brandy
svařené víno - hot wine
víno (červené, bílé) - wine (red, white)
voda - water

BEER

In Europe, the Czech Republic is synonymous with great beer, so there's no need to tell a European to drink the beer when he goes to the Czech Republic. In fact, he most likely is going there for the beer. But with Americans, it's a different story, because Czech beer has been available in American stores and bars only in the last few years. So you still see the odd American bellying up to a Prague bar and ordering a bottle of Heineken when he could be having a Pilsner Urquell on draft for half the price, which begs the question: Why drink an average Dutch beer, or any other foreign beer for that matter, when you're in the heart of the greatest beer-producing country in the world? It would be like going to France and ordering a California wine.

Having produced beer since the 11th century, the Czechs have come as close as anyone will get to perfecting it. Indeed, what wine is to France, beer is to the Czech Republic. Nothing gives Czechs a sense of pride for their country quite like beer does, and it shows in the amount that they drink. Per capita, Czechs average 153.6 liters per year, making them the biggest consumers of beer in the world. (However, that doesn't quite meet the daily allowance of 35 beers that the famous Czech writer, Jaroslav Hašek, recommended his countrymen drink.)

You can hardly deny the Czech gift for brewing beer when you take that first swill from a glass of Pilsner Urquell, Budvar, or any other great Czech beer. With no heavy carbonation, no stark bitterness, and no additives, Czech beer goes down like liquid velvet, leaving a flavorful malty coating around your mouth and on your upper lip. Licking the suds from your lips, you can understand why Czechs like a good inch of creamy head on their beer, through which the rest of the beer flows like nectar.

Most beer made in the Czech Republic is of the **pilsner** (bottom-fermented) variety, which is what most major breweries in America make so unsuccessfully. In fact, the Czech town of **Plzeň** is where the variety originated in 1842, from where it spread to Germany, England, and eventually America. That original bottom-fermented beer is today sold as **Pilsner Urquell**, or *Plzeňsky Prazdroj* as the Czechs know it.

So what makes Czech beer so sensational? One reason is that Czech brewers are rigidly traditional in their brewing methods, methods that have been employed since the 13th century. Not once have they fathomed the idea of substituting chemicals for the natural ingredients that come out of Bohemia's ground. And why should they, when the very best hop for making beer, the Saaz (Žatec) Red, grows abundantly and exclusively in Bohemia?

Czech brewers are also particular about the kinds of water they use. Only the softest, most natural waters will do. One brewery in South Bohemia, called **Regent**, is so concerned about the water factor in its beer that it has been using the same well since 1379, the year the brewery began production.

For good or bad, Czech brewers have rarely fallen out of line with those traditional methods and embarked on producing anything other than lagers. Consequently, you won't find the various wheat, fruit, or other perfume beers produced in Germany and Belgium. Czech brewers stick to either light (*světlé*) or dark (*tmavé*) beers, the preference being for light. If you're turned off by stodgy German dark beers, then you may like the dark beers made in the Czech Republic. They are not as heavy, and are generally sweeter than their German counterparts.

On every beer label and at every pub counter you'll see a number indicating the degree of the beer, which is according to the Czech version of the Balling scale – something used in measuring fermentation. Usually the degree is at either ten or twelve. Rest assured, this does not indicate the alcohol content. A ten-degree beer has about a four percent alcohol content, while a twelve-degree has a five percent. The higher degree, the more alcohol. So watch out for those 14, 16, and even 18-degree beers, which can knock you out in no time.

PUB PROTOCOL

Most pubs in the Czech Republic serve one and only one brand of beer on tap. There is a science good pubs use in treating and serving beer, a science involving the conditions in which you store the beer and the sort of pipes through which you draw it. So one pub might serve a better Pilsner Urquell or Budvar than the next. (See the listing of Prague pubs for the best places to get a Pilsner Urquell.)

When you go to a pub, expect to share a table or bench. A pub wouldn't be a pub if you were cordoned off into booths with no opportunity to meet fellow beer guzzlers. Almost all pubs have waiters who'll come and take your order.

*At the pub, beer comes in two sizes. The regular size is a half-liter. To order this, all you need to say is **pivo, prosím**, which means "beer, please." The second size is one-third of a liter, for which you say **malé pivo**, meaning small beer. Most pubs serve only light (**světlé**) beer, while others also serve dark (**tmavé**). If you want a mixture of the two, ask for **řezené**.*

If a Czech beer is served properly, the beer host will fill the glass three or four times and let the foam settle until there is a nice frothy head sitting above the glass rim. So be patient for that first one.

*After you order one, there's usually no need to order another, because the waiter keeps plopping them down one after the other until you pay up and stagger home. Each time the waiter brings a beer around, he'll leave a mark on a slip of paper. (You can always tell how long the guy next to you has been sitting at the pub by how many marks are on his slip.) When you're ready to pay, simply say **zaplatím, prosím**, which means, "I'll pay, please," and the waiter will add up your marks and bill you accordingly.*

A Short Guide To Beers in the Czech Republic

In the Czech Republic, there are three major breweries that export their beer all over the world. These are **Pilsner Urquell**, **Budvar**, and **Staropramen**. But there are also countless breweries that distribute their beer only in the immediate region of the brewery. Of course, Prague is the best place in the country to sample a wide-variety of Czech beers. Still, not every Czech beer is available there. Hence, one of the joys of traveling around the Czech Republic is sampling the regional beers, which can be just as good as if not better than the three biggies. Czechs are extremely loyal to their local brewery, and in most small town pubs you can only get the local brew. So come prepared to branch out from the nominal glass of Pilsner Urquell or Budvar and consume whatever the locals are quaffing.

The following list of major Czech beers is certainly not the definitive guide to Czech beer, but it does give you a good place to start. All of these beers are found in Prague. You'll have to discover for yourself the hundreds of other beers found around the country.

Bernard - A hoppy beer brewed in the South Moravian town of Humpolec, Bernard is becoming increasingly more popular in Prague.

Braník - Named for the Prague suburb in which it is brewed, this is lighter but more bitter than most Czech beers.

Budvar (Budweiser in German) - A creamy beer brewed in the South Bohemian city of České Budějovice, Budvar bears no resemblance whatsoever to the liquid of the same name processed in St. Louis. The Anheiseur-Busch Brewing Company has tried repeatedly to buy out Budvar. But Budvar owners, God bless 'em, refuse to be taken over by an American company, knowing full well it would mean the end of their traditional brewing methods and the beginning of more cost-effective methods that would surely jeopardize the quality of their beer.

Flek - This thick caramel beer has been brewed and served exclusively at Prague's U Fleků beer hall since 1399.

Gambrinus - A personal favorite, Gambrinus is made in Plzeň by the Pilsner Urquell brewery. A bottle of the ten-degree is just the ticket on a hot summer day.

Krušovice - This sweet, caramel-accented dark beer is some of the best of its variety in the republic. Also comes in light, which isn't as flavorful.

Pilsner Urquell *(Plzeňsky Prazdroj in Czech)* - The original pilsner beer copied with little success by just about every major brewery in America. Brewed since 1842 in Plzeň, this is perhaps the legitimate king of all beers, and with good reason.

Radegast - A newcomer to the nationwide Czech beer market, Radegast has quickly become one of the most popular beers in the Czech Republic. It's now widely marketed throughout the Czech and Slovak republics, and should soon break into the American market.

Regent - For my money, this is some of the best beer made in the Czech Republic. The brewery in the South Bohemian town of Třeboň has been making the smooth stuff since 1379.

Samson - České Budějovice's second beer, it's a bit lighter than Budvar and almost as good.

Starobrno - Brewed in Brno, this beer doesn't cut the mustard as compared to other Czech beers.

Staropramen - This beer brewed in the Smíchov district of Prague has a somewhat bitter aftertaste, making it not one of the most desirable around, even though it is exported worldwide.

Velkopopovický kozel - A favorite in Prague pubs, this is fairly bitter as far as Czech beers go. Saying the name is almost as fun as drinking the beer.

Velvet - Produced by Pilsner Urquell, the newest beer to hit the Czech market. Rather weak stuff compared to most Czech beers.

WINE & SPIRITS

Though they enjoy the occasional night in a pub drinking beer, Slovaks tend to head more frequently to the *vináreň* (wine bar) for a glass or two of *víno*. That's because they produce so much of the stuff that it's uncouth to drink anything else. Same goes for Czechs living in South Moravia, which has been in the business of producing wine ever since German and French vines were imported to the Czech lands in the 14th century.

If you're accustomed to drinking French or even Californian wines, you probably won't find anything too exciting about Moravian or Slovak wines. The whites tend to be overly fruity, much like some German and Austrian wines, and the reds tend to be somewhat lackluster, lacking the full-bodied taste that the Czechs have perfected in their beer production. But if your tastebuds are not so refined, then you should be pleased by the wines served at any upscale restaurant.

Thought private vineyards have been established, most wines produced in the two republics are done by large cooperatives. Labels on the bottle, therefore, are rather imprecise, showing you the type of wine and the town or region in which it was produced. Some labels don't even have the vintage printed on them, which can make choosing a bottle problematic, to say the least. But just like anywhere else in the republics, the price of any given bottle is a good indication of the quality of wine.

In Moravia, wine is produced mainly in the southeastern area, in particular the regions of **Paláva** and **Moravské Slovácko**. Here you can find hundreds of private wine cellars (called *vinné sklípky*) pouring the best wine you're bound to get in the Czech Republic. But if you're just in the shop looking for a good bottle to take with you, safe bets for reds are the musky *Vavřinec* and the fruity *Frankovka*, preferably produced in the town of Mikulov or Valtice. As for whites, *Tramín* is a sweet and spicy wine produced fairly well in the Moravské Slovácko. Something a little dryer would be *Müller-Thurgau* or *Rulandské bílé*.

The two major wine-growing regions in Slovakia are along the **Small Carpathians** in western Slovakia and along the border with Hungary to the south. Vineyards in West Slovakia stretch all the way down to Bratislava, producing a decent white called *Venušíno čáro* and a below-par red called *Kláštorné*. But the best Slovak wine comes from the **Tokaj region**, where a big concentration of ethnic Hungarians produce wines almost identical to the ones produced across the border in Hungary. Some good dry white wines to try here are *Furmint* and *Tokaj*.

As for the hard stuff, the Czech Republic produces some unique concoctions, not least of which is an herbal spirit called *Becherovka*. Made in the spa town of Karlovy Vary, Becherovka is said to be the town's 13th spring, which people drink after slurping down the town's 12 less palpable mineral waters. When served cold, it's good stuff, but some Americans can't help but think of it as fancy mouthwash. Czechs, on the other hand, believe it to be a cure-all for just about any stomach malfunction.

Another interesting spirit found in both republics is *fernet*, a potent, bitter booze that's best when mixed with tonic (a drink Czechs call *bavorák*). There are a couple of *fernet* producers, but only **Fernet Stock** is worth ordering. Like in most central and eastern European countries, *slivovice* (or *slivovic*) is big in the two republics. Said to have originated in Moravia, slivovice is a plum brandy that'll make your face clinch up. The mass producer of this fiery stuff is the Moravia-based **Jelínek**. Slovaks and Moravians, however, prefer to drink slivovice when it's home-brewed and properly aged.

12. BEST PLACES TO STAY

It's tough coming up with the best places to stay, as there are many memorable hotels and inns that could easily fit the bill. Here are my picks for those places in the two republics that, for reasons of quality, value, service, beauty, and overall ambience, are a cut above the rest.

PRAGUE

HOTEL SAVOY, *Keplerova 6, 110 00 Prague 1 (tram #22 from Malostranská metro station to Pohořelec stop). Tel. 02/243 024 30, fax 02/243 021 28. Rates for executive/deluxe rooms: 7,820/9,280 Kč. Credit Cards: AE, MC, DC, V. 61 rooms. Restaurant.*

And you thought Prague was cheap? Well, think again. But if you want to splurge, this hotel at the top of Hradčany is the place to do it. Part of the Vienna International Hotels & Resorts chain, the Savoy is set behind a yellow Art Nouveau facade, which is the only bit of authenticity left of the building. The interior was completely gutted in 1993 to make room for the handsome wood fixtures, marble floors, and expansive dining room atrium that now compliment the building. A nice touch is the library, where high tea is served every afternoon by an open fireplace.

Each of the individually decorated rooms comes with a marble bathroom, three telephones (one in the bathroom, of course), fax machine, satellite television, VCR, and a complimentary mini-bar. Definitely ask for a room in the rear of the hotel on the second level or above so you can have a view over Hradčany. The hotel also has what's called a "relax center," complete with whirlpool, sauna, fitness center, masseuse, and beauty salon. But the best part of the hotel is the friendly, English-speaking service.

In keeping with the hotel's formidable accommodations, the Savoy's restaurant offers a refined menu altered daily and revamped monthly. But you can expect something along the lines of elder sauce over a deer terrine and chestnut dumplings or spring lamb medallions smothered in garlic sauce. The expansive atrium dining room, reverberating with the sound of background piano music, makes for romantic dining. On Sunday, the hotel offers a jazz brunch with a buffet and a live jazz band. Tip-top, English-speaking service goes along with the multilingual menu. But like the rest of the hotel, the restaurant is more Vienna than Prague.

PENSION U RAKA, *Černiská 10/93, 118 00 Prague 1 (tram #22 from Malostranská metro station to Pohořelec stop). Tel. 02/351 453, fax 02/353 074. Rates for singles & doubles: 5,600/6,200 Kč. Credit Cards: AE, DC, MC, V. 6 rooms. No restaurant, but breakfast is included in rates.*

You can hardly believe that this pension, carved out of a 400-year-old cottage, is in the middle of Prague. Located down the hill from the Loreto among Hradčany's narrow, twisting lanes, U raka makes you feel like you're in some village in the countryside, a feeling that's compounded by the pension's abundance of wood fixtures, its fireplaces, and its Japanese style garden.

Even though U raka is billed as a pension, it has that homey, intimate touch that makes it feel more like a bed and breakfast. Antiques, original art work, and great ceramic ware abound. If you feel like splurging, go for the apartment, which comes with its own fireplace. But be sure to book a room as much as three to four months in advance for this small gem. Private parking is available.

SOUTH BOHEMIA

HOTEL RŮŽE, *Horní 153, 381 01 Česky Krumlov. Tel. 0337/711 141, fax 0337/711 128. Rates for single/double: 1,490/2,180-2,380 Kč. Credit cards: AE, MC, V. 50 rooms. Restaurant and café.*

Built as a Jesuit college during the Renaissance and converted to a hotel in 1889, this is one of the oldest and classiest hotels in Bohemia. Legend has it that the sgraffitoed hotel, which looks more like a chateau than an old college, was built on a ancient Celtic sacrificial site, prompting all sorts of ghost stories having to do with the hotel. Many of the spacious rooms come with the original wood ceilings, as well as an unfortunate bit of outdated furniture. But you can ignore that small minus when surrounded by so much opulence.

At press time, the hotel was closed for renovation. When it reopens in the spring of 1999, the hotel will have a lot more to offer, including a swimming pool, sauna, fitness center, travel center, beauty salon, and, thankfully, a new interior design the owner says will be as close as you can get to the Renaissance period. Expect prices to go up.

If your budget doesn't allow you one of the high-end rooms, ask to stay in one of the historical Jesuit cells, which don't come with their own baths. The hotel arranges tours of the town and of the area, including a "night visit" in which a guide dressed in medieval garb escorts you to haunted places around town. The hotel also features the occassional concert and other cultural events.

The first-rate **Rožmberk Restaurant** in the hotel will set you back between 160-300 Kč. The mostly Czech dishes, such as the roast beef with a creamy lemon sauce and the roast venison smothered in a red wine sauce, come beautifully presented and wonderfully served by the restaurant's deft servers.

WEST BOHEMIA

VILLA BUTTERFLY, *Hlavní třída 655, 353 01 Mariánské Lázně. Tel. 0165/484 100, fax 0165/762 10. Rates for single/double: 1,530-3,910/2,070-4,140 Kč. Credit cards: AE, DC, MC, V. 100 rooms. Restaurant.*

The lap of luxury in Mariánské Lázně, this hotel was recently reconstructed and made into one of the choicest places in town. Its two bright yellow wings, designed in a sort of contemporary Art-Nouveau style and topped by some avant-garde statues, nearly dominates the town's main street. Though the rooms are extremely comfortable, they're somewhat on the generic side – not at all as unique as the hotel's beautiful two-tiered marble lobby. All rooms come with satellite television, minibar, direct-dial telephones, and hairdryers. Definitely ask for a room overlooking the park. The hotel, true to its 1920s style, has a games and reading room, and presents the occasional classical performance and ballroom dance in it's small concert hall. Staff can arrange for you to play golf or tennis.

The hotel's superb **La Fontaine** restaurant (price range 250-500 Kč) is a great place to splurge. Serving French and international cuisine in an ultra-formal setting, you can feast yourself on beef tournedos with green pepper sauce, turkey medallions topped with curry, or crab meat in a salmon pillow. Efficient, multilingual service makes the experience all the more gratifying.

HOTEL EMBASSY, *Nová louka 21, 360 01 Karlovy Vary. Tel. 017/322 1161, fax 017/322 3146. Rates for single/double: 1,500-2,000/2,380-3,250 Kč. Credit cards: AE, DC, MC, V. 18 rooms. Restaurant.*

Of all the places to stay in Karlovy Vary, this small, family-run hotel is one of my favorites. Carved out of a pastel Baroque house, the hotel features a sunny atrium that does wonders for brightening up the old building. In the atrium is a small café that's perfect for a mid-afternoon beer or coffee.

There is a sense of grandeur that goes along with each of the large, individually-decorated rooms. They're decorated as they would have been in the 19th century, with old portraits of Karlovy Vary luminaries hanging on the walls. Every room is a winner here, but room number 202 with its old ceramic stove gets my vote for coziest. All rooms have direct-dial telephones, big bathrooms, and satellite television. Parking is free of charge. In keeping with the high standards of the place, the English-speaking service here is friendly and very accommodating.

The Restaurant Embassy (price range 200-600 Kč) is one of the oldest in Karlovy Vary, and maintains the high standards of the laudable hotel it occupies. Sumptuously-prepared dishes such as venison, Chateaubriand, and pasta with a salmon-cream sauce are served with flair under the restaurant's vaulted ceilings. If you got a hankering for lobster, the restaurant can prepare it with a two-day advance notice. And if you are a vegetarian, then you'll be thankful to find a wide assortment of vegetable and meat-less pasta dishes.

WEST SLOVAKIA

HOTEL TATRA, *M.R. Štefánika 2, 911 00 Trenčín. Tel. 0831/506 111, fax 0831/506 213. Rates for single/double: 2,200/3,200 Sk. Credit cards: AE, DC, V. 70 rooms. Restaurant.*

Located at the foot of the castle, the Hotel Tatra is a neo-Baroque confection looking all the more splendid after a recent restoration that took two years to complete. Slovakia's earliest written history happens to be inscribed just behind the hotel on a cliff face. It's a Latin inscription paying homage to Marcus Aurelius' victory over Germanic tribes in 179 AD, the year in which a Roman camp known as Laugaritio was stationed at this very site.

This is one of best hotels you could choose in the Slovak Republic. As you'll see, the Tatra is more than just a hotel, but a center of culture and food as well. The hotel strikes a unique introductory note in the lobby, where you'll find avant-garde paintings depicting the four humors. Off to the right of the lobby is the hotel's sunny Café Sissi, a favorite of the locals serving a bevy of cocktails and a variety of breakfast items such as scrambled and soft-boiled eggs and pastries. Off to the left is the Restaurant Tatra, the town's best restaurant decked out in pleasant earth tones and featuring a great menu of Slovak and international courses, including a tasty stuffed turkey breast drenched in a luscious gravy. The restaurant also has a salad bar that is sure to please North American travelers with a hankering for fresh vegetables. Prices at the restaurant run between 150 and 300 Sk.

In the basement of the hotel, the Victoria Wine Cellar is the place to go for a casual meal. The cellar features a different menu and a different style of cuisine every month or so. Some recent menus have featured French, American, and even Mexican specialties. During the evening, your meal is accompanied by a folk quintet playing heart-bleeding Romany songs. Prices at the wine cellar run between 50 and 150 Sk. And don't forget the terrace in the back of the hotel, where you can sit in the company of the Roman inscription hanging on the cliff face.

As for the accommodations, you can expect smartly decorated rooms outfitted with writing desks, tasteful art work, big comfortable beds, satellite television, mini-bar, and direct-dial telephones. The service, from the reception desk to the restaurants, is tip-top. In fact, the whole place seemingly operates in a service-oriented fashion, which is rare in the two republics. None too surprising, the hotel is run by a joint Slovak-Canadian hotel management company.

EAST SLOVAKIA

HOTEL SATEL, *námestie Majstra Pavla 55, 054 01 Levoča. Tel. 0966/ 512 943, fax 0966/514 486. Rates for single/double: 1,250/1,900 Sk. Credit cards: AE, DC, MC, V. 21 rooms. Restaurant.*

Not many hotels in Slovakia are as beautiful as this one. The building itself is a gem, featuring a pastel Baroque façade and intriguing vaulted ceilings. But the hotel's star attraction is its stunningly beautiful Renaissance courtyard, replete with delicate arcades, ornate ironwork, and a small fountain. Here you can have your breakfast, lunch, or dinner, or just sit back and soak it all in over a cocktail from the bar's huge drink menu.

The spacious, sunny rooms are nothing short of gorgeous, outfitted with polished wood floors, dark wood furniture, tasteful impressionist paintings, satellite television, and direct-dial telephones. It's hard to decide whether to take a room in the front of the hotel, offering a view of the main square, or in the rear, offering a view of the hotel's awesome courtyard. But you should be more than pleased wherever you end up. The hotel also has an excellent restaurant and a wine cellar hunkering down under a vaulted ceiling. All in all, a most memorable place to stay.

The restaurant at this hotel features a well-rounded menu of regional specialties such as venison steak topped with a red wine sauce or leg of pork smothered in a delectable cream sauce. If you're in the mood for something more formal, have a seat in the dining room, a regal setting with parquet floors, carved stone columns, and the town crest stamped on the ceiling. Or if you feel like coming to dinner in shorts and a tee-shirt, take a seat in the courtyard and dine by the fountain. Prices here range between 150-250 Sk.

13. PRAGUE

What is it that draws tourists by the hundreds of thousands to Prague? The answer to that question can been seen on people's faces as they walk across the **Charles Bridge**. Their faces speak of wonderment, and of disbelief that such a storybook city could actually exist in this day and age.

Prague is indeed a wonder.

But Prague reveals itself in many more ways than the glorious vista from the Charles Bridge. It reveals itself most magnificently from atop two castles more than a thousands years old – the **Prague Castle** and **Vyšehrad**. It reveals itself most colorfully from the middle of **Old Town Square** – festooned with a pastel symphony of architectural styles. It reveals itself most intimately along the sinuous medieval lanes that weave through **Staré Město** or **Malá Strana**. And it reveals itself most energetically from **Wenceslas Square**, where the city hustle reaches its peak.

As you've most likely heard by now, Prague escaped World War II largely unscathed. Consequently, Prague is astoundingly well preserved. It boasts so many historic houses, churches, palaces, towers, and other architectural treasures that it's enough to make your head spin, and enough to keep your itinerary completely booked for however long you stay. Certainly, you don't need to be a student of architecture to have a heyday in this city, where you're able to feast your eyes on just about every style introduced in Europe in the last thousand years: Romanesque, Gothic, Renaissance, Baroque, Historicist, even Cubist.

In fact, there's so much to see from the streets, bridges, parks, and squares that you could have a fine time in this city without ever stepping inside a church, palace, or museum. But you wouldn't want to do that because there's an equal wealth of fantastic sights to be had inside these churches, palaces, and museums.

But, by all means, don't feel as if you must take it *all* in. Prague is best appreciated at your leisure. And with so many wonderful sights so easily accessible by foot or by the great public transportation here, there's no need to feel pressed for time. So go ahead and take that empty seat in some outdoor café on **Old Town Square**, because it's the best way to absorb the life of that square. Go ahead and dive into some pub in **Malá Strana** (the Lesser Quarter) for a glass of Pilsner Urquell, because it's the best place to meet the locals and to sample the beer.

Like any major destination, Prague is not always wine and roses. In the summer and during the Christmas holiday, tourists clog the narrow lanes and choke the Charles Bridge. When that happens, the city can feel like one gargantuan theme park.

But it's not too difficult to avoid all the tourist hubbub by making an effort to get off the beaten path, the path being the one that takes you from Wenceslas Square, through Old Town Square, across the Charles Bridge, and up to the Prague Castle. You'll read it again and again in these pages: Drop the map and go where your instincts tell you. You never know where a little aimless wandering may lead you. It could lead to a peaceful, enclosed garden affording a spectacular view of the Prague Castle, or through an alluring medieval alley where there is no sign of modern life.

Another way to avoid the tourist flood is by doing some of your sightseeing after the sun has gone down. This is especially true of Prague Castle, which all but turns into a graveyard when the tour groups have retired to their hotels and all that's left are the castle guards. Though you won't be able to get inside the churches and palaces, you can still wander the grounds, stand in silent awe of **St. Vitus Cathedral**, and take in the twinkling lights of the city sprawled out before you.

Also, do try to get out of the historic center and visit some of the surrounding districts, where you'll have a much greater chance of finding a more reasonably priced hotel or restaurant, and a much greater chance to see how Praguers live, as very few of them these days can afford living in the touristy areas of town.

ORIENTATION

Prague is not only in the middle of **Bohemia**, but in the middle of Europe as well. It lies 320 kilometers (198 miles) northwest of Vienna, 500 kilometers (310 miles) east of Frankfurt, and 340 kilometers (211 miles) south of Berlin.

One of the things that makes Prague so terrific is that it is built on and around hills, seven of them to be exact. They are not just bumps on the landscape, nor are they peaks, but honest-to-god hills that afford infinite perspectives of the city, either from the bottom or top of them.

Running through it all, cutting the city more or less in half, is the **Vltava River** (pronounced VALtava), also known in German as the

Moldau. People who come to Prague for the first time are amazed to find such a mighty river flowing through the city. Indeed, it does take four or so minutes to walk across the river via one of the eight beautiful bridges that span the Vltava in the center of Prague. The river runs a fairly straight northward-bound course through Prague, swinging around one big bend before flowing out of the city.

The core of the city – where you'll be spending the majority, if not all, of your time – is comprised of four separate historical towns and one enclosed former ghetto, all of which are referred to today as districts. On the west side of the Vltava, occupying one of Prague's hills, is **Hradčany**, encompassing the **Prague Castle** and **St. Vitus Cathedral**. At the foot of the castle and spread out along the banks of the Vltava is **Malá Strana**, or the Lesser Quarter. On the east side of the river, directly across from Malá Strana, is **Staré Město**, or Old Town, engulfing the Old Jewish Quarter and former ghetto of **Josefov**. **Nové Město**, or New Town, is the largest of the four historical towns, shaped like a crescent around the south, east, and north sides of Staré Město. Nové Město is Prague's major business district and includes **Wenceslas Square**.

Creating a ring around the historic core of the city and included in the composition of "central Prague" are a number of 19th-century suburbs, among them **Vinohrady, Žižkov, Karlín, Holešovice, Bubeneč** and **Smíchov**. But the city limits don't end there; they reach further out to embrace several modern suburbs, characterized by legions of cinder block housing estates that the Communists were oh-so fond of building.

Prague is also divided into ten postal districts. You'll notice that addresses usually contain some number following "Praha," as in Praha 3 or Praha 9. But these postal districts are much too big to help in orientating yourself. Praha 1, as an example, takes up all of all the historic center. It's better to know the specific district of an address if you're catching a cab or attempting to track down a street by foot or by public transportation. Consequently, I've listed most everything by district.

Roughly 1,200,000 people live in Prague, but, with the tens of thousands of tourists invading the city each week, it can feel like a lot more. Only rarely does it climb over 85 degrees Farenheit in the middle of summer, so no need to worry about dying from the heat. Temperatures often fall below freezing during late autumn, winter, and early spring, so come well layered if you plan on being in the city during that time.

There are advantages and disadvantages to coming in the winter. The disadvantage is the cold, which can bite right down to your bones, especially if you're walking near the river. The advantages are fewer tourists, cheaper hotel rates, and greater room availability. It does snow often in Prague, and when that happens the city is truly a magical place to behold.

GETTING AROUND TOWN

First thing you'll need in this maze of ancient streets is a map, of which there are several choices. Most hotels provide maps of the city, as do some travel bureaus. If you're staying in town for three or four days, you most likely will not venture out of the historic center much. A good choice of maps then is Žaket's *Praha-historické centrum*.

If you plan on staying longer and venturing out of the center, then pick up Kartografie Praha's extensive 1:20,000 *Praha plán města*, offering a detail of the historic center, a street index, and public transportation routes for the entire city for about 30 Kč. You can buy either of these maps at any bookstore, several newsstands, and most hotels.

PRAGUE WALKING TOURS

I highly recommend taking one of the walking tours through the historic center of town, especially if you have just arrived and need a little guidance. Here are a couple agencies offering them:

Čedok, Na příkopě 18 (Můstek metro station); Tel. 02/241 976 43. Offers scores of different tours depending on the season.

Ghost Tour, ulice Armády 188; Tel. 02/651 7171. Explore Prague's spirit world and meet its legendary ghosts, such as the priest and the prostitute, the barber and his sharpened blade, and the vegetarian butcher. Check with the Prague Information Service (see "Practical Information" at the end of this chapter) for times and departure points.

One thing you need to be aware of when moving around Prague is the numerous pickpockets who generally prey in the more touristy areas, especially Wenceslas Square, Old Town Square, Charles Bridge, and the Prague Castle. Keep all your valuables (credit cards, cash, passport, etc.) in a money belt than can be tucked underneath your clothing. Take extra precaution when boarding trams and metros. And always stay alert, as these thieves have contrived many ways in which to divert attention away from your pockets.

By Foot

Prague, especially its historic center, was made for walking. You can walk straight through the historic center – from the National Museum at the top of Wenceslas Square to the Strahov Monastery at the top of Hradčany – in a matter of 30 minutes. But you wouldn't do that because there are so many intriguing lanes and mysterious alleys beckoning you to get off your intended route. Indeed, Prague wasn't built to get you from point A to point B as quickly as possible. It was built to get you from one point to another in the happiest, most roundabout way possible. So do come with some sturdy walking shoes. Hiking boots might even be a good idea, considering that you'll be walking on cobblestones 95 percent of the time. Oh, and do look out for dog poop on the sidewalk. Praguers love their dogs, and take them just about everywhere, including on the metro and trams and even in restaurants, pubs, and cafés.

By Metro

Most foreigners, when they come to Prague, remark that the Communists sure did one thing right in this city, which was build a fantastic metro system. The Soviet-designed system is indeed clean, fast, efficient, and safe. It's composed of three lines – **green** (line A), **yellow** (line B), and **red** (line C), which connect at various stations around the center and then shoot out to the suburbs. Metro stations are easy to identify by the "M" logo posted on the street above. A couple of key words to know when using the metro is *výstup* (exit) and *přestup* (connection).

Trains come about every four or five minutes during work hours on the weekdays, slackening off at night and weekends to about every eight minutes. Praguers are early risers, which means the trains start running at 5 a.m. The last train leaves its originating station at midnight.

Tickets, at 8 Kč and 12 Kč each, are dirt cheap, and can be purchased at any station by dropping coins into the yellow dispenser and selecting the appropriate ticket. With an 8-Kč ticket you can go four stations or less with one transfer. If you need to go more than four stations, then buy a 12-Kč ticket, good for 90 minutes (weekdays from 8 p.m. to midnight and 24 hours on weekends) or 60 minutes (weekdays from 5 a.m. to 8 p.m.). You can use the same ticket on the tram or bus. Validate your ticket by sticking it in the automated puncher at the top of the metro escalator.

You can buy a 24-hour (70 Kč), a three-day (180 Kč), a 7-day (250), or a 15-day (280 Kč) pass at many of the metro stations. But they are hardly worth it, unless you plan on riding the day away on the metro. Prague residents usually buy monthly passes, good with a special identification card you pick up from the metro offices.

Yes, you are on the honor system when you ride the metro, tram, or bus. Consequently, a lot of people chance it and ride, as they say here, "in the black." If you choose to join in on the freeloading and get caught, be prepared to shell out 200 Kč on the spot to the plain-clothes controller.

By Tram

Negotiating the scores of hairpin turns and tight curves along the cobblestone streets and lanes, the tram is well adapted to the ancient city, and a fun way to go. There are roughly 30 lines criss-crossing the city and running through the center of town. The regular day trams run about every five minutes during the work hours, slowing down to every ten to fifteen minutes at night and during the weekends. Timetables, posted at the stops, list each stop along the particular line. The day trams operate from 5 a.m. to midnight, while night trams (those numbered 51 through 58) operate from 11:30 p.m. to 4:30 a.m. All night trams stop at the Lazarská-Spálená intersection, located a block south of the Národní třida metro station in Nové Město. Trams take the same tickets as the metro. With the 8-Kč ticket, you can ride the same tram for no more than 15 minutes after validating the ticket. With the 12- Kč ticket, you can change to another tram or transfer to the bus or metro – as long as you get to your final destination in less than 60 minutes (weekdays from 5 a.m. to 8 p.m.) or 90 minutes (weekdays from 8 p.m. to midnight and 24 hours on weekends).

If you are nowhere near a metro station, you can buy a ticket from most newsstands and tobacco shops. To validate the ticket, stick it in the automatic puncher on board.

By Bus

Unless you get stuck staying in the boonies or have the urge to see the outskirts, then you probably will have no need to take the bus. The bus uses the same tickets as the tram and metro. Validate your ticket by sticking it in the automatic puncher. Schedules are posted at every stop.

Bus Tours

There are several bus tours around Prague, day or night. Prices range from 300 Kč to 1300 Kč, depending on the type and duration of the tour.
- **Čedok**, *Na příkopě 18 (Můstek metro station); Tel. 02/241 976 43*
- **Grayline-Cityrama**, *Štěpánská 21 (Můstek metro station); Tel. 02/249 112 89*
- **Koala Leisure Tours**, *Na příkopě 33 (Náměstí Republiky metro station); Tel. 02/242 226 91*
- **Prague Sightseeing Tours**, *Klimentská 52 (pick up at Náměstí Republiky); Tel. 02/231 4661*

Boat Tours

I know, it's the touristy thing to do. But after walking around so much, it's nice to put your feet up for a while and leisurely take in all the wonderful sights seen along the Vltava.

Cruises usually span a stretch between **Vyšehrad** and **Čechův most** (or Czech Bridge) and run only during the warm months. Prices for tours start at 200 Kč. Lunch and dinner cruises are also available for around 800 Kč.

• **Čedok**, *see "Bus Tours," above.*
• **Evropská Vodní Doprava**, *three boats anchored at Čechův bridge along the Na Františku embankment (north of Staroměstská metro station and in front of the Hotel Intercontinental); Tel. 02/231 0208.* Offers one-hour cruises, as well as two-hour lunch trips (with live music) and two-and-half-hour dinner trips (buffet and live music).
• **Pražská Paroplavební Společnost**, *anchored at Palackého bridge (take the Palackého exit at Karlovo Náměstí metro station); Tel. 02/298 309.* They also offer one-hour trips, as well as lunch and dinner cruises. But I recommend taking their two-hour trip to the Troja chateau and back (see the subheading for Troja under "Seeing the Sights").

By Taxi
Prague taxi drivers have perhaps the biggest racket going in the city. They are notorious for ripping off foreigners. I don't mean that they overcharge by a dollar here or there like American drivers sometimes do. I mean that Prague drivers will overcharge by as much as twice the legal rate, sometimes more. It's so bad that many foreigners living in Prague avoid cabs like the plague. Of course, there are times when there is just no other option.

But there are ways to circumvent getting overcharged. First, avoid hailing taxis from the street. Second, forget hiring a taxi from a stand at any of the major tourist hotspots, such as Wenceslas Square, Old Town Square, Charles Bridge, or Malá Strana Square. Some of the most corrupt drivers gravitate to these areas, preying on the most unknowing people in town – the tourists.

Your best bet, then, is to call a dispatcher at one of the two numbers given below. When you've reached your destination, ask the driver for a receipt (*paragon*) showing the price and number of kilometers driven. (By law, the driver is obliged to give you one.) At press time, a ride officially cost 12 Kč per kilometer. And a ride from the airport to Wenceslas Square (more or less the very center of Prague) should be around 250 Kč with luggage.

If you're forced to hail a taxi on the street or hire one from the stands outside one of the metro stations, make sure that the meter is on. If not, get out. Another taxi will come along soon enough, for there is no shortage of taxis in Prague. If you don't suspect that the driver has overcharged you, give him a 10 to 15 percent tip.

Here are two reliable taxi companies that can get you around town or to the airport. Dispatchers usually, but not always, speak English.
• **AAA**, *Tel. 02/33 99*
• **Rony Taxi**, *Tel. 02/692 1958*

By Car

You've come to Prague to relax, enjoy the sights, and drink some good beer. Right? Then forget trying to get around town by car. A guarantee: you will get lost. Remember that the historic center of Prague acquired its present layout centuries before the invention of the automobile. Therefore, there is no logical grid system to help you get from point A to point B. In the historic center, indeed in most of the city, you will rarely come across a two-way street, unless it happens to be a major thoroughfare. With the slightest curve in the road, many streets change names for no apparent reason. The worst part of driving in the city, however, is the added confusion of sharing streets with trams, which always have the right of way and can cut you off at any moment.

If you arrive by car, find some place to park it and then leave it there. Most hotels, no matter how small, usually have parking spaces, if not garages. But the availability is limited. So, when you make your reservation, ask the hotel to reserve a parking space for you as well. As for general parking in the city, follow the several blue "P" signs posted on your way into the center. Most of these lots cost about 25 Kč an hour, and are guarded by an attendant, to whom you pay.

As for parking on the street in the historic center, forget it. First of all, most of the street parking around the historic center is by permit only. Second, Prague police need little incentive to slap a boot on your tire and issue you a 500 Kč-charge for taking it off.

Finally, you run the extremely high risk in Prague of getting your car stolen. Car theft has skyrocketed in the last few years, to the point where many people I know have given up on the idea of even buying one. If you happen to be one of the unfortunate, you are plum out of luck, as there's very little the Czech police can, or care, to do about it.

To rent a car in Prague, try one of the following agencies:

- **Alamo**, *Prague Airport, Tel. 02/201 135 34*
- **Budget**, *náměstí Curieových 5/43 (Hotel Inter-Continental), Prague 1, Tel. 02/248 899 95*
- **Car Service** (with limousine service), *Výstaviště Exhibition Grounds, Prague 7, Tel. 02/201 036 25*
- **Europcar**, *Pařížská 28, Prague 1, Tel. 02/ 248 105 15*
- **Hertz**, *Karlovo náměstí 28, Prague 2, Tel. 02/297 836*
- **Avis**, *Prague Airport; Tel. 02/231 55 15*
- **Czechocar**, *5 května 65, Prague 4, Tel. 02/612 220 79*

By Bicycle

Are you crazy? Do you value your life?

Consider this: Prague streets are filled with drivers pretty much oblivious to pedestrians, which means they are totally oblivious to cyclists. Seasoned big-city bicycle couriers might have what it takes to negotiate Prague traffic. Those who are used to tooting around country roads or suburban streets should do themselves a favor and drop the idea of seeing Prague by bike. But there are a few parks in the city, especially Stromovka Park or Letná (see "Seeing the Sights"), that make for pleasant, easy-going cycling. (You can take your bicycle on the metro.)

Here are are some places that rent bikes:

• **A Landa,** *Šumavská 33, Prague 2, Tel. 02/242 561 21.* Rents mountain bikes.
• **Central European Adventure Tours,** *Pod útesy 8, Prague 5, Tel. 02/232 8879.* Rents bikes, provides transport, and suggests routes in and (better yet) out of the city.

WHERE TO STAY

Like all service-oriented industries in Prague, the hotel business is an emerging one, with new hotels and pensions popping up every few months or so. But Prague still has a long way to go to meet the overwhelming demand for accommodations put on the city. This is to say that you should always, no matter what, *book a room as far in advance as possible,* or you may end up staying in a real undesirable hotel and paying a pretty penny for it.

Until recently, you could divide hotels in Prague into two categories: luxury and fleabag. Hotel owners are now getting the idea that not everyone who comes to Prague is either a CEO of a major company or a student backpacker. Luckily, then, some mid-range hotels are popping up, and not just in the boonies either, but in the historic center of town. Mid-range in the historic center, however, means spending between $100 and $130 a night for a double room, while high-range means well over $200 a night. These rates, as do all of the rates listed below, include the 22 percent value-added tax.

No, accommodations are by no means cheap in Prague. If you had that idea when considering a trip to the Golden City, quickly drop it.

But you don't necessarily have to find lodgings in the heart of the city in order to get the most out of Prague. There are reasonably priced accommodations in several districts that are still considered "central Prague," and are a quick metro or tram ride to the historic center. (By "quick," I mean five or ten minutes.)

What follows is a range of choices, from the top of the line in the heart of Prague to alternative, cheaper stays just outside the heart. To help in making your choice, I've listed the hotels by district and added short descriptions of those districts. Unless otherwise noted, all rooms come with private baths, televisions (usually satellite), and direct-dial telephones. In many cases, the rooms feature a minibar, hairdryer, and a small safe for your valuables. Most rooms in Prague, even in the luxury hotels, are pretty small by American standards. But you didn't come all this way to live it up in your hotel room, did you? If you must have something larger, ask for an apartment or sometimes a junior suite.

PRAGUE'S BEST HOTELS

Of the hotels listed in this section, these are the cream of the crop, offering intriguing rooms and first-class service in the most ideal locations:

1. *HOTEL SAVOY, Hradčany*
2. *PENSION U RAKA, Hradčany*
4. *U KRÁLE KARLA, Malá Strana*
6. *HOTEL U TŘÍ PŠTROSŮ , Malá Strana*
7. *HOTEL U PÁVA, Malá Strana*
8. *HOTEL SAX, Malá Strana*
14. *HOTEL PAŘÍŽ , Staré Město*
15. *HOTEL CASA MARCELLO, Staré Město*

West of the Vltava – Hradčany & Malá Strana

Occupying a hill high above the Vltava, **Hradčany** is chock-full of Prague's most popular sights. First among them is the **Prague Castle**, encompassing **St. Vitus Cathedral** and a complex of palaces, museums, gardens, and churches. But Hradčany is more than just the castle. It extends westward up the hill, covering more gardens, a number of narrow twisting lanes, and additional fantastic sights, such as the **Loreto Church** and the **Strahov Monastery**.

At night, after the tourists have all moved down the hill and the spotlights have illuminated St. Vitus Cathedral, a heavy calm settles on Hradčany, and the area is transformed into one of the most peaceful places you can imagine.

Hugging the foot of the castle, and in places stretched out along the Vltava River, **Malá Strana** (the Lesser Quarter) is Prague at its most medieval. The quarter dates back to the 13th century and holds some of Prague's most intriguing lanes, alleys, and staircases. Some great sights include the newly-renovated **Malá Strana Square**, the **Church of St. Nicholas**, the **Wallenstein Palace**, **Nerudova Street** (a section of the **Royal Way**), **Kampa Park**, and a host of beautiful Renaissance and Baroque houses. Of course, you can't forget the **Charles Bridge**, its west end providing a path straight into Malá Strana.

1. HOTEL SAVOY, *Keplerova 6, 110 00 Prague 1 (tram #22 from Malostranská metro station to Pohořelec stop). Tel. 02/243 024 30, Fax 02/243 021 28. Rates for executive/deluxe rooms: 7,820/9,280 Kč. Credit Cards: AE, MC, DC, V. 61 rooms. Restaurant.*

And you thought Prague was cheap? Well, think again. But if you want to splurge, this hotel at the top of Hradčany is the place to do it. Part of the Vienna International Hotels & Resorts chain, the Savoy is set behind a yellow Art Nouveau facade, which is the only bit of authenticity left of the building. The interior was completely gutted in 1993 to make room for the handsome wood fixtures, marble floors, and expansive dining room atrium that now compliment the building. A nice touch is the library, where high tea is served every afternoon by an open fireplace.

Each of the individually decorated rooms comes with a marble bathroom, three telephones (one in the bathroom, of course), Fax machine, satellite television, VCR, and a complimentary mini-bar. Definitely ask for a room in the rear of the hotel on the second level or above so you can have a view over Hradčany. The hotel also has what's called a "relax center," complete with whirlpool, sauna, fitness center, masseuse, and beauty salon. But the best part of the hotel is the friendly, English-speaking service. For the hotel's sensational restaurant, see *Where to Eat* below.

2. PENSION U RAKA, *Černiská 10/93, 118 00 Prague 1 (tram #22 from Malostranská metro station to Pohořelec stop). Tel. 02/351 453, Fax 02/353 074. Rates for singles & doubles: : 5,600/6,200 Kč. Credit Cards: AE, DC, MC, V. 6 rooms. No restaurant, but breakfast is included in rates.*

You can hardly believe that this pension, carved out of a 400-year-old cottage, is in the middle of Prague. Located down the hill from the Loreto among Hradčany's narrow, twisting lanes, U raka makes you feel like you're in some village in the countryside, a feeling that's compounded by the pension's abundance of wood fixtures, its fireplaces, and its Japanese style garden.

Even though U raka is billed as a pension, it has that homey, intimate touch that makes it feel more like a bed and breakfast. Antiques, original art work, and great ceramic ware abound. If you feel like splurging, go for the apartment, which comes with its own fireplace. But be sure to book a room as much as three to four months in advance for this small gem. Private parking is available.

3. HOTEL HOFFMEISTER, *Pod Bruskou 9, 118 00 Prague 1 (Malostranská metro station). Tel. 02/561 8155, Fax 02/530 959. Rates for singles/doubles: 4,437-5,916/5,278-6,873 Kč. Credit Cards: AE, DC, MC, V. 42 rooms. Restaurant.*

The first question that comes to mind at this hotel is: Who is Adolf Hoffmeister and what makes him so special as to name a hotel after him?

With friends such as Pablo Picasso, Milan Kundera, and Francois Mitterand (just to name a bare minimum), the caricaturist and painter Hoffmeister was apparently a celebrity of sorts in Prague during his time. Whoever he was, you can't get away from him at the hotel. His caricature drawings of just about every celebrity of the early 20th century fill nearly every spare inch of the walls, which isn't all that surprising considering that his son owns the hotel.

The rooms, with their gorgeous wood-inlaid furniture and bright color patterns, are smartly decorated and certainly luxurious, but a bit on the generic side. They don't, however, match up to their exorbitant price tags. Another problem with the hotel is that it's located on a street jammed with traffic at all hours of the day. Granted, the windows block out most of the noise, but the street puts a damper on the location, and doesn't make for the best of views. Besides the restaurant serving Czech and French food, the hotel has a classy brasserie-style café, a cellar wine bar, parking garage, and cars for rent.

4. **U KRÁLE KARLA**, *Úvoz 4, 118 00 Prague 1 (tram #12 or 22 from Malostranská metro station to Malostranské náměstí stop). Tel. 02/538 805, Fax 02/538 811. Rates for singles/doubles: 5,300/6,800 Kč. Credit Cards: AE, DC, MC, V. 19 rooms. Restaurant.*

Stained glass windows, original painted ceiling beams, and a sweeping spindle-shaped staircase all contribute to the regal, medieval decor at this small hotel located footsteps down from the castle gate at the top of Malá Strana. Before its Baroque reconstruction in 1639, the Gothic building belonged to the Benedictine monks.

Renovated in 1993, the place is exquisite in detail, from the floral designs on the brass balustrade on down to the figurines, statues, and paintings filling the hotel. Direct dial phones, satellite television, and a wealth of antiques come with each room. The three suites feature fireplaces and original wooden ceiling beams. The hotel's vaulted dining room is frescoed with colorful paintings, serving high class Czech dishes such as venison steak with juniper berries or roast duck with a creamy pepper sauce.

5. **HOTEL POD VĚŽÍ**, *Mostecká 2, 118 00 Prague 1 (tram #22 or 12 from Malostranská metro station to Malostranské náměstí stop). Tel. 02/533 710, Fax 02/531 859. Rates for singles/doubles: 3,900-4,500/5,300-6,100 Kč. Credit Cards: AE, DC, MC, V. 12 rooms. Restaurant.*

In the shadow of the Charles Bridge tower, this pink-and-cream Baroque house occupies a prime piece of real estate. But the hotel fails to deliver the kind of accommodations you would expect with such exorbitant rates. In spite of the stylish wood-inlaid furniture and the carved stucco ceilings, the rooms are bit on the drab side. If you choose to stay here, definitely ask for a room with a view of Charles Bridge. The restaurant offers mostly Czech food, but does have some international and Jewish specialties. Private parking is available.

6. HOTEL U TŘÍ PŠTROSŮ, *Dražického náměstí 12, 118 Prague 1 (tram #12 or 22 from Malostranská metro station to Malostranské náměstí stop). Tel. 02/573 205 65, Fax 02/573 206 11. Rates for singles/doubles: 4,000-4,400/ 5,400-6,000 Kč. Credit Cards: AE, DC, MC, V. 18 rooms. Restaurant.*

This hotel frescoed with three ostriches sits off to the side of the Charles Bridge – one of the best sites you could imagine in Prague. The hotel gets its peculiar name, meaning "At the Three Ostriches," from the 14th century, when the house belonged to a man who sold ostrich feathers. A foreign delegation, arriving with three ostriches as a present for King Charles IV, are said to have stayed at the house, hence the name. Later, it became the first coffee house in Prague.

But an illustrious past is not all that comes with the hotel. The rooms, a couple of which have their original painted beamed ceilings, find a comfortable medium between authenticity and modernity. Some of the rooms are a bit cramped and don't have much of a view, so request a room with a view of the Charles Bridge. The restaurant serves a wide range of game dishes underneath Renaissance beams. Be sure to reserve at least three months in advance for this gem.

7. HOTEL U PÁVA, *U Lužického semináře 32, 118 00 Prague 1 (Malostranská metro station). Tel. 02/573 207 43, Fax 02/533 379. Rates for singles/doubles: 4,900/5,300 Kč. Credit Cards: AE, DC, MC V. 11 rooms. Restaurant.*

Karel Klubal, owner of this hotel on Kampa Island and Hotel U Krále Karla (see above), gave this 17th century house a noble restoration in 1991. Stone columns and beamed ceilings add an air of authenticity, while the crystal chandeliers and historical paintings provide a dose of opulence. The colorful rooms, outfitted with handsome walnut furniture, come with all the expected amenities. Ask for a suite or room with a splendid view of the Prague Castle.

8. HOTEL SAX, *Jánsky Vršek 328/3, 118 00 Prague 1 (tram #12 or 22 from Malostranská metro station to Malostranské náměstí stop). Tel. 02/538 422, Fax 02/538 498. Rates for singles/doubles: 3,300/3,950 Kč. Credit Cards: AE, DC, MC, V. 22 rooms. Restaurant.*

Offering the best value for the location, Hotel Sax features a gorgeous atrium set behind a 17th century facade. The hotel is located up the hill and around the corner from the American Embassy, right in the thick of Malá Strana's medieval lanes. The rooms are cheerful and smartly furnished and the restaurant offers an international menu with weekly specials. The hotel, which opened in 1993, has already won a local award for being one of the ten best in the country. Deserving the award or not, the hotel comes highly recommended. Private parking is available.

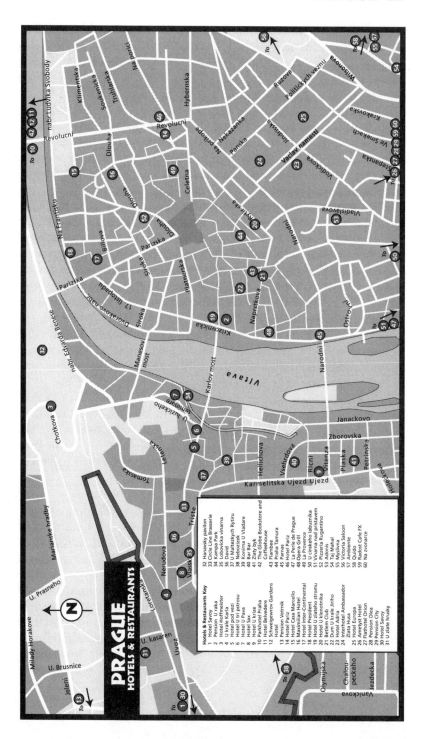

PRAGUE
HOTELS & RESTAURANTS

Hotels & Restaurants Key
1 Hotel Savoy
2 Pension U raka
3 Hotel Hoffmeister
4 U krale Karla
5 Hotel pod vezi
6 Hotel U tri pstrosu
7 Hotel U Pava
8 Hotel Sax
9 Hotel U krize
10 Parkhotel Praha
11 Hotel Belvedere
12 Schweigewrov Gardens Hotel
13 Pension Vetrnik
14 Hotel Pariz
15 Hotel Casa Marcello
16 Maximilian Hotel
17 Hotel Inter-Continental
18 Hotel President
19 Hotel U zlateho stromu
20 Hotel U klenotnika
21 Betlem Club
22 Dum U krale Jiriho
23 Hotel Adria
24 Interhotel Ambassador Zlata Husa
25 Hotel Europa
26 Ameryst Hotel
27 Flathotel Orion
28 Pension Olea
29 Pension City
30 Hotel Savoy
31 U zlate Hrusky
32 Hanavsky pavilon
33 Circle Line Brasserie
34 Kampa Park
35 Lobovicka vinarna
36 David
37 U Maltezkych Rytiru
38 Neboziziek
39 Konirna U Vladare
40 Bar Bar
41 Zlaty byk
42 The Globe Bookstore and Coffeehouse
43 Flambee
44 Praha Tamura
45 Parnas
46 Hotel Pariz
47 La Perle de Prague
48 Opera Grill
49 La Provence
50 U cinskeho labuznika
51 Vinarna nad pristavem
52 Pizzeria Rugantino
53 Adonis
54 Taj Mahal
55 Mystivna
56 Victoria Saloon
57 Ambiente
58 Quido
59 Radost Cafe FX
60 Na zvonarce

9. HOTEL U KŘÍŽE, *Újezd 20, 110 00 Prague 1 (tram #9 or 22 from Národní třída metro station to Újezd stop). Tel. 02/533 326, Fax 02/533 443. Rates for singles/doubles: 2,900/3,200 Kč. Credit Cards: AE, MC, V. 22 rooms. Restaurant.*

This hotel is a good alternative to the higher priced rooms closer to the foot of the castle and the Charles Bridge – both a mere two tram stops away. The 17th century building, at the base of the wooded Petřín Hill, was given a valiant renovation in 1995, and now sports handsome wood-beamed and vaulted ceilings. Interesting old maps of the Czech lands hang on the lobby walls, and in the restaurant you'll find a collection of funky art work.

The rooms are spacious and smartly outfitted with dark wood furniture. The double rooms facing the street afford a nice view of Petřín Hill, while the two-story apartments offer no view at all, except for the terrace that divides them from the main section of the hotel. The hotel has underground parking, which is good news in this part of Prague where parking is hard to come by.

Holešovice & Bubeneč

These two adjacent districts developed at the turn of century into well-to-do suburbs, but are now minutes away from the heart of Prague by tram or metro. Pretty Art Nouveau, neo-Renaissance, or neo-Baroque architecture fill the tree-lined streets.

Both districts are built around the edge of **Stromovka Park**, Prague's largest. At the northern edge of the park is the attractive **Výstaviště** – the city's exhibition grounds featuring a dancing fountain, amusement park, theater, and exhibit of sculptures. The newly opened **Trade Fair Palace** (housing the National Gallery's modern art collection) and the **National Technical Museum** are also located in this district.

10. PARKHOTEL PRAHA, *Veletržní 20, 170 00 Prague 7 (tram #12 from Nádráží Holešovice metro station to Veletržní stop). Tel. 02/201 328 62, Fax 02/243 161 80. Rates for singles/doubles: 3,420/4,100 Kč. Credit Cards: AE, MC, V. 245 rooms. Restaurant.*

A half-block away from the Výstaviště exhibition grounds, this monstrous concrete hotel is way overpriced when you consider its tacky decor, modular rooms, and overall lackluster appearance. The hotel is a target of tour buses, which makes things all the more impersonal. If you are willing to spend so much for a room, look into a smaller hotel further in the center.

11. HOTEL BELVEDERE, *Milady Horákové 19, 170 00 Prague 7 (Vltavská metro station). Tel. 02/374 741, Fax 02/370 355. Rates for singles/doubles: 1,900-2,350/2,700-3,150 Kč. Credit Cards: AE, DC, MC, V. 124 rooms. Restaurant.*

This mid-range hotel is not a bad choice for lodgings within the center. The plain rooms – outfitted with satellite television, direct-dial telephones, and showers – are nothing special, but are comfortable and functional. The hotel also has a parking garage, a bar, disco, and, unfortunately, a casino. The restaurant, serving basic Czech food, is nothing to get excited about, but does have a dance floor.

12. SCHWEIGEROV GARDENS HOTEL, *Schweigerova 3, 160 00 Prague 3 (Hradčanská metro station). Tel. 02/320 005, Fax 02/320 225. Rates for singles/doubles: 2,700-3,000/2,000 Kč. Credit Cards: AE, DC, MC. 12 rooms. Restaurant.*

This small, family-run hotel sits at the edge of Stromovka Park in a quiet neighborhood. The ten minute walk from the metro station is a bit inconvenient, but the proximity to the park makes it worth the effort. The plain but decent rooms are generously spacious and have satellite television, direct-dial telephones, and bathtubs with hand-held showers. The restaurant has an extensive menu with French and Italian specialties; in the summer seating moves out to the lawn.

Břevnov

A fairly long haul from the center, this part of town wouldn't be mentioned at all if it weren't for the 1,000 year-old **Břevnov Monastery** and for the following pension:

13. PENSION VĚTRNÍK, *U Větrníku 40, 162 00 Prague 6 (tram #18 from Hradčanská metro station to Větrník stop). Tel. 02/205 133 90, Fax 02/361 406. Rates for singles/doubles: 1,900/2,000-3,000 Kč. Credit Cards: MC. 6 rooms. Restaurant (for guests only).*

The affable owner, Miloš Opatrný, is half the reason for staying at this house that has been in his family since 1899. Before opening a pension in his home, Miloš made his living as a chef in Prague and, for a time, in Tokyo. Now he cooks solely for his guests, preparing whatever they desire for breakfast or dinner. (This can include sushi, by the way!)

If you can believe it, the tower adjoining this house dates back a thousand years, when it was part of the local Břevnov Monastery. The tower was later converted into a windmill, hence the pension's name which means just that. The rooms, all of which come with private showers, are decked out in dark woods and white walls, and are wonderfully cozy during chilly evenings. The alcoved dining room hunkers down below vaulted ceilings and is outfitted with a fireplace.

The pension is on a large plot of land, fully enclosed by a brick wall that provides a welcome bit of isolation in this not-too-attractive part of Prague. Here you can play tennis on the single court just steps from the pension. The commute, a 15 minute tram ride to the foot of Prague Castle, isn't so bad when you consider the pension's reasonable rates.

East of the Vltava – Staré Město & Josefov

Make no doubt about it. **Staré Město**, or Old Town, is the heart of Prague, a heart that pulses with the footsteps of thousands of tourists, shoppers, and students that march daily along its sinuous, cobblestone lanes where you'll find the majority of the city's best hotels, restaurants, pubs, and stores.

This is where the magnitude of Prague's beauty hits home, most forcefully inside **Old Town Square**, the keystone of the city where scores of people gather at the top of each hour for the procession of saints that make their rounds on the **Astronomical Clock**. Most of Prague's prettiest churches – including **Týn Church, St. Nicholas**, and **St. James** – cluster in this district, as do a hodgepodge of architectural designs, from Gothic on up through Cubism. **Josefov**, the Old Jewish Quarter, is included here, because Staré Město nearly engulfs it. The major attraction here, of course, is the thousands of teetering gravestones at the **Old Jewish Cemetery**, one of Prague's most poignant sights.

As you might guess, there's a steep price tag for staying in Staré Město, but it's almost worth it considering that the district comes as close as anywhere to fulfilling the fantasy that most North Americans have of old Europe. Yes, it's that extraordinary.

14. HOTEL PAŘÍŽ, *U Obecního domu 1, 110 00 Prague 1 (Náměstí Republiky metro station). Tel. 02/242 221 51 or 800/888-4747 (in U.S. and Canada only), Fax 02/242 254 75. Rates for singles/doubles: 7,200/7,800 Kč. Credit Cards: AE, DC, MC, V. 100 rooms. Restaurant.*

This is what Bohumil Hrabal had to say about Hotel Pařížin his novel *I Served the King of England*: "The Hotel Pařížwas so beautiful it almost knocked me over. So many mirrors and brass balustrades and brass door handles and brass candleabras, all polished till the place shone like a palace of gold. . . . Mr. Brandejs gave me a warm welcome."

Well, that was back in the 1930s, before the Communists got a hold of it and let it fall to pieces. Now it's in the proper hands of Antonín Brandejs, grandson of the aforementioned Mr. Brandejs – owner of the hotel before its nationalization in 1948. After more than $1 million worth of renovation, the hotel is beginning to reclaim its former glory, especially in its splendid Art Nouveau restaurant, café, and lobby, where Hrabal's words ring true to this day. (see *Where to Eat*.)

The triangular-shaped building boldly commands a corner in the old town, minutes away from Old Town Square and across the street from another Art Nouveau gem, the Municipal House (Obecní dům). Mosaics adorn the hotel's three-sided facade, its series of gables stretched along the two streets that meet in front of the hotel. Topped by a glowing bauble, a single spire lurches up from the hotel's roof. Hands down, the Hotel Paříž boasts the most beautiful exterior of any hotel in Prague. Many rooms await renovation, and don't live up to the hotel's fame. With time, I'm sure that will change. For now, they suffice, but don't shine like the rest of the hotel. The furniture is a tad out of date and the decor could use some sprucing up. Still, they are comfortable enough, and generously large. The hotel provides airport transportation and offers special golf packages (the course is out of town in Karlštejn).

15. HOTEL CASA MARCELLO, *Řásnovka 783, 110 00 Prague 1 (Náměstí Republiky metro station). Tel. 02/231 0260 or 800/888-4747 (in Canada or United States only), Fax 02/231 1230. Rates for singles/doubles: 6,600 Kč. Credit Cards: AE, DC, MC, V. 17 rooms. Restaurant.*

Casa Marcello, which has the same owner as Hotel Paříž, takes its name from the previous owners, a noble Italian family that settled in Prague in the 17th century. The building itself dates to the 13th century, when it was used as a dormitory for the Franciscan St. Agnes Convent, one of the oldest convents in Europe. In fact, the building's design comes from a small convent in Assisi, where the Franciscan order originated. Fully restored in 1995 and handsome all around, the Gothic hotel makes for intriguing lodgings in a silent pocket of Staré Město.

The rooms, a bit on the smallish side, come cheerfully outfitted with dark wood furnishings and large closets. Ideally, the double rooms would match the size of the junior suites, which have a small living room. It seems that all of the rooms have equally good views, with some facing St. Agnes Church and others facing St. Haštal Church. If you'd like to have a view of St. Agnes while soaking in the bathtub, ask for the rear corner room.

The hotel has a pleasant terraced courtyard, where you can take your breakfast from the Swedish buffet in the morning or sip on a beer in the afternoon. In the cellar is the stylish bar and the hotel's decently priced Venetian trattoria. A highly recommended place in a great location.

16. MAXIMILIAN HOTEL, *Haštalská 14, 110 00 Prague 1 (Náměstí Republiky metro station). Tel. 02/218 061 11 or 800/344-1212 (United States and Canada only), Fax 02/218 061 10. Rates for singles/doubles: 5,208-5,565/ 5,940-6,600 Kč. Credit Cards: AE, DC, MC, V. 72 rooms. No restaurant.*

Carved out of a turn-of-the-century house minutes away from Old Town Square and across the street from St. Haštal Church, this Austrian-owned hotel opened in 1995 and caters mostly to those here on business.

Case in point are the fax machines in each of the rooms. But if you're in town on pleasure, you won't be disappointed by the air-conditioned rooms and their French cherry furniture, sophisticated decor, and large bathrooms. This is one of the few hotels in Prague that provide non-smoking rooms. The hotel does not have a restaurant, but does have an espresso bar and offers a breakfast that's included in the rates. There is also has an underground parking lot, and they can rent cars for you and get you theater tickets. All in all, a very classy place.

17. HOTEL INTER-CONTINENTAL, *Náměstí Curieových 43/5, 110 00 Prague 1 (Staroměstská metro station). Tel. 02/248 811 18 or 800/327-0200 (United States and Canada only), Fax 02/248 100 71. Rates for singles/doubles: 8,250/8,950 Kč. Credit Cards: AE, DC, MC, V. 365 rooms. 2 restaurants.*

It's big, it's outrageously expensive, and, from the outside, it's ugly. Granted, it has a great location in Josefov, placing you minutes away from the Old Jewish Cemetery and Old Town Square. But the unbecoming 1960s architecture is, frankly, a blight in this most historic part of Prague.

Part of the illustrious chain of worldwide hotels, the Inter-continental opened its doors in Prague more than twenty years ago, making it the first high-powered, Western hotel in Communist Czechoslovakia to do so. (Just think of all the secret police swarming the place before 1989.) This is a place for moguls, movie stars, and political figures. It isn't a place for someone who wants to get a good taste of Prague.

In addition to all the obvious amenities, the hotel has two restaurants (one casual and one formal), a fitness center, swimming pool, masseuse, sauna, hairdresser, putting green, car rental, and airport transportation.

18. HOTEL PRESIDENT, *Náměstí Curieových 100, 116 88 Prague 1 (Staroměstská metro station). Tel. 02/231 7523, Fax 02/231 8247. Rates for singles/doubles: 3,890-6,320/4,220-6,695 Kč. Credit Cards: AE, DC, MC, V. 100 rooms. Restaurant.*

Just behind the Inter-Continental, the Hotel President is newer than its neighbor, a bit less pretentious, and a tad more interesting. The marble lobby features Greek busts and temporary exhibitions of local artists. In the back is the extravagantly-decorated casino.

The second-story restaurant, serving high-class Czech food, offers a stunning view of the Prague Castle from its dining room and balcony. Be sure to ask for a room with the same view.

The rooms are nothing to get excited about, but are huge compared to most in Prague. The hotel has a tiny fitness center, replete with masseuse and sauna. The hotel can also arrange for you to go on a sightseeing tour and can sell you theater tickets.

19. HOTEL U ZLATÉHO STROMU, *Karlova 6, 110 00 Prague 1 (Staroměstská metro station). Tel. 02/242 213 85, Fax 02/242 213 85. Rates for singles/doubles: 2,790-3,790/2,990-3,990 Kč. Credit Cards: AE, DC, MC, V. 22 rooms. Restaurant.*

On the Royal Way, steps from the Charles Bridge, this hotel couldn't have a more splendid location. The attractive green-and-white gabled facade, the vaulted ceilings, and the rough-hewn wood furniture all contribute to the "Prague experience" that this hotel has to offer. There is one drawback to staying in this ancient building: the double rooms, especially those facing the street, are minuscule. But those facing the courtyard are bit more bearable. The apartments, which come with lofts, are much more spacious, sleeping as many as four people. The checkerboard bathrooms come with either showers or bathtubs.

The hotel has a 24-hour restaurant serving international courses, either underneath the stars on the terraced courtyard or underneath the vaulted ceilings in the dining room. There's also a cheesy disco in the cellar.

20. HOTEL U KLENOTNÍKA, *Rytířská 3, 110 00 Prague 1 (Můstek metro station). Tel. 02/242 116 99, Fax 02/261 782. Rates for singles/doubles: 2,100-2,500/2,900-3,600 Kč. Credit Cards: AE, DC, MC, V. 10 rooms. Restaurant.*

This pink-and-white townhouse exhibits a collection of funky, surrealist art on the walls. It's this bit of offbeat decor that sets if off from other, stiffer hotels in the neighborhood. Located three minutes by foot from either Wenceslas Square or the Estates Theater, this small hotel has decent sized rooms outfitted with satellite television and showers. If you don't mind hiking the three flights of stairs, then you should be pleased with the attic rooms, which do receive plenty of sunlight and afford a cozy feel. The English-speaking service works hard to make you feel at home. Around the corner from the hotel is a huge outdoor market that's fun to browse in.

21. BETLEM CLUB, *Betlémské náměstí 9, 110 00 Prague 1 (Národní třída metro station). Tel. 02/242 168 72, Fax 02/242 180 54. Rates for singles/doubles: 1,600/3,400 Kč. No credit cards. 20 rooms. No restaurant.*

This hotel comes as a reasonably priced alternative to the swish hotels in Staré Město. If you can stand the rather unappealing furniture and the old carpet, then you should have a pleasant stay here. Rooms come with satellite television, direct-dial telephones, and private baths. The hotel sports an odd collection of stuff on its wall, from antique swords to inexplicable portraits of the Liechtenstein family. A nice part of the hotel is the bar, located in a 13th-century cellar.

The hotel takes its name from the Betlem Chapel across the street, where Jan Hus preached in the 15th century. The location – five minutes by foot from either the Charles Bridge, Old Town Square, or Wenceslas Square – is a great one. Parking is available for guests in front of the hotel. But take notice: the hotel does not accept credit cards.

22. DŮM U KRÁLE JIŘÍHO, *Liliová 10, 110 00 Prague 1 (Národní třída or Staroměstská metro station). Tel. & Fax 02/242 219 83. Rates for singles/ doubles: 1,500/2,600 Kč. Credit Cards: AE, MC, V. 8 rooms. No restaurant.*

As you would guess from the low price of the rooms, there's nothing extravagant about this bed and breakfast, except for its excellent location – just off the Royal Way, minutes away from either Old Town Square or the Charles Bridge. The spacious rooms are decent, however, and come with private showers and toilets. But beware of the attic room, which has no windows, only skylights. Though there is no restaurant, there are two pubs in the building, one Czech and one Irish, both of which serve food.

Wenceslas Square
     Wenceslas Square (Václavské náměstí) is the Czech Republic's version of the Champs-Elysées, and is the city's best glimpse at just how entrenched in capitalism Prague has become. All the signs of Western influence have reared their heads here, such as the two McDonalds, the scores of ultra-chic shops, and the several swish hotels. More like a short, broad boulevard than a square, Wenceslas Square bustles throughout the day and into the wee hours of the morning. Consequently, some of Prague's more undesirable elements emerge here, such as pickpockets and prostitutes. This isn't to say that the square is dangerous. It isn't, if you just use common street sense.
     In addition to the series of handsome facades, some other memorable sights include the stately **National Museum**, crowning the square right behind the gallant **statue of King Wenceslas**. But for my money, I'd choose a quieter neighborhood to stay in.

23. HOTEL ADRIA, *Václavské náměstí 26, 110 00 Prague 1 (Můstek metro station). Tel. 02/242 165 43, Fax. 02/242 110 25. Rates for singles/ doubles: 4,680/5,580 Kč. Credit Cards: AE, DC, MC, V. 66 rooms. Restaurant.*

This is one of the better choices on the square, as the service here ranks high above the other hotels. The hotel has recently been renovated, sporting a mirror lobby and hand-glazed walls in the hallways. The rooms are a tad small, but smartly decorated and outfitted with satellite television and direct-dial telephones. All the rooms facing the square are higher-priced apartments, but the view of the enclosed garden behind the hotel is actually nicer. The hotel's adequate wine restaurant, the Triton Club, hunkers down in a cellar dripping with stalactites and exhibiting stone carvings of eerie sea monsters. The hotel has private parking located across the square.

24. INTERHOTEL AMBASSADOR ZLATÁ HUSA, *Václavské náměstí 5-7 (Můstek metro station). Tel. 02/241 938 76, Fax 02/242 306 20. Rates for singles/doubles: 3,770-4,640/4,524-5,655 Kč. Credit Cards: AE, DC, MC, V. 172 rooms. Restaurant.*

This is definitely one of the posher hotels you could choose in Prague. Occupying two stately buildings at the west end of the square, the hotel caters mostly to those on business accounts, but that shouldn't distract you from the sunny, lofty rooms that come with all the expected amenities, including crystal chandeliers, terry-cloth robes, and fax machines. Do ask for a room with a view of the square, or else you'll have an undesirable view of backlots.

The hotel has two fine dining restaurants, a snack bar, café, wine bar, pub, and disco. In the Halali Restaurant, Romany violin players serenade guests. The hotel also has a flashy casino, which unfortunately tarnishes the intimacy of the place. The service is highly formal, to the point of being gruff.

25. HOTEL EVROPA, *Václavské náměstí 25, 110 00 Prague 1 (Můstek metro station). Tel. 02/242 281 17, Fax 02/242 245 44. Rates for singles/doubles with bathroom: 2,450/3,400 Kč. Rates for singles/doubles without bathroom: 1,450/2,400 Kč. Credit Cards: AE, DC, MC, V. 90 rooms. Restaurant.*

This is a hotel that may not please many Americans and Canadians. But it deserves a mention here because it is one of the most famous hotels in Prague, due to its Art Nouveau design, which is one of the best in Prague. Carved balconies, handsome mosaics, floral balustrades, and a heavy dose of ornamentation went into its construction between 1906 and 1908. The facade and the atrium still look great, but the rooms that have suffered from the ruinous "renovations" of the Communist era. The hotel has still to undo the damages.

The rooms are small, dingy, and a bit depressing, although clean. Most don't have private baths and none have television sets. But if you are looking to save some crowns and are willing to forfeit luxury for nostalgia, then choose this place. Even if you aren't staying here, be sure to stop in for a coffee and cake at the hotel's gorgeous café.

Vinohrady

Vinohrady is a peaceful, stylish district to the east and north of Wenceslas Square and Nové Město. The district rose mainly in the late 19th and early 20th century, and offers pretty, tree-lined neighborhoods filled with neo-Baroque and neo-Renaissance architecture, much of which is unfortunately in need of restoration. The heart of the district is **Náměstí Míru**, featuring the brick **St. Ludmilla Church**, the posh **Vinohrady Theater**, and the **National House of Vinohrady** with its gorgeous ballroom.

Throughout the district, there is no shortage of good restaurants and pubs. All the following hotels are within easy walking distance of Wenceslas Square and a quick shot by metro to Staré Město and Malá Strana.

26. AMETYST HOTEL, *Jana Masaryka 11, 120 00 Prague 2 (Náměstí Míru metro station). Tel. 02/242 541 85, Fax 02//242 513 15. Rates for singles/doubles: 4,140/5,220 Kč. Credit Cards: AE, DC, MC, V. 84 rooms. Restaurant.*

Located on a quiet, shady street, this new hotel offers ultra-comfortable accommodations behind a blinding white facade. Sophisticated decor bless each of the rooms that come with either showers or bathtubs, satellite television, direct-dial telephones, and mini-bars. Hallways double as galleries for local artwork. The restaurant features international cooking with a slant on Italian cuisine. Helpful service and international newspapers await at the reception. A very good choice for lodging, but way overpriced for the neighborhood.

27. FLATHOTEL ORION, *Americká 9, 120 00 Prague 2 (Náměstí Míru metro station). Tel. 02/691 0209, Fax 02/691 0098. Rates for studio/one-bedroom flats with living room: 2,230/2,960 Kč. Credit Cards: AE, DC, MC, V. 19 flats. No restaurant.*

This hotel of flats, owned by the Finnish OK-Tours travel agency, offers quite a good deal when you consider that you get an entire flat for a price that's less than most hotel rooms in Prague, the majority of which are half the size of those available at Orion. All flats come with a fully-equipped kitchen, including refrigerator and coffee maker. The flats also have satellite television, direct-dial telephones, and bathtubs with shower. A Finnish-style sauna is also available for guests. The OK-Tours office in the lobby can arrange sightseeing tours and excursions, tickets to the theater, and car rentals.

If you plan on staying a week or two in Prague or if you have brought the family, you have definitely come to the right place. But be sure to reserve well in advance, as the hotel has a steady stream of Finns staying here.

28. OLEA HOTEL, *Americká 18, 120 00 Prague 2 (Náměstí Míru metro station). Tel. 02/573 151 91, Fax 02/242 307 83. Rates for singles/doubles: 1,730/2,420 Kč. Credit Cards: MC, V. 7 apartments. No restaurant.*

Olea's seven apartments are not a bad deal when you consider that all of them have two rooms, two bathrooms, a refrigerator, kitchen space (but no stove), television, and telephones. The rooms are a somewhat threadbare and could use a little sprucing up, but are functional and reasonably comfortable. Service speaks English, and are quite accommodating.

29. HOTEL CITY, *Belgická 10, 120 00 Prague 2 (Náměstí Míru metro station). Tel. & Fax 02/691 1334. Rates for singles/doubles with bath: 1,000-1,590/1,621-2,220 Kč. Rates for singles/doubles without bath: 690-1,110/1,103-1,485 Kč. No credit cards. 19 rooms. No restaurant.*

Despite the ridiculous name, this isn't a bad choice for budget accommodations in a pleasant neighborhood well within the center. Seven of the 19 clean rooms come with private bath. All of them have a lot left to be desired when it comes to decor, but they suffice if you are looking for rates that are easy on the wallet. Note: The pension's telephone and fax numbers are likely to change. If the numbers don't work, you can also communicate through e-mail at: *hotel.city@telecom.cz.*

PRAGUE'S BEST BETS FOR BUDGET LODGING

And though they generally won't win any interior decorating awards or offer you a foot massage at the end of the day, the following hotels are your best bets for saving some money on accommodations:

11. HOTEL BELVEDERE, *Holešovice*
13. PENSION VĚTRNÍK, *Břevnov*
21. BETLEM CLUB, *Staré Město*
25. HOTEL EVROPA, *Wenceslas Square*
28. OLEA HOTEL, *Vinohrady*
29. HOTEL CITY, *Vinohrady*

WHERE TO EAT

In the last few years, Prague has experienced a gastronomic boom. It is no longer the bleak, culinary ghost town you heard about in the early 1990s. New restaurants, and by no means just Czech ones, have popped up in almost every neighborhood, offering a taste of cuisines from around the world, including those of France, Italy, Japan, China, the Middle East, and especially America.

Prague is not only serving up the exotic, but reinventing the domestic as well. A much bigger demand on the part of tourists and a wider accessibility to fresh ingredients have sparked something akin to a culinary rebirth on the burners in many Prague kitchens, which for years were stuck in a meat-dumpling-cabbage rut. Today, many Prague chefs demonstrate a graceful, creative, and health-conscious touch that was all but non-existent during the forty years of Communism.

In the early 1990s, the biggest complaint coming from Westerners visiting or living in Prague was the dirt-poor service. Service, thank god, has improved as well, but you still may encounter a server or two who may have more important things to do, like smoke a cigarette, than take your order. So bring some patience, and even a little humor.

With the vast improvement of quality has come a vast increase in prices, rivaling those at restaurants in any big American or Canadian city. Indeed, it wouldn't be hard to blow $80 or $90 on a dinner for two in Prague. But at the same time, you can still get away with paying four or five bucks for a large and very gratifying meal.

One word of wisdom: avoid restaurants on Wenceslas Square. Most of them offer nothing but a second-rate meal and a big check. Venture out, and explore the lanes and alleys where you just may find an intimate little place roasting a scrumptious goose, ladling a delicate mushroom soup, and pouring a fine Pilsner Urquell.

It's always a good idea to make a reservation, especially during the summer. Most, if not all, restaurants listed below will you get an English speaker on the phone. More of the haughtier restaurants charge you a cover charge, usually in the ballpark of 20 Kč. The 23 percent value-added tax is generally included in the price of meals.

So, *dobrou chuť* – bon appetit!

PRAGUE'S CLASSIEST RESTAURANTS

Of the restaurants listed in this section, here are the ones that rise above the others, presenting a solid menu, a classy atmosphere, good service, and the general makings for a memorable meal.

30. HOTEL SAVOY, Hradčany
31. U ZLATÉ HRUŠKY, Hradčany
32. CIRCLE LINE BRASSERIE, Malá Strana
36. DAVID, Malá Strana
37. U MALTÉZSKYCH RYTÍŘŮ , Malá Strana
45. PARNAS, Staré Město
47. LA PERLE DE PRAGUE, Staré Město
48. OPERA GRILL, Staré Město
49. LA PROVENCE, Staré Město

West of the Vltava – Hradčany & Malá Strana
30. HOTEL SAVOY, *Keplerova 6, 110 00 Prague 1 (tram #22 from Malostranská metro station to Pohořelec stop). Tel. 02/243 024 30, Fax 02/243 021 28. 900-1,400 Kč. Credit Cards: AE, DC, MC, V.*

In keeping with the hotel's formidable accommodations, the Savoy offers a refined menu altered daily and revamped monthly. But you can expect something along the lines of elder sauce over a deer terrine and chestnut dumplings or spring lamb medallions smothered in garlic sauce. The expansive atrium dining room, reverberating with the sound of background piano music, makes for romantic dining. On Sunday, the hotel offers a jazz brunch with a buffet and a live jazz band. Tip-top, English-speaking service goes along with the multilingual menu. But like the rest of the hotel, the restaurant is more Vienna than Prague.

31. U ZLATÉ HRUŠKY, *Nový svět 3 (tram #22 from Malostranská metro station to Pohořelec stop). Tel. 02/205 147 78. 500-1,000 Kč. Credit Cards: AE, MC, V, DC.*

The modest facade of this storybook cottage in the twisting lanes below the Loreto Church gives no indication of the extravagance that lies inside the entrance. The gilded sconces, damask-covered walls, and wood-carved fixtures make up a sensual environment in which to partake of something delicious from this restaurant's enormous, multilingual menu. Foie gras, caviar, and smoked salmon lie side-by-side with traditional Czech meals such as haunch of venison marinated in red wine, or goulash of wild boar with potato *knedliky* (Czech dumpling).

Believe it or not, the menu actually has a separate listing of snail specialties, including snail livers. There's an extensive list of white and red wines, but I'd stick to something red, perhaps a Cabernet. Top notch service reigns here. A great place for a special occasion. But be sure to make reservations.

32. HANAVSKÝ PAVILON, *Letenské sady 173 (in Letná Park; tram #18 from Malostranská metro station to Chodkovy sady stop). Tel. 02/325 792. 500-1,000 Kč. Credit Cards: AE, MC, V.*

Partly neo-Rococo, partly Art Nouveau, this pavilion was built for the Prague Jubilee Exhibition in 1891 and was later transferred to a ledge on Letná Park, where it now serves as a great restaurant. The pavilion pokes up above the trees and commands a stellar view of the Vltava River and Staré Město. The pleasure doesn't end with the view, but continues into the menu with a changing selection of Czech specialties that is bound to include all sorts of game dishes drenched in rich wine sauces. Reservations are required.

33. CIRCLE LINE BRASSERIE, *Malostranské náměstí 12 (tram #12 or 22 from Malostranská metro station to Malostranské náměstí stop). Tel. 02/530 308. 500-1,000 Kč. Credit Cards: AE, MC, V.*

One of the finer restaurants to have graced the Prague dining scene in recent years, Circle Line specializes in the freshest seafood around, especially shellfish. Lobster, crab, and oysters saddle up next to a fine selection of side dishes, among them baked polenta, garlic potatoes, and leek fondue. If you are not a seafood lover, you are still in luck with dishes such as sautéed filet mignon topped with a green peppercorn sauce or filet of lamb smothered in a curry sauce.

34. KAMPA PARK, *Na Kampě 8B (tram #12 or 22 from Malostranská metro station to Malostranské náměstí stop). Tel. 02/573 134 93. 500-1,000 Kč. Credit Cards: AE, V.*

A swish newcomer to Prague, Kampa Park sits at the waters' edge on Kampa Island – a stone's throw downstream from the Charles Bridge. (You can't miss the restaurant while on the Charles Bridge, thanks to the obnoxiously large sign.) The several bay windows afford fantastic views of the bridge and river. The menu veers away from Czech cuisine and presents a wider international fare, which includes a lot of excellent fish. A winner on the menu is the salmon baked in pesto sauce. Every Thursday the restaurant features a seafood buffet for the reasonable price of about $25. Kampa Park also has an American-style Sunday brunch.

35. LOBKOVICKÁ VINÁRNA, *Vlašská 17 (tram #12 or 22 from Malostranská metro station to Malostranské náměstí stop). Tel. 02/530 185. 500-800 Kč. Credit Cards: AE, MC, V.*

The Lobkovic family founded this wine restaurant 200 years ago so the locals could get a taste of the wine produced at the aristocrat's chateau in Mělník. Today, the restaurant, located up the hill from the American Embassy, provides a stellar decor indicative of its aristocratic roots and diplomatic surroundings. The menu, however, breaks free of the old ways and invites you to sample some mildly eccentric creations, such as free range chicken topped with crab meat and curry sauce or pork stuffed with cheese, garlic, ham, and eggs. The scrumptious fruit and cake desserts are invariably soaked in all sorts of liqueurs. Almost as impressive as the huge list of South Moravian wines is the list of Cognacs. Reservations are recommended.

36. DAVID, *Tržiště 21 (tram #12 or 22 from Malostranská metro station to Malostranské náměstí stop; restaurant can be accessed through a passage at Nerudova 13). Tel. 02/539 325. 300-600 Kč. Credit Cards: AE, V.*

Tucked away on one of Malá Strana's intriguing medieval lanes, David occupies two intimate rooms chock full of antiques. Unlike most Czech menus that run on endlessly, the one at David is more to the point, the point being straight-ahead contemporary Czech food. Delicate tomato soup, lamb chops with rosemary, roast saddle of lamb with spinach and cranberries, stuffed breast of duck with cabbage and plums all bless the á la carte and prix-fixe menus. Best to make reservations.

37. U MALTÉZSKYCH RYTÍŘŮ, *Prokopská 10 (tram #12 or 22 from Malostranská metro station to Malostranské náměstí stop). Tel. 02/536 357. 200-400 Kč. Credit Cards: AE, MC.*

This restaurant takes its name from the Knights of Malta, a quasi-religious society that ran a hospice in the house during medieval times. Occupying the ground floor and basement cellar of the house, the restaurant retains that medieval character with its vaulted ceilings, spartan decor, and alluringly dim lighting. On the opposite end of the spectrum is the thoroughly modern cuisine, such as turkey breasts stuffed with asparagus or perfectly seared steaks with caper sauce and almonds. Owner and hostess Nadia Černikova offers a warm welcome, and sees that her guests get the best possible service.

38. NEBOZÍZEK, *Petřínské sady 411 (tram #9 or 22 from Národní třída metro station to Újezd stop). Tel. 02/537 935. 200-500 Kč. Credit Cards: AE, MC, V.*

Half the fun of this restaurant is just getting there – in a glass-encased funicular that chugs up and down Petřín Hill (catch it near the Újezd tram stop). The restaurant occupies a chateau perched on the side of the heavily wooded hill, affording just about the best view you could ask for in Prague. The bird's eye perspective takes in Prague Castle and Malá Strana. But be sure to go after the sun goes down, when the spotlights bathe the castle and the spires of St. Vitus Cathedral. So, does the food match up to the view? Of course not. But the international courses – including the steak au poivre, roast duck with caraway seeds, and the Prague Castle pork – are still pretty good. Be sure to reserve a table, and definitely ask for one at the big bay windows.

39. KONÍRNA U VLADAŘE, *Maltézské náměstí 10 (tram #12 or 22 from Malostranská metro station to Malostranské náměstí stop). Tel. 02/538 128. 150-200 Kč. Credit Cards: AE, MC, V.*

This is the sister restaurant of the *vinárna* (wine restaurant) with the same name and location. Though the *konírna* (stable) may not be as snazzy as the *vinárna*, it offers many of the same items prepared by the same chef as the *vinárna*, but at a third the price. Some winners on the menu include a tender Weiner schnitzel and a rich and spicy goulash. Just off Malostranské náměstí, Konírna U Vladaře is a great value for the location.

40. BAR BAR, *Všehrdova 17 (tram #9 or 22 from Národní třída metro station to Újezd stop). Tel. 02/532 941. 150-300 Kč. Credit Cards: MC, V.*

Hunkering down in a quaint Malá Strana cottage, Bar Bar specializes in *palačinky*, the Czech version of crepes filled with your choice of vegetables, cheeses, meats, or fruits. Equally good are the mammoth-sized salads, especially the Greek salad. The gods are smiling down on you if the restaurant happens to be serving goulash soup on the day of your visit. It is some of the best I've had in the country. One drawback about this place is the sometimes slack service.

Smíchov
41. ZLATÝ BÝK, *Mělnická 13 (tram #9 or 22 from Národní třída metro station to Újezd stop). Tel. 02/537 544. 300-500 Kč. Credit Cards: AE, MC, V.*

Hungry? How does a whole roasted goose sound? Though you

would probably want to share it with three others, you can order it at this excellent upscale Czech restaurant. Other highlights from the menu include a hearty mushroom soup and stuffed pork tenderloin topped with a delicious rowanberry sauce. The restaurant is big on wild game, offering a unique lineup that includes quail eggs and pheasant.

Holešovice
42. THE GLOBE BOOKSTORE & COFFEEHOUSE, *Janovského 14 (Vltavská metro station). Tel. 02/667 126 10. 50-200 Kč. No credit cards.*

This funky English-language bookstore and café also serves some generous sized salads, luscious soups, and other comfort foods such as hummus, muffins, and brownies. Better to come here for lunch than dinner, as the café fills up nightly with all the ex-pats working on their great American novel.

GOOD CHEAP EATS IN PRAGUE

Searching for a good lunch or looking to go easy on the wallet for an evening? Then check out these restaurants:

39. KONÍRNA U VLADAŘE, Malá Strana
40. BAR BAR, Malá Strana
42. THE GLOBE BOOKSTORE & COFFEEHOUSE, Holešovice
52. PIZZERIA RUGANTINO, Staré Město
53. ADONIS, Nové Město
57. AMBIENTE, Vinohrady
58. QUIDO, Žižkov
60. NA ZVONAŘCE, Vinohrady

East of the Vltava – Staré Město & Nové Město
43. FLAMBÉE, *Husova 5 (Staroměstská metro station). Tel. 02/242 485 12. 2,000-2,500 Kč. Credit Cards: AE, MC, V.*

As the name indicates, the gimmick at this much-touted restaurant is the flaming main courses and desserts, drenched in sherry and set alight at your table in the posh 14th century cellar. Lamb ribs, beef sirloin, and chateaubriand top the menu at prices that would have most of us signing away the farm in order to afford. Flambée has perhaps the most suspicious-sounding dish I've seen in Prague: corn chicken with strawberry sauce. The service, however, is some of the best in the city, and fresh oysters are on the menu – a big plus in my book.

The restaurant is banking on being the first restaurant in the Czech Republic to receive a Michelin star, but I don't think that will happen anytime soon.

44. PRAHA TAMURA, *Havelská 6 (Můstek metro station). Tel. 02/242 320 56. 700-1,900 Kč. Credit Cards: AE, DC, MC, V.*
Have you come all the way to Prague to eat *sushi* and *sashimi*? If so, this is a damn good place to do it, considering how astoundingly fresh the fish is. Price-fixed menus start at 1,200 Kč and include seven or eight fantastic but tiny courses. Alternatively, you could order from the á la carte menu and end up spending a lot less.

45. PARNAS, *Smetanovo nábřeží 18 (any tram one stop from Národní třída metro station to Národní divadlo). Tel. 02/242 213 87. 600-1,000 Kč. Credit Cards: AE, MC, V.*
At the forefront of Prague's booming culinary scene, Parnas sets the standard for restaurants in this city. Polished wood fixtures, etched glass, and a bar made of green Cuban marble let you know that elegance reigns at this Art Nouveau restaurant. Occupying a section of the ground floor of the Lazansky Palace, in which Bedřich Smetana composed *The Bartered Bride*, Parnas sits just around the corner from the National Theater, making it a more than appropriate choice for a pre-theater dinner.

Some of the best seats in town are to be found at the window of Parnas, from where you have a view of the Vltava River, the Prague Castle, and Střelecký Island. The scrumptious *millefeuille* – a flaky puff pastry stuffed with spinach, mushrooms, and goat cheese – graces the list of starters, while grilled filet of Norwegian salmon with chopped coriander or the duck breast with pumpkin purée is on the formidable list of entrées. For dessert, try the luscious apple and orange crisp or the intense chocolate and hazelnut cake topped with a cognac sauce. The restaurant has an extensive list of wines, including a fine cabernet sauvignon from Valtice. Service is quick, deft, and multilingual. Be sure to reserve a table.

46. HOTEL PAŘÍŽ, *U Obecního domu 1, 110 00 Prague 1 (Náměstí Republiky metro station). Tel. 02/242 221 51. 500-800 Kč for fixed-price menus.*
It's hard to ignore the restaurant at this historic Art Nouveau hotel rendered so humorously by Bohumil Hrabal in his picturesque novel *I Served the King of England*. You can almost drink in the opulent, glittering decor stacked with mirrors, chandeliers, and marble fixtures. The big question is: does the food live up to the surroundings? The answer is a not-so-surprising no. The menu lacks imagination and the food often is only a half-step above what's served at cheaper restaurants.

But that doesn't mean you won't have an enjoyable meal from one of several price-fixed menus, which can include smoked salmon-and-mussel rolls or cones of Prague ham for starters, and Australian lamb cutlets, sirloin strips with Roquefort cheese, or baked goose as a main course. Tip-top service makes the experience all the more enjoyable.

144 CZECH & SLOVAK REPUBLICS GUIDE

47. LA PERLE DE PRAGUE, *Jiráskovo náměstí 6, 120 00 Prague 2 (Karlovo náměstí metro station). Tel. 02/219 841 60. 1,500-2,000 Kč. Credit cards: AE, MC, DC, V.*
You couldn't ask for a better atmosphere or view from a restaurant in Prague. Set atop the new "Dancing Building" on the banks of the Vltava, La Perle presents some of the best French cooking you're bound to get in Prague. The menu changes regularly, but you can look forward to haute cuisine such as snapper á la Provencal, tournedos de boeuf with Béarnaise sauce, and young rabbit in mustard sauce.

48. OPERA GRILL, *Karoliny Světlé 35 (Staroměstská metro station). Tel. 0602/203 962. 400-600 Kč. Credit Cards: AE, DC, V, MC.*
This intimately small restaurant around the corner from the Charles Bridge attracts a number of Czech luminaries and coddles its customers with antique armchairs, original paintings, and an impressive collection of Meissen porcelain. The hand-written menu features a fine selection of caviar and seafood, as well as such entrées as roast veal with Cumberland sauce or steak with rosemary and garlic. Best to reserve well in advance for this small gem.

49. LA PROVENCE, *Štuparstká 9 (Náměstí Republiky metro station). Tel. 02/232 4801. 700-1,000 Kč. Credit Cards: AE, MC, V.*
Offering a taste of Southern France just off Celetná street, La Provence is no place for a quiet dinner, especially late at night when the bar and upstairs nightclub become a target for a thoroughly loud and yuppy crowd. But if you eat early enough, then you should have no problem enjoying the bouillabaisse, grilled tuna, or *coq au vin rouge* from the nicely rounded menu. The decor, a mock-up of a French country bistro, is actually quite alluring, and may have you sticking around for a few drinks after dinner. Make sure to reserve a table a day or two in advance, however.

50. U ČÍNSKÉHO LABUŽNÍKA, *Vyšehradská 37-39 (Karlovo náměstí metro station). Tel. 02/249 114 77. 250-350 Kč. No credit cards.*
This is perhaps your best choice of Chinese food in a city that is littered with Chinese restaurants. Luscious sea vegetable soup, stir-fried vegetables piled high, and a formidable Beijing duck is served in a very exotic, very apropos setting.

51. VINÁRNA NAD PŘÍSTAVEM, *Rašínovo nábřeží 64 (Palackého náměstí exit at Karlovo náměstí metro station). Tel. 02/298 636. 175-300 Kč. Credit Cards: AE, MC, V.*
This unpretentious riverside restaurant fries, bakes, and broils fish, letting you choose how it will be seasoned. The result is usually light and flaky meat, perfectly cooked. Most of the fish is fresh-water, but there is cod and salmon on the menu as well. A popular place with the locals. Reservations are a good idea.

PRAGUE'S ILLUSTRIOUS CAFÉS

As a European capital, Prague sports its fair share of grand cafés (or **kavarny**) that were the haunt of the city's writers, artists, and composers. Though the prestige of these places have faded, they still make for enthralling spots to do some people watching while sipping on an espresso. Here is a selection of some of the most beautiful, and most historic:

Hotel Evropa, Václavské náměstí 25 (Wenceslas Square; metro to Můstek station). The delicious Art Nouveau décor – replete with big mirrors, marble pillars, and crystal chandeliers – draws a lot of posers, but that shouldn't stop you from drinking in the opulence of this place. Sidewalk seating is available when the weather cooperates.

Café Nouveau, in the Obecní dům at náměstí Republiky 5 (Staré Město, metro to Náměstí Republiky station). More Art Nouveau decadence is on display at this expansive café with a fountain. Servers make their rounds with a cake trolley. The cafe now glimmers even more after a thorough renovation completed in 1997.

Hotel Paříž, U Obecního domu 1 (Staré Město; metro to Náměstí Republiky station). If you don't have the funds to stay or eat at this illustrious hotel, then at least drop in here to get a load of the lavish (once more) Art Nouveau lamps, tables, and chairs.

Café Slavia, Národní 1 (Nové Město; any tram one stop from Národní třída metro station to Národní Divadlo). Across the street from the National Theater, this is perhaps the most famous café in Prague, having been the haunt of countless literary, artistic, and musical figures. Among the notable ghosts here are Bedřich Smetana and Antonín Dvořák. The Devětsil Group – a circle of painters, writers, and poets that included Karel Čapek, Nobel Prize-winner Jaroslav Seifert, and Vítězslav Nezval – used to mull over ideas and debate issues here. During the Communist times Slavia was one of the few literary cafés kept open, attracting dissidents by the dozen, among them one young playwright by the name of Václav Havel. (The Communist regime saw literary cafés as hotbeds for subversive ideas, and so found reason to shut most of them down.) In 1998, the cafe finally opened its doors after five years of renovation and ownership disputes. The place looks spit-shined through and through, and prices are thankfully still reasonable.

Café Savoy, Vítězná 1 (Malá Strana, tram #9 or 22 from Národní třída metro station to Újezd stop). Though mostly reconstructed and offering little authenticity, this café used to be a favorite of Franz Kafka's.

52. PIZZERIA RUGANTINO, *Dušní 4 (Staroměstská metro station).*
Tel. 02/231 8172. 150-250 Kč. No credit cards.

This stylish pizzeria just off Old Town Square packs 'em in night after night. In addition to the scores of delicious pizzas, the menu features a great selection of calzones and fresh salads. The bar serves a good Bernard beer to wash it all down. Best to reserve a table, or else you could be in for a long wait at the cash register. If you have trepidations about eating pizza in Prague, then you should know that the owner is from Northern Italy.

53. ADONIS, *Jungmannova 21 (Můstek or Národní třída metro station);*
Tel. 02/268 908. 80-200 Kč. No credit cards.

Hummus, falafel, puréed dips, gyros, spicy chicken, and other Middle Eastern specialties are served up at this popular café not far from Wenceslas Square. If you need to eat on the run, you can order to go.

Vinohrady & Žižkov

54. TAJ MAHAL, *Škrétova 10 (Muzeum metro station). Tel. 02/242 255 66. 400-800 Kč. Credit Cards: AE, MC, V.*

Located behind the National Museum up the hill from Wenceslas Square, Taj Mahal offers north and south Indian specialties such as papadum breads, onion bhajee, and a range of tangy tandori and curry dishes. Appropriately exotic decor and snappy service are a mainstay at this most enchanting restaurant.

55. MYSLIVNA, *Jagellonská 21 (Flora metro station). Tel. 02/627 0209. 500-600 Kč. Credit Cards: AE, MC, V.*

This restaurant, whose name means hunting lodge, makes no apologies that it thrives on game, and wild game at that. You know it from the moment you walk in. Trophy heads, skins, and stuffed birds brandish the walls. And in the corner is a fireplace where you would half expect to find a group of hunters swirling cognac in snifters, puffing on big cigars, and swapping stories of the day's hunt. Provincial and hearty are the key words for the menu that includes venison paté with quail eggs, hare in wine sauce, boar schnitzel with juniper berries, and saddle of venison stroganoff. But be prepared for a gamey taste, as not much on the menu is domesticated. All in all, a good value and a good place to sink your teeth into traditional Czech cuisine.

56. VICTORIA SALOON, *Seifertova 44 (tram #5 or 9 two stops from Hlavní nádraží metro station). Tel. 02/270 581. 200-300 Kč. Credit Cards: AE, MC, V.*

Got a hankering for a steak? Well, this is the place to satiate that carnivorous urge, especially if that urge is for a T-bone. Kitschy American old West decor sets the stage for the well-aged, well-seasoned Argentina-imported cuts.

57. AMBIENTE, *Mánesova 59 (Jiřího z Poděbrad metro station). Tel. 02/ 627 5922. 150-300 Kč. No credit cards.*

This relatively new restaurant brings in a nightly crowd for the "California-style cuisine" (whatever that means) that's offered on the menu. Tasty pasta dishes and deeply flavorful racks of ribs are served amidst a lot of Americana doo-dads and pictures of pop icons. For dessert, most definitely go for the sliced bananas and pineapples dipped in chocolate fondue. The bar pours Budvar, that excellent velvety beer from České Budějovice. Reserve well in advance for this gem.

58. QUIDO, *Fibichova 6 (Jiřího z Poděbrad metro station). Tel. 02/270 950. 150-300 Kč. Credit Cards: AE, MC.*

A classy Czech restaurant where the servers do everything but give you a back rub, Quido features a seemingly never-ending (multilingual) menu of just about every Czech specialty that's out there. With such a huge menu, don't be surprised if they happen to be out of what you order. Still, the crispy roast duck has been sensational in the past, as have the chicken livers. But, like a lot of upscale Czech restaurants, the food is inconsistent: the same item can be outstanding on some nights and just above par on others.

59. RADOST CAFÉ FX, *Bělehradská 120 (I.P. Pavlova metro station). Tel. 02/242 547 76. 100-300 Kč. No credit cards.*

This is one of the big American ex-pat hangouts. And no wonder, considering the Tex-Mex slant on the menu. Most everything is vegetarian, from the several salads on down to the pita bread sandwiches and wonderful soups. On weekends you can get a brunch that includes French toast, bagels, and huevos rancheros.

60. NA ZVONAŘCE, *Šafaříkova 1 (I.P. Pavlova or Náměstí Míru metro station). Tel. 02/242 527 75. 100-200 Kč. No credit cards.*

This restaurant makes for great outdoor dining on a large patio overlooking the Vltava River. Plzeň-style Czech dishes, including a decent *svíčkova* (slice of roast beef floating in a cream-based lingonberry sauce) and tasty little chicken livers, highlight the menu. But the food isn't so good as the sedate atmosphere under the trees. This is certainly the place to come on a warm summer night.

SEEING THE SIGHTS

The **Prague Castle, Charles Bridge,** and **Old Town Square** comprise the holy trinity of attractions in Prague. Indeed, many tourists see little else of the city other than these sights and what lies between them. But this is understandable, as these three places are spectacular enough to make most of us feel like we've died and gone to heaven.

So, why see more? Because you'll be extremely glad that you did!

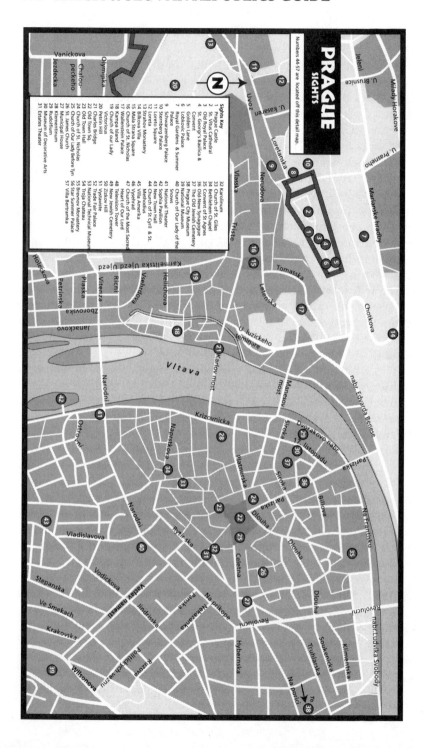

PRAGUE
SIGHTS

Numbers 44-57 are located off this detail map.

Sights Key
1 Prague Castle
2 St. Vitus Cathedral
3 Old Royal Palace
4 St. George's Basilica & Convent
5 Golden Lane
6 Lobkovic Palace
7 Royal Gardens & Summer Palace
8 Schwarzenberg Palace
9 Sternberg Palace
10 Loreto Square
11 Loreta
12 Strahov Monastery
13 Bilkova Villa
14 Mala Strana Square
15 Church of St. Nicholas
16 Wallenstein Palace
17 Kampa Island
18 Church of our Lady
19 Victorious
20 Petrin Hill
21 Charles Bridge
22 Old Town Sq.
23 Old Town Hall
24 Church of St. Nicholas
25 Church of Our Lady before Tyn
26 St. James Church
27 Municipal House
28 Klementinum
29 Rudolfinum
30 Museum of Decorative Arts
31 Estates Theater
32 Karolinum
33 Church of St. Giles
34 Bethlehem Chapel
35 Convent of St Agnes
36 Old-New Synagogue
37 The Old Jewish Cemetery
38 Prague City Museum
39 National Museum
40 Church of Our Lady of the Snows
41 National Theater
42 Sophia Pavilion
43 New Town Hall
44 Church of St Cyril & St. Methodius
45 Villa Amerika
46 Vysehrad
47 Church of the Most Sacred Heart of Our Lord
48 Television Tower
49 New Jewish Cemetery
50 Zizkov Hill
51 Vystaviste
52 Trade Fair Palace
53 National Technical Museum
54 Troja Chateau
55 Brevnov Monastery
56 Star Summer Palace
57 Villa Bertramka

There are hundreds of medieval alleys, lanes, and passages to be explored, especially in Malá Strana and Staré Město. Wander and get yourself lost, for you never know what you'll discover around each corner. (There's always a metro station or tram stop nearby to help get yourself back on track.) There are scores of parks and gardens – most notably the **Royal Gardens** (Prague Castle), **Petřín Hill** (Malá Strana), **Vyšehrad**, and **Stromovka** (Holešovice) – that offer an exquisite respite from the streets and present infinite views and perspectives of this majestic city. Finally, this city is chock full of good museums, many housing one segment or another from the National Gallery's inexhaustible art collection. The **Sternberg Palace** (Hradčany), the **St. Agnes Convent** (Staré Město), and the **Trade Fair Palace** (Holešovice) are just a few of the gorgeous venues for this collection.

The city of Prague was the only European capital to escape the ravages of World War II unscathed. What this means is that there are many hundreds of ancient houses, palaces, monuments, towers, and (especially) churches to be seen in this city. Obviously, there is no way anyone could tackle all of the significant sights during just one visit. So, if you are here for a week or two, content yourself with seeing only a fragment of them.

To make things a little tidier out of the cluster of attractions in and around the historic center, most sights are arranged below under their respective district, beginning with the historic center (where you'll find most of the sights below) and ending with those sights outside the historic center. In arranging your own sightseeing itinerary, it usually makes sense to concentrate on one district at a time, and to see that district on foot, instead of rushing around to various sights by metro or tram. You'll miss out on a lot if you do. Leave public transportation for getting to or from your hotel or for when you are just dead tired. (However, there are some districts, Nové Město in particular, that are just too big to conquer on foot. If that's the case, I'll tell you so.)

So enjoy yourself, and don't forget to pop into a pub now and again, or you'll never get a real taste of Prague.

INSIDE THE HISTORIC CENTER

Prague Castle Overview

Accessed from Malostranská metro station by taking tram #22 to Pražský hrad stop. Alternatively, you could walk up the Old Castle Steps just above the Malostranská metro station, climb up the New Castle Steps at the end of

Thunovská Street in Malá Strana, or walk up Nerudova Street – branching off Malostranské náměstí. All ways are scenic, but the tram is easiest.
The castle is open daily 5 a.m. to midnight from April to September and until 11 p.m. the rest of the year. Unless otherwise noted, the hours for the sights within the castle are Tuesday through Sunday 9 a.m. to 5 p.m. from April 1 to October 31 (until 4 p.m. November 1 through March 31). Most sites require individual tickets, costing between 50 and 80 Kč. A cheaper way to go is to buy a single, 100-Kč ticket from the information office (just west of the cathedral in the second courtyard). This ticket is good for St. Vitus Cathedral's older sections, the Old Royal Palace, St. George's Basilica, and the Powder Tower. For more information, call 02/243 733 68.

The mental picture that most of us carry of Prague, the one that seduces us into coming to this fantastic city and stays with us long after leaving it, is the view of the **Prague Castle** (Pražský hrad) from the Charles Bridge, from which the castle appears as a sheer wall of neo-Classical facades strung along a ridge, boldly fortifying its position high above the towers of Malá Strana. Part and parcel of that picture is **St. Vitus Cathedral**, thrusting out of the center of the castle and seemingly looming in midair. Altogether, it truly is one of the most magnificent sights there is.

I was standing smack dab in the middle of the castle one day and overheard an American tourist ask her tour guide, "So, where exactly is the castle?" Granted, this was a bit of a strange question, but an understandable one, for the Prague Castle is not an easy thing to grasp. It's better to think of it as a complex, or maybe even a town unto itself. The castle is composed of several palaces, a number of churches, a cathedral, a former convent, several gardens, three museums, numerous shops and galleries, four or so towers, a number of restaurants and cafés, and on and on. Yes, it's huge, so big in fact that the *Guinness Book of World Records* considers it the largest ancient castle in the world. So don't think you can just make a quick dash through it and tell your friends back home that you've been there. More than a thousand years have gone into its creation, demanding at least an afternoon of your time for it to unravel all its majesty.

No one is quite sure exactly which year the castle was founded, but around 880 or 890 AD seems to be the consensus. The Přemyslid **Prince Bořivoj** built the first fortification on the site, erecting a small stone chapel which has since turned to dust. The first ruler of Bohemia, **Vratislav I**, was coronated at the castle in 1085. Since then it has been the seat of every subsequent ruler of the Czech lands, from the Přemyslids to the Communists to President Václav Havel, whose office and administration today occupy the so-called Theresian buildings on the south wing.

Though most rulers have provided the castle with additions, adjustments, and facelifts (all in accord with the taste of the age), **Empress Maria Theresa** is most responsible for its present exterior appearance. She commissioned court architect **Nicolo Pacassi** to slap on the unbroken wall of Classical facades. (Many Czechs to this day smart at Pacassi's facelift, which wiped out a good deal of the castle's medieval and Renaissance appearance.) The last major architect to lend his hand to the castle's present appearance was the Slovenian **Josef Plečnik**, commissioned in 1920 by President T.G. Masaryk to give the castle a thorough renovation, a process that continues to this day.

Prague Castle's First & Second Courtyards

The most sensible place to start your tour of the castle is at the **first courtyard**, located at the west end of the castle just beyond the castle gate. This is the newest section of the castle, laid over the castle moat in the 18th century and lined with a serious of Rococo buildings. Greeting you at each side of the gate are the *Battling Titans* – sculptures by Ignác Platzer in which one titan is armed with a club and the other with a dagger, both poised to inflict a good deal of harm on their respective victims. A bit friendlier and known to crack a smile now and again are the two castle guards posted below the titans.

In line with his flair for the theatrical, President Havel commissioned Pissek, Oscar-winning costume designer for *Amadeus*, to design the castle guards' uniforms, which recall those worn during the First Czechoslovak Republic. The changing of the guard takes place at noon. But don't make any special effort to see this rather uninspiring affair.

To get to the **second courtyard**, follow the hordes through the Mannerist **Matthias Gate**, once a freestanding entrance that stood in the middle of the moat bridge, but now enclosed by one of Pacassi's Rococo buildings. ("Mannerist" refers to a short-lived style of art and architecture between the Renaissance and the Baroque periods.) Squatting in the corner of the courtyard to the right is the **Chapel of the Holy Cross**, formerly the treasury of St. Vitus Cathedral and now an **information office**. Stop here to buy a ticket to several of the sights around the castle or to hook up with a guided tour.

At the north end of the second courtyard is what remains of the Renaissance wing built by Rudolf II. In addition to the grand **Spanish Hall** and **Rudolf Gallery** (both closed to the public), the wing encompasses the old royal stables, now housing the **Prague Castle Picture Gallery**. Rudolf II amassed a sensational collection of paintings during his reign, but most of it was hauled away as war booty by the Swedes in 1648, transferred to Vienna and Dresden, or else sold off at a public auction in 1782. So what remains are the dregs, but some pretty impressive dregs at that, including a couple of Veroneses and a Rubens entitled *The Assembly of Olympian Gods*.

At the north end of the second courtyard is the western gate, leading to the Powder Bridge and the Royal Gardens, which we'll come to later, after we've seen everything that's inside the castle walls.

St. Vitus Cathedral

Continuing to the third courtyard, your first instinct will be to dive straight into **St. Vitus Cathedral** (Chrám sv. Vitá), which pervades the courtyard and soars above the castle skyline. But resist, and first take a walk around it so as to relish the exterior of what is the biggest church in the Czech Republic and one of the most stunning Gothic cathedrals in all of Europe.

You can attribute the existence of St. Vitus Cathedral to **Charles IV**, King of Bohemia and Holy Roman Emperor from 1346 to 1378. Having been educated in France and exposed to that country's Gothic feats, Charles commissioned French architect **Matthias of Arras** in 1344 to design and build Prague a cathedral, something that seemed appropriate in a city that had just become the seat of an archbishphoric as well as the new home of St. Vitus' relics.

Only the ambulatory and radiating chapels were completed before Matthias died, so the project was handed over to **Petr Parléř**, the most renowned architect in Central Europe in his day. Parléř employed a more flamboyant style, known as Bohemian Gothic, which departed wildly from the orthodox Gothic style of France. Parléř got as far as building the choir and south transept before he passed away in 1399.

Because of the ensuing Hussite Wars and the general lack of funds, the cathedral sat unfinished for the next 400 years, manifesting into a symbol of the Czech's thwarted quest for independence. In 1861, the **Union of the Completion of the Cathedral**, a group spawned from the Czech National Revival, put to work scores of the best Czech architects and artists, most notably **Josef Mocker**. St. Vitus was officially completed in 1929, exactly a thousand years after the first Romanesque rotunda was built on the site.

Starting out in front of the west facade (the one facing you as you enter the third courtyard), take note of the fourteen statues of saints and the three bronze-carved doors. Above the three doors are the depictions of three stories: that of the life of St. Adalbert on the right, the evolution of the cathedral in the center, and the life of St. Wenceslas on the left. Completed in 1929, this facade is the newest part of the cathedral.

The centerpiece to the south facade is the **Golden Door**, which was the main entrance to the cathedral for 500 years. The door is covered with red and gold mosaics that depict the Last Judgment. The wrought-iron railing over the door, made in 1954 and somewhat smacking of Communist influence, is adorned with decorative figures of various people at work, such as a butcher, blacksmith, and farmer. Soaring 90 meters (300 feet) above the Golden Door is the **main tower**, constructed by Parléř in the 14th century. The cupola topping the tower dates from 1770 and comes as another incongruent mark left on the castle by Pacassi.

Before finally heading inside the cathedral, continue around it so as to get a good look at the exterior of the original (eastern) section, supported by Matthias of Arras' flying buttresses. Also, get a load of the **gargoyles** – some of the more interesting ones you'll ever see on a cathedral. The figures include various hideous looking men and a crazy assortment of animals.

Now make your way inside St. Vitus. There's no admission charge for the new (western) section of the cathedral. But if you want to see the older section of the cathedral or ascend the main tower, you'll have to buy separate tickets from the office at the cathedral entrance.

Once inside, take a moment or two to piece together your thoughts after getting hit with the expansiveness of the cathedral's three lofty naves, its radiating ambulatory and choir, and its host of marvelous side chapels. A book could be devoted to all of the architectural and artistic treasures found here, so we'll have to stick to the highlights.

Built in the 19th and 20th centuries, the western portion of the ribbed vault and the western circuit of small side chapels follow Parléř's 14th-century idea for the cathedral. But the stained-glass windows, created by some of the best Czech Art Nouveau artists of the early 20th century, go against Parléř's intention that the cathedral bear only clear glass. Regardless of what Parléř would have wanted, the windows are some of the more interesting aspects of the cathedral, lending a fresh departure from the strict Gothic-ness of the rest of the church.

Two of the most noteworthy windows are František Kysela's *Creation of the World* (above the central western door) and Alfons Mucha's *Cyril and Methodius* (above the first chapel to the left). Another work you shouldn't miss is František Bílek's modernist **crucifix** (hanging to the right of Mucha's window), sculpted from three kind of woods and depicting an anguished Christ seemingly melting on the cross.

Cutting the cathedral more or less in half, the transept draws the line between the old and new sections of St. Vitus. Off to the left of the transept, note the **musical gallery**, which closed off the western end of the cathedral for 500 years.

Just beyond the transept on the south side is the **Chapel of St. Wenceslas**, which is probably the most celebrated chapel in the country. Built by Petr Parléř, the chapel pays homage to the country's patron saint, murdered by his pagan brother Boleslav the Cruel in 939. As legend has it, Boleslav had his brother's bones interred at the site of the chapel after converting to Christianity and repenting for his crime. Adorned with more than 1,000 semi-precious stones stuck to the gilded plaster, the chapel achieves a celestial effect, thanks to its handsome murals portraying the lives of St. Wenceslas and Christ. Hanging on the door to the chapel, the giant knocker is said to be the one St. Wenceslas clung to after being stabbed by his brother.

The door in the southeast corner of the chapel accesses a stairway that leads up to the **Royal Treasury**, containing the Bohemian crown jewels and the sapphire-studded gold crown of St. Wenceslas. The door to the treasury has seven locks, the keys to which are in the keeping of certain Czech officials, such as the president, the prime minister, and the mayor of Prague. Unfortunately, it is open one day out of every two years or so. But you can see replicas of the jewels at the museum in the Lobkovic Palace (see below).

Near the St. Wenceslas chapel, in the middle of the ambulatory, sits the **Tomb of St. John of Nepomuk**, unmistakable in all its gaudy excessiveness. Two tons of silver went into the creation of this tomb memorializing the man who is said to have been hurled off the Charles Bridge for not divulging the confession of King Wenceslas IV's wife. As the legend goes, stars miraculously appeared above the saint's head at the place where he drowned – hence the halo of stars that appear on the countless statues of this saint found in the Czech Republic. Apparently, John of Nepomuk didn't meet his death because of being tight-lipped about the queen's confession, but instead died under torture after taking the wrong side in an argument between the king and archbishop over the appointment of a certain abbot.

On the statue you'll notice one of the cherubs pointing to the carving of a tongue. In 1719, when the Jesuits opened up St. John's tomb so as to have his remains canonized, they found what they thought to be the saint's tongue. The tongue became the symbol of the saint's silence over the queen's confession, even though what the priests had found was in actuality a withered piece of St. John's brain.

Opposite St. John's tomb, the **Royal Oratory** perches magnificently above the choir. Built by Benedikt Ried in 1493 for **King Vladislav Jagiello** (conqueror of all the countries represented by the coat of arms hanging from the gallery), the oratory marks the culmination of the cathedral's Flamboyant Gothic style, a style initiated by Petr Parléř.

Smack dab in the middle of the choir is the **Royal Mausoleum**, bearing the reclining images of Ferdinand I (founder of the Hapsburg dynasty in Bohemia and Hungary in the 16th century), his wife Anna Jagiello, and their son Maximillian II – all of whom are buried in the cathedral.

More dead royalty are to be found in the **Royal Vault**, accessed via a staircase near the Royal Oratory. Here you'll find the remains of the original St. Vitus Rotunda, as well as a vault that contains the tombs of King Charles IV, his four wives, King George of Poděbrady, and Rudolf II – among other royal figures celebrated in Czech history. The richly ornate sarcophagi date from the 1930s.

During the warm months, be sure to climb to the top of the **main tower**, affording an unbeatable view of Prague and a look at the biggest bell in all of Bohemia.

Back outside the cathedral in the third courtyard you'll find a slender granite **monolith**, created by Plečnik in 1928 and dedicated to those who died in World War I. Also standing in the courtyard is a statue of St. George slaying a dragon. The statue, however, is a copy; the original stands in St. George's Convent. A staircase in the southeast corner of the courtyard leads to the garden called **Over the Ramparts** (Na valech), where you can soak in a stellar Prague vista.

Old Royal Palace

In the southeast corner of the third courtyard is the entrance to the **Old Royal Palace** (Starý Královský Palác), one of the oldest parts of the castle, with foundations dating back to 1135. The palace was the residence of princes and kings until the mid-16th century, when the Hapsburg built themselves newer quarters.

The most stunning aspect of the palace is the **Vladislav Hall**, one of the best offerings from the Late Gothic period at the castle. Here, you can feast your eyes on the complex stream of ribs supporting a vaulted ceiling that reaches nearly down to the floor. The wonderfully expansive and sunny space functioned as the site for banquets, coronations, and, more recently, for the swearing in of the republic's presidents. The size of the hall – 200 feet long, 50 feet wide, and 40 feet high – makes it easy to believe that it also served as a space for, of all things, jousting, which explains why you have the **Rider's Staircase** and its special horse steps off to the north side of the hall.

At the far end of the Vladislav Hall, you can survey the **All Saints' Chapel** from its gallery. Petr Parléř built the original chapel in 1370, at which time it stood separate from the palace. After a fire destroyed much of it in 1541, the chapel was reconstructed and attached to the Vladislav Hall.

In the southwest corner of the Vladislav Hall you can gain access to the **Ludvík Wing** and its series of fairly spartan rooms. Their importance is mainly due to an incident that happened in the furthest room on May 23, 1618. A angry mob of Protestant nobles, led by Count Thurn, marched to the castle on this day, steaming over pro-Catholic policies introduced by the Hapsburg Emperor Matthias. The Protestants stormed to the wing, finding there two of the king's counselors – Jaroslav Bořita of Martinec and William Count Slavata. An argument ensued, tempers flared, and the Protestants hurled the two royal counselors out the window and into the moat, which, in those days, was used as a dung heap. Known in history books as the second Prague defenestration, the incident supposedly ignited the Thirty Years' War, even though the two men survived.

Below Vladislav Hall at the bottom of the Riders' Staircase, the Romanesque and Gothic **Palace of Charles IV** offers a look at the foundations of the 12th century palace. The rather bare rooms feature some cannonballs left over from the Swedish siege of the castle during the Thirty Years' War and some models of how the castle looked at various stages of its evolution. Replicas of Parléř 's busts of Charles IV, his wives, and of the artist himself also are on display.

St. George's Basilica & Convent

If you exit the Old Royal Palace at the Old Riders' Staircase, you'll immediately walk out onto **St. George's Square** (Jiřské náměstí), partially enclosed by St. Vitus and by **St. George's Basilica** (Bazilica sv. Jiří). You are now at the center of Prague Castle. Though you wouldn't know it by the Baroque facade, the basilica is one of the oldest Romanesque structures found in Bohemia, and the most intact, thanks to the numerous restorations it has received since its completion in 912. The one long arcaded nave – made of white, undecorated stone – runs an expansive course to the choir, embellished with a Baroque double staircase. The remains of St. Ludmila, Bohemia's first Christian martyr (she was murdered by her daughter), lie here, as do two Přemyslid kings – Vratislav I and Boleslav II.

Adjacent to the basilica is **St. George's Convent** (Kláster sv. Jiří), the earliest religious establishment in Bohemia, founded in 973 by Mlada, the sister of Prince Boleslav II. The convent now houses a branch of the **National Gallery**, this one dedicated to Bohemian art from the Gothic period on up to 18th-century Baroque. *This branch of the National Gallery is open 10 a.m. to 6 p.m. daily except Monday.*

You can get a little overwhelmed by the sheer weight of the collection at this museum, which at times loses focus and elicits a ho-hum reaction to its works. But it is definitely worth a perusal, if not for the sensational Gothic collection, which includes mostly representations of the Madonna and Child – rendered by artists known only by their style and their location.

Hands down, the best of the lot is the so-called Master of Třeboň, his works exhibited on the first floor. In such paintings as his *Madonna of*

Roudnice, the artist lends a surprisingly humanistic touch to the mother and child, depicting them with ruddy cheeks and half-smiles. Also on this floor, keep an eye out for Petr Parléř's tympanum from the Týn Church (see Old Town Square), a work that defines the Late Gothic style and shows Parléř to be a master of it.

Not so clearly formidable but interesting in their own right are the vaguely erotic Mannerist paintings on the next floor up. With an overbearing amount of lukewarm Baroque works, this floor is where the museum begins to wain. But there are a few gems, such as the statues by Matthias Braun and a couple of paintings by Karel Skřeta.

Golden Lane

From the convent, walk a short ways down Jiřská Street and take your first left, leading you straight into one of the nicest surprises found at the castle – the **Golden Lane**, or Zlatá ulička. As the popular legend goes, this fairytale street of tiny squatting houses was occupied by alchemists during the reign of Rudolf II, a king who apparently had a penchant for the occult sciences. A little less intriguing, however, is that the lane was actually built for Rudolf II's guards, and was later occupied by goldsmiths. In 1955, the row of houses was completely renovated, and given new coats and colors of paint by the animation filmmaker Jiří Trnka.

No matter what the actual history is, the Golden Lane lends itself more than any other sight to Prague's mysterious aura, an aura perpetuated by one former resident of the lane, **Franz Kafka**, who lived at number 22 in 1917. Another famous Bohemian writer and a Nobel prizewinner, Jaroslav Seifert, lived here in 1917. Sadly, nobody lives on the lane anymore, as it has become completely stocked with giftshops.

At the near end of the lane is the **White Tower**, where you'll find a giftshop selling the gamut in medieval swords and other weaponry, as well as, if you can believe it, chastity belts (replete with lock and key).

At the far end of the lane is **Daliborka**, a tower that takes its name from its first and most infamous prisoner, Dalibor, who was a young Czech nobleman imprisoned and later beheaded for supporting a peasant uprising in the 15th century. As legend has it and as Smetana portrays it in his opera *Dalibor*, the nobleman learned to play the violin while a prisoner at the tower. His music could be heard all over the castle, seducing the townsfolk into pleading for his life and freedom – but all for naught, as was the case.

Lobkovic Palace

Back on Jiřská street and just inside the eastern gate of the castle is the **Lobkovic Palace** (Lobkovický palác), dating back to 1570 and now housing a branch of the **National Museum**, *Tel. 02/242 304 85*, this one devoted to Czech history. This is one of the better museums in which to get a grasp on the subject, but don't feel compelled to linger over all the exhibits, as most of them are rather tepid.

Some things that shouldn't be missed here are the stone-carved head of a man, dating back to the first or second century BC and considered one of the most impressive artistic works from the Celts; the replicas of the Bohemian crown jewels (the real ones are locked away in St. Vitus); and the sword of one Jan Mydlař, an executioner who lopped off the heads of 27 Protestants in Old Town Square in 1621. Look closely and you'll see the inscribed names of some of those executed by that very sword. If you don't understand Czech, be sure to pick up an English text in the museum's first room.

Opposite the Lobkovic Palace, the **House of Czechoslovak Children** (formerly the Burgraves Palace) is certainly the appropriate place in which to house the newly opened **Toy Museum** (hračky muzeum), a splendid place in which to set your kids, or the kid in you, free. The museum gives you a look at toys made by different cultures through the ages, starting with ancient Greece and leading up to the present-day Czech Republic. The Czechs take their wooden toy making quite seriously, and most of it is simply ingenious. Unfortunately, the museum isn't hands-on.

Powder Tower & Bridge

Now backtrack to the north side of St. Vitus Cathedral, where you'll find the entrance to the **Mihulka Powder Tower** (Prašna věž). Erected in the 15th century for defensive purposes, the tower became a bell workshop and later the laboratory for Rudolf II's alchemists. The museum – featuring exhibits on alchemy, bell-making, and castle life – is pretty boring, especially if you don't understand the strictly Czech explanations of the exhibits.

From the Powder Tower you gain access to the north gate of the castle, leading outside the castle walls to the **Powder Bridge** (Prašný most), a 16th century construction spanning over the **Stag Moat** (Jelení přikop), once used to raise wild game and now a picturesque ravine that is unfortunately closed to the public. On the opposite side of the bridge to the left, the **Riding School** was built by the French Baroque architect Jean-Baptiste Mathey and now functions as a space for temporary art exhibits. *It's open daily except Monday from 10 a.m. to 6 p.m.*

Royal Gardens & Summer Palace

Opposite the Riding School, you'll find the west entrance to the **Royal Gardens** (Královská zahrada), *open 10 a.m. to 5 p.m. daily except*

Monday, only from May 1 through September 31. The balmy manicured gardens, which double as an arboretum, go back to 1534, when Ferdinand I gave the orders for the creation of a Renaissance garden. Exotic flora, such as grapefruit and fig trees, somehow managed to thrive here at one time. And, as a matter fact, the first batch of tulips ever to be planted in European soil was done so right here, after which the Dutch picked up the idea. As fate would have it, every time the Prague Castle received a beating from the various invading armies, the gardens got wiped out. After a new layout in the 19th century and a restoration in 1918, the gardens now live up to their name, providing a soothing respite from the hubbub down in the city.

But there's more to the gardens than just nice trees and flowers. Spotted throughout are statues from the workshop of Mathias Braun, as well as a couple of fountains, one of which is called the **Singing Fountain** (Zpívající fontána) for the chimes it makes when the water flows into its bronze basins. On the south side of the garden, the Renaissance **Ball Game House** was once the site for an early form of tennis. Rebuilt after being destroyed in World War II, the structure features some pretty, allegorical sgraffito work.

WHAT IS SGRAFFITO?

Sgraffito is a term I use throughout this book. It's a technique of creating murals on buildings by scraping or etching an outer layer of white plaster to reveal a black layer of mortar beneath.

At the far end of the gardens, the **Royal Summer Palace** (Královský letohrádek) is considered to be the most genuine Renaissance structure outside Italy. Also known as the Belvedere (Belvéder), the palace cuts a sensational figure on the Prague skyline with its gallery of delicate arcades and its copper roof looking like the inverted hull of a ship. Built by Ferdinand I for his wife Anna in the 16th century, the palace now serves as a space for temporary art exhibits. *Open daily except Monday from 10 a.m. to 6 p.m.* Be sure to walk around to the southwest corner of the palace, where you can get a drop-dead view of the city and St. Vitus Cathedral.

Hradčany

See directions to Prague Castle. To gain access to the top of this district or to go directly to the Strahov Monastery, take tram #22 from Malostranská metro station to Pohořelec stop.

Hradčany arose as a sort of appendage to the castle, receiving official recognition as a "town" in 1320. Before the great fire of 1541, Hradčany consisted of little more than Hradčany Square (Hradčanské náměstí) and a few houses off the square. The fire, which wiped out most of Malá Strana and spread up the hill to the castle, allowed the church officials and the aristocracy to start with a clean slate and build the magnificent Renaissance and Baroque palaces that now fill the district. In 1529, Hradčany received the benefits of a royal town, apparent in the sheer majesty of the place.

Hradčany Square

Starting just outside the western castle gates in **Hradčany Square** (Hradčanské náměstí), you can't help but head straight to the square's stunning overlook, taking in Malá Strana's earth-toned roofs, Petřín Hill, and just about all of Prague east of the Vltava. Straight across from the overlook, you'll notice the American flag flying from a kiosk on the side of Petřín Hill. The land surrounding that kiosk is a vineyard, and belongs to the American Embassy, which sits just at the bottom of the hill.

If you can tear yourself away from the view, then head up the hill to the **Schwarzenberg Palace** (Schwarzenberský palác) at number 2, named for the last family to own it. Easily identified by its rich covering of sgrafitto and its imposing gables, the palace dates back to 1563, when Augustin Vlach built it for the aristocratic Lobkovic family. Today, the palace houses the **Museum of Military History**, showcasing the Czechs' long and sometimes dubious history of weapons production. In addition to the guns, cannons, and other arms, the museum features a great collection of tin soldiers and, obnoxiously enough, the largest mortar in the world. Even if you have no great interest in military matters, you should nonetheless have a look at the palace's sensational interior frescoes. *The museum is open from 9:30 a.m. to 4:30 p.m. Tuesday through Sunday; Tel. 02/536 488.*

Opposite the Schwarzenberg Palace, stunning for its half columns and pilasters, is the cream-colored **Archbishop's Palace** (Arcibiskupský palác), which has been the seat of Prague's archbishops since 1562. The only day in the year that the palace is open to the public is on the last Thursday before Easter (Maundy Thursday).

Accessed via a passageway running beside the Archbishop's Palace, the **Sternberg Palace** (Šternberský palác) serves as the venue for the National Gallery's collection of European art. The museum exhibits some of the country's best non-Czech art from the 15th to the 18th century. The first floor starts out with scores of Florentine triptychs, including not least those of Bernardo Daddi. The most formidable section of this floor however is the series of sanguine paintings by Dutch masters, highlighted by Breughel the Elder and his painting entitled *Haymaking*. On the second floor you'll find the indisputably most important work in the collection – *Feast of Rose Garlands* by Albrecht Durer, depicting the Virgin Mary enshrined by a host of luminaries such as the pope, the Holy Roman Emperor, and Durer himself (standing against the tree on the right). Another painting not to be missed is Rubens' *Murder of St. Thomas*, a rather bloody scene offset by hovering cherubs. *The Sternberg Palace branch of the National Gallery is open Tuesday through Sunday from 10 a.m. to 6 p.m; Tel. 02/245 105 94.*

One of the finer examples of sgraffitoed facades to grace Hradčany is the **Martinic Palace** at *Hradčanské náměstí 8* in the northwest corner of the square. The palace takes its name from the 17th century owner who was one of the unfortunates to be defenestrated from the Prague Castle. The formidable sgraffito work, which stretches into the courtyard, was discovered during a restoration in the 1970s, prompting director Miloš Foreman to choose this palace as the home for Mozart in the film *Amadeus*.

For a taste of Hradčany's medieval character, descend the hill along Kanovnická street, leading to what's called **Nový Svět**, or New World. This pocket of twisting lanes and adorable tiny houses slumping behind the stately palaces somehow manages to get bypassed by most tourists, making this an ideal place to take a stroll. The Dutch astronomer Tycho Brahe lived at Nový Svět 76 back in 1600, at which time the neighborhood was mostly composed of castle servants. Today, it remains residential, and free of the exchange offices and souvenir shops that have littered similar Prague neighborhoods.

Loreta Square

From Nový Svět head back up the hill to the second major square in Hradčany, **Loreta Square** (Loretánské náměstí), overwhelmed by the behemoth **Černin Palace** (Černínsky palác). The palace's original owner, Count Humprecht Černin, set his sights in 1669 on building himself a residence that rivaled the Prague Castle in majesty and pomp. Fickled as he was by the tastes of the day, he fired his first architect and hired Francesco Caratti to build him the gaudy pile that sent the Černin family into bankruptcy. With the establishment of the Czechoslovak First Republic, the palace was converted into the Ministry of Foreign Affairs, and later into the headquarters for the Nazi protectorate.

The third and saddest Prague defenestration occurred at the palace on March 10, 1948. Jan Masaryk, Minister of Foreign Affairs in the Gottwald cabinet and son of the founder of the First Republic, either jumped or was pushed to his death from the top floor of the palace.

Whether Masaryk's death was caused by suicide or murder has yet to be determined, but his anti-Communist stance in a Stalinist-influenced cabinet suggests that the regime had motive to silence him for good. Opposite the Černin Palace, counter-balancing the palace's severely secular appearance, is the **Loreta**, with its cheery yellow and cream-colored facade and its clock tower topped by a gorgeous onion dome. The facade and cloister of this religious complex is, however, merely a shell for the Loreta's star attraction – a replica of the **Casa Santa** (Holy House of the Virgin Mary), which, as legend has it, was carried by angels from Nazareth to the Italian village of Loreto just as the Turks were poised to sack the town and the house. Commissioned by Benigna Kateřina Lobkovic in 1626, the Prague Casa Santa is just one in 50 similar structures built in Bohemia during the Counter-Reformation.

The Prague replica, located in the arcaded Loreta courtyard, flourishes with an abundance of columns, Corinthian capitals, and niches containing numerous small statues of saints. You can also see a relief on the facade depicting the transfer of the Casa Santa to Loreto.

Opposite the Casa Santa, the **Church of the Nativity of Our Lord** (Kostel Narození Páně) features two skeletons, those of the Spanish saints Felicissima and Marcia – their appearances rather comically preserved by wax masks and nobleman's clothing. Even more bizarre is the bearded crucified woman rendered in the **Chapel of Our Lady Of Sorrows** (Kaple Panny Marie Bolestné), located in the southeast corner of the cloister. No, she is not some freak show martyr, but a Portuguese princess turned saint. As the story goes, her father promised her hand in marriage to the pagan king of Sicily. She prayed to God to save her from such a doomed marriage, and, low-and-behold, she woke up one morning sporting a luxurious beard. Furious that the marriage was called off, her father had her crucified.

From the courtyard, walk up the stairs to the Loreta **treasury**, filled with more monstrances than most of us would ever care to see. The most astounding, and ludicrous, of them is the solid silver *Prague Sun* (Pražské slunce), studded with no less than 6,222 diamonds. At the top of the hour, don't miss hearing the 27 Amsterdam-made bells chime out *We Greet Thee a Thousand Times*.

The Loreta is open daily except Monday from 9 a.m. to 4:30 p.m; Tel. 02/245 107 89.

Strahov Monastery

From Loretanské náměstí, continue up the hill along the arcaded Pohořelec street until you reach the entrance to the **Strahov Monastery** (Strahovsky Klašter); *Tel. 02/245 103 55,* founded in 1140 by Vladislav II as the first Bohemian site for the Premonstratensian order – a Catholic order established in the early 1100's by St. Norbet in France, who called for a greater devotion to the message of the Gospels. In 1783, the Strahov monks escaped Joseph II's decree disbanding monasteries by persuading Joseph that Strahov was an academic institution – something not far from the truth considering the thousands of books the monks had amassed. But the monks were not able to dissuade the Communists, who in 1952 threw most of the monks in prison and confiscated the monastery in an act of disdain for all religious institutions. After the events of 1989, the monastery was returned to the rightful hands of the order.

The reason for visiting the Strahov Monastery is the **library**, filled with more than a million books, manuscripts, and philosophical and theological treatises dating back to the 9th century. But there's more to the library than just books. Adorning the ceiling of the pilastered Philosophical Hall is the ethereal *Struggle of Mankind to Know Real Wisdom*, a fresco completed by Viennese painter Franz Maulpertsch in 1783. On the ceilings of the adjacent Theological Hall, Siard Nosecký added a series of allegorical frescos illustrating scenes from the Book of Proverbs. Unfortunately, you cannot relish these spectacular spaces from within, but have to view them from their respective entrances. *The library is open daily except Monday 9 a.m. to 5 p.m.*

Considering its fantastic library, it's no wonder then that the monastery also houses the **Museum of Czech Literature**. The museum displays the personal effects, manuscripts, and documents of the nation's great writers. *The musuem is open daily except Monday 9 a.m. to 5 p.m.; Tel. 02/245 111 37.*

One more part of the monastery you ought to see is the **Church of the Assumption of Our Lady** (Kostel Nanebevzetí Panny Marie), located around the corner from the library entrance. Originally built in 1143, the church nave and side vaults are cast in gold and ornamented with scores of frescos. Mozart supposedly improvised a sonata on the organ here.

At the far end of the monastery, at the bottom of the slope, don't miss the gorgeous view of Malá Strana and the castle. A path begins here, taking you through the Strahov Gardens.

Bílkova Villa

From Malostranská metro station, take tram #18 one stop to Chotkovy sady. You'll find the villa at the fork in the tram line. It's open daily except Monday from 10 a.m. to 6 p.m., but closes from October 16 to May 14.

Of all the artists to emerge from the Czech National Revival at the turn of the century, none were quite as unique as **František Bílek**, who designed this villa as a "cathedral of art" and as a residence for his family. A Christian mystic from South Bohemia, Bílek immersed himself in the works of Jan Hus and other Czech reformationists. He designed everything from houses to furniture to dishes. But it was his Symbolist statues and bas-reliefs, on exhibit at the villa, that have endowed the art world the most. Surprisingly, Bílek is hardly known outside his home country. But he did accrue quite a following during his day, earning the respect of none other than Franz Kafka.

The red-brick Bílkova Villa looks an awful lot like a Frank Lloyd Wright house, its unruly garden spotted with statues and its front porch ornamented with long shocks of corn. Inside, it's hard to decide if you've walked into an artist's workshop or a place of worship. One thing is for sure, you have definitely walked into the world of this great artist. Unbridled and acutely expressive, Bílek's statues and reliefs look as though they've been rendered in fits of religious ecstasy. One statue, however, stands out for its restraint, and for its shock value, and that's the *Virgin Mary of Golgotha*, perhaps the world's only representation of the Virgin Mary as an old woman. On exhibit are also some ceramics, drawings, and personal effects of the artist. Most tourists bypass this sensational museum, but you should definitely put it on your agenda.

After seeing the villa, head across the street to **Chotkovy sady**, Prague's first public park laid out in 1833. Here, you can lounge in the shade and take in some unparalleled views of the Vltava and its bridges and islands. The bizarre memorial in the middle of the park is to Julius Zeyer, a 19th Romantic poet. The carved marble figures are characters from his poems.

Malá Strana

This small Prague district is located on the west side of the Vltava River below the Prague Castle. Malostranská metro station puts you at the north end of the district. Take tram #12 or 22 one stop to Malostranské náměstí, the main square and heart of Malá Strana.

Of all the districts in Prague, none get so intriguingly medieval as **Malá Strana** (the Lesser Quarter), a pocket of the city hugging the foot of the castle and spread out along the western banks of the Vltava. The best thing to do here is get lost for an hour or so in the maze of sinuous cobblestone lanes and blind alleys curving and bending around aristocratic palaces, gabled houses, and enclosed gardens.

Even if you have never been to Prague, it's highly likely you have seen Malá Strana before. The district has been the location for countless films, including *Kafka*, *The Trial* (the most recent version), and *Amadeus*, in which Malá Strana served as 18th-century Vienna.

Malá Strana's history goes back to the 8th or 9th century as a market settlement and back to 1257 as a designated royal town. As fate would have it, it was largely destroyed by battles during the Hussite wars and again by the great fire of 1541. All this destruction paved the way (so to speak) for the emergence of a Renaissance town, built by scores of Italian architects and masons who lived along Vlašská (Italian) Street. But as the taste of the ages changed, so did Malá Strana.

The Catholic church and the Catholic aristocracy, wielding their power and riches after defeating the Czech Estates at the Battle of White Mountain, began building momentous churches and palaces, replacing the Renaissance character of the town with a Baroque one.

Malá Strana Square & the Church of St. Nicholas

The heart of Malá Strana and its main square is **Malá Strana Square** (Malostranské náměstí), enclosed by a wealth of newly restored palaces and pervaded by the district's main landmark – the **Church of St. Nicholas**. But before we head inside this gem of a church, let's take a look at Malá Strana's **former town hall**, now a restaurant and nightclub called Malostranská beseda, standing in the northeast corner of the square at number 21. The building itself is not so interesting as its history, for it was here that the famous "Czech Confession" was drawn up in 1575 by various Protestant groups demanding religious tolerance in the Czech lands. Rudolf II signed into law many of the document's terms, but his successor Matthias disregarded them, installing his own pro-Catholic policies. Outraged, the same assembly of Protestant groups met May 22, 1618, at the **Smiřický Palace** (*number 18 on the square*) and decided to march to the castle the next day and hurl the two Hapsburg counselors out the window, sparking the Thirty Years' War.

Hands down, the most intensely beautiful Baroque church in Prague is the one that dominates Malá Strana Square – the **Church of St. Nicholas** (Kostel Sv. Mikuláše), not to be confused with the St. Nicholas in Old Town Square. When viewed from the Charles Bridge, the muscular dome and soaring clock tower of St. Nicholas – somewhat grimy from the years of coal-smoke that only recently stopped choking Malá Strana – cuts such an alluring figure across the district skyline that you have to wonder for a moment if the scene is not some mammoth fresco.

In 1625, the Jesuits acquired the small Gothic church of St. Nicholas, after which they commissioned Krištof Dientzenhofer to build the imposing structure that would come to symbolize the order's widespread power in Bohemia. After Dientzenhofer passed away, his son Kilián Ignác and Kilián's son-in-law, Anselmo Lurago, took over the project, finishing it in 1755.

Inside the church, you can't help but feel like a "lesser person" beside the bulky pillars and underneath what is one of the largest frescoes in all of Europe – the *Apotheosis of St. Nicholas*, painted on the church ceiling by Viennese artist Johann Lucas Kracker. The fresco is not only astounding for its size (1,500 square meters), but also for its fusion with the church

CLASSICAL CONCERTS:
SOARING MUSIC IN SOARING SPACES

*The **Church of St. Nicholas** on Malá Strana Square is the venue for daily classical concerts, the tickets for which are on sale at a table standing just outside the church entrance. Another venue for classical concerts is just opposite the front of St. Nicholas at the **Liechtenstein Palace**, housing Prague's **Academy of Music**. The palace, named for the last aristocratic family to own it (the same family who lends their name to the small principality sandwiched between Switzerland and Austria) is a rather uninspiring pile extended across one side of Malá Strana Square. But inside the concert hall, you'll find a much more fragile beauty, creating a perfect setting in which to enjoy the daily concerts held here.*

*Finally, the **other Church of St. Nicholas**, located on the Old Town Square, also routinely holds concerts. Tickets can be purchased at the church entrance.*

architecture. Indeed, it is difficult to spot where the pillars and cornices end and the painting begins.

Almost as impressive is the richly adorned church choir, an expansive space lent an etherealness by the looming church dome and lent gravity by František Platzer's four superhuman statues of Greek saints. Coated with a shimmering glaze of gold is the statue of St. Nicholas, gesticulating ecstatically from above the pulpit. In the choir, check out the organ, notable not only for its 2,500 pipes, but also for the person who once played it – W.A. Mozart.

Around Nerudova Street

Running beside Malostranské náměstí up to the castle is one of Prague's most beautiful streets – **Nerudova ulice**, which forms part of the Royal Way through Prague (the historical route of the coronation procession). The cobble-stoned street is lined with scores of individual Renaissance or Gothic houses given Baroque facelifts. Most of the houses bear a symbol and a name. For instance, at number 31, three violins grace the facade of **"At the Three Little Fiddles"** (U tří housliček), a name that recalls that the Edlingers, a family of instrument makers, occupied the house from 1667 to 1748.

One of the more notable buildings on Nerudova, if only for the statues of two Moorish titans supporting the building, is the **Morzin Palace**, now housing the Romanian Embassy. Notice the doors, given a quirky design depicting day and night. Under the eaves, you'll also notice allegorical paintings depicting the four corners of the world.

Opposite the Morzin Palace, *at number 20*, the **Thun-Kolovrat Palace** features two outrageous sculptures of eagles made by Matthias Braun. This palace now houses the Italian Embassy, which at times opens an intriguing passageway beside the house, leading up to the **Castle Steps**. The **Church of Our Lady of Perpetual Succor** (Kostel Panny Marie ustavičné pomoci), *at number 24*, offers a nice respite from the throngs of tourists outside its doors. Further up Nerudova, *at number 33*, the **Bretfeld Palace** was once the setting for 18th-century high society balls, attended by the likes of Mozart and Casanova.

The house **"At the Two Suns"** (U dvou sluncŭ), *number 47*, was from 1845 to 1891 the residence of the street's namesake, Jan Neruda. This poet, journalist, and short-story writer captured the bohemian spirit of Malá Strana in works such as *Tales of the Malá Strana*. So great was his respect for Jan Neruda, the Chilean Nobel-prize winner Pablo Neruda took his pen name from the not-so-famous Czech.

From the top of Nerudova, you can either take the hairpin turn to the top of the Castle Steps, climb the winding staircase to the top of Hradčany Square, or continue up Úvoz street to the Strahov Monastery. Along Úvoz are some great views of Malá Strana, as well as another intriguing staircase squeezed in between two buildings leading up to Loreto Square.

More or less running parallel with Nerudova and situated closer to the castle ramparts is a corridor of lanes and blind alleys leading up to the Castle Steps (Zamecké schody). This is Malá Strana at its most engaging, and simply a good place to wander aimlessly. A good place to begin is just off Malostranské náměstí at the corner of Sněmovní and Thunovská streets. Strung along one side of Sněmovní is the former **Parliament House**, occupying the Thun Palace. This was the site of one the country's most momentous occasions: on November 14, 1918, the national assembly ousted the Hapsburgs from the Czech throne. On that same day, the creation of the Czechoslovak Republic became official, as Tomáš Garrigue Masaryk took office as president.

From Sněmovní head up Thunovská to the **Castle Steps**, hugging the castle ramparts above Malá Strana's red roofs. The intriguing steps, which have caught the imagination of countless movie directors, have unfortunately been blemished by a lot of senseless graffiti, as have a number of other sights in Prague.

Wallentstein Palace

Located directly behind Malostranská metro station between Letenská and Valdštejnská streets, the **Wallenstein Palace** (Valdštejnský palác) is Albrecht of Wallenstein's grand offering to himself. At the height of his power in the 17th century, Albrecht commanded the Hapsburg Imperial

168 CZECH & SLOVAK REPUBLICS GUIDE

army, a position that provided him with enough riches to buy up a huge chunk of Malá Strana, tear down 26 houses located on it, and build the largest palace in Prague.

A good example of Albrecht's self-importance is found in the palace's banquet hall, its ceiling covered with a representation of Albrecht himself as Mars, Roman god of war. (Albrecht's power, by the way, was not trusted by the Hapsburg rulers. In 1634, the Hapsburgs had him assassinated in his bed at Cheb for conspiring with the Swedes and Saxons.)

The Wallenstein Palace was built between 1623 and 1629 by Italian architects Andrea Spezza and Niccolo Sebregondi, who enhanced the interior with a good amount of tedious stucco work and a wealth of frescos. The Ministry of Culture occupies most of the palace, leaving one wing open to the **Komenský Pedagogical Museum** (Pedagogické muzeum Komenského), devoted to the 17th century Protestant teacher and theologian Jan Ámos Komenský (known in the west as John Comenius). Bishop of the Union of Czech Brethren, Komenský introduced the idea of nursery school, emphasizing the need for play in a child's education. Komensky was exiled to Holland after the defeat of the Protestants at the Battle of White Mountain.

In addition to Komenský's works, the museum has exhibitions on two other luminaries from Czech history – Tomáš Garrigue Masaryk and Jan Patočka. The entrance is at the far end of the courtyard, accessed via Valdštejnská street. *The museum is open 10 a.m. to 5 p.m. Tuesday through Sunday.*

The best part of the palace is, however, its enclosed **gardens** (Valdštejnská zahrada), entered through a small gate on Letenská street. Offering a piece of serenity away from the fast pace outside its walls, the gardens feature a large pond and an enormous Italianate arch, lending punctuation to a procession of sculptures. *The garden is open daily 10 a.m. to 5 p.m. May 1 through September 31.*

Other gardens in the immediate neighborhood worth checking out are located behind the walls of **Vojan Park** (Vojanovy sady), accessed from U lužického seminaře street. Established in 1248, Vojan is Prague's oldest park, and another wonderfully secluded place to put your mind at ease amidst the stands of trees, baby carriages, and strolling lovers. So secluded is this park that you could honestly live several years in Prague and never know about it. (It took me two years before catching on.)

Kampa Island

Kampa Island, a strip of land cut off from the rest of Malá Strana by Čertovka (the Devil's Channel), features a gorgeous main square, a few rustic water wheels, and a great riverside park. Kampa commands no must-see sights and thus makes no demands upon you, only that you find some peace of mind strolling through its leafy grounds.

The best approach to the island is by taking the double staircase down from the Charles Bridge, placing you in **Na Kampě náměstí** – a gorgeous square filled with sidewalk cafés, restaurants, and pubs. Here, you'll definitely want to sit down to a beer or coffee and relish the sight of the Prague Castle looming above. If you happen to have a bite to eat here, save a bit of your bread for the swans that congregate on the river bank just behind the square. They'll be most appreciative, as will you, standing at this perfect place in which to view the Charles Bridge.

From Na Kampě náměstí, go ahead and saunter into **Kampa Park**, a favorite with young Praguers, who come here on summer evenings to take part in acoustic jam sessions, stroll with their lovers, or just lie under the stars. Near the southern tip of the island, at Říční and Všehrdova streets, you'll find the **Church of St. John at the Laundry** (Kostel sv. Jana Na prádle), one of the oldest Gothic buildings in Malá Strana despite the peculiar name. Built in 1142, the church later was converted to a wash house, hence the title. Reconsecrated a house of worship by the Czechoslovak Hussite Church in 1935, St. John's features the faint remains of some 14th century frescoes.

Retrace your steps to the north end of Kampa Island and cross back over to the mainland via a narrow bridge providing a fine perspective of an old water wheel and a section of Malá Strana known as "Prague's Venice," so called for its buildings which seemingly emerge from the channel.

Just beyond the bridge is the **Lennon Wall** (Lennova zeď), lining Velkopřevorské náměstí (square) just opposite the French Embassy. John Lennon's pacifist message rung a vital chord with young Praguers living under the belligerent wing of the Soviet Union. Though it may be completely wiped out in the next few years, a graffiti rendering of John Lennon appeared on the wall after his death in 1980, simultaneously becoming an homage to the musician and a symbol of protest against the Communist government. (On the night of the anniversary of his death, dissidents would gather at the wall and wait for the police to forcibly remove them.) Since 1989, hundred of letters and postcards have arrived in Prague addressed simply to the "John Lennon Monument, Prague." Postmen have diligently gone ahead and attached them to the wall.

Around the corner from Velkopřevorské náměstí, **Maltézské náměstí** is another pocket of solitude footsteps away from the tourist hubbub along Mostecká street. The square takes it name from the Knights of Malta, an order of crusaders originating in France. The order is responsible for the **Church of Our Lady Under the Chains** (Kostel Panny Marie pod řetězem), located just off the square on Lázenská lane.

Though the present church dates to the early 17th century, the foundations date back to 1169, making them the oldest in Malá Strana. The church's two Gothic towers (built in 1385) provide a momentous portal through which you enter the enclosed, overgrown garden.

Tržiště & Vlašska Streets
The buildings on these two streets suffered some pretty serious dilapidation during the Communist era, and have only recently sprung back to life with new renovations. But they amount to what is another intriguing pocket of Malá Strana.

Around the corner from the intersection of Malostranské náměstí and Karmelitská street begins Tržiště. Half way up is the **Schönborn Palace**, occupied with a good bit of tight security by the **American Embassy**. Franz Kafka rented an apartment in the palace in 1917 (before it became an embassy).

Further up the hill, Tržiště turns into Vlašska (Italian) street, named as such for the large community of Italian architects and masons that settled on the street back in the 16th century. On your left, just as the street begins, is yet another **Lobkovic Palace**, this one now occupied by the **German Embassy**. The palace, built between 1703 and 1713 by one of the resident Italians, was besieged in the summer of 1989 by thousands of East Germans demanding West German citizenship. They took refuge in the embassy gardens until the Czechoslovak government capitulated and organized special trains taking them across the border to West Germany. The episode prompted the mass East German exodus that brought about the fall of the Iron Curtain later that year.

The best view you can get of the palace is not from the front, but from around the side of the English gardens, laid out by Václav Skalník in 1793 – by which time he had already become noted for his gardens in the spa town of Mariánské Lázně (Marienbad). The gardens are not open to the public, but you can stroll around outside its walls, decorated with two handsome sculptures of Persephone and Orietyia. Or you could continue up Vlašska, which eventually turns into a narrow romantic lane leading to the sloping **Strahov gardens**, a good place to take a breather on a park bench and enjoy a fine view of Malá Strana.

Karmelitská to Újezd
Just off Malostranské náměstí, *at Karmelitská 25*, is the gorgeous Baroque **Vrtbov Garden** (Vrtbovská zahrada), a breathtaking vision of balance and symmetry stretching up the side of Petřín Hill. The garden, laid out by F.M. Kaňka in 1720, features a series of delicate terraces adorned with urns and the occasional statue by Matthias Braun. At the top of the garden is an observation deck, affording yet another inspiring view of Malá Strana and the Prague Castle.

A little farther down Karmelitská on the same side of the street is the **Church of Our Lady Victorious** (Kostel Paní Marie Vítězné), a rather uninspiring Baroque structure initially built by the Lutherans but later confiscated by the Catholic Carmelites after the Battle of White Mountain. The main attraction here is the wax statuette of baby Jesus called the **Infant of Prague** (Pražské jezulátko), brought from Spain in 1555 by one of the Lobkovic brides and donated to the church in 1628. Thousands of pilgrimage makers turn up here each year to get a glimpse of the little statue that is said to have performed several miracles, like protecting the city against the plague and later against destruction in the Thirty Years' War. One German prior, E.S. Stephano, spread the word of the statue's miracles in the 18th century, starting a cult following throughout the Christian world. Since then, the statue has become the recipient of 60-some costumes from around the world, to be worn according to the religious calendar. One costume, made of a gold brocade, was donated by Empress Maria Theresa in 1742.

Three or four blocks down, at *Újezd 40*, is the **Michna Palace** (Michnův palác), a well-worn pile dating back to 1580. The front facade isn't all that impressive, and doesn't give you much of an idea of the breadth of this place. A better view is from the rear, accessed by walking around the sgraffitoed side of the palace. Today, the palace houses the Sports Faculty of the Charles University and the **Museum of Physical Education and Sport** (Muzeum tělovýchovy a sportu), which seems like an appropriate function for the building considering it was once owned by the Sokol Gymnastics Association.

Formed in Prague in the late 19th century, the Sokols fused the ideas of sport and Czech nationalism, emphasizing the need for strong body and strong mind. One million strong in 1947 and banned by the Communists in 1948, the Sokols are now making a comeback. At the museum you can learn more about them, and the rest of the history of Czech sports.

Petřín Hill

This steep, overgrown hill bulges high above the city, offering stupendous views of Prague from its zig-zagging lanes lined with tall trees and spotted with a number of interesting sights. There are several routes up Petřín Hill from Malá Strana, but the funnest way is up the funicular railway (*lánova dráha*), located just opposite the Michna Palace at the Újezd tram stop (*tram #12 or 22 from Malostranská metro station or #9 or 22 from Národní třída metro station). The funicular runs daily from 9:15 a.m. to 8:45 p.m. and takes the same ticket as the metro and tram.* The four-minute ride stops midway up the hill at the Nebozízek Restaurant (see *Where to Eat* above) and then continues to the top.

As you go up the funicular, you'll notice a long wall running along the ridge and descending down the hill. The so-called **Hunger Wall** (Hladová zeď), stretching from the Strahov Monastery to Újezd, was completed in 1362 under Charles IV, who ordered its construction so as to simultaneously provide work for the poor and fortify Malá Strana. At the top of Petřín Hill, you exit the funicular terminus to a nice surprise – a pretty rose garden laid out in front of the **Štefánik Observatory and Planetarium** (Štefánikova hvězdárna), offering the public a glimpse at the stars during various nighttime hours, which depend on the season and the weather conditions.

To the right (north) of the terminus, the Baroque **Church of St. Lawrence** (Kostel sv. Vavřince) sits, curiously enough, within a recess in the Hunger Wall. Built between 1735 and 1770 on top of some Romanesque remains dating back to 1135, the church features a ceiling fresco depicting the alleged founding of the church in 991. The fresco glorifies the bringing of Christianity to the pagans who supposedly practiced their rituals on Petřín Hill. (To this day, the hill is the site of mock Pagan bonfires, done more in the spirit of fun than seriousness.) The church grounds are lined with stations of the cross, reaching its conclusion at the **Calvary Chapel**, located next to the church and adorned with some bombastic sgraffito work portraying Christ's resurrection.

Standing in front of St. Lawrence is a neo-Gothic bastion, housing the so-called **Maze** (Bludiště), named for its room full of wacky mirrors. The structure, along with its diorama of the battle between Praguers and Swedes in 1648, was built for the 1891 Prague Jubilee Exposition and was later moved to the hill.

Built for the same exposition and also relocated to the top of Petřín is a miniature copy of the **Eiffel Tower**, erected as a sign of the close cultural ties between Prague and Paris at the time of the exposition. Though only one-fifth the size of the actual Eiffel, this 62-meter (203-foot) copy still affords an unbeatable view of Prague and the surrounding forests and hills.

From the Eiffel Tower, you can continue along the Hunger Wall to the Strahov Monastery at the top of Hradčany.

Charles Bridge

Spanning over the Vltava River between Malá Strana and Staré Město, the Charles Bridge is easy to find by following the hordes of tourists down from the castle via Nerudova and Mostecká streets or away from Old Town Square via Karlova street. The nearest metro station on the Malá Strana side is Malostranská, while the closest station on the Staré Město side is Staroměstská.

Again and again, you've probably heard it said: the **Charles Bridge** is the most beautiful bridge in Europe. I will take that one step further and say that the Charles Bridge (Karlův most) has to be counted as one of the most beautiful bridges in the world, if not *the* most beautiful. Certainly, there are few so old as this one dating back to 1402, and hardly any that provides such a breathtaking view of a hovering castle, a soaring cathedral, and innumerable towers and spires thrusting through the skyline. Add to that view a procession of looming statues lining the bridge, and what you come up with is something to restore your faith in the works of man. It is simply that awesome.

After the old Judith Bridge got washed away in a flood in 1357 and the two towns of Malá Strana and Staré Město found themselves without a link, Charles IV commissioned his castle and cathedral architect, Petr Parléř, to build a new stone bridge, one to withstand the temperamental waters of the Vltava River (which it has done ever since). For more than 400 years after it was built, the "Stone Bridge" (as it was known until it took Charles' name in 1870) served as the only link between Prague's two sides. Made of sandstone blocks, the somewhat crooked Charles Bridge is 1,700 feet long and 30 feet wide and is supported by 16 pillars. One good legend surrounding its construction is that the masons added egg yolk to the mortar, which is the assumed reason behind its endurance. Supposedly, towns from all over Bohemia donated eggs to the effort, not least that of the town of Velvary. But Velvary, fearing the eggs may break on the way to Prague, sent them hard-boiled. The town has been the brunt of jokes ever since.

What makes the Charles Bridge so exceptional is, of course, the statues lining it. The first statue to decorate the bridge was the bronze crucifix, erected not long after the bridge's completion. Replaced again and again, the present crucifix dates back to 1628 and has a plaque inscribed with "Holy, Holy, Holy God" in Hebrew. Apparently, a Jewish man was forced to pay for the plaque in 1695 after being found guilty of desecrating the crucifix.

The first statue to go up on the north side of the bridge is the one of St. John of Nepomuk, the Vicar-General of the diocese of Prague who was allegedly bound, gagged, and hurled from the Charles Bridge for not revealing the queen's confession when ordered to by King Wenceslas IV (see the description of St. John's tomb in the St. Vitus Cathedral). The statue, located roughly midway across the bridge, features a bronze relief on its pedestal rather humorously portraying St. John being tossed to his death in the Vltava – something that never actually happened. Legend has it that if you rub the relief you are sure to return to Prague someday, which is why the bronze looks so shiny compared to the rest of the sooty statue. The rest of the 22 brooding statues of saints come mainly from the workshops of Matthias Bernhard Braun and Maximillian Brokoff, added to the bridge between 1698 and 1713. But most of these have been replaced over the years with copies of the originals.

On the Staré Město side, the **bridge tower** lends perfect punctuation to the procession of saints. This Gothic masterpiece is the work of Petr Parléř, who adorned the east side with the sculpted faces of Charles IV (on the left) and Wenceslas IV. The severed heads of the nobleman executed in Old Town Square after the Battle of White Mountain were trophied here for ten years. The tower was later the site of the last battle in the Thirty Years' War, in which a hastily organized group of students and local Jews took on the invading Swedish army. *You can climb the tower for 30 Kč, daily from 10 a.m. to 6 p.m.*

On the Malá Strana side of the bridge are two defensive Gothic towers of unequal height, connected by an arch that spans over the bridge and serves as an alluring gateway to the Lesser Side. The smaller tower is a left-over from the old Judith Bridge. The taller one, an imitation of Petr Parléř's tower on the opposite side of the bridge, went up in 1464 during the reign of King George of Poděbrady. You can climb it for the same price and during the same hours as the Staré Město tower.

Unfortunately, the bridge loses some of its captivating powers during the peak of the tourist seasons, when a creeping herd of sightseers fills the bridge to capacity, stopping now and again to check out the wares of souvenir hawkers or to watch some buskers (street performers) playing all kinds of music from classical to Dixieland jazz. With so many people rubbing shoulders, the bridge is easy pickings for pickpockets, so make sure all your valuables are securely tucked away. The best solution to this hassle is to show up early in the morning. Better yet, if you happen to be out bar hopping nearby in the wee hours of the night, make the effort to pass over the bridge. You may just find yourself in solitary awe of this stunning structure.

Staré Město

There are three possible metro stations placing you in or nearby Staré Město: Staroměstská, which locates you a few blocks west of Old Town Square; Můstek, which places you on the eastern edge of the district; and Národní třída, which puts you just outside the southern edge.

The effect Staré Město (literally meaning "Old Town") has on its visitors is absorption; it lures you in, inviting you to wander through its maze of sinuous alleys, to tread its cobblestone lanes, and get lost in all its mystery. Staré Město compels, seduces, and eventually convinces you that this is as authentic as Europe gets. This is also where Prague comes alive, where tourists, students, and shoppers mingle in vibrant proximity to one another, feeding off one another's high-pitched moods.

The history of Staré Město goes back to the 10th century, when it was founded as a marketplace. By the 12th century, it had evolved into an important center of commerce, drawing a melting pot of peoples from Germany, Flanders, Burgundy, and Piedmont, who came to take part in the growing economy fostered by the royal court at the Prague Castle. It was during this period that Staré Město began to take shape, looking not so different back then as it does today.

A great period of Staré Město's growth occurred during the reign of Charles IV, whose title of Holy Roman Emperor made Prague the most important city in Europe. Charles granted the town the right to build a town hall, which meant that Staré Město now had a good amount of self-jurisdiction and could go ahead with more ambitious development, which it did with an intensely Gothic flair. After several floods and a devastating fire in 1689, the town was literally raised, done so by simply building on top of older Gothic buildings. Staré Město then received a largely Baroque face, facilitated by the Counter-Reformation which took Prague by storm after the defeat of the Protestant Czech Estates at the Battle of White Mountain.

Some must-sees in Staré Město include the **Old Town Hall** and its **Astronomical Clock**, the churches of **St. Nicholas** and **Our Lady before Týn**, the **Municipal House**, the **Museum of Decorative Arts**, the **Bethlehem Chapel**, and the **Convent of St. Agnes**.

Old Town Square

Get off at Staroměstská metro station and walk three blocks east (away from the river) on Kaprova street.

The beating heart of Staré Město and of Prague itself is **Old Town Square** (Staroměstské náměstí), sporting a hodgepodge of Gothic, Renaissance, Baroque, and Art Nouveau facades festooned with a brilliant array of colors. You can't help but gape while strolling this wonderful plaza, uplifted by the sound of classical music coming from CD shops, the clank of the souvenir coin minters, and the sight of horses and carriages providing rides through the old town.

Old Town Square has been the site of some of Prague's most historic events, going back to 1422 and the execution of Jan Želivsky, a Hussite preacher who instigated Prague's first defenestration and whose death sparked off the Hussite Wars. On June 21, 1621, Old Town Square once more became the site of carnage, when 27 Protestant nobleman were beheaded following the defeat of their troops at the Battle of White Mountain. In more recent history, Prague suffered some of its only damage during World War II when the Nazi SS, in a last moment of nihilistic destruction, set fire to the Old Town Hall on May 8, 1945, as the Russian army approached Prague and battles between Germans and

Czechs raged on the streets. The day after the fire, Russian troops marched into the square, liberating Prague.

Three years later, on February 21, 1948, **Klement Gottwald** stepped to the balcony of the Kinský Palace and proclaimed that Czechoslovakia was now a Communist country. And on August 21, 1968, Soviet tanks rolled into the square, squashing the Prague Spring and putting an end to Czechoslovakia's "Communism with a human face."

Another momentous occasion to hit Old Town Square was the unveiling of the **Jan Hus Statue**, which took place on July 6, 1915, commemorating the 500th anniversary of the martyr's death at the stake. The Art Nouveau statue, the work of Ladislav Šaloun, takes center stage in the square and portrays Hus' followers and enemies all languishing at the feet of the man himself, boldly standing in all the moral certitude credited to him ever since he and his martyrdom became a symbol of national identity for the Czechs. The inscription along the base of the statue include Hus' last words uttered at the stake: *Pravda zvítězí* – "Truth shall overcome" – a maxim chanted by students during the Velvet Revolution of 1989.

For three years after its unveiling, the statue stood side-by-side a Marian column, erected in the 17th century as an offering of thanks to God for the Hapsburg victory in the Thirty Years' War. It was only a matter of days after the declaration of Czechoslovak independence that a mob toppled the column, leaving Hus as sole occupant of the country's most revered square.

Jutting into the square is a row of houses that make up the **Old Town Hall** (Staroměstská radnice). Lacking funds to build a new structure to serve as a town hall, the newly formed municipality gradually bought up the six houses, starting out with the purchase of the Wolflin House, at the far end, in 1338. Petr Parléř added a magnificent Gothic tower to the Wolflin house in 1381. Eventually, the town hall came to include all the houses stretching across to the arcaded **Dům U minuty** (House At the Minute), featuring some gorgeous sgraffito work. Bought by the municipality in 1896, this was the last house to be included in the town hall row, before which it served as a residence for Franz Kafka's family.

As mentioned before, the town hall was one of the few buildings damaged during War World II, when it was set alight by a desperate Nazi army in the closing days of the war. The complex was mostly saved, except for the Wolfin House's Gothic chapel and the north wing of the town hall, which is now marked by a grassy space. Parléř's chapel, however, has been meticulously reconstructed and can be seen on your way up the tower.

Today, the Old Town Hall serves as a gallery for temporary exhibitions and as an information and ticket office, through which you must enter to gain access to the tower. For 30 Kč or so, you can climb to the top and get a spectacular view of the city. *Hours of the tower are daily from 9 a.m. to 5 p.m.*

On the east side of the tower, check out the plaque inscribed with the names of the 27 Czech noblemen publicly executed in front of the town hall after the Battle of White Mountain. White crosses on the paving show you exactly where the beheadings took place.

But the big attraction at the Old Town Hall is the world-famous **Astronomical Clock** (orloj), constructed in 1490 by one Master Hanuš. One of Prague's greatest small delights, it never fails to lure a big group of tourists at the top of each hour for its show, the beginning of which is signalled by the skeletal figure of Death pulling a rope and ringing a bell. At that moment, two small windows open and a procession of the 12 Apostles make their rounds, bowing to all those gawking at this mechanical wonder.

LEGEND OF THE ASTRONOMICAL CLOCK

As the story goes, the Old Town officials recognized that Master Hanuš's astronomical clock was one-of-a-kind, and would be the source of envy of every other town in Europe. To insure that Master Hanuš could never duplicate another such device in (God forbid) another town, the officials sent three men to his workshop one night. The men seized the clockmaker and stuck his face to the fire, blinding him. For years after the incident, Master Hanuš sat an idle man, filled with hate for the town officials who paid for his glorious gift by rendering him blind.

Near his death, the old clockmaker hobbled to the clock one day, assisted by one of his apprentices. Hanuš told the officials that he, with the help of his guide, would do some fine tuning to the clock. As instructed, his guide led him to the most integral part of the clock. At the peak of the clock's hourly performance, Hanuš reached in and jiggled the works. The Apostles, in the middle of their rounds, came to a grinding halt, as did the rest of the clock. That night, Hanuš passed away. It wasn't until 70 or so years later that the clock was repaired, as there was no one at the time of Hanuš's death who understood its workings.

Besides ringing the bell, Death holds an hour glass, turning it over each hour to remind you of your fleeting existence on earth. In addition to Death, there are three more anxieties of medieval Praguers represented on the clock and activated each hour: Greed as the Jew shaking his moneybags, Vanity as the dandy admiring himself in the mirror, and the fear of pagan invasion as the turbaned Turk shaking his head. Standing resolutely still throughout the hourly performance are four figures below – the Philosopher, Astronomer, Angel, and Chronicler. Once all the apostles have made their appearance, the cock flaps its wings and crows, the windows close, and Death sets the hourglass sands running once again.

The face of the clock itself depicts the universe as it was thought to work in medieval times. Earth is at the center, around which the sun, moon, and zodiacs revolve. A little hand, attached to the sun by a short arm, points to the Roman-numeraled hour of the day (adjusted for daylight savings) and to a Gothic numeral reading the traditional Bohemian measuring of time (where each day begins at sunset).

Below the clock is a calendar wheel adorned with bucolic scenes of Bohemian agrarian life. The hand on the calendar indicates which day it is and which saint the day is in honor of. The calendar wheel on view today is, however, a copy of the original painted by Josef Mánes in 1866 during the Czech National Revival and now hanging in the Prague City Museum (see Nové Město).

The **Church of St. Nicholas** (Kostel sv. Mikuláše) used to hide in the shadow of the north wing of the Old Town Hall. Since the Nazis burned the wing down, the cream-colored church and its smattering of blackened statuary have stood exposed in all its lavish glory in the northwest corner of Old Town Square. In four short years, Kilián Ignác Dientzenhofer constructed the church on the site of a Gothic chapel before going on to help his father build the equally brilliant but more indulgent St. Nicholas Church in Malá Strana.

The exterior, a fantastic vision of balance and symmetry graced with two towers and a central cupola, is thankfully as impressive as the surprisingly upbeat, sunny interior, where your eyes will first direct you to what has to be one of the largest chandeliers hanging in Prague. After getting over the size of the crystal beast, take a good look around and note the playfulness of Dientzenhofer's design, especially his abundance of balconies, pediments, and cornices – all of which gives the church a rather theatrical appearance. Also, be sure to check out the elliptical openings providing an interesting view up the inside of the two towers. Belonging to the Czech Hussite Church, St. Nicholas is yet another site for regularly held classical concerts, for which you can buy tickets at the church entrance.

Just off the main portion of the square, adjacent to St. Nicholas Church, is the **Franz Kafka Exhibition** (Expozice Franze Kafky), a rather kitschy affair documenting Kafka's life in Prague. The location of this small private museum is a good one, considering it was Kafka's birthplace. *Hours are 10 a.m. to 6 p.m. Tuesday through Friday and 10 a.m. to 5 p.m. on Saturday.*

Continuing on the east side of the Old Town Square, be sure to take note of the busy facade gracing the **Kinský Palace** (Palác Kinských) *at number 12.* Designed by Kilián Ignác Dientzenhofer, illustrious architect of both churches of St. Nicholas in Prague, the palace facade is perhaps the greatest example of the Rococo style found in the city. In February 1948, Klement Gottwald stood from the palace balcony and delivered a speech to a crowd of thousands in Old Town Square announcing that the country was now under complete control of a Communist government. Far from that unfortunate bit of the palace's history now, the building houses a branch of the **National Gallery**, this one devoted mainly to changing exhibitions of the state's graphic art collection. *Hours are 10 a.m. to 6 p.m. Tuesday through Sunday; Tel. 02/248 107 58.*

On the right side of the ground floor of the palace, you'll find the **Franz Kafka Bookshop** (Knihkupectví Franze Kafky), run by the Kafka Society. The palace is more than an appropriate setting for such a venture, considering that Kafka attended school here and that his father once ran a haberdashery out of its ground floor.

Oddly adjoined to the Kinsky Palace, **House at the Stone Bell** (Dům U kamenného zvonu) hid behind a second-rate Baroque facade of gooey plaster until the 1960s, at which time the building was stripped down to its original sandy-colored Gothic core. Today, the building serves as an excellent location for the **Prague City Gallery**, with excellent temporary modern art exhibits. *Open daily except Monday from 10 a.m. to 6 p.m.*

Perhaps the most indelible sight from Old Town Square, the one that makes it on just about every Prague tourist brochure, is that of the **Church of Our Lady Before Týn** (Kostel Panny Marie před Týnem), thrusting out from its barricaded position behind the arcaded Týn School. The exterior of "Týn Church" and its pair of spiky Gothic towers do indeed cut a sensational figure on the Staré Město skyline, best seen from the Old Town Hall Tower.

Through the eyes of the Czechs, the Týn Church is one of the most historically significant churches in Bohemia, mainly due to its connections with the Hussite movement in the 15th century. Several pivotal Hussite reformers preached here, and George of Poděbrady, the last Czech and only Hussite king, attended his first mass as king here, donating to the church a statue of himself and a huge golden chalice, which was the symbol of all the Hussite sects in and around Bohemia.

After the Battle of White Mountain in 1626 and during the mad dash to wipe out all vestiges of Protestantism in Prague, the chalice was taken down, as were most of the Gothic furnishings that hinted of the church's Hussite past. The interior was, for the most part, "Baroquefied," especially when it came to the high altar, now adorned with a painting by the famous Baroque artist Karel Škréta depicting the Assumption and Holy

Trinity. The interior does, however, offer up some of its Gothic origins, most notably the north portal and canopy, which comes from the workshop of Petr Parléř.

At the fifth pillar on the right, don't miss the tombstone of one Tycho Brahe, Rudolf II's famous court astronomer who apparently had quite a wild streak. He arrived in Prague sporting a gold nose, as he had apparently lost his own in a duel. As legend has it, he died in 1601 from a burst bladder, experienced during one of Rudolf's many royal benders that Tycho used to glady participate in.

In the church, also note two tiny windows near the third chapel on the south side. These windows once looked in from a bedroom on Celetná Street, the same bedroom inhabited by a young Franz Kafka.

A quick jaunt behind Týn Church along Stuparská street (branching off at the beginning of Celetná) and then along Malá Štuparská places you at the front of **St. James' Church** (Kostel sv. Jakuba), dating back to the 14th century. The church's worn, sooty facade does no justice to its sensational nave – a breathtaking space lined with soaring honey-colored pilasters, meticulously-carved capitals, and an abundance of statuary set on ledges, balconies, and cornices. Along the ceiling are luminous scenes from the life of the Virgin Mary, leading your attention to the high altar painting depicting the martyrdom of St. James. The painting itself, however, is nothing compared to its opulent gilded frame, topped by an enormous monstrance and surrounded by gilt cherubs. The tomb of Count Vratislav of Mitrovice (Lord Chancellor of Bohemia in the 18th century), located on the left side of the choir, offer more bombastic opulence you can relish here.

Upon leaving the church, look to the left of the main door. Here, you'll notice something a bit startling, to say the least: an actual human hand. It was taken from a thief who tried to steal the jewels from the statue of the Virgin Mary. Legend has it that the Virgin herself caught the thief in the act and snatched his wrist, her grip so tight that the thief had to have his hand lopped off.

Along the Royal Way

If you follow the Royal Way in the direction we take below, then get off at Náměstí Republiky metro station, placing you a block north of the Powder Tower. If you go the opposite direction and start at the square at the east end of the Charles Bridge, then get off at Staroměstská metro station, walk a block west on Kaprova, and then three blocks south along Křížovnická Street.

A series of handsome cobblestone lanes, stretching from the Powder Tower at the eastern edge of Staré Město to Křížovnické náměstí at the western edge, takes in part of the so-called **Royal Way** (králová cesta), the traditional route of the coronation procession continuing across the

Charles Bridge and on up to the Prague Castle. The route, cutting Staré Město more or less in half, was established by the first Bohemian dynasty, the Přemysls, and was followed by every subsequent king of Bohemia on up to Emperor Ferdinand I in 1836. Besides its historic value, the Royal Way is simply a beautiful walking tour that you can take of Staré Město.

Begin at the **Powder Tower** (prašna brána), its construction started in 1475 by Matěj Rejsek at the site of one of Staré Město's original gates. It was to be a part of King Vladislav Jagiello II's royal court, but the king decided he would be better off at the Prague Castle after the mayor of Staré Město got himself tossed out a window by an angry mob in 1483. The tower sat uncompleted until the 19th century, when Josef Mocker put the finishing touches on the upper story and added the steeple. He also invited some of the country's best sculptors – such as Šimek, Seeling, and Čapek – to adorn the east and west walls with the faces of the kings of Bohemia. The tower's name, by the way, comes from its function as a gunpowder magazine in the 18th century.

Set next to the Powder Tower is perhaps Prague's greatest architectural achievement of the 20th century – the **Municipal House** (Obecní dům). The idea for the Municipal House as a cultural center for the Czech community in Prague came at the zenith of the Czech National Revival at the turn of the century, involving 30 or so of the greatest artistic talents at hand in the country – among them architects Antonín Balšanek and Karel Osvald Polívka, painters Alfons Mucha and Maximillian Švabinsky, and sculptors Bohumil Kafka and Ladislav Šaloun. Only such a glorious building could rightly replace the remains of the court of Bohemian kings, which was used from 1383 to 1483. But with such an amazing line-up of architects and artists at work on the project, you too could put your conscience to rest and feel good about burying the past to make way for this momentous building.

The bulbous-shaped exterior, topped with pointed copper domes and sprinkled with scores of faces peering from the facade, features Karel Špillar's stunning mosaic entitled *Homage to Prague*, set between two of Šaloun's allegorical sculptures representing the repression and rebirth of the Czech nation. Moving inside under a decorative glass and wrought-iron awning, you are then confronted with a thoroughly Art Nouveau, thoroughly sensuous interior, outfitted with a café, restaurant, and the **Smetana Hall** – the largest concert hall in the city, where the **Prague Spring Music Festival** traditionally kicks off each year with a rendition of Smetana's *Má vlast* (My Country). Also part of the interior are six fabulous salons, all decorated with the paintings of none other than Alfons Mucha, hands down the most well-known Czech painter of the 20th century.

Running west from the Powder Tower directly to Old Town Square, **Celetná** is one of Staré Město's oldest lanes, originally part of the ancient commercial route into the town square, later a section in the Royal Way. The name of the lane derives from *calta*, a pretzel-like cake made by the many bakers who lived here in the 14th century.

Today it is a glorious pedestrian lane, lined with a pastel symphony of Baroque facades covering a mainly Gothic score of houses. But there is an exception, and that is the **House at the Black Madonna** (Dům U černé Matky boží), *located at number 34 at the corner of Ovocny trh*. Built by Josef Gočár in 1911-1912, the house is one of the better examples of Cubist architecture in a city that made a good go of the style during the four years preceding World War I. The building houses a gallery for temporary exhibitions. *Open daily except Monday from 10 a.m. to 6 p.m.*

From the end of Celetná, cut through Old Town Square (see above) past the Astronomical Clock to **Malé náměstí**, or Little Square. At the center of the square you'll notice a well dating back to 1560, enclosed by a pretty Renaissance wrought-iron railing and topped with a gilded Lion of Bohemia. But the biggest eye-catcher in the square is the delightful **Rott House** *at number 3*, formerly the residence of Jan Pytlích, who printed the first Bible in Czech in 1488. The house was later taken over by the Rotts, a family of ironmongers who had the facade smothered in floral designs and scenes of artisans and farmers at work. Also be sure to poke your head inside the Baroque lékárna (pharmacy) *at number 13*, indicative of the long history of pharmacies occupying the square since 1353.

Exit Malé náměstí in the southwest corner of square and then take your first right onto **Karlova**, another gorgeous lane unfortunately filled to capacity with curio, crystal, and toy shops. There's a lot of tourist traffic stuffing this narrow lane, which means pickpockets are on the prowl here. So watch your goods.

At *Hussova 19-21*, on the corner of Karlova, is the **Czech Museum of Fine Arts** (České muzeum výtvarných umění), a terrific venue for temporary exhibits of top-notch, 20th-century Czech artists. *Open Tuesday through Sunday from 10 a.m. to 12 p.m. and from 1 to 6 p.m.*

A door down on Hussova, **U zlatého tygra** (see the section on Prague pubs, below) is one of Prague's most famous pubs. Definitely see if there is a free place, so you can sample a glass of the sensational Pilsner Urquell served here.

Further down Karlova, a long wall on your right forms the southern flank of the **Klementinum** – a mammoth complex that includes three churches, more than 30 houses, four courtyards, and the National Library.

The Jesuits arrived in Prague in 1556 at the request of Ferdinand I, who wished to further entrench the influence of the Catholic faith in

Bohemia at a time when Protestantism was sweeping through the kingdom. The king donated the St. Kliment Church (see below) to the priests, who proceeded to buy up a huge chunk of land in the neighborhood, tear down 30 or so houses, and, over the next century, build themselves a college that covered an area second in size only to that of the Prague Castle. The Jesuits had only a few years to relish their construction in its completion before they were booted from the country by Josef II and the Klementinum handed over to Charles University.

From Karlova, you can enter into the Klementinum courtyards through a small gate and come out in front of the Charles Bridge on Křížovnické náměstí. This little jaunt off the beaten path comes as a welcome bit of solitude away from the tourist hubbub on Karlova. But about all you can do at the Klementinum is walk through the courtyards and visit the churches (the entrances to which are on Karlova and on Křížovnické náměstí; see below). Unfortunately, the frescoed Rococo halls that make up the National Library are closed to the public. But you can see some pictures of them just inside the entrance to the library.

The Klementinum also houses the stunning **Chapel of Mirrors**, a Baroque confection studded in gilt and adorned with ethereal murals. Inlaid mirrors reflect all the opulence. Your only opportunity for seeing the chapel is by attending one of the classical recitals held there daily. Not a bad concession to have to make, considering it's one of the most beautiful spaces in the city where you could attend a recital. Buy your ticket at the entrance on Karlova street.

Forming part of the Klementinum "wall" along Karlova is one church and one chapel. **St. Clement Church** (Kostel sv. Klimenta) was owned by the Dominicans before the Jesuits moved in and had the church rebuilt to plans by the Baroque master Kilián Ignác Dientzenhofer. Inside, you'll find lofty cupolas, statues by the infamous Matthias Braun, and a set of monumental frescoes portraying the life and death of St. Clement, who was bound to an anchor and thrown overboard into the Black Sea. Nowadays, the church belongs to the Greek Orthodox Church, offering a liturgy in Old Church Slavonic.

Next to St. Clement is the **Italian Chapel of the Assumption of the Virgin Mary** (Vlašská kaple Nanebevzetí Panny Marie), built between 1590 and 1597 by and for the Italian artisans who worked on the Klementinum. Technically still owned by the Italian government, the chapel features the only oval ground-plan in Bohemia.

Just around the corner, facing the Charles Bridge on Křížovnické náměstí, is the **Church of the Holy Savior** (Kostel sv. Salvátor), its sooty facade peppered with 15 statues forming a sort of halo around the church. Completed in 1601, the church was modeled after Il Gesu in

Rome, its three-naved interior garnished with an icing of stucco work and a busy ceiling fresco entitled *The Four Corners of the World*. Fronting the north side of Křížovnické náměstí, the **Church of St. Francis Seraphinus** (Kostel sv. Františka Serafinského) belongs to the Knights of the Cross with a Red Star, a Bohemian order of crusaders founded in the 12th century. Built by Jean-Baptiste Mathey in the 17th century, the church soars up from its purple marble pilasters to a single breathtaking dome frescoed with Reiner's *Last Judgment*, an ethereal painting of writhing bodies suspended in midair.

From Křížovnické náměstí, head south underneath the skyway and pass through the short gauntlet of minuscule shops selling everything from NBA uniforms to diamonds. Shortly, you'll come out at **Novotného lávka**, site of Staré Město's former mill now lined with chic bars, cafés, and a disco. At the end of the short lane, seated under a drooping weeping willow, is a statue of Bedřich Smetana, the country's foremost nationalist composer. The name for his most famous work comes from the river that flows to the statue's side – the Vltava (or Moldau in German).

Behind the statue, housed in a tall neo-Renaissance building, is the small **Smetana Museum**, mostly exhibiting the composer's personal effects, which should be of interest only if you are a hardcore Smetana fan. *Open daily except Tuesday from 10 a.m. to 5 p.m.* Besides the museum, the lane is simply a good place to snap some photos of the Charles Bridge and the Prague Castle, or to just take a breather on the bench and watch to the river flow by.

Rudolfinum & The Museum of Decorative Arts

Take the metro to Staroměstská station, walk a block west (towards the river), take your first right, and then go one block to Jana Palacha náměstí.

Proudly reigning over Jan Palach Square on the banks of the Vltava is the **Rudolfinum**, also known as the House of Artists (Dům umělců). The grand neo-Renaissance exterior is enshrined with statues of the world's great composers, among them Handel, Bach, Mozart, Beethoven, and Schubert. Completed in 1884 by Josef Zítek and Josef Schulz (both of whom are also responsible for the National Theater), the Rudolfinum emerged as part of the wave of civic projects sparked by the Czech National Revival of the late 19th and early 20th century.

It served as an art gallery, music conservatory, and concert hall for the Czech community until it was transformed into the seat of the Czechoslovak parliament in 1918. In 1946, it reverted to its original cultural purpose, and now is a major venue for classical concerts in Prague, as well as the home of the Czech Philharmonic Orchestra.

JAN PALACH SQUARE

Jan Palach Square (Jana Palacha náměstí) has only been named as such since 1989, before which it was called Red Army Square. The square is named after the Charles University student who, on January 16, 1969, set himself alight on the steps of the National Museum in protest of the Soviet invasion of Czechoslovakia. A tram conductor put out the flames, but not before Palach had suffered burns to 85 percent of his body, killing him four days later and turning him into a martyr of the Czechoslovak struggle against Soviet domination. Just off Jan Palach Square, at the north end of the front arcade of the Charles University Philosophical Faculty, is a rather disturbing memorial to the self-immolated martyr – his death mask.

The street which runs into Jan Palach Square from the north, 17. listopadu (17 November), originally commemorated the date on which Prague students were killed in an anti-Nazi rally in 1939. Exactly 50 years from that date students took to the streets in honor of the anniversary. They were clubbed and beaten by the police, precipitating mass protests and the imminent downfall of the Communist government.

Enter the **Galerie Rudolfinum**n on the west side of the building along Alšovo nábřeží; it's a space for temporary exhibitions featuring artists from around the world. *The gallery is open Tuesday through Sunday from 10 a.m. to 6 p.m.* On the east side, along 17. listopadu street, is the box office, selling tickets to the regularly scheduled concerts held at the Rudolfinum's **Dvořák Hall**, outstanding for its gorgeous colonnades.

Just off Jan Palach Square, the **Museum of Decorative Arts** (Uměleckoprůmyslové muzeum. or UPM), *17. listapadu 2, Tel. 02/248 112 41*, is perhaps one of the most unique museums that Prague has to offer, but, strangely enough, it's usually abandoned. Granted, it takes some of us a little prompting to get excited over porcelain, glassware, furniture, jewelry, dishes, and other household items on exhibit at the museum. But even those with little interest at the outset may find themselves lingering over a chair, a glass, or even a bowl.

The museum, a work of decorative art in itself, was completed in 1901 by Josef Schulz (see Rudolfinum and National Theater) at a time when European artists and intellectuals were combating the dissipation of aesthetic values in a fast-moving industrialized world. The idea was to amass examples from the peak of European design throughout the major artistic ages, an effort that has been so proliferative that the museum now has a collection that far outweighs what it can possibly exhibit at any one time.

The museum starts off in a room just above the entrance, where you'll find temporary exhibitions from the museum's overflowing catalogue. From there, go up the gorgeously painted staircase to the second floor, housing the museum's permanent exhibition in four rooms – each dedicated to a period in design. (Be sure to pick up your English text giving you the low-down on most items in each room.) In the first room you can feast your eyes on French and Italian Renaissance furniture, tapestries, and books.

In the second room, with its fantastic painted ceiling, there is some elegant gilded furniture and glassware from the early Baroque period in Bohemia. The third room takes the proverbial wedding cake, with its sumptuous exhibit of late Baroque and Rococo designs, which include some outrageous grandfather clocks, writing desks, and ebony-inlaid escritoires. The fourth room (which, by the way, has a great view of the Old Jewish Cemetery) features Classical and Empire designs, most notably a secretaire with a false perspective etched into the wood and a very curious crib with a snake suspended over it.

The gods are shining on you if the top floor happens to be open, which it rarely is for some unknown, infuriating reason. Here you'll find the early 20th century collection, incorporating Art Deco vases with Cubist chairs and secretaires. After taking in the exhibit, dive into the museum's funky café for an espresso. You'll be accompanied by a lot of Charles University students. *The museum is open daily except Monday from 10 a.m. to 6 p.m. and costs 50 Kč.*

Southern Staré Město

This portion of Staré Město is a three-pointed wedge hemmed in by Celetná and Karlova streets to the north, Smetanova nábřeží to the west, Národní to the south, and Na příkopě to the east. We start at the Estates Theater (Stavovské divadlo), accessed by taking the metro to Můstek, exiting on Na příkopě street, and then taking the first left on Havířská, at the end of which you'll find the theater.

This quarter of cobblestone lanes, sinuous alleys, and hidden passageways is Staré Město at its most medieval. Renovation has only recently begun on most of its buildings, so there's an extremely weathered look about the place, giving it an authentic, charming feel. More than likely, you'll get lost in the maze. But getting lost is the best way to discover this romantic corner of the old town.

We begin at the **Estates Theater** on Ovocný trh (Fruit Market), a brilliant green and white neo-Classical pile completed in 1783 by Count Nostitz-Rieneck, who lent his name to the theater until he sold it to the Czech Estates, the traditional nobility of Bohemia. The theater lives large in the eyes of hard-core Mozart fans, who know it as the venue for the premier of two of the composer's operas – *Don Giovanni* in 1787 and *La Clemenza di Tito* in 1791. The Estates, with its gold-laden interior and neo-Renaissance decorations, is the only opera house left unaltered from Mozart's day, which is why Miloš Foreman chose to shoot most of the opera scenes for his film *Amadeus* here.

To the west side of the Estates Theater, the **Karolinum** – **Charles University** – is the oldest university in Central Europe, occupying at its inception this Gothic house *at Železná 9*. Founded in 1348 by King Charles IV and modeled after the Sorbonne in Paris, the so-called University of Prague rose mainly as a center of study for noble Czechs, though it included a sizable enrollment of Germans, Poles, and Scandinavians. At the urging of Jan Hus, rector of the university in the early 15th century, King Wenceslas IV slashed the voting rights of the non-Czech students, infuriating the Germans so much that they went and formed their own university in Leipzig.

The university remained a bastion of Hussite ideas up until the Battle of White Mountain in 1622, when the Hapsburgs handed the university over to the Jesuits in their pursuit to wipe out all vestiges of Protestantism in the Czech lands. However, with the expulsion of the Jesuits from Bohemia in 1773, the university reclaimed the building, its Faculty of Letters going on to become a key player in the Czech National Revival in the 19th century. Once Czechoslovakia gained its independence in 1918, the university became officially known as Charles University.

Unfortunately, the Karolinum isn't the most stunning building today, thanks mostly to damages rendered during World War II and a rather harsh remodeling afterwards. Today, the faculties of Charles University have several locations throughout Prague, and its original home is used mainly for ceremonies. You can however see some traces of its Gothic origins, including a pretty oriel window on its east side, as well as its vaulted ground floor, housing a private gallery of contemporary Czech art.

From the Karolinum, head down Havelská street past the hemmed-in **St. Havel's Church** (Kostel sv. Havla, also known in English as St. Gall's), built in a Gothic style at its founding in 1232 but later given the obligatory Baroque makeover. Jan Hus and his radical disciple Konrad Waldhauser preached at this church in the 14th century, and in the 18th century the Order of the Discalced Carmelites moved in, building themselves a monastery next door.

The church was once the centerpiece of a medieval market stretching from Ovocný trh to Uhelný trh. In fact, the market used to make up most of the historic town of St. Havel, which grew shoulder to shoulder with Staré Město in the 13th century. What remains of that market today is the open-air **Havelská Market** (*trh*), accessed by continuing down Havelská street and forging the stream of tourists flowing between Old Town and Wenceslas squares. Selling everything from toys to tomatoes, the market's 50 or so booths buzzes daily with the excited chatter of Praguers doing their favorite activity of comparison shopping. The selection of fruits and vegetables is one of the best in the city, and if you are not in the shopping mode, you can still make a good time of it people watching, of which there is no end here.

From the market continue further down Havelská until you reach **Uhelný trh**, site of a former coal market (hence the name which means exactly that). Jutting out on the west side of the square is the former residence of František Dušek, a composer who was by no means as successful as his friend Mozart, who stayed with Dušek at this house for a short while in 1787.

From Uhelný trh head down Martinská street, at the end of which you'll find the **Church of St. Martin-in-the-Walls** (Kostel sv. Martina ve zdi), an intriguing structure closed in by surrounding buildings. The church's south-facing wall once formed part of the old fortification built around Staré Město, hence the name. Erected in the 12th century, the church got a Gothic face-lift a century later, which thankfully didn't deprive the church too much of its essentially Romanesque character that remains intact to this day.

In the history of the Reformation, this church was a pivotal one, setting the stage for the first-ever Hussite communion of *sub utraque specie*, that is, the taking of both bread and wine by both the clergy and congregation (a basic demand of the Hussite movement from which the Utraquist church took its name). St. Martin's now belongs to the Evangelical Church of Czech Brethren, a community formed by radical Hussites in the 15th century. Unfortunately, the church is open for services and the occasional concert only.

Down the lane from St. Martin's, hang a right on Na perštýně street. Off to the left, dominating the corner of Bartlomějská, is the blunt-grey former **Trade Union Building**, its stern facade recalling the Communist days when art had to be in praise of the workers. This is where the first Communist president of Czechoslovakia, Klement Gottwald, strategized his rise to power in 1948. After the Communist takeover, the building, along with the row of houses lining Bartlomějská, housed the notoriously-detested secret police, the *Státní bezpečnost* (better known as the StB). Suspected "enemies of the state" were regularly dragged to this gloomy section of Staré Město for severe StB interrogations, some of which ended in death.

A former student of mine, who played drums for an alternative rock and roll band in the 1980s, related to me some frightening stories of being hauled off to the secret police station for his involvement in a group that made music deemed subversive by the secret police. Years after the official dissolution of the StB, the former Trade Union Building and the rest of Bartlomĕjská still made him jumpy, and understandably so. In the 1950s, the Communist government confiscated the buildings lining Bartlomĕjská from a group of Fransican nuns. Since 1989, the nuns have reclaimed their property, and have subsequently rented out a bit of space to Penzion Unitas, which places guests in converted StB jail cells. For a little extra, you can sleep in the very cell where Václav Havel was forced to spend a night under interrogation.

From Na perštýnĕ, head a short block up Husova street, where you'll find the **Church of St. Giles** (Kostel sv. Jiljí), one of the few churches in Staré Mĕsto to have retained its Gothic exterior, which was built in the late 14th century borrowing French techniques of the age. Like countless other churches around Prague, St. Giles received a thoroughly Baroque interior during the Counter-Reformation, a time in which the church was handed over to the Dominicans. Imprisoned during the Communist era, the Czech Dominicans reclaimed the church in 1989, and have since restored much of the church back to its former glory.

Awash in a glaze of white and gold and sporting one too many cherubs for my taste, the nave is lined with bulky square pillars, supporting a lofty vaulted ceiling. As part of the church's Baroque renovation in 1733, Václav Vavřinec Reiner adorned the ceiling with a series of *trompe l'oeil* frescoes, most notably the one over the central nave entitled *The Triumph of the Dominicans over Heresy*. It was perhaps this ingratiating painting that earned him a burial spot in this Dominican church.

Retrace your steps along Husova and then take your first right into **Bethlehem Square** (Betlémské námĕstí), a handsome plaza lined with restaurants, cafés, bookshops, and a pub or two. A rather grisly legend has it that mothers took their unwanted children to the square and dumped them into the old fountain.

The square takes its name from the white **Bethlehem Chapel**, its two high gables towering over the square. As the cradle of the Czech Reformation, this is perhaps the most important place of worship in the city, at least in terms of Czech history. Czech reformers of the early 15th century were denied permission to build themselves a church, so they went ahead and built themselves in 1402 the largest chapel in Bohemia, with a capacity of more than 3,000.

Jan Hus (also known in the West as John Huss) preached here every day from 1402 to 1414, delivering his sermons not in the church-dictated Latin, but in the language of the common folk – Czech. Indeed, it was the common folk – the clerics, artisans, and workers – that filled the church daily to hear Hus' egalitarian message and sing the hymns (some written by Hus himself) that were an integral part of the Hussite service. Hus eventually had to answer for his radical ideas at the Council of Constance in 1415, where he was excommunicated, charged with heresy, and burned at the stake.

However, the reformist precedence set by Hus at the Bethlehem Chapel continued well into the 16th century, when Thomas Müntzer, leader of the German Peasant Revolt, delivered a sermon at the chapel. After the Battle of White Mountain, the chapel fell into the hands of the Jesuits and, in the late 18th century, was mostly demolished.

In a strange twist of history, the atheist Communist government decided in 1950 to reconstruct the chapel going on old drawings and on remnants of the original walls that were still standing. (The Communists believed that the Hussite movement was a forerunner of their own egalitarian ideology, and wanted to make that point clear by rebuilding the chapel.) What you see today is pretty much the fruit of that effort, an effort that proved to be quite successful in matching the model with the original.

The chapel is a strangely austere space, differing from Catholic churches in that the focus is on the pulpit rather than on the altar. Except for a few medieval illuminations on the walls, there is nothing else in the way of decoration. The chapel is, however, a welcome surprise after the bombastic excess of most of the Baroque churches in the city.

Upstairs from the chapel, you can inspect the original preachers' quarters, now filled with an exhibit chronicling the evolution of the Czech Reformation, the history of the Bethlehem Chapel, and the life and death of Jan Hus. A reproduction of an interesting historical painting shows the symbolic development of the Reformation, with John Wycliffe striking a spark, Hus lighting a candle, and Martin Luther wielding a torch. *The Bethelem Chapel is open daily 9 a.m. to 5 p.m. Admission costs 30 Kč.*

At the far end of Bethlehem Square, the **Náprstek Museum** (Náprstkovo muzeum) exhibits a surprisingly good collection of North American, South American, African, and Australian ethnographic items – culled by the museum's founder Vojta Náprstek, a 19th century industrialist who emigrated to the United States following his involvement in the 1848 revolution. Having amassed a respectable collection of Native American artifacts and American high-tech gadgets, he returned ten years later to convert his family brewery into a museum. (His technological collection now sits in the National Technical Museum.)

Today, the museum displays, among other things, a wide range of African masks and drums, South Pacific idols, and Southeast Asian puppets. Of particular interest to Americans is the collection of American coins, dating back to the mid-19th century. As a native Utahn, I was pleasantly surprised to find a decent collection of Anasazi pottery from my own part of the country. *The museum is open daily except Monday from*

9 a.m. to 12 p.m. and from 12:45 to 5:45 p.m. Admission costs 20 Kč; Tel. 02/242 145 37.

From Bethlehem Square, head down Betlémská street and hang a left one block on Karoliny Světlé to the tiny **Rotunda of the Holy Cross** (Rotunda sv. Kříže), one of the oldest buildings in Prague and one of the city's few remaining Romanesque structures. Built in the 12th century and restored in 1876, the rotunda features the remains of some Gothic mural paintings, but the only time you'd be able to see them is during Mass, *which is at 9:30 a.m. and 5:30 p.m. on Sunday and at 5 p.m. on Tuesday and Friday.* A friend of mine once tried to attend Mass here, but the priest didn't show up at the appointed time. Like a true Praguer, my friend decided to dive into a pub down the street instead of wait around. Much to his surprise, he found the priest sipping on a beer there, completely oblivious to the time and a tad sauced.

Convent of St. Agnes
A maze of twisting lanes surrounding the convent is likely to have you going around in circles. The best way to avoid getting lost is by starting out at Old Town Square, from where it's a fairly straight shot to the convent. Take Dlouhá street beginning in the northeast corner of the square and follow it straight into Kozí street and then U obecního dvora street. You'll find the entrance to the convent at U milosrdných 17. The convent, housing the National Gallery's collection of 19th century Czech art, is open daily except Monday from 10 a.m. to 6 p.m. Tickets cost 70 Kč.

What survives of the **Convent of St. Agnes** (Klášter sv. Anežký) makes it Prague's oldest Gothic structure. It was founded by the Fransican Order of the Poor Clares in 1233, with King Wenceslas I's sister, Anežka (Agnes), appointed its first abbess. In an effort to thwart the spread of Hussitism, Catholic officials beatified Agnes in the 19th century. And in 1989, one crucial week before the Velvet Revolution, Pope John Paul II invited a delegation of Czech Catholics to a special mass held at St. Peter's in Rome, where Agnes was then canonized.

The two churches and cloister that make up the convent were closed down in 1782 in accordance with Josef II's decree dissolving monasteries and convents. Used as a workshop and a squatters' haven for the next hundred years, the convent suffered major dilapidation, but was saved from utter ruin by the Union for the Restoration of St. Agnes, organized in 1892. Serious restoration, however, has only taken place in the last few decades, mostly in the 1980s.

Today, the convent's ground floor and its intriguing vaulted archways serve as space for temporary exhibits held by the **National Gallery**. Upstairs, you'll find the gallery's permanent exhibit of 19th-century

Czech art. The works on display constitute a period in the Czech National Revival, a movement in which Czechs came to terms with their cultural identity. Hence, you'll see a number of paintings and sculptures depicting legendary Czech figures such as St. Agnes, St. Wenceslas, and the lovers Břetislav and Jitka.

If you're a fan of sweeping Romantic landscapes filled with castles and sanguine scenes of village life, then you have definitely come to the right place. There's no short supply of this genre, made big in Bohemia by the likes of Josef Navrátil, Antonín Mánes, and Mánes' son Josef. If, however, you find all this romanticism a bit too sappy for your taste, then you may have more appreciation for the works in the latter section of the museum, where you'll find a group of late 19th century works more appealing to contemporary sensibilities.

Something to look out for is a sensational duo of paintings by the Symbolist painter Maximilian Spirner entitled *Madness, Hatred, and Death* and *Love, Idea, and Life* – a startling depiction of two opposite states of mind. Also be on the lookout for Spirner's sensuous femme fatales in his *Nymphs of a Spring*.

Josefov

*Josefov, or the Old Jewish Quarter, lies to the northwest of Old Town Square and includes only a handful of streets located to the west of Pařížská, to the north of Kaprova, and to the east of 17. listopadu. The easiest way to the **State Jewish Museum** (Státní Židovské Muzeum) box office, selling tickets to all the attractions in Josefov, is to take the metro to Staroměstská station, head east on Kaprova (away from the river), swing left on Maiselova, and then take your second left on U starého hřbitova. The State Jewish Museum – an umbrella title for the synagogues, museums, town hall, and cemetery of the former ghetto – is open daily except Saturday from 9:30 a.m. to 6:00 p.m., April through September; and from 9:00 a.m. to 4:30 p.m., October through March; Tel. 02/248 100 99.*

*   **Matana**, a travel agency at Maiselova 15 in Josefov, Tel. 02/232 1954, offers guided bus tours of the Old Jewish Quarter and of other Jewish sights around Prague, including Kafka's grave at the New Jewish Cemetery. The price is 650 Kč per person. They also sell tickets to the Josefov sights.*

Josefov & the Jews of Prague - A Short History

As far back as the 10th century, Jews have lived in Prague, the first colony settling at the foot of the Prague Castle. Throughout the centuries they were to subject to various degrees of persecution and favor, depending on whoever happened to be ruler of Bohemia at the time.

Přemysl Otakar II, a 13th-century king way ahead of his time, extended religious freedom to the Jews and banned forced baptisms and anti-Semitic acts. However, it was during that same century that the

Vatican issued directives segregating Jews from Christians, forcing the Jews of Prague to set up residence within the confines of a walled ghetto, the site of which is present-day Josefov. The Jews suffered arbitrary pogroms, as they had from the outset of their time in Prague, but none worse than the one on Easter in 1389, when 3,000 Jews were killed.

During the reign of **Rudolf II** (1576-1612), life for the Prague Jews took a drastic turn for the better, as the emperor afforded the Jews professional, economic, and political opportunities that had yet to be seen in the rest of Europe. Mayor of the ghetto **Mordechai Maisel** became Rudolf's finance minister, and eventually the richest man in Prague, financing the redevelopment of the Jewish quarter and adding several new synagogues and a town hall. With a better quality of life came an intellectual golden age, cultivating the minds of the famous chronicler **David Gans** and one Judah Löw Bezalel, better known as **Rabbi Löw** (both of whom are buried in Josefov's cemetery). Heavyweight theologian and student of the kabbalah, Rabbi Löw was the legendary creator of the *golem* – a mythical monster made of mud and brought to life by placing a *chem* (a parchment inscribed with a holy sign) on the beast's mouth.

It was **Emperor Joseph II** who, in his Toleration Edict of 1781, banned the dress code which had been in effect since the 11th century and allowed Jews and other non-Catholics to attend state-run schools. In honor of the enlightened ruler, the Jews named the ghetto Josefov, even though it wasn't until 1848 that the walls of the ghetto came down and Josefov became a regular borough of Prague.

In the wake of the walls' destruction, Jews were free to set up residence outside the former ghetto, which they did in droves, leaving behind the poorer Jews to be bombarded in their quarter by Prague's down-and-out – meaning Gypsies, beggars, prostitutes, drug addicts, and so on. The former ghetto fell into squalor, prompting city officials to make a case against its unsanitariness and recommend its demolition.

Starting in 1893, the ghetto was annihilated, save six synagogues, the cemetery, and the town hall. In its place rose block after block of tall, swish Art Nouveau houses, the most haughty of which were lined up on the newly-built **Pařížská třída** (Paris Avenue). Not everyone was happy about this paving over of the past, as Kafka writes in a letter to G. Janouch: "The hidden nooks and crannies, the secret passageways, the blind windows, the grubby courtyards, the noisy taverns, the sinister inns live on inside us.... The insalubrious Jewish Old Town is a lot more real than the hygienic new town that surrounds us."

With the Nazi occupation of Prague on March 15, 1939, the dark ages were once more upon the Jews, as they were stripped of their right to work, subjected to a curfew, and once again forced to wear the Star of

David. In November 1941, the first group of Jews were herded onto a train and transported to **Terezín** (Theresienstadt), a newly converted ghetto 60 kilometers (37 miles) northwest of Prague. Of the 50,000 Jews that lived in Prague just before the Nazi occupation, some 37,000 perished at Terezín or in other concentration camps (if you want to visit the town of Terezín, see Chapter 16, *North Bohemia*, for more details). The majority of Prague Jews who survived the Holocaust emigrated to Israel or America, while only about 8,000 resettled in Prague, most of whom ended up emigrating anyway once it became clear that Stalinist Czechoslovakia had about as much tolerance for Jews as Nazi Germany did. Sadly, after a history almost as old as the city itself, only a few thousand Jews live in Prague today.

One question, however, remains: Why were the remnants of Prague's historic ghetto – the synagogues, town hall, and the intriguing old cemetery – spared when other ghettos around Europe were eradicated in the Nazi pursuit to wipe out the Jewish people? The answer is a grotesque one: Hitler designated Prague's ghetto as the site for the planned "Exotic Museum of an Extinct Race." Consequently, the Germans ransacked synagogues around Europe and deposited the goods in Prague.

Though only a fraction of what the Germans had amassed, the collection of sacred Jewish artifacts on exhibit in the synagogues that constitute the State Jewish Museum is considered the largest in Europe. But the main attraction here in Josefov is the mind-bending **Old Jewish Cemetery,** with its melancholic heap of teetering tombstones.

Josefov's Synagogues, Town Hall, & Museums

At the corner of Pařížská and U starého hřbitova, the jagged gables and steep roof of the A-framed **Old-New Synagogue** (Staronová synagóga) rise from a submerged foundation, which predates the raising of Staré Město (done so to prevent flooding) and hence sits below street level. Completed in 1275, it is the oldest functioning synagogue in Europe and one of Prague's earliest Gothic structures. Because Jews were not allowed to become architects in the 13th century, builders of the nearby Franciscan St. Agnes Convent most likely constructed the synagogue, gracing it with its unique ribbed vaulting.

You enter the synagogue below a brilliant tympanum, decorated with a fig tree blooming with fruit and leaves. You then pass through two low-ceilinged chambers, the second of which is where women watch the exclusively male services. The focus of the main hall is the *bimah*, enclosed by a wrought-iron grille. On the east wall is the Holy Ark containing the Torah scrolls, and to the rear is a glass case filled with tiny lightbulbs, individually lit on the anniversary of a Jewish luminary's death (including Kafka's). Also on display is a red ragged flag, a gift to the Jewish community from Emperor Ferdinand III for helping in defending Prague against the Swedes in the Thirty Years' War.

Opposite the Old-New Synagogue to the south, the **Jewish Town Hall** (Židovská radnice) was one of the projects funded by the wealthy Mordechai Maisel. Erected in 1586 and given a pink Rococo facade in the 18th century, the building now houses the Shalom Kosher Restaurant, as well as a kosher lunch stand. You'll notice on the north-facing wall a clock in Hebrew, whose hands, like the Hebrew script, read right to left.

Behind the town hall on Červená street is the **High Synagogue** (Vysoká synagóga), so called because its prayer room is upstairs. Its expansive vaulted hall now houses a museum mainly devoted to Jewish textiles dating from the 16th to the early 20th century. The curtains, mantles, Torah bindings, and other draperies – mostly made in Jewish communities throughout Bohemia and Moravia – give evidence as to why these two regions are considered the very best in embroidery.

On U starého hřbitova street, where the road bends to the north, you'll find the **Klaus Synagogue** (Klausova synagóga) set into the wall surrounding the Old Jewish Cemetery. The Baroque building, erected at the end of the 17th century, houses a collection of Jewish prints and manuscripts, many of which come from the first Jewish publishing house north of the Alps – operating right here in Josefov from the 16th to the 19th century.

Catercorner to the Klaus Synagogue, the neo-Romanesque **Ceremonial Hall** (Obřadní síň) features the heartbreaking drawings from the clandestine children's art classes held in the attics and cellars of the Terezín ghetto during the Holocaust. The drawings speak volumes of the daily horror these children confronted, and give you some idea of how they managed to get by. A highly recommended exhibit you should not miss.

From the Ceremonial Hall backtrack to Červená street. Swing right and head two blocks to *Maiselova 10*, where you'll find the **Maisel Synagogue** (Maiselova synagóga) set a little ways back from the sidewalk. The original Renaissance synagogue, founded and funded by Maisel in 1591, burnt down in 1689 when French troops set fire to Staré Město. At the turn of the 20th century the less extravagant neo-Gothic structure rose in its place. Today, it houses a permanent exhibition of silver artifacts used in Jewish services, most of which has been culled from Jewish communities from around the Czech lands.

Around the corner from the Maisel Synagogue and sticking out from the cemetery wall is the comely **Pinkas Synagogue** (Pinkasova synagóga), built in the flamboyant Late Gothic style of the 16th century. In 1959 it was converted into a memorial for the 77,297 Bohemian and Moravian Jews who perished in the Holocaust. The complete list of victims, including their date of birth and date of disappearance, was inscribed on the walls, only for it to go to ruin at the hands of the Communists. The memorial has only recently been restored, along with the rest of the building.

The Old Jewish Cemetery

At the time of writing, the entrance to the Old Jewish Cemetery was at the Pinkas Synagogue on Široka street. But it's possible that it may revert back to the gate located between the Klaus Synagogue and the Ceremonial Hall on U starého hřbitova.

From 1493 to 1787, this small plot of land was the final resting spot of the Jewish Quarter's inhabitants, who had no choice but to bury their dead within the caged-in space of the ghetto. Far and above Prague's most poignant sight, the heap of 12,000 crumbling tombstones teetering on mounds and resting upon each other at the **Old Jewish Cemetery** (Starý židovský hřbitov) is a hard-hitting reminder of the Jewish plight in Prague and of their heroic dignity in the face of such intolerable living conditions.

The number of tombstones doesn't come close to the number of people buried in what is Europe's oldest existing Jewish cemetery. Some 100,000 graves lie here, superimposed on one another as many as 12 layers deep.

The oldest stone still standing, dating back to 1439 (but recently replaced with a replica), belongs to Avigdor Karo, court poet to Wenceslas IV and survivor of the 1389 pogrom. On some of the Hebrew-inscribed tombstones you'll find a lengthy text detailing the lives of the more prominent deceased, such as Mordechai Maisel and Rabbi Löw, whose graves are given quite a bit a fanfare in the cemetery.

The cemetery is on the itinerary of just about every tourist group coming to Prague, which can do more than anything to spoil the melancholic spell of the place. Best idea, then, is to arrive as soon as the cemetery opens.

Many people come to the cemetery looking for Franz Kafka's grave. But let me remind you that the cemetery was closed in 1787, a good century before the birth of the illustrious writer. Kafka is buried rather inconspicuously at the New Jewish Cemetery in the district of Žižkov (see below).

Pařížská Třída

Stretching from Old Town Square to the Vltava River through the heart of the old ghetto is Prague's swankiest street – **Pařížská třída** (Paris Avenue), a bevy of five-story Art Nouveau houses outfitted with more towers, turrets, and spires than you can shake a stick at. The architecture reflects Prague's turn-of-the-century infatuation with Paris' bourgeois character. Having decayed quite a bit during the Communist era, the houses are beginning to sport their original glory nowadays as chic clothing shops, antique stores, and airline ticket offices move into the ground floors.

The avenue, if looking down it towards the river, directs your line of sight to a rather strange object on the top of the hill – a giant red **metronome**. Put up as a publicity stunt by the Kotva department store in 1992, the metronome sits at the very site of the world's largest **Stalin Statue**, blown to smithereens in 1962.

Nové Město

Forming an arc around Staré Město, Nové Město is the largest of the four districts which make up the historic core of Prague, covering an area from Národní třída (National Street) south to Vyšehrad and from Wenceslas Square north to the main train station. There are several jumping off points along the metro and tram lines, which should be used to save yourself some long hikes from sight to sight. Respective stations are mentioned with individual areas and sights.

Literally translated as "New Town," Nové Město is as new as the year 1348, when it was founded by **King Charles IV** to make room for a booming population that came along with the city's temporary status as the capital of the Holy Roman Empire. Ambitious city planning incorporated expansive markets areas (later turned into Wenceslas and Charles squares), wide streets, and long thoroughfares that were all far ahead of their time.

Unfortunately or not, Nové Město met a fate similar to that of Josefov. Its buildings, with the exception of a handful of churches and other key historic structures, were demolished at the end of the 19th century to make way for new buildings of just about every modern style imaginable, including Cubism. But the layout of the streets have hardly changed a bit since the town was erected in 1348. It is, for the most part, a business district, but you will find some intimate lanes and alleys to get lost in and some neat passageways shortcutting through long blocks of office buildings.

The obvious heart of Nové Město is **Wenceslas Square**, a place where you can take care of most of the practical details of changing money, buying maps, and buying silly souvenirs for the less-appreciated friends back home. Some other good choices of sights here include the **Prague City Museum, Church of Our Lady of the Snows, National Theater, Masaryk Embankment, New Town Hall**, and **Villa Amerika**, all of which are described in the following sections below.

Prague City Museum
This museum sits just outside the Florenc metro station at Na poříčí 52.
Open daily except Monday from 10 a.m. to 6 p.m; Tel. 02/242 231 80. Entry is
a very reasonable 20 Kč. Be sure to ask for an English text at the ticket office.

First, a word of advice: see this museum after you've gotten to know Prague a little. The exhibits here are only of interest if you have some first-hand experience with the city.

Set in a pretty neo-Renaissance mansion at the north end of Nové Město, the **Prague City Museum** (Muzeum hlavního města Prahy) offers several excellent perspectives of the city, kicking off on its first floor with an historical rundown of Prague from prehistory up to the Battle of White Mountain in 1620. Capitals, cornices, frescoes, statues, and other bits and pieces representative of the architectural and artistic trends throughout the ages have been culled from historic sights around Prague, offering a well-rounded look at the development of the city.

But the fun part begins as you step up to the second floor and get a look at the meticulously detailed panorama of Prague, painted by Antonio Sacchetti on the museum staircase. The perspective is from the Charles Bridge tower (Malá Strana side), and scans everything just north of the Charles Bridge around to the Prague Castle. But the fun doesn't end there, not in the least, for you still have yet to feast your eyes on Antonín Langweil's 1:480 scale model of Prague.

The detail of the buildings and streets is stunning, and best viewed with binoculars (if you happened to have brought yours). What's truly remarkable about the model is that it shows how *little* the city has changed since the model was designed in the early 19th century. There are, however, some big exceptions that also make the model interesting to look at, most notably Josefov, which was torn down and rebuilt at the turn of this century.

In the same room as the model you can also inspect Josef Mánes' original calendar wheel from the Astronomical Clock at Old Town Hall. Executed in 1866, the wheel features a series of bucolic agrarian scenes.

Wenceslas Square
Take the metro to either Muzeum station, placing you at the top of the square
directly in front of the National Museum, or to Můstek station. The Můstek
station on line A has two exits, one letting out at the bottom of Wenceslas Square
(follows signs posted as Můstek) and the other letting out in the middle of the
square (follows signs posted as Václavské náměstí).

There's no doubt about it: **Wenceslas Square** (Václavské náměstí) bustles, it's broad sidewalks a raging torrent of shoppers, tourists, students, and business folk all getting to where they're going as quickly as possible. This is no place for a leisurely stroll. But if you want to feel the pulse of Prague, then look no further, because Wenceslas Square is where it's beating.

When I arrived in Prague in 1991, the square had already been pegged as the city's commercial hotbed – the Times Square or Picadilly Circus of Prague, if you will. Coca-Cola, Pepsi, and Fuji signs proudly flashed from the top of the square's rundown buildings as a sort of brash reminder that Capitalism had won over the bankrupt forces of Communism. It was only a matter of time before Wenceslas Square became the venue for all those bits of Americana you thought you had left at home: McDonald's, Kentucky Fried Chicken, and cinemas showing big Hollywood productions. It was also only a matter of time before the seedier aspects of a free society – gambling, prostitution, strip joints, and drug dealing – made its appearance on the square. (But don't get the impression that Wenceslas Square is a treacherous place to be; it isn't. I would, however, avoid walking here alone in the wee hours of the night.)

More like a broad, sloping avenue than a square per se, Wenceslas Square started out as a horse market in the 14th century, its two ends enclosed by gates to keep in the horses and keep out invaders. Throughout the ages it has been the site of political and social unrest, especially during the national uprisings of 1848, when a huge Mass was held here to rechristen the old horse market Wenceslas Square, in honor of the Czech patron saint that had come to symbolize the identity of the Czech nation. In 1918, it again saw a series of demonstrations in support of Czechoslovak independence, the establishment of which was cause for even bigger celebrations held at the square.

On a more depressing note, Soviet tanks roared into Wenceslas Square in August of 1968. Confrontation between Czech citizens and the Warsaw Pact soldiers turned violent, as the National Museum was raked with gunfire. (The Soviet commander, much to the later amusement of the Czechs, apparently mistook it for the Parliament building.) Throughout the following months protests occurred on the square on a regular basis, culminating in **Jan Palach** setting fire to himself on the steps of the National Museum in January 1969. The next day 200,000 people showed up at the square and held a vigil for the Charles University student who died three days later in a hospital. Apparently, Communist officials realized the power that demonstrations in Wenceslas Square had, and so built a motorway running across the front steps of the National Museum, limiting access to the square.

It would then seem logical, and appropriate, that the revolutionary events of that fateful month of November 1989 would find their focus on Wenceslas Square. After students demonstrating on Národní třída were clubbed by the police on November 17, some 250,000 angry people converged here night after night to call for the resignation of the Communist government. From the balcony of the Melantrich Building, **Václav Havel** delivered his quintessential sober speeches, evoking memories of the Soviet tanks that rumbled through the square 21 years before and of the subsequent self-sacrifice of Jan Palach. **Alexander Dubček**, ousted president of Czechoslovakia at the time of the Soviet invasion, also stepped to the balcony and continued a speech that was interrupted by Soviet officials back in August 1968. Of course, all these protests and speeches (later to be known as the **Velvet Revolution**) eventually facilitated the downfall of the Communist regime in Czechoslovakia.

We'll begin at the top of the square, commanded by the **statue of St. Wenceslas** (sv. Václav) astride his muscular horse. A statue of the 10th century Duke of Bohemia and the country's patron saint has stood in Wenceslas Square since 1680, but this one, done by Josef Myslbek, dates back to 1912. Surrounding Wenceslas, subject of the Christmas carol *Good King Wenceslas* (though he never was a king), are smaller statues of Bohemia's five other patron saints – Procope, Adalbert, Vojtěch, Wenceslas' grandmother Ludmilla, and his sister Agnes.

During every political upheaval since its unveiling, the statue has been plastered with sloganed posters and flags, and to this day is the favored Prague soapbox. In front of the statue, where Jan Palach collapsed after setting himself alight, is a small shrine to him and others who perished fighting against Communist oppression.

Looming behind the statue (though you'll have to use the metro underpass to get there) is the **National Museum** (Národní muzeum), designed by Josef Schulz and erected in 1885 during the Czech National Revival. The museum's gilt-framed glass cupola rises up between two bulky, outstretched wings, appearing like a crown at the top of Wenceslas Square.

Unless you have a great urge to view countless displays of stuffed animals, rocks, and fossils (all of which are explained exclusively in Czech), then you probably should skip the bulk of the museum and instead head up the grand staircase to the "pantheon," where you'll find some 48 busts and statues of the most prominent political, intellectual, and artistic figures from Czech history. Part and parcel of this hall of fame are the murals of Czech legend and history, rendered with a healthy bit of drama by the painters Václav Brožík and František Ženíšek. *The National Museum is open daily except Tuesday from 9 a.m. to 5 p.m. (until 9 p.m. on Wednesday); Tel. 02/242 304 85. Admission is 40 Kč.*

Midway down Wenceslas Square, *on the right at number 25,* is the square's most handsome building, the Art Nouveau **Hotel Evropa**. The building's facade and the café inside are about as sumptuous as architecture gets in this city. It was built between 1903 and 1906 to designs by Bendrich Bendelmayer and Alois Drýak, and until it's neglect in the

Communist era, it was *the* place to stay in Prague. It's well worth diving into the café for a coffee, so as to soak in the marble and chandelier-strewn interior and the oval upstairs gallery. But try not to mind the posers next to you. Opposite the Hotel Evropa, the **Melantrich Building** *at number 36* takes its claim to fame from the events of November 1989, when Havel and Dubček stood from its balcony to deliver speeches to the hundreds of thousands amassed on the square below.

On the left side, taking up the entire block between Štěpanská and Vodičkova, is the **Lucerna Palác**, outfitted with a cinema, café, and a handsome tiered ballroom where Prague's high school-level students hold their annual balls. Václav Havel, grandfather of the president, built the palace at the turn-of-the-century; it now belongs to the president and his brother. The neo-Renaissance **Wiehl House**, *at number 34*, built in 1896, is adorned with Mikolaš Aleš' pretty sgraffito work depicting Czech legends.

The slender **Peterka House** (Peterkův dům) *at number 12* was Jan Kotěra's first work, designed at the tender age of 28 having just returned from Vienna, where he studied under Otto Wagner, one of the great Vienna Secessionists.

Tomáš Baťa, the millionaire shoe magnate and great patron of the avant-garde in Czech art, funded the construction of **Dům obuv** (House of Shoes) *at number 6*. It was built in 1929 by the renowned Constructivist architect Ludvík Kysela, whose first venture with this style is noted next door *at number 4*. Dům obuv recently returned to the hands of the Baťa family, and is now a **Baťa department store**, selling a good selection of very reasonably priced shoes.

Na Příkopě

If you hang a right at the bottom (west end) of Wenceslas Square, you'll find yourself on Na příkopě, lined with a gauntlet of swank clothing shops, restaurants, bookstores, and banks.

Meaning "on the moat," **Na příkopě** (along with Národní and Revoluční streets) form the old fortifications of Staré Město. The moat was filled in at the end of the 18th century, but still marks the dividing line between Staré Město and Nové Město.

During the 19th century, Na příkopě was the favored haunt of the German literary set, frequenting the cafés that occupied the ground floor of a series of haughty bourgeois houses. Unfortunately, little remains now, as most of the houses were demolished in the 1930s to make way for a number of severe looking institutional buildings.

The **Dorfler House**, *number 7*, is one of the exceptions. Graced with whimsical floral designs and gilt urns, the Art Nouveau facade is an attractive one. Another exception is the **Sylva-Taroucca Palace**, *number*

10. It was completed by Kilían Ignác Dientzenhofer in 1751, making it the oldest building on the street. The Rococo facade, adorned with a number of carved decorations by Ignác Platzer, is outstanding, especially in comparison to the modern designs of the neighboring buildings. Even if you don't need to exchange money or cash a traveler's check, you should still take the opportunity to dive into **Živnostenka banka,** *number 20,* for a look at its outrageous interior, awash in Art Nouveau murals and gilt sculptures that attest to the financial strength of Prague at the turn of the century. You should also nip into the **Státní banka** *at number 3-5* for a peek at its polished granite interior sporting two competing styles of the early 20th century – Art Nouveau and Classicism.

If the Art Nouveau architecture has you intrigued, then you should definitely pay a visit to the newest museum to grace Prague's New Town, **the Alfons Mucha Museum** *– just off Na příkopě at Panská 7.* The museum pays homage to perhaps the greatest Art Nouveau European painter with a somewhat threadbare exhibit of his paintings, posters, and graphic art. *Open daily from 10 a.m. to 6 p.m.; Tel 02/628 4070. Admission is 100 Kč.*

Národní třída

At the bottom of Wenceslas Square, swing left (south) on 28. října street, which shortly lets out on **Jungmann Square** *(Jungmannova náměstí) and the east end of Národní třída. Alternatively, you could take the metro to Národní třída station and walk a few blocks east.*

This square, forming the east end of **Národní třída** (National Avenue), seems as good a place as any to pay tribute to Josef Jungmann (1773-1847) – writer, translator of Shakespeare and Goethe, and all-around star of the Czech National Revival. As a telling sign of his importance, his statue is situated so it looks down the street that has been so pivotal in the development of Czech culture.

But before you head down Národní, pop into the **Church of Our Lady of the Snows** (Kostel Panny Marie Sněžné), the entrance to which is just behind the Jungmann statue. When its construction began in the 14th century, Charles IV had intended it to be the most glorious church in Prague, a place worthy of coronations. But money for its ostentatious design quickly ran out after the completion of its choir. Its intended scale was minimized as the centuries rolled on and the church's construction didn't.

A compromise between its original and its later designs, the final result is rather odd. It's a short church, but a tall one at that. In fact, its nave is higher than that of St. Vitus Cathedral. And its altar, soaring up from the floor nearly to the ceiling, is the biggest you'll find in this corner of Europe. After coming out of the church, hang a sharp left into the gardens, laid out by the Franciscan monks to whom the church belongs.

The gardens are a surprisingly peaceful respite away from the traffic on Wenceslas Square.

Back on Jungmann Square, you'll notice quite a harsh, sooty building dominating the corner of Národní and Jungmannova. Built in the 1920s by Pavel Janák and Josef Zasche for an Italian insurance company, the **Adria Palace** purposely resembles a Venetian palace. Until a few years ago, the palace was the home of **Laterna Magika** (Magic Lantern), a multimedia theater combining live music, actors, dancers, and projected images. The theater was in the spotlight when it became the headquarters for the **Civic Forum** during the revolutionary events of November 1989. (More or less headed by Václav Havel, Civic Forum or *Občanské fórum* was the umbrella organization composed of various anti-Communist groups that brought the Communist government down in 1989.) The theater company, Divadlo za branou, has occupied the building since Laterna Magika moved to its new location at Nová Scéna (see below).

Farther down Národní, *underneath an arcade at number 16*, is a plaque inscribed with "17.11.89," the date on which a squad of riot police attacked 50,000 students on Národní without provocation. The incident occurred during a peaceful rally held by the Communist youth movement in commemoration of the 50th anniversary of the killings of anti-Nazi demonstrators. Five hundred people were reported to have been injured, 100 arrested, and one killed (though the death was later retracted), all of which sparked mass protests and the imminent downfall of the Communist regime.

A little way down on the opposite side of the street is a pair of sumptuous Art Nouveau houses both designed by Osvald Polívka, the first of which, *at number 7*, is the **Viola Building** (formerly the Prague Insurance Company). In addition to Ladislav Šaloun's decorative sculptures, the facade sports five oval windows on the top floor, around which "PRAHA" is handsomely spelled out. You'll also note some pretty mosaics that say what the old insurance company could help you with, which includes *život* (life), *kapitál* (capitol), *důchod* (income), *věno* (dowry), and *pojišťuje* (insurance).

Next door, the **Topič House** exhibits some of the same wrought-iron ornamentation, but in a more restrained, geometrical fashion that is more indicative of the German influence on Art Nouveau. Between the wars, the house was occupied by Borový, a publisher that specialized in French literature, but has more recently been the home of Československý spisovatel, the official publisher of the Czechoslovak state.

Across the street, you can't miss the one building that most Praguers love to hate – the **Nová Scéna**, or New Stage, which was an extension of the National Theater when it opened in 1983 but has since 1990 been the home of Laterna Magika, the multimedia theater company mentioned above. Typical of Communist planning and architecture, the whole ensemble looks rather like a giant mushroom wrapped in tinfoil, looking all the more ridiculous in the shadow of the grand **National Theater** (Národní divadlo).

More than any building in Prague, the National Theater represents the pinnacle of the Czech National Revival of the 19th century, when Czechs gleaned a cultural identity for themselves under the thumb of the Austrian Empire. When plans for the theater came up in 1849, Bohemians and Moravians of all social classes put up the money for its construction. Not a wit was donated (or wanted) from the Hapsburgs or German aristocracy, as the theater was to be *by* and *for* the Czech community.

On May 16, 1868, 50,000 people gathered to watch several Czech luminaries, such as František Palacký and Bedřich Smetana (who composed a special *Prelude* for the ceremony), lay the theater's foundation stones – hauled to Prague from numerous historic sites across Bohemia and Moravia. As fate would have it, the theater that emerged in 1881, designed by Josef Zítek, staged only a dozen or so performances before a fire ripped through it a few months after its doors opened. So, once more money poured in from around the Czech lands, and within two years the theater was rebuilt, this time to designs by Josef Schulz (who went on to build the National Museum).

The result is truly magnificent, and a worthy monument to the Czech people. Aptly nicknamed the "Golden Chapel on the Vltava," the neo-Renaissance theater rises up along Corinthian pilasters and big bay windows. Plunked down on the roof is a giant dome, topped by a decorative gilt railing. Above the front entrance, Greek gods in horse-drawn chariots launch from the theater's eaves, and a line of allegorical statues looks down upon us lowly souls on the street.

The exterior promises an equally brilliant interior, and it delivers from the stage all the way through to the restrooms. Just about every artist that ever gets mentioned in connection with the Czech National Revival lent their touch to the interior, surprising you with some adornment or another around every corner. Some details to take note of are the grand foyer's 14 lunettes (painted by Milolaš Aleš and inspired by Smetana's *Má vlast*) and the ceiling of the auditorium, where František Ženíšek rendered an ethereal painting depicting the allegories of the arts.

Over the stage are the words *Národ sobě* (translated loosely as "the nation for the nation"), the crowning dictum of this great theater that today is used mainly as the venue for ballets, operas, and the occasional play (see *Nightlife & Entertainment* below). If you need to get to the National Theater in a rush, take the metro to Národní třída station and then take any tram one stop to Národní divadlo.

From the Masaryk Embankment to Palacký Square

If you follow the course we take below, then follow the above directions to the National Theater. If you want to begin at Palacký Square, then take the metro to Karlovo náměstí station and exit at Palackého náměstí.

Running alongside the National Theater and following the river south, the **Masaryk Embankment** (Masarykovo nábřeží) is lined with a riot of handsome neo-Renaissance, neo-Baroque, and Art Nouveau houses topped with a symphony of gables, turrets, and spires. Looking out to the Vltava, the houses bathe in a twilight glow each evening as the sun sinks behind Petřín Hill, making it a romantic spot for a sunset stroll. (The embankment, by the way, used to be named after Klement Gottwald, the first Communist president of Czechoslovakia.)

One of the more outstanding buildings in this row of houses is the **Goethe Institute**, a German cultural center that replaced the East German Embassy after the two Germanies reunified. The facade is a curious marriage of neo-Baroque and Art Nouveau, made all the more delightful by Ladislav Šaloun's sculpted ornaments.

Just opposite the institute is a little bridge crossing over to **Slav Island** (Slovanský ostrov), named after a big Slav congress held here in 1848. You can hire a row boat and catch some great views of the Prague Castle while paddling around the island and along the embankment.

Dominating the island is the bright yellow **Sophia** (Žofín) **Pavilion**, Prague's premier dance and concert hall during the mid-19th century. Some of Europe's biggest names in music, including Berlioz and Liszt, used to perform here. The pavilion lost its esteem once the Rudolfinum was built, but it still continues to host the occasional concert and ball, and sometimes an impromptu evening brass performance from its rear balcony. On the south side of the pavilion is a lively terrace restaurant – a good place to rest your feet, watch the river flow by, and sip on a beer. (The food here, though reasonably priced, is only so-so.)

Spanning across the channel at the south end of the island (accessed by continuing down Masaryk Embankment) is the **Mánes Gallery**, a superb venue of temporary cutting-edge exhibitions housed in a stark white Functionalist building that strikes an odd chord when compared to the opposing row of fin-de-siecle houses. *The gallery is open daily except Monday from 10 a.m. to 6 p.m; Tel. 02/295 577.* Rising behind the gallery is the Gothic **Šítovsky Water Tower**, built in the 15th century as part of an old mill and topped with an interesting onion dome at the end of the 18th century.

Standing at the end of Masaryk Embankment in Jiráskovo náměstí (Jirásek Square) is the newest addition to Nové Město – the so-called **Dancing House** (or, as Praguers have come to know it, the "Fred and Ginger House"). When you get an eyeful of this structure, which does indeed look like a couple dancing, you'll get the gist of its name and nickname. Designed by American Frank Gehry and Yugoslav Vlado Milunič, the Dancing House raised more than just eyebrows when its construction began in 1995. Many Praguers, including Václav Havel (whose flat is located in the adjacent building), voiced their disdain at such an ultra-modern construction taking its place in (and effectively dominating) a fairly historic, turn-of-the-century neighborhood.

But this argument, which has probably been expressed a thousand times before in Prague, did not thwart construction of this office building, the top floor of which is a swanky restaurant. (See details on the restaurant under "Where To Eat."). The building is quirky. It appears as if it were rendered for a cartoon, its windows arbitrarily placed around its circular facade. I, for one, think it's a fresh piece of architecture.

Though he hasn't lived there for a few years now, **Václav Havel's apartment** faces the river on the top floor of the slender building *at Rašínovo nábřeží 78*. He chose to stay put at his humble abode rather than move to the castle in the early years of his presidency, during which time he was known to walk to work now and again. He still refuses to reside in the castle, and instead lives in a house on the outskirts of town.

One more bridge down, set a little ways off Rašín Embankment (Rašínovo nábřeží), is **Palacký Square** (Palackého náměstí), an expansive concrete space that has become a favorite of skateboarders in recent years. The focus here is Stanislav Sucharda's **monument to František Palacký**, the infamous 19th century Czech historian and leader of the Czech National Revival. Though it received a chilly reception at its unveiling in 1912, the statue holds up quite nicely to contemporary tastes. It's a rather dizzying affair of writhing bronze bodies swarming around the enormous seated figure of Palacký himself, appearing quite perturbed at all the silly business happening around him.

Charles Square & Environs
Take the metro or tram to Karlovo náměstí (Charles Square) station.

When Nové Město was laid out in the 14th century, **Charles Square** was intended as the heart of the new town. It was originally a livestock market, and for some reason or another Charles IV saw fit to display the crown jewels each May at the center of it.

At over seven hectares (17 acres), Charles Square is the largest square in Prague. But it doesn't feel like a square per se, mainly because it was transformed into a park and dotted with manicured gardens, fountains, and statues in the mid-19th century. Today, it's a pleasant spot where students go to read, lovers take strolls, and dog-owners let their pets romp. Unfortunately, it isn't the quietest of spaces, thanks to the heavy traffic buzzing on the streets surrounding and bisecting the square.

Forming the northern end of the square, identified by its tall Gothic tower, is the **New Town Hall** (Novoměstská radnice) – "new," that is, when it was completed in 1377. Its big claim to fame is a bit dubious, for it was here that Prague's first defenestration took place on July 30, 1419. Fitfully riled after listening to a fiery sermon by the radical Hussite preacher Jan Želivský, a mob of peasants stormed the town hall, demanding the release of men imprisoned for their Hussite beliefs. When the Catholic town officials refused, the peasants rushed the building and hurled three of Wenceslas IV's counselors and seven burghers out the window, sparking the Hussite Wars and setting a new precedence in Prague for expressing political disfavor. As the story goes, King Wenceslas IV suffered a stroke upon hearing the news, kicking the bucket two weeks later as result.

Access to the New Town Hall is limited to the gallery occupying the east side of the structure. Temporary exhibitions from the massive collection of the Museum of Decorative Arts are held here daily except Monday from 10 a.m. to 6 p.m.

Nearby is the **St. Ignatius Church** (Kostel sv. Ignáce), *on the east side of Charles Square, at the corner of Ječná,* built in the 1660s by Carlo Lurago for the Jesuits. Modeled after Il Gesu in Rome, the church features a gorgeous facade adorned with gilt-haloed statues, with St. Ignatius himself standing at the apex. Inside, through the enormous stone portal, you'll find a soaring nave smothered with frescos and lined with sculpted vaults – all leading up to Jan Jiří Heinsch's brooding painting of St. Ignatius over the high altar.

Getting slightly off the square, head straight down from St. Ignatius and continue on Resslova street, where you'll find the **Church of St. Cyril and St. Methodious** (Kostel sv. Cyrila a Metoděje) a block down from the square on the right. Built in the 1730s by Kilián Ignác Dientzenhofer, the sooty structure has been the center of the Czech Orthodox Church since the 1930s, even though it was originally built for retired Roman Catholic priests who lived in the adjacent building. During World War II, the church was the scene of a harrowing event in the Czech resistance against the Nazis; it was the last hiding place of the seven Czech and Slovak paratroopers involved in the assassination of Reinhard Heydrich, the Nazi Protector of Bohemia and Moravia. The seven were part of plot formulated by the Czechoslovak government-in-exile in London as a way to establish Czech resistance.

The paratroopers managed to wound Heydrich with a grenade as he was on his way to work on May 27, 1942. But the mission, the only Allied attempt to assassinate a leading Nazi, proved to be successful, as the protector died eight days later from shrapnel wounds. Of course, there was hell to be paid for killing the most powerful Nazi in the Czech lands, and the village of **Lidice**, west of Prague, was annihilated in retailiation on the day following Heydrich's funeral.

It wasn't until June 18 when the seven agents were betrayed, and found hiding in the crypt of the Church of St. Cyril and St. Methodius. The Nazis tried everything to drive them out, riddling the church with gunshot, throwing explosives at it, and even flooding it. Instead of being taken prisoner, the agents committed suicide. Bishop Gorazo, leader of the Czech Orthodox Church, was subsequently executed for giving the assassins refuge.

In commemoration of the event, a plaque devoted to the seven agents hangs on the south facade of the church, just above some bullet holes left over from the Nazi siege. The crypt, in which the agents hid, has been turned into a small museum detailing the event and recounting Prague's days under Nazi terror.

Today, it houses a good museum called **National Monument to the Victims of the Heydrich Terror**, telling the story of the Czech resistance and the Nazi occupation of Prague. *It's open daily except Monday from 10 a.m. to 4 p.m.*

South of Charles Square, *at Vyšehradská 49*, the **Emmaus Monastery** (Klášter Emauzy) was established in 1372 by a Croatian order of Benedictine monks. With the support of the pope, Charles IV ordered the creation of the monastery and sanctioned its use of the Old Church Slavonic liturgy in hopes of bridging the gap between the Eastern and Western churches. By 1419 the monastery had fully embraced the teachings of Jan Hus, becoming the one and only Hussite monastery. Of course, the monastery fell prey to the Hapsburg quest to wipe out Protestantism in Bohemia after the Battle of White Mountain, and the monastery was handed over to a group of Spanish Benedictines.

The monastery's Gothic church, **St. Mary's** (Kostel Panny Marie), sports the two twisting towers you may have noted standing at Palacký Square. These were finally added in the 1960s after a stray Allied bomb landed on the church during World War II. Inside the church there's not a whole lot worth noting, but the attached cloisters do feature some intriguing, faded frescoes dating back to the 14th century. *Hours of the church and cloister are supposedly 10 a.m. to 5 p.m. Tuesday through Sunday, although this hasn't always been the case.*

Opposite the monastery on Vyšehradská, the **Church of St. John on the Rock** (Kostel sv. Jana na Skalce) was built in 1730 by, who else, but Kilián Ignác Dientzenhofer. The church is one of the finer testaments to the Baroque style found in Prague, outfitted with a series of arches, balconies, and oval windows that effectively broaden the dimensions of the interior and give it a bit of theatricality. Worth checking out at the altar is the statue of St. John of Nepomuk, executed by Maximilian

Brokoff to serve as a model for the statue he sculpted for the Charles Bridge.

A block or so down on Na slupi is Prague's smallish **Botanical Gardens** (Botanická zahrada), laid out in 1897 on a series of ascending terraces and later acquiring a number of green houses. The flora here won't knock any socks off, but it is a good place to take a stroll and clear your mind. *It's open daily from 10 a.m. to 5 p.m. (until 4 p.m. in November and December); Tel. 02/297 941.*

Villa Amerika
From Karlovo náměstí station walk up Ječná or take the tram (#4 or #22) to Štepánská stop. Hang a right onto Ke Karlovu (one block up from Štepánská), where you'll find the villa on the left at number 20. If you are not in the area of Charles Square, the easiest way to get here is to take the metro to I.P. Pavlova station, cross Sokolská, veer left onto Kateřinska, and take another left on Ke Karlovu. The villa's Dvořák museum is open daily except Monday from 10 a.m. to 5 p.m.; Tel. 02/298 214. Admission is 30 Kč.

Few tourists make it this far off the beaten path, something which makes **Villa Amerika** all the more special. If there ever were an adorable Baroque house, this would have to take the wedding cake (something which the house looks a bit like). Built by Kilián Ignác Dientzenhofer (did this guy ever take a break?) for Count Michna of Vacinov, the villa is a sumptuous affair designed in the style of French country houses. Today, the villa houses a museum dedicated to the most renowned Czech composer of all time – **Antonín Dvořák** (1841-1904).

A villa named after America is more than an appropriate place to celebrate the man who wrote the *New World Symphony* and who was the first European composer to truly recognize the value of (and incorporate in his own works) the musical strains found in the United States. The museum recounts the life of Dvořák (including his stints in New York City and Spillville, Iowa) through old photographs and a number of his personal effects, among them his viola, piano, and a gown given to him when he received an honorary degree from Cambridge. With his music playing in the frescoed rooms of the villa and spilling out into statue-spotted garden, you can't help but feel a little giddy here.

About a quarter-mile away from Villa Amerika, at the southern end of Ke Karlovu, is perhaps the most exotic-looking church in Prague, and certainly the one with the longest name. **Our Lady of the Assumption and the Emperor Charlemagne** (Kostel Nanebevzetí Panny Marie a Karla Velikého) is easy to spot because of its bright red, nipple-shaped domes. The church, founded by Charles IV in 1350, is designed after Charlemagne's tomb in Aachen, and quite an engineering feat to boot. The ribbed vault, added to the church in the 18th century, has no central pillar supporting it, which made many 18th-century Praguers suspect that the architect, Bonifác Wohlmut, was in cahoots with the devil. Next to the church is the **Police Museum**, which is actually not a bad little museum. It chronicles the history of Czech crime and criminology, and is quite frank in its depictions of certain crimes. *It's open daily except Monday from 10 a.m. to 5 p.m.*

Be sure to check out the view from the church, which perches above the Botič Valley at the south end of the Nusle Bridge. The bridge is an impressive structure, replete with six lanes of traffic on top and a metro line underneath. If you've got it in you, go ahead and cross the bridge to the ancient fortification of Vyšehrad (see below), about a ten-minute walk from the church.

Vyšehrad

Vyšehrad is located beyond the southern tip of Nové Město overlooking the Botič Valley and the Vltava River. Take the metro to Vyšehrad station, head west past the Palace of Culture, and then follow signs. Another possible route is to take tram #18 or #24 from Karlovo náměstí to Na slupi station and then climb up the tree-studded slope to the top.

If Prague has a soul, it would have to reside at this ancient citadel perched upon a crag high above the city. For it was here that Prague, mythical Prague that is, was born. As the legend goes, **Vyšehrad** (meaning "high castle") is where the wise chieftain **Krok** built a castle in the 7th century. Krok had three daughters, the youngest of which was **Libuše**. She prophesied that a great city, a *threshold*, would emerge in the river valley below Vyšehrad. (*Praha*, Czech for Prague, means "threshold.") Capitulating to the male aversion of a female leader, Libuše elected as her husband and king a ploughman by the name of **Přemysl**. They were married at Vyšehrad, founding the Přemysl dynasty and the kingdom of Bohemia.

Unfortunately, history isn't so romantic as that, but archaeological evidence does suggest that Vyšehrad (then known as Chrasten) was founded in the early 10th century and that **Boleslav II** (972-99) was the first Přemysl to set up residence here. What is clear is that **Vratislav II** left Hradčany and came to live at a palace he built at Vyšehrad in the 11th century, at which time a town rose within the castle fortifications. Subsequent rulers stayed on until 1140, when Vladislav II moved back to the Prague Castle.

After that, Vyšehrad was pretty much left to rot until the 14th century, when **Charles IV** recognized its defensive value and incorporated Vyšehrad into his new town, Nové Město. A wall was built across the Botič Valley, establishing Vyšehrad as the southern gate to the town. A century later, the fortifications were wiped out in the Hussite Wars, again rendering the fortress a ruin. For the next two hundred years Vyšehrad served as a small township, and in the mid-17th century the Hapsburgs had the whole place rebuilt into a fortified barracks, adding the curtain walls at the base of the castle.

With the dawning of the Czech National Revival, Vyšehrad drew a new lease on life, as historians and artists waxed poetic about its significance as a symbol of Czech nationhood. It's no wonder then that Smetana chose Vyšehrad as the setting for his opera *Libuše* and that this opera was performed at both grand openings of the National Theater. It also makes sense that Vyšehrad would become the site of the **national memorial cemetery** in the 1880s.

Transformed into a park in the 1920s, Vyšehrad is today a wonderfully meditative place, offering unequaled views of Prague and a chance to take a breather away from the city bustle. A good time to come is around sunset, so as to watch the sun go down behind the Prague Castle and glint off the rooftops and steeples below.

The Vyšehrad Complex

Begin at the **Tábor Gate** (erected in 1655), on the south side of the complex and most easily accessed from the Vyšehrad metro station. Just inside the gate are the remains of the Gothic Špička Gate, as well as a tennis stadium that hugs the castle ramparts. You then proceed through yet another gate, a swirling Baroque affair named after Leopold I and making for a grand entrance to the park.

Off to the right is the **Rotunda of St. Martin** (Rotunda sv. Martina), erected by Vratislav II sometime around 1150. This is Vyšehrad's oldest standing structure, though it received a new door and its frescoes in the 1870s. A little ways down the K rotundě lane is a rather ho-hum museum chronicling the history of Vyšehrad. *It's open from 10 a.m. to 5 p.m. late spring to early fall.* At the end of the lane, on a small patch of grass beside the Church of St. Peter and St. Paul, are Josef Myslbek's four enormous statues depicting mythical figures connected with Vyšehrad, including Libuše and her ploughman-cum-ruler Přemysl (in the northwest corner). In the southeast corner is the vaguely lurid statue of Šárka and Ctirad, the tragic lovers.

With its twin towers soaring from its hilltop position, the **Church of St. Peter and St. Paul** (Kostel sv. Petra and Pavla) is Vyšehrad's landmark building, but a rather dull one at that. Its Romanesque foundations go back to the 11th century, on top of which Charles IV built a Gothic church that has since been altered so many times that it hardly resembles its original design. Josef Mocker, who gave it a neo-Gothic facelift in the 1880s, is most responsible for its current appearance. Be sure to check out

THE MYTH OF SÁRKA & CTIRAD

As the story goes, a war between men and women ensued after the death of Libuše. The women's army came up with a plot to kill Ctirad, commander of the men's army. They chose Šárka, the most beautiful woman in the female army, to act as a decoy. They tied her up naked to a tree and waited for Ctirad to be lured into the trap. But when Šárka laid eyes on Ctirad, she fell madly in love, as did Ctirad. Alas, Ctirad was knocked off anyway. So mad was Šárka's love for Ctirad that she took off for a nearby cliff and jumped to her death. The canyon into which she supposedly flung herself, located near the airport on the northwest outskirts of town, is now called Divoká (or "wild") Šárka.

the three spanking-new doors at the front of the church, emblazoned with the Bohemian and Moravian coats of arms.

If there were one single good reason for making the trek to Vyšehrad, it would have to be the little graveyard to the north side of the church. Established as a **national memorial cemetery** in the 1880s, the graveyard serves as the final resting spot for the most celebrated Czech figures from the last hundred years or so. A telling sign of this country's priorities is that most of the people buried here were either artists or intellectuals. Very few war heros, few politicians, and not a single Communist were given the honors.

Enclosed on two sides by a pretty arcade, the small cemetery harbors a dense concentration of gravestones, statues, and busts that make up a small museum unto themselves. At the entrance is a directory of the most notable figures buried here, among them the writers Božena Němcova, Jan Neruda, and Karel Čapek (who gave us the word "robot") and the composers Antonín Dvořák and Bedřich Smetana. (The Prague Spring Musical Festival begins each May 12 with a procession from Smetana's grave to the Municipal House in Staré Město.)

Dominating the east side of the cemetery is the *Slavín* (roughly "Place of Glory"), a huge monument crowned by a sarcophagus and a statue representing Genius. Designed by Antonín Wiehl, the monument is the final resting spot for 50 leading lights from the 20th century, including the painter Alfons Mucha, the sculptors Josef Myslbek and Ladislav Šaloun, and the opera singer Ema Destinová.

From the cemetery, follow the ramparts around the edge of Vyšehrad. The overlooks, taking in the Botič and Vltava river valleys, offer some stunning views of the city, though at times a little overwrought with smokestacks. One of the better overlooks is on the west side facing the river. It perches on top of a crag just above the old guard tower ruins – known quite nicely as "Libuše's bath." By this time you'll probably be in need of a rest and a beer, which you can get at a little outdoor pub behind the overlook.

If you came by way of the Vyšehrad metro station, I would recommend leaving at the opposite end of the fortress by way of the **Brick Gate** (Cihelná brána), where you'll find within the casemates a good exhibit (in English) on the construction of Vyšehrad and how it was incorporated into the defensive plan of Prague. From the gate, head down to the river embankment, where you can catch a tram back towards the center of town.

Cubist Architecture at the Foot of Vyšehrad

Leaving (or coming) to Vyšehrad by way of the Brick Gate will also give you the opportunity to check out the cluster of **Cubist buildings** hugging the foot of the old fortress. Nowhere else but Prague (and especially this neighborhood) will you find so many examples from this short-lived movement in architecture. In fact, Cubist architecture is completely unique to the Czech Republic. (No, it never took hold in the Cubist cradle of Paris, or anywhere else for that matter.) But in the four short years leading up to World War I, Bohemian architects such as Pavel Janák, Josef Gočár, and Josef Chocol found a way to duplicate in their structures the prismatic shapes and geometric forms laid down on canvas by Braque and Picasso.

Perhaps the most striking example of Czech Cubism is Chocol's five-story **apartment block** *at Neklanova 30*, just down from Vratislavova street (take your first right after coming down from the Brick Gate). The angular position at the corner of the block exposes the full thrust of the masonry walls, which are broken up into diamond shapes that reveal the Cubist-trademarked contrast between light and shadow.

From here, head back up to Vratislavova and follow it down to Vnislavova. After inspecting Chocol's apartment block you should be able to recognize the cluster of less successful attempts at Cubist design lining these streets. But also pay attention to the extravagant Art Nouveau houses here, noteworthy because it was exactly this ornamental style against which the Cubists rebelled.

At the bottom of Vnislavova and to the left *at Libušina 3* is a Cubist townhouse by Chocol. And round the corner, *at Rašínovo nábřeží 6-10* (near the tunnel under Vyšehrad), is yet another Chocol design, this one called **rodinný trojdům** (or three-family house) – a long structure with three independent dwelling spaces.

OUTSIDE THE HISTORIC CENTER

The following districts and sights are not in the heart of Prague, but most are easy enough to get to by metro, tram, or bus. We'll begin to the east of the historic center and work our way around it counter-clockwise.

Vinohrady

This large district borders Nové Město to the east. There are several metro stations, mentioned below in connection with individual sights.

Built on the site of royal vineyards dating back to the 14th century, **Vinohrady** was *the* place to live in the late 19th and early 20th century, luring to its neighborhoods some of the country's biggest celebrities. It still is one of the nicest districts in Prague, but the vast majority of the old bourgeois houses have yet to be restored, making the district a little worse for wear.

The heart of Vinohrady is **Náměstí Míru** (Peace Square), accessed by taking the tram or metro to the station with the same name. Rising from the middle of it is the neo-Gothic **St. Ludmilla Church** (Kostel sv. Ludmily), flanked by a circle of structures of every "neo" style imaginable, including the grand neo-Renaissance **National House** (Národni dům) and the neo-Baroque **Vinohrady Theater** (Divadlo na Vinohradech).

From Náměstí Míru, take the metro one stop to Jiřího z Poděbrad station, located below a beautiful square with the same name. All Praguers knows this square – lined with a barrage of Art Nouveau and other fin-de-siecle houses – by the "big clock church" that dominates it. More formally known as **Church of the Most Sacred Heart of Our Lord** (Kostel Nejsvětějšího Srdce Páně), it does indeed sport an enormous, translucent clock set within its thrusting, rectangular tower.

Designed by Josef Plečnik (the Slovenian responsible for much of the Prague Castle's restoration early this century), the L-shaped church is the city's most eccentric bit of architecture, and also its most controversial. Note the little crosses set within the brickwork, as well as the crazy planetary-shaped lamps above the congregation. Also, don't miss the life-like Jesus suspended above the altar and backed by what appears to be a sunflower. If you have any interest at all in modernist architecture, do check out this gem.

From náměstí Jiřího z Poděbrad, head down Slavíkova street and hang a left on Polská to **Riegrovy Sady**, a nice hilltop park flanked by rows of Art Nouveau townhouses and graced with fine views of the city below (including an excellent one of the Prague Castle).

Žižkov

Touching the northeast corner of Nové Město, the district of Žižkov borders Vinohrady to the north and east. Again, metro stations are listed below with individual sights.

Named after Jan Žižka, the tough-as-nails military leader of the Taborites, **Žižkov** is an equally tough district that emerged from the depths of a narrow valley at the turn of the century. Since its beginnings, Žižkov has been the proletarian district of Prague, its identity sharpened in conflicts with the bourgeois neighbors up the hill in Vinohrady. More or less as a result of its working class roots, Žižkov evolved into a Communist enclave (for years known as "Red Žižkov") long before the party even took control of the country.

Except for a few scattered sights, there ain't a whole lot of attractions in this somewhat seedy part of Prague. But if you have an adventurous streak in you, take tram #9 or #5 from Hlavní nádraží metro station up the hill one or two stops and then just wander. This section of the district is built on a steep slope and has some wild cobblestone streets running in diagonal directions. It's a safe place during the day, and a very lively one at that, but I've always been a bit uncomfortable walking alone here late at night.

The one landmark in Žižkov that never fails to draw attention and a lot of remarks (usually negative) is the **Television Tower** (Televizní věž), soaring 216 meters high (708 feet) and visible from just about anywhere in Prague. Up close this steely, futuristic tower overwhelms. It thrusts up like a missile, and looks like something straight out of the film *Brazil*.

What makes matters worse is that it was built on the site of a Jewish cemetery, most of which was cleared away to make room for it. Of course, it was the Communists who erected the eye-sore back in the 1970s, done so mainly with the intent to block out Western television and radio transmissions.

For an unreasonable 50 Kč you can ride up the high-speed elevator to the viewing platform, from where you can look right out past the city limits. But it's sort of like looking at Prague from an airplane, where you're just too high to appreciate much of anything other than the layout of the city.

To see what's left of the **Jewish cemetery** that the Communists destroyed in constructing the big steel beast, head to the north side of the square. The Prague Jews buried their dead here from 1787 (the year the cemetery in Josefov closed down) until 1890. To get to the tower and cemetery, take the metro to Jiřího z Poděbrad and walk a few blocks northeast. Just look up and you should have no problem finding your way.

On the east side of Žižkov is Prague's main cemetery, **Olšany** (Olšanské hřbitovy) – founded in 1680 for victims of the plague. It's an enormous green space laid out under the canopies of huge trees, bisected with cobblestone lanes, and stacked with monumental gravestones of just about every style through the ages. Perhaps the most notable of the deceased here is Jan Palach, the university student who set fire to himself in protest of the Soviet invasion. Officials hastily carted Palach's remains off to his hometown in 1974 to thwart demonstrations at the cemetery. But in 1990 he was reinterred here. To get to the front of the cemetery, take the metro to Flora station and walk a short ways east to the main entrance. Turn right at the main entrance and walk roughly 55 yards to Palach's grave.

If you walk eastward through the cemetery you'll eventually come out opposite the **New Jewish Cemetery** (Nový židovský hřbitov), opened in the 1890s when the one at the television tower filled up. This over-grown, rundown cemetery is a rather sad, thought-provoking place, especially after strolling through the manicured Christian graveyard across the street. The reason most people make the trek here is to see Franz Kafka's grave. He is buried next to his parents, both of whom outlived their son. A plaque, inscribed with the names of Kafka's three sisters who died in concentration camps, hangs here as well. The front entrance of the cemetery is just outside the Želivského metro station. Kafka's grave is to the right of the entrance, along the front wall.

Wedged between Žižkov and the district of Karlín is **Žižkov** (or **Vítkov**) **Hill**, the site of the infamous Battle of Vítkov, in which the ridiculously outnumbered Taborite army, commanded by the one-eyed Jan Žižka, gave a thrashing to Emperor Sigismund of Luxembourg and his papal forces. (The Taborites were a radical group of orthodox Hussites from Tábor in South Bohemia.) An enormous bronze statue of Žižka himself, mounted upon his mighty steed, stands at the crest of the hill. So big is this statue that UNESCO considers it the largest of the equestrian variety.

From the statue is yet another stunning view of the city, taking in just about all of the historic center. But Žižkov Hill has a creepy, abandoned feel to it, mainly due to the austere **National Memorial** that rises up behind the Žižka statue. Completed in 1932 as a monument to the new nation of Czechoslovakia, the memorial was shanghaied by the Commu-nists and turned into a mausoleum for presidents Gottwald, Zápotocký, and Svoboda. (Gottwald's body was mummified Lenin-style. Report-edly, he was mostly plastic by the time they finally reinterred him and the rest of his gang somewhere else.) The memorial has been closed for years now and is slowly decaying away; apparently no one wants to be bothered with it.

The easiest way to Žižkov Hill is take the metro to Florenc station, walk under the railway bridges, and then climb up the lane, U památníku. On your way up is the **Army Museum** (Armádní Muzeum), this one devoted to the history of the Czechoslovak army and to Czech resistance in World War II. It used to be a glorification of the Warsaw Pact's might, but is now a bit more objective in its presentations. *It's open Monday through Friday from 9 a.m. to 5 p.m.*

Holešovice

Squeezed into a big bend on the Vltava River, the district of **Holešovice** may look a little run down, but it still demonstrates a bit of its turn-of-the-century charm when you get off its busy thoroughfares and onto its tree-lined side streets. It's a desirable district to live in, mainly because it sits between two enormous parks – **Letná** to the east and **Stromovka** to the west. Here, you'll also find two museums well worth checking out – the **Technical Museum** and the **Trade Fair Palace** (exhibiting the National Gallery's modern art collection).

But we'll begin at **Výstaviště**, the city's main exhibition space and fairgrounds located on the east side of Stromovka Park (take tram #12 one stop from Nádraží Holešovice metro station). It's a vast space filled with a crazy-quilt assortment of buildings and architectural styles going back to 1891, the year Výstaviště opened for the Terrestrial Jubilee Exposition. Dominating the grounds is the grandiose wrought-iron and glass **Palace of Industry** (Průmuslový palác), sporting a jumble of cupolas and towers. In humble contrast is the neo-Baroque **Lapidarium**, a repository of statues, sculptures, columns, tombstones, and fountains culled from around Central Bohemia.

The Lapidarium's collection, amounting to 415 items dating from the 11th to the 19th century, is stuffed into eight smallish rooms, making it an intriguingly chaotic place, and a somewhat poetic one at that. Here you'll find several statues retired from the Charles Bridge, as well as bits and pieces of the Marian column that stood in Old Town Square (until it was pushed over by a mob in 1918). Also from the Old Town Square is the Renaissance Krocín Fountain, torn from the square in 1862. (Some of its pieces, believe it or not, were inexplicably found in the foundations of the gas-works in Žižkov when the plant was demolished in 1932.) *It's open Tuesday to Friday from 12 to 6 p.m. and on weekends from 10 a.m. to 12:30 p.m. and 1 to 6 p.m.*

Something else you might want to check out at Výstaviště is the **Maroldovo Panorama** – a 360-degree diorama of the Battle of Lipany in 1434, a pivotal event in Czech history in which the royal Utraquist forces gave a beating to the Taborites (a group of radical Hussites from South

Bohemia). *It's open Tuesday to Friday from 2 to 5 p.m. and on the weekend from 10 a.m. to 5 p.m.*

Výstaviště is *the* place to be on a summer weekend, when Praguers show up by the tram-load to go for spins on the amusement park rides, gobble sausages and candy, and listen to some good ol' Bohemian beer-swilling music. (Beer drinking is also on the agenda, but that goes without saying.) They also come to watch the **Křižík Fountain** (Křižíkova fontána) dance hourly to recorded music. This happens only in late spring and summer, *Tuesday through Friday from 6 to 9 p.m. and on weekends from 3 to 9 p.m.* But it's best to come after the sun goes down so as to see the fountain in all its spotlighted glory.

After all the excitement and commotion of Výstaviště, it may be time for a stroll in **Stromovka Park**, the largest and prettiest in Prague. Originally the royal hunting grounds, Stromovka is a wonderful lush oasis filled with old oaks, ashes, elms, and weeping willows and dotted with lakes fed by the Vltava River via a network of canals built in 1584. There's some wildlife here as well, including red squirrels, rabbits, redpolls, gray-headed woodpeckers, and tree creepers. If you are up to the 45-minute walk, go ahead and follow the signs to the Troja chateau and zoo (see below), taking you across a pretty stretch of the Vltava by way of Císařský ostrov (Emperor's Island). Otherwise, definitely head to the next featured attraction.

Perhaps the most exciting event to happen to the Prague cultural scene in the last few years has been the reopening of the **Trade Fair Palace** (Veletržní palác) as the new venue for the National Gallery's gigantic **modern art collection** (sbírka moderního umění). *It's open Tuesday through Sunday from 10 a.m. to 6 p.m. and costs a rather steep 80 Kč. From Výstaviště, catch any tram heading east and go one stop. Or catch tram #12 from Nádraží Holešovice metro station and go to Veletržní stop.*

Designed by Josef Fuchs and Oldřich Tyl, the glass behemoth was on the cutting edge of Functionalist architecture when it was completed in 1928. The palace served its namesake purpose for 36 years until it was gutted by a fire one night in 1974. Until reconstruction began in the 1980s, the building sat an empty shell. It finally opened in 1995 as a sensational and much-needed setting for the National Gallery's impressive collection of 20th century works by Czech, French, and other European masters.

When you first walk into the palace, you can't help but feel a little overwhelmed by the sheer expanse of the place, its hollow core soaring seven stories up to a glass dome. The collection, however, takes up only three of the floors, but three very wide floors at that. The best way to tackle it then is to take the elevator to the third floor and work your way down.

The third floor kicks off with the works of Antonín Slavíček, whose brooding cityscapes of Prague recall Monét's impressionist views of London. Not well-enough represented is the Symbolist František Bílek, who is one of the most outstanding sculptors of this century (at least in my humble opinion). The tree is not just a source of the material he employs in his sculptures, but is a main component in the overall, naturalist effect of his works. Case in point is his *Parable of the Great Decline of the Czechs*, an ecstatic work carved from a huge, raw chunk of wood and depicting a woman stretched below two unattached feet.

Also keep an eye out for the works of Bohumil Kubišta, who, in paintings such as *St. Sebastian*, came to define Czech Cubism, a style that is by no means merely an off-shoot of French Cubism, but rather a distinct style pursued and enhanced by the likes of Emil Filla, Josef Čapek, and Václav Špála – all of whom are well-represented here on the third floor. On the opposite wing don't miss Toyen's "Artificialist" paintings or Zdeněk Pešanek's crazy neon-lit torsos.

Greeting you at the beginning of the gallery's collection of 19th and 20th century French art on the second floor is Rodin's *St. John the Baptist*. Here you'll get a look at the original works of virtually all the Modernist masters who worked some time or another in France. Five or six paintings by Picasso (most notably his *Violin, Glass, Pipe, and Ink*) grace the collection, as does Van Gogh's stunning-as-usual *Green Wheat*. More daring, however, is the European collection around the corner, crowned by Gustav Klimt's kaleidoscope of writhing women entitled *Virgin* and complimented by Egon Schiele's anguished *Pregnant Woman and Death*. Opposite are a couple of intriguing Prague cityscapes by Oskar Kokoschka, who perhaps understood better than any the power of Prague's hilly perspectives.

In other sections of the museum are the changing exhibits of artists at work today. The art is up-to-the-moment contemporary, so much so that you're likely to see the artists themselves putting the finishing touches on their work as they set it up to be viewed. Indeed, the place is a living art space, one you would want to return to again and again if given the chance.

One more museum in Holešovice that I highly recommend is the **National Technical Museum** (Národní Technické Muzeum) at the western edge of Letná Park. Even if you have merely a passing interest in automobiles, you should get a kick out of the cars in the museum's enormous transport exhibit. Some of the gems include a 1939 armored Mercedes-Benz and a no-less-impressive 1935 Czech-made Tatra 80 built for President Masaryk. But the big knockout is the Russian 1952 Zavod Imeni Stalina (or ZIS), a beast of a car that only Stalin could have looked comfortable riding around in. Near the automobiles, you'll a find a sensational pair of Art Nouveau locomotive cars, built for Archduke Franz Ferdinand (who was assassinated before he had a chance to enjoy riding in them). Every other hour, starting at 11 a.m., the museum offers tours through a coal mine replica. In other sections of the museum you can inspect some old timepieces, cameras, and astronomical instruments, including two sextants that Tycho Brahe used back in the 16th century. But the real kicker at the museum is located in the film technology section, where you'll find the notorious shoes and walking stick of none other than Charlie Chaplin. (Chaplin himself formally presented these items to Czechoslovakia in honor of the country's resistance against Nazi fascism.) *The National Technical Museum is open daily except Monday from 9 a.m. to 5 p.m.; Tel. 02/373 651. Admission is a mere 30 Kč. Easiest way to get there is to take tram #1 or 25 from Vltavská metro station to Letenské náměstí stop and then walk east on Nad Štolou and Muzejní streets.*

Right out the front door of the museum is **Letná**, an immense green plain stretching above the Vltava between Hradčany and Holešovice. Přemysl Otakar II was coronated here in 1261, and for centuries it was the favored encampment site for armies invading Prague. Letná was also the focus of the Communist-era May Day parades, in which thousands were more or less mandated to join in and show their Red pride. But Letná served just as well in November 1989 as the location for a 750,000-strong demonstration supporting the country-wide strike which brought the Communist government down. Ever since a million people congregated here to see the Pope in April 1990 (after Poland, the Pope's first visit to a former Eastern bloc country), things have been pretty quiet.

It almost goes without saying, but more picture-perfect views of Prague await along the eastern edge of the park, especially from the curious red **metronome** – best approached by heading down Pařížská street from Old Town Square and crossing to the other side of Czech Bridge (Čechův most). As a publicity stunt, the Kotva department store set up the thing not long ago on a huge concrete plinth which at one time supported the biggest and most notorious **Stalin monument** ever built.

Six hundred men worked furiously on the 14,000-ton, 98-foot giant to have it ready for its unveiling on May 1, 1955 – the day after which its designer, Otakar Švec, committed suicide. Though Krushchev would denounce his predecessor a year later, the monument stayed put until 1962, when it was finally given a proper death by dynamite. Today, the remaining plinth is covered with graffiti, and, like so many of the old Communist monuments, is a favorite of skateboarders.

There's one more peculiar item sticking up through the trees in Letná, and that's the **Hanavský pavilón**. Originally built for the 1891 Jubilee Exhibition, this neo-Rococo (some would say Art Nouveau) pavilion was relocated here from Výstaviště in 1898, later becoming a fine restaurant (see a listing for the pavilion under *Where to Eat* above).

Troja

Take the metro to Nádraží Holešovice and hop on bus #112 to the last station, dropping you off at the chateau and zoo entrances. The bus ride takes about ten minutes. Alternatively, in the summer, you could take a boat from Palackého most (bridge) to Troja (see "Boat Tours" under "Getting Around Town" above). From April 1 through October 31, the chateau is open daily except Monday from 10 a.m. to 6 p.m. The rest of the year it's open on Saturday and Sunday only, from 10 a.m. to 5 p.m. The zoo is open daily 9 a.m. to 6 p.m.

Lying north of Holešovice on the other side of the Vltava, the suburb of **Troja** has the feel of a little village, and a rather posh one at that. Its lanes and streets are lined with pretty villas and make you feel as if you've left Prague altogether, even though you are still well within the city limits.

The big attraction here is the **Troja Chateau** (Trojský zámek), a bulky 17th-century pile sporting all the Baroque extravagance of its day. The Frenchman Jean-Baptiste Mathey, influenced by his native land's Renaissance castles, built the chateau as a summer residence for Count Šternberk, who liked the location because of its close proximity to the royal hunting grounds across the river (now Stromovka Park). Its bright red-and-white striped exterior is offset by the chateau's sooty balustrade, upon which gods, titans, and giants of stone battle it out.

In order to get inside you'll have to join a guided tour. The big stunner of the interior is the **Imperial Banqueting Hall**, smothered in murals giving all-holy praise to the Hapsburgs and their finest achievements, including Leopold I beating the Turks at Kahlenberg. The chateau also exhibits more of the National Gallery's collection of 19th century Czech paintings, including some by Václav Brožík, Maximilian Pirner, and Mikoláš Aleš. But the real attraction at the chateau are its French-style **gardens**, laid out in or about 1700 in a star-shaped plan.

Across the street from the chateau, covering a steep hillside, is the city's fairly large **zoo**. Though it's getting better, the zoo is in pretty bad shape, its animals looking somewhat neglected the last time I was there. But if you have brought your children along, then you should be able to make a good time of it. There's a fun funicular running to the top of the hill.

And, in addition to all the usual zoo animals, there are some rare Przewalski horses, indigenous to the steppes of Mongolia and successfully bred here. Outside the entrance is a jolly beer garden.

Břevnov Monastery
   Take either tram #22 from Malostranská metro station or tram #8 from Hradčanská metro station to Břevnovský klašteř stop. The exhibit at the monastery is open daily except Monday (weekends only in the winter) from 10 a.m. to 2 p.m.
   Founded in 993, the Benedictine **Břevnov Monastery** (Břevnovsky klašteř) was established jointly by Duke Boleslav II and St. Adalbert, Bishop of Prague. Having recently celebrated its 1,000-year anniversary, it's Bohemia's oldest monastery, though you wouldn't know it by its outward appearance. It's been rebuilt several times, most recently between 1708 and 1745, when Krištof Dientzenhofer turned it into a thoroughly Baroque affair, adding the single-naved **Church of St. Margaret** (Kostel sv. Markéty), with scores of carved pilasters, oval skylights, and *trompe l'oeil* frescoes.
   But the highlight of the monastery just may be the crypts, where you can see the original foundations of the monastery, as well as a few skeletons. Also, don't miss the **Theresa Hall**, with its sweeping fresco entitled *The Miracle of St. Gunther.* Cosmas Asam, considered one of the finest German fresco artists in the 18th century, executed it.
   Jan Patočka, a famous Czech dissident, is buried in the monastery graveyard. He died in 1977 under interrogation by the StB (secret police), the same organization that used the monastery for storage during the Communist years.

Star Summer Palace
   From Hradčanská metro station, take tram #1, #2, or #18 to Heyrovského náměstí stop, located at the main entrance to the park surrounding the palace. The palace and its museum are open daily except Monday from 10 a.m. to 5 p.m. Entry is 20 Kč.
   In 1556, Archduke Ferdinand of Tyrol built the **Star Summer Palace** (Letohrádek Hvězda) inside the royal game reserve that had been established by his father, Emperor Ferdinand I. The Renaissance palace, designed according to the archduke's plans, is shaped like a six-pointed star (hence the name), and is a grand sight when you approach it along one of the forest-lined boulevards radiating from the palace.
   The palace now serves as a fairly decent museum devoted to two stars of the Czech National Revival: writer **Alois Jirásek** (1851-1930) and artist **Mikolaš Aleš** (1852-1913) – both of whom received their main inspiration from Czech myths. Even if you don't have an interest in these two men, then you still might appreciate the palace's wonderful stucco work and frescoes depicting Greek myths, or its exhibition on the Battle of White Mountain, which took place only a mile or so away. The palace is also a good excuse for getting out of the city and wandering around the

old hunting grounds, which makes for good biking in the summer and good cross-country skiing in the winter.

Villa Bertramka

From Anděl metro station, take tram #4, 7, or 9 one stop to Bertramka. The villa at Mozartova 169 is a quick walk from there; just follow the signs. The Mozart museum is open daily from 9:30 a.m. to 6 p.m.; Tel. 02/543 893. Tickets cost 50 Kč.

A lush oasis in the midst of the gritty, chimney-laden district of Smíchov, **Villa Bertramka** would probably have found itself under a factory if it hadn't several times lodged one **Wolfgang Amadeus Mozart**. The villa itself, a yellow country manor built in the 17th century, is no great shakes, but if you are a Mozart fan (like who isn't?), then you probably will get a thrill out of the little museum here.

Mozart became smitten with Prague when he first visited in 1787. He attended a performance of *The Marriage of Figaro* at the Estates Theater and heard at its conclusion a rapturous round of applause, prompting him to remark, "My Praguers understand me." Delighted with his success in Prague, he returned later that year and stayed with his friend and fellow composer František Dušek at Bertramka, where he completed the overture for *Don Giovanni* on the night before the opera's premier at the Estates Theater. In September 1791, Mozart again stayed at Bertramka, where he composed *La Clemenza di Tito* for the coronation of Leopold II as king of Bohemia. (Mozart completed the opera in a record-breaking 18 days.) Ill by the time he returned to Vienna, Mozart died December 5, 1791. Mozart was given a pauper's burial in Vienna. But in Prague, some 4,000 people showed up at Malá Strana's St. Nicholas Church to lament his death and hear a performance of his *Requiem Mass*. It would take another 50 years or so before Vienna would afford such an event in honor of the composer.

The little museum at Bertramka recounts Mozart's days in Prague, and pumps his music through the rooms as you take in some autographed compositions, old letters written from and about Prague, and an old hammer piano that he supposedly played. You can even set your eyes on a lock of his hair. When there, check out the schedule of concerts held at the villa, some of which are held outside on the lawn.

Zbraslav Monastery & Sculpture Museum

The village of Zbraslav is located ten kilometers (six miles) south of Prague, but still within the municipal boundaries. You can take a regular city bus there (#129, #241, #243, or #255 to Zbraslavské náměstí stop) from Smíchovské nádraží metro station. The convent's sculpture museum is open April through November, daily except Monday from 10 a.m. to 6 p.m. Tickets cost 20 Kč.

Not many tourists make it this far, but that doesn't mean it's not worth making the trek to this little village and its pretty **Zbraslav Monastery** on the banks of the Berounka River. In the 14th century, the Cistercians founded the monastery at the site of King Přemysl Otakar II's old hunting lodge. (For a time, the convent church served as a mausoleum for the last of the Přemysl line.) All but completely destroyed in the Hussite and Thirty Years' wars, the monastery was enlarged in the 18th century, receiving a colorful array of Baroque buildings that form a U-shape around a big grassy courtyard, today spotted with items from the National Gallery's collection of sculptures from the 19th and 20th centuries.

Though somewhat depleted since the opening of the National Gallery's branch at the Trade Fair Palace, the monastery is still the best place in the republic to view sculptures. All the Czech greats are well represented here, not least Josef Myslbek, who executed the statue of St. Wenceslas on Wenceslas Square. Ladislav Šaloun, sculptor of the Hus monument on Old Town Square, is also given pride of place, as is Otto Gutfreund, one of the first artists in Europe to embrace a Cubist style.

NIGHTLIFE & ENTERTAINMENT
Prague Pubs
If you haven't experienced a *hospoda* or *pivnice* (both meaning pub) in Prague, then you haven't experienced Prague culture. It's that simple. In a pub you can saddle up next to a lawyer, a janitor, a writer, a construction worker, or anyone else from the cross-section of Prague society and hear their stories, all the while enjoying a superb glass of beer. There's never any problem finding a pub, because they are in every neighborhood, virtually on every street.

Men always outnumber women in pubs, which isn't to say that pubs are male-exclusive. They aren't, whatsoever. Why more men than women go to the pub is an age-old question to be taken up in another book. But suffice it to say that, as a woman, you would probably get a few strange looks if you sat alone in a pub. If you sat down accompanied, no one would bat an eyelash (unless, of course, you and your company stand out as foreigners in an all-Czech pub).

If you happen to have a big aversion to cigarette smoke, then you probably won't be able to stand more than one beer in most Czech pubs, if that. Unfortunately, the only word of advice I can offer to people who detest the smell of smoke is: endure.

You can get a meal at most pubs around Prague, though some of them serve merely cheese and cold cuts. Pubs are usually open daily from the early morning (yeah, a lot of Czechs like a cold one for breakfast) and

IRISH PUBS IN PRAGUE

Prague has its fair share of the Irish, who seem to be doing nothing more these days than opening pubs in this city. All of the following Irish pubs serve a decent meal. Guinness is always on tap of course, as is one or two Czech beers.

***James Joyce Pub**, Liliová 10 (Staré Město). Near the Charles Bridge just of Karlova street. Overpriced and more American than Irish.*

***Molly Malone's**, U obecního dvora 4 (Staré Město). Tel. 02/231 6222. Between Pařížská street and the St. Agnes Convent. The best of the lot, Molly Malone's is a real cozy place, replete with fireplace, wood floors, and traditional folk melodies.*

***Scarlett O'Hara's**, Mostecká 21 (Malá Strana). Tel. 02/534 793. Near the Charles Bridge. Just about every Irish beer is served at this pub decked out with a lot of old Hollywood posters.*

close at 11 p.m. A half-liter mug in Prague can run you anywhere from 12 Kč in a regular neighborhood pub up to 60 Kč at a real touristy place like U Fleků (see below). If you see a pub with prices set this high, chances are that the only Czechs in the place will be the people serving beer.

Here are some well-known and not-so-well-known pubs in the historic center, listed by district. But, by all means, don't hesitate in trying a pub outside the center; there are, after all, thousands of them, many quite good.

Hradčany & Malá Strana

BARÁČNICKÁ RYCHTA, *Na tržiště 22. Just off Malostranské náměstí at the bottom of the castle steps.*

This tiny place, serving an excellent Pilsner Urquell, is just barely off the beaten path, which means it's a favorite with the locals.

U ČERNÉHO VOLA, (At the Black Bull), *Loretánské náměstí 1. Above the castle, kiddy corner to the Loreto.*

Big tables, frescoed walls, and a friendly local clientele make this a personal favorite. Excellent dark and light Velkopopovicky beer on tap.

U KOCOURA, (At the Tomcat), *Nerudova 2. Just off Malostranské náměstí.*

One of the few remaining historic pubs on a street that used to be lined with them, the vaulted U kocoura pours some of of the best Pilsner Urquell in Prague. The Beer Party bought the pub in 1992 to ensure its existence – thankfully so, or else there would probably be another crystal shop here instead.

U SCHNELLŮ, *Tomášská 2. Just off Malostranské náměstí.*
Having served the likes of Tsar Peter the Great and Archduke Ferdinand, U Schnellů has an illustrious history, to say the least. This is more of a restaurant than a pub, but I'd come just for the Pilsner Urquell.

Staré Město
U DVOU KOČEK (At the Two Cats), *Uhelný trh 10. Off the west end of Wenceslas Square.*
Serves up a mean Pilsner Urquell, but at night becomes a hangout for pimps and prostitutes who are on break. Best to go during the day.
KRUŠOVICKÁ PIVNICE, *Široka 20. Off Pařížská street near Old Town Square.*
This pub feels more like a German beer hall, attracting a lot out-of-towners. It's worth going for the velvety dark Krušovice, some of the best dark beer made in Bohemia.
U MEDVÍDKŮ (At the Little Bears), *Na Perštýně 7. Near Národní třída metro station.*
More a restaurant than a pub, U medvídků originated in the 14th century. Now it serves a creamy Budvar, drawing mostly tourists who will pay for their overpriced beer.
U VEJVODŮ, *Jilská 4. Close to Národní třída metro station.*
The vaulted ceilings provide the right atmosphere in which to enjoy Prague's own Staropramen beer.
U ZLATÉHO TYGRA (At the Golden Tiger), *Husova 17. Between Charles Bridge and Old Town Square.*
This is what Bohumil Hrabal, novelist and regular at U zlatého tygra, had to say about this pub in his book *I Served the King of England*: "This noisy inn is a little university, where people, inspired by the beer, relate stories and events which hurt the soul, while over their heads there rises the great question mark of absurdity and human existence in the form of cigarette smoke." If you're still wondering who this Hrabal guy is, he's the one in the picture shaking hands with President Clinton. The picture hangs above the very table where Clinton washed down his (reportedly) first beer as president, done so in 1994 with who else but Havel and Hrabal. Clinton couldn't have chosen a better beer (or a better pub) in which to break his abstinence. The Pilsner Urquell, stored in the pub's 13th century cellars and served here for more than 130 years, is probably the best in Prague. Unfortunately, chances are never any good that you'll find a seat. Try anyhow.

Nové Město
U FLEKŮ, *Křemencova 11. In the web of lanes west of Národní třída metro station; look for the big clock out front.*

You'd be hard pressed to find a single Czech among the 900 or so people U Fleků can accommodate in its several rooms and out in its pretty beer garden. It's Prague's most famous pub, and understandably so, because the caramelized Flek beer brewed and served here (and nowhere else) is sensational. The small brewery has been in operation since 1499, and since 1843 it has been malting a limited, daily ration of the luscious stuff that now draws Germans by the busloads. Last I checked, a beer here was 60 Kč – about five times the average price in Prague.

JÁMA (The Hollow), *V jámě 7. Just south of Wenceslas Square off Štěpánská street.*

Owned by a couple of enterprising Americans, this pub is plastered with rock posters, drawing a surprising number of Czechs (as well as a lot of Anglophobes). It's one of the few places in Prague pouring Regent, a fantastic beer from South Bohemia.

U KALICHA (At the Chalice), *Na bojišti 12. Five minute walk south of I.P. Pavlova metro station.*

At the beginning of *The Good Soldier Švejk,* Jaroslav Hašek's ribald novel set during World War I, a secret policeman arrests the dimwitted Švejk at this pub, kicking off Švejks' adventures in the war. Having been mentioned in what is perhaps the most famous novel written by a Czech, U kalicha milks it for all it's worth. If there ever were a tourist trap in Prague, this is it. It's so bad that you can actually have your picture taken to look as though you're being taken away by Imperial Guards – just as Švejk was in the novel.

Classical Music, Opera, & Ballet

With so many performances happening each day in Prague, the problem is not finding something to see; it's choosing something from the barrage of options. One way you might want to narrow down your choices is by deciding what venue appeals to you the most. Indeed, half the fun of a performance could be just sitting back in a plush chair and soaking in the sensational decor or stellar architecture of a theater. Or it could be the thrill of seeing a symphony or opera performance at the theater where that same symphony or opera premiered.

For instance, what better place to see one of the regularly-held productions of *Don Giovanni* than at the **Estates Theater**, the same theater in which Mozart first presented this opera back in 1787. Or what better place to see a Dvořák symphony or a Smetana opera than at the **National Theater** or at the **Rudolfinum**, two houses where both these composers debuted and conducted many of their works.

But if you are more concerned with the quality of the music, then you can't go wrong with the **Czech Philharmonic Orchestra** or with the **Suk Chamber Orchestra**, led by violinist **Josef Suk**. Considering Suk is the

GETTING TICKETS & INFORMATON

First, you need to know what's happening in Prague during the time of your stay. So, pick up a copy of the English-language weekly, The Prague Post, offering listings of musical performances, plays, and films presented around town. (You'll find a copy of the newspaper at any newsstand in the city center.) Another good source is the monthly Praha magazine, available at most tourist information offices and hotels.

Though most theaters and concert halls sell their own tickets, it sometimes saves time to drop by one of the many ticket outlets around the city center, many of which are conveniently located in tourist information offices. Most hotels also sell tickets. Here are some locations in the historic center where you can get tickets to just about anything, but bear in mind that tickets are often cheaper at venue box offices.

•Bohemian Ticket International, Václavské náměstí 27 (Wenceslas Square). Tel. 02/242 272 53. Second location: Na příkopě 16 (Staré Město); Tel. 02/242 150 31.

•Ticketpro, Salvátorska 10 (Staré Město) and on the web (www.ticketpro.cz). Tel. 02/248 140 20. Prague's largest computerized ticket service. You can reserve tickets on the web and pay when you arrive.

•Prague Tourist Center, Rytířská 12 (Staré Město). Tel. 02/242 122 09.

grandson of a famous violist and composer (whose name was also Josef Suk) and the great-grandson of **Antonín Dvořák**, you could rightly say Suk has music in his blood.

During his stay in Prague, my father remarked that you could come to this city and a have wonderful time doing nothing but going to classical performances. He may be right, considering the wealth of breathtaking venues in Prague that allow you to go concert-hopping. At all hours of the day and into the evening, you can hear small chamber pieces perform works by Bach, Vivaldi, Mozart, Beethoven, or Dvořák (among other great composers) at dozens of churches and palaces – fantastic for both sight and sound – around the historic center.

What makes these concerts at the churches and palaces so nice is that, first, you don't need to worry about wearing your best duds and, second, you don't need to spend an outrageous amount on tickets. There are more than enough teenagers hired to stand out in the tourist traffic and hand out flyers to these concerts, so you should have no problem finding out about when and where the performances are happening. As always, you can always refer to The Prague Post for a city-wide overview. Usually, tickets go on sale three hours before showtime at the entrance to the respective venues.

But if you are looking to do the evening up in style and soak in some opulence (which will cost you anywhere from 500 to 2,000 Kč for tickets), look for performances held at one of these illustrious theaters, all of which but the State Opera House are described in the section above entitled *Seeing the Sights*:

ESTATES THEATER (Stavovské divadlo), *Ovocný trh 6 (Staré Město).* Tel. 02/242 285 03. *Near Můstek metro station.*

Presents performances of classical music, operas, and ballets in a gorgeous, newly renovated setting. Plays are performed here as well, for which there is a simultaneous headphone translation.

NATIONAL THEATER (Národní divadlo), *Národní třída 2 (Nové Město).* Tel. 02/249 126 73. *Near Národní třída metro station.*

The cultural heart of the republic and the number one venue in Prague for concerts, operas, ballets, and plays.

RUDOLFINUM, *Náměstí Jana Palacha (Staré Město).* Tel. 02/248 933 52. *Near Staroměstská metro station.*

Home of the Czech Philharmonic Orchestra, this is another cultural landmark in Prague, presenting strictly classical concerts.

STATE OPERA HOUSE (Státní opera), *Wilsonova 4 (Nové Město).* Tel. 02/242 276 93. *Near Muzeum metro station.*

Symphonies and ballets are also held at this magnificent theater built by Prague's German community in the 19th century.

PRAGUE SPRING FESTIVAL

There's always some sort of music festival happening in Prague, but none is more prestigious than the **Prague Spring** *(Pražské jaro). It traditionally kicks off on May 12 (the anniversary of Bedřich Smetana's death) with a performance of Smetana's Má vlast (My Homeland) and wraps up on June 3 with a rendition of Beethoven's Ninth Symphony. Orchestras, chamber pieces, and soloists from all over the world perform at scores of theaters, churches, palaces, gardens, and courtyards around the city.*

It's becoming a huge event with foreigners, one you should reserve for up to five months in advance. To order and purchase tickets, contact **TIKETPRO a.s.,** *Salvátorská 10, 110 00 Praha 1, Czech Republic (Tel. 420/2/248 140 20, Fax 420/2/248 1021). For more information about the festival, contact* **MHF Pražské jaro,** *Hellichova 18, 118 00 Praha 1, Czech Republic (Tel. 420/2/573 204 68, Fax 420/2/536 040).*

ŽOFÍN, *Slovansky ostrov (island next to the National Theater)*.
Another illustrious house where both Berlioz and Liszt presented their works in the mid-19th century. This is more a big ballroom than a theater per se. Josef Suk and his orchestra often perform here.

Film
The Czechs have a long and respectable tradition of filmmaking, spawning the likes of Oscar-winning directors Miloš Foreman, Jiří Menzel, and Jan Svěrak (winner of the 1997 "Best Foreign Film" for *Kolya*). But, as is the case all over Europe, Prague is nowadays inundated with American movies, its cinemas screening only a scant number of domestic releases.

You can always tell how well an American film does at American box offices by how long it takes to arrive in Prague after its release in the United States. If a film does well in America, then it will take three to six months to show up in Prague. If it's a flop, then you can count on about a month.

Most of the American or British films shown in Prague are in English with Czech subtitles, but it's always best to play it safe than sorry and make sure the film is listed as having *české titulky* (Czech subtitles). There are about 30 cinemas (*kino*) in Prague, the nicest of them clustered on Wenceslas Square. Tickets run you about 70 Kč each, a bargain at around $2.50. As usual, pick up a copy of *The Prague Post*, providing a full line-up of that week's screenings, including information on times, places, directions, and whether a film is in English.

Though American productions dominate Prague screens, there are a fair number of Czech films that have recently wheedled their way in. Having recognized that Prague is chock-full of Americans and other Anglophones, Czech studios have actually began subtitling an occasional film or two in English. Look for them as having *anglické titulky* (English subtitles).

Praguers are crazy about all films, no matter how old they are. Indeed, it's easier in Prague to see an old American release on the big screen than it is in any American city. One good place to see old films is **Dlabačov film club** at *Bělohorská 24* (tram #22 to Malovanka stop), which has a nominal yearly membership fee you must pay in order to buy a ticket. *The Prague Post* has also gotten into the film club act, screening classic Czech films with English subtitles at *Bartlomějská 11* (metro to Národní třída station).

Theater
Theater in Prague has always played an essential role in maintaining and cultivating Czech culture and language, especially during the 400

years of Austrian rule. It makes sense then that several theaters in Prague would serve as nerve centers for the revolutionary events of November 1989, and that the Czechoslovak people would elect a playwright, **Václav Havel**, as their president.

Even though Czech audiences are big on American dramatists like **Arthur Miller, Sam Shepard**, and even **Woody Allen**, don't expect to find much available in English. But there are two English-language theater companies in Prague, **Misery Loves Company** and **Black Box Theater**. Their productions are held at **Divadle v Celetné**, *just off Old Town Square at Celetná 17, Tel. 02/248 127 62*. Again, check the listings in *The Prague Post*, which gives you a rundown of plays in English, plays with English supertitles, or plays with simultaneous headphone translations.

Two venues offering translations are:

DIVADLO MINOR, *Senovážné náměstí 28 (Nové Město). Tel. 02/242 574 84. Near Můstek metro station.*

THE ESTATES THEATER, *Ovocný trh 6 (Staré Město). Tel. 02/242 285 03. Near Můstek metro station.*

But if you happen to have a big interest in Czech theater, then look for these illustrious houses presenting plays in Czech only:

DIVADLO ABC, *Vodičkova 28 (Nové Město). Tel. 02/242 159 43. Near Můstek metro station.* This was an anti-fascist theater in the years preceding World War II. Havel got his start here in 1958.

DIVADLO NA ZÁBRADLÍ (Theater on the Ballustrade), *Anenské náměstí 5 (Staré Město). Tel. 02/242 219 33. Near the Charles Bridge.* Havel wrote his plays for this absurdist theater during the 1960s. Today, it also offers pantomime performances.

DIVADLO NA VINOHRADECH, *Náměstí Míru 7 (Vinohrady). Tel. 02/257 041. Near Náměstí Míru metro station.* Gorgeous neo-Renaissance theater where many notable directors and playwrights work.

Multimedia, Black Light, & Puppet Theater

Prague's multimedia theater incorporates dance, opera, music, and film. There are so many lights, sounds, and images that language hardly enters into the spectacle. Consequently, most people who go to these shows are tourists. The same goes for black light theater, which is a lot like multimedia, but uses more pantomime and even less words.

Puppetry has a been a wildly popular art form in Bohemia ever since troupes from England and the Netherlands introduced the idea to the Czechs in the 17th century. But for the hordes of puppet shops around the city, there's sadly only a couple of puppet theaters.

Expect to pay around 500 Kč for tickets at these theaters:

DIVADLO ZA BRANOU II, *Národní třída 40 (Nové Město). Tel. 02/ 242 296 04. Near Národní třída metro station.*

This multimedia theater is the former home of Laterna Magika (see below), offering the same sort of extravaganzas as its predecessor.

THE IMAGE THEATER, *Pařížská 4 (Staré Město). Tel. 02/232 9191. Just off Old Town Square.*

Black light theater geared towards tourists.

MAGIC THEATER OF THE BAROQUE WORLD (Zázračné divadlo barokního světa), *Celetná 13. Tel. 02/232 2536. Just off Old Town Square.*

Huge marionettes perform Baroque operas on beautifully-crafted stages.

NOVÁ SCÉNA, *Národní třída 4 (Nové Město); Tel. 02/249 141 29. Next to the National Theater.*

The new home of **Laterna Magika** (Magic Lantern), the original multimedia theater company in Prague.

NATIONAL MARIONETTE THEATER (Národní divadlo marionet), *Žatecká 1 (Staré Město). Tel. 02/232 3429. Near Staroměstská metro station.*

Mozart's *Don Giovanni*, brought to life with puppets, has been playing here for years now.

TA FANTASTIKA, *Karlovo náměstí 8 (Nové Město); Tel. 02/242 290 78.*

More black light theater.

Jazz

Ever since Louis Armstrong blew everyone away when he played here in the 1940s, Praguers haven't been able to get enough of jazz, even though the Communists all but banned it during their 40-year stint. Although Prague ain't quite on par with New Orleans or New York when it comes to jazz, it's still pretty good, and may just impress an aficionado or two.

One musician who is sure to impress is **Jiří Stivín**. The guy can play just about any wind instrument you put in his hands, and he is a great showman to boot. Don't miss him if he happens to playing while you're in Prague.

The love affair that Praguers have with this music makes it all the more unfortunate that jazz in Prague has become a tourist commodity, meaning most jazz clubs charge what tourists are willing to pay and not what the average Praguer is able to afford. But there are still a few reasonably priced venues charging between 40 and 60 Kč, where you can see the same musicians as in some of the more touristy, higher-priced joints that charge up to 150 Kč.

PRAGUE NIGHTLIFE

A lot of foreigners, especially young Americans, come to Prague and find themselves so overwhelmed by the nightlife that they see very little of the day-life. Yes, it's easy to wind up living a nocturnal life in all the bars, clubs, and discos at hand just about everywhere in the city. What makes things even more enticing is that prices of drinks and cover charges amount to peanuts compared to what you pay in the States.

But there are some things you should bear mind before you set out. Remember that the metro and the regular day trams stop running at midnight. So make sure that you can get home by night tram if you are not in walking distance of your hotel (for more on night trams, see "Getting Around Town"). There's never any problem finding a taxi at any hour of the night. But avoid hiring one from a stand outside a club or disco – places where the more dubious taxi drivers know they can easily wind up with a tipsy tourist who'll shell out whatever they are overcharging. If you must take a cab, then hail one off the street. Better yet, order one from AAA, Tel. 3399. Chances are much greater that you'll wind up with an honest driver.

As usual, consult The Prague Post's weekly calendar of events to see what's on.

Here are some of the clubs, touristy and not-so-touristy. Gigs get going at around 8 or 9 p.m.:

AGHA-RTA JAZZ CENTRUM, *Krakovská 5 (just off Wenceslas Square). Tel. 02/242 129 14. Closest to Muzeum metro station.*

This place draws a good number of foreigners who are in-the-know. It's hard to find a seat on most nights, however.

JAZZ CLUB U STARÉ PANÍ, *Michalská 9 (near Old Town Square). Tel. 02/242 300 71.*

This new club presents an impressive line-up of musicians, including the indomitable Milan Svoboda.

JAZZ CLUB ŽELEZNÁ, *Železná 16 (just off Old Town Square). Tel. 02/242 125 41.*

A cabaret-style club in a brick cellar. A great place, reasonably priced all around.

MALOSTRANSKÁ BESEDA, *Malostranské náměstí 21 (opposite St. Nicholas Church in Malá Strana). Tel. 02/539 024. Tram #12 or 22.*

This second-floor club presents a hodgepodge of bands, from rock to ska to jazz. Jiří Stivín plays here about once a month.

REDUTA JAZZ CLUB, *Národní třída 20 (Nové Město). Tel. 02/249 122 46. Metro to Národní třída metro station.*

This is the most famous jazz club in the city, with prices to match. Bill

Clinton hung out here with Václav Havel in 1994, tooting his obligatory version of *My Funny Valentine*. The club has been milking the occasion for all it's worth ever since.

Nightclubs & Discos

Prague, thank god, doesn't yet sport the kind of clubs and discos where people cue up around the corner on the off-chance that they won't be turned away by knuckleheaded bouncers. I'm sure that day will come, but for now what you have are a lot of cheesy discos playing either top-40 fluff or that pounding industrial-techno-rave whatever-you-call-it music that Europeans seem to be oh so fond of. Steer clear of discos on Wenceslas Square, unless you have the urge to hang out in meat markets where prostitutes make the rounds.

There are, however, a couple of places around town where you can boogie down in a fairly classy environment. Though doors open usually around 8 p.m., things don't get hopping until 11 or 12 and don't let up until the crack of dawn.

"A" KLUB, *Milíčova 32 (Smíchov). No phone. Tram 5, 9, or 26.*

Tastefully-furnished club decked out with the art work of female artists, catering mostly to lesbians. Fridays, women only, unless escorted by a man.

CORONA BAR, *Novotného lávka 9 (Staré Město). Tel. 02/210 822 08. Next to the Charles Bridge.*

Sip on some excellent sangria, munch on some tapas, and go mambo.

LÁVKA, *Novotného lávka 1 (Staré Město). Tel. 02/242 147 97. Next to Charles Bridge.*

Sit out on the terrace and have a romantic view of the Charles Bridge. The small dance floor is neon-lit, which makes everyone look like they have horses' teeth.

MUSIC PARK, *Francouzská 4 (Vinohrady). Near Náměstí Míru metro station.*

This place should be renamed Prostitute Park for all the ladies of the night who assemble here. Three or four bars, a lot of trippy lights on the dance floor, and head-pounding techno music make it a popular place.

U STŘELCE, *Karolíny Světlé 12 (Nové Město). No phone. Close to Národní třída metro station.*

Gay, lesbian, and straight club in a den-like hideaway, featuring a transvestite cabaret.

RADOST, *Bělehradská 120 (Vinohrady). Tel. 02/242 547 76. Near I.P. Pavlova metro station.*

As American ex-pat central, Radost is the trendiest place in town, attracting the beautiful people of Prague. The disco spins techno, funk,

and industrial. There's a pretty good restaurant and a funky café here as well (see *Where to Eat*). Open-mike poetry on Sunday night.
ROCK CAFÉ, *Národní třída 20 (Nové Město). Tel. 02/249 144 16. Around the corner from Národní třída metro station.*
Though it has two bars, a dance floor, and a stage where live rock acts perform a few times a week, Rock Café is not the most inspiring place to dance, mainly because they play so many classic rock tunes we've heard a thousand times before. Who in the world wants to dance to "Stairway to Heaven?"
ROXY, *Dlouhá 33 (Staré Město). Tel. 02/248 109 51. Three or four blocks off Old Town Square.*
The atmosphere here is straight-up cyberdelic, attracting the most innovative DJs in town.

Rock
When the president of the Czech Republic treats visiting rock stars such as **Lou Reed, The Rolling Stones,** or **Paul Simon** as if they were heads of state, then you should have some idea what rock music means to the post-revolution Czech Republic and what it meant to pre-revolution Czechoslovakia. Music made by the likes of **John Lennon, Frank Zappa,** and especially the **Velvet Underground** lent expression to generations of Czech dissidents, not least Havel himself.

This is how the president put it to Lou Reed in an interview published by *Musician* magazine: "Rock music, underground music, in particular one record by the Velvet Underground (*White Light/White Heat*), played a rather significant role in the development of democracy in our country. . . ." Nowadays, the Czech taste for Western music isn't so refined as back in the pre-Velvet Revolution days, something which American Top 40 has made damn sure of. But there is a thriving rock scene in Prague, supported by bands such as **Půlnoc** (an offshoot of the **Plastic People of the Universe**), **Garaž, Pražky Vybĕr,** and **Hudba Praha**. Try to catch any of these bands if you can.

You also might get a kick out of one of the many "revival" bands performing in Prague. Something akin to the "Legends" acts in Las Vegas, these revival groups don't just play cover songs of the bands they worship; they impersonate them as well. Just how well can a bunch of Czech guys can do the Cure, the Doors, or the Velvet Underground (just to name a few of the bands they impersonate)? I wouldn't know. I've never had a tad bit of interest. But I do hear they're "as close to the real thing that you can get."

Most of the following rock clubs double as discos, so they stay open until the crack of dawn. Gigs kick off at around 8 or 9 p.m. Cover charge is usually in the ballpark of 60 Kč if there is a band, 40 Kč if there isn't.

BELMONDO REVIVAL CLUB VLTAVSKÁ, *Bubenská 1 (Holešovice). Tel. 02/791 4854. Near Vltavská metro station.*

How can you say no to a club named after Jean-Paul Belmondo, the cult hero of French film? This is an enormous, cavernous place, drawing big names in Czech music.

BATTALION, *28. října 3 (Nové Město). Tel. 02/201 081 47. Near Můstek metro station.*

Upstairs is a lounge, serving cheap mugs of Pilsner Urquell. Downstairs is a smoky cave, where bands play mostly ska or punk.

KLUB ÚJEZD, *Újezd 18 (Malá Strana). Tel. 02/538 362. Tram #9, #12, or #22 to Újezd stop.*

Upstairs is a classy bar, in the cellar is a smoky pub, and in the middle is a small room with a tiny stage where punks bands thrash.

LUCERNA MUSIC BAR, *Vodičkova 36 (on Wenceslas Square). Tel. 02/ 242 171 08. Metro to Můstek station.*

In the basement of the grand ol' Lucerna Palace, this club is an intriguing place, serving up rock, blues, and reggae.

MALOSTRANSKÁ BESEDA, *Malostranské náměstí 21 (opposite St. Nicholas Church in Malá Strana). Tel. 02/539 024. Tram #12 or 22.*

The best all-around club in Prague. Jazz, funk, ska, blues, folk, and rock – they got it all, at about half the price as anywhere else in this city.

PALÁC AKROPOLIS, *Kubelíkova 27 (Žižkov). No phone. Closest to Jiřího z Poděbrad metro station.*

This was a cinema before František Skála, a well-known artist from Prague, gave it an sandstone-cave appearance and added some bizarre designs of mutant people and floating sperm. The best Czech bands are on the schedule, and once in a while you can catch a well-known alternative band from England or America. The decor next door at the Akropolis pub is equally outrageous, equally cool.

SPORTS & RECREATION

Praguers aren't exactly health nuts. A lot of them get all the exercise they need by lifting the beer mug from table to mouth. But they do love sports of all kinds, soccer and hockey topping the list.

Fitness Centers

Most of the big hotels in Prague have a fitness center of some sort, offering treadmills, lifecycles, weights, massages, and tanning beds (solariums, as they're known here.) One of the bigger and better fitness centers is at the **Hotel Inter-Continental** *at náměstí Curieovych 43 (west end of Pařížská street in Josefov).* As with most of the hotel fitness centers, you don't need to be a guest to use the equipment, but you will have to pay around 100 Kč an hour.

Here are some other fitness centers around town:

ERPET GOLF CENTER, *Strakonická 510 (Smíchov). Tel. 02/245 116 05. Metro to Smíchovské nádraží.*
This big golf center offers a wide array of modern fitness equipment and free weights, as well as a sauna and a whirlpool. Rates run 200 Kč an hour.

THE PYRAMID HOUSE OF RECREATION (Dům rekreace pyramida). *Tel. 311 3241. Tram #22 to Malovanka stop.*
An old trade-unionist hotel with a big fitness center and swimming pool.

SPORTOVNÍ AREÁL MASOPOL, *Libušská 320 (Libuš district). Tel. 02/619 117 86. Bus #113 or 171 from Kačerov metro station.*
A big sports complex, replete with swimming pool, weights, saunas, massage, and tennis courts.

Golf

Yep, Prague has a 9-hole, par-72 golf course. It's in the western suburb of Motol, behind the **Hotel Golf** *at Plzeňská 103. Tel. 02/644 3828.* Take tram #9 from Anděl metro station. You can rent golf clubs and carts there. Green fees are around 700 Kč. If you are looking for something nicer and a bit more challenging, then you may want make the excursion to the 18-hole golf course in **Karlštejn**.

At the **Erpet Gold Centrum,** *Strakonická 510 in Smíchov, near Smíchovské nádraží metro station. Tel. 02/245 116 05,* you can practice your strokes at its indoor driving range.

Horse Racing

Steeplechases and hurdles take place May through October at **Velká Chuchle**, a pretty racetrack on the southwestern outskirts of Prague. There's country music on the loudspeakers and plenty of cheap beer to keep you happy between the races. If you are feeling lucky, go ahead and place a bet on a horse.

Races are on Sunday, starting at 2 p.m. Take bus #172 or 453 from Smíchovské nádraží metro station to Velká Chuchle stop.

Ice Hockey

The Czech Republic has been known to produce some of the world's best hockey players, a good many going on to play in the NHL, not least one Jaromír Jágr, now with the Pittsburgh Penguins. Canadian friends of mine who are big hockey fans say that the level of play in Prague comes surprisingly close to that of NHL games.

The best team in Prague is **Sparta Praha**. You can see them play September through April at the **sportovní hala** (sports hall) *at the*

Výstaviště exhibition grounds in Holešovice (tram #12 one stop from Nádraží Holešovice metro station). Another big team to watch for is **Slavia Praha**, skating in the district of Vršovice (tram #4 or 22 from Náměstí Míru metro station to U Slavie stop).

Games usually take place on Tuesday and Friday nights, and sometimes Sunday afternoon. You can buy tickets, usually dirt cheap, at the stadium box office on the day of the game. Look to the sports page in *The Prague Post* for a weekly rundown of matches.

Jogging

If you would like to keep your regimen going while in Prague, then take to the parks where the air is cleaner, like Petřín Hill in Malá Strana, or Stromovka or Letná in Holešovice (see *Seeing the Sights*, above). Running on the streets is not a great idea; the traffic makes it a bit dangerous and the diesel-polluted air is not ideal for your lungs.

Soccer

Like most Europeans, the Czechs are fanatic about soccer. Their season runs from September to December, and from March to June. The top team in the country, **Sparta Praha**, battles it out at the **Sparta stadium** – *opposite Letná field in Holešovice (a five-minute walk from Hradčanská metro station)*. You can buy tickets at the stadium just before the games. Don't worry about tickets selling out, because it never happens.

Other big teams around Prague are **Slavia Praha**, **Bohemians**, and **Dukla Praha** (the army team). Slavia plays in the district of Vršovice *(tram #4 or #22 from Náměstí Míru station to U Slavie stop)*, as do the Bohemians *(same tram to Vršovice náměstí stop)*. Dukla plays further from the center in the district of Dejvice *(tram #20 or #25 from Dejvická metro station to the end of the line)*. Again, consult *The Prague Post* for game times.

Swimming

Plavecký stadión (Swimming Stadium), a huge complex just south of the city center in the district of Podolí, has an indoor pool and Olympic-size outdoor pool. *Take tram #3 from Karlovo náměstí metro station to Dvorce stop. You'll find it on the river embankment on Podolské nábřeží.* **Výstaviště** exhibition grounds in the district of Holešovice also has an indoor and outdoor pool. *Take tram #12 one stop from Nádraží Holešovice.* **Erpet Golf Centrum** (see *Golf*, above) also has two outdoor pools.

If you are willing to head to the northwest outskirts of town, you'll find a nice outdoor pool and a reservoir for swimming at **Divoká Šárka**, a large natural park with rugged cliffs, thick forests, and nice views. *Take tram #26 from Dejvická metro station to the end of the line.*

Tennis

Letná Park in Holešovice *(take tram #1 from Vltavská or Hradčanská metro to Letenské náměstí stop)* has nice public outdoor clay courts opposite the National Technical Museum. **Tenis aréal Strahov**, in Strahov *(take Bus #149 or #217 from Dejvická metro station to Koleje Strahov stop)* has more public outdoor courts. And, if you want to play at a prestigious club with clay courts where the Škoda Czech Open is held in May, head to **TJ Slavoj Praha** in Ostrov Štvanice, the island between northern Nové Město and Holešovice. *Tel. 02/231 1270. Metro to Vltavská station.*

SHOPPING

What to buy in Prague? The obvious choice is crystal and glass, something which Bohemia is notorious for. Consequently, you can hardly turn a corner in the historic center without running into a crystal and glass shop. Just as pervasive are wooden toy and puppet shops, which are always fun to browse and play in. Less obvious things to buy in Prague, but generally superb nonetheless, are antiques and ceramics.

The big shopping districts are in the thick of the real touristy areas, especially along the **Royal Way** in Staré Město and Malá Strana. You can also find just about anything that's available in Prague on **Wenceslas Square** and on the adjoining **Na příkopě** street.

It usually pays off to do a little comparison shopping before you open the wallet. This is especially true when it comes to buying crystal and glass. Like I said, crystal shops are everywhere, so you'll never have a problem finding enough places in which to compare prices.

Here are some places where you can begin your spree, listed by what they sell. Most of the individual shops listed below will package and mail your purchase home.

Antiques *(anticky)*
• **Antique**, three locations: *Václavské náměstí 17 (Wenceslas Square). Tel. 02/ 240 091 66. Křížovnická 1 (Staré Město). Tel. 02/231 1625. Karlova 8 (Staré Město). No Tel.*
• **Art Décoratif**, *Obecního domu (Staré Město). Tel. 02/220 023 50. In the Municipal House at náměstí Republiky.*
• **Art et Decorations**, *Pařížská 21. Tel. 02/232 4587. Just off Old Town Square.*
• **U Keplera**, *Karlova 4 (Staré Město). Tel. 02/242 282 07. Near Charles Bridge.*

Ceramics *(keramika)*
• **Galerie U sv. Jiljí**, *Husova 8 (Staré Město). no Tel. Near Old Town Square.*
• **Keramika**, *Karlova 26 (Staré Město). no Tel. Near Charles Bridge.*
• **Lidová Řemesla**, *Melatrichova 17 (Staré Město). Tel. 02/216 324 11. Off Old Town Square.*

Crystal & Glass (*krystal, sklo*)
Like I said before, you won't have any problem finding crystal shops in the historic center of Prague. But here are few to get you started:
• **Bijouterie Czech Crystal,** *Jilská 24 (Staré Město). Tel. 02/266 933. Near Old Town Square.*
• **Lord Crystal,** *Husova 8 (Staré Město). No Tel. Near Charles Bridge.*
• **Kerpet,** *Staroměstké náměstí 27 (Old Town Square). Tel. 02/242 297 55.* Offers a big selection of porcelain as well.
• **Moser,** *Na příkopě 12. Tel. 02/242 112 93. Near west end of Wenceslas Square.* The biggest of the lot, Moser also sells porcelain and silver-plated goods.

Department Stores (*obchodní dům*)
All of the following stores, except for Baťa, have good supermarkets (*potraviny*) in their basements, in addition to all the typical things you'd find in a department store.
• **Baťa,** *Václavské náměstí 6 (Wenceslas Square).* Besides the great selection of very reasonably priced shoes, Baťa sells a lot of other goods, such as clothes, cosmetics, and luggage. There's a Gap store on its top floor.
• **Tesco (Máj),** *Národní třída 26 (Nové Město). Metro to Národní třída station.*
• **Kotva,** *náměstí Republiky 8 (Staré Město). Closed Sundays. Metro to Náměstí Republiky station.* The biggest of them all.
• **Krone,** *corner of Wenceslas Square and Jindřišská (Nové Město).*

English Language Bookstores
There are scores of bookshops (*knihkupectví*) on **Wenceslas Square** and on **Na příkopě** street (extending from the west end of Wenceslas Square) that sell maps of all sorts. They also offer books in English, which are usually either coffee-table books or Czech novels translated into English. For a much wider selection of English titles, check out these two bookstores, both of which have very nice cafés.
• **The Globe,** *Janovského 14 (Holešovice). Tel. 02/667 126 10. Metro to Vltavská station. (See the section on Where to Eat.)* This American ex-pat center has a good selection of magazines and a big supply of Central and East European books translated into English. You can trade and buy used books here as well.
• **U knihomola,** *Mánesova (Vinohrady). Tel. 02/627 7767. Metro to Jiřího z Poděbrad.* In addition to its excellent selection of new titles from abroad, this international bookstore offers a wide array of unique coffee-table books.

Fashion
As you can imagine, Prague isn't exactly the center of the world when it comes to fashion. But there are a fair number of swank shops where you can find the latest in European and American designs. Look for them on the streets radiating from Old Town Square, especially along **Pařížská** and **Celetná** streets. **Wenceslas Square** and **Na můstku** street (which extends from the west end of Wenceslas Square) are also good places to explore.

If you're real serious about doing some clothes shopping, then head to the **Vinohradská tržnice**, the closest thing to a mall in Prague, located east of Wenceslas Square *at Vinohradská 50*. But don't expect to find much there if you are on a budget.

Open Markets
In the first three or four years following the end of Communism, all of Prague appeared to be one giant open market. Free-market capitalism isn't so rampant these days, but you can still find a concentration of outdoor vendors at just about any pedestrian square in the city. The biggest and most enjoyable one is the **Havelská trh**, *located between Wenceslas and Old Town squares along Na můstku street.* Here you'll find one of the city's best selection of fruits and vegetables, as well as a number of souvenir items, including puppets and wooden toys.

Puppets (*loutka*)
You hardly need a guidebook to tell you where to find puppets (or marionettes) in Prague. Just keep your eyes open when you walk from Old Town Square to the Charles Bridge or when you walk down from the Prague Castle along Nerudova street. But the shop with the biggest selection of puppets I've seen is away from these areas. It's called **Fantazie Kuběnova**, and it's located between Wenceslas and Old Town squares *at Rytířská 19, Tel. 02/264 130*. It has a second, smaller location at *Karlova 10, near the Charles Bridge in Staré Město.*

Wooden Toys (*dřevěné hračky*)
Again, Prague has no shortage of shops selling the ingenious wooden toys made in Bohemia. The biggest shop I've seen is the **Česky Národní Podnik** cooperative at *Karlova 26, near the Charles Bridge in Staré Město.* But the prices are better at **Havelská trh** (see *Open Markets*, above).

EXCURSIONS & DAY TRIPS AROUND CENTRAL BOHEMIA

Is Prague's diesel-infused air starting to wear on you? Is the fast pace of the city bending your nerves a little? If so, then don't hesitate to get out of the city for a day, because there's some wonderful things to be seen that will bring you back in much better spirits.

If you've been to the outskirts of Prague and seen the legions of concrete housing estates encircling the city, then it's hard to imagine that an idyllic countryside awaits beyond the city limits. But you can go ahead and put your doubts to rest, because the rest of Central Bohemia harbors little of the tasteless development Prague's suburbs experienced under Communism. What it does harbor are thick forests, grassy plains, weaving river valleys, and a sprinkling of some of the republic's most beautiful castles, such as **Karlštejn**, **Křivoklát**, and **Konopiště**.

Another pleasant surprise that Central Bohemia offers is **Kutná Hora**, featuring one of the republic's most sensational cathedrals. Kutná Hora is a bit of a haul from Prague, so I've mentioned a couple of hotels you should be comfortable staying at if you choose to spend the night (which I heartily recommend).

Most of the following destinations are easily accessible by public transportation. But if you are short on time or would like someone else to do the navigating, then look into the bus tours offered by the agencies listed at the beginning of this chapter under *Getting Around Town*. Čedok has the biggest range of them, with tours going to Česky Sternberk, Konopiště, Karlštejn, and Kutná Hora.

The nice thing about these tours is that some of them visit several castles and towns in one day. But, be fair-warned that they are pricey, usually in the ballpark of 1,000 Kč. When you compare that to the 22 Kč-train ticket to Karlštejn or the 26 Kč-train ticket to Konopiště, then these bus tours make little sense unless you are truly pressed for time.

Sázava Monastery

Set above the lazy Sázava River, the **Sázava Monastery** (Sázavsky klášter) was founded in the 11th century by Prince Oldřich as the Bohemian center for Orthodox Christianity. Later, the monks began building a huge Gothic church here, but they were kicked out of Bohemia before they had a chance to finish it. Though the original sandstone nave of the church is still intact, the rest of the monastery was harshly rebuilt in the Baroque style, and eventually transformed into a chateau in the 19th century. But there are some other traces of the monastery's Gothic origins worth checking out, such as the chapter hall, where some faded 13th-century frescoes hang on for dear life.

The tours of the monastery take you through a number of uninspiring Rococo rooms with exhibits on archaeological research and on the Old Church Slavonic that the monks employed at the monastery. Be sure to pick up an English text, or you won't get much out of the strictly Czech tours. *The monastery is open daily May through August except Monday from 8 a.m. to 5 p.m. and on weekends only in April and September from 9 a.m. to 4 p.m.* The monastery is 55 kilometers (34 miles) southeast of Prague, but difficult to get to by public transportation. By car, take E65 towards Brno and get off at the Sázava exit. Otherwise, go by by train from Prague's Hlavní nádraží to Čerčany (on the line going to Benešov), where you must take another train to the station of Sázava Černé Budy. The monastery is a 15 minute walk from there. If you don't have to wait long for the connection at Čerčany, then the trip from Prague to the monastery should take roughly an hour-and-a-half, costing about 31 Kč.

Český Šternberk

The best thing going for this castle 60 kilometers (40 miles) southeast of Prague and a stretch of the river down from the Sázava Monastery are its sweeping views of the Sázava River valley. The fortress itself, commanding a stellar position on top of a sheer cliff, is truly something to behold as well. Other than that, there's not a whole lot going for this castle, owned throughout the centuries by the aristocratic Šternberk family.

Besides the Gothic fortifications, there's little to attest for its 13th-century origins, as most of it received a harsh Baroque facelift in the 17th and 18th centuries. But I would recommend going to the castle anyway, if only for the stunning approach to the castle through the steep and winding Sázava valley, densely packed with fir trees and punctuated with limestone crags. But if you are pressed for time and don't have your own wheels, then don't bother with the two-hour train ride from Prague.

The castle is open May through September daily except Monday from 9 a.m. to 5 p.m., and in April and October on weekends only from 9 a.m. to 4 p.m. By car, head southeast on E65 towards Brno and exit at Český Šternberk. Take the same trains as to the Sázava Monastery (see above), but continue on to the Český Šternberk *zástávka* (a stop after Český Šternberk station), which is 30 minutes down the line from Sázava Černé Budy station.

Konopiště

To say that the last owner of Konopiště Castle, Archduke Franz Ferdinand, had an obsession with hunting would be an understatement; a mania would be closer to the truth. Case in point are the 9,000 sets of antlers and other trophies hanging on the walls of this neo-Gothic castle founded in the 13th century. If the hordes of antlers don't turn your stomach, then perhaps the stuffed crocodile, fruit bowls made of elephant toes, or the drink table made of an elephant's leg will.

Yes, old Franz felt quite at home among heads, hooves, teeth, and other animal body parts, which is perhaps why he seemingly did nothing else but hunt. He supposedly averaged 22 kills a day, bringing up a grand total of 300,000 animals he did away with before a Sarajevo assassin did away with him and his wife in 1914.

There are three different tours of the castle (explained at the ticket office) in which you can view the Archduke's odd assortment of Chinese vases, Meissen porcelain, Italian cabinets, and, of course, weapons. But it's difficult to even pay attention to the genteel items with all the taxidermist work abounding in just about every room.

For my money, I'd skip the tours altogether and go for a stroll through the 220 hectares (543 acres) of lush grounds, dotted with pretty lakes, a sensational rose garden, and a number of statues. You might even see a deer or two that has learned that it's now safe to venture into the park.

The castle is open daily May through August from 9 a.m. to 6 p.m., in September until 5 p.m., and in October and November until 3 p.m.

Tickets for a tour in English costs around 70 Kč, in Czech 20 Kč. Konopiště lies 40 kilometers (25 miles) south of Prague. To get there by car, take highway 603 to E55 and then take the exit to Benešov. Signs then point the way to Konopiště. Otherwise, the best way is by train from Prague's Hlavní nádraží to Benešov u Prahy, from where it's a two kilometer walk to the castle. Trains run about every hour for the hour-long trip that costs 26 Kč.

Karlštejn

After the Prague Castle, **Karlštejn** is the most-visited castle in the Czech Republic, mainly because of its close proximity to where all the tourists are – in Prague, of course. Granted, the castle is quite breathtaking when you first lay eyes on it. But when you begin walking through town and pass by the gauntlet of tour buses, souvenir shops, and currency exchange outlets on your way up to the castle, then you can't help but feel as if the village of Karlštejn and its castle have lost a great deal of its authenticity. If you've been in Prague for any amount of time, then you perhaps are numb to these forces of manic tourism. But the idea is to get out of Prague, right?

If you are still intent on going, then try to make it there early in the morning, before the tour buses show up and the guided castle tours sell out, which they do quite often during the high season.

What makes the sight of this cliff-top castle so breathtaking is its staggering height. Seen from the village it hovers above, it appears completely impregnable, which is probably why King Charles IV chose it as the treasury for the imperial crown jewels after having commissioned Matthias of Arras to build it 1438. In addition to stowing away the jewels here, Charles IV used the castle as a secret retreat from the pressures of Prague, never allowing even his wives to accompany him there.

From the outside, the castle looks remarkably well intact, with kudos given to the all-out restoration it received in the 19th century. But the inside is a letdown after the exhaustive climb up to the box office in the main courtyard. Tours take you through a number of palatial rooms, which have only the barest of furnishings and a couple of tepid exhibits on the restoration work. But the gorgeous views from the windows, taking in the surrounding green hills, are almost worth the price of admission.

Things do get a bit more interesting in the **Marian Tower** (Marianská věž), where you can set your sights on Charles' private quarters and on the tiny **Church of Our Lady** (Kostel Panny Marie). Charles locked himself away in the tower during his retreats to Karlštejn, taking only the most urgent of messages through a little peep hole that the guide will point out to you.

Unfortunately, the best part of the castle hasn't been open to the public for years now. I'm speaking, of course, about the **Chapel of the Holy Rood** (Kaple sv. Kříže), located in the upper reaches of the Great Tower. With its gilt walls, 2,000 or so semi-precious stones, and frescoes by Master Theodoric (the most accomplished Bohemian painter of the day), the chapel is one big jewelry box. The imperial crown jewels were in safekeeping here until the 15th century, but now reside in St. Vitus Cathedral.

Tours last about thirty minutes and run every 20 minutes or so, but not always in English. If you want to join an English tour, you'll have to pay 100 Kč, as compared to 30 Kč for a tour in Czech. *The castle is open daily except Monday – from 9 a.m. to 6 p.m. in May and June, until 7 p.m. in July and August, until 5 p.m. in April and October, and until 4 p.m. the rest of the year.*

But there's more to do in the village of Karlštejn than just see the castle. There's an 18-hole, par-72 **golf course** that opened in 1994. It's a beautiful course, set along the banks of the Berounka River and offering a number of perspectives of the castle. Green fees are 1,200 Kč Monday through Thursday, 1400 Kč Friday through Sunday. If you didn't bring your golf clubs, you can rent them here. For more information or to reserve a tee time (which you should do at least a week in advance), *call 0311/947 16.*

Karlštejn is 28 kilometers (17 miles) southwest of Prague. If you go by car, take E50 and exit at the sign for Karlštejn. Otherwise, go by train from Prague's Smíchovské nádraží. Trains depart every half-hour for the 30-minute ride. Tickets cost 22 Kč.

Křivoklát

When you go by train, the first sight of **Křivoklát Castle** (30 miles west of Prague) hits you as you come out of a pitch-dark tunnel, providing a fairly dramatic introduction to this formidable castle hidden around a bend in the Berounka River valley. Though not as immediately appealing as Karlštejn, Křivoklát holds its own special intrigue, without the crowds of Karlštejn to go along with it.

The castle dates back to the 13th century, when the Bohemian royalty used it as a hunting lodge. But it got its present Gothic appearance in the 15th century, when Vladislav II had it turned into a jail for political prisoners. (One of these prisoner was Edward Kelley, the infamous Irish alchemist under Rudolf II who jumped to his death from the castle tower in an attempt to escape.)

Having passed through various noble families since then, the castle is remarkably well-preserved, especially when you consider that it still has fragments of the old hunting lodge from the time of King Přemysl Otakar II and has one of the few late-Gothic chapels in the Czech Republic to have never been altered. With its meticulous wood carvings and murals of angels bearing instruments of torture, the chapel is indeed one of the highlights of the tour, as is the enormous King's Hall, counted as the second biggest secular Gothic hall in Bohemia, after Vladislav Hall in the Prague Castle.

The castle is open daily except Monday from 9 a.m. to 5 p.m. June through August, 9 a.m. to 4 p.m. in May and September, and from 9 a.m. to 3 p.m. October through December. Closed from January 1 to April 31.

One of the nicest things about Křivoklát is getting there by the slow train that chugs its way through the heavily-wooded narrows of the Berounka River valley. Hop on one of the trains departing every half hour from Prague's Smíckovské nádraží to Beroun, and then change to another train going in the direction of Rakovník. The ticket from Prague to Křivoklát is 38 Kč. You should have no problem getting there in under an hour and a half. Because the train from Prague to Beroun stops in Karlštejn, it's feasible (and recommended) to hit Karlštejn Castle and Křivoklát both in one day. By car, head due west out of Prague on the E50 motorway, exit at Lány, and then follow signs to Křivoklát.

Kutná Hora

Located 65 kilometers (40 miles) east of Prague, **Kutná Hora** comes as quite a revelation to those who thought that Prague has always had the monopoly on beauty, power, and culture in the region. For about two centuries, Kutná Hora was the second most important city after Prague, and was well on its way to rivaling the capital in terms of beauty. Though it can no longer live up to its glorious past, Kutná Hora is still one of the most beautiful towns in Bohemia, and is certainly the most rewarding excursion you could make from Prague. With all its beauty and tranquility, you may even want to consider staying the night (which is why I've listed a couple of hotels and restaurants).

The story of Kutná Hora goes something like that of a boomtown in the American West, except that Kutná Hora's boom began in 1260, the year silver deposits were discovered in the area. The discovery prompted people from all over the kingdom to make a dash for the site, where a makeshift town was thrown up to serve the needs of the miners. In 1308, King Wenceslas (Václav) II brought in a group of Italian minters and established the Royal Mint near the mines, suddenly turning this shanty town into a center of Bohemian power. Ambitious town planning ensued, and construction on one of Central Europe's grandest cathedrals was begun, all of which enticed King Wenceslas IV to move the royal residence here in 1400. By that time, Kutná Hora had become one of Europe's richest and biggest towns, pumping out a third of all silver mined in Europe and minting the most valuable currency in Central Europe (called the *groschen*).

But, by the mid-16th century, the mines had reached a depth of 600 meters, which made it no longer possible to extract the silver in such profitable amounts as before. Whatever was dug up in Kutná Hora didn't amount to much anyway, as compared to the bountiful amounts of silver that was being shipped in from the New World at that time. The last draw came when the Thirty Years' War rolled around, wiping out the mining operations and bringing to a close Kutná Hora's days of power and importance.

But vestiges of Kutná Hora's heyday still remain, most notably in the form of **St. Barbara's Cathedral** and the **Italian Court**. There's also the ghoulish **All Saints' Chapel** in the suburb of Sedlec, filled with hundreds of thousands of human bones arranged into decorative patterns. It's almost too hard to believe, but Kutná Hora is relatively free of crowds, which makes it all the more enjoyable for a visit.

Kutná Hora's historic center sits above the **Vrchlice River**. Like any great medieval town, Kutná Hora has a maze of lanes and alleys that are fun to get lost in. But you won't be lost for long in the small historic center, because there are signs at just about every corner pointing you in the direction of the major attractions around town.

Arrivals & Departures

In Prague, there are a couple of buses departing each morning from Želivského metro station and a few in the afternoon from Florenc station. For exact times, contact the Prague Information Service (see Practical

Information in the *Prague* chapter), or call ČAD. The trip takes about an hour and a half and a one-way ticket costs 35 Kč. The bus station in Kutná Hora is a 5 minute walk north of the center.

By car from Prague, take highway 12 all the way there. It takes about an hour to get there. A slower, but more scenic route is along highway 333. Parking is no problem in and around town.

A train departs Prague's Hlavní nádraží (main station) each morning at 9:13 for Brno, stopping at Kutná Hora's Hlavní nádraží along the way. The ride takes a little more than an hour and costs 32 Kč. From the main train station in Kutná Hora, which for some reason is in the suburb of Sedlec, it's a good 20 minute walk west to the center of town. (Turn right as you come out the station, take your first left, and then go straight on for about a mile.) Alternatively, you could wait for a regional ČAD bus that goes roughly every hour from the front of the train station to the bus station (which is the closest you'll get to the center). Pay the driver when you get on board.

Getting Around Town

In and around the historic center, your only option is to go by foot. These places might come in handy if you're interested in taking a tour or going to spend some time around town:
•**Culture and Information Center** (two offices), *Palackého náměstí and Havličkovo náměstí (inside the Italian Court). Tel. 0327/512 378.* Sells booklets, arranges tours of the town, and can help with bus and train schedules.
•**Komerční banka**, *Tylova 9.* Place to change money.

Where to Stay

HOTEL U VLAŠSKÉHO DVORA, *28. října 511, 284 01 Kutná Hora. Tel. 0327/514 618, Fax 0327/4627. Rates for single and double: 990-1,290 Kč. Credit cards: MC, V. 8 rooms. Restaurant.*

This small, new hotel just off the main square (Palackého náměstí) should definitely be your first choice of accommodations in Kutná Hora. The cozy, generous-sized rooms are simply but smartly decorated with attractive wood furniture and slanted ceilings and outfitted with satellite television and direct dial telephones. Service is quite friendly and does speak some English. In addition to the very good restaurant (see below), the hotel has a sunny café and an intriguing cellar wine bar.

HOTEL MĚDÍNEK, *Palackého náměstí 316, 284 01 Kutná Hora. Tel. 0327/2741, Fax 0327/2743. Rates for single/double: 800/1,300. Credit cards: AE, MC, V. 50 rooms. Restaurant.*

Right on the main square, this hotel doesn't cut it when it comes to providing comfortable lodging. Rooms are minuscule, furniture is outdated, and the carpets look as though they should have been replaced 10 years ago. The restaurant, serving uninspiring Czech food, is nothing special either.

HOTEL U HRNČÍŘE, *Barborská 24, 284 01 Kutná Hora. Tel. 0327/2113, no fax. Rates for single and double: 800 Kč. Credit cards: MC, V. 14 rooms. Restaurant.*

By the small appearance of this cute hotel in the center of town, you can hardly believe that it has as many as 14 rooms. What comes as a bigger surprise is that the rooms are not cramped (though not huge either). Though the furnishings and decor could definitely use some updating, the rooms do suffice if you plan on just staying the night. The hotel does have a decent restaurant with a pleasant summer terrace.

Where to Eat
HOTEL U VLAŠSKÉHO DVORA, *28. října 511. Tel. 0327/514 618, Fax 0327/4627. 150-200 Kč.*

Not only does this hotel have the best rooms in town, but also the best restaurant. Checkerboard floors and big bay windows make for a nice decor in which to feast on nicely prepared steaks, game dishes, or chicken livers. Service is quick, deft, and usually multilingual.

RESTAURANT U GROŠE, *Kollárova 313. Tel. 0327/75330. 100-200 Kč. No credit cards.*

Downstairs is a very nice pub with vaulted ceilings and three beers on tap, and upstairs is the restaurant, its bowtie-clad waiters serving up solid Czech dishes.

PIZZA NAVONA, *Palackého náměstí 90. 75-150 Kč. No credit cards.*

If you're fed up with Czech food, then have one of the decent, thin-crust pizzas baked here. But I'd stay away from the pasta dishes. The restaurant has a nice outdoor deck on the main square, which just may be the place for a midday coffee or beer.

Seeing the Sights

Your introduction to the illustrious history of Kutná Hora begins at **Vlašsky dvůr** (the Italian Court), *located just west of Palackého náměstí (square) on Havlíčkovo náměstí.* Originating as Wenceslas II's royal seat, the court went on to become Bohemia's one and only mint, run by a team of Italian craftsmen (hence the name). As if he needed to actually sit on top of the kingdom's money source, Wenceslas IV later had his royal palace built above the workshops where the minters were pounding out the Prague groschen, for its time the most valuable currency in Central Europe. When the mint ceased to exist in the early 18th century, the building was converted into the town hall, which it still is to this day.

Unfortunately, there's not a whole lot to attest for the Italian Court's original appearance, thanks to a heavy-handed 19th century restoration. The 25-minute tour of the Italian Court kicks off in the treasury, where you can view some samples of the old coins minted here, including the Hapsburg *tolar* – from which we get the name, dollar. The tour then moves up to Wenceslas IV's Audience Hall, decorated with murals depicting two crucial events in Czech history: the election of Vladislav II Jagiello as King of Bohemia in 1471, and the famous meeting between Jan Hus and Wenceslas IV in which Czechs were given administrative power at Charles University.

The tour ends in the Chapel of St. Wenceslas and St. Ladislav, which is mostly a reconstruction of the chapel that was built here in 1386. The only thing that remains from the original chapel is the oriel window, but that's overshadowed by the gorgeous Art Nouveau wall paintings and stained-glass windows. *Guided tours of the Italian Court run on demand Tuesday through Sunday from 9 a.m. to 5 p.m. Tickets cost 40 Kč for a tour in English.*

Just behind the Italian Court, the **Church of St. James** (Kostel sv. Jakuba) is the town's oldest church, dating back to 1420. It sits at the edge of a slope just above the abandoned mines, which has caused the church tower to lean a bit. Unfortunately, the church is only open during services.

From the church, head up the pretty Ruthardská lane to **Hrádek** (the "Little Castle"). Originally conceived as a fortress, Hrádek was taken over in 1490 by the administrator of the royal mines, Jan Smíšek. He transformed the little castle into a regal palace with funds he procured by doing some illegal silver mining from just below the building. These days Hrádek houses the **Museum of Mining History**, with a fairly good exhibit on the tools and equipment used by miners during the Middle Ages. But the best part comes when you don a miner's white coat and helmet and step down into some of Smíšek's old mines. *The museum is open daily except Monday from 9 a.m. to 5 p.m.*

Up the hill, a short promenade lined with gesticulating saints provides a dramatic approach to what is arguably the most beautiful Gothic church in Central Europe – **St. Barbara's Cathedral** (Kostel sv. Barbora). Financed by the miners of Kutná Hora and dedicated to the patron saint of mining, the cathedral was originally designed by John Parleř, who was appropriately-enough the son of Petr Parleř, architect of the St. Vitus Cathedral in Prague. Work was begun on the cathedral in 1380, but was put off when the Hussite Wars broke out and again when the town had depleted its supply of silver and simply didn't have the money to complete it. So, it wasn't until 1905 that the finishing touches were put on St. Barbara's.

Holding a precipitous position at the top of the Vrchlice River valley, the cathedral rises up along a series of spiky flying buttresses, supporting three tent-like domes that pierce the air with their needle-thin spires. Inside, the gravity of the exterior gives way to an interior infused with a brilliant light that pours in through the clear, arched windows of the central nave and through the Art Nouveau stained glass. The Gothic brilliance of the cathedral hits home when you peer up at the ribbed ceiling vaults, woven into shapes of flowers, petals, and stars and stamped with the coats of arms of miners' guilds and local nobility.

Surrounding and leading up to the main altar are eight ambulatory chapels smothered in frescoes depicting, among other things, the miners and minters of Kutná Hora at work. The details of this cathedral go on forever, and you could happily spend a couple hours inspecting every last bit of beauty, which you can do *daily except Monday from 8 a.m. to 5 p.m. Admission costs 30 Kč.*

With St. Barbara's Cathedral situated next to it, it's easy to pass by the **Jesuit College** without giving it much thought. The hulking Baroque pile, which looks more like a severe chateau than a school, has a floorplan in the shape of an "F," designed that way in honor of Emperor Ferdinand II.

From the rear of the cathedral, climb up the steps to Na valech street and hang a right. A short ways up is a terrace pub where you can drink a glass of the local beer while taking in a fine view of the cathedral. Afterwards, continue along Na valech and then take a right on Husova street down to the Gothic **Stone Fountain** (Kamenná kašna), which looks more like a mini-fortress than a place to store water. Further down Husova and then up Lierova street, you'll run into the sculptured facade of the **Stone House** (Kamenny dům), one of the few remaining Gothic houses in Kutná Hora. It houses the good **Museum of Arts and Crafts**, with exhibits stressing locally-crafted silverware. *It's open Tuesday through Sunday from 9 a.m. to 5 p.m.*

Before calling it a day in Kutná Hora, you should make the slight excursion to the suburb of **Sedlec**, which is where Kutná Hora's main train station is located. Buses run to Sedlec from the main bus station about every hour. (You can get exact times from the Cultural and Information Center on Palackého náměstí.) Or you can take the 20 minute walk there along Na Náměti street. (Just follow the signs to the train station from the center.)

Along the main road in Sedlec is the **Church of Ascension of the Virgin** (Kostel Nanebevzetí Panny Marie), part of the former Cistercian monastery that was founded here in 1142. The church, originally built in a French Gothic style, was given a Baroque restoration by Giovanni Santini, whose forté was marrying the Gothic with the Baroque. Unfortunately, the church is under renovation for the next century or so, so you'll have to content yourself with admiring the elongated, T-shaped exterior fronted by a pretty Gothic window. Just so you know: the rest of the defunct monastery currently houses the Tabac tobacco factory, previously state-controlled but now owned by Philip Morris.

Somewhat apropos of a suburb with a huge tobacco factory, Sedlec's main attraction is the **All Saints' Chapel** (Kaple Všech Svatých), its interior decorated with the bones of some 40,000 dead people. In the 13th century, a monk brought back a handful of holy dirt from Golgotha and scattered it over the Sedlec Monastery's graveyard, after which it became a favored final resting spot of Central European nobility. With all the wars and plague epidemics striking this part of Europe, it didn't take long for bones to start piling up at the graveyard. In 1870, the church authorities commissioned František Rint, a local wood carver, to do something with all those pestering bones. So he did something creative with them. He started out by assembling them into the shape of four bells, which now sit in each corner of the little chapel. From there, Rint's imagination ran wild, as he festooned the church with garlands of bones, designed a monstrance of bones, and fashioned the Schwarzenberg coat of arms out of bones. But his crowning achievement was the chandelier, in which he utilized every single bone in the body.

The chapel isn't as creepy as it sounds. In fact, it may strike some people as being somewhat humorous. *The chapel is open Tuesday through Sunday from 9 a.m. to 12 p.m. and from 1 to 4 p.m. Admission costs 20 Kč.*

PRACTICAL INFORMATION FOR PRAGUE

Changing Money

American Express and the major banks listed below charge the lowest commission. Forget patronizing the "Change" outlets littering the historic center, most of which charge an outrageous commission. And whatever you do, don't do business with guys who come up to you on the street offering "change, change." It's illegal to do so, and chances are you'll end up with a pile of worthless old Czechoslovak bills.

Places to exchange money include:

• **American Express**, *Václavské náměstí 56 (Wenceslas Square). Tel. 02/242 277 86. Open Monday to Friday from 9 a.m. to 6 p.m. and on Saturday until 3 p.m.* American Express travelers' checks are cashed free of commission here.

• **Česká obchodní banka**, *Na příkopě 14 (Staré Město). Metro to Můstek station. Open Monday through Friday from 7:30 a.m. to noon and from 1 to 3:30 p.m.* There's also a cash machine here that takes MasterCard and Cirrus.

• **Komerční banka**, *Na příkopě 28 (Staré Město). Metro to Náměstí Republiky* *station. Open Monday through Friday from 8 a.m. to 7 p.m. and on Saturday from 9 a.m. to 2 p.m.* You can use your MasterCard or Cirrus card at a machine here as well.

• **Živnostenská banka,** *Na příkopě 20 (Nové Město). Metro to Můstek station. Open Monday through Friday from 8 a.m. to 6 p.m.* Cash advance is given here with Visa or MasterCard.

Embassies

• **American** – *Tržiště 15 (Malá Strana). Tel. 02/573 206 63. Metro to Malostranská station.*

• **Australian** – There is no Australian embassy in Prague, but Australians can go to the British embassy for emergency help.

• **British** – *Thunovská 14 (Malá Strana). Tel. 02/573 203 55. Metro to Malostranská station.*

• **Canadian** – *Mickiewiczova 6 (Dejvice). Tel. 02/243 111 08. Metro to Dejvická station.*

• **Slovak** – *Pod hradbami 1 (Střešovice). Tel. 02/320 521. Metro to Dejvická station.*

Laundromats

• **Laundry Kings,** *Dejvická 16 (Dejvice). Tel. 02/312 3743. Metro to Hradčanská station.* Self-service and full-service.

• **Laundryland,** *Londýnská 71 (Vinohrady). Tel. 02/251 124. Metro to I.P. Pavlova.* Not recommended.

• **Prague Laundromat,** *Korunní 14 (Vinohrady). Tel. 02/255 541. Metro to Náměstí Míru station.* Self-service and full-service. The best of the lot, run by a nice couple from Seattle.

Libraries

• **American Center for Culture and Commerce,** *Hybernská 7a. Tel. 02/242 310 85. Metro to Náměstí Republiky station.* American books, newspapers, and magazines.

• **The British Council,** *Národní třída 10. Tel. 02/249 130 48. Metro to Národní třída station.* British books, newspapers, and magazines.

Medical Services

In case of a life-threatening emergency, call an ambulance at 155. The following clinics have English-speaking doctors and staff:

• **Na Homolce Hospital Foreigners Clinic,** *Roentgenova 2 (Motol). Tel. 02/529 221 46 or 529 221 91. Bus #167 from Anděl metro station to Na Homolce stop.* This is one of the best hospitals in Prague, geared mainly towards foreigners. It has a dental clinic inside.

• **Charles University International Clinic,** *Karlovo náměstí 32 (Nové Město). Tel. 02/249 043 47. Metro to Karlovo náměstí station.*

•**First Medical Clinic of Prague**, *Na perštýně 10 (Staré Město)* – *metro to Národní třída station; and Vyšehradská 35 (Nové Město), metro to Karlovo náměstí station. Tel. 0603/555 006 for both locations.*

Places of Worship
The *Prague Post* publishes a weekly list of services in English. Here is where some of them are happening:
•**Church of Jesus Christ of Latter-day Saints** (Mormon), *Milady Horákové 85/95 (Holešovice). Tel. 02/243 222 15. Metro to Hradčanská station.*
•**Church of St. Joseph** (Roman Catholic), *Josefská 4 (Malá Strana). Tel. 02/ 530 218. Metro to Malostranská station.*
•**International Baptist Church of Prague**, *Vinohradská 68 (Žižkov). Tel. 02/206 119 57. Metro to Flora station.*
•**Prague Christian Fellowship** (Interdenominational), *Ječná 19 (Nové Město). Tel. 02/575 300 20. Metro to Karlovo náměstí station.*
•**Welcoming Shabbat/Beth Simcha** (Jewish Liberal), *Vězeňská 9 (Josefov). Tel. 02/248 123 25. Metro to Náměstí Míru.*

Post Office
The **main post office** (*hlavní pošta*) is at *Jindřišská 14*, just off Wenceslas Square. Its postage, telegram, and fax services are open 24 hours, while its international telephone service is open daily 7 a.m. to 11 p.m. You can mail a package here if it weighs less than two kilograms. If it isn't, then you'll have to take it to the **customs post office** (*Celnice-pošta*) at *Plzeňská 139* in the district of Smíchov *(take tram #4, #7, or #9 from Anděl metro station to Klamovka stop)*. It's open weekdays from 7 a.m. to 3 p.m.

Tourist Information Offices
•**Čedok**, *Na příkopě 18 (Nové Město). Tel. 02/241 971 11. Near Můstek metro station*. Offers basic tourist information and concert tickets and issues train and bus tickets. Also arranges sightseeing tours and excursions all over the Czech Republic. Čedok has several offices in Prague. Here are a few others: *Pařížská 6 (just off Old Town Square), Rytířská 16 (Staré Město),* and *Praha-Ruzyně airport.*
•**Prague Information Service** *(Pražská informační služba, or PIS), in the Old Town Hall on Old Town Square. Tel. 02/244 822 02.* This is the most helpful of all offices in Prague, with information on just about everything, from concerts to accommodations to guided tours. There's also a ticket office here where you can get tickets to just about any cultural event happening in the city.
•**Prague Tourist Center**, *Rytířská 12 (Staré Město). Tel. 02/242 122 09. Near Můstek metro station*. Tickets, accommodations, and a wealth of other information available here.

14. SOUTH BOHEMIA

Having escaped (for the most part) the ravages of World War II and the callous industrial development of the Communist regime, South Bohemia treats you to a glance of the Czech Republic at its most idyllic. Walled towns absorb you into their curved, medieval streets and lanes. Imposing castles rise majestically over verdant river valleys, providing views of hills that softly undulate across the horizon. Scores of natural and artificial lakes, especially around **Třeboň**, spot the countryside like scattered pieces of crystal. Flowing through and enhancing all this beautiful scenery is the **Vltava River**.

Yes, it can be desperately romantic here, so much so that it might have you running back to Detroit or Newark for a good dose of the industrialized world. With the exception of the Temelín nuclear power plant and a few smokestacks sticking up here and there, South Bohemia is conspicuously lacking in industry. Even the region's sole "city," **České Budějovice**, has very little industry compared to the rest of the country. Instead it has a gorgeous old town and a notably provincial appeal for a town of 200,000.

BEER IN SOUTH BOHEMIA

The dominant beer in this part of the Czech Republic is far and above **Budvar** *(or Budweiser, as is it's known in German). I'm not talking about that stuff processed in St. Louis. I'm talking about the creamy, mild beer brewed in České Budějovice. But Budvar isn't České Budějovice's only beer, nor is it the town's oldest. There's also* **Samson**, *nearly as impressive as Budvar but slightly more bitter.*

Regent, *one of Bohemia's oldest and most respected beers, is brewed close to České Budějovice in the town of Třeboň. This brewery, meaning the beer and its facility, goes back to 1379 and still uses water from its original spring. Finally, there's* **Eggenberg**, *a less inspiring beer based in Český Krumlov.*

South Bohemia is known as the "Land of the Rose," after the all-powerful **Rožmberk family**, whose symbol was the five-petalled rose. Ruling much of South Bohemia from the early 13th century until 1611, the Rožmberks established below their castles some of South Bohemia's most graceful towns, such as **Český Krumlov** and **Rožmberk nad Vltavou**. Later, the Bavarian **Schwarzenbergs** acquired a number of fortresses in South Bohemia and turned them into fairytale castles. Among the castles in their possession were **Hluboká, Krumlov**, and **Třeboň**.

In the 15th century, South Bohemia became the epicenter for the anti-Catholic Hussite movement, which gathered furious momentum after their leader, Jan Hus, was burned at the stake for heresy. The radical wing of the Hussites, known as the Taborites, retreated from Prague and built the stronghold of **Tábor** to serve as their religious and strategic base. The Taborites, led by the one-eyed Jan Žižka, not only targeted the Catholics, but anyone who had the misfortune of being wealthy. The Taborites spread their wrath throughout the region, and many a nobleman saw his property go up in smoke.

Though still thawing from the forty-year Communist freeze, South Bohemia is waking up to its potential as a popular tourist destination. Hotels, usually installed in comely historic houses, now grace nearly every historic town square. Restaurants are finally getting away from the tedium of meat, dumplings, and cabbage and offering a greater range of dishes, including a surprising number of vegetarian meals. (In this part of Bohemia, fish and game are your best bets.) And beer . . . Well, South Bohemian beer has always been good, at least for the last 600 years or so.

SOUTH BOHEMIA FINDS & FAVORITES

Vila Černý Leknín in Tábor (see Where To Stay in Tábor)
The walled city of Třeboň and tours of its 14th century brewery,
Regent *(see Třeboň)*
The Rococo ballroom in the **Krumlov Castle** *in Český Krumlov*
Hotel Růže in Český Krumlov
Vinárna U Šatlavy (see Where To Eat in Český Krumlov)

Tábor

If it were not for its impressive location on top of a hill looking down at the Lužnice River and Jordán Lake, **Tábor** might not cut it as a worthwhile destination. Though the town has done a nice job in restoring its main square, **Žižkovo náměstí**, the old town's side streets are a catastrophe, looking like the town has yet to clean up from the last war.

But there are some inspiring views, especially from the top of **Kotnov Tower**, where gently rolling hills and tree-studded slopes are a comforting sight. You can also have an interesting time getting lost in the zigzagging lanes or exploring the underground tunnels.

Tábor takes its claim to fame as the former spiritual and military center of the radical wing of the Hussite movement, called the Taborites. Spurned by the martyrdom of Jan Hus, a group of Hus' followers came here in 1420 to build a stronghold against the Catholics. At that time Tábor was nothing more than the abandoned Kotnov Castle (of which only one tower now remains). The town, named after a hill mentioned in the Bible, was designed with warfare in mind, and for 17 impressive years the Taborites, led by **Jan Žižka**, defended themselves against the Holy Roman Empire's onslaughts, until they were finally defeated by the moderate Hussite King George of Poděbrady.

The best time to come to Tábor is in mid-September, when the **Tábor Meeting** takes place. Representatives from all the towns named Tábor (there are quite a number in the United States) converge here for a celebration of its Hussite past. The old town turns into a medieval village. Townsfolk don the garb of the age and old-time markets hawk a good bit of arts and crafts. You're bound to see a lot of jousting, and maybe even a battle or two. For specific dates, call **Infocentrum**, *Tel. 0361/252 385*.

ORIENTATION

Built around the banks of the Lužnice River in the hills of the northeastern region of South Bohemia, Tábor is 88 kilometers (55 miles) south of Prague and 60 kilometers (37 miles) north of České Budějovice.

ARRIVALS & DEPARTURES

By Bus

Buses run several times a day from Prague's Florenc station, costing about 50 Kč and taking about an hour. The bus station is a ten minute walk east of the old center.

By Car

Tábor's close proximity to Prague makes it a feasible day trip if you've got a car. Roads from Prague to Tábor are in fairly good condition and take you through some pretty pastoral scenery. Take E50 to E55. Once in Tábor look for the well-marked blue P signs, which will direct you to a parking lot on the outskirts of the old town.

By Train

Several trains run each day between Prague's Hlavní nádraží and Tábor, taking roughly two hours and costing about 40 Kč. Trains between

Tábor and České Budějovice run about 10 times a day, costing about 30 Kč for the hour-long trip.

GETTING AROUND TOWN

The best way to get around is most assuredly by foot. The small size of the town rules out any need for taking public transportation.

WHERE TO STAY

HOTEL KAPITÁL, *9. května 617, 390 01 Tábor. Tel. 0361/256 096, Fax 0361/252 411. Rates for single/double: 980/1,550 Kč. Credit cards: AE, V. 24 rooms. Restaurant.*

Newly remodeled hotel carved out of a pink 19th-century house. The rooms are somewhat sparely furnished, but the smart decor will make you feel right at home. Unfortunately, the hotel is bait to a lot of tour buses, which can sometimes ruin the "smallness" of a small hotel like this one. Private parking is available for guests.

HOTEL PALCÁT, *9. května 2467, 390 01 Tábor. Tel. 0361/252 901, Fax 0361/252 905. Rates for single/double: 790/1,550 Kč. Credit cards: AE, V. 50 rooms. Restaurant.*

One of the ugliest structures I've seen in Tábor, this Communist-era hotel is situated close to the old town. Rooms have very little personality, if any at all. Book a room here only as a last option.

VILA ČERNY LEKNÍN, *Přiběnická 695, 390 01 Tábor. Tel. 0361/256 405, Fax 0361/252 574. Rates for single/double: 1,200/1,500 Kč. No credit cards. 9 rooms. No restaurant.*

Just outside the old town, this black, imposing villa-turned-pension is a hop, skip, and a jump down from the Kotnov Tower. Though nice inside, the interior is not as impressive as the spooky black exterior, which looks like something out of an Edgar Allen Poe story. The view of the surrounding countryside from its rear rooms is nothing less than spectacular. Doubling as a gallery, the pension exhibits some fairly decent local art. If you can stay anywhere in Tábor, stay here.

WHERE TO EAT

HOTEL KAPITÁL, *9. května 617. Tel. 0361/256 096. 100-200 Kč.*

Featuring a huge menu of South Bohemia specialties reasonably priced. Venison tops the menu here, and is usully quite good when topped with a heavy mushroom sauce. Risotto, strangely enough, has also found its way into the menu. The decor is a bit tacky, but the service is speedy and friendly – two qualites you can't take for granted in this town.

RESTAURANT PONTE, *in the Oskar Nedbal Theater (Divadlo Oskara Nedbala), Palackého ulice. Tel. 0361/253 785. 70-150 Kč. No credit cards.*
On the first floor of the biggest theater in town, the Ponte serves up continental fare that may not win any awards but ranks high above most restaurants in town. A pretty good choice for dinner is the trout with walnuts sprinkled on top. Service is generally top-notch and decor borders on the surreal.

BESEDA, *Žižkovo náměstí 5. No telephone. 60-180 Kč. No credit cards.*
This restaurant with the rather generic name that means "gathering place" dishes up a lot of rather generic Czech dishes, which means meat, cabbage, and knedlíky. A lot of tourists flock here since it is on the main square. Expect rude service and a lot of smoke under the vaulted ceiling. But there is one plus: the restaurant serves a mean Budvar.

SEEING THE SIGHTS

If you've come by bus or train, then you've landed at the best place to start your tour. Across the street from the two stations at the east end of 9. května street is *Husovo náměstí*, where you'll find the **statue of Jan Hus**, the town's most revered man. Sculpted by František Bílek at the turn of the century, the statue captures the intense fervor Hus arouses in Tábor, the most Protestant town in the country. Kafka apparently regarded it as one of his favorite statues.

Continue westward down 9. května street towards staré město, or old town, which begins on Palackého street once you reach the other side of *náměstí Fr. Křižíka*. The old town has a series of steep, circulating dusty streets and lanes, meant to disorient the enemy. (This tactic has the same effect on tourists today.) Strolling down Palackého past the neo-Renaissance **Oskar Nedbala Theater**, you'll eventually end up in **Žižkovo náměstí**, a colorful square filled with centuries worth of architecture, from late Gothic up to Baroque. Here is where people came in the 15th century to forfeit all their possessions in order to become a true Hussite.

In the middle of the square is a **statue of Jan Žižka** and **a copy of a peasant wagon**. Why of all things, you ask, would a wagon be sitting in the middle of the square? If it weren't for these meager little vehicles, the Taborites would probably have never held off the Holy Roman Empire as long as they did. Old Žižka himself came up with the idea that if you mounted cannons on the wagons, then you could have roving artillery, and thus have a mobile advantage over your enemy. The first tank, if you will.

Behind the statue of Žižka is the late Gothic **Church of the Transfiguration of Our Lord on Mt. Tábor** (Kostel Proměnění Páně na Hoře Tábor). But the most impressive of all the buildings on the square is the **town hall** (radnice), completed in 1521, in which you'll find the **Hussite**

Museum, chronicling the movement that shook Europe and hinted of the coming Reformation. The museum contains a number of paintings, documents, and archaeological finds, as well as a veritable arsenal of weapons, all of which are seemingly meant to do no less than mangle the Catholic enemy. A great painting of the one-eyed Žižka adorns the walls. Offered at the museum are guided tours of a section of the town's **underground passages**, a network of linked cellars used during the Hussite wars in the case of fire or if the enemy had breached the town walls. *The museum is open Tuesday through Sunday from 8:30 a.m. to 4 p.m.*

Another opportunity for visiting an underground cellar can be had at **Galerie Lucina**, just below the main square *at Kotnovská 137.* (Look for a sign on the south side of the main square pointing the way.) This gallery specializes in local art and ingenious wood toys you've probably grown accustomed to seeing in the Czech Republic. But the best reason to come here is to see what owners Marko and Olga Lucinovi have done with their ancient cellars. With the idea of seducing you into buying one of their sculpted crystals, they've added mood lighting and new age music. Yes, it's a bit hokey, but it is one of the more unusual experiences available in Tábor. *Open weekdays 10 a.m. to 6 p.m. and Saturdays 9 a.m. to 10 p.m.*

Taking Klokotská down from Žižkovo náměstí, you'll soon run into the town's only existing town gate, the 15th century **Bechyně Gate**. Standing next to it, the **Kotnov Tower** is what remains of the old Kotnov Castle, built before the Hussites appeared in the 15th century. All but the tower was destroyed in a fire in the 16th century. In true Czech fashion, a brewery was built on the site of the castle, holding to one Czech proverb that says, "Better a live brewery than a dead castle." (In this case, however, both the castle and the brewery are dead.) If you've got it in you, take the eight flights of stairs to the top of the tower, where a spectacular panoramic view of the surrounding tree-studded hills, the slithering Lužnice River, and the town's red roofs await. Be fair warned: If some of the staircases were any steeper, you'd have to call them ladders. The tower also features a museum, exhibiting a number of artifacts from the town and region. *The museum and tower are open Tuesday through Sunday from 8:30 a.m. to 4 p.m.*

Before calling it quits in the old town, go ahead and get yourself lost in the twisting lanes and alleys. (You won't be lost for long, I promise.) You may even find a quaint *hospoda*, or pub, to dive into and swill back a beer or two.

One more sight in Tábor that you might want to venture to is **Klokoty**. From the Bechyně Gate, go about a kilometer northwest across the meadows. At the gate you'll be able to see the church's nine green onion domes, poking out amidst the surrounding pines. Though admittance to the church is not allowed, it's well worth the pleasant stroll to get an eye-full of this graceful, unassuming church and monastery built during the Counter-Reformation.

NIGHTLIFE & ENTERTAINMENT

The neo-Renaissance theater, **Oskara Nedbala**, at Palackého presents a number of contemporary and classical plays. Behind the east side of náměstí Fr. Křižíka, **Orion Rock Club** features live acts on the weekends and a disco on week nights. It's also not a bad place to belly up for a glass of Regent beer.

DAY TRIPS & EXCURSIONS

Train buffs shouldn't miss hopping on the puny electric train running daily during the summer from the Tábor train station to the spa town of **Bechyně**. Built in 1902, this train line was the first narrow gauge service in the Austro-Hungarian Empire. Even if trains aren't your thing, you might want to go along for the 24 kilometer (15 mile) ride anyway, at least to have the opportunity of going across the bridge that spans the Lužnice gorge. If you're going by car, head southwest through Čenkov and follow the signs there.

One of the first settlements in South Bohemia, Bechyně perches on the edge of the gorge. The town, about a ten minute walk southwest of the train station, is well-known for its ceramics, which are featured at the **Alšova Jihočeská galérie** (South Bohemia Aleš Gallery), a former brewery in the main square, náměstí TG Masaryka. *Open 9 a.m. to 5 p.m. May through October.*

PRACTICAL INFORMATION

• **Agrobanka**, *náměstí Fr Křižíka 2840.* A bank where you can change money.
• **Čedok**, *9. května 1282, 390 01 Tábor. Tel. 0361/252 235.* Offers information on the town and can arrange tours of the area. Will also change your money.
• **Infocentrum**, *Žižkovo náměstí 2, 390 01 Tábor. Tel. 0361/253 339.* The most helpful of tourist offices in town, offering private accommodations, guide services, and a number of maps. Best chance for finding someone who can speak English.
• **Post Office**, *Žižkovo náměstí.*

České Budějovice

Even though **České Budějovice** is South Bohemia's principal city, don't believe that it's horrendously large, or even industrial. Quite the contrary. One of the first things you'll notice here is that everyone seems to be riding bicycles. Though not an important fact in itself, it does give you some idea of the pace of life, which is much slower than you'd reckon, considering the city has a population of over 200,000. The unusually wide streets and number of pedestrian (and bike) zones allow for moments just to happily stroll, which you should do a lot of in this great city.

České Budějovice got its start when **King Přemysl Otakar II** decided in the middle of the 13th century that he needed to wield greater power in South Bohemia, so as to keep in check the powerful Vítkovici family, who were at the time expanding their domain over much of the region. The king chose a piece of land at the confluence of the Vltava and Malše rivers, a place that had strategic and economic advantages. He handed the city plans over to a group of Dominican priests, who were also to build a monastery there. And the city was born.

The town eventually accrued its wealth from its position on the old salt route between Linz and Prague, later from its silver mines located just outside town. Despite being so close to the eye of the Hussite storm, České Budějovice remained a bastion of Catholicism during the Hussite wars, which was probably why it was given the privilege of secretly holding the Bohemian crown jewels and royal archives during the Thirty Years' War. A fire in 1641 destroyed much of České Budějovice's medieval character. From the ashes rose a predominately Baroque town, which has survived to this day.

Today, the city is renowned for its **Budvar** (Budweiser) beer, a light and creamy malt that goes down like silk – not at all like its American counterpart with the same name.

For all its history and all its beauty, České Budějovice doesn't offer a whole lot to keep its visitors occupied. But it's well worth your time just to wander through the old town and soak in the life around the gorgeous **náměstí Přemysla Otakara II**. Another must-see is **Hluboká Castle**, located only 10 kilometers outside České Budějovice.

ORIENTATION

Located at the marshy confluence of the Vltava and Malše rivers, České Budějovice is about 120 kilometers (74 miles) south of Prague and 40 kilometers (25 miles) north of the Austrian border.

ARRIVALS & DEPARTURES

By Bus

Costing about 120 Kč, buses from Prague are quicker than trains, taking about three hours. Buses depart Prague's Florenc bus station about every two hours. The bus station, across the street from the train station, is a ten minute walk east of the old town.

By Car

No problem getting here by car, as the roads are in good condition. From Prague take E-50 to E-55. Parking, restricted to the perimeter of the old town, can be a problem, as there aren't very many lots. If you park on the streets outside the center, don't forget to put some change into the meter, or else you'll be getting the boot.

By Train

Several trains run daily between Prague's Hlavní nádraží station and České Budějovice, taking about three-and-a-half hours and costing around 100 Kč. The train station is a ten minute walk east of the old center.

GETTING AROUND TOWN

The efficient bus system is the only form of public transportation in České Budějovice, but it does stop running at midnight. Taking a taxi is only a good idea in a pinch, as you run the risk here (like anywhere else in the country) of getting overcharged because you're a foreigner. Most likely you'll be able to get around just fine on foot.

As of yet, no one rents bicycles. But if you've brought your own, you'll definitely want to join the locals on two wheels. If you need to rent a car, Čedok (see *Practical Information*, below) can help you arrange it.

WHERE TO STAY

HOTEL ZVON, *náměstí Přemysla Otakara II 28, 370 01 České Budějovice. Tel. 038/731 1383, Fax 038/731 1385. Rates for single/double: 1,395/2,430 Kč. Credit cards: AE, MC, V. 75 rooms. 3 restaurants.*

If the newly renovated Hotel Zvon has anything going for it, it's certainly the location – right on the main square. Occupying three colorful houses, the hotel is a gem. The plush rooms are spacious and chock-full of all the amenities. Be sure to ask for a room with a view of the square. The staff is ultra-professional and English is spoken here. Several possible tours and excursions are offered. But stay away from the restaurants, which for some reason can't seem to achieve the same high standard as the rest of the hotel.

HOTEL MALÝ PIVOVAR, *ulice Karla IV. 8-10, 370 21 České Budějovice. Tel. 038/731 3285, Fax 038/731 3287. Rates for single/double: 1,590/1,990 Kč. Credit cards: AE, MC, V. 28 rooms. Restaurant.*

Totally renovated in 1994, this hotel sits in an 18th century former brewery located just off the main square. Some of the rooms are furnished using the structure's original beams, a welcome bit of authenticity. The hotel's wine bar hunkers down in a Gothic cellar that survived the disastrous fire of the 17th century. Fine restaurant offering top-notch Czech specialties.

U SOLNÉ BRÁNY HOTEL, *Radniční ulice 11, 370 01 České Budějovice. Tel. 038/635 4121, Fax 038/635 4120. Rates for single/double: 690/1,420 Kč. Credit cards: MC, V. 12 rooms. Restaurant.*

This adorable small hotel, also located just off the main square, is hemmed in at the corner of the block, offering not much in the way of any view. Though somewhat lacking in imagination, the rooms are comfortable, but not worth their rates.

HOTEL U TŘÍ LVŮ, *ulice U tří lvů 3a, 370 01 České Budějovice. Tel. 038/599 00, Fax 038/597 80. Rates for single/double: 1,100/1,490 Kč. Credit cards: AE, MC, V. 36 rooms. Restaurant.*

An attrociously ugly structure that looks as though it was built to house offices rather than hotel rooms. But the interior is another story. If you can get over the liberal use of purple in the decor, then you should have a perfectly comfortable stay. Parking is available right in front of the hotel. The restaurant feautures a number of hearty German dishes reasonably priced. President Václav Havel apparently enjoyed a meal here, as pictures at the hotel makes sure to let you know.

HOTEL GOMEL, *Pražská 14, 370 04 České Budějovice. Tel. 038/731 1390, Fax 038/731 1365. Rates for single/double: 1,800/2,500 Kč. Credit cards: AE, MC, V. Restaurant.*

As one of the tallest (and ugliest) buildings in town, Gomel is a somewhat daunting, if not sleazy hotel strictly catering to those with a business account. The hotel's strip joint gives you some idea of what's going on here. Rooms don't come close to being worth their rates. Same goes for the overpriced menu at the restaurant. Try to avoid this one.

HOTEL BAKALÁŘ, *Masarykova 69, 373 41 Hluboká nad Vltavou. Tel./ fax 038/965 516. Rates for singles/doubles: 720/1,080 Kč. Credit cards: AE, MC, V. 10 rooms. Restaurant.*

Located 10 kilometers north of České Budějovice in Hluboká nad Vltavou (see *Excursions*, below), the Bakalář is carved out of a cute 19th building that actually looks like a graduate's cap. Simple yet stylish rooms, friendly service, and the best restaurant in this tiny town make the Bakalář a good alternative to staying in the big city to the south.

WHERE TO EAT

With the exception of Hotel Zvon and Hotel Gomel, all the hotels listed above have fine restaurants.

U LÍBUŠE, *Kněžská 26. Tel. 038/552 11. 100-200 Kč. Credit cards: AE.*

This stylish restaurant serves a host of continental and South Bohemia dishes, including a nice selection of steaks. The upstairs of the restaurant is a Vienna-style cafe, a nice place to have a glass of wine or an aperitif before going downstairs for dinner. Impeccable service makes dining here all the more memorable.

U PANÍ EMY, *Široká 25. No telephone. 70-150 Kč. No credit cards.* The vaulted ceilings at U Paní Emy create an intimate atmosphere where a lot of locals like to gather. International dishes, including a passable curry chicken, are on the menu. Service is a bit slow, but you won't mind hanging out and a enjoying a bottle of Moravian wine from the big wine list.

MASNÉ KRÁMY, *Krajinská 13. Tel. 038/326 52. 60-150 Kč. No credit cards.* A landmark in České Budějovice. Yes, it's touristy, but not so bad as to keep the locals away. The interior, one big basilica-like structure with little alcoves set off to the side, was formerly a meat market dating back to 1554. The Southern Bohemia menu includes a lot of fish and venison, as well as the restaurant's signature dish – the brewery-style goulash. Of course everything tastes better when washed down with a glass of the local Budvar, 1,500 liters (390 US gallons) of which gets consumed here each day. Apparently, a group of crazy Austrians from Linz liked the place so much they created a society called "Friends of Masné Krámy," and have made a point of coming here at least once a year.

RESTAURACE JIHOČESKÁ CHALUPA, *Husova třida. Tel. 038/459 88. 100-200 Kč. No credit cards.* A favorite with the locals, this restaurant with the name that means "South Bohemian Cottage" serves colorful regional favorites such as roast duck and broiled carp.

SEEING THE SIGHTS

What better place to start than smack dab in the middle of České Budějovice at **náměstí Přemysla Otakara II**, the town's main square and, at 133 square meters, the largest plaza in the Czech Republic. Surrounded by a series of Gothic, Renaissance, and Baroque houses, the square's centerpiece is **Samson's Fountain**, a Baroque creation depicting Samson killing a lion.

But the building that definitely stands out the most is the 1555 **town hall** (*radnice*), which got a Baroque facelift in 1730 and, just recently, a new coat of shiny blue paint. You'll have an easy time spotting the building because of the incongruous gargoyles sticking out of the facade. In front of the radnice you can hire a horse-drawn carriage to tug you around the old town.

Just off náměstí Přemysla Otakara II at the corner of Kanovnická and U Černé věže is the 16th-century **Black Tower** (Černá věž), one of a few structures in town to survive the 1641 fire. If you are feeling fit, climb the

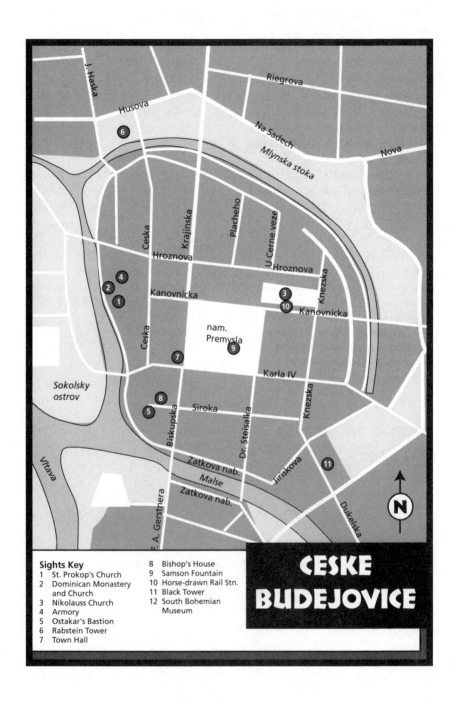

Sights Key
1 St. Prokop's Church
2 Dominican Monastery and Church
3 Nikolauss Church
4 Armory
5 Ostakar's Bastion
6 Rabstein Tower
7 Town Hall
8 Bishop's House
9 Samson Fountain
10 Horse-drawn Rail Stn.
11 Black Tower
12 South Bohemian Museum

CESKE BUDEJOVICE

200 stairs to the top, where you can look out across the city and get a bird's eye view of the main square. *Open daily except Monday 9 a.m. to 5 p.m.* Right next to the Black Tower is the **Cathedral of St. Nicholas** (Chrám sv. Mikuláše), which was originally built at the end of the 13th century but has since burned so many times that it's hard to tell just how old it is. It's worth your time to stick your head in and get a look at the gorgeous altar.

From the Black Tower, head three blocks west on Hroznová and take a left onto Česká, where you'll find the entrance to the **Old Dominican Monastery** and the **Church of the Virgin Mary's Sacrifice** (Bývalý klášterní kostel Obětování P. Marie). Built into the town wall, the monastery dates back to the time of the town's inception. The Gothic painting of the Virgin Mary at the main altar of the church was brought here from Italy in 1410.

Next to the monastery stands the austere, high-gabled **Salt House** (Solnice), which was the town's armory before it became a storage space for the precious salt traveling along the Linz-Prague route. The three chiseled faces on the gable involve a legend about a group of thieves caught red-handed in the Salt House.

From the Salt House, wind around the corner and take a stroll on the banks of the River Malše along the original town walls. After a hundred meters or so you'll be able to get a good look at another early structure from the town's beginnings – the **Iron Maiden** (Železná panna), a 15th century prison tower named after the prison's favorite instrument of torture.

Continue further upstream along Zátkovo nábřeží, cross Dr. Stejskala street, and head down Jirsíkova until you reach the **Museum of South Bohemia** (Jihočeské muzeum) at the corner of Dukelská. Through artifacts, documents, and models, the museum introduces you to the region's history, going back to the Celts and the first Slav tribes. In addition to the human history, the museum has a number of natural history exhibits, including the largest collection of mushrooms you'll ever care to see. *The museum is open Tuesday though Sunday 9 a.m. to 12 p.m. and 1 p.m. to 6 p.m.*

Train buffs might want to check out the tiny **Museum of the Horse-drawn Railway** (Památaky koněspřežní železnice), about a ten minute walk south of the center *at Mánesova 10.* The museum and its collection of paraphernalia from the days of the earliest railway are housed in what the brochures tout as the oldest railway station in Europe. *Open daily except Monday from 9 a.m. to 5 p.m. Closed December through February.*

NIGHTLIFE & ENTERTAINMENT

For drama and opera, check out the comely **South Bohemian Theater** (Jihočeské divadlo) *on Dr. Stejskala street.* The **Hotel Malý Pivovar**

hospoda (see *Where To Stay*) is a rip-roaring pub serving Samson beer (what else). You're more likely to rub elbows with a local than with someone staying at the hotel.

Club New York, *in the basement of an apartment house located opposite Hotel Gomel on Pražská*, is the absolute center of nightlife in České Budějovice, with thumping industrial music, three bars, and a lot of people cramming the dance floor.

EXCURSIONS & DAY TRIPS
Hluboká Castle

It's easy to understand why **Hluboká Castle** is the third-most visited castle after Prague Castle and Karlštejn. Its numerous towers and turrets would almost have you believe that it was rendered in a Walt Disney studio. But you can attribute the present appearance of the castle to the all-powerful Bavarian family who owned a great chunk of South Bohemia for several centuries – the Schwarzenbergs, who acquired the 13th-century castle in 1661 and stayed there until 1947.

No doubt will you see the resemblance between Hluboká and Windsor Castle. In the early 19th century, the Schwarzenbergs made several trips to England, where they became enraptured by Windsor's grandeur. They decided to convert their actual Gothic castle into a romanticized version of a Gothic castle, which they more or less completed in 1855. In addition to a major facelift, the castle got an English-style garden and an adjoining riding school.

In order to enter the castle you have to join a guided tour. Unfortunately, most of them are in Czech and German, with the (very) occasional English tour thrown in for good measure. The castle's gorgeous interior is worth the tour, even if you can't understand the guide. *The castle is open daily except Monday, from 8 a.m. to 5 p.m. June through August, from 9 a.m. to 5 p.m. during May and September, and from 9 a.m. to 4 p.m. during April and October. Czech tours cost 30 Kč, while English and German ones cost 80 Kč.*

Set in the former riding school, **South Bohemian Aleš Gallery** (Alšova jihočeská galéria) has an interesting collection of 16th century Czech religious works, a number of paintings by Dutch masters, and a changing exhibition of Czech modernist art. *Open Tuesday through Sunday 8 a.m. to 6 p.m.*

Hluboká Castle sits above the quaint town of Hluboká nad Vltavou, about a 10 kilometer (6 mile) drive from České Budějovice. Take E49 six miles northwest out of town and then follow signs to Hluboká nad Vltavou. If you don't have your own car, the best way of getting from České Budějovice to Hluboká nad Vltavou and back is most definitely by bus, which leaves several times a day from the main bus station in České Budějovice and drops you off below the castle.

PRACTICAL INFORMATION

• **Čedok**, *náměstí Přemysla Otakara II 39, 370 01 České Budějovice. Tel. 038/ 521 27, Fax 038/731 2771.* Offers tours of the area, changes money, and can help with renting a car.

• **G-Sports Turistické Informační A Mapové Centrum**, *náměstí Přemysla Otakara II 2, 370 01 České Budějovice. Tel. 038/731 2840, Fax 038/525 89.* Arranges private accommodations, sells the gamut in maps, and is the most helpful overall. Can arrange tours of the town and area. English spoken here.

• **Main Post Office**, *Pražská 69.* Open 24 hours.

Třeboň

Although it is quite easy to see all the sights that **Třeboň** has to offer in one afternoon, you may want to consider hanging your hat here for a day or two. This little spa town in the lake region of South Bohemia is a good base for hiking or biking, thanks to the number of tranquil forests and trails beginning at the very edge of town.

Entirely surrounded by the original 16th-century walls, the old town of Třeboň, with its cluster of mostly Renaissance houses, numbers only a few streets and gates. The centerpiece of the old town, **Masarykovo náměstí**, is so narrow that you may be inclined to think of it as a wide street, and not a town square.

Třeboň's roots go back to the early 12th century, when it was founded as a market settlement on the Hungary-Bavaria trade route. **Petr Vok**, legendary party animal and the last in the Rožmberk line, built a chateau here in the 16th century. The **Schwarzenbergs** took over as town owners in 1660, deciding they would make their final resting spot at a church a little ways outside town, now the **Schwarzenberg Mausoleum**.

One of the stranger chapters of Třeboň's history happened during the Nazi occupation of Czechoslovakia. Hundreds of ethnically "pure" German women were brought to a camp established on the banks of the Svět pond, where they mated with an elite group of Aryan men so as to produce the perfect Aryan child. Apparently, the German women were forbidden to even speak with Czech men, as this would somehow "contaminate" their offspring. Bohumil Hrabal, the great post-World War II Czech writer, gave an hilarious depiction of this camp in his fantastic novel, *I Served the King of England*.

Třeboň is better known around Bohemia as the site of the **Regent brewery**, producing a beer that many consider one of Bohemia's finest. Believe it or not, Regent, which dates back to 1379, still uses water from the original spring, located in the middle of Svět Lake.

A good time to come to Třeboň is late August or early September, the time when ponds are drained to allow the carp to be harvested. Song, dance, and lots of beer swilling accompanies the occasion. For exact dates, call the **Information and Cultural Center**, *Tel. 0333/ 3776.*

ORIENTATION

Lying in the heart of the **Třebonsko** region and in the midst of 600 linked ponds, Třeboň is 24 kilometers (15 miles) east of České Budějovice and roughly 120 kilometers (74 miles) south of Prague.

ARRIVALS & DEPARTURES

By Bus

Buses run almost hourly between České Budějovice and Třeboň and cost about 25 Kč. The bus station is a five minute walk northwest of the center, with plenty of signs to point you in the right direction.

By Car

Třeboň is a 20 minute drive from České Budějovice on E49/E551. Parking is easiest near the bus station on the northwest corner of town.

By Train

Going by train from České Budějovice will only give you a headache, so forget it. The Vienna-Prague train stops in Třeboň, making it quiet easy to travel by train if you're coming down from the capital. The train station is a five minute walk east of the old town.

GETTING AROUND TOWN

Everything is easily accessed on foot, so there's no need to take any public transportation, of which there's little to speak of in Třeboň. You can hire a cab from either of the three hotels listed below.

WHERE TO STAY

HOTEL ZLATÁ HVĚZDA, *Masarykovo náměstí 107, 379 01 Třeboň. Tel. 0333/757 111, Fax 0333/757 300. Rates for single/double: 800-1,420/1,600- 3,200 Kč. Credit cards: AE, MC, V. 38 rooms. Restaurant.*

Excellent location right on the main square. Although the furniture could use some updating, the rooms are pleasant enough, but way overpriced. Be sure to ask for a room overlooking the square, or else you might get stuck with a depressing view of their not-so-romantic court-yard.

HOTEL BÍLY KONÍČEK, *Masarykovo náměstí 97, 379 01 Třeboň. Tel. and Fax 0333/721 213. Rates for single/double: 720/960 Kč. Credit cards: V. 10 rooms. Restaurant.*
The dank, tacky interior is a disappointment after admiring this 1544 fortress-like house from the outside. The hotel rents bicycles to its guests and can arrange horseback riding excursions.
PENSION SIESTA, *Hradební 26, 379 01 Třeboň. Tel. and Fax 0333/ 2324. Rates for singles/doubles: 360/720 Kč. No credit cards. 6 rooms. No restaurant.*
It's hard to resist this adorable villa that sits just outside the town walls and on the banks of a canal. No need to worry about your privacy; all rooms come with private bath and shower, plus a television. Flower boxes in the window and the big terrace out front help to make this a top pick in Třeboň.
HOTEL REGENT, *Lázeňská ulice 1008, 379 01 Třeboň. Tel. and Fax 0333/721 149. Rates for single/double: 721 396 Kč. Credit cards: AE, MC, V. 42 rooms. Restaurant.*
Another ugly Communist-era leftover offering rooms with run-down furniture and characterless rooms. But it does rent bikes and has the good fortune of being located behind a tennis club.

WHERE TO EAT
ŠUPINA BAR, *Valy 155. Tel. 033/2500. 80-200 Kč. No credit cards.*
Like all restaurants in town, they specialize in fish, especially the carp that is raised just around the corner from the restaurant. But Šupina prepares their fish with a bit more creativity and a bit more spice than the other restaurants in town. A very popular place with the locals, which means a table is hard to come by on certain nights. But they do have a bar pouring the beer made right across the street at the Regent brewery.
HOTEL BÍLY KONÍČEK, *Masarykovo náměstí 97, 379 01 Třeboň. Tel. and Fax 0333/721 213. 50-150 Kč.*
This restaurant at this hotel is a favorite with the locals, dishing up tasty South Bohemian specialties with an accent on fish, of course. But there is plenty else to order if you are not a fish eater or if you have no intention of joining in on the local specialty, carp.
HOTEL ZLATÁ HVĚZDA, *Masarykovo náměstí 107, 379 01 Třeboň. Tel. 0333/757 111, Fax 0333/2604. 60-200 Kč.*
You don't need to be a genius to guess what's on the menu here. Brasserie-style seating and deft service make for a decent dining experience.
U ČOCHTANA, *Březanova 7/I. No Tel. 80-190 Kč. No credit cards.*
Intimate place where the emphasis is, once more sadly, on fish.

SEEING THE SIGHTS

Once inside the town walls, you'll have no problem finding your way to the main square, **Masarykovo náměstí**. All roads and lanes inside the old town lead to this square festooned with brightly-colored Renaissance and Baroque houses. Be sure to check out the 1544 **Hotel Bílý Koníček** and its battlement facade.

For a look at the interior of the Renaissance **chateau** built by Petr Vok, buy your tickets (40 Kč) at the box office that is located about 200 meters beyond a gate entered opposite Březanova at the west end of Masarykovo náměstí. The lavish rooms, part of the castle complex, have an impressive collection of porcelain and furniture from the days when Vok threw his notoriously wild parties. *May through September, it's open Tuesday through Sunday from 9 a.m. to noon and from 1 p.m. to 4:30 p.m. Open weekends only in April and October.*

From Masarykovo náměstí, head down Žižkovo náměstí to reach the **Regent brewery** (pivovar), started in 1379 and one of the oldest in Bohemia. The Information and Cultural Centre (see *Practical Information below*) can arrange tours of the brewery, taking you through the process of beer making that has been in employed for centuries.

From the brewery, it's a few short steps out of the old town and to the shores of the **Svět pond**. A walking path continues around the pond to the other side, where you'll find the 1877 **Schwarzenberg Mausoleum** (Schwarzenberská hrobka), poking up through the trees in the middle of a park, U hrobky. Several members of this noble family rest in the cellar of this comely neo-Gothic church. The pretty, ten minute walk from Třeboň around the shores of the pond is well worth the trip, even if you find the Mausoleum no great shakes. Tours, unreasonably priced at 50 Kč, are in Czech only. English speakers have to settle for a horribly written text. *It's open Tuesday through Sunday, May through September, from 9 a.m. to 11:30 a.m. and 1 p.m. to 4 p.m.*

NIGHTLIFE & ENTERTAINMENT

The cavernous but classy **Rock Club Torpedo**, *Zámek 110*, sits in a cellar lodged in the town walls at the Svinenská gate, just off Masarykovo náměstí to the west. The club, more like a pub, is also the best place to throw back a Regent beer or two.

You can catch a flick at **Kino Světozor**, *Masarykovo náměstí 146*.

SPORTS & RECREATION

The Svět and Opatovicky ponds are the sites for all sorts of water sports – swimming, fishing, sailboarding, and so on. There are two public swimming areas on the Svět, one at the north end (**U Světe**) and one at the southern end (**Ostende**). For information on renting canoes or acquiring a fishing license, contact the Information and Cultural Centre (see *Practical Information* below).

They can also help out with renting bicycles or going on a horseback ride, two great ideas considering the number of paths that venture out into the woods and to outlying ponds and lakes. An interpretive bike trail, following foot paths and asphalt roads, takes you 39 km (24 miles) around the town of Třeboň.

PRACTICAL INFORMATION

• **Agrobanka**, *Palackého náměstí 37/II*. Bank that will change your money.
• **Information and Cultural Centre**, *Masarykovo náměstí 103, 379 01 Třeboň. Tel. 033/721 356*. Extremely helpful agency that can help with just about every aspect of your stay in Třeboň. Come here for bus and train schedules.
• **Post Office**, *Seifortova 588*.

Český Krumlov

Český Krumlov is one of Bohemia's most popular tourist spots. You won't find this all that surprising when you get a look at this medieval town rising from the Vltava River's gooseneck meanders. Imposed on by a clifftop castle and punctuated by a round, 13th-century tower, Český Krumlov enchants like no other town in the Czech Republic.

Although Slav settlement of Český Krumlov goes back to the first half of the 8th century, the town didn't start taking shape until the **Krumlov family** established a small fortification here in the early 13th century, which they soon handed over to their distance relatives, the **Rožmberks**. Over the next few centuries, the Rožmberks developed the town from a backwater village into a cultural and political center. **Vílem and Petr Vok**, the last in the Rožmberk line, gave the castle and building facades a Renaissance facelift, but thankfully did not alter the medieval character of the town (actually two towns then, Krumlov and Latrán, built on opposite sides of the river).

As things went with most of South Bohemia, the **Schwarzenbergs** eventually ended up owning the castle and town. They peppered Český Krumlov with a few Baroque structures, but left it at that. Their greatest contribution, however, was endowing the castle with a number of spectacular Rococo designs, including the castle theater and ballroom – two must-sees when in Český Krumlov. So renowned was the castle's artistic integrity that it received the nickname of "Little Vienna."

Today, Český Krumlov is the one of the best-preserved towns in Europe. Adding Český Krumlov to the World Heritage List in 1992,

UNESCO apparently thinks so as well. With so many architectural gems, the town has sold off a whopping 250 of its Renaissance and Baroque houses to private businesses, which means that almost every house now has some kind of service geared towards the hordes of mostly Austrian and German tourists.

The best days to be in Český Krumlov are June 16–18, when the **Festival of the Five-Petalled Rose** (Slavnost pětilisté růže) is in full swing. Folk music, street theater, chess matches (involving people as chess pieces), and jousting are all part of the spectacle that originated during the Prague Spring of 1968, but was subsequently banned by the Communists.

ORIENTATION

Český Krumlov sits on the banks of the **Vltava River** in the foothills of the **Šumava Mountains**, 25 kilometers (15 miles) southwest of České Budějovice and 140 kilometers (87 miles) south of Prague. The streets and lanes of Český Krumlov are quite confusing, made all the more so by the Vltava River, which swings around the town, resuming its course downstream virtually at the same spot it left off.

But the small size of the town rules out the possibility you'll be lost for long. Keep your eyes out for the castle and its tower, which will help you get your bearings. Two major thoroughfares are Látran and Horní streets, both leading to the main square.

ARRIVALS & DEPARTURES

By Bus

Buses run nearly hourly between České Budějovice and Český Krumlov, taking 30-45 minutes and costing less than 25 Kč. From Prague, you'll have to make a connection in České Budějovice. The bus station is a ten minute walk east of the town center.

By Car

If you are driving from České Budějovice, take E55 south and then follow signs. From Prague, go via České Budějovice. Parking is by permit only within the city center, so go ahead and dump your car at one of several, well-marked parking lots on the outskirts of the old town.

By Train

Trains from České Budějovice to Český Krumlov are far less efficient than buses, but they do run about seven times daily during the weekdays (about three times daily on the weekends). From Prague, you'll have to make a connection in České Budějovice. From the center, the train station is a 20 minute hike on the north side of town – all the more reason to take the bus.

GETTING AROUND TOWN

Everything is well-centered around the castle, which makes walking the best way of getting around town. But you can hail a cab easy enough in the old town or order one from one of the hotels.

WHERE TO STAY

HOTEL RŮŽE, *Horní 153, 381 01 Český Krumlov. Tel. 0337/711 141, Fax 0337/711 128. Rates for single/double: 1,490/2,180-2,380 Kč. Credit cards: AE, MC, V. 50 rooms. Restaurant and café.*

Built as a Jesuit college during the Renaissance and converted to a hotel in 1889, this is one of the oldest and classiest hotels in Bohemia. Legend has it that the sgraffitoed hotel, which looks more like a chateau than an old college, was built on a ancient Celtic sacrificial site, prompting all sorts of ghost stories having to do with the hotel. Many of the spacious rooms come with the original wood ceilings, as well as an unfortunate bit of outdated furniture. But you can ignore that small minus when surrounded by so much opulence.

If your budget doesn't allow you one of the high-end rooms, ask to stay in one of the historical Jesuit cells, which don't come with their own baths. The hotel arranges tours of the town and of the area, including a "night visit" in which a guide dressed in medieval garb escorts you to haunted places around town. The hotel also features the occassional concert and other cultural events.

At press time, the hotel was closed for renovation. When it reopens in the spring of 1999, the hotel will have a lot more to offer, including a swimming pool, sauna, fitness center, travel center, beauty salon, and, thankfully, a new interior design the owner says will be as close as you can get to the Renaissance period. Expect prices to go up.

HOTEL KONVICE, *Horní 144, 381 01 Český Krumlov. Tel. 0337/711 611, Fax 0337/711 327. Rates for double only: 1,300 Kč. Credit cards: AE, V. 5 rooms. Restaurant.*

Outfitted with gorgeous period furniture, original wood ceilings, shiny parquet floors, and Egon Schiele prints, the rooms at this small hotel just off the main square are exquisitely tasteful. The hotel service provides a warm reception, and takes good care of their guests. The restaurant prepares a number of tasty continental dishes and has an extensive wine list (it is after all a *vínarna*, or wine bar). When the weather is nice, seating moves to the terrace on the roof, affording an excellent view of the castle, river, and red roofs of the old town. Best to reserve way in advance for this small gem.

U ZLATÉHO ANDĚLA, *náměstí Svornosti 10, 381 01 Český Krumlov. Tel. and Fax 0337/2473. Rates for single/double: 790/1190 Kč. Credit cards: AE, MC. 4 rooms. Café.*

"At the Golden Angel" offers bright, airy rooms (all with private bath) in the rear of a Baroque house on the main square, which you sadly can't see from the rooms.

HOTEL KRUMLOV, *náměstí Svornosti 14, 381 01 Český Krumlov. Tel. 0337/711 565, Fax 0337/3831. Rates for single/double: 1000/1550 Kč. Credit cards: AE, MC, V. 33 rooms. Restaurant.*

The two things going for this hotel are its location (right on the main square) and its elegant Renaissance facade. Like a lot of hotels carved out of old buildings, Krumlov has forfeited a lot of authenticity in its restoration. Although clean and functional, the rooms lack personality. Friendly service, however, and a pretty good pub.

BOHEMIA GOLD HOTEL, *Park 55, 381 01 Český Krumlov. Tel. 0337/ 613 23, Fax 0337/613 22. Rates for single/double: 2,450/2,860-4,260 Kč. Credit cards: AE, MC, V. 9 rooms. Restaurant.*

A handsome structure that used to be the dormitory for the Jesuit college, this hotel is located a stone's throw away from the Vltava River. But that doesn't exactly make up for the gaudy, gold decor of the rooms, which seem better suited in Las Vegas than in Bohemia. Having said that, the hotel has great service and an excellent restaurant, and can probably assure you a very pleasant stay.

PENZION VE VĚŽI, *Latrán 28, 381 01 Český Krumlov. Tel. & Fax 0337/ 711 742. Rates for single/double: 1,300-1,800 Kč. No credit cards. 2 rooms. Café.*

You can't deny the novelty of this pension built into a Renaissance guard tower. The two strangely-shaped rooms share a bathroom and shower, as there isn't a whole lot of space to work with here. A romantic place to stay nonetheless.

WHERE TO EAT

ROŽMBERK RESTAURANT, *Horní 153. Tel. 0337/5481. 160-300 Kč.*

Crisp, table-clothed dining goes without saying at this nicest of hotels in Český Krumlov. The mostly Czech dishes, such as the roast beef with a creamy lemon sauce and the roast venison smothered in a red wine sauce, come beautifully presented and wonderfully served by the restaurant's deft servers.

CAFFÉ VERDI, *Náměstí Svornosti 3. Tel. 0337/2246. 70-150 Kč. No credit cards.*

This stylish Italian restaurant serves tasty, individual thin-crust pizzas and some excellent Italian gelato. One of the few, good alternatives to Czech food in Český Krumlov. Seating moves out to the main square when the weather cooperates. You'll definitely want to come here to at least have a cappucino and soak in the sights.

VINÁRNA U ŠATLAVY, *145 Šatlavská. No telephone. 50-100 Kč. No credit cards.*

This wine bar, hidden in a cellar just off the main square, is most definitely the coziest place in town. But don't come here expecting privacy. Everyone sits at two or three huge tables, making it a bit difficult when someone has to go to the bathroom. Steaks and other meats are prepared over an open fire and washed down with wine straight from the cask. There's no electricity here, only the big fire and candles. A truly unique place you should not miss.

NA LOUŽI, *Kájovská 66.Tel. 0337/5495. 60-150 Kč. No credit cards.*

This small pub dishes out some hearty goulash and pours a nice glass of Eggenberg. The wood-studded interior, recently renovated, lends a warm and cozy feeling. Tables are set up outside when the weather's nice. A good place for lunch or just to have a beer.

BOHEMIA GOLD HOTEL, *Park 55. Tel. 0337/613 23. 120-300 Kč.*

If you can stomach the over-the-top, gold decor and the ultra-formal service, then you should be able to enjoy a meal from the restaurant's huge menu. Servers, no doubt trained at one of the restaurant and hotel schools around the republic, do much of the food preparation at your table, making your dining experience into one big production. The food, especially the pan-seared duck and the steak au poivre, is extremely good. Prices are quite reasonable, escpecially when you consider the coddling service. Nice dress is certainly recommended.

KRČMA MARKÉTA, *in the chateau garden up the hill from the castle. Tel. 0337/3829. 70-200 Kč. No credit cards.*

Medieval song and dance and servers dressed in period garb are all part of the novelty at this Renaissance pub serving chicken, beef, and game over an open fire. Realy touristy, but can be a hoot.

SEEING THE SIGHTS

What better place to start than at **Krumlov Castle,** which you can access by taking Latrán to the Red Gate (Červená brána) and walking up the hill. At the entrance to the castle you'll be greeted by three brown bears, who have traditionally been kept in the castle's dry moat since the 16th century. Just beyond the entrance bridge you'll enter into the first of three courtyards, where you'll see a ticket office selling admission to the 54-meter-high (178 feet) **castle tower** (hrádek), built in the late 13th century but later modified to Renaissance taste. There are 162 steep steps to the top, where you can get a spectacular panoramic view of the town and the surrounding city.

Between the second and third sgraffitoed courtyards you'll find the ticket office for the castle. There are two tours to choose from. One is of the older sections of the castle mostly built by the Rožmberks. But if you have to choose only one, then take the other tour, which takes you through a number of Baroque rooms and, most importantly, through the **Rococo ballroom**. Painter J. Lederer covered the ballroom's walls with a cast of characters living it up at a ball. He went so far as to paint peasants looking in through the windows and admiring the class of people inside. Also make sure to get a load of the guards at the doorway, who always have their eye on you, no matter where you stand.

On the other side of the covered bridge (most Na Plášti) is the castle's **Rococo theater** (zámecké divadlo), the oldest castle theater in Europe, retaining most of its original 18th-century backdrops, props, and costumes. Occasionally, plays are performed here, which are about the only times you can go inside. Check with Infocentrum (see *Practical Information*) for a schedule of perfomances. After climbing the hill through the castle you'll want to catch your breath in the **chateau gardens**, above the theater next to the riding school and summer palace. *May through August the castle is open daily except Monday from 8 a.m. to noon and 1 to 5 p.m. In April and September it opens at 9 a.m.*

Retrace your steps back down to Latrán, take a right, and then continue across the bridge into **Inner Town** (vnitřní město). From the bridge it's a straight shot into the main square, **náměstí Svornosti**, where the focal point is the 1716 **Marian Plague Column** (Mariánský sloupek). You'll definitely want to soak in the square's regal Renaissance and Baroque houses from one of the several outdoor cafés.

Up the hill from the main square and just off Horní is **St. Vitus Church** (Kostel sv Víta), its spires sticking up through the skyline at the top of Inner Town. The church, from the 14th century,began as a Gothic construction, but was given a Baroque interior in the 18th century. Vílem Rožmberk is buried inside the walls next to his third wife, Maria Bádenská. A little further up the hill, *at Horní 152*, the **Regional Museum** (Okresní muzeum) tells the story of Český Krumlov from prehistoric days on up to the 19th century. It also has an eclectic collection of local folk art and a detailed, ceramic model of the town. *The museum is open daily except Monday from 10 a.m. to 12:30 p.m. and 1 p.m. to 6 p.m.*

As you've probably already noticed by all the Egon Schiele posters sticking to the walls around town, there is a museum in Český Krumlov devoted to this Viennese painter who spent less than a year here in his mother's hometown. During his time in Český Krumlov he produced a number of townscapes that now hang in the **Egon Schiele Centrum**, *Široka 70-72*, just down from náměstí Svornosti. Set in a former brewery built in 1578, the museum houses a permanent collection of original

Schiele paintings, as well as a changing exhibit of 20th century art. *Open daily 10 a.m. to 6 p.m.*

NIGHTLIFE & ENTERTAINMENT

During the summer, catch a play at the outdoor **Revolving Auditorium** (Otáčive Hlediště), above the castle in the chateau garden. Fortune is shining upon you if you happen to be in town during a performance at the **Castle Theater** (see *Seeing the Sights*). Definitely do not miss this once-in-a-lifetime opportunity of seeing a play presented in one of the oldest theaters in Europe. For ticket and schedule information for either of these venues, contact Infocentrum *(see Practical Information)*.

Get a taste of the local brew at **Pivnice Eggenberg**, a beer hall housed in the former ice room of the Eggenberg brewery at *Latrán 27,* or at Na Louží hospoda (see *Where to Eat*).

SPORTS & RECREATION

What better way to see the mountains and foothills surrounding Český Krumlov than by canoe down the Vltava River. **Vltava,** *Kájovská 62, Tel.* 0337/711 978, is a travel agency that rents canoes and provides the transportation. Putting in at Český Krumlov, you can get out at Zlatá Koruna, Dívči Kámen, or Boršov. Or you can choose a trip starting upstream at Vyšší Brod, Rožmberk, Záton, or Větřní and letting out at Český Krumlov.

Prices range from 400 to 800 Kč, depending on the length of the trip. Beginners should have no problem negotiating the Vltava's easy waters.

DAY TRIPS & EXCURSIONS

Zlatá Koruna

Downstream from Český Krumlov is one of the best-preserved Gothic structures in Bohemia, **the Cistercian Monastery** (Cisterciácky klášter) in the tiny village of **Zlatá Koruna** (Golden Crown). Originally called Saintly Crown of Thorns, the monastery was established in 1263 by Přemysl Otakar II in an effort to outdo his rivals, the Rožmberks, who had just finished building a monastery at Vyšší Brod. Although the Hussites gave it a good thrashing during the Hussite Wars, Zlatá Koruna lives on in all its Gothic majesty in spite of past attempts to give it a Baroque character. Highlights of the monastery included its rib-vaulted **cathedral** and the **Museum of South Bohemian Literature** (Památník písemnictví jižních Čech).

From June through the August the monastery is open daily except Monday from 8 a.m. to noon and from 1 to 5 p.m. In April, May, September, and October it's open from 9 a.m. to 4 p.m.

Zlatá Koruna is about a 15 minute drive northeast of Český Krumlov. Get on the main road heading to České Budějovice and then follow signs. If you don't have a car, it's easiest getting to Zlatá Koruna from Český Krumlov by bus. Check at Infocentrum (see *Practical Information*) for times of departure, which always depend on the season.

Rožmberk Nad Vltavou

Eighteen kilometers (11 miles) south of Český Krumlov, this quaintest of quaint villages hugs the banks of the Vltava River and sits in the shadow of the imposing **Rožmberk Castle**, commanding a hilltop position over the scenic valley. As the name suggests, Rožmberk Castle served as headquarters for the all-pervasive Rožmberks until their extinction in the 17th century.

Jakobín Tower, the oldest existing part of the castle dating back to the 13th century, is all that remains of the so-called Upper Castle after it was destroyed by fire in 1522. Lower Castle, on the other hand, lived on to get a Renaissance makeover and become a reward for the French general Karel Buquoy for his role in fighting against the Hussites. The Buquoy family apparently went to great lengths in reminding their guests that they descended from an illustrious cadre of Crusaders, filling one of the rooms with a number of paintings of fictitious heroes from the Holy Wars. They also seemingly had a keen interest in instruments of torture, as you'll see on one of the regularly scheduled tours that takes you through the Lower Castle. In addition to the rooms filled with torture instruments, the **Banquet Hall** and its gorgeous Italian frescoes are a definite highlight in the tour. *From June through August the castle is open daily except Monday from 9 a.m. to 5 p.m., until 4 p.m. in May and September, and on weekends only in April and October.*

If you don't have a car, the best way of getting to Rožmberk nad Vltavou is by bus; around ten of them leave daily from Český Krumlov and continue on to Vyšší Brod, the next excursion destination.

Vyšší Brod

The reason for coming to this tiny town on the Vltava is its blinding white **Cistercian monastery** (Cisterciácký Klašter), established by Vok of Rožmberk in 1259 and finally completed in the late 14th century. The monastery managed to stay intact in spite of two assaults the Hussites waged on it in the 15th century. Petr Vok, the last of the Rožmberks and victim to excessive alcohol and drug use, was given his final resting spot under the monastery's presbytery. The monastery subsequently changed hands to the Eggenbergs, and later to the Schwarzenbergs. The Communists confiscated it in 1950 and threw the Cistercian monks in jail.

Back in Cistercian possession, the monastery now offers tours of the 13th-century **Chapter House** (Kapitulní síň), an amazingly well-preserved Gothic structure considering that its roof is supported by a single beam. But the highlight of the tour comes at the end, when you step through the secret bookcase entrance and into the monastery's dazzling Rococo **library**, filled with 70,000 volumes and inlaid with enough gold to buy yourself a yacht or two. *The monastery is open May through September daily except Monday from 8:30 a.m. to 5 p.m., and to 4 p.m. in April and October.*

Vyšší Brod is 23 kilometers (14 miles) south of Český Krumlov and a mere 8 kilometers (5 miles) from the Austrian border. Running several times a day, buses are easy enough from Český Krumlov, stopping at Rožmberk nad Vltavou on the way.

PRACTICAL INFORMATION

• **Čedok,** *Latrán 44, 381 01 Český Krumlov. Tel. 0337/711 406, Fax 0337/2062.* Sells maps, organizes tours, changes money, and can help with finding accommodations.

• **Infocentrum,** *náměstí Svornosti 1, 381 00 Český Krumlov; Telephone/fax 0337/711 183.* This very helpful office sells maps and books, can arrange private accommodations, and provides train and bus schedules. It also sells tickets to cultural events happening in town.

• **Investiční banka,** *náměstí Svornosti 5.* A bank where you can change money.

• **Post Office,** *Latrán 193.*

15. WEST BOHEMIA

The Czech Republic is a country jam-packed with cities, towns, and villages, which is why it comes as such a big surprise to find a region as scarcely populated as **West Bohemia**. Of course, it's not like driving through the American West and not seeing a sizable town for hours on end. But, considering its location in the heart of Europe, West Bohemia is astoundingly rural, not to mention wonderfully green, with nearly half its land area covered in dense forests. Consequently, it's one of the more sedate regions you could choose to visit in the two republics.

Part and parcel of this sedate atmosphere is West Bohemia's many spa towns, in particular the spa triangle of **Karlovy Vary, Mariánské Lázně,** and **Františkový Lázně**. Set like jewels in a pillow of lush, wooded hills, Karlovy Vary and Mariánské Lázně are definitely the two star attractions in the region, featuring exquisite turn-of-the-century architecture that reflects their illustrious pasts as two of Central Europe's most fashionable retreats.

But for all their beauty, the spa towns lack excitement (especially Františkový Lázně), mainly because their aim is to provide the most relaxed atmosphere possible for their patients, who come to drink and bathe in the mineral waters, undergo any number of questionable treatments, and take long, constitutional walks in the surrounding woods. (For more information on arranging spa treatments, see "Spas" in the *Sports & Recreation* chapter.)

Thankfully then, there are alternative destinations, such as the captivating town of **Cheb** and the romantic, walled village of **Loket nad Ohří**, both of which make rewarding day trips from Karlovy Vary or Mariánské Lázně. We also can't forget the region's main city of **Plzeň**, a destination that's a must for beer connoisseurs. Yes, it's an industrial town, but it does have a pretty historical center that makes it worth spending the night.

Plzeň

If you are on a beer pilgrimage through the Czech Republic, your most important stop would have to be the industrial town of **Plzeň** (Pilsen), perhaps the mecca of beer brewing in Europe. The beer-making tradition of this city goes back to 1295, the same year **King Václav II** founded the town as the administrative center for the region (which it still is) and granted a handful of burghers the exclusive right to make beer.

Throughout the ages, beer was made in all quantities and forms in Plzeň, most of it served upstairs from whichever basement it was brewed or stored in. But it wasn't until 1842 that Plzeň became world-renowned for its beer, the year Plzeň citizens were on the brink of rioting over the swill its brewers were pumping out.

Under fire to produce something satisfactory, a group of brewers joined forces and came up with the first bottom-fermented beer the world had yet seen. Having appeased the demanding tastes of the Plzeň beer-guzzlers, this light golden beer, generically known as Pilsner (or Pils), went on to grab the attention of brewers everywhere, including America, where just about every major brewing company today produces this type of beer with rather unfortunate results. Luckily for us, the original Pilsner beer is with us today in the form of **Pilsner Urquell**, or Plženský Prazdroj as the Czechs know it. (To make it's point, the original Pilsner brewery eventually had to tack on the German name of *urquell* and the Czech name of *prazdroj*, both of which mean "original source.")

Of course, Plzeň means more than just beer. To Czechs, it also means **Škoda**, one of the largest employers in the country, founded in 1859 in Plzeň as a small iron foundry. Transformed during World War I into a weapons manufacturer, Škoda and its many plants in Plzeň were later incorporated into the Nazi war machine, which was why American forces were compelled to bomb the city on December 20, 1944. (Plzeň was later liberated by General Patton's Fifth Army.) Having produced the unsound Soviet-designed nuclear reactors used in all the Warsaw Pact countries, Škoda today concentrates its efforts on building cars, locomotives, and industrial machinery (the auto plant is in the nearby town of Mladá Boleslav). Considering that Volkswagen loaned Škoda a whopping $1 billion for development, you could rightly say that the German car company now has a big stake in Škoda.

In spite of the many factories and smokestacks, Plzeň is still a rewarding destination for teetotalers and beer guzzlers alike. Beer enthusiasts will have a heyday walking through the town's terrific **Brewery Museum**, touring the **Pilsner Urquell brewery**, and quaffing the three different beers made in Plzeň. Students of architecture will also find something of interest in the original Gothic layout of the historical center and in the many Renaissance buildings preserved there. With a population of 175,000, Plzeň is the fourth largest city in the Czech Republic, which makes it a lively enough place to spend the night or make the easy day trip from Prague.

By the way, the big **Plzeň Beer Festival** (Pivní slavností) happens here in early October. Call the **City Information Center**, *Tel. 019/723 6535*, for exact dates.

ORIENTATION

Located 84 kilometers (52 miles) west of Prague, Plzeň sits at the confluence of four rivers – the **Mže**, **Radbuza**, **Berounka**, and **Uhlava**. The streets in the historic center are laid out in their original Gothic checkerboard fashion, which makes it easy to find your way around.

ARRIVALS & DEPARTURES

By Bus

Buses leave Prague's Florenc station roughly every 45 minutes for the two hour journey. (Fast train is quicker). Tickets cost about 66 Kč and seat reservations are not necessary. The central bus station in Plzeň is a 15 minute walk west of the city center along Husova street or a couple of minutes on tram #1 or #2.

By Car

From Prague, head east on E50 all the way to Plzeň. The drive takes less than an hour. Look for the blue "P" signs after you've been directed into the *centrum* from the highway. If you park on the street, make sure you feed some money into the meter. For some confounding reason, the meters run only until 10 p.m., after which the police will slap a boot on your tire if you're still parked on the street. Most hotels do have private parking for their guests.

By Train
This is the best way to go if you don't have your own wheels. But make sure you get on a fast train (*rychlík*) or a Eurocity (EC) train, both of which take about an hour-and-a-half as compared to two hours by slow train (*osobní vlak*). Trains depart Hlavní nádraží and Smíchovské nádraží in Prague roughly every hour and tickets cost 53 Kč.

The main train station in Plzeň is conveniently located five minutes east of the historic center. When you walk out the front door of the train station, hang a right, then take your first left (through the vestibule under the intersection), and then go straight on Americká street.

GETTING AROUND TOWN

There are three forms of public transportation in Plzeň: tram, bus, and trolley bus – all of which take the same ticket you can buy at most kiosks, newsstands, and *tabacs*. Don't forget to validate them on board. If you are arriving and departing by train and plan on sticking to the compact historical center, then you'll probably have no need to use public transportation. But you can hail a cab easily enough from the street if the need ever arises.

WHERE TO STAY

HOTEL CONTINENTAL, *Zbrojnická 8, 305 34 Plzeň. Tel. 019/723 5292, Fax 019/722 1746. Rates for single/double without bathroom: 540/660 Kč. Rates for single/double with bathroom: 1,560/2,160 Kč. Credit cards: AE, MC, V. 55 rooms. Restaurant.*

As was the case of countless gorgeous Central European hotels built in the early 20th century, the Hotel Continental was stripped of its fine furnishings at the hands of Communist directors, who by and large destroyed the interior refinement of this once opulent hotel. Though American and new owner George Janaček still has miles to go before the hotel captures its former glory, the alterations done to it since George took over have been noble, especially in the restored rooms, which are some of the nicest I've seen in the Czech Republic. You can hardly believe you're in the same hotel when you walk from the dank, unrestored hallways into a room shining with Art Deco furniture and original art work. (George has a storeroom of antique furniture and a full-time employee refurbishing it.)

But most rooms have yet to be transformed, and are still stuck in the earlier days of Communist tackiness. So definitely ask for one of the new rooms, one of which is an enormous office suite filled with all the high-tech amenities traveling business people need. Room rates come with a first-rate breakfast buffet. And with prior notice, George can arrange cultural, hunting, and fishing excursions for his guests. For more on the hotel's excellent restaurant and café, see *Where to Eat*, below.

THE INCREDIBLE HISTORY OF THE HOTEL CONTINENTAL

In the spring of 1993, I happened to meet George Janaček in a tiny, obscure village just outside Plzeň, where I was with a friend visiting her mother, an elderly woman who had once worked at the hotel. When George arrived at the house to say hello to this old friend of the family's, I had the distinct feeling of having seen him somewhere before. It turned out that George and I were not only both from Utah, but that we had spent some time doing work for the same magazine back in Salt Lake City.

That night, he related the incredible history of the Continental, which has been in his family since 1929. The grand Hotel Continental is more than a hotel – it's a legacy, with a noble and fascinating history. In the heady days of the First Republic, it was one of the most illustrious hotels in Czechoslovakia, its crystal and damask opulence luring the likes of Ingrid Bergman, Jack Benny, and Marlene Dietrich.

It was owned by Emanuel Ledecky and his young wife Eugenie. On December 20, 1944, a stray American bomb ripped through the hotel, killing 100 people inside, including Emanuel. Eugenie, who happened to be out of town visiting her dying mother when the bomb struck, was left a young widow and the owner of a hotel that was in ruins, but still standing. When American forces liberated the town, they used it as their headquarters. After the Americans had gone, Eugenie set to work rebuilding the hotel, but her efforts were rendered futile with the advent of Stalinism in Czechoslovakia. So she and her newly-wedded husband Jiří Janaček (George's father), sailed for America in 1946, relinquishing the hotel to the Communist powers.

By the time the Velvet Revolution rolled around, Eugenie had of course given up all hope of ever reacquiring the hotel, which is why it came as a shock when her son George called her one day to tell her that she was entitled to ownership of the hotel, made possible by the country's post-revolution restitution laws. A photographer from Salt Lake City, George had covered the Velvet Revolution for Life magazine, afterwards deciding to settle in his parents' homeland. In her 80s by now, Eugenie decided to claim ownership of the hotel and then sign it over to George.

Now a Czech citizen, George has the near-impossible task of restoring the hotel, a task that is a far cry from George's old occupation of shooting photos in the Utah desert. As for Eugenie, she has come back from the U.S. to live in the hotel that she left in 1946.

PENSION CITY, *Sady 5. května 52, 301 14 Plzeň. Tel. 019/226 069, Fax 019/222 976. Rates for single/double: 850/1,300 Kč. No credit cards. 10 rooms. No restaurant.*

This family-run pension is a decent alternative to the big hotels in town. Rooms are somewhat plain but come with satellite television and private bath, although rooms number four and five have their baths and toilet inconveniently located down the hall (avoid these rooms). Private parking is available.

HOTEL CENTRAL, *Náměstí Republiky 33, 305 31 Plzeň. Tel. 019/722 6757, fax 019/722 6064. Rates for single/double: 1,125-1,412/1,910-2,548 Kč. Credit cards: AE, DC, MC, V. 72 rooms. Restaurant.*

Right on Plzeň's main square, the modern Hotel Central has rooms that are rather generic, but are comfortable nonetheless. Though the rooms look perfectly clean, I had to wonder about the maids' attention to detail when I saw one of them in a hotel suite smoking a cigarette and watching a German soap opera on television. If you do stay here, definitely ask for a room with a view of the square. In addition to the restaurant, the hotel has a private garage, a small fitness center, sauna, and nightclub.

PENSION BÁROVÁ, *Solní 8, 305 31 Plzeň. Tel. 019/723 6652, no fax. Rates for single/double: 510/850 Kč. No credit cards. 3 rooms. No restaurant.*

The three rooms at this 16th-century house just off the main square are cozy and generously large. Each room has a private bath and television. If you don't like big hotels or their prices, this is a good choice. Private parking is not available, unfortunately.

HOTEL SLOVAN, *Smetanovy sady 1, 305 28 Plzeň. Tel. 019/722 7256, Fax 019/722 7012. Rates for single/double without private bath: 580/900 Kč. Rates for single/double with private bath: 1,380/1,800 Kč. Credit cards: MC, V. 109 rooms. Restaurant.*

The stucco and gilt lobby with its grand staircase is the most impressive thing about this late 19th-century hotel a few blocks south of the main square. But that's where the opulence ends. The rooms that have been renovated are smartly furnished, while those that haven't are typically drab. The ugly restaurant serves basic Czech fare that I wouldn't go out of my way to try. Private parking is available.

HOTEL VICTORIA, *Borská 19, 320 22 Plzeň. Tel. 019/722 1010, Fax 019/276 621. Rates for single/double: 1,100/1,850 Kč. Credit cards: AE, V, MC. 30 rooms. Restaurant.*

This hotel isn't so conveniently located as the ones listed above. It's a kilometer south of the historic center, accessed by taking tram #4 from Sady Pětatřicázníků street to Borská street. Rooms are decent and functional, but way overpriced.

WHERE TO EAT

HOTEL CONTINENTAL, *Zbrojnická 8. Tel. 019/723 5292. 150-250 Kč.*

When George Janaček took over the hotel, his first priority was the restaurant. He built a new kitchen, remodeled the dining room, and revamped the menu. The menu now features tangy Chicago-style barbecue ribs and a hulking chili burrito, both of which are godsends for Americans who have had their fill of Czech food.

For something a bit more refined, try the rabbit medallions with chips of garlic or the shark with mustard sauce. The big bay windows offer a nice view of the newly-laid out park in front of the hotel. Top-notch service and very reasonable prices to boot.

U SALZMANNŮ, *Pražská 8. Tel. 019/723 5855. 130-200 Kč. No credit cards.*

Founded in 1637, this is the oldest pub in Plzeň, something the place never lets you forget. With its wood-studded furnishings and big windows, the newly remodeled rooms are made to look as they did at the turn of the century. Despite being a touristy place, it does the job of drawing a good Pilsner Urquell and Purkmistr (another local brew). Standard, overpriced Czech fare is on the menu. You'd be better off stopping here for lunch or just a beer than you would for dinner.

RESTAURANT ASIA, *Veleslavínova 26. Tel. 019/220 073. 150-300 Kč. Credit cards: AE, DC, MC, V.*

The very exotic decor makes this one of the swankiest Chinese restaurants I've seen in the Czech Republic. But the Czech waiters dressed up in Chinese garb do look a bit ridiculous. The menu (in English) here is immense, offering a lot of seafood such as curried mussels and swordfish steak. Though the food won't astound connoisseurs of Chinese cuisine, it does do the trick of satisfying an empty stomach.

KRÁLOVSKÁ ROSSO VINÁRNA, *Pallova 12. Tel. 019/722 6473. 200-400 Kč. Credit cards: AE, MC, V.*

This is perhaps Plzeň's premier restaurant, but it unfortunately doesn't live up to its good reputation now that its original chef is gone. French food such as escargot, frog legs, and flaming meats are on the menu, as are a lot of traditional Czech dishes. The intimate setting, under the vaulted ceiling of this 16th century house, is the best aspect of the place.

RESTAURANT NA SPILCE, *U Prazdroje 1. Tel. 019/706 2754. 150-300 Kč. No credit cards.*

This restaurant/beerhall right on the grounds of the Pilsner Urquell brewery claims to be the biggest of its kind in the Czech Republic. For being such a touristy place, the basic Czech food is surprisingly good. But how can you go wrong when you've got an endless supply of some of the best beer in the world? **MORAVSKÁ VINARNÁ,** *Bezručova 4. Tel. 019/723 7972. 150-200 Kč. No credit cards.* This favorite of the locals serves up some paprika-laced Moravian specialties, washed down with glasses of Moravian wine. **CAFÉ 21,** *Prokopova 21. Tel. 019/285 258. 100-250 Kč. Credit cards: AE, MC, V.* This classy place resembling an English pub features a tasty chicken steak with sage and a couple of good pasta dishes. Some juicy steaks are on the menu, including one drenched in an herb-butter sauce.

SEEING THE SIGHTS

The logical place to start is smack dab in the middle of town at **náměstí Republiky,** Plzeň's bustling main square. Thrusting up from the middle of the square is **St. Bartholomew's Cathedral.** Built in the late Gothic style of the 14th century, the cathedral is strangely distanced from the buildings outlining the square, giving you plenty of space to soak in the cathedral's soaring rusted steeple – at 103 meters (338 feet), the highest in Bohemia. If you've got what it takes to go up 298 steps, then go ahead and climb the church tower for the best view you'll ever get of the flat city. Inside on the main altar, you'll find the Plzeň madonna, a Gothic statue dating from 1390.

Surrounding the square is a hodgepodge of architectural styles that date right up to the 1960s. But the style that dominates is Renaissance, stated most eloquently by the pretty 16th-century **town hall** (radnice), which is just behind the obligatory plague column. Plzeň's finest piece of architecture, the town hall is topped by three fanciful gables and smothered in sgraffito that was added early this century. On the opposite side of the square are similar Italianate buildings with spiky gables cutting a pretty outline of the square.

From náměstí Republiky, it's a short walk west along Pražská street to the town's medieval water tower, used at one time as part of the town's fortifications. Standing opposite is the Gothic **Butchers' Stalls** (Masné krámy), fronted at each end by two distinct battlement facades. The elongated halls of the structure now house the **West Bohemian Gallery** (Západočeská galerie), exhibiting an excellent collection of contemporary Czech art. *It's open Tuesday through Friday from 10 a.m. to 6 p.m., on Saturday until 1 p.m., and on Sunday from 9 a.m. to 5 p.m.*

From the Butchers' Stalls, walk back towards náměstí Republiky and then swing right on Perlová, where you'll come to a handsome Renaissance building *at number 65*. Believe it or not, this is the entrance to the **Plzeň Historical Underground**, a subterranean maze of medieval cellars and passageways. The earliest of the cellars dates back to the 14th century, when they were most likely used for storing beer. Over the years, people threw their rubbish in them, which has left a treasure trove for modern-day archaeologists.

On exhibit are many of those artifacts, including a good bit of pottery and pewter, as well as some Czech glass dating back to the 14th century. All in all, there are an estimated 11 kilometers of passageways under the town, but only 500 meters are open to the public. Be sure to bring a sweater even in the dead of summer, because it gets cold down there. *In April, May, October, and November, tours run Wednesday through Sunday from 9 a.m. to 5 p.m. From June through September they run the same hours daily except Monday. Tickets cost 30 Kč.*

Right around the corner *at Veleslavínova 6* is the city's star attraction – the **Brewery Museum** (Pivovarské Muzeum), the oldest and best of its kind anywhere. The museum's location is a good one when you consider that it's set within an old brewer's house and next to a Gothic malthouse. Through paintings, photographs, and old beer paraphernalia, the museum traces the history of beer making and consumption in the city of Plzeň, which in itself is a good microcosm for beer drinking worldwide.

In addition to all the instruments for making beer the old-fashioned way, there's a mock-up of a 19th century Czech pub that shows you how little beer drinking customs has changed in the Czech Republic over the centuries. Upstairs is a humorous picture gallery of all the illustrious and not-so-illustrious people caught in the act of swilling the town's beer or visiting the Prazdroj brewery. There's even a great one of President Clinton sitting in a Prague pub quaffing a beer alongside President Havel and writer Bohumil Hrabal. *The museum is open daily except Monday from 10 a.m. to 6 p.m. Entrance is 40 Kč, with which you get a well-written English text.*

From the Brewery Museum, retrace your steps back to náměstí Republiky and then cut across to Solní street, at the end of which you'll find a couple of handsome Art Nouveau facades by Mikuláš Aleš, a leading figure in the Czech National Revival at the turn of the century. From there, bear left on Sady Pětatřicázníků street to the **Great Synagogue** (Velká Synagoga). Built in 1892 in the neo-Renaissance style, this is the biggest synagogue in Central Europe, which is strange when you consider that the number of Jews living in Plzeň at the time of its construction was only about 2,000 – marginal compared to the number of Jews living in Warsaw or Prague at that time. After decades of neglect, it's finally being restored, and most likely will still be under scaffolding by the time you visit.

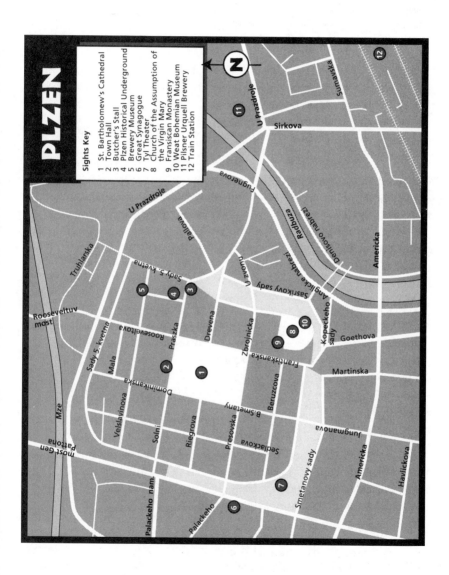

PLZEN

Sights Key

1 St. Bartholomew's Cathedral
2 Town Hall
3 Butcher's Stall
4 Plzen Historical Underground
5 Brewery Museum
6 Great Synagogue
7 Tyl Theater
8 Church of the Assumption of the Virgin Mary
9 Fransiscan Monastery
10 Weat Bohemian Museum
11 Pilsner Urquell Brewery
12 Train Station

292 CZECH & SLOVAK REPUBLICS GUIDE

Diagonal to the synagogue is the stately **Tyl Theater**, built at the turn of the century and named for Josef Kajétan Tyl, who composed the Czech half of the Czechoslovak national anthem. Today it presents plays, operas, and ballets.

Running just behind the theater is Smetanovy sady, a long strip of grass and trees spotted with the occasional statue, including one of Bedřich Smetana, the famous composer who once taught in Plzeň. By now, you've probably noticed that the old historical center has a green ring around it, which is a pleasant surprise in a city that is, for the most part, industrial. Half-way down, swing a left on Františkánská street, where you'll see the **Church of the Assumption of the Virgin Mary** (Kostel Nanebevzetí Panny Marie) off to your right. Gothic at its core, this church contains an extremely curious crucifix. Whoever created it went against the orthodox image of Christ, giving him a scraggly mustache rather than the obligatory full beard. He hangs from the cross with only one hand and one foot nailed to the cross.

Adjoining the church, the **Franciscan Monastery** (Klášter Františkánů) houses a section of the West Bohemian Museum, this one devoted to Gothic and Baroque statues culled from churches in the region. But the highlight at the monastery is the tiny **St. Barbara's Chapel** (Kaple sv. Barbory), not once altered since it was constructed in the 13th century. Under its gorgeous ribbed vaults are some faded frescoes that date back to 1460.

Just behind the monastery at the corner of Kopeckého sady and Šafaříkovy sady, the **West Bohemian Museum** (Západočeské muzeum) occupies a handsome neo-Baroque pile built as part of the Czech National Revival. On exhibit are number of medieval artifacts, handicrafts, and a lot of stuffed animals. If you're short on time, don't feel bad about missing this one. *It's open daily except Monday from 10 a.m. to 6 p.m.*

Last but not least is the **Pilsner Urquell Brewery** (Plzeňský Prazdroj pivovar), across the Radbuza River *at U Prazdroje 7, Tel. 019/706 2632.* From the West Bohemian Museum, follow the river downstream and cross the first bridge you come to. Fronting the brewery are the grand arches that have adorned the Urquell label since 1892, the year the arches were erected in commemoration of the brewery's 50th anniversary.

The one-hour tour first takes you through the brewing house, where you can see the old methods of brewing with direct heat. Then you descend into the cavernous historical cellars carved out of sandstone, which is where the beer is fermented. A slick video introduces you to some of the more technical aspects of brewing the beer. Of course, the tour wouldn't be complete without sampling some of the wonderful product. If that hasn't quenched your thirst, then head to the beerhall, Na Spilce, on the brewery grounds. There's a gift shop here where you can buy some souvenirs for your beer buddies back home. *Tours are given daily from 8 a.m. to 3 p.m.* Best would be to first call the brewery at the number above to set up an appointment, so you don't end up waiting around for the next tour.

NIGHTLIFE & ENTERTAINMENT

If you've come to Plzeň, then drinking some of the local brew is most likely a high priority on your list of things to do. Like any city in the Czech Republic, there's no shortage of pubs. In addition to **U Salzmannů** and **Na Spilce** (see *Where to Eat*, above), you can throw back a glass of Urquell at **Na parkánu**, right next door to the Brewery Museum *at Veleslavínova 4*. There's also **U Žumbery** *at Bezručova 14*, pouring a fine Gambrinus (another beer by the Urquell brewery) and seating folks in their nice summer garden.

A good place to drink good beer and hear live or recorded rock tunes is **Rock Club 21** *at Prokopova 21*, part of the good Café 21 (see *Where to Eat*).

For something a little more highbrow, you could catch a ballet or opera at the gorgeous **Tyl Theater**, at the corner of *Smetanovy sady and Pětatřicázníků*. For ticket information, *call 019/224 256* or go to the theater box office.

Or, if you just feel like taking in a movie, you can do so at **Kino Hvězda** at *Pražská 35* or **Kino Eden** at *Rejskova 10*.

PRACTICAL INFORMATION

- **City Information Center Plzeň**, *náměstí Republiky 41. Tel. 019/723 6535.* Offers maps, guides, brochures, and souvenirs.
- **Komerční banka**, *at the corner of Kopeckého sady and Anglické nábřeží.* Changes money.
- **Kreditní banka**, *náměstí Republiky*. Also changes money.
- **Post Office**, *just off náměstí Republiky on Solní street.*

Mariánské Lázně

Cradled in a narrow, tree-strewn valley, **Mariánské Lázně** (Marienbad to the Germans) is a gem of a town, sporting a bevy of fin-de-siecle architecture in and around its genteel spa. Comparatively speaking, it's a new town, founded as a spa in 1817 by local abbot **Karel Reitenberger** and German doctor **Josef Nehr**.

By the end of the 19th century, it had become the chic retreat for the European rich and renowned, attracting the likes of **King Edward VII**, **Frédéric Chopin**, and **J.W. Goethe** – the compulsive spa-goer who, at the age of 72, fell in love with the 16-year-old daughter of a Marienbad hotelier.

Indeed, the town has had an inspiring effect on artists, prompting **Wagner** to compose *Lohengrin* and **Nikolai Gogol** to write *Dead Souls* here. **Franz Kafka**, who seemingly never gave himself the chance to see the light of day, shared a happy sojourn here with his lover **Felice Bauer** shortly before he died. Even **Mark Twain** was compelled to make his way here during his European travels.

After falling into decay during the Communist era, Mariánské Lázně has made a comeback, and in a big way. With the exception of a few facades, the entire spa area of town looks as though it has been renovated. There is no shortage of hotels in Mariánské Lázně. In fact, there would seem to be nothing *but* hotels. There is no shortage of Germans either, who show up by the bus-load to partake of the curative mineral waters in and around the **Colonnade**, the centerpiece of the spa.

For all of Mariánské Lázně's beauty, there is a lack of things to do here. But you could happily wile away a day admiring the architecture, strolling through the town's several beautiful parks, and hiking up the tree-studded slopes that engulf the town. One of the spa sanatoriums – Nové Lázně, see *Sports & Recreation* below – does offer walk-in spa treatments, which is a good idea if you've been walking all day and are in need of an elaborate bath and a heavy-duty massage.

ORIENTATION

Mariánské Lázně is 162 kilometers (100 miles) west of Prague and 74 kilometers (49 miles) west of Plzeň. It sits in the midst of the beautiful **Slavkov Forest** (Slavkovský les), a hilly protected landscape region responsible for the town's crisp, clean air.

Lined with scores of hotels, restaurants, shops, and cafés, **Hlavní třída** (Main Avenue) is the town's main drag, stretching from the train station to the spa area. There's no problem finding your way around this small town, limited in size by the encroaching hills.

ARRIVALS & DEPARTURES

By Bus

From Prague's Florenc station, six or seven buses depart every day for the three-and-a-half-hour journey that costs 95 Kč. From Plzeň, buses go about as often and cost 30 Kč for the hour-long ride. The bus station in Mariánské Lázně sits just in front of the train station at the bottom of Hlavní třída street. It's about a ten minute walk or a quick ride on trolley bus #5 to the spa area.

By Car

From Prague, head east through Plzeň on E50 and then cut north on Highway 21 once you come to Stříbro. The drive should take about two-and-a-half hours, depending on traffic. I wouldn't dare park on the streets in Mariánské Lázně for fear of automatically getting a boot on your wheel. Instead, park at one of the pay lots at the top or bottom of Hlavní třída street.

By Train

Eight or nine fast trains depart Prague's Hlavní nádráží and Smíchovské nádráží each day for the three-and-a-half-hour trip that costs 95 Kč. These same trains stop in Plzeň. The Mariánské Lázně train station is a ten minute walk or a quick ride on trolley bus #5 to the spa area up the hill. If you're traveling between Karlovy Vary and Mariánské Lázně, train is the way to go. It's a bit slower than the bus, but well worth it because of the beautiful scenery taken in along the way.

GETTING AROUND TOWN

Walking is the main activity here, and it's easy enough to get around town on foot. Trolley buses run up and down Hlavní třída, but you'll probably never have any use for them unless you're going to or coming from the train station. There are no tickets for the buses; just drop 5 Kč in the slot on board. Taxis are easy enough to hail from the street or order by calling *Tel. 0165/2708*.

WHERE TO STAY

VILLA BUTTERFLY, *Hlavní třída 655, 353 01 Mariánské Lázně. Tel. 0165/484 100, Fax 0165/762 10. Rates for single/double: 1,530-3,910/2,070-4,140 Kč. Credit cards: AE, DC, MC, V. 100 rooms. Restaurant.*

The lap of luxury in Mariánské Lázně, this hotel was recently reconstructed and made into one of the choicest places in town. Its two bright yellow wings, designed in a sort of contemporary Art Nouveau style and topped by some avant-garde statues, nearly dominates the town's main street. Though the rooms are extremely comfortable, they're somewhat on the generic side – not at all as unique as the hotel's beautiful two-tiered marble lobby. All rooms come with satellite television, minibar, direct-dial telephones, and hairdryers. Definitely ask for a room over-looking the park.

The hotel, true to its 1920s style, has a game room and reading room, and presents the occasional classical performance and ballroom dance in its small concert hall. Staff can arrange for you to play golf or tennis. For more on the hotel's superb La Fontaine restaurant, see *Where to Eat* below.

HOTEL EXCELSIOR, *Hlavní třída 121, 353 01 Mariánské Lázně. Tel. 0165/622 705, Fax 0165/625 346. Rates for single/double: 1,590-2,390/1,990-2,990 Kč. Credit cards: AE, DC, MC, V. 60 rooms. Restaurant.*
This hotel is yet another swank place right on the main street. The hotel's untasteful rooms don't match up to their high prices, but they are generously large, and do come with all the expected amenities. The receptionist can arrange a tee time at the nearby golf course and reserve you a tennis court in town. You can also take a sauna or have a massage here.

HOTEL BOHEMIA, *Hlavní třída 100, 353 01 Mariánské Lázně. Tel. 0165/623 251, Fax 0165/622 943. Rates for single/double: 1,100-1,800/1,600-2,300 Kč. Credit cards: AE, DC, MC, V. 77 rooms. Restaurant.*
Recently renovated, this grand Victorian hotel built in 1904 now offers spacious, sunny rooms outfitted with crystal chandeliers, satellite television, and direct-dial telephones. But the decor is somewhat tacky, and can even be bombastic at times. The hotel staff can arrange just about any activity for you, such as golf, tennis, and even cross-country skiing.

HOTEL POLONIA, *Hlavní třída 50, 353 01 Mariánské Lázně. Tel. 0165/ 622 452, Fax 0165/622 4785. Rates for single/double without private shower: 700/950 Kč. Rates for single/double with private shower: 1,080-1,430 Kč. No credit cards. 80 rooms. Restaurant.*
This old hotel still awaits renovation, which means its furniture and fixtures are outdated by about 20 years. Though its rooms are overpriced, this is about the cheapest hotel you'll find in town.

HOTEL PALACE, *Hlavní třída 67, 353 01 Mariánské Lázně. Tel. 0165/ 622 222, Fax 0165/624 262. Rates for single/double: 1,190-2,550/1,870-3,400 Kč. Credit cards: AE, DC, MC, V. 40 rooms. Restaurant.*
Carved out of a yellow, turn-of-the-century house opposite the spa, the Hotel Palace offers bright, cheerful rooms washed in pastel colors and neo-Baroque furniture. But the bright pinks and cutesie fixtures just might turn you off, as it did me. This hotel does have unbeatable views of the main street and of the Colonnade. The hotel also features a spa facility, offering its guests (according to the hotel brochure) "electrotherapy, leg waxing, and magnetotherapy." The English-speaking service is quite good. The restaurant, serving tasty international specialties, has outdoor seating with a nice view of the spa.

HOTEL ZVON, *Hlavní třída 68, 353 01 Mariánské Lázně. Tel. 0165/622 015, Fax 0165/623 245. Rates for single/double: 1,400-2,500/1,800-3,500 Kč. Credit cards: AE, MC, V. 120 rooms. Restaurants.*
Right next door to Hotel Palace, Hotel Zvon occupies three Art Nouveau houses opposite the spa at the top of the main street. The hotel's brownish, drab rooms unfortunately don't live up to their rates. As for now, the rooms in the front do come with great views of the Colonnade,

but that may not be the case when the planned hotel across the street is built. Hotel staff is friendly and can arrange activities such as golfing, tennis, coach tours of the area, and sightseeing flights. The hotel also has a small fitness center.

HOTEL MAXIM, *Nehrova 141, 353 01 Mariánské Lázně. Tel. and Fax 0165/620 786. Rates for single/double: 1,060/1,770 Kč. Credit cards: AE, DC, MC, V. 22 rooms. Restaurant.*

Footsteps away from the Colonnade, this hotel features a grand staircase punctuated by Greek statues. The dining room, serving Czech and international food, is another grand affair. The rooms are not so lavish, but are comfortable enough, and outfitted with satellite televisions, decent-sized bathrooms, and high ceilings. Prices are fairly reasonable here.

HOTEL HELGA, *Třebízského 428/10, 353 01 Mariánské Lázně. Tel. and Fax 0165/762 41. Rates for single/double: 1,628/1,813 Kč. Credit cards: AE, MC, V. 25 rooms. Restaurant.*

This intimate, family-run hotel carved out of an Art Nouveau mansion lies a short, comfortable distance away from the main street and all the tourist hubbub going on around the spa. Though recently renovated, the hotel is somewhat drafty, but that shouldn't deter you from feeling at home among the rooms' nice mahogany furniture and tasteful decor. If you're in town with the family, then I would highly recommend staying in one of the hotel's apartments.

When the weather cooperates, the restaurant serves excellent Czech meals out on its big terrace. And when it's cold outside, you can sit by the fireplace in a neat, 1920s-style tea room. Service, though not English-speaking, is very friendly, and can arrange for you to go golfing, play tennis, or go on a horseback ride.

WHERE TO EAT

LA FONTAINE, *in the Villa Butterfly Hotel, Hlavní třída 655. Tel. 0165/ 484 100. 250-500 Kč.*

If you're out to splurge, there's no better place in town to do it than at this restaurant serving French and international cuisine in an ultra-formal setting. Feast yourself on beef tournedos with green pepper sauce, turkey medallions topped with curry, or crab meat in a salmon pillow. Deft, multilingual service makes the experience all the more gratifying.

PIZZERIA U MÜLLERŮ, *Na průhonu 24. Tel. 0165/3764. 60-150 Kč. No credit cards.*

At this brasserie-style restaurant you can get passable pasta dishes and a pretty good pizza. Look for this restaurant down the hill from the only stoplight in town, which is near the bottom of the main street.

RESTAURANT NEW YORK, *Hlavní třída 233. Tel. 0165/3033. 90-200 Kč. No credit cards.*
With dishes such as "Wall Street steak" and "Tribeca sirloin," you can get an idea of what this restaurant tries to be. But it forces the New Yorker thing and turns out being Czech. I got a kick out of the place anyhow because of its Manhattan nick-knacks and exposed brick walls. Unfortunately, the main dishes are not up to snuff, but you can have a made-to-order salad and a tasty falafel. Food is served here until 2 a.m., just in case you get the late-night munchies. This is also the liveliest night spot in town, serving 70 different kinds of cocktails to a mostly local crowd.

CLASSIC RESTAURANT & CAFÉ, *Hlavní třída 131/50. Tel. 0165/ 622 807. 120-200 Kč. Credit cards: AE, DC, MC, V.*
Serving up some scrumptious vegetarian dishes, a very tasty rumpsteak, and a wide variety of salads, Classic Restaurant is a good choice if you're looking for skilled service, thoughtful preparations, and a snazzy atmosphere. The bright and cheerful café – serving French, British, and American-style breakfasts – is a perfect place to grab a bite to eat in the morning. You can also get a good cappucino or espresso here.

ČESKÝ DVŮR, *Hlavní třída 650/36A. 150-400 Kč. No credit cards.*
Czech food is the specialty here, but you wouldn't know it by some of its starters, which includes lobster soup, turtle soup, and artichokes with Hollandaise sauce. Entrées such as roast duck and smoked pork are, however, more in line with the national cuisine. The place is a bit on the touristy side, drawing mostly German day-trippers, but the food and floral atmosphere makes it a good place to eat anyhow.

U ZLATÉ KOULE, *Nehrova 26. Tel. 0165/2691. 150-400 Kč. Credit cards: AE, MC, V.*
Set in an old monastery, this restaurant calls itself the "National Restaurant." Yeah, the place is overly pretentious, but you will get one of the better Czech meals to be had in Mariánské Lázně, which means top-notch cuts of meat, thick and rich sauces, and hearty soups. The brassy atmosphere is particularly attractive, featuring some neat old photos on the wall.

CAFÉ PANORÁMA, *Pod Panoramou 7. Tel. 0165/5321. 100-200 Kč. Lunch only. No credit cards.*
This café on top of the hill to the west of the main street is a good place to stop off for lunch on a tromp through the woods. Serving standard Czech fare, the café has a pleasant outdoor terrace set amidst tall pines. Unfortunately, it's not open for dinner.

KOLONÁDA KAVÁRNA, *Hlavní třída 122.*
When in any of the spa towns of West Bohemia, you won't be able to escape the *Kolonáda oplatky* – big round wafers meant to be eaten with the

less-palpable mineral waters. You can buy 'em fresh and warm at this café.

SEEING THE SIGHTS

The unavoidable place to start your stroll through town is right on the main street, **Hlavní třída**. Festooned with turrets, towers, and balconies, this is where the fin-de-siecle architecture reaches fever-pitch. Here, you can do some window shopping or just gawk at the architecture.

Stop first at the **Chopin Museum** (Muzeum F. Chopina), *Hlavní třída 47*, established in commemoration of the Polish composer who stayed at this very house in 1836 on his way from Paris to Warsaw. Here, you can sit and listen to some old, scratchy recordings of the composer and have a look at some of his personal effects. *It's open daily from 10 a.m. to noon and from 2 to 5 p.m.*

Sprouting from the surrounding hillsides are more late 19th-century buildings, many of them lined up on Ruská street – up the hill from Hlavní and accessible by any number of staircases. There are a couple of churches on this street that you would hardly expect to find in this part of the world. At *number 347/9* is the red-and-yellow-striped **St. Vladimír's** (Kostel sv. Vladimíra), a Russian Orthodox church built at the turn of the century in a Byzantine style. Inside are the obligatory icons, as well as an iconostasis (a screen dividing one part of a church from another) that's said to be the largest work of porcelain in the world.

Up the street is the red-brick **Anglican Chapel** (Anglikánsky kostelík), a prim neo-Gothic structure erected in 1879 with funds from the English royalty who used to retreat to the spa here. These days you can catch an occasional classical concert here. For ticket and scheduling information, contact the Culture and Information Center (see *Practical Information* below).

On the opposite side of the valley is the **spa** proper, the centerpiece of which is the neo-Baroque **Colonnade** – a demure, cast-iron structure with ribbed vaults smothered in ethereal paintings. Here you'll see a lot of aging Germans slurping on their ceramic beakers, filled with the two kinds of mineral waters that spring up under the Colonnade. Another kind of mineral water springs up at the **Křížovy pramen** (Cross Spring), located under a church-like pavilion at the north end of the Colonnade.

Two or three times a day you can hear live classical or oom-pa-pa music at a bandstand under the Colonnade. And every two hours you can catch the **Singing Fountain** (Zpívající fontána) spray up its waters in synch with recorded classical favorites. Unless you happen to be in the neighborhood, I wouldn't make any great effort to see the fountain do its thing. It's entertaining for about two minutes.

Just down the hill from the Singing Fountain is a monument commemorating the American liberation of Mariánské Lázně, which occurred on May 6, 1945. This part of the spa, stretching down to Hlavní třída, is one in a series of landscaped parks surrounding the town. Dotted with the occasional statue, the parks were laid out by Václav Skalník in the late 19th century so as to provide the most genteel of settings in which to imbibe the mineral waters that bubble up at various sites around town. There's a map at the south end of the Colonnade that shows you where each of the 12 or so springs are located. Any giftshop in town should also sell maps to help you find your way around if you feel like quaffing "the Cure." But, I warn you: Drinking the mineral waters is not like sipping on a bottle of Perrier. Some of them are extremely salty, and hardly what you would call refreshing.

Up the hill from the Colonnade are some more extravagant fin-de-siecle buildings, not least those around the manicured **Goethe Square** (Goethovo náměstí). In a building where Goethe stayed during his last visit to Mariánské Lázně, *at number 11,* is the **Municipal Museum** (Mětské Muzeum), with exhibits documenting the town's German origins and explaining the American liberation at the end of World War II. An English-narrated video about the history of the town is shown every hour. *The museum is open daily except Monday from 9 a.m. to 5 p.m.*

Opposite the museum is the **Church of the Assumption** (Kostel Nanebevzetí Panny Marie), its bright interior designed and decorated in a gorgeous neo-Byzantine style.

NIGHTLIFE & ENTERTAINMENT

There are couple of good music festivals happening in Mariánské Lázně in the summer. One is the **International Music Festival** in late June and another is the week-long **Chopin Music Festival** in mid-August. For exact dates and ticket information, contact the Culture and Information Center (see *Practical Information* below).

Ballroom dancing has traditionally been the nighttime activity at most any spa found in Central Europe. Mariánské Lázně is no exception. Several hotels around town, including **Villa Butterfly** and **Hotel Palace** (see above), offer ballroom dancing, as does the big **Casino** *at Reitenbergerova 95.*

Where the locals usually go for a late-night drink is **Restaurant New York** (see *Where to Eat*), serving 60 different cocktails and a good glass of Gambrinus beer. If you're desperate, you could try hanging out at one of the hotel nightclubs, but those are usually terribly boring. Other than that, you'll be hard pressed to find much in the way of excitement in this town. (The only cinema in town had closed when last checked.)

SPORTS & RECREATION

You figure that since you're in a spa town, there should be no problem of popping into some sanatorium for a mineral water bath. Unfortunately, that's not necessarily the case, because almost all the sanatorium spas are for patients suffering from some ailment or another. But **Nové Lázně** (New Baths) *at Reitenbergerova 53* does offer walk-in spa treatments. You can soak in a "carbonic bath" for about 320 Kč and have a massage for 230 Kč.

Part of the spa cure is walking, something which Mariánské Lázně has made a delight to do. There are dozens of color-marked trails weaving through the town's landscaped parks and through the surrounding hills. At the Cultural and Information Center (see *Practical Information*) or at any giftshop you can pick up a map showing you the different trail routes and the various springs and cafés found along the way. The trails are well-signposted, so you should have no problem getting around. Don't forget to bring a cup of some kind in case you want to imbibe the mineral waters.

Golfers will be glad to know that the best golf course in the country, **Golf Club Mariánské Lázně**, is located a few miles outside town on the road to Karlovy Vary. In fact, this is one of the oldest courses on the European continent, hosting the professional **Czech Open** each summer. If you want to try the course out, then have your hotel receptionist reserve you a tee time. Or you can do it yourself by calling the club *at Tel. 0165/4300*. Green fees will run you about 1,000 Kč. You can rent golf clubs there if you haven't brought your own.

If you want to play some tennis, try the **tenisové dvorce**, *Anglická 10, Tel. 0165/2495*, or at the top of *Chopinova street, Tel. 0165/4086*. Your hotel receptionist can usually make a reservation for you.

PRACTICAL INFORMATION

• **České obchodní banka**, *Hlavní třída 51* and **Komerční banka**, *Hlavní třída 132*. Both change money.
• **Culture and Information Center**, *Hlavní třída 47. Tel. 0165/622 474, Fax 0165/625 892*. This is the place to get maps, train and bus schedules, and just about any information you need regarding the town.
• **Marianex Tourist Center**, *Nehrova 27. Tel. and Fax 0165/624 202*. A guide service offering tours of the area.
• **Post Office**, *Poštovní street (near the main bus stand, just off Hlavní)*.

Karlovy Vary

Of all the spa towns in the Czech Republic, **Karlovy Vary** (Karlsbad) stands out as the most grandiose. Here, you'll find a parade of Revivalist and Art Nouveau buildings strung like pearls along the winding Teplá River and overlooked by legions of mansions and villas sprouting from the pine-strewn hillsides above. This is one of the most popular tourist destinations in the Czech Republic, and it shows in the summer, when the spa promenade is jam-packed with sight-seers gaping at the sheer elegance of the place.

Karlovy Vary is the biggest spa town in the Czech Republic, and the oldest. Legend has it that **King Charles IV** discovered the first of the spa's 12 mineral springs while on a hunting expedition, during which his dog fell into the spring chasing down a deer. From this legend comes the original German name of Karlsbad (or "Charles Spring"). In truth, the springs had already been discovered by the time Charles came around. But he did build a hunting lodge here and grant its German settlers certain royal privileges that helped the town eventually turn into one of the most fashionable retreats in Europe.

Royal figures such as **Tsar Peter the Great, Frederick I of Prussia**, and **Empress Maria Theresa** took the waters here, as did countless composers, including **Bach, Beethoven, Brahms, Wagner, Tchaikovsky**, and **Dvořák** – whose *New World Symphony* made its European debut here in 1884. And of course, the poet **Goethe** (a man who never met a spa town he didn't like) could never get enough of the place.

Unfortunately, you can't just drop into town and expect the full nine yards of mineral water baths, electrotherapy, and all the other "medicinal" treatments on the menu in Karlovy Vary. Prior arrangements need to be made with spa hotels (many of which are listed below under *Where to Stay*).

But you can drink to your heart's content the 12 different kinds of mineral waters tapped along the spa promenade and under the ornate and not-so-ornate colonnades. Or you can just forego the water altogether and indulge in the local herbal spirit called *Becherovka*, known in Karlovy Vary as the 13th spring.

ORIENTATION

Karlovy Vary sits amidst the verdant hills of the **Slavkov Forest** 122 kilometers (76 miles) west of Prague, 83 kilometers (51 miles) northwest of Plzeň, and 47 kilometers (29 miles) north of Mariánské Lázně. The spa proper, with its three-kilometer promenade and its many colonnades, winds its way up the narrow **Teplá River** valley, while the business center of town sits to the north, where the Teplá spills into the **Ohře River**. Chances are you'll stick to the spa proper, in which case you'll have no problem finding your way around.

ARRIVALS & DEPARTURES

By Bus

Karlovy Vary is a possible day trip from Prague by bus (but not by train). Regular ČAD buses depart Prague's Florenc station about 10 times a day for the two-and-a-half-hour trip that costs about 80 Kč. Reservations from Prague are a good idea, especially at the height of the tourist season. The bus terminal for long-distance arrivals and departures in Karlovy Vary is at Dolní nádraží, near the corner of Bechera and Západní streets. You can make bookings or get information at the **ČAD office**, *náměstí Republiky 7, Tel. 017/322 3662.*

By Car

Karlovy Vary is a two hour journey from Prague. Just head east all the way on E48. From Plzeň, head northwest on E49. The spa proper is strictly a pedestrian zone. Pay lots around the spa are clearly signposted. Some hotels do offer private parking, but usually for a fee.

By Train

Going by train from Prague or Plzeň is a hassle, so you're best off avoiding it. But if you're traveling to or from Mariánské Lázně, then train is the way to go. The slow, scenic train to Mariánské Lázně departs every hour or two from Dolní nádraží (Lower Station) – on the south side of the Ohře river near the corner of Bechera and Západní streets. The train to Cheb departs every 90 minutes or so from Horní nádraží (Upper Station – the main station), which is up the hill on the north side of the river.

GETTING AROUND TOWN

Much of Karlovy Vary, especially in and around the spa, is closed off to auto traffic. So you will be doing a lot of walking, like it or not. If you want to take a cab, call **Centrum Taxi**, *Tel. 017/322 3236* or **Willy Taxi**, *Tel. 017/294 44.* It makes no sense whatsoever to get around by car in Karlovy Vary.

But if you want to see some of the surroundings, you can rent a car at **Autorent**, *central office at Dubová 8, Tel. 017/322 2528.*

WHERE TO STAY

Along the Promenade

GRANDHOTEL PUPP, *Mírové náměstí 2, 360 91 Karlovy Vary. Tel. 017/310 9111, Fax 017/322 4032. Rates for single/double: 4,000/5,000-6,500 Kč. Credit cards: AE, DC, MC, V. 111 rooms. Restaurant.*

Rich, are we? How about the presidential suite for a cool $800? Outside Prague, you won't find a hotel more exclusive (or more expensive) than the Grandhotel Pupp, serving Europe's elite since it was founded in the early 18th century by the confectioner Johann Georg Pupp. But for all its esteem, I can't help but think that the hotel gets by on its historical significance alone. Of course, the old Communist directors managed to give it a half-baked restoration that appears in the lackluster appearance of its "de Luxe" rooms and hallways. The staff doesn't seem to be up to snuff either, the receptionists offering what you would hardly call a warm welcome when you first enter the hotel.

Obviously, all the amenities of a five-star hotel are offered here. But if you're willing to spend so much on a room, I would take my money elsewhere, somewhere where you're going to get more out of it.

HOTEL DVOŘÁK, *Nová louka 11, 360 21 Karlovy Vary. Tel. 017/322 4145, Fax 017/322 2814. Rates for single/double: -3,400/3,600-5,200 Kč. Credit cards: AE, DC, MC, V. 74 rooms. Restaurant.*

Another exclusive, expensive hotel on the promenade, the Austrian-managed Dvořák is not so overtly pretentious as the Pupp. This is a spa hotel, offering its guests the full range in spa treatments, which can include carbonic baths, hydrotherapy, and massage. Despite the musical notes on the bedsheets, the rooms are nothing to get excited about, nor are they quite up to the standards you would expect for such exorbitant rates. But you do get the privileges of using the hotel's fitness center, swimming pool, and sauna. You're also treated to a big buffet breakfast. The restaurant serves a lot of healthy, low-fat foods prepared by an Austrian chef.

HOTEL HELUAN, *Tržiště 41, 360 01 Karlovy Vary. Tel. and Fax 017/ 257 57. Rates for single/double: 3,050/3,200 Kč. Credit cards: AE, DC, MC, V. 15 rooms. Restaurant.*

The centrally-located Heluan offers very tasteful rooms outfitted with wood floors, rough-hewn furniture, and high, stucco ceilings. All of the rooms come with a nice view of the promenade. The very friendly service can help you with getting a tee time at the local golf course or reserving a tennis court. They can also help you get tickets to the theater. In addition to its good restaurant, the hotel has a wine bar, pizzeria, and summer beer terrace. All in all, a very fine hotel.

HOTEL EMBASSY, *Nová louka 21, 360 01 Karlovy Vary. Tel. 017/322 1161, Fax 017/322 3146. Rates for single/double: 1,500-2,000/2,380-3,250 Kč. Credit cards: AE, DC, MC, V. 18 rooms. Restaurant.*

Of all the places to stay in Karlovy Vary, this small, family-run hotel is one of my favorites. Carved out of a pastel Baroque house, the hotel features a sunny atrium that does wonders for brightening up the old building. In the atrium is a small café that's perfect for a mid-afternoon beer or coffee.

There is a sense of grandeur that goes along with each of the large, individually-decorated rooms. They're decorated as they would have been in the 19th century, with old portraits of Karlovy Vary luminaries hanging on the walls. Every room is a winner here, but room 202 with its old ceramic stove gets my vote for coziest. All rooms have direct-dial telephones, big bathrooms, and satellite television. Parking is free of charge. In keeping with the high standards of the place, the English-speaking service here is friendly and very accommodating. For more on the hotel's excellent restaurant, see *Where to Eat*, below.

HOTEL KOLONÁDA, *I.P. Pavlova 8, 360 01 Karlovy Vary. Tel. 017/ 313 1111, Fax 017/322 8045. Prices for single/double: 1,260-1,710/1,620-2,610 Kč. Credit cards: AE, MC, V. Restaurant.*

The Hotel Kolonáda is actually two hotels joined into one. On one side is the Otava Hotel, on the other the Patria. There are no differences in price between the two, but the Patria is a bit more intimate, and nicer. Rooms in both hotels come with satellite television, telephones, and mini-bar. The Atria has an attractive cellar restaurant serving Czech basics under vaulted ceilings.

JESSENIUS SPA HOTEL, *Stará louka 36, 360 90 Karlovy Vary. Tel. 017/322 8122, Fax 017/322 3227. Rates for single only without private shower: 600-700 Kč. Rates for single/double with private shower: 850-900/1,300-1,500 Kč. Credit cards: AE, DC, MC, V. 50 rooms. Restaurant.*

Occupying two bright pink buildings, the Jessenius offers very nice antique-filled rooms, some of which have a balcony view of the promenade (there's an extra charge for these rooms, as these are the only ones with telephone and television.) The hotel does offer its guests the full range in spa treatments, which the brochure says will help with, among other illnesses, "hyperlipoproteinemie." If you know what that is, you should be awarded a free room!

SPA HOTEL ASTORIA, *Vřídelní 23, 360 01 Karlovy Vary. Tel. 017/322 8224, Fax 017/322 4368. Rates for single/double: 500-750/1,000-1,500 Kč. Credit cards: DC, V. 89 rooms. Restaurant.*

Occupying two gorgeous Art Nouveau buildings opposite the Mill Colonnade, the Astoria may not win any interior design awards, but the rooms are comfortable enough, and a bargain to boot. Definitely ask for a room with a balcony and view of the colonnade. The hotel offers the full range of spa treatments to its guests. But you don't have to take the treatments in order to stay here.

VILLA BASILEIA, *Mariánskolázeňská 4, 360 01 Karlovy Vary. Tel. 017/ 322 4132, Fax 017/322 7804. Rates for single/double: 480-720/800-1,200 Kč. No credit cards. 6 rooms. No restaurant.*

Set at the south end of the promenade, this small pension occupies a pretty turn-of-the-century villa on the banks of the Teplá River. Though not far from the center of the spa, it is comfortably removed from the crowds. The generously large rooms all have private baths, big windows, lace curtains, and a lot of personality. Ask for a room overlooking the river, so as you can hear the sound of it when you go to bed at night.

Off the Promenade
    HOTEL MIGNON, *Sadová 55, 360 01 Karlovy Vary. Tel. 017/322 2508, Fax 017/322 1531. Rates for single/double: 1,280-1,600/1,520-1,900 Kč. 13 rooms. Restaurant.*

Also set in a pretty turn-of-the-century villa, the Hotel Mignon has an excellent hillside location minutes away from the promenade and footsteps away from the forest. Surrounding it are other sensational villas that make up this gorgeous neighborhood. Because of the unattractive, outdated furnishings, the rooms unfortunately don't live up to the prime surroundings or their rates. But some of the rooms have a great view of the glimmering Russian Orthodox Church across the street.

    HOTEL-GARNI SIRIUS, *Zahradní 3, 360 01 Karlovy Vary. Tel. 017/322 2310, Fax 017/234 69. Rates for single/double: 1,105-1,280/1,460-1,720 Kč. Credit cards: AE, MC, V. 24 rooms. No restaurant.*

Carved out of a green, neo-Baroque house, this hotel has small, plain rooms, which are comfortable nonetheless. The locale, just off the north end of the promenade, is a good one. The receptionists can arrange for you to play golf, go on a horseback ride, and, believe it or not, play paintball. There's no restaurant here, but there is a small bar in the lobby.

WHERE TO EAT
    PROMENÁDA, *Tržiště 31. Tel. 017/322 5648. 250-600 Kč. Credit cards: AE, MC, V.*

This is one of the classier restaurants in town, offering a thankfully short, to-the-point menu that features such items as smoked salmon, steak medallions with rosemary and Roquefort sauce, and roasted duck. The provincial decor, candle-lit tables, and accomplished service make the dining experience all the more gratifying. A highly recommended place if you feel like splurging.

    RESTAURANT EMBASSY, *Nová louka 21. Tel. 017/322 1161. 200-600 Kč.*

One of the oldest in Karlovy Vary, this restaurant maintains the high standards of the laudable hotel it occupies. Sumptuously prepared dishes such as venison, Chateaubriand, and pasta with a salmon-cream sauce are served with flair under the restaurant's vaulted ceilings. If you got a hankering for lobster, the restaurant can prepare it with a two-day advance notice. And if you are a vegetarian, then you'll be thankful to find a wide assortment of vegetable and meatless pasta dishes.

ZÁMECKY RESTAURACE KAREL IV, *Zámecký vrch. Tel. 017/322 7255. 200-500 Kč. Credit cards: AE, MC, V.*

Set in an old tower overlooking the promenade, this restaurant has a great view from its outdoor terrace, where you can get any number of Czech or international dishes. Unfortunately, the cuisine here lacks originality, and therefore seems way overpriced to me.

HELUAN, *Tržiště 41. Tel. 017/257 57.150-300 Kč.*

The wood-studded setting is appropriate for a restaurant specializing in game. Venison steak, roast duck, and wild boar come prepared in a provincial style. The animal skins and trophy heads hanging on the wall, however, don't make for the most appetizing of decorations.

STEAK HOUSE FORTUNA, *Zeyerova 1. Tel. 017/291 97. 120-300 Kč. Credit cards: AE, MC, V.*

This restaurant in the business part of town carries the American theme a bit too far, but it is a comfortable place that lures a lot of locals to its big booths and long bar. Needless to say, the menu features an extensive list of steaks, which are surprisingly tender and well-prepared. The restaurant also bakes one of the better pizzas to be found in Karlovy Vary. Unfortunately, the service here is extremely slack.

U ŠVEJKA, *Stará louka 10. Tel. 017/231 36. 120-300 Kč. No credit cards.*

Named after the hapless protagonist in the novel *The Good Soldier Švejk,* this restaurant is somewhat touristy, but its uncompromising Czech food comes as a good value on the promenade, where prices for meals are rather expensive. Try the spicy goulash served with some very fresh, very light *knedliky.*

METRO CAFÉ, *T.G. Masaryka 27. Tel. 017/295 55. 100-200 Kč. No credit cards.*

This is another affordable restaurant serving fairly decent Czech standards such as roast pork, fried cheese, and a few kinds of steaks. But you are probably better off stopping here for lunch rather than dinner.

PIZZERIA HELUAN, *Tržiště 41. Tel. 017/257 57. 100-200 Kč. No credit cards.*

Set in the Hotel Heluan, this tiny joint in the middle of the spa area bakes a very satisfying thin-crust pizza that's just the ticket for lunch.

SEEING THE SIGHTS

Along the Promenade

If you've come from Prague, you'll most likely find yourself at the north end of the spa, which stretches up the Teplá River valley along a wide promenade lined with a riotous array of Belle-Epoque buildings. Unfortunately, that's not the first impression you get of the spa from the north end, thanks to the Communist-era highrise Thermal Hotel – a pink elephant if there ever were one. But once you get past it, then you can begin to gain a full appreciation of the spa's sumptuous architecture. The first in a series of colonnades lining the promenade is the wrought-iron **Sadová kolonáda** (Park Colonnade), one of many works on the promenade built by the Viennese team of Helmer and Fellner in the late 19th century. With ivy growing around it, the genteel, white-washed colonnade looks straight out of a plantation in the American South.

A short distance up the river is Karlovy Vary's landmark sight – Josef Zítek's grandiose **Mlynské kolonáda** (Mill Colonnade). This sweeping, neo-Renaissance structure is supported by cornice-topped columns and topped with graceful statues depicting each month in the year. Under it is where you can partake of five different mineral waters right at their source. (There's a special beaker made especially for taking these tepid waters, sold at any nearby giftshop. You may also want to take along a bottle of plain water to chase the salty stuff down.)

At the first big bend in the river is a stunning Art Nouveau house called **Dům Zawojski**, completed in 1900 and recently renovated. Just opposite, Fellner and Helmer's **Tržní kolonada** (Market Colonnade) has also recently undergone renovation, which means that you can now fully appreciate its relief depicting Charles IV's discovery of the first spring at Karlovy Vary. Just beyond the Tržní kolonada is the Art Nouveau **Zámecká kolonáda**, overlooked by the **Zámecká věž** (Castle Tower), built on the site of Charles IV's hunting lodge, which burned down in 1604.

A little further up the promenade is another unfortunate modern addition to the spa – **Vřidelní kolonáda** (Sprudel Colonnade), which looks and feels more like a shopping mall than anything. Encased in a glass room within the colonnade is the **Vřidlo** (Sprudel in German), Karlovy Vary's biggest and hottest spring gushing more than 2,550 gallons of water every hour. In the glass room you're meant to inhale the vapors of the spring, which splashes a good 15 feet up into the air. In the next room is a line of taps from which you can drink the stuff after it's cooled down a bit.

Showing its cream-colored face up the hill from the Vřidelní kolonáda is the **Church of the Mary Magdalene** (Kostel sv. Maří Magdaléna), a work by the master Baroque architect Kilián Ignátz Dientzenhofer, whose fantastic churches are seemingly found on every corner in Prague. With its oval-shaped balconies and windows, the sunny interior is typical of the architect's theatrical style.

Back down on the promenade along the parallel lanes of Stará louka and Nová louka, the newly rediscovered chic-ness of Karlovy Vary hits home. Get a taste of it (and some pretty good cake) at the swish **Elefant**

Café, reminiscent of the heady days when Central Europe's elite used to converge in Karlsbad. Next, nip into the **Moser Shop**, *Stará louka 40*, for a look at Europe's top-of-the-line glassware.

If the glass at the Moser Shop doesn't whet your appetite, then check out the **Karlovy Vary Museum**, *Nová louka 23*, across the river. In addition to tracing the development of glassware in Bohemia, the museum tells the story of Karlovy Vary's history and introduces you the geology and wildlife of the region. *It's open Wednesday through Sunday from 9 a.m. to noon and from 1 to 5 p.m.* Afterwards, take a look at how the other half lives at the gargantuan **Grandhotel Pupp**, Karlovy Vary's first hotel dating back to the beginning of the 18th century. You can't miss the hotel, because it pretty much dominates everything for miles around.

Past the Pupp Casino, the **Vitězslav Theater** is another architectural confection by the duo Helmer and Fellner. If you ask at the box office, you may be able to get a peek inside at the frescoes, executed by a group of Viennese artists that included one Gustav Klimt, whose erotic paintings went on to startle Victorian sensibilities.

Finally, peruse the modest collection of 20th-century Czech art at the **Karlovy Vary Art Gallery**, *Goethova stezka 6*. Among the notable artists represented here are Kubišta, Špala, and Čapek. *It's open daily except Monday from 9:30 a.m. to noon and from 1 to 5 p.m.*

Into the Hills

Part of the Karlovy Vary experience is of course venturing into the hills of the Slavkov Forest, its slopes beautifully studded with beeches and oaks. If you're feeling fit, go ahead and ascend the steep 1.5-kilometer trail starting just behind the GrandHotel Pupp. If you are not up to it, then take the funicular (also behind the Pupp) to an old lookout tower called **Charles' View Point** (the trail goes there, too). Here you can take in a sensational view of the spa.

Another good view is to be had a half-kilometer northeast of the midway stop on the funicular. Here, the **Deer's Leap statue** (Jelení skok) perches on top of a rock jutting from the hillside. The statue represents the legendary stag flushed out by Charles IV's dog. Nearby is the **Peter the Great Memorial**, erected in commemoration of the Russian Tsar who visited the spa in 1711 and again in 1712.

When you come down from the hills, be sure to pay your respects at the **Karl Marx statue** across the street from the Russian Consulate at the top of Sadová and Petra Velikého streets. The old bourgeois himself used to frequent the spa with his daughter near the end of his life.

Near the top of Sadová is a mesmerizing sight – the golden **St. Peter and St. Paul Russian Orthodox Church**, completed in 1897 and financed by the Russian nobility that used to sojourn here. Modeled after the

Byzantine church in Ostankino, Russia, this church is topped by five gleaming onion domes and covered with sumptuous Art Nouveau murals. From there, descend the hill by way of Sadová street, lined with rows of handsome villas and townhouses.

NIGHTLIFE & ENTERTAINMENT

For a list of goings-on, pick up the monthly, multilingual *Promenáda* magazine, with a schedule of concerts, films, and performances happening around Karlovy Vary. You can buy a copy at the **Kur-Info office**, *located in the center of the spa at the Vřídelní kolonada (Sprudel Colonnade)*.

A Bohemian spa wouldn't be a Bohemian spa without the obligatory oom-pa-pa music. In Karlovy Vary, you can hear it live at the **Mlynská kolonáda** (Mill Colonnade) **bandstand** almost every day at 4:30 p.m. Classical concerts take place at various hotels and churches, including the **GrandHotel Pupp** and the **Church of Mary Magdalene** (addresses above).

You can hear live rock and do some dancing at **Klub Propaganda**, *located in the business part of town at Jaltská 7*.

There are several places to catch a flick in and around the spa. The **Hotel Thermal** *at the north end of the promenade* has a cinema, as does the **Hotel Richmond** *at Slovenská 3*. Other cinemas include **Kino Čas** *at T.G. Masaryka 3* and **Kino Drahomíra** *at Vítězná 48*.

If you're a hardcore film-goer, then you'll want to be in town during the month of July, when the town hosts the **International Film Festival**. In recent years, it has become a fairly high-profile event, drawing some major European and American stars. For exact dates and ticket information, contact Kur-Info (see *Practical Information* below).

SPORTS & RECREATION

The ugly **Hotel Thermal** at the north end of the promenade does have one nice thing about it – an outdoor, **spring-fed swimming pool** that's set high above the spa, providing a nice view up the promenade. And you don't need to be guest to use it.

Of course, there's hiking galore in this part of West Bohemia. Pick up a map of trails at any bookstore on the promenade or at Kur-Info (see *Practical Information* below). If you want to spend the day hiking, then you might want to consider huffing the 17 kilometers (10.5 miles) to the storybook village and castle, **Locket nad Ohří** (see *Day Trips & Excursions* below). The trail, marked in blue, crosses over the Ohře river before passing by the enormous pillar rocks of the **Svatošské skaly**. You can pick up the blue-marked trail at the top of the funicular running behind the Grandhotel Pupp.

For a round of golf at the 18-hole **Karlovy Vary Golf Club**, *Tel. 017/ 240 11*, ask your hotel receptionist to reserve you a tee time or call the club directly yourself. The golf course is east of town on the highway going to Prague. Green fees will run you about 800 Kč.

DAY TRIPS & EXCURSIONS

Few villages in the Czech Republic get so desperately romantic as **Loket nad Ohří**, 10 kilometers (6 miles) west of Karlovy Vary. The walled, hilltop village – its lanes lined with narrow, storybook houses – hugs a castle on an elbow of the Ohří River, providing a setting that's just too beautiful to be true. Here, you'll want to stroll along the town's curving square, náměstí Masaryka, and take in the rows of narrow facades, one of the most beautiful being that of the neo-Gothic **Hostinec Bílý kůň**.

Afterwards, climb up to the hill for a look at the impressive Gothic castle, perched precipitously high above the village and affording a sensational view of the red rooftops below. The castle dates back to the 12th century, when Vladislav II had a Romanesque fortress built on the site, of which only a tower and fragments of a rotunda remain. In the 14th century it was rebuilt according to the late Gothic style of the era and has changed little ever since (at least from the outside).

Loket and the surrounding villages have for centuries been in the business of producing ceramics. Inside the castle, you can have a look at some of the ornate wares in its good **ceramics museum**. Unfortunately, you have to settle for a short text in English that offers little explanation of the items on view. The museum also exhibits some medieval artifacts discovered at the castle. *The museum is open Tuesday through Sunday from 9 a.m. to noon and from 1 to 5 p.m.*

From Karlovy Vary, Loket is a 20 minute bus ride from stand #4 or #8 at the regional bus terminal on Varšavská street. Tickets cost no more than 10 Kč. But the best way to go is on foot (see *Sports & Recreation*, above).

PRACTICAL INFORMATION

• **Česká Spořitelna**, *T.G. Masaryka 14*, and **Komerční Banka**, *Tržíště 11*. Two banks where you can change money.
• **Kur-Info**, *Vřídelní kolonáda (half-way up the promenade). Tel. 017/322 4097, Fax 017/322 4667*. The town information office, where you can pick up maps, brochures, and general information. They can help you find accommodations in town, too. Pick up the monthly *Promenáda* magazine here, with information on just about every aspect of town.
• **Post Office**, *T.G. Masaryka 1*.

Cheb

Historically speaking, **Cheb** (*Eger* in German) is a German town, its existence owing to the German immigrants who settled it in the 11th century. At the cross-roads of Bohemia and Bavaria, Cheb grew into a center of trade between the two kingdoms, which played tug of war with the town until Bavaria finally handed it over to Bohemia in 1322 in lieu of a debt that it owed Bohemia. Hoping to placate the merchants of Cheb, the Bohemian kings granted the town suzerainty in return for a chunk of the riches that the town generated. In fact, Cheb remained self-governing well into the 19th century, which is part of the reason why the German majority resented their incorporation into the Czechoslovak Republic in 1918 and why they later desired to be part of Hitler's Third Reich.

As a result of that desire and their fascist leanings, the Germans of Cheb were forcibly expelled from the country, reducing the town's pre-war population of 45,000 to a staggering 18,000 by 1950. The town, with a current population of 32,000 Czechs and Romanies, has seemingly not bounced back since the Germans were kicked out. Nowadays, the only Germans in town are the ones passing through.

Despite its sordid history, Cheb is an intriguing place, one bypassed by most tourists on their way to the nearby spa towns. You too will probably want to make Cheb a day trip from either Mariánské Lázně or Karlovy Vary. But I would recommend staying the night so as to get a feel of the medieval streets after the sun goes down.

ORIENTATION

Situated on the **Ohře River** 168 kilometers (104 miles) west of Prague and 46 kilometers (28 miles) southwest of Karlovy Vary, Cheb is an easy place to find your way around in. The center of town and its main square is náměstí Krále Jiřího z Poděbrad, located at the end of Svobody street.

ARRIVALS & DEPARTURES

By Bus

From Prague's Florenc station there are four buses departing each day for Cheb, taking about the same amount of time as the train. The ride takes four hours and costs about 100 Kč. The bus station in Cheb is in front of the train station at the end of Svobody street. It's a ten minute walk down Svobody to the town's main square.

By Car

Easiest from Prague is to head west on E48 all the way to Cheb via Karlovy Vary. Parking is usually not a problem on the streets. Just follow the blue "P" signs and put money in the meter (or pay the attendant).

By Train

Several express trains depart Prague daily for Cheb, stopping in Plzeň and Mariánské Lázně along the way. Tickets cost about 100 Kč, and the ride takes roughly four hours. The train station is at the end of Svobody street, from where it's a 10 minute walk straight ahead to the center of town.

GETTING AROUND TOWN

There's no reason for taking public transportation (bus) in Cheb. But if you do, buy your tickets at any newsstand and validate them on board. You can usually catch a cab on the street or on the main square.

WHERE TO STAY

HOTEL HVĚZDA, *náměstí Krále Jiřího z Poděbrad 4-6, 351 01 Cheb. Tel. 0166/422 549, Fax 0166/422 546. Rates for single/double: 500-700/1,000 Kč. Credit cards: AE, MC, V. 30 rooms. Restaurant.*

Clean and functional are about all you can say about the rooms at this decrepit old hotel on the main square. But they are about the best you'll get in this town, with its terrible lack of accommodations.

HOTEL HRADNÍ DVŮR, *Dlouhá 12, 350 02 Cheb. Tel. 0166/422 006, Fax 0166/422 444. Rates for single/double without private bath: 430/680 Kč. Rates for single/double with private bath: 990/1,190 Kč. Credit cards: AE, MC. 21 rooms. Restaurant.*

Just off the main square on one of Cheb's intriguing lanes, this old hotel also has very basic rooms that are comfortable nonetheless. The English-speaking receptionist is awfully friendly, and will cater to your needs. Again, your choices are slim in a town that has only two hotels.

WHERE TO EAT

ZLATÉ SLUNCE, *náměstí Krále Jiřího z Poděbrad 38. No Tel. 80-200 Kč. Credit cards: MC, V.*

On the main square, this cellar restaurant serves up Czech basics on one side of the restaurant and grilled meats such as steak and chicken on the other.

RESTAURACE DELA, *Kamenná 22. Tel. 0166/225 96. 150-200 Kč. Credit cards: MC.*

Just down from the main square, Dela dishes up a spicy stroganoff and a good roast pork smothered in mushroom sauce. Classy atmosphere and good service to boot.

STAROČESKA RESTAURACE, *Kamenná 1. Tel. 0166/422 170. 100-200 Kč. No credit cards.*

This restaurant on the main square serves a lot of Czech standards that won't knock your socks off but will satisfy an empty stomach. It's probably a better choice for lunch than for dinner.

SEEING THE SIGHTS

If you arrive at the bus or train station and proceed down Svobody street, your first impression of Cheb isn't the greatest. Many of the buildings are either dilapidated or boarded up, plus there seems to be an inordinate amount of drunks staggering around, especially in front of the train station. But don't worry, there is relief to be found at the end of Svobody, where you'll find the town's main square, **náměstí Krále Jiřího z Poděbrad**, named after the 15th-century Czech king who often visited the town for negotiations with Saxon rulers.

The commercial heart of the region for more than seven centuries, the sloping square dates back to the 12th century, though most of the buildings come from the 16th. With their steep roofs and earth-toned facades, the Gothic buildings look as though they've been lifted from an illustrated children's book – a notion that becomes harder to deny when you see the bundle of tall houses teetering at the bottom of the square. Called **Špalíček** (or *Stöckl* in German), these houses were built in the 16th century by Jewish merchants and now appear to be on the verge of collapsing in on each other.

On the square you'll want to peruse a couple of very good museums. First is the **Cheb Art Gallery**, housed in the Baroque **Old Town Hall** (stará radnice), *at number 16*. The ground and top floors are devoted to temporary exhibitions, while the middle floor is taken up by the permanent collection of modern and contemporary Czech art. Cubist renderings by Václav Špála and Josef Čapek are on view, as are some intriguing Prague cityscapes by Antonín Pracházka. There's also a tiny room filled with historic bas-reliefs that you'll want to check out. *The gallery is open daily except Monday from 9 a.m. to 5 p.m. Tickets are 20 Kč.*

Behind the Špalíček at the bottom of the square is the **Cheb Museum** (Chebské Muzeum), housed in the pink Renaissance **Pachelbel House** (Pachelblův dům). In this house, **Albrecht von Waldstein** (or Wallenstein), the commanding Hapsburg general during the Thirty Years' War, was assassinated in 1634. In wiping out the Protestant rebellion in Bohemia, the general had confiscated more than 100 estates from the Czech nobility. Suspecting that Waldstein was conspiring with the Swedes to create his own kingdom, Hapsburg Emperor Ferdinand I put a reward out on the general's head. To claim that reward were an Irishman, Scotsman, and Englishman. Through numerous paintings and a mock-up of the bedroom where the murder took place, the museum tells the story of that night in 1634 when Waldstein was woken from his sick bed and slain by the three men.

The museum also features a lot of Waldstein's possessions, such as his horse (stuffed) and several of his portraits. On top of that, there's a number of items dealing with the history of the town, including the axe of the last Cheb executioner, Karl Huss, who also happened to be an artist (his paintings, dementedly cheerful, are on view, too). Be sure to check out this great museum, *open daily except Monday from 9 a.m. to noon and from 1 to 5 p.m. Tickets are 30 Kč.*

Just behind the museum, the hulking **Church of St. Nicholas** (Kostel sv. Mikuláše) features two captivating Romanesque towers that were part of the church when it was originally built in the 13th century. In the 18th century, the church was expanded in the Baroque style, but it still retains the plan of a Romanesque basilica, which makes it an intriguing structure. Step inside for a look at the frescoes on the columns.

Perched above the Ohře River in the northwest corner of the historic center is the **Cheb Castle** (Chebsky hrad). The Holy Roman Emperor and crusader, Frederick I Barbarossa, had the castle built in 1167 as a stronghold for the empire's eastern front. Though mostly in ruins now, the castle is well worth a visit mainly because it's one of the few Romanesque fortresses you'll see in Bohemia.

You enter the castle past the boxy **Black Tower** (Černá věž), a somewhat ominous structure affording a nice view of Cheb's rooftops below. But the real attraction at the castle is the chapel in the northeast corner. The austere chapel has two stories, it's bottom floor built in the early Gothic style and its second floor built in the late Gothic style. Take note of the carved granite pillars that rise up in the middle of the chapel, supporting a beautiful vaulted ceiling. Behind the chapel you can get a look at the walls of the old Romanesque palace, its carved capitals and arched windows still intact.

For an impressive perspective of the castle fortifications, stroll down the hill to the riverbank. *The castle is open daily except Monday from 9 a.m. to 6 p.m. June through August, until 5 p.m. in May and September, and until 4 p.m. in April and October.*

NIGHTLIFE & ENTERTAINMENT

U kata at *Židovská 17* is a nice pub with pool tables. **Country Club**, a pub and restaurant at *Křížovnícká 4*, has a lot of Americana items on the walls and pours the excellent local brew, Platan. You can watch a movie at **Kino Svět**, *at Májová 29.*

PRACTICAL INFORMATION

•Čedok, *Májová 31. Tel. 0166/433 951.* You can get information on the town here.

•**Komerční banka**, *Obrněné brigády 20*. A bank where you can change money. There's an ATM machine here.
•**Post Office**, *náměstí Krále Jiřího z Poděbrad 38*.

Františkový Lázně

Of the three big spa towns in West Bohemia, **Františkový Lázně** (Frazenbad) is definitely the least inspiring. The problem is in the appearance of the town itself, its symmetrical streets lined with repetitive neo-Classical buildings all painted the same yellowish color. It's much smaller than Karlovy Vary and Mariánské Lázně, and much flatter, affording none of the great views that the other two spa towns do.

But if you're intent on seeing the place, I'd make it a day trip from Karlovy Vary, Mariánské Lázně, or Cheb.

ORIENTATION

Františkový Lázně is 5 kilometers (3 miles) north of Cheb and 6 kilometers south of the nearest German border crossing at Vojtanov. You'll have no problem finding your away around the tiny town and its streets, laid out in a grid plan. There are more than enough signs to point you in the right direction.

ARRIVALS & DEPARTURES

By Bus

From Cheb, there is a bus to Františkový Lázně departing every 20 minutes or so and costing about 5 Kč. From Prague, there are five or six daily buses, stopping in Mariánské Lázně along the way. Tickets cost about 100 Kč and the ride lasts about four hours. From Karlovy Vary, there are two or three departures daily.

The bus terminal in Františkový Lázně is at the corner of Anglická and Americká streets, from where it's a two minute walk to the spa area.

By Car

From Cheb, head north on E49 and then follow signs.

By Train

There is a train that leaves Prague's Hlavní nádraží every morning at 9 a.m. for Františkový Lázně. The train station is at the end of Nádražní street, from where it's a five minute walk to the center of town.

WHERE TO STAY/WHERE TO EAT

HOTEL TŘÍ LILIE, *Jiráskova 17, 351 01 Františkový Lázně. Tel. 0166/ 942 970, Fax 0166/942 970. Rates for single/double: 1,800/3,100 K. Credit cards: AE, MC, V.* This is the most luxurious place in town, offering large, smartly furnished rooms that come with satellite television and direct dial phones. The restaurant is a good one, serving international specialties that are somewhat overpriced.

HOTEL SLOVAN, *Národní třída 5, 351 01 Františkový Lázně. Tel. 0166/ 12, Fax 0166/542 843. Rates for single/double: 800-1,000/1,100-1,600 Kč. Credit cards: V. 20 rooms. Restaurant.* This genteel-looking hotel isn't a bad option when you consider the reasonable rates. Though the rooms have outdated furniture and could certainly use some sprucing up, they are clean and functional. The Slovan offers several dining options. There are two ornate cafés, a grill, and a *vinárna* – all of which are decent enough for lunch or dinner.

SEEING THE SIGHTS

The cultured, neo-Classical character of Františkový Lázně hits home along **Národní třída**, the spa's main boulevard dotted with potted palm trees. You can inspect the building where Beethoven stayed in 1812 *at number 7.* At the south end of the boulevard, the town's main spring of **Františkův pramen** is covered by a neo-Classical rotunda that is no great shakes.

One block east on Jiráskova, you can feast your eyes on a number of stately mansions fitted with pretty wrought-iron balconies. This street provides a nice line of focus for the **Church of the Raising of the Sun** (Kostel Povýšení sv. Kříže), one of the few churches in Bohemia built in the Empire style. Around the corner, *at Dr. Pohoreckého 8,* is the **Municipal Museum** (Mětské Muzeum), featuring ho-hum exhibits on the history of the spa and some amusing renderings of patients being subjected to some harsh 19th century treatments. *It's open on the weekdays from 9 a.m. to 5 p.m. and on the weekends until 4 p.m.*

PRACTICAL INFORMATION

•**Čedok,** *Národní třída 5. Tel. 0166/942 210.* This is the place to pick up tourist information.
•**Česká spořitelná,** *Ruská street.* Change money here.
•**Post Office,** *Boženy Nemcové street.*

16. NORTH BOHEMIA

North Bohemia has the rather unfortunate reputation as being the armpit of the Czech Republic. Surely enough, the region is heavily industrialized. Fueled by the brown coal dug out of the **Krušné hory** (Ore Mountains), the factories of North Bohemia's industrial towns – such as Ústí nad Labem, Teplice, and Most – pump out a disastrous level of sulphur dioxide that has wreaked havoc on the mountains and forests of the northern Czech Republic, been the cause of countless birth defects, and shaved years off the life-span of the citizens who have to breathe the muck. Indeed, the situation hits home each winter when the Prague newspapers print photographs of children going to school wearing gas masks.

Though Communist mismanagement is mostly to blame for making this region one of the most polluted in Europe, the leaders of the former regime can't be held entirely responsible. The Hapsburgs laid the corner-stone in the late 19th century, when they made this region into the industrial center of the Austro-Hungarian Empire – an occurrence which thrust Czechoslovakia onto the World League's list of ten most industrialized nations when the country was formed back in 1918.

Although the country's current politicians have paid a lot of lip service to the absolute necessity of cleaning up North Bohemia, most aren't willing to appropriate the adequate funds to do so, nor are they willing to put their necks out on a limb and pass laws that would mean placing more workers out on the street. However, the situation is getting better. The burning of brown coal is being phased out, as other sources of energy are being sought out and used.

So, are there any incentives for venturing into North Bohemia? Absolutely – because not all of North Bohemia is covered with smoke-stacks blighting the scenery. Case in point is the graceful, uplifting town of **Litoměřice**, which makes for a great day trip from Prague and provides the much-needed relief after visiting its neighbor to the south – the former Jewish ghetto of **Terezín**. Another good incentive for getting up north is the city of **Liberec**, with its gorgeous main square, town hall,

---

NORTH BOHEMIA FINDS & FAVORITES
Ghetto Museum in Terezín
*The town of **Litoměřice***
Hotel Roosevelt in Litoměřice
Gallery of Fine Arts in Litoměřice
Hotel Zelené Údolí in Liberec
Hotel Ještěd in Liberec
***Town Hall** in Liberec*

---

and mountainous surroundings. There's also what's been dubbed misleadingly as **Česky Švýcarsko** ("Czech Switzerland"), referring to a mountainous, 35-kilometer (22-mile) strip of land on the German border, dotted with more of the republic's unique "rock cities."

Terezín

Before the Nazis put Terezín to use for their own lunatic purposes, Terezín was quite a normal Czech town that happened to occupy a former fortress. Erected by Emperor Josef II in the 1780s and named for his mother Maria Theresa, Terezín and its Main and Small fortress were intended as bulwarks to protect the Austrian Empire against Prussian attack from the north. As it turned out, the fortresses were never put to use in battle, and the Main Fortress was eventually transformed into a town. Built at the same time as the Main Fortress, the Small Fortress became a prison for military and political enemies of the Hapsburg monarchy.

When the Germans took over the Czech lands in 1939, they immediately recognized the role that the fully fortified town of Terezín and its prison could play in carrying out their "final solution." In June 1940, the first prisoners arrived at the Small Fortress. And in October 1941, the 3,500 Czechs living within the Main Fortress were all expelled to make way for the 60,000 Jews who would be interned here by the end of 1942. When you consider that this garrison town was built for an army of 5,000, you can imagine the egregiously overcrowded conditions that existed in the new ghetto.

Terezín served mainly as a way-station for Jews being sent to extermination camps. Out of the 140,000 European Jews deported to Terezín during the war, 87,000 were later herded onto trains bound for the gas chambers. The Nazis didn't need to bother with condemning 35,000 of the Jews who were interned here, because they died at Terezín by suicide, disease, or starvation.

Terezín also served as a smokescreen for the sadistic practices that the Nazis were engaged in at the fully-fledged extermination camps. The town was made to appear self-governing. It had its own city council, its own bank, its own shops, and its own schools. But it was all a charade, meant to fool the world into thinking that the Nazis were actually benevolent in their treatment of the Jews. The ploy proved to be successful, as indicated by the positive reports filed by delegates of the Red Cross following their two visits to Terezín.

Despite the appalling conditions Jews endured at Terezín, something extraordinary occurred at the ghetto. With so many Jews amassed here from across the European continent (many of whom were prominent artists, intellectuals, and musicians), a thriving cultural life took shape, with clandestine concerts, puppet shows, art lessons, and literary discussions taking place in the basements and attics of the barracks.

Though you can't exactly call Terezín an "attraction," it is perhaps the most thought-provoking destination you could choose on your travels through the Czech Republic. Less than 90 minutes away from Prague, it makes for a rewarding day trip from the capital.

ORIENTATION

Roughly 60 kilometers (37 miles) north of Prague, Terezín (referred to as the **Main Fortress**, or Hlavní Pevnost) sits on the west bank of the **Ohře River**. The **Small Fortress** (Malá Pevnost) is on the other side of the Ohře, about a ten minute walk east along the highway to Prague.

ARRIVALS & DEPARTURES

By Bus

There are three or four buses that leave each morning from Prague's Florenc station and three that go back in the afternoon. The ride takes about an hour and 15 minutes and costs 50 Kč. The bus from Prague makes two stops in Terezín. One is just beyond the Small Fortress and the other is at the town's main square, opposite the Ghetto Museum.

Mantana, a travel agency in Prague, offers transport from Prague and guided tours of Terezín in a mini-van. Contact them at *Maiselova 15, 110 00 Prague 1, Tel. 02/232 1954*.

By Car

From Prague, take highway E55 all the way there. There's a huge lot just outside the Small Fortress where you can park your car.

By Train

There nearest train station to Terezín is two kilometers south in the village of Bohušovice, so it's best to just take the bus.

GETTING AROUND TOWN

Unless you catch the ČAD bus that runs between the Small Fortress and the main square in town, your only option is to take the 10 minute walk (or drive) from the Small Fortress into town.

WHERE TO STAY

I can't think of a less attractive place to spend the night than in a former concentration camp. There is only one hotel here anyway, and it looks rather seedy. So forget spending the night in Terezín and head three kilometers (two miles) north to the very delightful town of **Litoměřice** (see below), where you'll find several good places to stay.

WHERE TO EAT

U HOJTÁSŮ, *Komenského 152. Tel. 0416/922 03. 100-200 Kč. No credit cards.*

You probably won't exactly have the appetite for a multi-course meal while in Terezín, so the decent Czech fare served at this restaurant near the Ghetto Museum should suffice for lunch.

There's also a restaurant at the **Small Fortress** in what used to be the Germans' mess hall. Needless to say, not many people go there to eat.

SEEING THE SIGHTS

Main Fortress

The **Main Fortress** refers to the town proper of Terezín, set within four kilometers of red-brick fortifications that form an intricate star shape around the town. Certainly, the fortifications appear to be absolutely impregnable, which makes them the most impressive sight in town. But they don't look so ominous these days, thanks to local greenthumbs who have made gardens out of the old moats.

As a garrison town, Terezín was laid out to a severe grid plan around a leafy main square, now called náměstí Československé armády (Czechoslovak Army Square). Lining the streets are rows of neo-Classical administrative buildings and block-houses originally used as barracks but later as spaces in which to cram more and more Jewish prisoners.

At the corner of the main square and Komenského street is the **Ghetto Museum** (Muzeum ghetta). Thoughtfully laid-out and remarkably embracing, the museum tells the story of Terezín during World War II, starting out on the ground floor with a look at the drawings done by children in the clandestine art classes. The children's art is particularly startling, allowing you a glimpse at how they came to terms with the horror they witnessed every day. Upstairs, the museum moves into the history of the ghetto, documenting it through photographs, artifacts, newspaper clippings, paintings, and letters. As you peruse the displays, you're introduced to some of the Terezín survivors, who have given harrowing accounts of their time in the ghetto on video.

After you've looked over all the exhibits, step into the cinema for a viewing of the propaganda film, *Hitler Gives the Jews a Town*, shot at Terezín and spliced with more interviews of the ghetto survivors. This insightful museum is *open daily 9 a.m. to 6 p.m. Tickets are 70 Kč.*

Small Fortress

A ten minute walk east of the Main Fortress along the road to Prague, the Small Fortress comes closer to the picture most of us have of a concentration camp. The former prison has a sprawling network of fortifications, but on a scale that's easier to grasp than the Main Fortress. You can either walk through the prison by yourself (which costs 70 Kč) or join one of the guided tours (120 Kč), some of which are led by Terezín survivors.

You approach the fortress past the **National Cemetery**, filled with 10,000 victims exhumed from the mass graves at the Small Fortress, the Terezín ghetto, and the Litoměřice concentration camp. Inside the walls and to the left, you walk under a sign bearing the ridiculing Nazi slogan, *Arbeit Macht Frei* ("work makes you free"), on your way through a series of dusty courtyards lined with prison cells where prisoners were stuffed by the hundreds. You then walk through a seemingly never-ending underground tunnel built into the fortifications (claustrophobes should turn back and go around the other way), which lets out at the execution grounds, where some 250 Jewish prisoners were shot to death. Nearby are the former mass graves.

After watching a documentary on Terezín at the prison cinema (built in 1942 for the SS guards' entertainment), you then proceed into another courtyard, surrounded by solitary confinement cells and overlooked by a tiny guard station at the entrance. Back outside the courtyard is the **prison museum**, housed in the former SS barracks and providing more details of the sadistic treatment the prisoners of Terezín underwent.

The Small Fortress is open daily from 8 a.m. to 4:30 p.m. October 20 through March 31, until 5 p.m. in April, until 6 p.m. May through September, and until 5 p.m. October 1 through October 19.

PRACTICAL INFORMATION

Both the Ghetto Museum and Small Fortress offer a large selection of English-language pamphlets and books on Terezín. They also offer guided tours of the Main and Small fortresses. For more information, *call 0416/922 25 or fax 0416/922 45.*

Litoměřice

After acquainting yourself with the atrocities that occurred at Terezín, you will surely be in need of some uplifting. Thankfully then, the delightful town of Litoměřice is just up the road.

Přemyslid princes founded Litoměřice as an administrative center back in the tenth century. It was a logical choice, considering that the site had already been fortified a century earlier by a Slavic tribe. In 1057, **Prince Spytihněv II** set up an ecclesiastical college here, after which German colonists flooded in to take advantage of its prime trading location at the confluence of the Ohře and Labe rivers. In no time, Litoměřice turned into one of Bohemia's richest towns, sporting a wealth of Gothic and Renaissance architecture along the town's winding lanes.

When the Reformation hit Bohemia, Litoměřice embraced the Hussite cause, for which it paid dearly in the Thirty Years' War, when Hapsburg forces marched in and pummeled the town. Of course, having given itself over so easily to Protestantism, Litoměřice was forced to endure a heavy Counter-Reformation, brought on by the Jesuits who established a bishopric here in the mid-17th century. The Jesuits set to work redeveloping the town, commissioning Litoměřice native **Octaviano Broggio** to design new Baroque churches and rebuild the Gothic ones that got trashed in the war.

Litoměřice's present appearance is a grand testament to Broggio's work. You can't turn a corner in town without running into something he had a hand in building. In addition to the fine architecture and intriguing medieval lanes, the town has a fine setting at the base of the **Central Bohemian Mountains**, which makes for a fine backdrop to this great destination.

ORIENTATION

Litoměřice sits at the confluence of the **Labe** and **Ohře** rivers three kilometers (two miles) north of Terezín and roughly 63 kilometers (39 miles) north of Prague.

ARRIVALS & DEPARTURES

By Bus

There are three or four buses that depart each morning from Prague's Florenc station, stopping at Terezín along the way. The trip takes about 90 minutes and costs around 50 Kč. A bus runs roughly every hour from Terezín's main square to Litoměřice, costing 6 Kč. The bus station in Litoměřice, which is adjacent to the train station, is a five minute walk east of the town center.

By Car
Take highway E55 all the way there from Prague. The drive should take you no more than an hour and 15 minutes. There's parking available right on the main square of Mírové náměstí.

By Train
There's no sense in taking the train to or from Prague. It requires too many time-consuming changes. But if you're coming from or going to Děčín, train is your only option, and a good one at that, with departures every 90 minutes or so. Tickets cost about 45 Kč for this beautiful journey along the Labe River and through the Central Bohemian Mountains. The train station in Litoměřice is a five minute walk east of the main square at the end of Dlouha street.

GETTING AROUND TOWN
You'll have no problem getting around this small town on foot. Public transportation is pretty much non-existent anyway. If you require a taxi (which might be a good idea if you're coming from or going to Terezín), call 0416/2698 or just hail one from the main square in Litoměřice.

WHERE TO STAY
HOTEL SALVA GUARDA, *Mírové náměstí 12, 412 01 Litoměřice. Tel. & Fax 0416/732 506. Rates for single/double: 900/1,300 Kč. Credit cards: AE, MC, V. Four rooms and three apartments. Restaurant.*
Carved out of a striking Renaissance building on the main square, this hotel underwent a very successful restoration in 1994 that preserved a good deal of the building's historic character. The sunny rooms – replete with satellite television, new furniture, and tasteful art – come with a great view of the square. In addition to its superb restaurant, the hotel has an art gallery and a handsome ballroom where dances and other cultural events take place.
HOTEL ROOSEVELT, *Rooseveltova 18, 412 01 Litoměřice. Tel. 0416/ 733 590, Fax 0416/733 593. Rates for single/double: 800/1,200 Kč. Credit cards: AE, MC, V. 32 rooms. Restaurant.*
This is an extremely pleasant hotel located in a neighborhood filled with turn-of-the-century mansions, one of which the hotel occupies. The comfortable, smartly decorated rooms come with brass beds, slanted ceilings, new carpet, satellite television, and direct-dial telephones. The hotel sits above the historic center, providing a nice view of the spires poking through the skyline. In addition to the great restaurant, the hotel has a wine bar (with dance floor), sauna, tiny fitness center, an enclosed parking lot, and a terrace with an amazing view over town.

PENSION U PAVOUKA, *Pekařská 7, 412 01 Litoměřice. Tel. 0416/734 409, no fax. Rates for double only: 900 Kč. No credit cards. 4 rooms. Restaurant.* This is simply a restaurant which rents out rooms to tourists. But the rooms, which do come with private baths, are decent enough, though a bit spartan. The pension has a good location, between the main square and Cathedral Hill.

HOTEL HELENA, *Želetická 10-12, 412 01 Litoměřice. Tel. & Fax 0419/ 739 002. Rates for single/double: 800/1,200 Kč. No credit cards. 12 rooms. Restaurant.*

Though the rooms here are quite comfortable, the hotel has a lousy location – right on the main highway running between Litoměřice and Terezín. It's about a 20 minute walk south of Litoměřice center, which puts it out of range of the good restaurants and good sights. Make a reservation here only if none of the above places work out.

WHERE TO EAT

RESTAURANT SALVA GUARDA, *Mírové náměstí 12. Tel. & Fax 0416/732 506. 150-300 Kč.*

This is definitely the swankiest restaurant in town, serving up a nice selection of game dishes and a zingy tournedos with green peppercorn sauce. The vaulted ceilings add enchantment, but the rude service unfortunately mars the experience.

RADNIČNI SKLÍPEK, *Mírové náměstí 21. Tel. 0416/734 306. 100-200 Kč. No credit cards.*

Descend into the intriguing cellars of this laudable restaurant for a hearty Czech or Asian-Czech meal. Extremely gracious service and good prices make the dining experience all the better.

VINÁRNA BAŠTA, *Mezibranní 59/5. Tel. 0416/732 346. 150-250 Kč. No credit cards.*

The best thing going for this wine restaurant is its setting – within an old town bastion. The standard Czech fare is nothing to get excited about, but should suffice for lunch. You'll find this restaurant cat-a-corner to the train station.

HOTEL ROOSEVELT, *Rooseveltova 18. Tel. 0416/733 590. 150-250 Kč.*

The high standards of this fine hotel are maintained at the restaurant, featuring appetizers such as lobster cocktail and escargot and entrées such as steak au poivre and shark topped with chips of garlic. Very friendly service and good prices to match.

SEEING THE SIGHTS

Mírové Náměstí & Around

If you arrive by bus or train, then the first sight you'll see of the historic center are the remains of the old town fortifications, including a squat bastion that's now a restaurant. Proceed up the hill along Dlouha street to the town's handsome main square, **Mírové náměstí**. Where Dlouha meets the square is a bundle of attractions.

First is an ominous four-story **Gothic tower**, each of its four corners fitted with spiky turrets. The tower is attached to the **All Saints Church** (Kostel všech svatých), and together they make for a rather incongruous ensemble. A hybrid church if there ever were one, All Saints started out as a Romanesque basilica in the early 13th century, but was converted into a Gothic church sometime around 1480. Then in 17th century, Octaviano Broggio gave it a Baroque restoration, adding to it the present slender facade. The musty, stucco-ridden interior bears more of Broggio's touches, including a series of chapels leading up to the marble altar.

Opposite the church is the square's most striking building – the Renaissance **Old Town Hall** (stará radnice). Its series of spade-shaped arcades draws your attention upward to the rows of bristling gables and the syringe-like copper tower thrusting from the roof. The building now houses the ho-hum **District Museum of Local History and Geography** (Okresní vlastivědné muzeum), *open daily except Monday from 10 a.m. to 5 p.m.* The museum is worth a quick perusal if only for the Renaissance stone staircase and the original panel ceiling in the council hall.

Along the south side of the square, *at number 12*, is another comely Renaissance building called **Dům U Černého orla** (House at the Black Eagle), its gabled facade smothered in black and white sgraffito depicting scenes from the Bible. These days it houses the hotel and restaurant, Salva Guarda (see above). A few doors down *at number 15*, the blue **Dům U kalicha** (House at the Chalice) features an enormous chalice-shaped copper dome plunked on top of its roof. The 16th-century burgher who owned the house apparently wanted to clearly state his Hussite beliefs when he added the chalice, which is the symbol of the Hussites.

You'll find the town's superb **Gallery of Fine Arts** (Galerie výtvarného umění) *at Michalská 29*, occupying an ornate 16th-century house just off Mírové náměstí. The gallery's permanent collection includes a little bit of every style, from Gothic to Renaissance to Modernist. But where the museum really shines is in its collection of Naive art, the only such collection in the republic. The paintings and wood sculptures have been culled from villages around the Czech Republic, and are truly representative of the rich folk traditions of this country. Another highlight at the museum is the set of 16th-century panels by the anonymous Master of

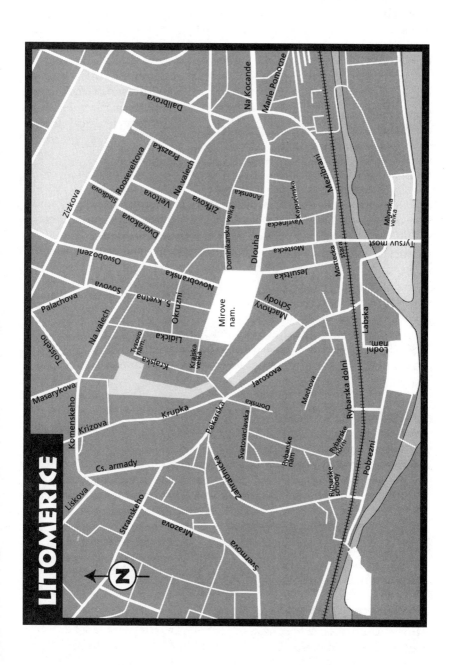

Litoměřice, the most praised Bohemian artist of the Renaissance whose work also graces St. Vitus Cathedral in Prague. *The museum is open Tuesday through Sunday from 9 a.m. to 6 p.m. Admission costs 16 Kč.*

Cathedral Hill

In the southwest corner of the old town rises **Cathedral Hill** (Dómský vrch), accessed from Mírové náměstí by walking to the end of Michalská and then taking a left on Krajská. Going up the hill, you can't miss **St. Wenceslas Church** (Kostel sv. Václava) sticking its cylindrical dome above the rooftops. Perhaps Broggio's finest work, the newly restored church has a dynamic facade adorned with stucco pilasters and cornices (hard to appreciate because of the church's cramped quarters).

From there, it's a short climb up to **Dómské náměstí** (Cathedral Square) – a spartan, grassy enclosure that looks more like a compound than a square. Dominating the square is the hulking **St. Stephen's Cathedral** (Katedrála sv. Štěpána). Originally conceived in the 11th century as a Romanesque basilica, the cathedral was given its present appearance in the 17th century. The single-nave interior, typical of early Baroque design, is lined with side chapels leading up to main altar, which is adorned with paintings by Karel Škréta, one of the more renowned Bohemian artists of the time.

Attached to the cathedral by an arch is a soaring belfry, erected in the 1880s. Behind the church is the **Bishop's Palace**, a dull 17th-century pile looking extremely weathered at the edge of Cathedral Hill's fortifications.

NIGHTLIFE & ENTERTAINMENT

A rowdy, old pub you might want to try is **Pivnice Kalich**, just off the main square on Lidická street. It pours the good local beer called, fairly enough, Litoměřice. You can catch a film at **Kino Máj**, *on the corner of Rooseveltova and Sovova*, or at the **open-air cinema** (summer only) on Střelecký Island, *just behind the train station on the banks of the Labe River.*

SPORTS & RECREATION

For a game of tennis, try the leafy clay courts also on Střelecký Island. Have your hotel receptionist book you a court, or just show up. For outdoor swimming, try the pool on Písečný Island.

PRACTICAL INFORMATION

- **Investiční banka**, *Mírové náměstí 11.* You can change money here.
- **Litoměřice Information Center** (Městské Informační Centrum), *Mírové náměstí 15. Tel. 0416/732 440.* Sells maps and brochures to the town,

can help find you accommodations, and provides bus and train schedules.

•**Post Office**, *two blocks north of Mírové náměstí on Osvobození street.*

Děčín

In terms of attractions, there's really not much going for this sprawling port city on the Labe River. The town **castle**, an ominous 18th-century pile built on top of a rocky crag, has been closed to the public ever since 1968, the year the Soviet army took it over and used it as their barracks. Despite rumors of it being restored, the castle stands closed.

But Děčín does have a couple of decent hotels and restaurants that make the city a good base for exploring **České Švýcarsko** (see below). And if you got time to kill, then it may be worth your while to have a look around at its historic center or take the chairlift to top of **Shepherd's Wall**, a sheer cliff topped with a tiny chateau.

ORIENTATION

Děčín sits just 13 kilometers (nine miles) south of the German border and roughly 115 kilometers (71 miles) north of Prague. Děčín has two distinct centers, **Děčín** itself and **Podmokly**, which are divided by the **Labe River**. On the east side of the river is Děčín, the historic part of town where you'll find better accommodations and better restaurants.

On the west side is Podmokly, the modern part of town where the train and long-distance bus stations are located. The two town centers are not really within walking distance of each other, so you'll need to take the bus or a cab between the two (see *Getting Around Town*).

ARRIVALS & DEPARTURES

By Bus

Three buses run daily from Florenc station in Prague to Děčín, taking about two-and-a-half hours and costing about 70 Kč. If you're heading to. But if you're heading to České Švýcarsko, bus is your most convenient form of public transportation. The long-distance bus station is on the Podmokly side at the corner of Podmokelská and Hankova.

By Car

From Prague, head north on E55 to Lovosice, highway 30 to Ústí nad Labem, and then E442 to Děčín. The drive should take you about two hours. The most central parking lot is on Masarykovo náměstí – the main square on the Děčín side.

By Train

Fast trains go back and forth from Prague's Hlavní nádraží to Děčín about seven times a day. The journey takes about two hours and costs 75 Kč. The main train station is on the Podmokly side of town on Čs mládeže street.

If you're coming from Litoměřice, you may end up at the minor train station, Děčín-vychod (Děčín-East), located on the east side of the river. In that case, it's a five minute walk north on 17. listopadu street to the historic center.

GETTING AROUND TOWN

Most buses run back and forth between the train station and Masarykovo náměstí (the main square on the Děčín side). When you board the bus, drop 7 Kč into the meter and wait for your ticket to come out. If you'd rather not deal with the bus, taxis are easy enough to catch at stands in front of the train station or at Masarykovo náměstí.

WHERE TO STAY

HOTEL ČESKÁ KORUNA, *Masarykovo náměstí 60, 405 01 Děčín. Tel. 0412/220 93, Fax 0412/222 71. Rates for single/double: ,250/1,716 Kč. Credit cards: DC, MC, V. 45 rooms. Restaurant.*

This hotel is carved out of a pretty Baroque house right on the main square of the historic center. In spite of the hotel's pretentious character, the rooms here are not up to snuff when you consider their rates. Furnishings are tacky, the carpets need to be changed, and the bathrooms are cramped. But the hotel does have a laudable restaurant (see below).

HOTEL FAUST, *U Plovárny 43, 405 00 Děčín. Tel. 0412/222 50, Fax 0412/262 67. Rates for single/double: 700/1,100 Kč. Credit cards: V. 21 rooms. Restaurant.*

This hotel sits on the edge of a pond just below the castle. The rooms are simply but smartly furnished and come with satellite television and direct-dial telephones. Definitely ask for a room with a view of the pond. The hotel also has a decent restaurant and a big deck where you can eat or just have a coffee.

PENSION NELA, *U starého mostu 111/4, 405 01 Děčín. Tel. 0412/235 66, no fax. Rates for single/double: 540/900 Kč. No credit cards. 8 rooms. Restaurant.*

This quiet pension has the feel of a bed and breakfast. It has a nice garden replete with chickens and dogs. Rooms are spacious and even a bit cozy, and come with private baths. Ask for a room in front so you can have a view of the castle. The restaurant, open to guests only, serves a nice variety of game dishes.

PENSION KARIN, *Ruská 52, 405 02 Děčín. Tel. 0412/532 046, no fax. Rates for double only: 850 Kč. No credit cards. 10 rooms. No restaurant.* Just up the road from the train station in Podmokly, this pension has atrociously ugly rooms that are way overpriced. The place is hardly inviting, considering you have to be buzzed through an iron gate in order to get in. But rooms do come with private bath and satellite television. Even still, book a room here only if you're in a pinch.

WHERE TO EAT

HOTEL ČESKÁ KORUNA, *Masarykovo náměstí 60. Tel. 0412/220 93. 150-250 Kč.* Though the hotel itself isn't anything too great, its restaurant serves probably the best food in town in a very classy, chandelier-strewn dining room. The menu features a lot of exotic dishes, such as Ukrainian-style pork liver, and some good Czech standards, such as roast goose. The restaurant also features a big buffet for breakfast.

RISTORANTE PALERMO, *U Plovárny 45/5. Tel. 0412/226 54. 80-150 Kč. Credit cards: MC.* This place has a nice deck on the castle pond where you can enjoy any number of good, thin-crust pizzas. Service is top-notch and the clientele is usually pretty young. But this is probably a better choice for lunch than dinner.

VINÁRNA CHALOUPKA U KAPLIČKY, *Březová 13. Tel. 0412/267 00. 100-200 Kč. No credit cards.* If you happen to be staying at Pension Nela, then stroll over to this quaint wine restaurant serving up some eccentric but tasty Czech dishes, such as breast of chicken topped with a slice of peach and melted cheese (which, surprisingly enough, is not too bad).

ARIZONA RESTAURANT, *Husova náměstí 36/9. Tel. 0412/238 19. 100-200 Kč. No credit cards.* If you're looking for a place to eat on the Podmokly side of town, this is probably your best choice. Located near the train station, this restaurant goes for the American southwestern theme. But the only thing southwestern about the thoroughly Czech food are the ridiculous names. For some reason, this place is popular with the local bodybuilders, who sit around the bar and grunt a lot.

SEEING THE SIGHTS

Děčín Side

The uncontested centerpiece of town is the **Děčín Castle**, commanding its position on a rocky pedestal above the Labe River. King Václav III founded the castle in 1305 to protect the northern border of Bohemia.

After a Renaissance reconstruction and a Baroque facelift, the red and white castle now appears as an enormous, well-fortified chateau. Certainly, its most gorgeous exterior feature is its majestic tower, overlooking the river on the west side.

As I said, the castle has been closed ever since 1968, the year the Soviet Union decided to use (and abuse) it as barracks for their soldiers. Despite rumors of being restored, the castle is still closed. So you'll just have to content yourself with a stroll through the castle **Rose Gardens** (Růžová záhrada), a pretty Baroque affair laid out at the side of the castle and accessed through a gate on Dlouhá jízda street (the street stretching up to the castle.)

The gardens – *open May through October daily except Monday from 10 a.m. to 5 p.m.* – afford a nice bird's-eye view of U brány ulice, perhaps the nicest street in Děčín. From the garden, walk down the footpath to the **Church of the Holy Cross**, a red and white Baroque confection topped with a handsome dome and a line of statuary. Chances are the church will be closed. But if it isn't, step inside for a look at its fading frescoes.

Podmokly Side

About a block north of the train station at Čs mládeže 1 is the town's **Regional Museum** (Okresní muzeum), with great exhibits on the history and evolution of the Děčín Castle and its former royal and aristocratic owners. Those with a penchant for boats and navigation will get a kick out of the exhibits on shipping along the Labe River, which springs from the Krkonoše Mountains in North Bohemia, flows across Bohemia into Germany (where it's called the Elbe), and empties into the North Sea near Hamburg. *The museum is open Tuesday through Sunday from 9 a.m. to noon and from 1 to 5 p.m.*

For something a bit more thrilling, take the chairlift to the top of the sheer cliff called **Pastýřská stěna** (Shepherd's Wall), where you'll find a neat, cream-colored chateau and a breathtaking view of the castle below. The chateau has a café, which means you can have a coffee or something light to eat as you look out as far as the eye can see. To get to the chairlift (*vytah*) from the museum, continue down Čs mládeže street under the railway bridge and then hike the steps to the lift. If you're coming from the Děčín historic center, cross over Tyršova bridge and then take a left on Labské nábřeží to the chairlift.

PRACTICAL INFORMATION

Note: A rather annoying thing about Děčín is that it has no tourist information office or any travel agencies that can give you substantial information on the town or region. Best idea then would be to pop into a hotel and make your inquiries at the reception desk.

•**Čs. Obchodní banka**, Podmokly side, *in front of the train station at Zbrojnická 18.* A bank where you can change money.

•**Komerční banka**, Děčín side, *Masarykovo náměstí* . You can change money here.

•**Post Office**, Děčín side, *corner of náměstí Svobody and 17. listopadu;* Podmokly side, *just south of the train station on Poštovní street.*

České Švýcarsko

Though I wouldn't count it as a must-see on your travels through the Czech Republic, **České Švýcarsko** (or "Czech Switzerland") does offer a pleasant respite from the cities and big towns of Bohemia. The hyperbolic name (there's nothing Swiss about the place), coined none-too-surprisingly by Czech artists of the Romantic era, refers to a 35-kilometer-long (22-mile) strip of densely forested mountains, dewy pastures, and precipitous gorges all stretched along the border with Germany. But what really draws the hordes of Czech and German tourists here are the numerous "rock cities" – unique clusters of sandstone cliffs, bridges, and other formations that bear a slight resemblance to those you'd find in the American Southwest.

Of course, the main activity at České Švýcarsko is hiking, of which there is plenty to do. Feasibly, you could catch the region's highlights – including the natural sandstone bridge of **Pravčická brána** and the dramatic depths of **Kamenice Gorge** – on a day hike. And when you get tired of hiking, you can go on a boat trip up or down the **Kamenice River** through the Kamenice Gorge.

ORIENTATION

The hub, if you will, of České Švýcarsko is **Hřensko**, located right on the German border 12 picturesque kilometers (seven miles) down the **Labe River valley** from Děčín. At an elevation of 115 meters (377 feet), the town sits at the lowest point in the Czech Republic. Though it has a pretty, rock-strewn location at the confluence of the **Kamenice** and **Labe** rivers, Hřensko is no place to hang around in for long.

Lining the streets is vendor after vendor hawking T-shirts, stuffed animals, gnome statues, and a lot of other unsightly crap. And on the road from Hřensko to Děčín are a lot of high-heeled women selling, at any time of day, something of an entirely different nature to German men.

So, if you want to avoid all this nonsense, head for **Mezní Louka**, **Mezná**, or **Vysoká Lípa** – three tiny villages in the hills of České Švýcarsko. Mezní Louka is located 11 kilometers (seven miles) east of Hřensko near Pravčická brána natural bridge. Two kilometers south of

Mezní Louka is the village of Mezná, with a beautiful setting overlooking the Kamenice Gorge. And six kilometers (four miles) east of Mezní Louka is Vysoká Lípa, located near some old castle ruins and another natural bridge called Malá Pravčická brána.

ARRIVALS & DEPARTURES

By Boat
The nicest possible way to travel between Děčín and Hřensko is by boat through the narrow Labe River valley. Unfortunately, the boat runs only on weekends April through September, costing 50 Kč each way. Times of departure are likely to change, so check at the boat terminal to confirm times. The boat terminal in Děčín is slightly downriver from Tyršův most (Bridge) on the east side of the Labe and a few blocks west of Masarykovo náměstí. The terminal in Hřensko is at the turnoff for Kamenice Valley.

By Bus
A private bus company called Fobus has the only bus line through České Švýcarsko. The bus originates at the ČAD bus station (stand #3) on the Podmokly side of Děčín, but you can catch it at 2. Polské armády street (next to the big pond below the castle). From Děčín, the bus goes to Hřensko and Mezní Louka and then turns around at Mezná. Buses go back and forth about eight times a day. The ticket from Děčín to Mezná costs 80 Kč.

By Car
From Děčín, head north on highway 261 to Hřensko. There you can park along the river embankment. But remember to put some coins in the meter. From Hřensko turn east up to Mezní Louka or Mezná, where you'll find plenty of free parking. But there is no parking at all between Hřensko and Mezní Louka.

By Train
Sorry, there are no trains into České Švýcarsko.

GETTING AROUND THE AREA
If you want to get to some of the sights in a hurry, then catch the Fobus bus that comes along every one to two hours. It stops at Hřensko, then Tří prameny (closest stop to Pravčická brána natural bridge), Mezní Louka, and ends up at Mezná (closest stop to Kamenice Gorge). Tickets cost no more than 10 or 12 Kč, depending on how far you're going. Just tell the driver where you want to go and he'll hand you a ticket with the price printed on it.

There's also a boat service taking you up or down the Kamenice River (but only May through mid-September). There are three different landings where you can get on or off. The furthest up the river is three kilometers down from Mezní Louka (accessed via the blue-marked trail). The middle landing is a steep two kilometers down from Mezná. And the bottom landing is two kilometers up the river from Hřensko. Each stretch costs 30 Kč. Boats come along about every 30 minutes.

WHERE TO STAY/WHERE TO EAT

Note: Throughout České Švýcarsko, especially in Mezná and Vysoká Lípa, are scores of private houses with rooms for rent. Most are quite cozy and quite cheap, though they don't always come with private baths. Just look for the sign that says, "*Zimmer frei*" (room available). In Hřensko are a number of hotels, most of which are listed below. But, if your aim is to get away from it all, head for Mezní Louka, Vysoká Lípa, or Mezná, none of which have the tourist crowds you find in Hřensko.

HOTEL LABE, *Hřensko 13. Tel. & Fax 0412/912 88. Rates for single/ double: 450/900 Kč. Credit cards: MC. 13 rooms. Restaurant.*

This is a handsome old hotel set against a big rock pinnacle at the point where the Kamenice River empties into the Labe. Though cheerfully decorated with nice rugs and bright paintings, rooms are a bit cramped and do not come with television or telephones. Definitely ask for one of the rooms on the top floor. That way you can have a nice view of the Labe River valley. The restaurant serves standard Czech fare with prices ranging from 80 to 200 Kč.

RESTAURACE U LEOPOLDA, *Hřensko 125. Tel. 0412/982 89. 100-200. Credit cards: MC, V.*

If you're going to eat dinner in Hřensko, do it at this restaurant with seating outside on the Kamenice River or inside in the tastefully decorated café. The kitchen uses old Czech recipes and fresh ingredients in preparing any number of flavorful dishes.

MINIHOTEL & RESTAURANT OÁZA, *Hřensko 40. Tel. 0412/913 33, no fax. Rates for single/double: 360/700 Kč. No credit cards. 2 rooms. Restaurant.*

Of the two rooms here, ask for number two, which is in a real cozy attic studded with wood. The basic Czech meals here are gratifying, but will probably suit you better for lunch than dinner.

HOTEL U LÍPY, *Hřensko 35. Tel. 0412/912 17, no fax. Rates for double only: 425 Kč. No credit cards. 12 rooms. Restaurant.*

This is another venerable old hotel right on the Kamenice River. Rooms are very basic, but functional nonetheless. Again, food here is very Czech – satisfying, but not particularly memorable.

HOTEL MEZNÍ LOUKA, *Mezní Louka 76. Tel. & Fax 0412/912 89. Rates for single/double without private bath: 250/340 Kč. Rates for double only with private bath: 800 Kč. No credit cards. 158 rooms. Restaurant.*

Located at the turnoff to Mezná (about 10 kilometers east of Hřensko), this rustic, old hotel with jagged gables and ornate iron work has probably seen better days. But it still enchants – from the outside, at least. The interior looks like it was last renovated in the 1960s, though it still makes for a pleasant place to shack up for the night. In addition to the mediocre restaurant, the hotel has a very pleasant outdoor terrace where you can get a good glass of Louny beer. From the hotel, you can easily walk to either Kamenice Gorge or the natural sandstone bridge called Pravčická brána.

HOTEL HUBERT, *Mezná 76. Tel. & Fax 0412/912 92. Rate per person: 300 Kč. No credit cards. 28 rooms. Restaurant.*

This hotel in Mezná caters mostly to big groups, so there are only two double rooms and no single rooms. All of the rooms are very basic, and none of them come with private bath. (Unfortunately, this is the case with all accommodations in Mezná.)

U MAREŠŮ, *Mezná 21. Tel. 0412/912 93. Price per person: 180 Kč. No credit cards. 8 rooms. Restaurant.*

It's too bad that none of the rooms at this pension have private baths, because the old wood house has a wonderfully rustic appeal that makes you want to stay a few nights. But if you came to enjoy the great surroundings, then you should be able to get by without the conveniences of a toilet or shower in your room. The restaurant, serving hearty chicken and steak dishes in a woody dining room, is a good one.

SEEING THE SIGHTS

If you plan on doing some heavy-duty hiking, then get a hold of a good map to the area, preferably Kartografie Praha's 1:50,000 *Českosaské Švýcarsko* (Czech-Saxon Switzerland), which is available at bookshops in Děčín or at tourist shops in Hřensko.

A good trail that allows you to see České Švýcarsko's best sights all in one day is the one marked by a green slash. It begins in Hřensko and follows the road three kilometers (1.8 miles) up to Tří prameny bus stop, from where it's a two kilometer (1.2 mile) walk to **Pravčická brána**. (Alternatively, you could take the Fobus bus from Hřensko to Tří prameny.)

With a width of 30 meters (98 feet) and a height of 21 meters (69 feet), Pravčická brána is Europe's largest and most impressive natural bridge. Just as impressive is the top-of-the-world view from the bridge, taking in a good bit of České Švýcarsko's rolling hills.

From Pravčická brána, the trail straddles the German border before veering southward to **Mezní Louka**, four kilometers (2.5 miles) from the bridge. In Mezní Louka, you can grab a bite to eat or have a beer at the venerable hotel there.

South of Mezní Louka is the gorgeous **Kamenice Gorge**, a dramatic slot in the mountains draped in pines and studded with mossy cliffs. Snaking through it are the clear waters of the **Kamenice River**, with a boat service going up or down it from May to mid-September (see *Getting Around The Area*, above).

About four kilometers (2.5 miles) east of Mezní Louka along a foot trail (beginning across the street from the hotel) is another natural bridge, this one called **Malá Pravčická brána**. A kilometer beyond the bridges are some castle ruins you may want to check out as well.

PRACTICAL INFORMATION

A good source of information on České Švýcarsko is a little **tourist office/exchange outlet** *in Hřensko, located at the turnoff for Kamenice Valley.* You can pick up maps and get times of departure for boats going to Děčín.

Liberec

Rolled out in the sweeping Nisa River valley, the once-rich city of **Liberec** comes as quite a revelation to those who venture this far north. Yes, it is an industrial town, and has been since the Hapsburgs made it the center of the textile industry in the Austrian Empire. But it was this industry, plus its glass works, that allowed the town to prosper, and become for a short time the second biggest city in Bohemia in the mid-19th century.

With all the money pouring in, Liberec blossomed into a gorgeous city, erecting such superb buildings as the stunning **Town Hall** and adding to its streets a wealth of turn-of-the-century architecture that rivals that found in the big spa towns of Karlovy Vary and Mariánské Lázně.

These days, it looks as though Liberec is reclaiming much of its former glory after falling into decay during the previous decades. A good deal of restoration in recent years has brightened up the town, and turned it into a popular destination with neighboring Germans. Even without the tourists, Liberec is a lively city, its cobblestoned center bustling with students, shoppers, and workers at all hours of the day. Liberec also serves as a good base for seeing the gorgeous landscape of **Česky ráj** (see Chapter 17, *East Bohemia*).

ORIENTATION

Located 109 kilometers (68 miles) north of Prague, Liberec lies within the broad Nisa River valley at the base of the **Jizera** (Jizerské) **Mountains**. Liberec is only 30 kilometers (19 miles) northwest of Turnov, the northern gateway to Česky ráj.

ARRIVALS & DEPARTURES

By Bus

This is the easiest way to travel between Prague and Liberec. Buses depart Prague's Florenc station about every two hours for the two hour journey. Tickets cost 70 Kč. You may want to make a reservation to insure a seat on the bus. The bus station in Liberec is at the corner of 1. máje and Na rybničku streets – a block down from the train station in the southwest part of town.

To get to the center, walk down 1. máje street and then up Pražská to the town's main square, náměstí dr. E. Beneše.

By Car

From Prague head north on E65 through Mladá Boleslav and Mnichovo Hradiště and then north on highway 35 to Liberec. The drive should take no more than two hours. The closest parking lot to the main square is two blocks west on Sokolovské náměstí (square).

By Train

In order to go by train from Prague to Liberec, you'll have to change trains in Turnov, which is really a waste of time. (Take the bus instead.) But if you're already in Turnov, then definitely take the pretty, hour-long ride through green meadows and densely forested hills to Liberec. Trains leave about every hour and tickets cost about 20 Kč. Outside the train station in Liberec, hop on any of the trams heading north or walk five minutes down 1. máje street to Soukenní náměstí (where you'll see a lovely, orange K-mart). From there, it's a quick jaunt up Pražská to the main square.

GETTING AROUND TOWN

Tram is the main form of public transportation. You can buy the 6 Kč tickets from machines at the tram stops or from any newsstand.

WHERE TO STAY

HOTEL ZELENÉ ÚDOLÍ, *Zelené údolí 3, 463 11 Liberec. Tel. 048/513 3891, Fax 048/513 3893. Rates for single/double: 1,100/1,530 Kč. Credit cards: AE, MC, V. 24 rooms. Restaurant.*

This is a gorgeous hotel set on a big, leafy plot of land. You can play tennis, go for a swim in the outdoor pool, cook out on the garden grill, or go fishing in a nearby lake. The plush, smartly decorated rooms come with satellite television, VCRs, direct-dial telephones, and nice views of the surrounding yard. The restaurant maintains the same high standards with creative Czech and international meals served in a glass-encased sun room or out on the big deck. What's truly amazing about this place is that it has the services of a big resort, but it still feels like a small, quaint hotel. A wonderful place all around.

HOTEL PRAHA, *Železná 2/1, 460 01 Liberec. Tel. 048/510 2655, Fax 048/511 3138. Rates for single/double: 1,490/1,980 Kč. Credit cards: AE, MC, V. 35 rooms. Restaurant.*

This grand Art Nouveau hotel sits right on Liberec's main square. Greeting you in the lobby is a marble fountain adorned with a mural of Eve handing Adam the apple. Up the old-style elevator and down the hall to your room, the classy decor stays the same, taking you back to the heady days of the 1920s. But, as is the case with many rooms, that's where the nostalgic experience ends. Though the rooms are nicely furnished with dark woods and satellite television, they're a bit of a let-down after admiring the rest of the hotel. The furniture and carpets are lackluster, and the bathrooms are in need of renovation.

Still, it's a wonderful hotel, with a good restaurant, stylish café, private parking, and information desk. Oh, remember to ask for a room with a view of the square, so you can gawk at the sensational town hall.

GRANDHOTEL ZLATY LEV, *Gutenbergova 3, 461 27 Liberec. Tel. 048/510 4086, Fax 048/423 407. Rates for single/double: 1,150-1,570/1,745-1,990. Credit cards: AE, MC, V. 80 rooms. Restaurant.*

Another venerable Art Nouveau hotel, Zlaty lev came out of the Communist era in pretty sorry shape. Nowadays, the hotel is gradually being restored, offering its guests accommodations in dour, un-renovated rooms or in sunny, renovated rooms. (Of course, the renovated rooms are more expensive). On the ground floor is a chandelier-strewn café where you can sit in a cushy armchair while having a coffee. The hotel's "French" restaurant is not really French, but it does serve up some Czech and international dishes that are well-prepared. Top-notch service is a mainstay at this hotel located across the street from the town chateau – about a five minute walk east of the main square.

HOTEL EDEN, *Chrastavská 13, 460 01 Liberec. Tel. 048/510 8430, Fax 048/510 8420. Rates for single/double: 1,180/1,260 Kč. Credit cards: AE, MC, V. 27 rooms. Restaurant.*

A five minute walk west of the main square, this newish hotel provides comfortable lodging in decent-sized rooms outfitted with satellite television, direct-dial telephones, and tiled bathrooms. You might want to ask for a room in the rear of the hotel, away from the loud, busy street the hotel is located on.

HOTEL U JEZÍRKA, *Masarykova 76, 460 01. Tel. 048/424 221, Fax 048/ 424 220. Rates for single/double without private bath: 400/750 Kč. Rates for single/double with private bath: 550/800 Kč. No credit cards. Restaurant.*

Located footsteps away from the zoo in Liberec's handsome turn-of-the-century neighborhood, this hotel is carved out of á neat, neo-Gothic house and is your only decent choice of budget accommodations in Liberec. Rooms are very basic, but clean and functional. To get there, take tram #1, #2, or #3 from the center to the Zoo stop.

HOTEL JEŠTĚD, *Horní Hanychov, 460 08 Liberec. Tel. 048/510 4291, Fax 048/510 4295. Rates for single/double: 500/900 Kč. Credit cards: AE. 15 rooms. Restaurant.*

This is perhaps the most unique hotel you could choose to stay in the Czech Republic. The hotel occupies a television and radio transmitter that looks like one giant cone (or space capsule). It sits atop the summit of Ještěd, a lone mountain on the southwest outskirts of Liberec. On a clear day, the panoramic view stretches across the border into Poland and Germany. Thankfully, that view can be yours from your room at this funky hotel. Rooms are pretty plain, but well worth it when you consider not only the view, but the cordial service, the decent rates, and the stories you'll have for your friends back home.

To get here, take tram #3 from the center of town to the end of the line (Spáleniště stop) and then follow signs to the cable car (*lánovka dráha*), which runs up and down Ještěd mountain from 6 a.m. to 10 p.m. every day, year-round. See below for more on the hotel's restaurant.

WHERE TO EAT

ZLATY DŽBÁN, *Lazebnický vrch 16. Tel. 048/202 00. 120-250 Kč. Credit cards: AE, V.*

Just off the main square, this is one of the classier restaurants in the center, presenting a wide range of game and poultry dishes smothered in luscious sauces. The wood-beam ceilings and the diligent, tuxedoed waiters make the dining experience all the more eventful.

RESTAURANT RADNICE, *náměstí Eduarda Beneše. Tel. 048/422 901. 100-200 Kč. No credit cards.*

Hunkering down in the vaulted cellars of the town hall, this restaurant serves up an honest Czech meal of meat and dumplings, washed down with a cold glass of Budvar.

KAVÁRNA POŠTA, *náměstí Eduarda Beneše. Tel. 048/208 52. 100-200 Kč. No credit cards.*

You want to talk about opulence, then check out this striking café with its neo-Classical decor and glittering chandeliers. It's no wonder tour buses pull up to the front door of this place and unload German tourists. But this is not to say the Czech food is anything special; it's not. In fact, it's mediocre. But you'll want to come here anyway for a coffee and cake so as to get a load of the place. **RESTAURANT DULI**, *Moskevská 4. Tel. 048/510 0738. 100-200 Kč. No credit cards.*

This two-story restaurant off the main square has pleasant outdoor seating on its rooftop, where you can chow down on any number of good chicken or pork dishes prepared with an Asian slant.

PIVNICE U SALAMANDRA, *Pražská 13/19. Tel. 048/286 34. 80-200 Kč. No credit cards.*

This classy cellar pub just down from the main square has three big, loud rooms decorated with old photographs of Liberec. The bar pours a fine glass of Gambrinus beer and the kitchen prepares hearty Czech standards to go with it.

HOTEL JEŠTĚD, *Horní Hanychov. Tel. 048/340 21. 100-200 Kč.*

If the view doesn't grab you, then the outlandish decor and crazy mirrors will. As expected, the Czech food served here is pretty mediocre, but the setting is just too memorable to be missed, especially if you happen to eat here when the sun is sinking into the mountainous horizon.

SEEING THE SIGHTS

The most telling feature of Liberec's former wealth is its bustling main square, **náměstí Eduarda Beneše** – named after the second president of Czechoslovakia. Festooned with enough gables, spires, and turrets to start a war, the square is perhaps one of the most beautiful in Bohemia. In fact, if you've ever been to Belgium, you may find some slight similarities between náměstí E. Beneše and Le Grand-Place, Brussels' main square.

Surely enough, the **Town Hall** (radnice) would not look out of place in Flanders whatsoever. This neo-Renaissance gem, modeled after the town hall in Vienna, rises up along lofty arcades and decorative reliefs and culminates in a trio of towers piercing through Liberec's skyline. With this magnificent edifice looming above you and all the rest of the square's fin-de-siecle architecture beckoning your attention, you'll definitely want to join the groups of teenagers loitering in the square or else grab a coffee at one of the outdoor cafés.

Hiding behind the Town Hall is another fine testament to Liberec's turn-of-the century grandeur – the **F.X. Šalda Theater**, adorned with stucco decorations and topped with a row of allegorical statues (including Apollo and his dolphins). Maybe if you bribe the attendant (or buy a ticket to one of the plays, ballets, or operas performed here), you can have a look at the theater curtain, painted by a young Viennese artist by the name of Gustav Klimt, who later went on to startle Europe with his renderings of writhing women.

If you can tear yourself away from náměstí E. Beneše, then head down Moskevská and take your first left for two blocks to the town's 16th-century **chateau**, dubbed the "Glass Castle" because it houses the largest display of glass in the world. The big Czech firm, Glassexport, uses the display to entice buyers from abroad. Sadly, the display is not open to the public, but you can catch glimpses of it if you walk around the chateau through the surrounding park.

Behind the chateau, at the east end of the park, is the **Regional Gallery** (Oblastní galerie), housing a formidable collection of 19th-century French landscapes and 17th-century Dutch and Flemish paintings (among them a token Rembrandt). The gallery also exhibits a good number of modern Czech paintings and sculptures, including a room-full of Cubist works by the likes of Josef Čapek and Bohumil Kubišta. *The museum is open daily except Monday from 9 a.m. to 6 p.m.*

If you're upset that you can't see the glass display at the chateau, then console yourself with the fine collection of historical glass at the **Museum of North Bohemia** (Severočeské muzeum), housed in a gorgeous, Romantic-style mansion located northeast of the main square on Masarykovo street. In addition to the collection of glass, the museum delves into the city's other big industry, textiles. Here, you can also get a taste of the ceramics, jewelry, and furniture produced in the region. *The museum is open on Tuesday from noon to 5 p.m. and Wednesday through Sunday from 9 a.m. to 5 p.m.* To get there from the main square, walk 15 minutes along 5. května street to Masarykovo or jump on tram #1, #2, or #3 to Muzeum stop.

Since you've already come out this far, then you might as well walk farther down Masarykovo and dream of living in one of the turn-of-the-century mansions and villas that fill this lush neighborhood. (Liberec, by the way, is dubbed the "City of Rhododendrons," a nickname that hits home in this neighborhood.)

And while you're at it, why not take a stroll through the **zoo** and **botanical gardens**, located a tram-stop away from the museum or another five minutes on foot. The oldest and best in the republic, the zoo has a couple of white tigers than may be worth the price of admission. The botanical gardens, noted for its orchids and cacti, will round off your tour of Liberec nicely.

NIGHTLIFE & ENTERTAINMENT

For a night at the opera, ballet, or theater, see what's happening at the **F.X. Šalda Theater,** *just behind the Town Hall on náměstí E. Beneše.* There's a box office in the theater where you can buy tickets. Whatever the performance is, it's worth attending so as to inspect the theater's interior, replete with a sweeping staircase, marble balustrade, and a curtain painted by none other than Gustav Klimt. If you really want to do the evening up in style, sashay into the ultra-ornate **Kavárna Pošta** afterwards for a coffee and dessert (see *Where to Eat*).

For something a little more low-brow, head to the newly-restored cellars of **Pivnice U Salamandra,** pouring a damn fine glass of Gambrinus beer. Or if you just want to take in a movie, see what's on at the **kino** *at Soukenné náměstí, down from the main square at the end of Pražská street.*

EXCURSIONS & DAY TRIPS
Ještěd

On top of the isolated **Ještěd** peak, in the southwest outskirts of town, is a bizarre sight – a silver, cone-shaped tower that looks like a giant space capsule. So, you ask, what purpose does this thing serve? Well, it's two things at once: a transmitter and a hotel. Whatever it is, it's pretty cool, and worth the slight effort to get to (see directions under Hotel Ještěd, above. It should take you all of 30 minutes to get to from the town center.)

Even if you can't appreciate the structure that won architect Karel Hubáček the Perret Award in the 1970s, you won't be disappointed by the eagle's-eye view that takes in all of Liberec and stretches across to Germany and Poland.

PRACTICAL INFORMATION
- **Čedok,** *Revoluční 66.* A place where you can change money and get some information on the region.
- **Information Center** (Informační Centrum), *náměstí E. Beneše 1. Tel and fax 048/510 1709.* A very helpful office offering a good selection of brochures about the town. The English-speaking staff can help with you accommodations and train and bus schedules.
- **Knihkupectví-Antikvariát,** *Pražská 14.* This is a neat book store with new and used books in English and a fine selection of maps.
- **Post Office,** *behind the Town Hall on náměstí E. Beneše.*

17. EAST BOHEMIA

Of all the regions in the Czech Republic, East Bohemia is probably the most diverse when it comes to landscape. Crowning the region at its northern end are the **Krkonoše Mountains**, the highest in the Czech Republic. In the northeast of the region, a bundle of romantic hills sprouting sandstone pinnacles make up what is called **Český ráj** (or Czech Paradise). As you move southward, the mountains and hills give way to the flat, verdant basin of the **Labe River**, which springs from the Krkonoše and flows southward through East Bohemia before heading westward for Germany and the North Sea.

Though East Bohemia boasts some nice scenery, its towns have a hard time rivaling those found in other parts of the country. **Hradec Králové** and **Pardubice**, the two big cities in the region, do have appealing historic centers that warrant a couple of hours of your time. But they aren't really tourist-friendly places, offering little in the way of good accommodations or good restaurants. If you're short on time, consider leaving these towns for the stopover on your way elsewhere.

For my money, I would concentrate my efforts on Český ráj, where a convenient railway line and hiking trail network afford a good look at this truly idyllic region dotted with "rock cities" and sprinkled with majestic castles. **Jičín** and **Turnov** – two sizable but moderately attractive towns – serve as bases for touring Český ráj. Of these two, Turnov has the handier location and the better sights, offering a much better selection of hotels and pensions.

Beyond Český ráj rise the Krkonoše Mountains, accessible from Prague in under two-and-half-hours, making it a popular hiking and skiing retreat for Praguers. But honestly, I can't fully recommend spending your well-earned vacation time in these mountains, swamped as they are with unsightly hotels and largely devastated by the effects of acid rain.

EAST BOHEMIA FINDS & FAVORITES
Gallery of Modern Art in Hradec Králové
Hotel Lázně Sedmihorky in Český ráj
Hotel Korunní princ in Český ráj
The rock cities of Český ráj

Hradec Králové

Hradec Králové dates back to the 9th century, when a small fortress was built here by the feudal Slavníkov family. It wasn't long afterwards that the Přemysl rulers got a grip on it, after which the fortress was beefed up into a full-fledged castle and the town made into the regional capital – a status it has kept ever since.

With its advantageous position at the confluence of two rivers, the town grew rich as a major center of trade, and by the end of the 13th century it had turned into the second biggest town in Bohemia and had become the residence of widowed Bohemian queens, hence the name of the town which means "Queen's Castle."

When the Reformation hit Bohemia, Hradec Králové rose as a fervently Hussite town, for which it paid dearly during the Thirty Years' War. Sadly, the castle was demolished, as were many of the town's Gothic buildings. But the immense town fortifications remained standing well into the 19th century, when it was finally decided to pull them down in order to expand the town.

So, at the beginning of the 20th century, a "new town" took shape according to the plans laid out by some of the most illustrious Czech architects of the era, in particular **Jan Kotěra** and his student **Josef Gočár**. As a result, Hradec Králové now has two radically distinct sides to it: Staré Město, the historic old town that grew within the town walls; and Nové Město, Kotěra and Gočár's progressive new town.

What makes Hradec Králové an interesting day out is the contrast in these two parts of town. Though you may not appreciate the uniformity and occasional severity of the new town, it is well worth a look anyhow because it represents one of the great urban projects of the First Czechoslovak Republic. In case you don't find anything attractive about the new town, then you should find some relief in the attractive old town, which has the quintessential Bohemian hodgepodge of Gothic, Renaissance, and Baroque buildings. It also boasts one of the best art museums in the country, the **Gallery of Modern Art**.

ORIENTATION

Hradec Králové sits at the confluence of the **Labe** and **Orlice** rivers 101 kilometers (63 miles) east of Prague, which means it's a feasible day trip from the capital by car, train, or bus. Hradec Králové's historic old town (Staré Město) sits on a hill between the two rivers, while its new town (Nové Město) stretches to the west beginning on the banks of the Labe River.

There are also plenty of signs to point you in the right direction. Ignore the sign pointing to an information office; there no longer is one here.

ARRIVALS & DEPARTURES

By Bus

A bus departs Prague's Florenc station about every hour-and-a-half. The ride takes 90 minutes. Tickets cost 50 Kč. The bus station in Hradec Králové lies just in front of the train station on the western edge of Nové Město. It's about a five minute walk east to the heart of Nové Město and another five minutes to Staré Město via Puškinova and Gočárova streets.

Take trolley bus #2, #3, or #7 to the edge of Staré Město if you don't feel like walking.

By Car

From Prague, head east all the way on highway E67. The ride should take about an hour and 15 minutes. A good place to park in town is along the Elbe River embankment at the border of Nové Město and Staré Město. There's also parking in Velké náměstí, the main square of Staré Město.

By Train

There are eight or nine fast trains that go daily from Prague's Hlavní nádraží to Hradec Králové. The rides takes about 90 minutes and costs around 55 Kč.

See "By Bus" above for directions from the train station into the center of town.

GETTING AROUND TOWN

Tickets for the trolley buses and regular buses cost 7 Kč and can be purchased at just about any newsstand around town. Validate them on board.

Staré Město is mostly a pedestrian area, with buses stopping at various stations around it. If you've arrived by train or bus, you can catch a taxi easy enough at the train station or at the nearby Hotel Černigov.

WHERE TO STAY

PENZION U JANA, *Velké náměstí 137, 500 01 Hradec Králové. Tel. 049/ 241 55, no fax. Rates for single/double: 1,000/1,300 Kč. Credit cards: MC, V. 5 rooms. Restaurant.*

Right on Staré Město's main square, U Jana beats the other places in town in providing comfortable, spacious rooms. The building itself dates back to the 17th century, but the pension and its restaurant and bar have been completely modernized, unfortunately bearing little of the house's age. The brightly lit rooms, each of which has their own private bath, come with black and brown furniture and slanted ceilings. Definitely ask for a room with a view of the square. The service is friendly and quite accommodating. For more on the good restaurant, see *Where to Eat,* below.

PENZION U SVATÉHO LUKÁŠE, *Úzká 208, 500 01 Hradec Králové. Tel. 049/521 0616. Rates for single/double: 1,000/1,300 Kč. Credit cards: MC, V. 4 rooms. Restaurant.*

Located just off the main square, this pension is the only other choice for lodgings in Staré Město. Outfitted with old furniture and tacky decorations, the four rooms don't live up to the pension's nice location, nor do they live up to their rates. Rooms come with private baths, satellite television, and direct-dial phones. But I'd book a room here only in the case Penzion U Jana is full. The attractive restaurant serves a wide variety of steaks and venison dishes on its terrace and its attractive dining room.

HOTEL ČERNIGOV, *Riegrovo náměstí 1494, 500 03 Hradec Králové. Tel. 049/581 4111, Fax 049/329 98. Rates for single/double: 1,500/1,990 Kč. Credit cards: AE, MC, V. 70 rooms. Restaurant.*

This big hotel opposite the train station caters mostly to those on business accounts who don't mind getting overcharged for the character-less rooms. But the rooms do come with direct-dial telephones and satellite television, plus the English-speaking service is quite good.

HOTEL ALESSANDRIA, *třída SNP 733, 500 03 Hradec Králové. Tel. 049/415 21, Fax 049/428 74. Rates for single/double:1,100/1,470 Kč. Credit cards: AE, MC, V. 50 rooms.*

This ugly high-rise hotel on the east side of town is just too far away from any of the sights or from any decent restaurants to make it worth your while. But if this turns out to be your only option, hop on bus #6, #12, #22, or #23 and you can't miss it.

WHERE TO EAT

RESTAURACE U RADNICE, *Velké náměstí 39. Tel. 049/235 18. 180-400 Kč. Credit cards: AE, DC, MC, V.*

The crisp tablecloths, smart decor, and discreet service makes this the classiest place in town, delivering traditional Czech meals prepared in a creative manner. A fair number of seafood dishes, including grilled salmon, grace the menu, as do three or four luscious soups, like the excellent cream of asparagus.

PENZION U JANA, *Velké náměstí 137. Tel. 049/241 55. 120-300 Kč.* The restaurant here has a casual, woody decor and a nice skylight that helps brighten the place up. The restaurant dishes out colorfully prepared Czech dishes such as grilled chicken breast topped with melted cheese and asparagus. The service is good and the prices are right.

RESTAURACE ASIE, *Eliščino nábřeží 17. Tel. 049/551 3902. 100-150 Kč. Credit cards: AE, MC, V.*

An appropriately exotic decor sets the stage for specialties from just about every Asian country, including Thailand, Korea, and the Philippines. Of course, the food is not exactly authentic, since many crucial vegetables that go into Asian cooking are just not available in the Czech Republic. But the chicken chow mein and curry pork are surprisingly good. You'll find the restaurant right along the embankment on the east side of the river.

PIZZERIA PINOCCHIO, *Masarykovo náměstí. Tel. 049/424 11. 80-150 Kč. No credit cards.*

This is a great place to stop off for lunch. It has a semi-hip decor, drawing a young crowd who go to chow down on the thin-crust pizzas and passable pasta dishes.

SEEING THE SIGHTS
Staré Město

Occupying the only hill for miles around, **Staré Město** (Old Town) features a hodgepodge of Gothic, Renaissance, and Baroque buildings that have only recently regained some purpose after decades of neglect. The old town centers itself around two adjoining squares – **Velké náměstí** and the much smaller **Malé náměstí**. The most intriguing architectural aspects of Staré Město are, however, found on Velké náměstí. Unfortunately, the arcaded square is now one big parking lot, its beauty marred by the rows of cars and the traffic streaming in.

At the west end of Velké náměstí is an assembly of five towers. Two of these towers rise up from the **Church of the Holy Spirit** (Kostel sv. Ducha) – a Gothic, brick church built in a style that's more common to Silesia than Bohemia. After admiring the beautiful jagged towers and the cone-shaped roof, you may find its plain, whitewashed interior and uninteresting vaulted nave a let-down.

Right next to the church is the **White Tower** (Bílá věž). Though having long ago lost its whiteness, the 68-meter (223-foot) free-standing tower built in 1608 is topped by a handsome Renaissance belfry – the

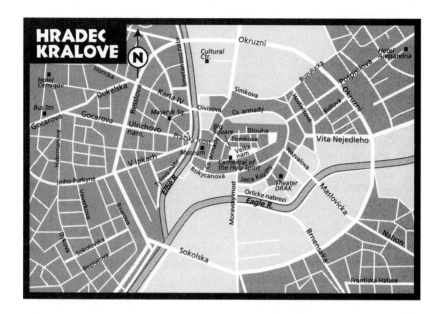

work of Italian craftsmen who settled here in the 16th century. If you have the energy, climb the tower steps for the best view you can get of Hradec Králové.

Whatever impact the yellow and cream-colored **town hall** (radnice) has on the square is certainly undermined by the White Tower and Church of the Holy Spirit soaring up next to it. But it is a pretty Renaissance structure nonetheless, its two ends topped with identical towers. Also worth a peek is the row of **former canons' houses** to the south of the Church of the Holy Spirit, their charming, gabled facades recently given shiny new coats of pastel paint.

On the south side of the square, step into the **Church of the Assumption of the Virgin** (Kostel Nanebevzetí Panny Marie) for a look at its newly-restored interior. Built as part of the adjacent Jesuit college in the 17th century, the church is predictably filled with stucco decorations and gleaming gilt cherubs. What isn't so predictable are the oval balconies and beautiful trompe l'oeil mural just behind the altar, both of which add a pleasingly theatrical feel to the church.

Opposite the church is Hradec Králové's star attraction – the **Gallery of Modern Art** (Galerie moderního umění). Before 1995, the year the National Gallery finally opened the big modern art museum in Prague, this was probably the best venue for modern Czech art in the country. It still is one of the best museums in the republic, exhibiting paintings and sculptures by the most formidable Czech artists of the early 19th and 20th centuries. The Secessionist building, designed by Osvald Polívka in 1910, is a work of art in itself, its interior revolving around an oval shaft topped by a glass roof.

The ground floor has temporary exhibitions, while its two upper floors and rooftop gallery house the museum's permanent collection. In keeping with the architectural style of the building, the first floor is given over mainly to Secessionist art, including a couple of obscure paintings by Alfons Mucha and some wood carvings by František Bílek. You can also survey some of Maximilián Pirner's provocative nymphs and an early self-portrait of Bohumil Kubišta.

The second floor moves directly into the Czech avant-garde, with Cubist paintings by Josef Čapek and the surreal, ink drawings of Josef Šíma. Also keep an eye out for Zdeněk Sklenař's frantic scribblings, which appear to have been done on wax. On the sunny top floor, you can inspect some of the art that the Communist regime banned from museums, such as the internationally acclaimed collages of Jiří Kolář. After you've taken in all the art, step out on the museum's balcony for a great view of the square. *The museum is open Tuesday through Sunday from 9 a.m. to noon and from 1 to 6 p.m. Tickets for the permanent collection cost 20 Kč and tickets to the temporary exhibit cost 10 Kč.*

Nové Město

From the northwest corner of Velké náměstí, head down V kopečku street to Československé armády street, across which begins Nové Město (New Town). This part of town was laid out from 1910 through the 1920s and bears the hallmarks of some of the country's leading architects, not least Jan Kotěra and his student Josef Gočár. Kotěra's **Hotel Bystrica**, at the corner of Čs armády and Palackého, is one of the earlier efforts of this ambitious new town.

The sumptuous Art Nouveau hotel was one of the most fashionable during the First Republic, though it now sits abandoned despite rumors of it being restored and reopened. Some of the hotel's former beauty is still detectable beneath the layer of grime caked on the facade, especially on the north side, where some beautiful sculptures still cling on for dear life.

In much better shape is the **East Bohemia Regional Museum** (Krájský muzeum vychodních Čech), on the river embankment a half-block down from the old hotel. The red-brick museum is another stylish work by Kotěra, who added his signature dome to the roof. Greeting you at the door are two brawny, bare-chested men seated on thrones. Inside, you'll find nothing as elaborate as the outside, but there are a couple of good exhibits featuring old photographs, some arts and crafts from the region, and a really great model of Hradec Králové and its fortification system in 1865. *It's open Tuesday through Sunday from 9 a.m. to noon and from 1 to 5 p.m.*

Before heading over to the west side of the river, stroll downriver along the embankment to **Jiráskovy sady**, a beautiful park laid out at the confluence of the Labe and Orlice rivers. Here you can saunter past a couple of rose gardens and have a look at a wooden Uniate church relocated here from the Ukraine in 1935.

When Kotěra died at the end of World War I, the planning of Hradec Králové's new town was put in the hands of his student Gočár, a formerly Cubist architect who by that time was keen on establishing a particularly Czech style in architecture called Rondo-Cubism. You can inspect some products of this style on the west side of the Labe, accessed by crossing the Kotěra-designed **Prague Bridge** (Pražský most).

The biggest of Gočár's projects was the **State Grammar School** (Statní gymnázium), to the rear of náměstí Svobody just after you cross over the Prague Bridge. Not exactly what you would call beautiful, the red brick facade has the shape of an open book, beyond which extend a symmetrical series of wings. A bit more inviting is Gočár's **Ambrosian Chapel** (Ambrožů sbor), past the State Grammar School on V lipkách street. The functionalist church features a lot of the architect's tell-tale sharp angles, which are accentuated by its site at a fork in the road.

In terms of town planning, Gočár's major work was the pastel-colored **Masarykovo náměstí** (Masaryk Square), two blocks north of the State Grammar School. The expansive, semi-circular square is a bit on the severe side, despite its orderly gardens and rows of trees. But it's well worth a look anyhow.

NIGHTLIFE & ENTERTAINMENT

For a listing of cultural events and films in Hradec Králové, pick up the *Kam* booklet at any newsstand or at the Gallery of Modern Art.

The **Hradec Králové Philharmonic Orchestra** performs *at Eliščino nábřeží 777, Tel. 049/611 491*. The **Church of the Holy Ghost** *on Velké náměstí* and the **East Bohemian Regional Museum**, *Eliščino nábřeží 465*, also hold the occasional concert.

If you'd like to sample the favorite regional beer called Krakonoš, head for the **Pod věží** pub at the west end of Velké náměstí. For a bigger selection of drinks or a glass of Guinness, try the dimly lit **Irish Pub**, *V kopečku 85*, just down from Velké náměstí. Or, if you just want to catch a film, go to **Kino Centrál** or **Kino Alfa** in Nové Město.

PRACTICAL INFORMATION

•**Informační centrum**, *Havlíčkova 836 (Nové Město). Tel. 049/551 1650.* Sells maps and can help find you accommodations.

•**Komerční banka,** *Masarykovo náměstí (Nové Město).* A place to change money.
•**Post Office,** *just north of Velké náměstí on Tomkova street (Staré Město).*

Pardubice

One name you can't escape while in **Pardubice** is **Pernštejn**. That's because this aristocratic Moravian family owned the town and region from 1491 onwards, endowing Pardubice with a Renaissance chateau and a wealth of Renaissance buildings. For its time, Pardubice was said to be the loveliest town in Bohemia. Unfortunately, the aesthetic beauty that the Pernštejns achieved was largely annihilated when the Swedes ripped through town during the Thirty Years's War. But there is a sufficient amount of Renaissance architecture to tickle your fancy.

As East Bohemia's second biggest city after Hradec Králové, Pardubice has always been in competition with its neighbor to the north. Though Hradec Králové has the more attractive "new town," Pardubice has the more appealing, better-preserved historic center. But Pardubice is short on things to see and do, so you may want to consider it as an excursion from Hradec Králové (under thirty minutes away) or as a day trip from Prague (under two hours away).

Pardubice's big claim to fame is its annual **Great Steeplechase**, occurring at the town's enormous course since 1874. It takes place in early October, at which time it's impossible to find a vacancy in town. (For more on the steeplechase, see *Sports & Recreation*, below.)

Pardubice's dubious claim to fame is that it is home to Semtex, maker of the plastic explosives that were used by the world's terrorists in the 1980s.

ORIENTATION

Pardubice lies at the confluence of the **Labe** and **Chrudimka** rivers 22 kilometers (14 miles) south of Hradec Králové and 103 kilometers (64 miles) east of Prague.

ARRIVALS & DEPARTURES

By Bus

Buses depart hourly from Prague's Florenc station. The two hour ride costs about 60 Kč. Every half hour, buses depart Hradec Králové for Pardubice, a 30 minute trip that costs about 15 Kč. The bus station is at the west end of Palackého street, about a ten minute walk west of the historic center along Míru and Paleckého streets.

If you don't feel like walking from the bus station to the historic center, then jump on any bus heading east.

By Car

From Prague, head about 60 kilometers east on motorway E67 and then follow signs southeastward to Pardubice along highway 36. The drive takes about 90 minutes. From Hradec Králové, just take highway 37 south. It should take you about 15 minutes to get there. There's a big parking lot at the intersection of Hradecká and Míru. Look for it as you drive into the center of town.

By Train

This is the fastest way to go from Prague. Trains depart Hlavní nádraží about every 90 minutes and get to Pardubice in under an hour and 45 minutes. Tickets cost around 60 Kč. Trains go back and forth between Hradec Králové and Pardubice roughly every 45 minutes. The ride takes about 30 minutes and costs 20 Kč.

The train station in Pardubice is across the street from the bus station (see above).

GETTING AROUND TOWN

Bus and trolley-bus are your two options of public transportation. Buy your tickets at any newsstand and validate them on board. There's no problem getting around on foot inside the compact historic center. In fact, it's the only way you can get around.

WHERE TO STAY/WHERE TO EAT

HOTEL AND BISTRO 100, *Kostelní 100, 530 02 Pardubice. Tel. 040/511 179, Fax 040/518 825. Rates for single/double: 1,000/2,000 Kč. Credit cards: MC, V. 6 rooms. Restaurant.*

Located in the historic center of town, Hotel 100 certainly likes to deal in round numbers. Unfortunately, those numbers are a little steep. But the hotel does offer some of the nicest lodgings in town, providing comfortable wood-beamed rooms with satellite television, mini-bar, and nice tiled bathrooms.

The hotel can rent mountain bikes, reserve you a tennis court, or arrange a horseback ride. The bistro is also quite good, specializing in Moravian food and wine served in the vaulted dining room or out on the terrace.

ZÁMECKÁ, *Zámecká 17, 530 02 Pardubice. Tel. 040/515 893, Fax 040/516 925. Rates for double/triple only: 3,000/4,000 Kč. Credit cards: MC, V. 3 apartments. Restaurant.*

Carved out of a pink Baroque house at the gate to the chateau, this restaurant/pension is swank through and through. The building recently underwent restoration, which would have been completely successful if the owners hadn't decided to put in an atrium plastered with mirrors, which has the unwanted effect of making the place feel like a disco. Despite this tasteless addition, the pension features three plush apartments (there are no regular rooms for rent), which are smartly furnished with parquet floors, a living room, beautiful art work, and brass-framed beds.

No less fancy is the restaurant, its tuxedoed waiters serving exquisitely prepared Continental dishes such as beef tournedos and chicken cordon-blue under an attractive vaulted ceiling. (Prices for meals range from 150 to 300 Kč.)

RESTAURACE U ČÁPA, *Zámecká 24. Tel. 040/514 028. 60-140 Kč. No credit cards.*

With its newly renovated vaulted ceilings and woody atmosphere, this restaurant has a nice, homey feel to it. The solidly prepared Czech meals are nothing to get too excited about, but the bar does pour three of the best Czech beers made – Budvar, Pilsner Urquell, and Gambrinus. You'll find this restaurant at the gate to the chateau.

HOTEL LABE, *Masarykovo náměstí 2633, 530 02 Pardubice. Tel. 040/ 517 286, Fax 040/517 281. Rates for single/double: 1,590-1,790/1,680-1,890. Credit cards: AE, MC, V. 190 rooms. Restaurant.*

This modern high-rise hotel is a five minute walk west of the historic center. You can't miss it when you drive into town. The brown, lackluster rooms here look as though they haven't been updated since the hotel was built in 1985. But they come with all the amenities of a three-star hotel, including satellite television, direct phones, and minibar. The hotel also has a sauna you can roast in. The receptionists can arrange private tours of the town and region. In addition to the restaurant, the hotel has a café and snack bar serving, of all things, Finnish food.

SEEING THE SIGHTS

If you arrive by bus or train, you'll approach the historic center along the bustling Míru street, jam-packed with shops and shoppers. Just outside the main gate to the old town, the traffic-filled **náměstí Republiky** (Republic Square) has a few choice buildings surrounding it that will certainly grab your attention.

One is the **East Bohemian Theater** (Vychodočeské divadlo), with a handsome Art Nouveau facade adorned with two colorful mosaics. One of them depicts Libuše founding Prague and the other shows the one-eyed Žižka leading the Hussites into battle. On the opposite side of the square, the **Church of St. Bartholomew** (Kostel sv. Bartoloměj) strikes an alluring pose with its jagged gables and needle-thin steeple. The church was founded in the late 13th century, but was burnt down by the Hussites in 1421. It got its present appearance when it was rebuilt at the beginning of the 16th century.

From the church you can simply stroll right into the old town. But you'll get the more ceremonious effect if you backtrack and pass under the Gothic **Green Tower** (Zelená brána), festooned with a riotous amount of baubles, spikes, and flags. As you pass through the tower gate, you enter into **Pernšteynské náměstí**, definitely the prettiest square in East Bohemia. The square has a very intimate feel to it, mainly because it's completely enclosed by tall Renaissance and neo-Classical buildings. The facades are topped with a playful ensemble of gables that cut a wave-like figure on the skyline.

The most intriguing of the square's facades, found on the east side, features a plaster relief showing Jonah at the moment of being swallowed by the whale. This 18th-century building, called **Dům U Jonáše**, was created by Jakub Teply, who was also responsible for the saint-shrouded plague column at the center of the square.

From the square, stroll down Pernštynská klašterní lane to the town chateau, surrounded by a series of picturesque ramparts now used as a park. The Renaissance chateau, covered in trompe l'oeil sgraffito and topped with tiny gables, has been under renovation for years now, and looks as though it will continue to be for a few years more. For now, you'll have to content yourself with seeing the small collection of 19th- and 20th-century Czech art housed in one of the restored wings.

NIGHTLIFE & ENTERTAINMENT

For a list of happenings around town, pick up the *Kam* booklet at the Pardubice Information Center (see *Practical Information* below). Classical music is performed at **Dům hudby**, *Sukova třída 1260*. Tickets can be purchased at the box office there.

The best place to go for a beer in town is *U čápa* (see *Where to Eat*, above.) You can catch a film at the cinema in the train station.

SPORTS & RECREATION

The first thing that comes to a Czech mind when you mention the town of Pardubice is horse racing. Indeed, Pardubice has one of the most well-known steeplechase courses in the world. Races take place here every other weekend and tickets are available at the stadium.

The biggest race of the year is the international **Great Pardubice Steeplechase** in early October. For ticket and schedule information, contact the Pardubice Information Center (see *Practical Information* below). To get to the course, take bus #4 or #14 two kilometers outside town.

PRACTICAL INFORMATION

• **Agrobanka,** *náměstí Republiky.* This is a bank where you can change money.
• **Information Center** (Informační centrum), *třída Míru 60. Tel. 040/233 39, Fax 040/207 37.* Has information and brochures on the town and region.
• **Post Office,** *corner of Míru and Na hradku streets.*

Český ráj (Czech Paradise)

Czech poets, painters, and sculptors have always waxed poetic about this region, and it's easy to see why. **Český ráj** (or Czech Paradise) is a pocket of rolling hills blanketed in thick forests and bucolic meadows, dotted with lakes and sprinkled with ruined castles. But the best part about this region are the so-called "rock cities" (*skalní město*), named after the soaring sandstone pinnacles that congregate along the ridge of the hills. Yes indeed, the landscape is desperately romantic, so much so that you may even get a little teary-eyed looking at it all.

There are two gateways to Český ráj, the towns of **Jičín** and **Turnov.** Jičín lies at the southeast corner of Český ráj, while Turnov sits at the north end about 30 kilometers (19 miles) northeast of Jičín. The two towns are connected by a rickety train that slowly chugs its way through the Libuňka River valley, stopping at tiny villages within easy walking distance of the rock cities, castles, and other sights.

Though some people may beg to differ, I think Turnov makes the better base for exploring Český ráj. It's a more attractive town and affords better access to Český ráj's best sights. Turnov also offers a much better selection of hotels and pensions. But Jičín is a fairly attractive town in its own right, and does warrant an hour or two of your time (that is, if you're in the mood to see a town).

ORIENTATION

Both Jičín and Turnov lie roughly 100 kilometers (62 miles) northeast of Prague, with Český ráj spread out between the two towns. Both Jičín and Turnov are small towns, whose streets are easy to navigate.

ARRIVALS & DEPARTURES

By Bus

The best way to get from Prague to Jičín or Turnov is by bus. There are seven or eight daily departures from Prague's Florenc station. The ride to either town takes an hour-and-a-half, costing about 55 Kč. The bus station in Jičín is at the corner of 17. listopadu and Šafaříkova streets –

about a two minute walk down the hill from the main square. The bus station in Turnov is in front of the main train station (see *By Train*, below).

By Car

From Prague, take E65 north and exit at Mladá Boleslav for Jičín. To Turnov, take E65 all the way there. Parking is generally not a problem on the streets of both towns. Just be sure to put some coins in the meter.

By Train

Jičín is on a minor railway line, which makes getting here from Prague a big hassle. From Hradec Králové, there is a slow train that goes directly to Jičín in about an hour-and-a-half. It leaves every hour and costs 40 Kč. The train station in Jičín is on Fugnerova street, about a ten minute walk southeast of the historic center.

Three or four trains run daily between Prague's Hlavní nádraží and Turnov. The trip takes roughly three hours and costs 75 Kč. (Better is just to go by bus.) The station in Turnov is on the west side of the Jizera River just off Nádražní street. It's about a ten minute walk into the center of town along Nádražní and Palackého streets. Signs point the way.

GETTING AROUND

As I said, the most relaxing and scenic way of getting around Český ráj is by the train that ambles its way along the Libuňka River between Jičín and Turnov. The train makes several stops at villages along the way, from where you can pick up a trail to one of the rock cities or other sights above the villages; specifics are given below under *Seeing the Sights*. There's also a bus that runs every two hours between Jičín and Turnov (departing and arriving in front of the respective train stations) and stops at places that the train doesn't service. Prachovské skály, the largest of the rock cities, is one such destination that you can get to only by bus or car.

If you're a real go-getter, you could feasibly walk your way through Český ráj from Jičín to Turnov (or vice versa) along the red-marked trail. At 32 kilometers, this would, however, take you a couple of days. A fine day hike would be to take the train to Ktová station, climb up to **Trosky Castle**, and then head for the rock city of **Hrubá Skála** and its chateau, from where you can either walk the four kilometers back to Turnov or hop on the next train. Trails are always well-signposted, showing you directions and distances.

WHERE TO STAY

Note: In just about every village between Jičín and Turnov are houses with private rooms for rent. Just look for the signs that say *zimmer frie* or *ubytovna*. Otherwise, consider these following hotels and pensions:

PENSION BOHEMIA, *Markova 303, 506 01 Jičín. Tel. & Fax 0433/244 31. Rates for one apartment: 1,700-2,100 Kč. Credit cards: MC. 7 apartments. Restaurant.*

Located 10 minutes north of the historic center, this pension offers ultra-comfortable, three- and four-bedroom apartments with private bath, satellite television, and mini-bar. Relax in the sauna or have the receptionist arrange for you to play tennis or go fishing. The restaurant is quite good, serving up local fish and game specialties.

HOTEL PAŘÍŽ, *Žižkovo náměstí 3, 506 01 Jičín. Tel. 0433/227 50, Fax 0433/245 10. Rates for single/double room: 720/900 Kč. Rates for single/double apartment: 900/1,080 Kč. No credit cards. 60 rooms. Restaurant.*

This is the most central hotel in Jičín. Unfortunately, the bare rooms don't have an ounce of personality, and are only suitable if you're in a pinch. The apartments are a tad nicer, and they do come with television and telephone (whereas the normal rooms don't). The restaurant does, however, serve a nice breakfast, but you'll have to put up with MTV blaring on the television.

HOTEL LÁZNĚ SEDMIHORKY, *516 62 Karlovice u Turnova. Tel. 04396/916 112, Fax 04396/916 158. Rates for single/double: 470/940 Kč. No credit cards. 50 rooms. Restaurant.*

This hotel is carved out a breathtaking neo-Gothic chateau in the rock city of Hrubá Skála (see *Seeing the Sights*, below.) Needless to say, its location in the thick of Český ráj's beauty is an ideal one. But don't think that just because the hotel occupies a chateau that it's something grandiose. It's not, as you can tell by the modest room rates.

Rooms, most of which have a sensational view of Česky ráj, are fairly simple and straightforward, but comfortable nonetheless. What's really great about this hotel are the services it provides. These include guided walking tours of the area, horseback riding, mountain bike rental, and airplane rides. The hotel also presents cultural events such as folk dancing and fencing.

HOTEL KORUNNÍ PRINC, *náměstí Českého ráje 137, 511 01 Turnov. Tel. & Fax 0436/242 12. Rates for single/double: 900/1,260 Kč. Credit cards: MC. 23 rooms. Restaurant.*

Carved out of a yellow turn-of-the-century building, this hotel on Turnov's main square is perhaps the nicest you'll find in the region. Rooms are smartly decorated with dark wood furniture, new carpet, and tasteful art, and are outfitted with direct-dial telephones, mini-bars, satellite television, and generously large bathrooms. Certainly ask for one of the sunny corner rooms with a nice view of the square (room 117, for instance). The English-speaking service is quite accommodating, and can help you plan your day in Český ráj. For more on the restaurant's interesting menu, see *Where to Eat*.

PENZION EDEN, *Palackého 179, 511 01 Turnov. Tel. 0436/233 69, no fax. Rates for single/double: 450/900 Kč. No credit cards. 4 rooms. No restaurant.*

This place doubles as a fitness club and pension. Here you can play tennis, lift weights, rent a mountain bike, and then relax in a sauna. Rooms, though a little plain, have modern furnishings and are quite comfortable. But the best aspect of this place is that it was built around a huge tree. How's that for an eco-minded decision?

HOTEL SV. JANA, *Hluboká 142, 511 01 Turnov. Tel. & Fax 0436/233 25. Rates for single/double: 400/700 Kč. No credit cards. 8 rooms. Restaurant.*

The rates at this hotel just down from Turnov's main square are almost too good to be true. Granted, the rooms are not the fanciest in town, but they are perfectly clean and comfortable, and do come with private baths (but no television or telephone). The Swiss owners are quite nice, but will mostly hike their rates before long.

ALFA PENSION, *Palackého 211, 511 01 Turnov. Tel. 0436/213 38, Fax 0436/237 00. Rates for single/double: 400/700 Kč. No credit cards. 10 rooms. Restaurant.*

The rates at this centrally located pension are also quite reasonable. Again, the rooms are nothing special, but are certainly clean, functional, and even a bit cozy. Rooms do come with private bath, but not a television or telephone. The pension serves an American-style breakfast in its classy restaurant.

WHERE TO EAT

RESTAURACE VOLF, *Husova 39, Jičín. Tel. 0433/215 38. 75-200 Kč. No credit cards.*

The restaurant's wood-studded decor makes for a very pleasant ambience in which to sample local chicken and fish specialties. Unfortunately, the wait staff here can be gruff.

U MATĚJE, *Nerudova 46, Jičín. Tel. 0433/226 41. 120-200 Kč. No credit cards.*

I got a kick out of this place because of its country-western decor. The specialty here is fish and game, well-indicated by the guns and trophy heads hanging on the walls. Here you can chow down on venison (prepared five different ways) while listening to some good ol' Czech country music and throwing back a glass of Budvar. Very friendly service and a loud local clientele make things all the more eventful.

HOTEL KORUNNÍ PRINC, *náměstí Českého ráje 137, Turnov. Tel. & Fax 0436/242 12. 150-300 Kč.*

This laudable hotel maintains its high standards at its restaurant. Sit at any one of the comfortable high-back booths and enjoy a tender steak, a nicely prepared roast pheasant, or a slice of kangaroo. Yes, kangaroo. You'll find that listed below fried ostrich under "Australian Specialties."

SV. JANA, *Hluboká 142, Turnov. Tel. & Fax 0436/233 25. 60-150 Kč at the bistro. 130-200 Kč at the restaurant. No credit cards.*
Downstairs at the intimate little bistro you can have a tangy mixture of chicken, onions, and green peppers. Upstairs in the formal restaurant or out on the terrace, you can dine on any number of solidly prepared German and Czech dishes.

SEEING THE SIGHTS OF THE CZECH PARADISE

Jičín

The Hapsburg general **Albrecht von Waldstein** (or Wallenstein) conquered **Jičín** in the early stages of the Thirty Years' War and planned on developing the town into the capital of the empire he was conspiring to create. But development of Waldstein's capital was cut short when he was assassinated in Cheb.

But he did manage to endow the town with a pretty square in the 1620s, now appropriately called **Valdštejnovo náměstí.** Each side of the square is lined with pretty arcades fronting an impressive collection of late Renaissance houses. Providing a dramatic entrance into the square is a Gothic gate tower, whose red-roofed gallery provides a panoramic view of the town. As you walk through the gate, it's easy to pass by **St. James Church** (Kostel sv. Jakuba) without noticing it, mainly because it has no steeple attracting your attention. The exterior bears a number of Renaissance flourishes, but the inside is strictly Baroque bombast.

Dominating the south side of the square is Waldstein's palatial **chateau,** built by the same Italian architects that crafted the square. These days the chateau serves as a regional museum with ho-hum exhibits on local history, archaeology, and arts and crafts. If the museum doesn't interest you, then at least step inside the courtyard for a look at the sensational rows of arcades.

Prachovské skály

Of course, the real reason for being in Jičín is to be on your way to the rock cities of Český ráj, the biggest of which is **Prachovské skály,** located about 6 kilometers (3.7 miles) northwest of Jičín. Here, you can wander through the maze of sandstone rock towers thrusting out of a thick growth of fir trees. Understandably, this is a popular spot with rock climbers, who gravitate here from all over Central Europe in the summer.

There are a couple of ways you can get here. One is to hike it from the Motel Rumcajs in Jičín. From the main square, go north on Palackého street, swing left on Jiráskova, and then follow Kollárova to the motel, from where it's a mild eight-kilometer (five-mile) hike to the rocks. Or you can hop on a bus there, departing from the front of the Jičín train station about every two hours. The Jičín information center, located in the chateau on Valdštejnovo náměstí, can give you exact times of departure.

Trosky Castle

A definite highlight on your tromp through Český ráj are the ruins of **Trosky Castle**, its twin Gothic towers perched on basalt pinnacles and visible for miles around. The castle was built sometime in the late 14th century, and passed hands from local gentry to local bandits who pillaged nearby villages. You can get a sense of the local humor from the names of the two towers. The taller, more shapely one is called Panna (Virgin) and the lower, more decrepit one is called Bába (Granny). You can't climb to the top of either, but you can walk along the saddle that connects them. Even from there, the view is no less than stunning.

The best way to get to Trosky from either Jičín or Turnov is by train to the village of Ktová, from where it's a two-kilometer (1.2-mile walk) to the castle ruins along the green-marked trail.

Hrubá Skála

Perhaps the most beautiful rock city in Český ráj is **Hrubá Skála**, about five kilometers south of Turnov above the village that's also called Hrubá Skála. Here you can have a blast getting lost in the labyrinth of sandstone pinnacles and bluffs, climbing up and down the narrow staircases chiseled out of the rock, and peeking in at the scores of crevices.

Augmenting this intriguing landscape is a majestic chateau, occupying a precipitous site among the rocks. The chateau was once a Gothic castle owned by, who else, but General Albrecht von Waldstein. Following Waldstein's assassination, the castle-turned-chateau fell into the hands of the Aehrenthal family, who owned it up until 1945. In the 19th century, it was reconstructed into the Gothic castle-esque chateau you see today. With its dramatic setting, you can understand why there have been so many Czech films shot here. The chateau recently underwent restoration and now serves as a hotel and recreation center (see Hotel Lázně Sedmihorky, above).

Take the train from either Turnov or Jičín to the village of Hrubá Skála, from where it's a quick walk to the rock city and chateau. Or walk the five-kilometers (three-miles) from the Turnov Město railway stop along the red-marked trail.

Valdštejn Castle

Nearby is yet another majestic sight – the **Valdštejn Castle**, a Gothic fortress built in the 13th century. Before General Waldstein (Valdštejn) acquired the castle, it was used as a Hussite stronghold during the

Hussite Wars. The castle is now mainly in ruins, but is still a magnificent sight, as is the castle's 18th-century bridge lined with Baroque statues. *You can have a look around the old castle daily except Monday from 9 a.m. to 4 p.m. May through August and on weekends only in April and October.*

From Turnov, you could easily hit Valdštejn Castle and Hrubá Skála all in one afternoon on foot. Pick up the red-marked trail at the Turnov Město railway stop, from where Valdštejn Castle is a two-kilometer (1.2-mile) walk. Continue on the red-marked trail for another three kilometers (1.8 miles) to Hrubá Skála. And if you're tired of walking, then take the train from Hrubá Skála village back to Turnov or Jičín.

Turnov

The town of Turnov has a lovely setting amidst Český ráj's hills, which makes up for its dearth of interesting architectural sights. But the town, which sweeps up the hills on both sides of the Jizera River, is more picturesque than Jičín, and is certainly livelier. The main square in town is called **náměstí Českého ráje**, which is where you'll find the comely neo-Renaissance town hall, as well as a number of shops and restaurants.

Just off the main square is the **Český ráj Museum**, *Skálova 71*. Rock hounds will get a kick out of the scores of semi-precious stones unearthed from around Český ráj and exhibited here. In addition to the stones are some decent jewelry displays, as well as exhibits on local history. The museum also displays a sweeping panoramic painting called *The Defeat of the Saxons below Hrubá Skála*, done by Mikuláš Aleš (an artist who adorned many Art Nouveau facades in Prague). *The museum is open daily except Monday from 9 a.m. to 6 p.m. May through September and until 4 p.m. the rest of the year.*

Turnov's landmark sight is the **Church of the Virgin Mary** (Kostel Panny Marie), just up the hill from the main square and visible from points throughout the valley. Up close, the three-naved church is nothing special, but the unfinished tower is definitely something strange. The church is open for services only.

A nice change of pace from Turnov's busy streets is the chateau of **Hruby Rohozec** on the northern outskirts of town. To get there, cross over to the west side of Jizera River via Palackého street and follow Bezručova street to the chateau. Striking a dramatic pose high above the Jizera River, the chateau started out as a Gothic castle and later turned into the Renaissance gem you see today.

On one of the hour-long tours, you can get acquainted with many of the palatial rooms while checking out the exhibits on interior design from the last four centuries. *The chateau is open daily except Monday from 9 a.m. to 5 p.m. May through September and until 4 p.m. in April and October.*

NIGHTLIFE & ENTERTAINMENT

Jičín turns into dullsville when the sun goes down, so seeing a film may be the thing to do if you're staying the night. You can do so at a cinema that's just off Valdštejnovo náměstí below the tower gate. Or you can try boogying at the disco that's ten minutes northeast of the center, *at Revoluční 836 just past the Hotel Start.* There's also a decent pub with terrace seating closer into town *on Revoluční.*

In Turnov, you can catch a film at the Městské kino, *Žižkova 1276.* Or you can try your luck with a folk, rock, or classical concert happening at the town theater, *Markova 311 just off the main square.* Go to the Turnov Information Center (see *Practical Information,* below) for a schedule of concerts. For a taste of the local brew, try the upstairs restaurant at *Alfa Pension* (see "Where to Stay").

Hotel Hrubá Skála, *Tel. 0436/916 281,* holds the occasional cultural event such as folk dancing and fencing.

PRACTICAL INFORMATION

• Česká spořitelna (Turnov), *náměstí Českého ráje.* A bank where you can change money.
• Jičín Information Center, *Valdštejnovo náměstí 1. Tel. 0433/243 90.* The English-speaking staff here supplies basic information on the town and region, sells maps to Česky ráj, and can give you the time of bus and train departures.
• Turnov Information Center, *Dvořákova 1. Tel. 0436/255 00.* English-speaking staff supplies information on the town and region, sells tickets to cultural events, gives information on train and bus services, helps with finding accommodations, and sells maps.
• Komerční banka (Jičín), *Valdštejnovo náměstí.* Change money or get cash from an ATM machine here.
• Jičín Post Office, *Šafaříkova street.*
• Turnov Post Office, *náměstí Českého ráje.*

Krkonoše

The Krkonoše (or Giant Mountains) span across the northeast corner of Bohemia along the Polish border. They're the highest mountains in the Czech Republic, crowned by the 1,602-meter Sněžka and patched with forests of spruce trees. The reason I say "patched" is because some 25 percent of the Krkonoše forests have been ravaged by acid rain. Pollutants from North Bohemian and East German smokestacks accumulate in the rain clouds, drift into the high peaks of the mountains, and dump their lethal toxins on the ground. In their weakened state, the trees fall prey to insects. And, as has been the government's practice for decades, large swatches in the forest are clear-cut with the haphazard intention of stopping the spread of the insects. When you come across one of these huge, dead gaps in the forest, you can't help but feel saddened.

But this hasn't stopped the Krkonoše resort towns from booming at the exact time ecologically sound planning was needed most. Nor has it stopped hordes of Czechs, Germans, and Dutch skiers and hikers from filling up the hotels and lodges that litter the resorts such as **Špindlerův Mlýn**, **Harrachov**, and **Pec pod Sněžkou**. Granted, the Krkonoše does offer the best skiing in the Czech Republic and some of the cheapest lift tickets on the continent (which is probably the biggest incentive for so many people skiing here).

But these resort towns get swamped with people, which means parking is scarce (and expensive), lift lines are long, and the slopes are veritable anthills. Thus, it makes little sense for American or Canadian skiers to come all this way for conditions that are just not up to snuff. Message: Head for the Tatras in Slovakia, instead.

Hiking in the **Krkonoše National Park** can be enjoyable if you stay low in the valleys, as most of the acid rain damage has occurred in the higher elevations, especially on top of the peaks. If you intend on doing some serious hiking, then get a hold of a map showing the color-marked trails, such as Kartografie Praha's 1:50,000 Krkonoše map. You can find it at just about any bookstore, hotel, or information office. Also, be sure to take precautions.

Though the elevations of Krkonoše are not so extreme, they do get a lot of cold wind and a lot of rain. The Krkonoše also tend to get extremely foggy, which creates a high risk of hypothermia. So dress warm and bring along rain protection, no matter what time of year it is.

ORIENTATION

As I mentioned, the Krkonoše Mountains run along the northeastern border of the Czech Republic right up against Poland. In fact, **Sněžka** (the highest peak in the range and the country) sits right on the border. So, if you go to the top of this mountain, you'll see Czech and Polish guards holding the borders.

The so-called gateway to the Krkonoše is the town of **Vrchlabí**, located at the southern base of the mountains roughly 130 kilometers (80 miles) northeast of Prague. **Špindlerův Mlýn**, the biggest and most central resort town in the Krkonoše, is 15 kilometers (nine miles) up the Labe River valley from Vrchlabí. The other big resort, **Pec pod Sněžka**, is about 30 kilometers (19 miles) to the northeast of Vrchlabí.

The **Labe River**, which flows across the Czech Republic and Germany before emptying into the North Sea, originates in the Krkonoše just above Špindlerův Mlyn and flows down past Vrchlabí.

ARRIVALS & DEPARTURES

By Bus

Bus makes the most sense from wherever you originate. There are eight to ten buses that depart each day from Prague's Florenc station for Vrchlabí, many of which continue on to Špindlerův Mlýn. The ride takes two-and-a-half hours and costs about 90 Kč.

From Vrchlabí, buses run every hour or so to Špindlerův Mlyn and Pec pod Sněžkou. The bus station in Vrchlabí sits next to the train station. To get from either station into the center of town, cross the river and then take your second right on Slovanská street, which eventually turns into Krkonošská (the town's main street).

By Car

From Prague, head north on E65, exit onto highway 16 at Mladá Boleslav, drive through Jičín, and then follow signs to Vrchlabí. Plenty of signs in Vrchlabí point the way up to Špindlerův Mlýn. Head east on highway 14 and then follow signs up the valley to Pec pod Sněžkou from Vrchlabí.

By Train

Taking the train from Prague to Vrchlabí requires a lot of time-consuming changes. Stick to the bus. Unless you're driving, biking, or hiking, bus is the only way to get around the mountains.

WHERE TO STAY/WHERE TO EAT

Note: The Krkonoše are littered with mountain chalets (called *bouda* in Czech) offering accommodations in the summer. Usually, they're located at the top of some mountain trail or chair lift. Some can be pretty crude, while others can be quite luxurious. Walk-in possibilities at these chalets aren't very good, especially during weekends.

It's best to go to one of the tourist information offices (see *Practical Information* below) and have them book a room for you. Otherwise, consider these following hotels:

HOTEL LABUŤ, *Krkonošská 188, 543 01 Vrchlabí. Tel. 0438/229 64, Fax 0438/220 75. Rates for single/double: 1,000/1,575 Kč. Credit cards: AE, MC, V. 25 rooms. Restaurant.*

Centrally located on Vrchlabí's main street, this newly-renovated hotel offers smartly decorated rooms with stylish furniture, satellite television, and direct-dial telephones. However, the rooms are somewhat cramped. Outfitted with comfortable booths and shiny brass fixtures, the restaurant is one of the finer ones in town, offering nicely prepared Czech and international courses. Meals run between 150 and 300 Kč.

HOTEL SABI, *Krkonošská 255, 543 01 Vrchlabí. Tel. 0438/234 77, no fax. Rates for single/double: 900/1,200 Kč. No credit cards. 10 rooms. Restaurant.* At the north end of the main street, this small hotel offers clean rooms with comfortable beds and simple furnishings. The restaurant dishes up tasty chicken dishes and decent grilled meats at around 100 Kč.

HOTEL HARMONY, *Bedřichov 106, 543 51 Špindlerův Mlýn. Tel. 0438/969 111, Fax 0438/937 67. Rates for single/double: 2,000/2,700 Kč. Credit cards: AE, MC, V. 100 rooms.* This sprawling, concrete hotel high above Špindlerův Mlyn is frankly an aberration on the mountainous landscape. To make matter worse, it sits opposite a hillside that's been devastated by acid rain. If you have any environmental concerns at all, then you'll probably be too incensed at the whole situation to even want to set foot in the place. Nevertheless, this is a four-star hotel, offering plush rooms with all the expected amenities. The hotel also has a sauna, masseuse, fitness center, indoor tennis, squash, and a cinema. It also rents skis and mountain bikes.

HOTEL HUBERTUS, *č.p. 20, 543 51 Špindlerův Mlýn. Tel. 0438/932 39, Fax 0438/930 16. Rates for single/double: 1,500/1,800 Kč. Credit cards: MC, V. 18 rooms. Restaurant.* This is definitely one of the cozier hotels you could choose in the Krkonoše. It's located smack dab in the middle of the resort town on the banks of the rushing Labe River. The folkish design of the wooden hotel is typical of the Krkonoše, but the stylish, contemporary rooms are not. Like every hotel restaurant in town, Hubertus serves all the Czech standards, but in a very pleasant wood-studded dining room. Prices for a meal range anywhere from 150 to 200 Kč.

HOTEL START, *Bedřichov 17/B, 543 51 Špindlerův Mlýn. Tel. 0438/ 933 05, Fax 0438/939 56. Rates for single/double: 1,200/1,600 Kč. Credit cards: AE, MC, V. 30 rooms. Restaurant.* This stark white hotel commands a good position over town. Rooms are suitably outfitted in wood, and come with nice furniture, satellite television, and direct-dial telephones. The hotel has a range of facilities, including a sauna, fitness center, and pool table. You can rent skis and mountain bikes here as well.

HOTEL NECHANICKÝ, *Bedřichov 43, 543 51 Špindlerův Mlýn. Tel. & Fax 0438/932 63. Rates for single/double: 1,000/1,300 Kč. Credit cards: V. 20 rooms. Restaurant.* Dating back to 1929, this venerable, rustic hotel was given an impressive restoration in 1993. The hotel provides cozy lodging in rooms decked out with dark wood furniture, tile bathrooms, satellite television, and direct-dial telephones. The restaurant is one of the better ones in town, offering solidly prepared Czech fare with prices ranging between 150 and 300 Kč.

HOTEL HORIZONT, *542 21 Pec pod Sněžkou. Tel. 0439/962 121, Fax 0439/962 378. Rates for single/double: 800/1,130 Kč. Credit cards: AE, MC, V. 150 rooms. Restaurant.*
You can't miss this high-rise hotel because it stick outs like a soar thumb in the village of Pec pod Sněžkou, marring the impressive view of Sněžka peak from the village. But it does have some of the most comfortable rooms you'll find in Pec.
PENSION LESNÍ PRAMEN, *č.p. 155, 542 21 Pec pod Sněžkou. Tel. & Fax 0439/962 348. Rates for single/double: 800/1,020 Kč. No credit cards. 12 rooms. No restaurant.*
This lodge-like pension is a bit more digestible than the Hotel Horizont, offering cozy rooms with private baths.

SEEING THE SIGHTS
Vrchlabí
As the gateway to the Krkonoše Mountains, **Vrchlabí** sees a lot of German tourists drive in and quickly drive out of town. The town mainly serves as a base or point of transfer for exploring other parts of the Krkonoše, because there's really not much at all to encourage you to hang around.
Vrchlabí is cut in half by one long main street called **Krkonošská,** along which you'll find all the services you need. While you're driving or walking down Krkonošská, take note of the town's 16th century **chateau,** which apparently has a window for each day of the year. Around it is a grassy park with a small zoo if you feel like taking a stroll. You also might want to pop into the Krkonoše Park Service's two **museums.** One of them, located just off náměstí Míru on Husova street, has a small exhibit on the ecology of the Krkonoše. The other, located on náměstí Míru near the park information center, has displays on local history and folk arts. *Both are open Tuesday through Sunday from 8 a.m. to 4 p.m.*

Špindlerův Mlýn & Environs
Located in the heart of the Krkonoše, at the point where seven valleys meet, Špindlerův Mlyn must have been a beautiful mountain village before large tracts of surrounding forest were felled and atrocious-looking hotels thrown up to accommodate the hordes of tourists.
Unfortunately, there's not much of a chance to get away from it all here, even if you take the chairlift up to the top of 1,235-meter **Medvědín** peak, which has suffered badly from the acid rain. The lift ride up and down costs 50 Kč.
A better idea is to hike to the **source of the Labe River** along the blue-

marked trail (starting at the north end of Špindlerův Mlýn). The trails takes you past huge boulders and along rushing river water up to Labská bouda (chalet), from where it's another 800 meters to the source (called *pramen Labe* on the maps). It should take you about three hours to reach the source from Špindlerův Mlýn. If you want to make more of a day-hike out of it, return to Špindlerův Mlýn on the red trail via Horní Mísecky and Medvědín for a round trip of about six hours.

Pec pod Sněžkou

The village of Pec pod Sněžkou, which means "Pec under Sněžka," serves mainly as a base for ascending the 1,602-meter (5,255-foot) Sněžka, the highest and most impressive-looking peak in the Czech Republic. The rocky, bald-faced mountain rises well beyond the timber-line, providing Pec with a dramatic backdrop. Of course, the reason to be in Pec is to be on your way up Sněžka, which can be done two ways: by foot or chair lift. By foot, it's a semi-strenuous, six-kilometer (3.7-mile) hike to the top along the green-marked trail, which begins near the Hotel Horizont. If you're not feeling that fit, then take the chairlift (called *lanovka* in Czech). A round-trip ticket costs 65 Kč and the ride takes 30 minutes each way.

The Czech-Polish border runs right across the summit of Sněžka. It's rather humorously marked by rock cairns, and looked over by a brigade of friendly-looking Czech and Polish guards. A chairlift comes up from the Polish side as well, so you'll hear a pleasant mix of Czech, Polish, and German tongues as you look out across the Krkonoše.

PRACTICAL INFORMATION
• **Čedok** (Vrchlabí), *Krkonošská 203. Tel. 0438/211 31.* This is an invaluable tourist office that can help you arrange accommodations all over the Krkonoše. They also sell maps.
• **Komerční banka,** (Vrchlabí), *Krkonošská 177.* Change money here or get cash from an ATM machine.
• **Park Information Center** (Vrchlabí), *náměstí Míru. Tel. 0438/210 11.* Provides maps and brochures to the Krkonoše National Park.
• **Pavilion Tourist Shop** (Špindlerův Mlýn), *in the central pavilion. Tel. 0438/933 64.* The friendly Dutch-Czech couple who own the place can help with accommodations in Špindlerův Mlyn and give good advice on where to go hiking and skiing.
• **Veselý Výlet** (Pec pod Sněžkou), *near the bus stand.* Get advice here on accommodations, camping, or hiking.

18. SOUTH MORAVIA

Like South Bohemia, South Moravia boasts some of the Czech Republic's most idyllic scenery in an environment that (for the most part) is free of the industry that plagues North Moravia. Indeed, the region's geography – the densely forested hills of the **Bohemia-Moravian Highlands** to the west or the limestone outcroppings of the **Pavlov hills** to the south – suffices as one of the best reasons to venture into South Moravia.

Another great reason yo visit are the scores of charming towns that seemingly litter this part of the republic, among them **Slavonice**, **Mikulov**, and **Kroměříž** – all gracefully rendered with twisting cobblestone lanes that draw you into expansive, colorful squares. Far and above the best of these towns, **Telč** treats its visitors to a perfectly-preserved Renaissance plaza, making it a crucial destination for anyone traveling in the Czech Republic. At the opposite end of the spectrum, impressive in its own right, is the factory town of **Zlín**, a veritable museum of modernist architecture.

The centerpiece of the region and the country's second largest city, **Brno** may not enchant like some of its neighboring towns, but it does contain a handful of intriguing sights, and serves as a good base for exploring the network of limestone caves at the **Moravian Karst** or for visiting the dramatically Gothic castle of **Pernštejn**.

An unsuspecting feature of South Moravia is its huge cluster of elegant chateaux, most of which were owned at one time or another by the aristocratic **Liechtensteins**, the same family that now lends its name to the small principality squeezed in between Switzerland and Austria. Offering the best glimpse of the Liechtensteins' former glory, the chateaux of **Valtice** and **Lednice** sit amidst a verdant track of landscaped grounds spotted with the occasional neo-Classical temple, arch, or statue.

Incidentally, these two chateaux and the neighboring town of Mikulov put you smack dab in the middle of South Moravia's great wine-producing region of **Pálava**, the perfect area in which do some biking or hiking on the trails that make up part of the **Czech Greenways** system.

SOUTH MORAVIA FINDS & FAVORITES

the **Church of St. John of Nepomuk** in Žďár nad Sázavou (see "Excursions"under Jihlava)

Telč's **Renaissance main square**, náměstí Zachariáše z Hradce (see Telč)

the sgraffitoed **old town of Slavonice** (see "Excursions" under Telč)

Restaurant and **Pension Havelka** (see Znojmo)

Hotel Rohatý Krokodýl (see Mikulov)

the **landscaped grounds** between Valtice and Lednice (see Valtice and Lednice)

the **Archbishop's Chateau** (see Kroměříž)

South Moravian Wines

It's difficult to paint a clear picture of South Moravian wines because almost none of those sold in markets and restaurants are produced by private vineyards. Instead, the wines are produced under large cooperatives and labeled by variety, location of the vineyard (region or town), and year. Most of the wines produced on the 13,000 hectares (32,000 acres) of vineyards in South Moravia are a fruity white, resembling those made across the border in Austria.

But the best wines are usually offered straight from the cask at the hundreds of private wine cellars dotting the Pálava and Slovácko regions (see Mikulov, Valtice, and Lednice). Unfortunately, most cellars are not open to the public. But many hotels and tourist offices can arrange visits for you. Some excellent wines to look out for is the musky red *Frankovka* produced in Valtice or the delicately sweet *ryzlink vlašský* produced in the Mikulov area.

TYPES OF SOUTH MORAVIAN WINES

– and their German or French equivalent –

Rulandské bílé (pinot blanc)

Ryzlink vlašský (Welschriesling)

Rulandské šedé (pinot gris)

Frankovka (Blaufränkisch)

Chardonnay

Veltínské zelene (Grüner Veltliner)

Müller Thurgau

Neuburské (Neuburger)

Sylvánské zelené (Sylvaner)

Tramín červený (Traminer)

Brno

As the Czech Republic's second-biggest city, **Brno** certainly doesn't inspire as much gawking as Prague does, nor does it get as downright gorgeous as some of its neighboring towns in South Moravia. But this city of 400,000 maintains a vibrant center replete with enough shops, watering holes, and excellent museums and galleries to keep you happily occupied for a day or two.

Like Prague, Brno developed into a melting pot of races, cultures, and religions. Rhinelanders, Flems, and Jews (among others) gravitated to Brno, joining the Slavic natives congregated in settlements below the two castles – the long-gone **Brno Castle** (seat of the Přemysl princes and the Margaves of Moravia) and the still-existent **Špilberk Castle**. In 1243, Brno gained its city charter, and these disparate settlements gelled into a single town now noted for having a long history of social and cultural tolerance, something that was by no means common in most Czech cities during the middle ages.

Brno hasn't always been the capital of Moravia. During the Thirty Years' War, Brno successfully staved off a two-year attack by the mighty Swedish forces, after which the town was given capital status as a reward for doing what most towns in the Austro-Hungarian Empire couldn't do – beat the Swedes. From the ashes of the war rose a largely Baroque town that didn't acquire a sizable population until the end of the 18th century, when it became the center of textiles in the empire.

Today, Brno is the country's center for exhibitions and trade fairs, some 38 of them held each year at the functionalist **Výstaviště** (Exhibition Grounds). During these fairs, hotels jack up their prices, sometimes doubling them. Obviously, you want to steer clear of Brno during these times, when rooms are not only exorbitantly expensive, but hard to come by. (Any of the tourist offices listed below under *Practical Information* can tell you if there happens to be a fair at the intended time of your stay.)

ORIENTATION

Located 196 kilometers (122 miles) southeast of Prague and about 100 kilometers (62 miles) north of Vienna, Brno sits in a basin along the Svratka and Svitava rivers. However you arrive, make sure to get specific directions to wherever you're going or to at least have a map, because the streets around the center, which run in a maze-like fashion, make you want to rip your hair out.

Keep an eye out for the two hilltop landmarks, the Špilberk Castle and the Peter and Paul Cathedral, both of which can help you gain your bearings in the city. Knowing the two streets that form a ring around the old town, **Husova** and **Koliště**, can also help you get around.

ARRIVALS & DEPARTURES

By Air

Air Ostrava, *Tel. 02/240 327 31*, offers flights between Prague's Ruzyně airport and Brno's Tuřany airport. One-way tickets cost around 1,300 Kč and return tickets cost around 2,000 Kč. You can also fly with **ČSA**, *Tel. 02/201 043 10 in Prague.*

By Bus

Buses depart almost hourly from Prague's Florenc station, taking about two-and-a-half hours and costing about 100 Kč. You'll find the main bus station two kilometers south of the city center on the corner of Zvonařka and Plotní.

If you can, take the privately-owned **Čebus**, leaving Prague's main train station (Hlavní nádraží) and dropping you off in the center of Brno, opposite the Grandhotel near the train station. Though it's a bit more expensive (125 Kč), it's faster, more convenient, and more comfortable than the public bus. *Call 02/422 100 46 to make reservations.*

By Car

From Prague, Brno usually takes about two hours via E50/65. But traffic can be insane at times, especially during some of the major trade fairs. Parking lots are scattered throughout the city center. Just keep an eye out for the blue "P" signs.

By Train

Trains from Prague, departing several times a day from either Hlavní nádraží or Nádraží Holešovice, take 3 to 4 hours and cost around 100 Kč. The main train station in Brno sits on the southern edge of the city center on Nádražní street.

GETTING AROUND TOWN

In and around the city center, you can manage getting most anywhere on foot. Otherwise, tram is the way to go. Most of them congregate in front of the main train station, running through the city center and to outlying suburbs. Buy your tickets from news kiosks or *tabaks* and validate them using the punching gadget on board.

Taxis are easy enough to hail on the street, or you can order one from **AB Radio Taxi**, *Tel. 05/666 666*. The **Hertz** office, *Tel. 05/421 228 42*, at the Hotel International (see *Where to Stay*, below) is the place to rent a car.

WHERE TO STAY

A word of warning: expect as much as a two-fold increase in the hotel rates listed below if there happens to be a trade fair going on at the time of your stay!

GRANDHOTEL BRNO, *Benešova 18/20, 657 83 Brno. Tel. 05/423 212 87, Fax 05/422 103 45. Rates for single/double: 2,400/3,600 Kč. Credit cards: AE, DC, MC, V. 110 rooms. Restaurant.*

The grande dame of the city, the Grandhotel dates back to 1870. But it's the hotel's Art Nouveau annex with a painting depicting the legendary *Judgment of Paris* that steals the show. Though completely renovated in 1988, there's somewhat of a lackluster appearance about this place, inside and out. The furniture in the rooms is a bit outdated, as are many of the fixtures. Of course, you receive all the special amenities and excellent service that come with such pricey rates, but that doesn't make up for some of the tacky rooms. (Beware of some of the rooms on the fourth floor, which have no windows, only skylights.)

Having said that, the Grandhotel is your best bet for big hotel lodgings in a city where the majority of four-star hotels are really quite dismal. Disappointingly, the hotel houses a casino, something that seems out of place in such a historic and respectable place as this. If you do stay here, take advantage of the personalized tours of Brno and the area. One great tour they offer is to South Moravia's wine cellars, something you shouldn't miss if you stay here. In addition to the tours, the hotel has a fitness center and sauna, and can even arrange a spin on Brno's Grand Prix race track in your own car or a rented one.

HOTEL PEGAS, *Jakubská 4, 602 00 Brno, Tel. & Fax 05/422 112 32. Rates for single/double: 1,100/1,670 Kč. Credit cards: AE, MC, V. 14 rooms. Restaurant.*

Recently renovated, this small hotel, smack dab in the center is your best alternative to the ugly, pretentious hotels catering to business accounts. Rooms are somewhat small, but have personality, which is more than you can say than about 95 percent of the rooms in this city. Downstairs is a restaurant/pub, popular with the locals and serving beer made right on the premises.

HOTEL SLAVIA, *Solniční 15/17, 622 16 Brno. Tel. 05/423 212 49, Fax 05/422 117 69. Rates for single/double: 2,000/2,379 Kč. Credit cards: AE, MC, V. 78 rooms. Restaurant.*

This stately-looking hotel festooned with flags and located almost dead center in the city appears promising from the outside, but inside is another story. A glum, dark interior is found throughout the hotel, from the lobby up to the rooms, which have terrible yellow wallpaper that looks as though it could start peeling off at any moment. If you've ever seen the film *Barton Fink*, you know what I mean.

HOTEL INTERNATIONAL, *Husova 16, 659 21 Brno. Tel. 05/421 221 11, Fax 05/422 108 43. Rates for single/double: 1,900/2,500 Kč. Credit cards: AE, MC, V. 262 rooms. Restaurant.*

Since having been taken over by Best Western, the hotel has improved its standards, but is still fairly generic-looking. The building itself, situated just below Špilberk Castle, is a squatting concrete structure of the sort the Communists were so fond of building.

Sure, the rooms are certainly comfortable and come with the expected amenities like satellite television, direct-dial phones, and fax service. But with pastel carpets and drapes, the decor takes the cake for tackiness. Like most of the hotels around town, this one has a casino.

HOTEL CONTINENTAL, *Kounicova 6, 657 64 Brno. Tel. 05/415 191 11, Fax 05/412 112 03. Rates for single/double: 1,200/2,580 Kč. Credit cards: AE, MC, V. 220 rooms. Restaurant.*

Another blight on the Brno skyline, the grey Hotel Continental and its 15 floors tarnish the pleasant neighborhood it sits in just outside the old town. Desperately plain rooms, gruff receptionists, and a lousy restaurant add up to a hotel you shouldn't waste your time on.

HOTEL SLOVAN, *Lidická 23, 659 89 Brno. Tel. 05/413 212 07, Fax 05/412 111 37. Rates for single/double: 1,100/1,690 Kč. Credit cards: AE, MC, V. 102 rooms. Restaurant.*

This big hotel is a bit more digestible than its neighbor, Hotel Continental. Some of the rooms, outfitted for the most part with new furniture and bright colors, are actually quite pleasant, but you wouldn't know it by the dark, almost spooky hallways. The receptionists are extremely friendly, and are willing to give you some advice on seeing the town and eating elsewhere other than the unpromising hotel restaurant.

U KRÁLOVNY ELIŠKY, *Mendlovo náměstí 1a, 602 00 Brno. Tel. 05/432 168 98, no fax. Rates for single/double: 500/750 Kč. No credit cards. 6 rooms. Restaurant.*

This cozy pension is set in a former section of the Augustinian monastery. Simple but smartly decorated rooms under vaulted ceilings come with private baths. This is another good alternative to the big, impersonal hotels littering the city. The pension is a ten minute walk or five-minute tram ride southwest of the center.

HOTEL VORONĚŽ I, *Křižkovského 47, 603 73 Brno. Tel. 05/431 411 11, Fax 05/432 120 02. Rates for single/double: 1,170-3,033/1,600-4,125 Kč. Credit cards: AE, MC, V. Restaurant.*

Another big, ugly hotel catering to the folks attending fairs across the street at the Exhibition Grounds (Výstaviště), Voroněž offers functional, clean lodgings that certainly wouldn't win any awards for its decor. But it does run a reputable restaurant serving traditional Moravian dishes in an out-of-place cottage located adjacent to the hotel.

HOTEL BOBY, *Sportovní 2a, 602 00 Brno. Tel. 05/727 2133, Fax 05/412 120 15. Rates for single/double: 2,800/3,200 Kč. Credit cards: AE, MC, V. Restaurant.*

Let's just say that the glitzy Hotel Boby would have no problem fitting into Las Vegas' Strip. This plush hotel is part of the greater Boby Centrum, home of a soccer stadium, shopping center, movie theater, fitness center, pool hall, bowling alley, roller-skating rink, three discos, and a car wash. (Welcome to the new Central Europe.) Ultra-comfortable rooms don't afford much in the way of views, but come with all the modern amenities, such as direct-dial telephone, satellite television, and faxes.

The one problem with Hotel Boby is that you have to take a bus and tram to get there from the center of town. (Take tram #1 or #18 to the Hrnčířská stop and then a trolley bus one stop to Zimní Stadion.) With so much happening at the hotel, you may be tempted to just skip the old town altogether. But if you can resist the temptation and endure the inconvenience, then you should have a pleasant stay here.

WHERE TO EAT

STOPKOVA, *Česká 5. Tel. 05/422 110 94. 100-250 Kč. Credit cards: AE, MC, V.*

Stopkova's gorgeous sgrafittoed facade and vaulted interior draw a lot of tourists. The German-accented Czech cuisine, such as the wiener schnitzel and the rest of the fried meats, looks better than it tastes. But the real reason to come is for the Pilsner Urquell served here, something the restaurant has been doing since 1880.

ITALIA BAR, *just off náměstí Svobody on Zámečnická. 70-150 Kč. Tel. 05/422 125 70. No credit cards.*

This upbeat café bakes a mean thin-crust pizza and steams the best cappucino in town.

U RUDÉHO VOLA IRSKÁ HOSPODA, *Kobližná 2. Tel. 05/422 147 71. 120-200 Kč. Credit cards: MC, V.*

The best thing going for this Irish pub is its polished wood fixtures and circa-1930 group photos of happy-go-lucky Irishmen. Billed as Irish though looking suspiciously Czech, the hearty meat and potato dishes are generously large, doing the trick of filling an empty stomach. The handsome bar pours Guinness and Kilkenny at a price that's two to three times as much as Czech beers. Eat here, but leave the beer drinking to Czech pubs.

MODRÁ HVĚZDA, *Šilingrovo náměstí 7. Tel. 05/422 152 92. 100- 350 Kč. Credit cards: MC, V.*

This restaurant, just up the street from the Cabbage Market, offers a wide variety of solid international dishes, served up in a classy atmosphere in an historic part of town. Come here if you're in need of a late-night meal. It's open until 1 a.m.

HRADNÍ VINÁRNA ŠPILBERK, *in the Špilberk Castle. Tel. 05/432 145 28. 100-400 Kč. Credit cards: MC, V.*

This top-notch Moravian restaurant treats its guests to live cymbal music and an extensive selection of Moravian wines. The restaurant utilizes a number of alcove-like rooms which make for intimate dining. Deft service goes along with the crisp decor. Try the succulent game dishes, often served with robust wine sauces.

LA BRASERIA, *Pekařská 80. Tel. 05/432 145 28. 120-300 Kč. Credit cards: MC, V.*

The aroma of herb-laden sauces wafting under the vaulted ceilings is enough reason to come here. By the number of Italians frequenting this trattoria, it's not too hard to figure out that La Braseria serves the most authentic Italian food you're bound to get for miles around. A huge selection of antipasta, pasta, and entrées grace the menu. The one disappointment here is the slack service.

VINÁRNA U KRÁLOVNY ELIŠKY, *Mendlovo náměstí 1a. Tel. 05/432 125 78. 100-300 Kč. No credit cards.*

Moravian cymbal music, impromptu sword fights, and solid local cuisine are all dished up in an intriguing wine cellar once belonging to the Augustinian monastery. The emphasis here is traditional Moravian food, which differs from other Czech cuisine in that it's heavily influenced by Hungarian cooking. That means a liberal use of paprika and sugar, even on the vegetables. The restaurant also gives you the opportunity to sample as many as 32 different wines from around South Moravia, but don't feel pressured to try all of them. Garden seating is available in the summer.

RISTORANTE DIANA DA SANDRO, *Štefanikova 30. Tel. 05/412 12552. 100-200 Kč. No credit cards.*

This snappy Italian eatery bakes a fine lasagna and serves a number of decently-priced pasta dishes. The bar is a welcome place for solo travelers to eat or just have an espresso. But the restaurant is a good haul north of the city center.

SEEING THE SIGHTS
The Old Town

We'll start at the newly-restored, Art Nouveau **train station**, itself a worthwhile sight at the south end of the city center on Nádražní. From there go through the tunnel and climb the stairs up to **Masarykovo ulice**, a major pedestrian thoroughfare leading into the core of Brno. Although decayed for the most part, this cobblestone street is Brno at its finest. Students and shoppers – munching on pizza or licking ice cream cones

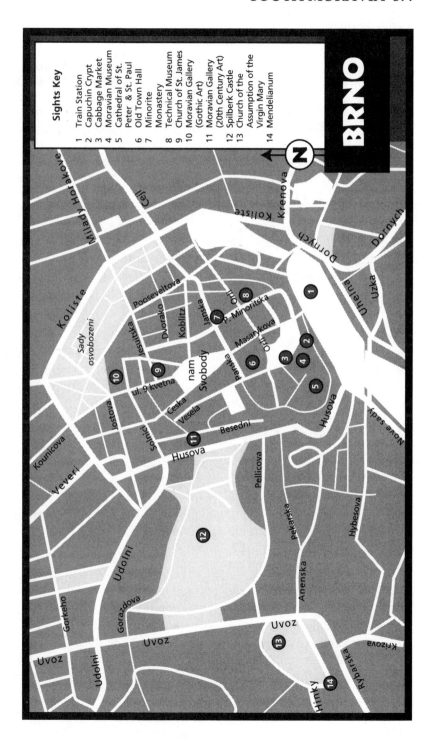

BRNO

Sights Key

1 Train Station
2 Capuchin Crypt
3 Cabbage Market
4 Moravian Museum
5 Cathedral of St. Peter & St. Paul
6 Old Town Hall
7 Minorite Monastery
8 Technical Museum
9 Church of St. James
10 Moravian Gallery (Gothic Art)
11 Moravian Gallery (20th Century Art)
12 Spilberk Castle
13 Church of the Assumption of the Virgin Mary
14 Mendelianum

– keep it filled at all times of day with the sound of laughter and idle chatter.

A little ways up Masarykovo swing left into **Kapučinské náměstí** (square), where you'll find the **Capuchin Crypt** (Kapučinská Hrobka) in the basement of the **Capuchin Monastery**. Definitely not for those with a weak stomach, the macabre attraction here is no less than 150 corpses, mostly monks mummified in air-tight caskets or strung out in little alcoves.

Two signs, one in Latin and one in Czech, announce, "What we are, they once were, what they are, we will be." A sound word of wisdom, indeed. Until the 18th century, the well-to-do apparently paid hefty sums in order to have the privilege of rotting next to the heaven-bound monks, as well as have tourists come centuries later and get a salacious thrill out of viewing their empty stares. Hours for this somewhat ridiculous, if not memorable, attraction are: *Tuesday through Saturday from 9 a.m. to noon and from 2 to 4:30 p.m. On Sunday you can catch it from 11 to 11:45 a.m. and from 2 to 4:30 p.m.*

From the crypt, head a little ways north to the bustling **Zelný trh** (Cabbage Market), a square where the vendors are thankfully selling more than just cabbage these days. There's a buzz of entrepreneurship here, where hundreds of the self-employed set up their tables around the 1695 **Parnas Fountain**, which would probably be a better sight if there were some water coming out of it. Apparently, water did once fill its basin, from which live carp were sold.

Housed in the handsome **Dietrichstein Palace** at the top of the square is the **Moravian Museum** (Moravské zemské muzeum), showing a number of temporary exhibitions and a wealth of permanent prehistoric artifacts uncovered in the Brno region, including the 25,000-year-old Venus of Věstonice. *The museum is open Tuesday through Sunday from 9 a.m. to 6 p.m. (until 4 p.m. in the winter).*

From Zelný trh, climb Petrská to the **Cathedral of St. Peter and St. Paul** (Katedrála sv. Petra a Pavla), its needle-thin spires poking up through the skyline from the top of Petrov hill. The best features of this rather uninspiring cathedral reconstructed in the 19th century are the meticulous stained-glass windows behind the altar and the unfinished *Stations of the Cross*, a downright avant-garde work constructed by Jiří Marek in the 1950s using aluminum.

Before making your way down Petrov hill, take a stroll through **Denisovy Sady**, a small park accessed by descending the steps behind the cathedral. Here you'll find a great view of the city and of surrounding hills, as well as an obelisk commemorating the end of the Napoleonic Wars.

FOR BRNO'S NOON BELLS, TIMING IS EVERYTHING!

If you happen to hear the cathedral noon bells chime at 11 o'clock, don't reset your watch thinking you gained an hour somewhere along the way to Brno. The reason for the noon bells ringing an hour early alludes to a legend involving the Swedish siege of Brno in 1645. Low on manpower and even lower on morale, the Swedish general Tortennson declared one day that if Brno couldn't be captured by 12 noon he would call it quits and retreat. At 11 o'clock the Swedes were on the verge of finally seizing Brno. In a literal eleventh-hour fit of desperation, the bellringer rang the noon bells an hour early, prompting Tortennson to call off the siege. The town was saved, and the noon bells have rung an hour early ever since.

From Petrov Hill, retrace your steps down to Zelný trh and cross the square to Radnická. A half-block up on the left is the entrance to the 13th century **Old Town Hall** (stará radnice), the oldest secular structure in Brno. A marvelous panoramic view of the city awaits at the top of its observation gallery. But first be sure to check out the Gothic doorway as you enter the building. Just above the Statue of Righteousness you'll notice a number of twisted pinnacles. Anton Pilgram, who later went on to build St. Stephen's Cathedral in Vienna, left this rather symbolic mark on his portal when the town council paid him less than the amount negotiated.

Something that's not hard to miss, if only for its incongruent appearance, is the **Brno dragon** (Brněnský drak), hanging from the entrance ceiling. What is actually a stuffed Amazon River crocodile was a gift to Brno from Archprince Matyaš in 1608. Numerous legends have turned this plastic-looking beast into a dragon, and one of the town mascots.

The second of Brno's mascots, the **Brno wheel** (Brněnské kolo), hangs here as well. Legend has it that Jiří Birek, a cabinet maker from Lednice, bet a friend in 1636 that he could cut down a tree, carve a wheel from it, and roll it some 45 kilometers to Brno – all in one day. He succeeded, and the town council proudly gave it a special place in town hall. An addendum to this legend states that, after Birek performed his feat, the locals suspected him of being in cahoots with the devil. No one dared patronize his business anymore and Birek died a poor man.

Take a left out of the Old Town Hall to Panská, cross Masarykova to Jánská, and then swing right onto Minoritská. Dominating one side of the block is the **Minorite Monastery**. Founded in 1230, this is the only monastery in Moravia where the monks still occupy medieval quarters. Of particular interest here is the **Church of St. John** (Kostel sv. Janů) and the adjacent **Loretto chapel** – two of the finer testaments to the Baroque era you'll find in Brno.

Continue down Minoritská to the former Franciscan convent at *Josefská 1*, now housing the **Technical Museum** (Technické muzeum). Its exhibits on hydrology, electronics, computers, cars, and so on probably won't peak the interest of those inclined towards more abstract subjects. But the 1890 Panorama, a rotating stereoscope showing multiple postcard pictures of sights around Central Europe, is almost worth the price of admission. *The museum is open weekdays from 9 a.m. to 6 p.m. and weekends from 10 a.m. to 4 p.m.*

With all this walking around, it's time to take a load off your feet and grab a coffee. And the place to do it is at one of the outdoor cafés on **náměstí Svobody**, or Freedom Square. Though not breathtakingly beautiful, the town's main square is Brno's liveliest spot and is easy enough to find by following the wave of traffic to the end of Masarykovo. A mishmash of architectural styles from several centuries fill this square, packed full of students during the demonstrations of 1989.

As you enter the square from Masarykovo, look to your left and keep an eye out for the dirty Renaissance facade of **Schwarz Palace** (Schwarzův palác), still riddled with bullet holes from the last world war. On the opposite side at **Dům u čtyř mamlasů**, or "House of the Four Stupid Boys," is something of a less serious nature. Built by a wealthy Jewish industrialist in the 19th century, the facade of this house shows four ogres holding up the building with one hand while trying to keep their private parts covered with the other.

A rather drab example of functionalist architecture, **Moravská banka** (now called Komerční banka) in the northwest corner of the square is just one of several designs by Bohuslav Fuchs dotting the city. And let's not forget the obligatory **plague column**, erected in 1680 out of thanks to God for saving the town from the Swedes.

Just off náměstí Svobody is a fairly interesting **Ethnographic Museum** (Etnografické muzeum), *at Koblížna 1*, showcasing the folk traditions of Moravia through costumes, ceramics, and housing. *Open Tuesday through Sunday from 9 a.m. to 6 p.m.*

Back on náměstí Svobody, turn right on ulice 9. května to the **Church of St. James** (Kostel sv Jakub), a rather ordinary-looking 13th century structure where Raduit de Souches, French leader of the Brno defense in 1697, is buried. Not ordinary whatsoever is a figure of man positioned above a Gothic window on the south side of the church. The man is sticking out his bare bottom in a gesture implying, "Kiss my . . . ." Well, you get the picture. The story behind what is locally known as "The Immoral Little Man of St. James" is that it was put there by a brash sculptor who wanted to send a message to the priests on Petrov Hill, who at that time were building the cathedral. Apparently, there was some animosity between the two parishes and the young sculptor wanted it to be known just how he felt about his rivals.

A little farther down ulice 9. května street and off to the right is one branch of the **Moravian Gallery** (Moravská galerie), *at Moravské náměstí 1a*, this one devoted to Gothic and Baroque Moravian art. *Open Tuesday through Sunday from 10 a.m. to 5 p.m.* Next door is **St. Thomas Church** (Kostel sv. Tomáše), part of the Augustinian monastery founded in 1350. The original Gothic church was nearly pulverized during the Swedish siege, but was rebuilt later on to suit the Baroque tastes of the day.

To reach the other two branches of the Moravian Gallery, go east on Solniční and then take a left on Husova, serving as the western boundary of the old town. Standing next to each other with a garden in between, *at Husova 14*, are two handsome neo-Renaissance buildings, the first exhibiting 20th century Czech art and the second applied arts from the Renaissance on up to the 19th century.

If you have time to tour only one, make it the former, which has one of the finest collections of Modernist Czech art in the republic, including the Cubist works of Bohumil Kubišta and Josef Čapek. *Both are open Tuesday through Sunday from 10 a.m. to 5 p.m.*

Špilberk Castle

A little farther south down Husova are a number of paths leading up the hill through a park to **Špilberk Castle**, a rather mundane-looking citadel that would be hard to recommend if it weren't for its views of the city and surrounding countryside. Occasional residence of Czech kings, this 13th-century castle stood up to the Swedes during the Thirty Years' War, after which it was rebuilt into one of the greatest fortifications under Hapsburg rule.

In the 18th century, the Austro-Hungarian rulers turned it into a fortress prison, throwing the most dangerous criminals into the lower stories (known as the dark chambers) and rebels of the monarchy into the less-severe upper stories. It became known as "Prison of the Nations" for its international list of inmates. The French briefly occupied the castle during the Napoleonic Wars, as did the Nazis during World War II.

You can take a self-guided tour of the former prison, housed in the castle's casemates (*kasematy*) – the dank, dark corridors below the garrison. The tour of these creepy passages, introducing you to prison life and a number of sadistic instruments of torture apparently never used at Špilberk, is something claustrophobes will certainly want to bypass. *The casemates are open Tuesday through Sunday June through September from 9 a.m. to 6 p.m., in April and May to 5 p.m., and in March and October to 4 p.m. Tickets cost 30 Kč.*

On the east side of the castle is a museum with temporary exhibitions usually devoted to some historical aspect of Špilberk. Hours should be the same as the casemates.

Staré Brno
Though you wouldn't know it by all the all the modern buildings, the **Staré Brno** district (Old Brno) was the site of the first Slav settlement in Brno. Retrace your steps down from Špilberk Castle, continue south on Husova, and then take a right on Pekařská, where you can catch any one of the trams heading east or take the ten minute walk to **Mendlovo náměstí** (the heart of Staré Brno) and the **Church of the Assumption of the Virgin Mary** (Kostel Nanebevzetí Panny Marie).

Out of all the churches in Brno (and God knows there's a lot of them), this is Brno's finest testament to the Gothic age. The Czech Republic's oldest painting on wood, the 13th-century *Black Madonna*, finds its place here among a wealth of other darkly melancholic paintings and sculptures adorning the breathtaking interior.

Around the corner from the church is the **Mendelianum**, *at Mendlovo náměstí 1*, a tiny museum occupying a space in the 14th-century Augustinian monastery. Most of you have probably heard of Gregor Johann Mendel (1822-84), the humble monk whose experiments with garden peas and bees paved the way for the discovery of genetics. Mendel's experiments took place right here at the monastery's gardens, which is now part of the museum. The beehives used in Mendel's work are also on display, as is the monastery's richly decorated library. *Open weekdays from 8 a.m. to 5 p.m. (until 6 p.m. in July and August).*

At the station on Mendlovo náměstí hop on tram #1 or #18 to the mammoth **Výstaviště** (Exhibition Grounds), a veritable shrine to functionalist and constructivist architecture. Finished in 1928 for the Contemporary Culture in Czechoslovakia exhibition, Výstaviště brought together the vanguard of Czechoslovak architects to help design and build it.

The result is a complex of pavilions that champion the use of geometrical figures, offering a dizzying array of symmetrical lines and shapes that maintain their novelty to this day. The biggest and most captivating of them all, the **Z pavilion** (actually built in the years following World War II), has a soaring steel dome with a 122-meter (400-foot) diameter – a powerful sight when looking at it from the inside.

Generally, you can walk around Výstaviště at your leisure, unless there's a trade fair going on, for which you'll have to pay an entry fee. But most of the fairs are really quite interesting.

Villa Tugendhat

Ludwig Mies van der Rohe, director of the Bauhaus art and architecture school, designed this stark white villa and its furniture for the Tugendhats, a wealthy Jewish family that owned a number of the city's textile factories. The design of the villa, finished in 1930, is state of the art functionalism – simple and elegant.

Built against a hillside, the house hides its breadth when viewed from the street, where only the pill-boxed top level is visible. In the so-called "living space," the walls and bookcases are paneled with strips of ebony or else covered with African onyx marble. The ultra-stylish furniture follows the same black-and-white motif, complimenting the rest of the interior furnishings. The villa, by the way, was where Václav Klaus and Vladímir Mečiar met to negotiate the break-up of Czechoslovakia.

The tour of the villa is well worth your time if you have the slightest interest in modern architecture. *Open to the public Wednesday through Sunday from 10 a.m. to 5 p.m.*

To get here from the north end of the city center, take tram #9 or #11 several stations to Zemědělská stop. To the left of the tram stop is Černopolní street, where you'll find the villa at number 45 – about a ten minute walk from the tram stop. For other information, *call 05/452 121 18.*

Janáček Museum

Counted as one of the three best Czech composers (including Smetana and Dvořák), Leo Janáček lived in this small house-turned-museum in 1893 and 1894. Photographs, original sheet music, and a piano belonging to the man himself are all part of the exhibit. The museum is a ten minute walk north of the old town at the corner of Smetanova and Kounicova.

NIGHTLIFE & ENTERTAINMENT

Rich in musical and dramatic traditions, Brno offers the gamut in performing arts. The venues for operas and ballets include the **Janáček Theater** (Janáčkovo divadlo) on Rooseveltova and the **Mahen Theater** (Mahenovo divadlo) a block away. Built in the 1960s and boasting the largest auditorium in the republic, the Janaček makes up in size for it what may lack in beauty. With its gorgeous sweeping staircase, inlaid gold, and gigantic chandeliers, the Mahen leaves a much better impression.

Built in the 1880s, the Mahen was the first theater in the Austro-Hungarian Empire to use electric light bulbs. You can buy tickets for performances at both these theaters and find out about the scores of concerts happening at churches around the city at an office located *at Dvořákova 11, Tel. 05/422 102 94.* For the best in experimental theater, check out the newly-restored **Divadlo Husa na Provázku** at the top of Zelný trh.

If the pounding industrial music at the Boby Centrum's three **discos** (see *Where to Stay*) were any louder, it would measure on the Richter Scale. You'll find all the makings for a night of debauchery at these dance clubs. There are several **cinemas** (*kino*) around the old town, including one on náměstí Svobody.

Of course, what would your stay in Brno amount to without checking out the local brew. Most of the pubs in Brno offer the local Starobrno, a below-par beer by Czech standards. **Pegas pivnice** (see *Where to Stay*) makes their beer, a light and dark, right on the premises. The caramelized dark was a bit too sweet for my taste, but I found a better one brewed and served at **Černehorská pivnice**, near the train station at the south end of Masarykova. This place has more of a down-at-its-luck appearance, but the ambience is Czech through and through. (That means a lot of cigarette smoke.)

Though hardly off-the-beaten path, **Stopkova** (see *Where to Eat*) serves one of the best mugs of Pilsner Urquell you're liable to get anywhere. The classiest pub in town, **U rudého vola**, *Kobližná 2*, unfortunately doesn't pour Czech beer, reason being is that it's an Irish pub (Irská hospoda). With Guinness and Kilkenny at three to four times the price of Czech beer, it's no wonder that most of the customers are drinking coffee.

SPORTS & RECREATION

Golf Club Brno, *Pompova 28, Tel. 05/336 209*, offers 9 holes of golf and rents golf clubs if you haven't brought your own.

At the end of August, the **Motorcycle Grand Prix** gets revving at Brno's grand prix track, located at the end of Masarykův okruh street. In September, **grand prix car racing** comes to the same track. For exact dates and ticket information, contact the Cultural and Information Center (see *Practical Information* below).

EXCURSIONS & DAY TRIPS

Slavkov U Brna

Slavkov, about 20 kilometers (12 miles) east of Brno, probably doesn't ring many bells with foreigners, but its German name of Austerlitz should. The Battle of Austerlitz, otherwise known as the "Battle of the Three Emperors," raged ten kilometers west of Slavkov on the foggy morning of December 2, 1805. Pitted against an Austrian-Russian alliance far outnumbering his French troops, Napoleon triumphed over Austrian Emperor Ferdinand I and Russian Tsar Alexander I.

Napoleon stalled his attack until the allies had established a position at the top of Pracký hill, where the French were able to force a split in the allied forces and wreak chaos in their organization. In a few short hours, the Russians and Austrians suffered the loss of more than 20,000 troops, five times what the French lost. Following the battle, the three emperors signed a peace treaty that put an end to the anti-Napoleon coalition.

A hundred years after the battle, the governments of Austria, Russia, and France donated the funds to build the **Monument of Peace** (Mohyla míru) on Pracký Hill, accessed by train (get off at the Ponětovice station) or by car (ten minute drive west of Slavkov.) The monument contains a tiny museum explaining how the battle played itself out. Every December 2 you can see a reenactment of the battle at the monument acted out by the Friends of the French Revolution.

Of interest in Slavkov is the **Slavkov Chateau** (zamek), where Napoleon himself stayed in the days preceding the battle and where the three emperors signed the peace treaty. This late-Baroque structure designed by Martinelli sports a number of gorgeous ceiling murals and houses the Chapel of the Holy Cross, adorned with precious Kounice paintings. *The chateau is open Tuesday through Sunday, June through August, from 8 a.m. to 5 p.m. In April, May, September, October, and November it's open from 9 a.m. to noon and from 1 to 4 p.m.*

To get here by car from Brno, take E462 east to highway 50. Otherwise, take one of the several daily trains that run from Brno directly to Slavkov, stopping at Ponětovice along the way. From Ponětovice station, it's a 25 minute walk to the battlefield and the Monument of Peace.

Moravian Karst

One of the wildest outdoor experiences to be had in the Czech Republic lies about 28 kilometers (17 miles) north of Brno in the **Moravian Karst** (Moravský kras), a spectacular area of precipitous canyons, underground ravines, and dead-end valleys. But the major attraction here is the network of limestone caves, some 400 of them, of which only four are open to the public. Grottoes of stalactites and stalagmites, the result of mineral-tainted rain water seeping through the ceilings of the underground caverns, give you the feeling of entering the jaws of earth.

The largest and most-accessible of the cave systems, **Punkevní jeskyně**, takes its name from the Punkva, an underground ravine running through part of the system. The tour, partially by boat, takes you through five chambers before letting out at the bottom of the so-called **Macocha Abyss** (Propast Macocha), a 140-meter-deep (459 feet) chasm formed when the ceiling of one of the caves collapsed. The ticket and information office for Punkevní jeskyně is at Skalní Mlýn; from there take the "ecological train" to the entrance of Punkvení. *Caves are open daily*

April through September from 7 a.m. to 4:30 p.m. and October through March from 7:30 a.m. to 2:30 p.m.
To reach Skalní Mlýn from Brno, take E461 north and follow signs to Blansko and then Skalní Mlýn. Buses and trains run several times a day from Brno to Blansko, where you'll need to catch a connecting bus to Skalní Mlýn. The Cultural and Information Center in Brno (see *Practical Information* below) can help help with bus and train schedules. The trip to the caves take a little more than an hour from Brno. In the summer months tour buses besiege Punkvení, which means you should try to get there as early in the day as possible. If you want to save yourself the hassle, join a Čedok tour *(see Practical Information)*. However you go, be sure to dress warm; the caves maintain a chilly temperature year-round.

Pernštejn
Whatever image you may have of a Gothic castle, **Pernštejn** may just furnish the closest match. Moravia's best-preserved Gothic structure, this 13th-century fortress and its intimidating walls poke out from its hilltop vantage point in all sorts of crazy angles, providing a sight that has not changed much at all since the 16th century, when the leading Moravian nobility, the Pernštejn family, gave the castle its final adjustment. The tour takes you through several centuries-worth of interior designs and provides a number of breathtaking views that are all well worth the 30 Kč admission. *May through August the castle is open daily except Monday from 9 a.m. to noon and from 1 to 5 p.m. In April and October it's open the same hours, but on weekends only.*
Pernštejn sits a little ways west of the town of Nedvědice, a little more than an hour drive northeast of Brno. Take E461 out of Brno and then follow signs to Kuřim, Tišnov, and finally Nedvědice. If you don't have a car, train works best to Nedvědice with a connection in Tišnov, costing no more than 30 Kč and taking about an hour from Brno.

Moravský Krumlov
Moravský Krumlov sits in a pretty pastoral valley on a bend of the Rokytná River. But that is not the reason to come here. Moravský Krumlov deserves a visit for its **Mucha gallery**, housed in the local chateau on the west side of town. Probably the most famous Czech artist outside the republic, Alfons Mucha (1860-1939) is best known for his commercial Art Nouveau posters, mostly work he accomplished in Paris while sharing a studio with Gauguin.
When the First Czechoslovak Republic was formed in 1918, Mucha changed courses, devoting himself to the national cause by designing the country's bank notes and stamps. But his greatest challenge, one that would seal his reputation as a master painter, are the 20 monument-size

canvases that make up the Slav Epic (Slovanksá Epoje), now hanging at the Mucha Gallery. Commissioned by an American millionaire, Mucha spent 18 years at work on these lusty scenes from Czech and Slav history. The paintings of blood-splattered battlefields, crazed priests, and medieval festivals signal a definite departure from his polite Art Nouveau days, to say the least. *The gallery is open April through October, Tuesday through Sunday, from 9 a.m. to noon and from 1 to 4 p.m.*

Moravský Krumlov lies about 30 kilometers (19 miles) southwest of Brno via a number of backroads. (You'll need a good local map for this one.) Otherwise, bus directly from Brno works best, as the train station is a good two kilometers from town.

PRACTICAL INFORMATION

• **Čedok,** *Nádražní 10-12. Tel. 05/423 212 67.* Travel agency located across the street from the train station that changes money, organizes sightseeing tours of the area, and sells international bus and train tickets.

• **Cultural and Information Center** (Kulturní a Informační Centrum), *in the Old Town Hall at Radnická 8, 658 78 Brno. Tel. 05/422 110 90, Fax 05/422 146 25.* The friendliest place in town. Besides selling maps and brochures and providing information on tours in the area, the office arranges private accommodations, sells theater tickets, and has train and bus schedules. Perfect English spoken here.

• **Komerční Banka,** *náměstí Svobody 21.* A bank where you can change foreign cash and travelers' checks.

• **Post Office,** *next door to the train station on Nadražní.* There's 24-hour international telephone service and poste restante available here.

Jihlava

There's not a whole lot to keep you entertained in **Jihlava**, hardly warranting more than three or four hours of your time. But it is a pleasant-enough city with a bustling old town and a number of pretty Renaissance and Baroque houses.

Following the discovery of silver ore in the 13th century, Jihlava was transformed from a tiny backwater settlement into one of the most important mining towns in all of Central Europe. A royal mint was established and mostly German speakers flocked here to work in the mines. The town grew into a "German island," and stayed that way until the end of World War II, when all Germans living in Jihlava were expelled. With the expulsion of the majority of the town's residents, so went most of the town's wealth – apparent in Jihlava's present down-at-its-luck appearance.

Nowhere in Moravia have the Communists shown such a shameful disregard for the architectural and aesthetic integrity of a town than they have in Jihlava. The Communist town council (apparently at the urging of one man) gave the go-ahead for the building of a coal-black, square-shaped department store right in the center of Jihlava's gorgeous town square, **Masarykovo náměstí** – a plaza that ranks as one of the largest in Central Europe. To add insult to misery, a group of medieval houses were torn down to make way for this blight.

Again, there's not a whole to see in Jihlava, which is why you should seriously consider making the excursion to **Žďar nad Sázavou**, where you'll find two of the finest Baroque creations in the Czech lands – the **Cistercian Monastery** and the **Church of St. John of Nepomuk**.

ORIENTATION

Jihlava is 84 kilometers (52 miles) northwest of Brno and 124 kilometers (77 miles) southeast of Prague, on the border of Bohemia and Moravia in the **Bohemia-Moravian Highlands** (Českomoravská vysočina).

ARRIVALS & DEPARTURES

By Bus

Running nearly every hour, buses from Prague (departing Florenc station) cost about 90 Kč and take an hour and a half. Buses from Brno also run nearly every hour, costing no more than 60 Kč and taking about 45 minutes. From the bus station, the old town is a five minute walk up Dvořákova.

By Car

Jihlava is six or so kilometers off E50/65 on E59. Parking is scattered throughout the city, so just look for the blue "P" sign.

By Train

Jihlava takes about an hour from Brno (50 Kč) and two hours from Prague (85 Kč, departing Hlavní nádraží). As many as ten trains run daily from both these cities. From the main train station, hop on trolley bus A for the two kilometer ride to the center.

GETTING AROUND TOWN

The only form of public transportation here are buses, which you'll probably never need to take unless you arrive in Jihlava by train. Taxis are easy enough to hail from the street or order from any hotel.

WHERE TO STAY/WHERE TO EAT

HOTEL ZLATÁ HVĚZDA, *Masarykovo náměstí 32, 586 01 Jihlava. Tel. 066/294 21, Fax 066/294 96. Rates for single/double: 900/1,160 Kč. Credit cards: AE, MC. 15 rooms. Restaurant.*

Things look promising from the outside of this 13th-century building with a sgraffitoed facade. But inside you can't help but feel a slight pang of disappointment, despite the pretty vaulted ceilings in the lobby and in the below-par restaurant. The glum hallways, spartan rooms, and cheap furniture indicate that the hotel has little to lavish on its guests.

HOTEL GUSTAV MAHLER, *Křížová 4, 586 01 Jihlava. Tel. 066/273 71, Fax 066/273 77. Rates for single/double: 1,290/1,540 Kč. Credit cards: AE, DC, MC, V. 24 rooms. Restaurant.*

This former monastery named after the Jewish composer who spent his childhood in Jihlava is pretty generic-looking inside and out. Though in dire need of some updating, rooms are comfortable enough and come with television and telephone. The restaurant serving Czech standards is nothing to brag about, but is one of the finer places in town.

GRANDHOTEL, *Husova 1, 587 52 Jihlava. Tel. 066/235 41, Fax 066/295 38. Rates for single/double: 890/1,290-2,000 Kč. Credit cards: AE, DC, MC, V. 31 rooms. Restaurant.*

Housed in an impressive Art Nouveau building, the stately Grandhotel offers functional rooms in dire need of some better decor. Like all the hotels in Jihlava, the Grandhotel caters to business people, as there are few people who ever come to Jihlava just to soak in the sights. Ask for one of the sunny corner rooms, affording a 90-degree view from the building's turret. Their restaurant serves a standard Czech fare of fried meats, potatoes, and dumplings.

SEEING THE SIGHTS

In spite of the atrocious pink elephant plopped down in the middle of **Masarykovo náměstí** (Masaryk Square), it's not too hard to appreciate the beauty and expanse of the town's main square, enclosed by a score of colorful Renaissance and Baroque houses and enriched by a couple of fountains. Step inside the **Church of St. Ignatius** (Kostel sv. Ignáce) for a look at the false perspectives on the church's frescoed ceiling and altar.

At the top of the square, *at number 58*, the **Highlands Museum** (Muzeum Vysočiny) has an exhibit of natural history and local folk arts and crafts, displayed in a number of rooms with vaulted, diamond-shaped ceilings. Around the corner *at Komenského 10,* the **Regional Highland Gallery** (Oblastní galérie Vysočiny) also boasts some fine Gothic spaces where you can view local contemporary art.

The museum and the gallery are both open Tuesday through Sunday from 9 a.m. to 5 p.m.

390 CZECH & SLOVAK REPUBLICS GUIDE

EXCURSIONS & DAY TRIPS

Žďar nad Sázavou

Tourists aren't exactly flocking to **Žďar nad Sázavou**, a bleak industrial town 30 kilometers (18 miles) northeast of Jihlava at the highest point in the Bohemia-Moravian Highlands. But there are two very good reasons to make a jaunt here: the **Cistercian Monastery** (Klášter Cisteriáků) and **Church of St. John of Nepomuk** (Kostel sv. Jana Nepomuckého) – two structures designed and built by one of the most celebrated architects of the Baroque era, Giovanni Santini. In 1702, Santini went to work on the monastery, building its **Church of the Virgin Mary** (Kostel Panny Marie) – a good example of Santini's signature style, in which he manages to marry the Gothic with Baroque.

In the stables of the former monastery complex is a small museum introducing you to Santini and his work in the Czech lands, as well as an exhibit on the history of book making. The monastery is a three-kilometer (1.8-mile) walk north of the train and bus stations. Local buses run about every hour from the adjoining stations to the monastery.

A bit closer to town is the Church of St. John of Nepomuk, atop the hill called Green Mountain (Zelená Hora). Shaped like a five-pointed star, this cemetery church has a bulbous dome topped by a single, slender spire. The church's star-shape is in keeping with the legend of St. John of Nepomuk, who had his tongue cut out in 1393 for not revealing a secret divulged to him by the queen. He was thrown off the Charles Bridge in Prague, and, as he sank, five stars were said to have appeared above his head, hence the church's shape and the hundreds of statues across Central Europe in which St. John's head is haloed with stars.

Allusions to the legend abound inside the church, where the pulpit's gilded relief illustrates St. John getting hoisted off the bridge by King Václav IV's soldiers. The church's murals get downright surreal (a la Salvador Dali). They show tongues suspended in celestial realms amidst clusters of stars. This is definitely one of the most unique churches you'll find in Czech Republic. (Follow signs to the church from the monastery.)

Žďar is on the Prague-Brno railway line, which makes it a good stopover if you're travelling by train between the two cities. From Jihlava, bus works best, with five or six buses departing daily (fewer on the weekends). The ride takes about an hour and costs around 40 Kč.

PRACTICAL INFORMATION

- **Česká Spořitelna,** *corner of Masarykovo náměstí and Křížová.* Bank where you can change money.
- **Post Office,** *corner of Masarykovo náměstí and Komenského.*
- **S.T.A.N.D.A. Tour Operator,** *Kosmákova 1, 586 01 Jihlava. Tel. & Fax 066/*

731 0700. A very helpful place arranging tours and providing information on the entire Jihlavsko region. English is spoken here.

Telč

If I were to choose the three best destinations in the Czech Republic, **Telč** would firmly sit alongside Prague and Česky Krumlov. Once you step into the town's arcaded main square, you'll have a hard time disagreeing, and a hard time leaving. The square, outlined with a bevy of gabled Renaissance houses, is so perfectly preserved that you almost have to doubt its authenticity and assume it's a movie set. The town **chateau** sits at the top of the triangular-shaped square and contributes its own Renaissance finesse to the picture-perfect old town.

The town dates back to the 14th century, when a regional marketplace was established here. But real prosperity and growth came when King George of Poděbrady granted Telč the privilege to sell salt, a right bestowed on few towns at that time. The **Lords of Hradec**, a branch of the all-powerful Vítkovec family who controlled much of South Bohemia at that time, built a castle here (later transformed into a chateau) and ruled over the town until their extinction in 1604.

After a fire wiped out all its Gothic buildings in 1503, Telč started anew, rebuilding the town into the Renaissance showpiece you see today. After visiting Telč, you'll understand why UNESCO added the town to the World Heritage list in 1992.

ORIENTATION

Telč sits in the southwest corner of Moravia in the **Bohemia-Moravian Highlands**, 156 kilometers (97 miles) southeast of Prague and 100 kilometers (62 miles) west of Brno. The tiny historic center, which pretty much consists of one oblong-shaped square, is nearly surrounded by two ponds, **Ulický** to the west and **Štepnický** to the east.

ARRIVALS & DEPARTURES

By Bus

From Prague to Telč, buses depart Florenc station three or four times a day for the three hour trip. Tickets cost about 120 Kč. If you can't find a bus going directly there, then buy a ticket to Jihlava and make one of the easy connections to Telč. Several direct buses run daily between Brno and Telč, taking roughly 90 minutes and costing about 50 Kč. The bus station is a five minute walk east of the town center.

By Car

From Prague, take E50/65 to E59. The roads are good all the way.

From Brno, head northwest out of town on E50/65, exit at Rosic, and then veer west all the way to Telč on highway 23. Parking should be no problem in or around Telč's main square.

By Train
Train doesn't work all that well unless you're coming from or going to somewhere in the vicinity, such as Dačice or Slavonice. The train station is a five minute walk southeast of the main square.

GETTING AROUND TOWN
You won't want to go any other way than by foot in this tiny town; all the sights and hotels are concentrated in or around the main square.

WHERE TO STAY
HOTEL NA HRÁZI, *Na Hrázi 78, 588 56 Telč. Tel. 066/721 3150, Fax 066/721 3151. Rates for single/double: 1,100/1,560-1,760 Kč. Credit cards: AE, DC, MC, V. 13 rooms. Restaurant.*

This brand new hotel built on top of a dam in between two ponds offers stylish rooms replete with direct-dial telephones, satellite television, and room service. Ask for a room in the front of the building, providing a view of St. James' spires rising above Ulický Pond. The restaurant dishes out a lot of interesting international dishes and the basement pub pours an excellent beer. The hotel is two minutes from the main square.

HOTEL TELČ, *Na Můstku 37, 588 56 Telč. Tel. 066/962 109, Fax 066/ 968 87. Rates for singles/doubles: 900-1,190/1,150-1,490 Kč. Credit cards: AE, V, DC, MC. 10 rooms. No restaurant.*

The first thing that catches your eye at the wonderful Hotel Telč is the hand-carved reception desk and the mural of Telč's main square. If that weren't enough, ceramic sculptures of mutant fish adorn the walls of the hotel. The sunny, smartly decorated rooms sport up-to-date furniture, satellite television, and direct-dial telephones.

HOTEL CELERIN, *náměstí Zachariáše z Hradce I/43, 588 56 Telč. Tel. 066/721 3580, Fax 066/721 3581. Rates for single/double: 950-1,600/1,200-1,800 Kč. Credit cards: AE, DC, MC, V. 12 rooms. No restaurant, but breakfast is included.*

Wedged in the corner of the main square, the bright yellow Hotel Celerin could use a bit more imagination in each of the individually decorated rooms. But no matter the decor, you can't go wrong with a room that has a view of náměstí Zachariáše z Hradce, which comes as the hotel's biggest advantage over the two other hotels listed above. The hotel can arrange a number of activities, including horseback rides, horse-drawn wagon rides, fishing, and even airplane rides.

HOTEL ČERNÝ OREL, *náměstí Zachariáše z Hradce 7, 588 56 Telč. Tel. & Fax 066/962 220. Rates for single/double: 800/1,000 Kč. Credit cards: AE, DC, MC, V. 30 rooms. Restaurant.*

Installed in the biggest building on the main square, Černý Orel comes as a big disappointment after admiring its battlement facade. I don't know if it's the ugly yellow wallpaper or the cheap red carpet that gives this place a depressing feel, but something certainly does. It is affordable however, and you do get what you pay for. Unfortunately, the rooms that face the square don't come with private baths, but they are cheaper as a result.

WHERE TO EAT

HOTEL NA HRÁZI, *Na Hrázi 78. Tel. 066/721 3150. 100-250 Kč. Credit cards: AE, DC, MC, V.*

This is the best restaurant in town (which isn't saying much), offering a huge menu of South Moravian and international dishes presented in a subdued, candle-lit atmosphere. Go with the pork chop smothered in a mushroom wine sauce. Snappy service and good beer to boot.

U ZACHARIÁŠE, *náměstí Zachariáše z Hradce 33. Tel. 066/962 672. 70-200 Kč. No credit cards.*

The menu here features an uninspiring host of Czech standards, such as pork or veal schnitzel, served in a smoky, pub-like atmosphere. You would be better off to eat lunch here and save dinner for another restaurant. You'll definitely want to stop here for at least a beer when the restaurant sets up tables out on the square. This is one of only two restaurants on the square, so expect a crowd.

HOTEL ČERNÝ OREL, *náměstí Zachariáše z Hradce 7. Tel. & Fax 066/ 962 220. 120-200 Kč. Credit cards: AE, DC, MC, V.*

Like the monotonously plain dining room, the menu here could use a good dose of creativity. Hopefully, the weather will allow you to sit outside on the square, where the restaurant has patio seating.

SEEING THE SIGHTS

Now that I've touted Telč as on heaven on earth, I have to admit that there isn't a whole lot to keep you occupied here, due to the small size of the town. But you can easily wile away a delightful hour just wandering around the arcades of **náměstí Zachariáše z Hradce** (Zacharias of Hradec Square) and perusing the shops and galleries there. All of the winsome, pastel-painted houses on the square sport individually designed gables, cutting an alluring figure on the town skyline.

Rising above it all in the northern corner of the square, the towers of **St. James Church** (Kostel sv. Jakuba) and the **Holy Name of Jesus Church** (Kostel Jména Ježíšova) lend punctuation to the breathtaking plaza. St. James was founded when the town was conceived in the 14th century, but it received a good beating at the hands of the Hussites. Right next to St. James, the Holy Name of Jesus arose in 1667 as part of the adjoining Jesuit College and was designed after Il Gesu in Rome.

After you've made your rounds of náměstí Zachariáše z Hradce, see when the next tour of the **Telč Chateau** begins. (Tours run about every hour in Czech and German only. If you don't understand either of these languages, you'll have to settle for a booklet sold at the ticket office.) Credit for the handsome chateau lies mainly with Zacharias of Hradec. Inspired by his trip to Genoa in the 1540s, he hired Italian architects Antonio Vlach and Baldassare Maggi to transform his fire-damaged Gothic castle into the finest Renaissance chateau in Moravia.

The most astounding aspect of the chateau is definitely its ceilings. Floral designs, faces, and animals decorate the star-shaped ceiling of the chateau armory. And on the Golden Hall's ceiling, 30 gilded octagonal panels show figures from Greek mythology. Another fantastic part of the tour is the Knights Hall's trompe l'oeil floor, made of artificial marble and appearing as though you are walking along attic beams. Also take note of the gorgeous frescoes on the treasury's walls.

When the tour is over, be sure to stroll around the manicured garden, where you'll find the entrance to the **Jan Zrzavý Gallery**, named for the famous 20th century Czech artist whose work is on exhibit here. Also be sure to check out the **Chapel of All Saints** and its stucco vaulted ceiling. The chapel's ornate wrought-iron railing, topped with four bears holding family crests, is something to marvel at as well.

The chateau is open Tuesday through Sunday, May through August, from 8 a.m. to noon and from 1 to 5 p.m. In April, September, and October it's open from 9 a.m. to noon and from 1 to 4 p.m.

You wouldn't know if you entered the old town from the south, but just outside the main square are **two ponds**, Štepnický to the east and Ulický to the west, separated by a large park just behind the chateau. A foot path follows the shore of Štepnický, leading to the south end of the square. But first take a stroll around the park for some impressive perspectives of the chateau and the two adjacent churches. You can access Štepnický and the park via Small Gate (Malá brana), located at the end of a narrow lane leading out of the northeast corner of the square.

NIGHTLIFE & ENTERTAINMENT

Unfortunately, Telč turns into dullsville after the sun goes down. There are no discos and no theaters to speak of. But if you want to throw back a Gambrinus beer or two with the locals, the place to do it is at the basement hospoda in **Hotel Na Hrázi** (see *Where to Stay*).

SPORTS & RECREATION

Located at the southern end of town, **Staroměstký Pond** is a good place to doff the togs and take a dip.

EXCURSIONS & DAY TRIPS

Slavonice

About every hour or so, a slow train departs Telč for **Slavonice**, another tiny Renaissance town that unfortunately hasn't been as well preserved as Telč, but remains an intriguing place nonetheless. About a kilometer from the Austrian border, Slavonice fell into decay during the Cold War, when most of the town's inhabitants were border guards posted along this section of the Iron Curtain. But the town is making a comeback, and people are once again recognizing Slavonice for the small gem that it is.

If you have a penchant for sgraffito, then you'll definitely have a fine time in Slavonice's old town. Scenes from Greek mythology, the Bible, and even the Apocalypse find a place on scores of the old town facades. Though a good number of the buildings have been restored, there's still a run-down look about Slavonice that is actually quite compelling. The uneven lanes, crumbling walls, and chipped buildings evoke a poetic authenticity that sometimes gets lost in the restoration of towns.

If you're staying in Telč, then I strongly recommend going by train, even if you have your own wheels. The slow train takes you through some beautiful woods and past idyllic countryside littered with tiny villages – all of which you'll enjoy much more chugging along in a train than zooming past in a car. It takes about an hour and costs no more than 40 Kč. By car, head due south through Dačice and then follow the signs.

PRACTICAL INFORMATION

• **Agrobanka**, *náměstí Zachriáše z Hradce 10*. A bank where you can change money.
• **Městske Informační Středisko**, *náměstí Zachariáše z Hradce 10, 588 56 Telč. Tel. 066/962 233*. Information office selling maps and guides and arranging private accommodations. They can also help with bus and train schedules.
• **Post Office**, *Staňkova 294*.

Jaroměřice nad Rokytnou

If you're traveling by car between Telč and Znojmo or Jihlava and Znojmo, you should make the slight detour to the massive **chateau** at **Jaroměřice nad Rokytnou**, just off E59 about 45 kilometers (28 miles) southeast of Jihlava and 30 kilometers (19 miles) northwest of Znojmo.

The red-and-cream striped chateau counts as one of the largest Baroque structures in Europe, made all the more impressive by a wealth of wildly extravagant rooms and halls. The man behind this bombastic construction was Johann Adam von Questenberg, who, like a lot of the super-rich at that time, rose to power with the fall of the Protestant Czech Estates during the Counter Reformation. The list of artists and architects involved with the Baroque reconstruction of the chateau in the 17th and 18th centuries reads like an Italian school roster. D'Angeli, Alfieri, Canoni, Caspar, Gionimo, and Seglioni among other Italians lent a hand, as did two stars from Vienna, Jakob Prandtauer and Johann Lukas von Hildebrandt.

The hour-long tour of the chateau takes you through several exquisite Rococo halls. Hall of the Forefathers (Sál předků) strikes a suitably noble chord with its muscular wood ceiling, while the Dance Hall (táneční sál) gets downright lavish with all its stucco designs. The splashy chateau theater, located in the English and French-style gardens, is notable for being the venue for the first Czech opera, František Míča's *The Origin of Jaroměřice* (*O původu Jaroměřic*). No less inspiring is the chateau chapel, lined with gilded, earth-tone pilasters supporting a dome filled with heavenly blue frescoes. *Group tours run May through September, Tuesday through Sunday from 8 a.m. to noon and from 1 to 5 p.m. In April and October the chateau is open same hours, but weekends only.*

If you don't have a car, the best way of getting to the tiny town of Jaroměřice nad Rokytnou is by bus from Znojmo, Jihlava, or Brno, with several daily departures from all three cities. Train is a hassle, as the closest station is two kilometers away in the village of Popovice.

WHERE TO STAY/WHERE TO EAT

HOTEL OPERA, *č.p. 996, 657 51 Jaroměřice nad Rokytnou. Tel. & Fax 0617/440 230. Rates for single/double: 445/700-900 Kč. Credit cards: AE, MC, V. 36 rooms. Restaurant.*

The cinderblock Hotel Opera is unfortunately your only choice of lodgings in this tiny town. The characterless rooms come with television, telephone, and private baths. One thing going for this hotel is its extremely friendly receptionists. The hotel has a pub, wine bar, and restaurant serving basic Czech food. If need be, you can change money here.

Znojmo

First, an anecdote. Having just arrived in **Znojmo** after an early morning train ride, I stopped into what looked like a decent place to have an espresso and a light breakfast before touring the town. Much to my chagrin, I watched several Austrian tourists, who had arrived after me, get served before I even had a chance to look at the menu. The service went from bad to worse. It took a full 30 minutes before I got my espresso, and another 20 minutes until the waitress finally got around to my food. Leaving this place (it's called Café U Michala, by the way, so you know which place to avoid), my blood was boiling and I was in no mood to enjoy my stay in Znojmo.

But once I walked around some more and chatted with a few of the locals, Znojmo began to grow on me. By mid-afternoon I had completely forgotten the escapade at the café. In the end, Znojmo won me over, despite my miserable introduction to it. Give it some time, and I think it will win you over, too.

Perched on a hillside and commanding a view of the Dyje River, Znojmo has a lot of history, starting as a fortification in the 7th century. As a border town, Znojmo was always close to the hearts of the Czech kings, if only for its strategic importance. So, in 1226, **King Přemysl Otakar I** named Znojmo a royal town, long before Brno, Olomouc, or any other town in Moravia was elevated to such a status. Being a royal town had its perks, and Znojmo benefitted from them, gaining a lot of trading and commerce advantages it otherwise wouldn't have had.

In serious need of across-the-board restoration, Znojmo's unkempt old town doesn't immediately impress like some others in Moravia, but there are some sights, such as the Gothic **Town Hall Tower** and the Romanesque **St. Catherine Rotunda**, that make a visit to Znojmo worth the effort. Staying the night is only worth it if you can book a room in one of the two pensions listed below. Otherwise, set out for Telč or Mikulov, where you'll find much better accommodations.

Finally, a note on the local snacks. The specialty in Znojmo is pickled gherkins – *kyselá okurka* – something you'll find on just about any menu in town. Also big in Znojmo is fried dough, or *langoš*, a Hungarian specialty sold at scores of stands around the city. The taste depends on the topping, which can run from jam (not bad) to garlic (interesting) to ketchup (absolutely disgusting).

ORIENTATION

Znojmo lies in the **Dyje Valley** along the **South Moravian borderlands** 65 kilometers (40 miles) southwest of Brno and 199 kilometers (123 miles) southeast of Prague.

ARRIVALS & DEPARTURES

By Bus

From Prague, bus is best, departing Florenc station two or three times daily. The ride takes three to four hours and costs about 140 Kč.

Make a connection in Jihlava if you can't get a bus directly there. Seven or so buses run daily between Brno and Znojmo, taking about two hours and costing about 70 Kč. The bus station, adjacent to the train station, is a 15 minute walk southeast of the old town at the bottom of a hill.

By Car
From Brno, take E461 to highway 54. From Prague take E50/65 to E59. Parking in Znojmo can be a problem. A safe bet is the parking lot at náměstí Republiky.

By Train
There are eight or so direct trains running daily between Brno and Znojmo. The trip takes two hours and costs about 120 Kč. The train station, located on Dr. Milady Horákové street, is about a 15 minute walk southeast of the old town at the bottom of the hill.

GETTING AROUND TOWN
Bus is the only form of public transportation in Znojmo, but you should have no need for it, as the old town is fairly manageable on foot. You can catch a cab easily enough on the street.

WHERE TO STAY/WHERE TO EAT
RESTAURANT A PENSION HAVELKA, *náměstí Mikulašské 3, 669 02 Znojmo. Tel. & Fax 0624/220 138. Rate for double only: 800 Kč. No credit cards. 2 rooms. Restaurant.*

Completely decked out in wood and decorated with fantastic folk paintings of saints, the restaurant and the two pension rooms hint of an old English inn. The friendly service makes you feel right at home, a feeling you already get from the cozy fireplace, by which you can eat a fine Moravian meal from the hearty menu. Indeed, the place gives you the impression of being in a small village or in the middle of the woods, even it is located at the side of St. Nicholas Church in the middle of Znojmo. It's a pity there are only two rooms, since they are the nicest ones in town. Be sure to book well in advance for this small gem.

HOTEL KÁRNIK, *Zelenářská 25, 669 02 Znojmo. Tel. & Fax 0624/226 826. Rates for single/double: 800/1,200 Kč. No credit cards. 9 rooms. Restaurant.*

This fairly new hotel in the center of town has small, characterless rooms that do the job of at least putting a roof over your head. Serving basic Czech cuisine, the hotel restaurant isn't a bad place to eat lunch.

PENSION KIM-EX, *Vinohrady 26, 669 02 Znojmo. Tel. & Fax 0624/222 580. Rates for single/double: 700/900 Kč. No credit cards. 3 rooms. No restaurant.*

Despite the peculiar name, this small pension is another good alternative to the grim Communist-era hotels in the city. Comfortable rooms come with private baths and some personality. **HOTEL DRUŽBA**, *Pražská 100, Znojmo 669 02. Tel. 0624/756 21, no fax. Rates for single/double: 700/900 Kč. Credit cards: MC, V. Restaurant.* Only if you must, book a room at this gloomy hotel north of the city center. The monotonously plain rooms are a bit depressing, and certainly not worth their rates.

SEEING THE SIGHTS

If you've just parked the car at náměstí Republiky or arrived by train or bus, hike up the hill along Videňská třída to náměstí TG Masaryka, the run-down main square you'll quickly want to escape, but not until you've taken a stroll through the **House of Art** (Dům Umění). The museum has temporary exhibitions of contemporary Czech art, as well as some interesting coins from the First Republic. A gregarious older gentleman happy to practice his English takes you through the exhibit. *Open daily from 9 a.m. to 5 p.m.*

Up the hill from the square on Obroková, you can't help but notice the Gothic **Town Hall Tower** (Radniční věž). With its eight needle-thin spires rising up in support of the pyramid-shaped pinnacle, the tower cuts a bold figure on the skyline, made all the more bolder when you consider that a bomb ricocheted off it during World War II and blew up the town hall. The view from the top takes in the entire old town and, on clear days, you supposedly can see all the way to the Austrian Alps. The tower is also a good place just to gain your bearings on the town. *Open daily from 8:30 a.m. to 4:30 p.m. during the high season and from 9 a.m. to 3:30 p.m. during the low season.*

Around the corner from the tower and off Kramářská in the old Chicken Market (*Slepičí trh*) is the entrance to the **catacombs** (*podzemí*). The underground cellars were once part of a 27-kilometer labyrinth of linked tunnels, used since the 14th century for defensive purposes and for storing wine. Tours of the catacombs, which go only with seven or more people, are open the same hours as the tower.

Back on Obroková, go farther up the hill and hang a quick left on a side street to Zelenářská and another left on Malá Mikulášská, placing you in front of the **Church of St. Nicholas** (Kostel sv Mikuláše). Though nothing to get excited about when standing on the outside, this Romanesque-turned-Gothic church boasts an expansive three-nave interior and an intriguing pulpit that's shaped like a globe. To the side of St. Nicholas, built into the old town wall and designed like a Romanesque rotunda, is the tiny Russian Orthodox **St. Wenceslas Chapel** (Kaple sv

Václava), which isn't as dramatic as the adjacent view of the Dyje River gorge and the tree-studded slopes rising from it. Same thing can be said about the **Znojmo Castle**, accessed by heading straight up the hill from St. Nicholas to the end of Přemyslovců street and then by following a foot path along the hillside. In true Czech fashion, many of the structures that once surrounded the castle were torn down in the 19th century to make way for a brewery. Consequently, there's not a whole to get excited about here, except for the **St. Catherine Rotunda** (Rotunda sv Kateřiny).

One of the republic's few remaining Romanesque structures, the rotunda is graced with frescoes dating back to the 12th century and illustrating the genealogy of the Přemysls, rulers of Bohemia and Moravia. If you can fathom it, the rotunda once served as a pig sty and later as a beer and dance hall. The rotunda was saved late in the mid-18th century when a group of concerned citizens raised holy hell over the structure's desecration. *The castle and the rotunda are open Tuesday through Sunday from 9 a.m. to 4 p.m..*

Near the entrance to the castle, *at Přemyslovců 6*, is the **South Moravian Museum** (Jihomoravské muzeum), housed in the former Minorite Monastery. *Open daily from 9 a.m. to 4 p.m.*, the museum has geological and archaeological exhibits that aren't all that exciting.

NIGHTLIFE & ENTERTAINMENT

There's not much happening in Znojmo, except for the occasional opera at the neo-Baroque **South Moravian Theater** (Jihomoravské divadlo) *at náměstí Republiky* and the even more occasional concert in the Church of St. Nicholas.

For a drink, try the **Bonsai Bar** *at the corner of Kramáská and Slepičí trh*.

EXCURSIONS & DAY TRIPS
Vranov nad Dyjí

Looking almost too stylish to be a castle, **Vranov nad Dyjí** rises majestically from its cliff-top position above the Dyje River. A former Gothic garrison protecting the Moravian border, Vranov was transformed into a palatial Baroque residence at the hands of Viennese architect J.B. Fisher von Erlach in the 17th and 18th centuries. Erlach's crowning achievement, shared with artist Johann Michael Rottmayr, is the **Hall of the Ancestors** (Sál předků) and its heavenly dome decorated with ethereal frescoes depicting the accomplishments of the Althans, the family who just so happened to commission the work. The other Baroque rooms, though not as impressive, give you a taste of when Maria Anna Pignatelli, a Spanish princess in the 18th century, lived here. *The castle is*

open Tuesday through Saturday from 9 a.m. to noon and 1 to 6 p.m. in July and
August; to 5 p.m. in May, June, and September; and to 4 p.m. on weekends only
in April and October.

The Vranov dam (*přehrada*), a 20 minute walk from town, is a good
place to take a dip and soak in the sun.

Several daily buses run directly Znojmo to Vranov, located 20
kilometers (12 miles) west of Znojmo. By car, head north out of Znojmo
on E59 and then follow signs west along backroads.

PRACTICAL INFORMATION

• **Komerční banka**, *náměstí Svobody 18*. Exchanges money.
• **Informační Středisko**, *náměstí T.G. Masaryk 22. Tel. 0624/224 369*. Books
private accommodations, arranges tours, and provides a wealth of
information on Znojmo.
• **Post Office**, *Horní náměstí 13*.

Mikulov

In the heart of the wine-producing region of Pálava, **Mikulov** hugs
the slopes of the **Pavlovské hills**, looking out across the plains into
Austria. With its crooked and gnarled lanes and a castle rising above it
all, this ancient Moravian border post, dating back to the 9th century,
offers a healthy dose of enchantment.

Mikulov has a particularly interesting history, thanks mainly to the
sizable Jewish and Anabaptist populations that mixed here early on in
the town's history. Jews arrived in the 14th century, and from the 16th
through 19th centuries they made up forty percent of Mikulov's population. As many as twelve synagogues once stood in the tiny village, as did
a Talmudic school, which counted among its students Rabbi of Prague
David Oppenheimer and Golem-creator **Rabbi Loew**.

Appearing a century after the Jews, the Anabaptists came directly
from their home in Switzerland, led by **Balthasar Hubmaier**, who was
later burned at the stake in Vienna as a heretic. Mikulov became the
center of Anabaptist learning, and eventually the site of its major schism.
Local nobility endured their "dangerous" ideas because they profited
from the Anabaptist trades of ceramics and medicines. But they expelled
them anyway in 1622 after years of pressure from the Hapsburg rulers.

Excluding two synagogues and an enormous cemetery, not much
remains of the Jewish legacy, and nothing remains of the Anabaptist one.
But Mikulov is well worth a visit anyway, and good place to bed down
for a night, offering two good hotel choices. The town also makes a good
base for exploring the Pálava region, which includes the next two
featured destinations, **Valtice** and **Lednice**.

ORIENTATION

Located 255 kilometers (158 miles) southeast of Prague and 55 kilometers (34 miles) south of Brno, Mikulov sits in the middle of the famous wine-producing region of **Pálava**, which is a designated UNESCO biosphere reservation.

ARRIVALS & DEPARTURES

By Bus

Bus works best from Brno, taking about an hour and costing 45 Kč. The bus station is next to the train station on Nádražní street, a 15 minute walk southwest of the town center

By Car

From Brno, take E461 all the way there. From Prague the fastest way is E50/65 to E461 via Brno. Parking is no problem around the small town.

By Train

From Prague, it's easiest is to hop on a train at either Nádraží Holešovice or Hlavní nádraží to Břeclav, about 4 hours away.

From Břeclav, a train runs every hour to Mikulov, less than 30 minutes away. When you buy your ticket (around 140 Kč) in Prague, be sure it's for Mikulov na Moravě, and not the Mikulov in Bohemia. From Znojmo, trains depart nearly every hour for the hour-long trip that costs 27 Kč. The train station in Mikulov is on the southwest side of town along Nádražní street – a ten minute walk from the center.

GETTING AROUND TOWN

Except for taxis, the only way to get around the small town of Mikulov is by foot. But some of the restaurants listed below are quite a ways from the center. You can order a taxi by calling *2426 or 2466*.

WHERE TO STAY

HOTEL ROHATÝ KROKODÝL, *Husova 8, 692 00 Mikulov. Tel. 0625/2692, Fax 0625/3695. Rates for single & double: 1,090-1,450 Kč. Credit cards: V. 13 rooms. Restaurant.*

The name of the hotel, meaning Hotel Horned Crocodile, gives you some indication of this quirky place located in the old Jewish ghetto. Avant-garde art hangs in the hotel gallery and decorate the gorgeous, wood-floored rooms. Ask for the room with the huge terrace, affording a great view of the Austrian plains. All the rooms are fully modernized, outfitted with handsome new furniture, direct-dial phones, and satellite television.

The restaurant serves excellent Moravian cuisine, dished out in huge portions and spiced up with plenty of paprika. Keep your eye out for the house specialty, roast horned crocodile. Also note the booths in the restaurant, which look like waves rolling across the wall. And don't miss the hotel mascot, the horned crocodile, hanging on the wall in the billiards room.

HOTEL RÉVA, *Česká 2, 692 01 Mikulov. Tel. 0625/3901, Fax 0625/2332. Rates for single/double: 700/1,200 Kč. Credit cards: MC. 14 rooms. Restaurant.*

Opened in autumn of 1995, this brand new hotel offers simple but cozy rooms just around the corner from the main square. As you would expect from a new hotel, Réva needs some time to work out the kinks, but the staff is more than willing to take care of its guests. Its restaurant serves fairly standard Czech fare in an upbeat environment that draws a lot of locals.

PENSION PRIMA, *Piaristů 8, 692 01 Mikulov. Tel. 0625/3793, Fax 0625/2383. Rates for single/double: 600/1,200 Kč. Credit cards: MC, V. 10 rooms. No restaurant.*

Located in a back lot down the street from the main square, this one-level pension looks a bit like an American motel. All the rooms are suitably comfortable, and come with private baths. But I would only book a room here if the two hotels in town are filled.

WHERE TO EAT

DIONYSOS, *Náměstí 1. Tel. 0625/31 32. 100-200 Kč. No credit cards.*

Occupying the ground floor of the historic town hall, Dionysos draws a lot of tourists because of its central location. But the food they bill as "wonderful home cooking" is rather lacking in imagination.

U NÁS DOMA, *1. května 577. Tel. 0625/2338. 100-250 Kč. No credit cards.*

You can bet that the hearty cuisine served here comes as close to real Moravian home cooking as you are going get in a restaurant, hence the name of this restaurant which means "at our home." Paprika-laced pork, mushroom-smothered game dishes, and a good variety of local wines are all part of the package. The service is quite attentive, making you feel... well, at home. The 15 minute walk from the center to the restaurant at the end of 1. května will help you work up an appetite for the generous portions.

RESTAURANT LÍPA, *Dukelská 32. Tel. 0625/2547. 120-250 Kč. No credit cards.*

Owner Anna Lípová prides herself on providing a fresh cabbage salad all year round. In a meat and potatoes country such as this one, that comes as a welcome surprise. Paní Lípová's concern for good ingredients carries over into the main course, where you'll find tender meats and tasty fresh potatoes. The summer terrace is a fine place to sip a glass of wine and enjoy the view of the surrounding hills.

SEEING THE SIGHTS

Start in the center of town at what's simply called **Náměstí**, or Square, where the focus is on a **plague column** built in 1732 and the **Pomona fountain** sculpted in 1680. In the southeast corner of the skinny L-shaped square, looking a tad out of place with its lofty columns and towers, is the **Dietrichstein Crypt** (Dietrichštejnská hrobka), formerly St. Anne's Church (Kostel sv. Anna). The ardently Catholic Dietrichstein family, who are most responsible for the development of the town, transformed the church into a mausoleum after a fire destroyed all but the presbytery and towers in the 18th century.

Poking up above the square to the north is a Renaissance clock tower, belonging to the **Church of St. Wenceslas** (Kostel sv Václava). Rebuilt in the 15th century after the Hussites destroyed the structure along with most of the town, the small airy church backed up against the castle walls has a vaulted ceiling with pretty Baroque stucco work.

Beckoning you all this time while walking around Náměstí is the **castle**, a steep, winding walk up the hill from the main square. Compared to other castles around the republic, Mikulov's is a pretty ho-hum affair, mostly because very little of the 13th-century structure is original. Before setting it ablaze during the final days of their occupation, the Nazis used the castle to horde works of art that they had looted from chateaux, castles, and churches across Central Europe.

The castle was rebuilt after the war and is now a regional museum, with exhibits on local history, archaeology, and geology. But the best aspects of the museum cover the folk traditions and viticulture of the Pálava region. Most amusing is the largest wine barrel in Central Europe, with a weight of 390 kilograms (862 pounds) and a capacity of 101,000 liters (26,260 US gallons). *Though not always the case, the museum is open Tuesday through Saturday, from 8 a.m. to 5 p.m. from May through September and from 9 a.m. to 4 p.m. in April and October.*

Retrace your steps back down to Náměstí, go up to Česka, and swing left around the castle to *Husova 13*, the site of one of Mikulov's two remaining synagogues, located in the old Jewish ghetto. (The other synagogue is in such a state of disrepair that it's not open to the public). Housing a museum devoted to the Jewish legacy in Mikulov, the newly restored **Dolní synagogue,** or *Altschul* (Yiddish for "Old Synagogue"), has a graceful vaulted ceiling supported in the center by four marble pillars. Photographs and drawings in the side galleries offer an intriguing look at Mikulov's Jewish ghetto and the synagogue prior to the 20th century. During the 40 years of Communism the synagogue was left to rot, which makes the successful restoration all the more impressive. *It's open daily except Monday.*

From the synagogue, go back up Husova street, take a left on Brněnská, and then make an immediate right up the hill to the entrance to the **Jewish cemetery**. Bigger than and nearly as old as the one in Prague, the cemetery was in continual use from the 15th century on up to 1939, when all Jews living in Mikulov were deported by the Nazis. Serving as a poignant reminder of Mikulov's Jewish past, the gravestones – some still firmly standing in neat rows and others lying in heaps – stretch across a sloped grove of wild plum trees. The vague, overgrown paths through the cemetery give you some idea of how infrequently people visit this place. It almost seems forgotten, which it pretty much was during Communist rule. You can't help but feel touched, and perhaps a little depressed. (Usually, the gate to the cemetery is locked, but you can get a key from the attendant at the synagogue.)

Just in case you're wondering, the strange tower standing above the cemetery at the top of Goat's Hill (Kozí vrch) is the remains of the castle's old **guard tower**, later transformed into the town's gunpowder store.

If you're feeling fit and have got a couple hours on your hands, hike to the top of the barren **Holy Hill** (Svatý kopeček), rising to the east of town opposite the castle. Not so much the Greek-style chapel as the view (especially during sunset) of Mikulov and the Austrian plains is worth the torturous climb to the top of this wind-swept, limestone hill that was supposedly once the site of pagan solstice rituals.

NIGHTLIFE & ENTERTAINMENT

You're in wine country, which means you should hunker down in one of the town's wine cellars. **Sklípek Arkáda** *at Vídeňská 37* treats you to a number of locally-produced wines straight from the cask. Depending on the day, the sklípek might be serving Welschriesling (Ryzlink vlašský), Grüner Veltliner (Veltínské zelené), or Müller Thurgau. If you're there on the right night, a Moravian folk band will have you up and dancing.

Unfortunately, most of the wine cellars in and around town are not open to the public. But the Regional Tourist Center (see *Practical Information* below) can arrange visits to some of them.

If wine and folk music ain't your thing, then try **Rock Club 1620** *at Koněvova 22*. Upstairs is a pub serving Pilsner Urquell and downstairs is a club featuring local rock acts. Movies are shown at **Kino Hvězda** *at Česká 4*.

PRACTICAL INFORMATION

• **Agrobanka, Česka spořitelna,** and **Ekoagrobanka** – *three banks located on the main square (Náměstí),* all of which change foreign currency.
• **Regional Tourist Center,** *Náměstí 32. Tel. & Fax 0625/2855.* Tourist information office for the entire Pálava region, selling all sorts of helpful maps and brochures to the area. The office also organizes sightseeing tours of Mikulov and the surrounding area, rents cottages in the Pálava countryside, and arranges evenings in private wine cellars.
• **Post Office,** *Česká 17.*

Valtice & Lednice

No other monuments in the Czech Republic offer such a grandiose testament to the former omnipotent power of the **Liechtenstein family** as do the chateaux of **Valtice** and **Lednice,** set seven kilometers apart in the thick of the wine-growing Pálava region, where limestone outcroppings, gently rolling hills, and sweeping valleys come together in a truly romantic manner. Indeed, the emphasis here is not so much on the two chateaux as it is on the 200 square kilometers (124 square miles) of landscaped grounds surrounding these two chateaux.

The largest such "designed landscape" in Central Europe and perhaps the world, the grounds are a designated UNESCO biosphere reserve, and simply a fantastic place to hike and bike. The oldest and largest collection of North American trees and plants in Europe dot the countryside, as do scores of so-called follies – neoclassic temples, manors, arches, and so on built in the 19th century. The best way of seeing the landscaped grounds is by either biking or hiking between the two chateaux.

The World Monuments Fund, a New York-based organization dedicated to the preservation of historical sites worldwide, is helping to finance the restoration of the Valtice chateau, the less grander and further deteriorated of the two chateaux. One way they raise funds for the restoration is by sponsoring an annual **summer festival** of jazz, modern dance, and Baroque music. Artists from around the world are invited to perform under the stars in the chateau courtyard or inside at various rooms sometime in mid-August. It's a great event, but one you'll want to plan well in advance for, as rooms are scarce throughout the summer in this part of the republic. *For specific dates of the festival and other information, call the chateau at Tel. 0627/944 23.*

THE LIECHTENSTEIN FAMILY HOLDINGS

For six centuries the Liechtensteins controlled a good chunk of the Czech lands, especially in South Moravia. Valtice and Lednice were only two of some 100 estates in the Czech lands belonging to the family, many of which were confiscated from the Protestant Czech Estates after their defeat at the Battle of the White Mountain in 1620. Officially, the Liechtensteins were employed as financial advisors to the Hapsburgs. Unofficially, they worked to outclass the Hapsburgs by gobbling up land and building ostentatious monuments to themselves. The party lasted until 1945, when the Communists accused the Liechtenteins of collaborating with the Nazis, stripped them of all their property in Czechoslovakia, and sent them fleeing to the principality that now bears their name.

Now that the Czech Republic is once again a democracy, the Liechtensteins want their land, castles, and chateux back – a vast amount of holdings that amount to ten times the area of present-day Liechtenstein. But the Czech restitution laws only apply to property confiscated in 1948 or after. Obviously, resolution over this matter will be tied up in court for a long time to come.

ORIENTATION

Located seven kilometers (three-and-a-half miles) south of Lednice, Valtice sits just north of the Austrian border roughly 70 kilometers (43 miles) south of Brno and 265 kilometers (164 miles) southeast of Prague.

ARRIVALS & DEPARTURES

By Bus

As many as seven buses a day run between Valtice and Lednice, taking less than 20 minutes and costing about 15 Kč. There's only one bus that runs daily from Brno to Valtice and Lednice, and that's only on working days. From Prague, forget it.

It's best, then, to go by train. The buses stop right in the center of both these towns.

By Car

From Brno, go roughly 45 kilometers south on E65, exit at Podivín, and then follow signs either to Lednice or Valtice. The trip should take no more than an hour.

From Prague, it's easiest to go via Brno.

By Train

Valtice sits on a minor rail line connecting Břeclav and Znojmo. Mikulov, a 15 minute ride from Valtice, is also on this line. But Lednice is not, which means it's impossible to travel directly between Valtice and Lednice by train.

From Prague and Brno, you'll have to make a connection in Břeclav, where separate trains run almost every hour to Valtice and Lednice. From Brno, it should take no more than two hours to reach either of these destinations. From Prague, expect to pay around 130 Kč for the four-to-five hour trip originating at either Hlavní nádraží or Nádraží Holešovice.

GETTING AROUND TOWN

The towns of Lednice and Valtice are both so small that you should have no problem getting around on foot. Of course, you could catch one of the eight or so buses that run between Valtice and Lednice each day. But you'll have a better time walking or biking between the two towns, if you have the time of course. On foot, it takes roughly three hours, much less of course by bike. Unfortunately, there are no shops that rent bicycles as of yet.

Some hotels, including Hotel Hubertus (see *Where to Stay*), rents bicycles to their guests. If you are not a guest at a hotel that rents bikes, check around anyway. Someone should come up with the bright idea sooner or later.

WHERE TO STAY/WHERE TO EAT

HOTEL HUBERTUS, *Zámek Valtice, 691 42 Valtice. Tel. 0627/945 37, Fax 0627/945 38. Rates for single/double: 850/1,020 Kč. Credit cards: AE, MC, V. 27 rooms. Restaurant.*

Carved out of a wing of the Valtice chateau, Hubertus certainly takes the cake for location. The vaulted ceilings, arcaded lobby, and the original wood beams in the restaurant are about all that remain of this wing's former glory. It's the cheap carpet, blah furniture, and general run-down look of the hotel that almost make you wish they could do something else with this piece of the architectural treasure.

Having said this, I do recommend staying here, if only for the expansive English gardens in back, of which there is a view from the hotel's rear rooms. The hotel also has a lot to offer its guests, including bicycle rentals, tennis, wine cellar visits, and guided hunting excursions. The restaurant's dining room, where you can get decent Czech food and the musky red wine produced right at the chateau, has gorgeous arched entryways and shimmering wood ceilings.

RESTAURANT ALBERO, *náměstí Svobody 12. Tel. 0627/946 15. 80-200 Kč. No credit cards.*

Located on Valtice's main square just below the chateau, Albero dishes out the best fresh fish in the region. Pleasant folk decor and always an upbeat local crowd (probably due to the excellent red Valtice wine served here) combine to make this a winner of a restaurant.

HOTEL APOLLON, *P. Bezruče 720, 691 42 Valtice. Tel. 0627/352 625, Fax 352 009. Rates for single/double: 400-880/880-2,750 Kč. Credit cards: AE, MC. 15 rooms. Restaurant.*

Opened in 1995 and set in a turn-of-the-century mansion, the hotel was formerly a hospital, but you would never know it by the outstanding renovation of the building. The exterior – with its single turret, yellow walls, and red roof – is no great shakes, but the interior and its downright sophisticated decor are a another story. Shiny wood floors, beautiful wood-carved furniture, and all the expected amenities (satellite television, direct-dial phone, and room service) make this one of the finer hotels in the region. The restaurant is strong on fresh vegetables, serving an international variety of dishes, made all the more enjoyable when eaten on the outdoor patio.

HOTEL HARLEKIN, *no street address, 691 44 Lednice. Tel. 0627/340 130, Fax 0627/340 166. Rates for single/double: 1,290/1,380 Kč. Credit cards: AE, MC. 50 rooms. Restaurant.*

With so many tourist buses parked outside the Hotel Harlekin, you can't miss this newest-looking of buildings in the tiny town of Lednice. Although nothing extravagant, the fully modernized rooms here are suitably comfortable, but a little generic. Helpful staff go out of their way to make sure guests have what they need. The restaurant offers decent Moravian specialties and live Moravian folk music.

HOTEL MARIO, *21. dubna 73, 691 44 Lednice. Tel. & Fax 0627/340 152. Rates for single/double: 1,000/1,250 Kč. Credit cards: MC, V. 10 rooms. Restaurant.*

This intimately small new hotel is your best bet for cozy lodgings in Lednice. Plush, stylish rooms come with satellite television, direct-dial telephones, and 24-hour room service. Friendly, English-speaking receptionists help you have a nice stay. The restaurant offers international courses quickly and skillfully served.

SEEING THE SIGHTS

Walking up the front steps to the forecourt of **Valtice chateau**, you can't help but feel a little overwhelmed by the perfect balance and symmetry of this Baroque chateau. The two wings have the effect of drawing you in, as does the path running in a straight line right down the middle of the forecourt to the gate, directly above which is the family crest and the clock tower. The effect is enhanced by two neoclassical statues of brawny men, placed in a spot that allows them to serve as a frame for the entire ensemble.

As the main residence of the Liechtenstein family, the Valtice chateau conjures a powerful feeling, to say the least. Credit for that feeling goes mainly to the architects Johann Fischer von Erlach and Domenico Martenelli, who turned this 12th-century castle into one of the finest Baroque chateaux in the Czech lands.

Tours of the yellow chateau, costing 30 Kč and lasting about 45 minutes, introduce you to bits and pieces of the furnishings left behind by the Liechtensteins when they fled from the approaching Soviet army in the closing days of World War II. The ornate show of wealth, though seriously depleted since the war, gets a bit ridiculous with the walls themselves, which were plastered using a stucco and gilt mixture containing 7.5 kilograms of gold. But the highlight of the tour comes near the end, when you catch a glimpse of the chateau chapel with its gorgeous porphyry pilasters and meticulously crafted adipose putty walls.

The view you get of the chapel, from a loge above it, is the same view the Liechtensteins would get as they sat observing mass. If mass got a little long or the sermon a little tedious, they could easily sneak out from the little compartment without anyone noticing. After a visit inside the chateau, make sure to go for a stroll around the English gardens outside. The tall trees, mangy grass, and statues popping up here and there have the makings for the most mawkish of romance stories, or at least a Thomas Hardy novel. *The Valtice chateau is open daily, except Monday, May through August from 8 a.m. to noon and from 1 to 5 p.m., and on weekends in April and October from 9 a.m. to 4 p.m. Tours cost 40 Kč. For more information, call 0627/944 23.*

If you don't have a car, then you can take a bus departing náměstí Svobody in Valtice nearly every hour for **Lednice**, taking about 15 minutes and costing 10 Kč. But if you take the bus or drive to Lednice, you'll be missing out (for the most part) on one of the most unique attractions in the republic – the landscaped gardens between the two chateaux known as **Boří forest** (*les*). The red-marked trail, unlike the arrow-straight road connecting Valtice and Lednice, winds gently and leisurely through the forest, embellished with scores of neoclassical **follies** and hundreds of varieties of trees and bushes. The walk or bike ride also may give you the opportunity to do some bird watching around the artificial lakes, where you might spot a laughing gull or heron.

So what exactly are these follies? Styled after the classical architecture in Greece, they are mostly temples and manors, with an arch, tower, or colonnade thrown in for good measure. When you walk from one chateau to the other, it becomes apparent what the Liechtensteins had in mind when they built the follies. They were meant to tickle the fancy of the Liechtensteins, who would set out on hunting trips and bask in their riches all along the way. They would perhaps have a picnic at one of the temples, take a rest at one of the colonnades, and spend the night at one of the manor houses.

The way to see most of the follies is to hike or bike the red-marked trail, beginning in Valtice at the train station. You'll wander past the former pheasantry called Belvedére Manor and then pass a series of temples named after Diana, Apollo, and the Three Graces. After about three hours on foot, you'll finally end up at **Lednice chateau**, the former summer palace of the Liechtensteins.

Like Hluboká Castle in South Bohemia, Lednice chateau prompts immediate comparisons to Windsor Castle, the flagship of the neo-Gothic movement that swept through Europe in the 1840s. The Liechtensteins took over Lednice in 1243, when it was actually a Gothic castle. The family had it rebuilt several times to suit the passing Renaissance, then Baroque, tastes of the day before settling on the present neo-Gothic bombshell on view today.

Tours of Lednice take in all the lavish interior glory of the chateau. Crystal chandeliers shimmer in rooms imbued with deep-red wall coverings and decorated with gold-inlaid Chinese cabinets. Most handsome of all, however, is the staircase, an exhaustive work with meticulous patterns hand carved into the rich wood. *The chateau is open daily, except Monday, May through August from 9 a.m. to noon and from 1 p.m. to 6 p.m., to 5 p.m. in September, on weekends in April and October from 9 a.m. to 4 p.m.*

Something else you'll want to check out at the chateau is the **greenhouse** (*skleník*), where a collection of exotic flora – such as palm trees, bougainvillea, and jasmine – thrive under a glass canopy. If you don't have the deepest interest in ornithology, nature conservation, or hunting weapons, then you should skip the **National Agricultural Museum** (Národní zemēldské muzeum), located next to the chateau museum. Much more impressive are the chateau's manicured **French gardens**, dotted with artificial lakes and containing 500 different varieties of trees and bushes from around the world. You'll have to stroll through the gardens anyway to get an up-close look at what has to be the oddest of follies at the Lednice estate – a Moorish-style **minaret**, soaring 62 meters (203 feet) above the garden.

PRACTICAL INFORMATION

You won't find any tourist offices in either Valtice or Lednice. The **Regional Tourist Center** in Mikulov (see *Practical Information* under

Mikulov above) handles most of the general business regarding tourism in the Valtice-Lednice area.

You can change money at **Hotel Apollon** in Valtice or at **Hotel Harlekin** in Lednice (see *Where to Stay* above).

Zlín

Now for something completely different – a factory town.

It may sound a little strange to recommend spending part of your Moravian travels in a city with no historic old town, no charming main square, and very few historic buildings. But there's something about **Zlín**, whether it's the city's melding of working and leisure space or its stark display of functionalist architecture, that makes this most modern of cities in the republic also one of its most fascinating.

It's impossible to speak of the history of Zlín without mentioning the name of **Tomáš Baťa**, the multi-millionaire shoe manufacturer and philanthropist who single-handedly funded and organized the development of Zlín from a tiny backwater village into a modernist metropolis. After reaping millions producing boots for the Austrian army in World War I, Baťa (pronounced "BOUGHT-ya") went to work on building his city, employing the country's most well-known planners and architects, most importantly **Jan Kotěra** and his disciple **František Gahura**. (Gahura headed the town's planning after Baťa rejected the designs by the famous French architect, Le Corbusier.)

Baťa's idea was to create a "garden town" for his workers, a town that supplied good housing and education and cultivated a healthy cultural and arts scene. Apparently, Baťa succeeded in doing just that. But he had only a few short years to enjoy the fruit of his labor, as he was killed in a plane crash in 1932. His son, also named Tomáš, took over, and continued to build the model factory town that his father had begun.

The main component of Zlín, its veritable heart, is the shoe assembly line. At the peak of its power just before World War II, the Baťa shoe company employed as many as 41,000 people in Zlín and another 23,000 worldwide. But, at the advent of the war, Tomáš Jr. uprooted the company and fled to Canada, taking his management team and establishing his own town just outside Ottawa, immodestly called Bataville.

When the Communists nationalized the company immediately following World War II, they not only renamed the factory, but also renamed the city in an attempt to erase its capitalist past. Zlín became **Gottwaldov**, after Czechoslovakia's first Communist president, **Klement Gottwald** (also known as the "Stalinist Butcher"). Of course, the new name could endure only as long as the Communist regime did, and sure enough the city became Zlín once more in 1990.

As for the Baťa shoe company, it has not reacquired the Zlín factory (renamed Svit by the Communists), but it has, through the republic's restitution laws, taken back a number of properties confiscated by the Communists, including the site of the original flagship store on Prague's Wenceslas Square, Dům obuvi (now a Baťa department store). And in just about every moderately-sized town in the Czech Republic, you can now find a Baťa shop or two, usually occupying the most modern of buildings in the main squares.

After years of blunderous Communist development, which included the emergence of the proto-typical cinder block housing estates, Zlín isn't the model factory town it once was. But there is enough left from the good old days to at least give you a feel for the Zlín Tomáš Baťa had in mind. Attractions include a couple of very good art museums, as well as a delightful shoe museum. But the real attraction in Zlín is its 1930s functionalist architecture – a style generally recognized by its hard edges, its shoe-box shapes, its red-brick infills, and its pervasive use of plate-glass windows. Like all avant-garde styles, Zlín's functionalist architecture won't appeal to everyone, but it is well worth your attention.

One more interesting tidbit on Zlín: it is the birthplace of one **Ivana Trump**. Born Ivana Zelníčková, Ivana Trump (or Trumpova, as the Czechs call her) shined on the 1972 Czechoslovak Olympic Ski Team and later on the pages of international fashion magazines before the tabloids had a feeding frenzy over her marriage and divorce to New York business tycoon Donald Trump.

ORIENTATION

Located 98 kilometers (61 miles) east of Brno and 292 kilometers (181 miles) southeast of Prague, Zlín straddles the banks of the **Dřevnice River** in a lush valley in eastern Moravia. Zlín's wide streets and long blocks make it easy to find your way around town.

ARRIVALS & DEPARTURES

By Bus

Buses run nearly every hour between Brno and Zlín, costing about 70 Kč and taking two hours. From Prague, buses cost about 175 Kč and run once a day, usually overnight. A better idea than taking this hellish six-and-a-half hour ride, dropping you off at a terrible hour in Zlín and stopping at every podunk town along the way, is to buy your ticket for Brno and then make a connection from there to Zlín. You probably won't save much time this way, but at least you won't have to travel in the dead of night.

The bus station is in the middle of the city, within easy walking distance of the hotels and sights listed below.

By Car

From Brno, head east on E462 and then E50. When you come to Uherské Hradiště, swing north on highway 55 and then east on 49. The trip should take no more than an hour-and-a-half. From Prague, the easiest route is via Brno. Parking lots are scattered throughout town. Look for the blue "P" sign. All hotels have private parking.

By Train

Because Zlín sits on a minor railway spur, getting to or from Zlín requires a change of trains at Otrokovice, 20 minutes west. From Brno, you'll have to make a change first at Veselí nad Maravou and then another one at Otrokovice. The journey should take about three hours and costs around 60 Kč. From Prague this requires a change first in Přerov and then Otrokovice. The trip costs around 200 Kč and takes about seven hours. Obviously, bus is a much easier way to go.

The little train station in Zlín sits behind the bus station, right in the middle of town and within easy walking distance of everything.

GETTING AROUND TOWN

Generally, you should have no problem getting around on foot. But if you need to, you can hop on a trolley bus or regular bus frequently running through the city center to outlying suburbs. Buy your ticket at any newsstand and validate it on board by sticking it in the puncher.

Taxis congregate in front of hotels and can easily be hailed on the street. But you run a good chance here, like anywhere else in the country, of getting overcharged for being a foreigner. You can rent cars at the Interhotel Moskva (see *Where to Stay* below).

WHERE TO STAY

INTERHOTEL MOSKVA, *náměstí Práce 2512, 762 70 Zlín. Tel. 067/836 1111, Fax 067/365 93. Rates for single/double: 1,200/1,700-2,000 Kč. Credit cards: AE, MC, V. Restaurant.*

This 11-story hotel is the biggest and most exclusive address in town. A great example of the 1930s architecture prevalent in town, the Moskva was designed by Vladimír Karfík, the architect responsible for the Baťa administrative building. Today, it caters mostly to those on expense accounts, so expect exorbitant prices. Flashy and somewhat tasteless decor runs throughout much of the hotel, but the rooms, though a bit lackluster, are fairly easy to digest. In addition to the casino, bar, café, and nightclub, the hotel offers massages, car rentals, horseback rides, plane rides, and can book tennis courts in town. Like a lot of big hotels in the republic, the receptionists are curt beyond belief.

HOTEL GARNI, *náměstí T.G. Masaryka 1335, 762 70 Zlín. Tel. 067/721 1941, Fax 067/366 60. Rates for single/double: 750/1,200 Kč. Credit cards: AE, MC, V. 70 rooms. Restaurant.*
A small version of its neighbor Interhotel Moskva, Garni overdoes it with the white neo-Classical decor. But the rooms are functional and clean, albeit a little tacky. The hotel has two bars and a billiards club and offers massages and hair styling. If you're in town on business, the hotel can also arrange interpreters for you.

HOTEL SOLID GOLD, *Tyršovo Nábřeží 486, 760 01 Zlín. Tel. & Fax 067/721 1950. Rates for single/double: 980/1,360 Kč. Credit cards: AE, MC, V. 12 rooms. Restaurant.*
Despite the ridiculous name, this small cream-and-white hotel is one of two good options in Zlín. Bright, airy rooms come with up-to-date furniture, direct-dial telephones, and satellite television. The new hotel has an intimately small restaurant, serving solidly prepared international courses. The hotel also has private parking and can arrange a game of tennis for you at one of the local private clubs. Friendly, English-speaking receptionists go out of their way to make you feel at home.

HOTEL SALOON, *Tyršovo Nábřeží 487, 760 01 Zlín. Tel. 067/721 0475, Fax 067/721 3575. Rates for single/double: 850/1,200 Kč. Credit cards: MC, V. 16 rooms. Restaurant.*
Right next door to Hotel Solid Gold, Hotel Saloon opened in the summer of 1995, after giving the turn-of-the-century building a handsome renovation. The theme of the decor throughout the hotel, as indicated by its name, is the American West (as captured in old photographs), a somewhat disorienting theme considering you are in the middle of a Czech factory town. The hotel has a fine restaurant serving mostly Czech food and offers guests use of their fitness center. Extremely friendly, English-speaking service on top of everything else makes this the best choice of accommodations in town.

HOTEL ONDRAŠ, *Kvitková 4323, 760 01 Zlín. Tel. 067/721 0603, Fax 067/721 1351. Rates for single/double: 900/1,230 Kč. Credit cards: MC, V. 21 rooms. Restaurant.*
Dank halls, characterless rooms, and a lousy restaurant amount to a hotel you should stay at only if you're desperate.

WHERE TO EAT
ZÁMECKÁ RESTAURACE, *Soudní 1. Tel. 067/394 67. 100-250 Kč.*
Housed in the town chateau, this restaurant has a fancy vaulted-ceiling interior with several rooms and alcoves. Mostly Moravian specialties, like paprika-laced pork cutlets or game dishes served with a rich cream sauce, fill the extensive menu. Be sure to try the mushroom soup;

it's a winner. The tuxedoed servers are ultra-formal, but a little slow on their feet.

INTERHOTEL MOSKVA, *náměstí Práce 2512. Tel. 067/836 1111. 130-250 Kč.*

The dining room on the third floor offers Italian and French cuisine, cooking that of course ends up tasting suspiciously like Czech food. The decor, with its sky-blue walls and gold-colored chairs and chandeliers, is overdone to the point of being gaudy.

HOTEL SOLID GOLD, *Tyršovo Nábřeží 48. Tel. & Fax 067/721 1950. 120-230 Kč.*

The restaurant offers mostly international dishes, but with an emphasis on Moravian cuisine. Discreet service in an intimate, candle-lit atmosphere makes this a romantic spot for dinner.

PIZZERIA U ČÁPA, *Benešovo nábřeží 2732. Tel. 067/303 91. 80-200 Kč. No credit cards.*

U Čápa bakes a tasty thin-crust pizza, of which there are 24 different kinds available. Other Italian specialties, like spaghetti and lasagna, top the menu, but I would stick to the pizzas. Filling up on a nightly basis, this is perhaps the most popular restaurant in town, which is not all that surprising considering it's also the most exotic. You'll find the restaurant right across the street from the hotels, Solid Gold and Saloon.

SEEING THE SIGHTS

The most reasonable place to begin is at the heart of the city – the shoe factory's **administrative building** (Správní budova Svit), the centerpiece of Baťa's works located on třída Tomáše Bati near the intersection with Březnická street. At the time of its completion in 1938, the 16-story building was the tallest in Czechoslovakia. Vladimír Karfík, a student of Le Corbusier and Frank Lloyd Wright before becoming chief architect of the Baťa company, designed the plate-glass and red brick building, a structure that could easily have found its way into New York or Chicago. The most unique aspect of the building is the director's office, built for Tomáš Baťa. It occupies an air-conditioned elevator so that it can place itself on any floor at any time.

The quirky **shoe museum** (obuvnické muzeum), near the administrative building *at třída Tomáše Bati 1970,* is a somewhat small affair, but a fun one at that. With an emphasis naturally put on Baťa shoes, the museum exhibits footwear worn around the globe at different periods of time, starting with the medieval age. A new section introduces you to the man behind the making of Zlín, Tomáš Baťa, Sr. *Open June through August weekdays from 8 a.m. to 4 p.m. and on Saturdays to 2 p.m. During the rest of the year it's open on weekdays only from 8 a.m. to 3 p.m.*

From the shoe museum, head east on Štefánikova to Gahurova and then walk up the hill. Commanding a position at the top of a long stretch of grass and trees, the **House of Arts** (Dům umění) *at náměstí T.G. Masaryka 2570* is perhaps the boldest example of the 1930s architecture in Zlín.

The concrete and glass building, shaped ironically or not like a shoebox, was designed by the head of city planning, František Gahura, as a memorial to Baťa after his death in 1932. The Communist city council, however, had it converted to a "house of arts" in 1953, significantly altering its original design. Inside, you'll find a concert auditorium downstairs and an art gallery upstairs with temporary exhibits of contemporary Czech artists. *The gallery is open Tuesday through Sunday from 10 a.m. to noon and from 1 to 5 p.m.*

BAŤA - SHOEMAKER & FILM PRODUCER

A huge benefactor of the avant-garde in all its mediums, Tomáš Baťa would probably not have been too upset that the building memorializing him was converted into a gallery now exhibiting the cutting edge of Czech art. Baťa himself employed the cutting-edge artists of his time, putting them to work on advertisements for his shoes. (After all, he was a businessman.) He even went so far as to build a Baťa film studio in order to produce commercials for his products. But as most Baťa enterprises went, the film studio moved beyond shoes and acquired a life of its own.

The studio branched out, and in the last 50 years has produced over 2,000 narrative films, documentaries, and, for the first time in Czech history, animation films. Incidentally, two of the three founding members of the studio, Elmar Klos and Alexander Hackenschmied, both went on to win Oscars: Klos for his film A Shop on the Promenade and Hackenschmied for his documentary work in America.

Continuing with the art tour of this factory town, our next stop is one of two branches of the **State Gallery** (Státní galerie). This one is housed in the House of Culture (Dům kultury), located down the hill from the House of Art, just off Gahurova třída and in front of the bus station. All of the best 20th-century Czech artists are represented here, including Mucha, Mánes, the surrealists Toyen and Jindřich Štýrský, and the cubists Josef Čapek and Bohumir Kubišta. The other branch of the State Gallery sits in the uninspiring town chateau, across the street from the House of Culture.

This branch, featuring temporary art exhibits, shares space with the **Regional Museum of Southeast Moravia** (Oblastní muzeum jihovýchodní Moravy). The folk artifacts – instruments, tools, and kitchen utensils – from the Slovácko and Haná regions are not as exciting as the photographs of early Zlín and the Baťa family lining the staircase walls. *Both branches of the State Gallery and the regional museum are open Tuesday through Friday from 9 a.m. to 5 p.m. and on weekends from 10 a.m. to 6 p.m.*

NIGHTLIFE & ENTERTAINMENT

The **House of Art** (see *Seeing the Sights* above) features frequent concerts by the world-class **Bohuslav Martin Philharmonic Orchestra**, while the **House of Culture** books folk, jazz, rock, and the occasional blues acts. **Disco Flip**, *near the corner of třída Tomaše Bati and Gahurova*, spins a lot of Euro-trash dance tunes, attracting hordes of Italian men, who come to Zlín looking for Czech mates. (Zlín, by the way, has the reputation in Italy for having an enormously disproportionate number of women, and hence a good place to find a wife.)

If you want to avoid this meat market, try the classy **Rock Club Golem**, *across the street at náměstí Práce 1099*, featuring nightly rock acts, four bars, and a great statue of the Golem monster, which blows smoke out its mouth when you feed him a token bought at the bar. The best place to catch a flick is most definitely the **Velké Kino** *at náměstí Práce*. Built in the 1930s as part of the Baťa film studio, Velké Kino means "Big Cinema," an appropriate name considering that it seats 2,000 movie-goers.

PRACTICAL INFORMATION

• **Komerční Banka**, *next to the town hall on náměstí Míru*. A good place to change money.
• **Informační Centrum**, *in the town hall on náměstí Míru. Tel. 067/721 0240*. Offers information on the town, books private accommodations, and sells maps.
• **Post Office**, *náměstí Míru*. International calls can be made here.

Kroměříž

Two great reasons for coming to this modestly enchanting town on the Morava River are its **chateau** and its lush **gardens**. As the residence of the **Archbishops of Olomouc** from the 12th to the 19th century, the Kroměříž chateau evolved into one of the grandest in Moravia. The chateau is enriched with a wealth of artwork from around Europe, outfitted with the finest furnishings from each era, and graced with an enormous garden that covers an area greater than that of Kroměříž's old town.

But there's more: the old town itself, with its winding pedestrian lanes chock-full of Baroque houses. Much of the old town's character, indeed the chateau's as well, belongs to the 17th and 18th centuries, when the town was rebuilt after being sacked by Swedish forces in the Thirty Years' War.

A word of warning: the hotel and restaurant situation in Kroměříž is quite dismal. So you may want to consider this destination as an easy day trip from Zlín or a more difficult one from Brno or Olomouc.

ORIENTATION

Nicknamed the "Athens of the Haná region," Kroměříž straddles the **Morava River** 33 kilometers (19 miles) northwest of Zlín, 60 kilometers (37 miles) east of Brno, and about 47 kilometers (29 miles) south of Olomouc.

ARRIVALS & DEPARTURES

By Bus

Kroměříž is a stop along one of the Zlín-Brno lines. Buses run nearly every hour, which makes Kroměříž a convenient stopover if you are traveling between the two cities. Buses to or from Zlín take 30 minutes and cost about 20 Kč, while the ones to and from Brno take about 90 minutes and cost around 60 Kč. Six or seven buses run daily between Olomouc and Kroměříž, taking about an hour and costing 45 Kč. The bus station is a five minute walk across the river from the old town.

By Car

From Brno, take E462 east past the Vyškov turn-off and then follow signs east along backroads. From Zlín head west on highway 49, north on 55 to Hulín, and then follow signs east. From Olomouc head south on highway 55 all the way to Hulín and then follow signs east. Parking should be no problem; just keep an eye out for the blue "P" signs.

By Train

In order to get anywhere, you first have to change either at Hulín (for trains going to Břeclav, where you change for Olomouc and Prague) or at Kojetín (for trains going to Brno). The train station, located behind the bus station, is a five minute walk east of the old town.

GETTING AROUND TOWN

The tiny size of Kroměříž rules out any need to take public transportation. No problem getting around on foot here.

WHERE TO STAY/WHERE TO EAT

HOTEL BOUČEK, *Velké náměstí 108, 767 01 Kroměříž. Tel. & Fax 0634/ 257 77. Rates for single/double: 1,280/1,660 Kč. Credit cards: AE, MC, V. 10 rooms. Restaurant.*

The only decent choice of accommodations in town, the Bouček offers rather spare rooms in serious need of some modern furniture. It does, however, have a great location – right on the main square and a two minute walk from the chateau. The service is friendly, and usually speaks English. The restaurant, offering a regular Moravian fare, is nothing to get excited about, but does the trick of filling an empty stomach.

RADNIČNÍ SKLÍPEK, *Kovářská 20. Tel. 0634/206 08. 100-200 Kč. Credit cards: MC.*

This stylish wine cellar just off Velké náměstí offers excellent Moravian game dishes smothered with heavy paprika sauces. Your best (and almost only) option for good food in Kroměříž, this restaurant is a favorite with the locals.

HOTEL OSKOL, *Oskol 3203, 767 01 Kroměříž. Tel. 0634/242 40, Fax 0634/242 46. Rates for single/double: 750/1,100 Kč. Credit cards: MC, V. Restaurant.*

This big Communist-era hotel suffices only in a last-ditch attempt to find a room. Otherwise, don't bother with the depressingly plain, over-priced rooms or the restaurant's mediocre food.

SEEING THE SIGHTS

No better place to start than at the town's Baroque gem, the **Archbishop's Chateau** (Arcibiskupský zámek), its entrance located just off Velké náměstí below the fantastic, tiered clock tower. The 90-minute tour, which runs every 45 minutes in Czech and German (ask the guide for an English text), starts out rather unpromisingly in the Hunters' Hall, filled with 80 pathetic trophy heads of deer. But things brighten up as you move to the Rococo Rose Room and later to the Tsar's Room, named for Tsar Alexander III, who arrived at the chateau in 1885 with, what else, but a painting of himself, which now takes pride of place in the room that bears his title.

Once inside the marble-studded Mansky Hall, adorned with murals by Rococo artist Franz Anton Maulpertsch, you can't help but feel the weight of the chateau's Baroque excessiveness, which comes to a climax in the phenomenal Assembly Hall, glittering with no less than 20 crystal chandeliers. In 1845, the Austrian Imperial Assembly met here while revolution raged back in Vienna. (The acoustics here are incredible, which makes this a grand place to see one of the classical concerts taking place here June through September.) The tour winds up in the Old Palace

Library, notable for its four intriguing globes presented to the Bishop of Olomouc by King Louis XIV of France. By the end of the tour, it may dawn on you that the whole place seems a little familiar. In that case, you've probably seen the film *Amadeus*, which shot several of its scenes inside the chateau.

After the tour, or if you have time to kill before the tour, walk through the **Chateau Picture Gallery** (Zámecká obrazárna), filled with Moravia's richest collection of paintings from the 16th and 17th centuries. A wealth of paintings by Flemish masters such as J. Breughel and David Ryckaert hang here, as does Sir Anthony Van Dyck's portrait of King Charles I of England and his wife Henrietta Maria. But the crown gem at the gallery is Tizian Vecelli's *Apollon and Marsyas*, completed by Vecelli at the age of 90. *From May through September, the chateau is open Tuesday though Sunday from 9 a.m. to 5 p.m. In April and October, it's open same hours, but on weekends only. Price of the tour is 50 Kč, while entry to the picture gallery is 20 Kč.*

Just outside the chateau entrance, the Gothic **Church of St. Moritz** (Kostel sv Mořič) was built in 1260, making it the oldest structure in town. It was about the only thing spared by the Swedes when they burnt the town down. Of interest inside the church is the Bishop Schrattenbach tombstone, a major Moravian work from the 18th century created by Ondřej Zahner, also known for his work on the Trinity Column in Olomouc. Farther up Pilařova street is the Baroque **Church of St. John the Baptist** (Kostel sv Jana Křtitele), its lofty dome sensuously decorated with murals depicting the baptism of Jesus.

Head back towards the chateau on Janská until you reach the haggard main square, **Velké náměstí**, decorated with the obligatory plague column and fountain. The **Kroměříž Museum** (Muzeum Kroměřížska), *at number 38*, features the work of Max Švabinský, born in Kroměříž in 1872. His forté was nude paintings, mawkishly rendered with an abundance of bright hues that do no service to his uninspiring style. Better than his paintings are the old Czechoslovak postage stamps on view here, some of which were done by Švabinský. *The museum is open daily except Monday from 8 a.m. to noon and from 1 to 5 p.m.*

At the bottom of the square, head down Vodní street and continue along Farní to the **Church of the Assumption of Our Lady** (Kostel Nanebevzetí Panny Marie). The church has a huge Gothic steeple, which is the only thing left of the original church that stood here before the Swedes ripped through town. From the church, a walk down Moravcova puts you in the **old Jewish ghetto**, at one time one of the largest in the Czech lands. But the only thing recalling the ghetto is the **Jewish Town Hall**, off to your left half-way down Moravcova. Serving as a local cultural center, the building offers little of its past.

Now that you've pretty much covered all that there is to see in the old town, it's time to go for a stroll in the lush **Chateau Gardens** (Zámecká zahrada), stretching from the rear of the chateau down to the Morava River. A few ponds, a pavilion here and there, and a lot of trees and flower beds fill 64 hectares (158 acres) of land, adding up to one of the largest historical green spaces in the country. You'll also find an aviary hidden amidst the shrubs, and perhaps a deer or two as well.

On the north end of the Chateau Gardens, about a 10 minute walk from the chateau, is the **Flower Garden** (Květná zahrada), created by the Liechtensteins in the 17th century. Perfectly manicured, this garden comes in blaring contrast to the unruliness of the Chateau Gardens. But what has brought you this far are not the flowers, but the garden's graceful neoclassical colonnade replete with 46 columns, all of which are topped with Roman busts.

NIGHTLIFE & ENTERTAINMENT

From June through September, Kroměříž hosts the annual **Summer Music Festival** (Kroměřížské hudební léto), with several performances taking place in the chateau's brilliant Assembly Hall. For ticket and schedule information, contact Eurotour Informačni Centrum (see *Practical Information* below).

PRACTICAL INFORMATION

•**Eurotour Informačni Centrum**, *Kovářská 1. Tel. 0634/212 19.* Offers maps, tours, and general tourist information.
•**Komerční banka**, *Tova ovského 2784.* Changes money.
•**Post Office**, *corner of Oskol and Denkova.* You can make international calls here.

19. NORTH MORAVIA

Nudging the borders of Poland and Slovakia in the eastern-most corner of the Czech Republic, **North Moravia** is not what you would call a tourist's paradise. This is one of the Czech Republic's most industrial regions, and probably its least popular with tourists.

Hugging the Polish border, the **Jeseníky Mountains** crown North Moravia, containing the region of **Silesia**, an historical province divided today by the Czech-Polish border. To the south, the **Beskydy** hills roll sedately into Slovakia, for centuries nurturing the **Wallachian culture**, its architecture on view at the outdoor museum in **Rožnov pod Radhoštěm**.

Ostrava, the region's administrative capital, carries the dubious honor of being the Czech Republic's biggest producer of coal and steel and, as a result, possesses some of the worst pollution in Europe. This is no place to spend a well-earned holiday, so we'll bypass it and concern ourselves with destinations that won't have you running for the next plane home. One place that certainly won't have you packing your bags so quickly is **Olomouc**, the second biggest city in the region and one of the best destinations you could choose in the Czech Republic.

There is some castle-hopping to do here as well. An easy day trip from Olomouc is **Šternberk Castle**, one of a deluge of castles in Central Europe formerly owned by the Liechtensteins. Off the beaten path in the foothills of the Jeseníky is **Bouzov Castle**, a grand affair with all the makings for fairy tales.

NORTH MORAVIA FINDS & FAVORITES
Hotel Gemo in Olomouc
Holy Trinity Column in Olomouc
Clock Museum in Šternberk Castle (see Olomouc "Excursions")
Wallachian Open-Air Museum in Rožnov pod Radhoštěm

Olomouc

Approaching **Olomouc** by car or bus, your immediate reaction may be: Why would anyone in their right mind recommend coming here? Indeed, Olomouc does not have the most attractive-looking outskirts. As is the case with several towns in the Czech Republic, legions of apartment blocks surround the town, giving no indication of the beauty that lies beyond their dull gray walls. But once you get past these concrete monoliths and into the old town, you'll most certainly have a change of heart.

The perfect description for Olomouc is its nickname, "a pearl on a green pillow." Practically surrounded by a ring of parks and gardens, Olomouc's old town consists of a maze of sloping streets, lanes, and staircases connecting six medieval market squares. The most impressive of these squares is **Horní náměstí**, where the momentous **Trinity Column** rises to unbelievable heights. Fountains and churches – structures Olomouc can't seem to get enough of – appear nearly everywhere you turn, making any comparisons to Rome or Florence seem plausible.

Legend has it that **Julius Caesar** founded Olomouc. Even without this wishful bit of thinking, Olomouc does have an air of importance about it. So it comes as no surprise to learn that Olomouc was the capital of Moravia from 1187 to 1641. But the Swedes gave it a good pounding during the Thirty Years' War, after which Olomouc lost its capital status to Brno. From 1777 to this day, Olomouc has maintained its esteem as the seat of an archbishopric.

Olomouc is also home to **Palacký University**, established by the Jesuits in the 16th century and now one of the three major universities in the Czech Republic. More so than any other place in the country, Olomouc is a college town, its cultural and social scene geared towards the throngs of students who converge here from around the country. Thanks to the university and its students, Olomouc offers a vibrant lifestyle, one you'll want to experience for at least a few days.

ORIENTATION

Located in central Moravia in what's called the **Haná** region, Olomouc is 77 kilometers (48 miles) northwest of Brno and 250 kilometers (155 miles) east of Prague.

ARRIVALS & DEPARTURES

By Bus

Bus works best between Brno and Olomouc, with ten or so buses departing daily. It costs about 50 Kč and takes roughly 90 minutes. The bus station in Olomouc is on Tovární street, about two kilometers southeast of the center. This is obviously too far to walk, so hop on any of the trams heading west, which will take you directly into the center.

By Car

Olomouc is about a 45 minute trip from Brno. Head northwest on E50/65 to E462. From Prague to Olomouc, you can either go via Brno or take E67 to E442 via Hradec Králové. Both routes take roughly three hours to drive. Parking is restricted in the center of Olomouc during the weekdays from 9 a.m. to 6 p.m., which means you need to buy a short-term "parking card" from any tabak, tourist agency, or hotel if you plan on parking in the center during this period.

By Train

Strangely enough, there are no direct fast trains between Brno and Olomouc. So, it's much easier to take the bus. But train works best between Prague and Olomouc, with ten a day (less on the weekends) arriving and departing at Prague's Hlavní nádraží (Main Station). It costs about 120 Kč and takes three-and-a-half hours.

The train station in Olomouc is at the end of Masarykovo třída, about a 20 minute walk east of the town center. Catch any of the trams heading west, which will take you into the center.

GETTING AROUND TOWN

The tram system is fairly efficient here, with several lines running through the old town and out to the suburbs. For 7 Kč you can buy a ticket from any of the cigarette and magazine kiosks, of which there is no short supply in Olomouc. Once on the tram, validate your ticket by sticking it in the automated puncher. You can buy one-, two-, or three-day passes for 25, 35, and 45 Kč respectively, but I doubt you'll be using the tram enough to make these passes worth your while.

Generally, you can get around just fine on foot, except in the case of getting to and from the bus and train stations. There's no problem hailing cabs on the streets or hiring one from any hotel.

WHERE TO STAY

HOTEL GEMO, *Pavelčákova 22, 772 00 Olomouc. Tel. 068/522 2065, Fax 068/28 625. Rates for single/double: 1,856/2,568 Kč. Credit cards: AE, DC, MC, V. 33 rooms. Restaurant.*

African cherry tree furniture, decorative tile floors, and original local art have gone into making this new hotel the most exclusive address in Olomouc. The hotel sits on the very edge of the old town on one of the town's busiest streets, which means traffic noises can sometimes get a little overbearing in the rooms that face the street. Otherwise, you can expect a comfortable stay in any of the rooms, which are smartly decorated with period furniture and outfitted with satellite television. The sun-lit lobby has a pleasant café – a good place to stop in for a drink and get a glimpse of the place.

I also highly recommend the restaurant, which sticks to the same high standards as the rest of the hotel.

HOTEL LAFAYETTE, *Alšova 8, 779 00 Olomouc. Tel. & Fax 068/543 6407. Rates for single/double: 1,700/1,800 Kč. Credit cards: AE, MC, V. 10 rooms. Restaurant.*

Located in a quiet neighborhood five minutes from the old town, this Art Noveau hotel is named after the French general imprisoned in Olomouc in the late 18th century. Sunny rooms are tastefully furnished with dark wood furniture. The hotel has private parking and offers carriage tours of the town. The restaurant in an English-style dining room serves Moravian specialties and even some passable French dishes.

HOTEL FLORA, *Krapkova 34, 772 00 Olomouc. Tel. 068/542 1201, Fax 068/542 1211. Rates for single/double: 1,400-2,200/1,500-2,300 Kč. Credit cards: AE, MC, V. Restaurant.*

Another Communist-era high rise slowly trying to spruce up its interior. Some rooms have been renovated (and are much higher priced as result), while others are still stuck in the year 1977. If you can help it, avoid this one.

HOTEL U DÓMU, *Dómská 4, 772 00 Olomouc. Tel. & Fax 068/522 0501, Rates for single/double: 1,000/1,200-1,600 Kč. Credit cards: MC, V. 6 rooms. No restaurant.*

This rather unassuming hotel sits on a silent side street just off the peaceful Wenceslas Square. The spartan but cozy rooms are nothing to get excited about, but they do come with satellite television. St. Wenceslas Cathedral looms overhead.

HOTEL PALÁC, *třída 1. máje 27, 772 00 Olomouc. Tel. 068/522 4096, Fax 068/522 3284. Rates for single/double: 625/1,650 Kč. Credit cards: AE, MC, V. Restaurant.*

About the only thing going for this glum place is its central location. Rooms are clean, but should only be booked in a pinch.

WHERE TO EAT

HOTEL GEMO, *Pavelčákova 22. Tel. 068/522 2065. 100-250 Kč.*

Gemo treats you to intimate dining indoors and out. The tuxedoed waiters deliver tender roast beef, spicy grilled chicken, and meticulously prepared appetizers – just a few of the items that make this a sure-fire place to have dinner.

MICHALSKÝ VÝPAD, *Blaženské náměstí 10 (corner of U výpadu and Michalské). Tel. 068/522 2563. 90-200 Kč. No credit cards.*

One of the most-respected restaurants in town, Výpad has a nice view of the park, Bezručovy sady, from its classy dining room. Moravian specialties, mostly rich game dishes doused in wine sauces, top the menu.

DU PIETRO TRATTORIA, *třída Svobody 34. Tel. 068/522 5858. 60-200 Kč. No credit cards.*

A pleasant surprise in Olomouc. What is even more surprising is that the Italian food actually comes pretty close to true trattoria fare. A big selection of anitpasta, pasta, and entrées grace the menu. But don't expect much from the service. Reservations are a good idea at this tiny place.

U ANDĚLA, *Hrnčířská 10. Tel. 068/522 8755. 70-175 Kč. Credit cards: MC, V.*

Set on a picturesque medieval lane around the corner from St. Michael's Church, "At the Angel" serves top of the line Czech food in a cozy setting that's popular with the students. Make sure to have some of the spicy fish soup; it's to die for.

CAFÉ CAESAR, *ground floor of the town hall on Horní náměstí. Tel. 068/522 987. 60-150 Kč. Credit cards: AE, MC, V.*

Set below the vaulted ceilings of the newly renovated town hall, this expansive café bakes an excellent thin-crust pizza. Some people in Olomouc like the pizza here so much that they are eating it for breakfast. The café also serves a mean cappucino.

VEGETKA, *Dolní náměstí 39. Tel. 068/522 6069. 70-180 Kč. Credit cards: MC.*

This mostly vegetarian restaurant deserves credit based on its existence alone. Unfortunately, their vegetarian dishes are uninspiring, mainly due to the lack of seasoning and the mundane ingredients used, such as carrots, potatoes, and mushrooms.

U MACHA, *Komenského 5. Tel. 068/522 5489. 60-150 Kč. No credit cards.*

Solid Czech fare done with a good amount of creativity and presented in a stylish setting. A good place to go for lunch.

SEEING THE SIGHTS

Just off 1. Máje at the end of Dómská, the tiny **Wenceslas Square** (Václavské náměstí) is a pocket of solitude in the northeast corner of the old town. The square bows down at the foot of **St. Wenceslas Cathedral** (Metropolitní chrám sv Václava), originally a Romanesque basilica consecrated in 1131. It was rebuilt again and again to suit the tastes of the ages before it was finally given a neo-Gothic appearance. The last members of the Přemysl dynasty are buried here, as are the remains of Jan Sarkander, a priest who was tortured three times and finally killed for not revealing a secret disclosed to him in confession. Descend into the crypt for a look at an exhibit of archaeological finds, church stamps, and an ostrich egg that was once used as ballot box in selecting bishops.

Around the corner of the cathedral you'll find the entrance to the **Přemysl Palace** (Přemyslovský palác), one of the country's great treasures dating back to the early 12th century. The short self-guided tour begins in the Gothic cloister, where a series of frescoes were added to the original walls in the 15th and 16th centuries. Up the stairs you'll come to the Bishops's bedroom and its Romanesque walls and windows, part of the original palace that went undiscovered until 1867. The spongolith (sponge-like) windows offer a fine glimpse at the sort of artistry that was produced during the Romanesque era. Back downstairs in the Chapel of St. John the Baptist are some more frescoes, these ones showing angels curiously wielding instruments of torture. *The palace is open Tuesday through Sunday from 9 a.m. to 12:30 p.m. and from 1 to 5 p.m.*

Next to the Přemysl Palace is the former **Chapter Deanery**, a Baroque house that became infamous when Wenceslas III, king of Bohemia and last of the Přemysl dynasty, was assassinated here in 1306. The building gathered more notoriety when Mozart stayed in 1767 and composed his Sixth Symphony in F-major here. Today, the deanery houses the university's Department of Fine Arts.

Retrace your steps down Dómská street, cross 1 Máje, and continue up to **Biskupské náměstí**, enclosed by a series of stately Baroque buildings, including the enormous **Archbishop's Palace** (Arcibiskupský palác), which was the setting for the coronation of Emperor Franz Joseph I in 1848. Further up the hill are the buildings housing Palacký University's Philosophical Faculty and its student center. An outdoor café in the rear of the student center is perched on top of the old fortress walls – a perfect place to sip an espresso and enjoy the view of the park down below.

Make your way down Křížkovského to the slanted **náměstí Republiky**, where the focal point is the 1709 **Triton's Fountain** (Kašna Tritonů), a fanciful depiction of dolphins, sailors, and a boy in a sea shell. Protruding into the square is the **Church of St. Mary of the Snows** (Kostel Panny Marie Sněžné), part of the old Jesuit college founded in 1573 to combat the rise of Protestantism in the region.

Directly across the street is the **Olomouc Museum of Art** (Olomoucký muzeum umění). A permanent collection of Italian paintings from the 14th through the 18th centuries and changing exhibits of contemporary local art hang in the handsome interior of this former convent and cloister. An added bonus for coming here is the opportunity to ascend the observation turret, providing a panoramic view of the town. *The museum is open Tuesday through Sunday 10 a.m. to 6 p.m.*

Continue down Denisova and veer right onto Pekařská, where you'll find the entrance to **St. Moritz Church** (Chrám sv Mořic), looking more like a fortress than a place of worship. Things get even more disorienting when you step inside to find an interior completely washed in pink. For all its inadequacies, the church can boast of having the largest organ in Moravia, complete with no less than 2,311 pipes.

From St. Moritz, all lanes lead to **Horní náměstí** (Upper Square), Olomouc's main square. Plunked down in the middle of the square is the immediately appealing **town hall** (radnice), a mostly Renaissance, hybrid structure dating back to 1378. Take note of the carved, free-standing staircase and the pretty oriel window hidden around back. But these things are overshadowed by the town hall tower, piercing the skyline with its gleaming baubles and jagged spires. Just below the tower is the **astronomical clock** (*orloj*), destroyed in World War II and then revamped under Communist scrutiny, as you'll notice by the ridiculous wooden proletarians (which replaced the clock's saints) who make their rounds at the top of the hour.

Stealing the show in Horní náměstí is the blackened **Holy Trinity Column** (Sousoší Nejsvětější trojice), a mammoth Baroque sculpture climbing 35 meters (114 feet) high. It's said to be the single biggest plague column in Central Europe, which is saying a lot, considering that just about every town in the former Austrian Empire has one.

Of course, the square wouldn't be complete without its **two Baroque fountains**, one depicting Hercules (looking incredibly fit for his age) and the other Caesar (gallantly mounted on his horse).

From Horní náměstí, climb the hill either along Michalská or Skolní – two of Olomouc's most intriguing medieval lanes both leading to **St. Michael's Church** (Kostel sv Michala), its three green domes commanding the Olomouc skyline. The interior, with its heavy Baroque ornamentation, packs a forceful load. If you ever get your jaws hoisted back up from the floor, crane your neck upwards toward the center dome, where you'll notice four heads peering down back at you. It's an amusing sight.

Head back down the hill along Panská to **Dolní náměstí** (Lower Square), which is somewhat of a disappointment after Horní náměstí. But this haggard, odd-shaped square does have the obligatory **fountains** (Neptune and Jupiter) and a Marian plague column. Something of interest here is the **Hauenschild Palace**, noteworthy for its oriel window depicting scenes from Ovid's Metamorphoses.

Cross Dolní náměstí to Kateřinská and then take a left on Aksamitova, which will lead you straight into **Bezručovy sady**, a wonderfully sedate place to take a stroll or have a picnic. The lush park, formerly the city moat, hugs the bottom of the old fortress walls and make you feel as if you've left town altogether.

A few blocks west of třída Svobody (Olomouc's main street running along the west side of the old town) are two more parks, **Čechovy and Smetanovy sady** – two more great opportunities to get away from the bustle and take a breather among the manicured gardens.

NIGHTLIFE & ENTERTAINMENT

Drápal, a bar *at the corner of Svobody and Havlíčkova*, presents a curious Caribbean decor and pours a number of beers, including Guinness. Always a lively crowd here. For something a bit more highbrow, check out the plays at the attractive **Moravian Theater** (Moravské divadlo) *on Horní náměstí*. The **Moravian Philharmonic Orchestra** performs at various venues around the city. The Center for Information, Culture, and Tourism (see *Practical Information* below) has a schedule of all cultural events happening in town and can even sell you tickets to them.

Catch a flick at either **Kino Central**, *just off náměstí Republiky on Denisova*, or at **Kino Metropol**, *corner of Zámečnická and Sokolská*.

For something more exciting, check out an outlandish techno club called **Depo No. 8**, at *náměstí Republiky 1*.

EXCURSIONS & DAY TRIPS
Šternberk

Just 15 kilometers (nine miles) north of Olomouc, the town of **Šternberk** sits at the base of the Jeseníky foothills and in the shadow of its big attraction, **Šternberk Castle**. Originally built in 1269 by the family with the same name, Šternberk eventually passed into the hands of the Liechtensteins, who adapted it to Renaissance and later to Romantic tastes. The tour of the castle palace, usually in Czech and German (English speakers have to settle for a terribly written text), is worth your while if you're a hardcore castle fan, or if you happen to have an interest in antique ceramic stoves, of which there is no short supply at Šternberk.

But the real reason to make the excursion to the castle is for its excellent **clock museum**, showcasing the evolution of timepieces from the first rudimentary Chinese alarm clocks on up to the outrageous designs of the Baroque era. Just in case you're wondering, the reason Šternberk has a clock museum is because the country's largest manufacturer of alarm clocks, Chronotechno, sits just below the castle, blighting what would otherwise be a great view of the town and countryside. *In April and October it's open weekends only from 9 a.m. to 4 p.m. Closed rest of the year.*

Something else you shouldn't miss while in Šternberk is the **Parish Church of the Annunciation of Our Lord** (Farní kostel Zvěstování Páně), with its handsome Baroque facade commanding a position above the town center.

If you're traveling by car from Olomouc, go 15 kilometers (nine miles) north on highway 46. Otherwise, it's easiest to get there by train, which runs nearly every hour and takes about 20 minutes. The castle and the town center are a good 20 minute walk east of the train station.

Bouzov Castle

When you first lay your eyes on the 14th-century **Bouzov Castle**, you would have expect to see Repunzel throwing down her hair from the castle's tower. Indeed, this 13th-century Gothic fortress has all the makings for fairy tales, which is why so many directors have chosen Bouzov as the location for their period films. Once a base for the Order of Teutonic Knights and the summer home of the order's Grand Master, the red brick castle lured the Nazi SS, who seized the fortress in World War II and made it their Czech headquarters – but not without looting it first.

Most likely the castle will still be under renovation when you visit. Only a handful of rooms are open to the public, and most of them are a letdown after having marveled at the castle's exterior. But the castle is worth the trip, if only to see it from the outside *The castle is open from 8 a.m. to 5 p.m. Tuesday through Sunday, May through September. In April and October it's only open during the weekends from 9 a.m. to 4 p.m. Call 068/544 6201 to confirm times.*

While at the castle you may want to consider hiking to **Javoříčko Caves** (Javoříčské jeskyně), a five-kilometer (three-mile) jaunt through the woods along the blue-marked trail. Receiving nary a tourist, the limestone karst caves are a good alternative to the ones near Brno. The caves are located near the village of Javoříčko, which was completely wiped out by the local SS in the last days of the war. If you don't feel like walking, you can catch the (very) occasional bus from the town of Bouzov to Javoříčko. By car, it's a four-kilometer drive south.

By car from Olomouc, go about 28 kilometers (17 miles) northeast on E442 and then follow signs to Bouzov. It should take about an hour to get there. Otherwise, bus is your only option, and an inconvenient one at that. You'll have to take a bus first to Litovel (leaving every hour or two) and then make a connection to the town of Bouzov. Count on about two-and-a-half hours from Olomouc to Bouzov.

Unfortunately, there are no hotels in Bouzov or in the immediate area, which makes this excursion from Olomouc only feasible if you have a car or if you leave Olomouc first thing in the morning.

PRACTICAL INFORMATION

• **Center for Information, Culture, and Tourism,** *on the north side of the town hall on Horní náměstí. Tel. 068/551 33 85.* Carries a good supply

of maps, helps with accommodations, and can give you bus and train schedules. English spoken here.
- **Komerční banka**, *down the hill from Horní náměstí on třída Svobody*. You can change money here.
- **Post Office**, *Horní náměstí*. You can make international calls here.

Rožnov pod Radhoštěm

Nestled in the hills of the Western Beskydy, the town of **Rožnov pod Radhoštěm** (Rožnov under Radhošť) is nothing special in itself. But the reason busloads of people target this town is because of its **open-air museum** (or *skansen*), featuring the story-book, wooden architecture that has made this region of **Wallachia** (Valašsko) infamous. Named for the Wallachians, who were semi-nomadic sheep herders that wandered into the Beskydy region in the 16th and 17th centuries, Wallachia has a rich history of folk artistry that comes alive in Rožnov's museum.

Rožnov's Wallachian Open-air Museum was the brain-child of **Bohumir and Alois Jaroněk**, brothers from the Moravian city of Zlín. Inspired by visits to several skansens around Europe (including the grandaddy of them all – the Stockholm Skansen), the Jaroněks set in motion the museum's development when they landed the **Wallachian Year**, a folklore festival celebrating Wallachian culture, in Rožnov. For the festival, they relocated the 18th-century wooden town hall from Rožnov's main square and a number of other folk structures from the area to the town's spa park. After the Jaroněks passed away, others took on the challenge, relocating or reconstructing Wallachian structures in the park. Today, the Wallachian Museum occupies three separate sites, which are actually three museums unto themselves.

Warning: hotels in and around Rožnov are completely booked up during the week of July 4th, when hundreds of Texans of Czech descent

THE WALLACHIANS

*The origins of the **Wallachians** are subject to a good deal of debate among anthropologists. But most believe that the Wallachians left Romania in the 10th century. They passed through the Ukraine and "colonized" the Polish and Slovak Carpathians, finally ending up in the Moravian Beskydy, joining the Slavs who had long before settled there. After years of intermarriage and a Hapsburg campaign aimed at eradicating their culture, the Wallachians have since lost their separate identity among the Moravians. But they did leave an indelible cultural mark in the form of their wood architecture and crafts, which can be seen on exhibit in Rožnov.*

invade the town for a week-long Independence Day bash. Country-western music, barbecues, and (if you can believe it) a rodeo are all part of the American festivities happening in this little Moravian town.

ORIENTATION

Located roughly 46 kilometers (29 miles) east of Olomouc and 265 kilometers (164 miles) southeast of Prague, Rožnov pod Radhoštěm sits in the **Western Beskydy** hills along the banks of the **Bečva River**.

ARRIVALS & DEPARTURES

By Bus

Bus is your only convenient option if you don't have a car. There are six daily buses from Brno (three hours), three from Prague's Florenc station (five-and-a-half hours), and two from Olomouc (hour-and-a-half). The bus station is a five minute walk west of the town center.

By Car

From Brno, take E462 to Olomouc and then E442 all the way to Rožnov. From Prague, you can either go via Brno or take E67 to Hradec Králové and then E442 all the way to Rožnov. Driving time from Brno is about two hours. Count on about four hours from Prague. Parking is widely available around the small town.

GETTING AROUND TOWN

The three sections of the Wallachian Open-air Museum are all within easy walking distance of each other. If need be, you can usually catch taxis in front of any of the hotels or at the train and bus stations.

WHERE TO STAY/WHERE TO EAT

HOTEL EROPLÁN, *Horní Paseky, 756 61 Rožnov pod Radhoštěm. Tel. 0651/558 35, Fax 0651/572 17. Rates for single/double: 1,150/1,580 Kč. Credit cards: AE, MC, V. 25 rooms. Restaurant.*

This is the only hotel in Rožnov worth a recommendation, as all the others are either dank cinder block highrises or fleebag hovels. The recently-built Eroplán, on the other hand, offers pleasant lodging and all the services you would expect from a high-class hotel, such as satellite television, tours of the area, and horse-drawn wagon rides.

The restaurant, serving above-par Moravian fare ranging from 100 to 200 Kč, is not great, but is your best bet in a town where the dining options are as dismal as the lodging ones. If you plan on staying during the high season, make sure to reserve a room well in-advance.

THE LAST GROSCHEN PUB (Hospoda na posledním groffi), *part of the Wooden Small Town (see Seeing the Sights below). Tel. 0651/545 17. 75-150 Kč. No credit cards.*

Here, you can get a number of good Moravian dishes and wash it all down with the excellent local brew, Radegast. Long tables and benches are set outside this cozy wooden chalet. A folk cymbal band plays here every Friday evening. Unfortunately, the pub is open only during the hours of the museum, which means for lunch or early dinner only (see hours for Wooden Small Town)

HOTEL TESLA, *Meziříčská 1653, 756 61 Rožnov pod Radhoštěm. Tel. 0651/545 35, Fax 0651/545 46. Rates for single/double: 700/1,100 Kč. Credit cards: MC. Restaurant.*

What can you expect from a cinder-block highrise hotel named after the electronics factory in town? The rooms are clean and functional, but should be considered a last option.

HOTEL TANEČNICA, *Pustevny, 756 57 Horní Bečva. Tel. 0656/835 341, Fax 0656/836 206. Rates for single/double: 1,200/1,470 Kč. Credit cards: AE, V. Restaurant.*

This large mountain lodge on the leeward side of Mt. Radhošť is a good 10 minutes by car from Rožnov, but is worth your while if Hotel Eroplán is booked up. Buses run here fairly often, depending on the season. It would be nice if the rooms were a bit more rustic, but as of yet they are somewhat characterless. See *Day Trips & Excursions* below for more on Mt. Radhošť and on how to get to Pustevny.

HORSKÝ HOTEL BIOCEL SOLÁN, *Karolinka, 756 06 Velké Karlovice. Tel. 0651/926 381, Fax 0651/926 385. Rates for double only: 1,000-1,240 Kč. No credit cards. 40 rooms. Restaurant.*

Providing a splendid view of the Beskydy hills from its ridge-top location, this mountain chalet offers a retreat from the tourist hubbub down below in Rožnov. Swimming pool, solarium, and massages are all part of the package. A tiny ski resort is five minutes away on foot. Hotel Biocel is a 25-minute drive east of Rožnov. Take Bayerova out of town and follow signs to Velké Karlovice. Only the occasional bus runs here, pretty much making this a viable option only if you have a car.

SEEING THE SIGHTS

The first part of the **Wallachian Open-air Museum** (Valašské muzeum v Přírodě) is what local brochures and signs call **Wooden Small Town** (Dřevěné městecko), but a better translation would probably be "Wooden Hamlet." This is the oldest part of the museum, where you can see the old town hall and Bill's chalet, both relocated from Rožnov's main square in 1925. Most picturesque, however, is the Church of St. Anne, modeled after the late Gothic wooden church found in the village of Větřkovice. An endearing example of Wallachian folk art are the museum's beehives, decorated with carved faces of men. These guys look a little surprised, as well they should, because the bees' enter and exit through their mouths. If you're in need of a little refreshment, don't miss having a beer or a sip of *slivovice* (peach brandy) at the museum's Wallachian *hospoda*, the Last Groschen. *Wooden Small Town is open daily, May 1 through June 30 from 8 a.m. to 6 p.m.; July 1 through August 31 until 7 p.m.; in September until 6 p.m.; and October 1 through November 15 from 8:30 a.m. to 5 p.m. December 15 to March 31 it's open Monday through Wednesday from 8:30 a.m. to 3:30 p.m., on Saturday until 1 p.m., and on Sunday from noon to 4 p.m.*

The second part of the Wallachian Open-air Museum is **Mill Valley** (Mlynská Dolina). As the name implies, this part of the museum devotes itself to the exhibition of water-powered Wallachian mills. Compared to the other parts of the skansen, this one isn't as endearing. But if you've got a real penchant for water-wheels, then it might be worth your while to check it out. *It's open daily April 1 through May 15 from 8:30 a.m. to 5 p.m., May 16 through August 31 from 8 a.m. to 6:30 p.m., and September 1 through October 15 from 8:30 a.m. to 5 p.m.*

The third and biggest part of the museum is the **Wallachian Village** (Valašská Dědina), a gorgeous representation of a shepherds' village that comes replete with live sheep and organic crops and orchards. The entrance is through a six-sided bailiff's barn, modeled after the one belonging to the family of the esteemed Czech historian, František Palacký. From there it's a climb up the hill past several adorable cabins, cottages, and houses that do no less than charm your socks off.

What makes things even more enchanting is the fine pastoral views of the surrounding hills. The whole idyllic effect, views included, leaves you gushing with nostalgia for the old days. *The Wallachian Village is open daily in May from 9 a.m. to 6 p.m., June 1 through August 31 from 8 a.m. to 6 p.m., and in September from 9 a.m. to 5:30 p.m.*

EXCURSIONS & DAY TRIPS

For a good look at the 1,129-meter (3,703-foot) **Mt. Radhošť**, drive or take the bus to the resort of Pustevny, where a four-kilometer hike to the top of the peak begins. Along the way to the summit you'll encounter the wooden totem of **Radegast**, the mountain pagan god that lends its name to the excellent local beer. The grimacing statue, which looks an awful lot like a Polynesian idol, is the work of Albin Polášek, a native of the area and former professor at the Academy of Arts in Chicago.

At the summit of Radhošť is something of another religion, a splendid wooden **Uniate chapel** named for the two men who brought Christianity to Moravia, Cyrillus and Methodius. Their statues stand behind the church.

Buses run regularly between Rožnov and Pustevny. By car it's about a ten minute drive. Take E442 east out of town and then follow signs.

PRACTICAL INFORMATION

- **Information Center,** *Nádražní ulice. Tel. 0651/53403.* This office sells books and maps, can help you find accommodations, and can give you the train and bus schedules.
- **Spořitelna Rožnov,** *Masarykovo náměstí.* You can change your money here.
- **Post Office,** *náměstí Míru.*

20. WEST SLOVAKIA

West Slovakia is where you'll most likely get your first taste of the **Slovak Republic**. But keep in mind that it's far removed from the eastern two-thirds of the country, most notably in terms of its landscape. Compared to the mountainous central and eastern regions, West Slovakia is relatively flat, tree-less, and otherwise not so appealing.

But there are some enticements for traveling through West Slovakia, number one being the capital city of **Bratislava**, which will surprise you with its attractive, manageable old town and its wealth of good restaurants and cafés. Other enticements include the castles of old Hungarian nobility, such as the ruins of **Devín** and **Čachtice**, the hulking bastion of **Červený Kameň**, and the cathedral-crowned castle in the town of **Nitra**.

> ### EXCHANGE RATE IN THE SLOVAK REPUBLIC
> *Remember to check the financial newspaper of your choice for the latest fluctuations in the dollar-crown exchange rate (or whatever currency you happen to have on you). But as a general reminder, the Slovak crown is roughly 35 Sk to the US dollar.*

All of West Slovakia's worthwhile destinations (with the exception of Nitra) are lined up to the northeast of Bratislava along the **Lesser Carpathian Mountains** and in the hilly **Váh River** valley, both of which come as a welcome bit of relief after the monotonous, flat expanses of the Danubian plain in the southern portion of the region, a part of the country that doesn't make for stellar traveling unless you're interested in seeing how Slovakia's Hungarian population lives.

The Lesser Carpathians is the setting for the quaint wine-tasting town of **Modra** and the aforementioned castle of Červený Kameň, while the Váh River valley sets the stage for Slovakia's most popular spa town of **Piešťany**, Čachtice Castle, and **Trenčín Castle** – one of the most magnificent castles in Slovakia located in the amiable town of **Trenčín**.

WEST SLOVAKIA FINDS & FAVORITES

Hotel No. 16, see "Where to Stay" in Bratislava
The Little Blue Church, see "Seeing the Sights" in Bratislava
Hotel Zlaty Kľúčik, see "Where to Stay" in Nitra
Hotel Tatra, see "Where to Stay" in Trenčín
Trenčín Castle, see "Seeing the Sights" in Trenčín

I would be hard pressed to recommend spending a considerable amount of time in any Western Slovak city or town other than Bratislava and possibly Trenčín. There's just too many grand sights awaiting in the central and eastern regions.

Bratislava

I had been living in Prague a few years before I finally made the jaunt down to **Bratislava**. Jaded as I was by Prague's remarkably preserved historic center, I had my doubts that I would find much of interest in a city that was subject to a redevelopment under Communism that was about as insensitive as the battles that raged in the city during World War II.

But once I had a chance to walk around Bratislava's Old Town and feel the vitality here, I put my trepidations to rest. I was so pleasantly surprised by the city that I ended up hanging around a day or two longer than I had originally planned. If you give it some time and drop the comparisons to Prague, I think you'll be pleasantly surprised by this small city on the **Danube** as well.

By its small geographical size and a population of a little more than 450,000, it's still somewhat difficult to conceive of Bratislava as the cultural, political, and economic center of a country. But once you get to know the youngest capital in Europe a bit, you have the feeling that Bratislava is finally coming into its own.

It's also hard to imagine that this city, with its strong Slovak nationalist identity, has truly belonged to Slovaks for only the last 80 years. In fact, if history has any claim to Bratislava, it would have to go to the Hungarians (or *Magyars*), who conquered the town in 906, when it was nothing more than the site of a Slav fortress under the Great Moravian Empire.

Under the expanding Hungarian Empire, **Pozsony** (as the town was first called by the Hungarians) evolved into a regional administrative center, becoming the most important town in the empire after Budapest, which makes it not that surprising to learn that **King Matthias Corvinus** established the first Hungarian university here in 1465, called the **Academia Istropolitana.**

In 1526, the Austrian **Hapsburgs** took control of the Bohemian and Hungarian lands, only to see Buda (of modern-day Budapest) taken over ten years later by the Turks. Capital status naturally fell to **Pressburg** (as Bratislava was known in German), kicking off the town's golden age, in which kings and queens were crowned at the **St. Martin Cathedral** and grandiose palaces were erected around the city. But when the Turks were driven off the Hungarian plain in 1783, the Hungarian capital reverted back to Buda, and Pressburg once again was relegated a provincial town.

Pressburg was thrust onto the world's stage following Napoleon's victory at the Battle of Austerlitz in 1805, when the Treaty of Pressburg was signed at the **Primate's Palace** and Austria was forced to relinquish much of its territory to the French. The Primate's Palace once again became the site of an historic occasion in 1848, when **Ferdinand V** signed into law the demand of the great Slovak nationalist, Ľudovít Štúr, that Slovak serfdom be abolished.

Life, however, didn't get much better for the minority of Slovaks living in Pressburg, as they were subject to harsh policies favoring Germans and Hungarians, who made up the majority of the 60,000 people living in Pressburg at the turn of the century. But that all changed in 1918, when Pressburg was incorporated into the newly formed Czecho-slovak Republic and Slovaks were given the upper political and cultural hand in Slovakia. In an effort to carve an identity for themselves in a city that had never really belonged to them, the Slovaks renamed the city Bratislava in honor of **Bratislav,** the last ruler of the Great Moravian Empire.

When Bohemia and Moravia were declared a Nazi protectorate in 1938, Bratislava found itself the capital of a newly formed Slovak puppet state, led by one **Jozef Tiso.** The **Slovak National Uprising** (Slovenské národné povstanie or SNP) managed to overthrow this fascist govern-ment, but the fight for freedom was promptly quashed by the Nazis, who ruled here during World War II until they were driven out from Bratislava by the Russians on April 4, 1945.

Bratislava boomed in the forty years of Communism, becoming the second biggest city in Czechoslovakia and a major industrial center. As a result, it acquired some of its most dour features, most notably the futuristic **SNP Bridge**, which links the center of the city to the utterly depressing and shockingly enormous housing estate of **Petržalka** on the south side of the Danube River.

With the divorce of Czechoslovakia on January 1, 1993, Bratislava became the capital of the independent Republic of Slovakia, and has, despite the odds, done well for itself. Though it's the most progressive city in Slovakia, Bratislava thankfully still hasn't completely succumbed to the forces of westernization like Prague has, nor has it been bombarded by tourists, experiencing none of the crowd-control problems that Prague, Vienna, or Budapest have.

Bratislava's historic **Staré Mesto** (Old Town) features a network of enchanting lanes lined with pretty Baroque houses and overlooked by an occasional tower, such as the most famous one here – **St. Michael's Tower**. But where Bratislava really shines is in its score of wonderfully unique museums, especially the ones located in the **Bratislava Castle**. Decorative arts, Slovak musical instruments, and antique clocks are all found in this none-too-inspiring castle that bulges up in the center of town.

You'll want to spend at least two days here soaking in the sights, maybe more if you're the kind who likes to wile away hours in excellent restaurants and snazzy cafés, of which there is no shortage in Bratislava.

ORIENTATION

Hugging the Austrian border in the southwest corner of Slovakia, Bratislava straddles both sides of the **Danube River** (called the *Dunaj* in Slovak) a mere 65 kilometers (40 miles) downstream from Vienna in the foothills of the Lesser Carpathian Mountains and on the edge of the Danubian plain. Prague is 321 kilometers (199 miles) to the northwest.

Where you'll want to spend the majority of your time is **Staré Mesto** (Old Town), the historic core of Bratislava located on the north side of the Danube. **Bratislava Castle**, the city's most indelible sight, rises up on the western edge of the Old Town. The city's second-most memorable sight, the massive **SNP Bridge**, stretches across the Danube just below the castle. If you use the bridge, castle, and river as your landmarks, then it's not hard to come to grips with the layout of Staré Mesto, as it is fairly compact and easily negotiated on foot.

ARRIVALS & DEPARTURES

By Air

Czech Airlines (or ČSA), *Tel. 02/201 043 10 in Prague and 07/361 073 in Bratislava*, has several daily flights between Bratislava and Prague, costing about 3,000 Kč (3,500 Sk).

Tatra Air, *Tel. 07/366 758 in Bratislava*, has flights from Bratislava to Prague and Košíce.

The tiny airport is eight kilometers (five miles) from the center of town, accessed by taking bus #28 from the main train station or by taking the Czechoslovak Airlines shuttle from their office *at Štúrova 13*.

Don't forget, Bratislava is less than 40 miles away from Vienna's Schwechat Airport, from where you can take a bus directly to Bratislava's main bus station.

By Boat
If you'd like to nip up to Vienna for a day, then consider taking a hydrofoil up the Danube from Bratislava's **river terminal** at *Vajanskeho nábrežie 2*. Boats depart Bratislava twice a day (and return twice a day) for the hour-long trip. The cost is around 650 Sk one-way and 950 Sk round-trip. Times of departure depend on the season.

During the same period there are several daily, hour-long cruises going up and down the Danube, costing about 40 Sk. The **Blue Danube travel agency**, *Panenska 7, Tel. . 07/533 1295*, has scheduling information and sells tickets for both cruises.

By Bus
Four or five buses run daily between Prague's Florenc station and Bratislava's main station. The four hour trip costs about 300 Kč (275 Sk). But you need to buy your ticket in advance at either of the stations.

The main bus station, where almost all regional and long-distance buses depart and arrive, is just east of the city center on Mlynské nivy street. Hop on bus #53 or #121 or on trolley bus #210 or #211 to take you into the Old Town.

By Car
Prague, Brno, and Bratislava are linked by the E65 motorway. Prague to Bratislava is about a three hour trip, while Brno to Bratislava takes about an hour. Parking is usually not a big problem; just look for the blue "P" signs. Almost all of the hotels listed below have private parking.

By Train
Trains depart Prague's Hlavní nádraží for Bratislava's Hlavná stanica roughly every two hours. The five-and-a-half journey costs about 400 Kč (350 Sk). There are two train stations in Bratislava. The main station – **Hlavná stanica** – where all international and most long-distance trains arrive and depart – is at the end of Štefánikova street, about a half-mile north of Staré Mesto. If you've just arrived at the main station, hop on tram #1 or #18 to get to the center.

The second station, **Nové Mesto stanica**, is about four miles northeast of the center on the #6 tram line. Most trains servicing nearby towns arrive and depart here.

GETTING AROUND TOWN

Walking is certainly the best (and only) way to get around Staré Mesto and up to the castle. But you may end up staying in a hotel that's a good stretch from the historic center, in which case you'll need to come to terms with Bratislava's fairly good public transportation system. It's made up of trams (numbered 1 through 12), buses (numbered from 21 on), and trolley buses (numbered in the 200s). At each stop you'll find a time table with a little map showing you where the tram lines and bus routes go. Most buses and trams start running at around 5 a.m. and stop at midnight. After midnight, your only option is a night bus (numbered in the 500s). Most of them originate at the main train station and stop at námestie SNP.

Trams, buses, and trolley buses all use the same ticket, purchased for 7 Sk from a little yellow dispenser found at most bus and tram stops. Be sure to validate your ticket on board by sticking it in the little gadget by the door and pulling back on the handle. If you don't have a validated ticket, be prepared to shell out 700 Sk to the plain clothes controller.

Taxi is a good way to go as well. There's never any problem finding one, and the drivers are fairly honest (not at all like their counterparts in Prague). There is an extra charge for taking a taxi late at night and for getting picked up somewhere. A reliable company with some English-speaking dispatchers is **Yellow Express**, *Tel. 07/531 1311*.

If you'd like to rent a car in Bratislava, you can do so from the **Hertz** offices at the Hotel Forum (see below) and Bratislava airport, from **Europcar** (*Tel. 07/534 0841*) in the lobby of Danube Hotel (see below), or from the better-priced **Slavocar** (*Tel. 07/521 3119*), near the bus station at *Prievozská 30*.

WHERE TO STAY

DANUBE HOTEL, *Rybné námestie 1, 813 38 Bratislava. Tel. 07/ 534 0833, Fax 07/531 4311. Rates for single/double: 5,636/6,380 Sk. Credit cards: AE, DC, MC, V. 280 rooms. 2 restaurants.*

This is one of the swankiest hotels in town, catering almost exclusively to Westerners. Its riverbank location is as central as you can get – a mere two minute walk from the National Theater. South-facing rooms look out onto the Danube, while west-facing rooms have a view of the castle. But there's noting particularly unique about this hotel. Sure, it has all the expected conveniences, such as a fitness club, swimming pool, and sauna, but it feels like your average Hilton. The fine dining restaurant, the Presbourg, is exceptional, however (see *Where to Eat*).

HOTEL PERUGIA, *Zelená 5, 811 01 Bratislava. Tel. 07/544 318 18, Fax 07/544 318 21. Rates for single/double: 4,280-4,880/5,080 Sk. Credit cards: AE, DC, MC, V. 14 rooms. Restaurant.*

This is the most intimate hotel n the center. This small hotel in the thick of Staré Mesto's lanes offers peaceful accommodations footsteps away from the town's major sights and best restaurants. The hotel's glass atrium, filled with all sorts of flora, can be enjoyed as you ride up the hotel's "panoramic elevator." All the rooms feature classy dark-wood furnishings, direct-dial telephones, and satellite television. The best rooms, however, are on the first floor to the rear. These come with a private, outdoor terrace. Friendly, English-speaking service abounds.

HOTEL DEVÍN, *Riečna 4, 811 02 Bratislava. Tel. 07/533 0851, Fax 07/533 0682. Rates for single/double: 3,500-4,300/4,900 Sk. Credit cards: AE, DC, MC, V. 101 rooms. Restaurant.*

Though it hasn't completely rid itself of its Communist-era furnishings yet, the Hotel Devín is still not a bad choice if you're looking for something central and reasonably priced. The white-washed rooms are cheery, especially if you get one facing the Danube. Yes, the hotel is located on the riverbank, right next door to the Hotel Danube.

BOTEL GRACIA, *Rázusovo nábrežie, 811 02 Bratislava. Tel. 07/544 324 30, Fax 07/544 321 31. Rates for single/double: 1,600/2,200 Sk. Credit cards: AE, DC, MC, V. 28 rooms. Restaurant.*

The novelty of sleeping in a boat anchored in the Danube River makes this a good choice of accommodations. Though somewhat cramped, the rooms are nicely outfitted, with big windows providing a great view of the river or of the Bratislava Castle. The boat is located just behind the Danube Hotel off Rybné námestie, with great access to the historic center.

HOTEL KYJEV, *Rajská 2, 07/322 041, Fax 07/326 820. Rates for single/double: 1,350-1,850/1,500-2,000 Sk. Credit cards: AE, MC, V. 180 rooms. Restaurant.*

This hotel, located minutes away by foot from Staré Mesto, occupies one of the tallest buildings in the city. And it's an eyesore. The rooms come with tacky furniture, but are clean and functional. The hotel is also a target for huge tour buses, which means there are always a lot of people milling around the lobby. But I would almost recommend staying here if only for the views, which take in just about all of the city.

HOTEL FORUM, *Hodžovo námestie, 816 25 Bratislava. Tel. 07/534 8115, Fax 07/531 4645. Rates for single/double: 4,900/5,900 Sk. Credit cards: AE, DC, MC, V. 230 rooms. Three restaurants.*

This is the most exclusive address in town, attracting mostly folks who are here on business. Like the Danube Hotel, it really has nothing unique going for it, other than rates that are far and above most hotels in town. Of course, you can expect all the Western comforts in each room, such as direct-dial telephones, satellite television, mini-bar, and what have you. There's also a nightclub, fitness center, swimming pool, sauna, and in-house masseuse.

The hotel's Forum Restaurant serves continental food; its Slovakia Restaurant serves local and national specialties; and its Budapest Restaurant serves Hungarian cuisine replete with live Hungarian folk music. There's a Hertz desk here if you need to rent a car. The hotel is located just outside Staré Mesto, within walking distance of just about everything.

CHEZ DAVID, *Zámocká 13, 811 01 Bratislava. Tel. 07/531 3824, Fax 07/ 531 2642. Rates for single/double: 1,770/2,770 Sk. Credit cards: AE, DC, MC, V. 8 rooms, 1 apartment. Restaurant.*

This small pension at the foot of the castle is a nice alternative to the big hotels in Bratislava. It's located just outside Staré Mesto in the heart of what used to be the Jewish quarter. Each of the threadbare but cozy rooms comes with a private bath, satellite television, and direct-dial telephone. If you'd like to stay in town for a while, then consider renting out the pension's apartment, which comes with a fully equipped kitchen. The hotel can arrange tours of Bratislava, especially ones dealing with the long Jewish history of the town. But the best thing about this pension is its excellent kosher restaurant (see *Where to Eat*).

HOTEL NO. 16, *Partizánska 16a, 811 03 Bratislava. Tel. 07/531 1672, Fax. 07/531 1298. Rates for single/double: 2,800/3,700 Sk. Credit cards: AE, MC, V. 14 rooms. No restaurant.*

Set in a quiet neighborhood high above Staré Mesto, No. 16 has more the feel of a bed and breakfast than a hotel. Though it's a bit of a hike from the center (about 15 minutes on foot), it's well worth the effort considering the good air and handsome villas surrounding the hotel, itself a recently built villa. Inside you'll find a beautiful, wood-studded lobby, with Slovak folk art hanging on the walls and a little fountain trickling by the staircase. (The lobby is where you sit down to a made-to-order breakfast and page through the English-language newspapers that the hotel provides for its guests.)

Each of the rooms is individually decorated, outfitted with wood ceilings, direct-dial telephones, cable television (with remote), huge windows, and ultra-comfortable beds. Definitely request room #5, a cozy nook with what has to be Bratislava's most romantic view of the castle. Other incentives for staying here are the tip-top, English-speaking receptionists and the affable owners, Braňo Hronec and Judita Vargová. All in all, this is the best hotel in Bratislava. Look for signs pointing the way on Štefánikova street as you come into the center of town from the main train station or from the E65 motorway.

HOTEL TURIST, *Ondavská 5, 826 47 Bratislava. Tel. 07/525 4844, Fax 07/543 8263. Rates for single/double: 800/1,050 Sk. No credit cards. 90 rooms. Restaurant.*

This is your best option for budget accommodations in Bratislava. Though it's well connected by tram, the hotel is a long, mile-and-a-half haul northeast of the center. The peach-colored rooms are pleasant enough, outfitted with balconies and satellite television (but no telephones). The whole place, in fact, looks a bit like an American motel.

WHERE TO EAT

PRESBOURG, *at the Danube Hotel, Rybné námestie 1. Tel. 07/534 0833. 800-1,000 Sk. Credit cards: AE, DC, MC, V.*

As you would expect from a French-owned hotel, the Alsatian food served here is superb. Scrumptious puff pastry with asparagus top the list of the starters, while roast pheasant with smoked bacon and deep-fried grapes grace the list of entrées. For dessert, go for the iced nougat stuffed with cherries; it's heavenly. Complimenting the food is live harp and guitar music.

KORZO, *Hviezdoslavovo námestie 11. Tel. 07/334 974. 200-400 Sk. No credit cards.*

Venison and steak prepared in a Slovak style are two excellent choices at this reputable cellar restaurant opposite the Danube Hotel. Live folk music and a salad bar are two other big enticements for eating here.

SPAGHETTI & CO., *Gorkého 1. Tel. 07/533 2303. 200-300 Sk. Credit cards: AE, MC, V.*

This restaurant cat-a-corner to the National Theater has gotten better over the years, and now serves perhaps the best pizza you can get in the historic center.

U LISZTA, *Klariská 1. Tel. 07/544 125 40. 175-300 Sk. No credit cards.*

Locals swear by this restaurant just off Michalská. Large portions of chicken, pork, and steak layered in thick sauces unfortunately don't measure up to the promising candle-lit atmosphere and the excellent service.

POD BAŠTOU, *Baštova 3. Tel. 07/533 1765. 200-400 Sk. No credit cards.*

Just around the corner from St. Michael's Tower, this fine wine restaurant hunkers two stories down in a vaulted, brick cellar. Offering an extensive list of Slovak wines from bottle and cask, this is as good a place as any to sample the local *víno*, which goes down well after a taste of the spicy stuffed ham rolls, venison medallions topped with a blackberry sauce, or the pork chops stuffed with peas, ham, and cheese.

PRAŠNÁ BAŠTA, *Zámočnícka 11. Tel. 07/533 4957. 100-200 Sk. No credit cards.*

A dimly lit, octagonal room outfitted with stained glass windows sets the appropriate mood for the excellent Slovak cuisine served at this wine restaurant footsteps away from St. Michael's Tower. Some winners on the menu are the Roquefort *placky* and the pork chop smothered with a creamy paprika and mushroom sauce.

BRATISLAVA CAFÉS

*The people of Bratislava take their café society quite seriously, as you can tell by the few number of empty seats in any given **kaviareň** (café). Most are quite elegant. Unfortunately, the most splendid of them all, the Café Roland, closed in 1998.*

Most cafés serve a light continental breakfast, some sort of dessert (be it a puffy cake or a sundae), or sometimes a full meal.

Here are a few you ought to dive into:

__Café Maximilián__, Hlavné námestie 2. This two-tiered café has a discreet, sophisticated feel. A good place to go after dinner for a coffee or a drink.

__Korzo Kaviareň__, Hviezdoslavovo námestie 11. This is a somewhat touristy place you might want to avoid, unless it's a nice day. In that case, go for the outdoor terrace, which has a nice view of the castle.

__Slamienka__, Obchodná 26. Bratislava artists and intellectuals come here to drink the Oriental and herbal teas and soak in the New Age atmosphere.

__Kaffee Mayer__, Hlavné námestie 4. This new, very classy cafe caters mostly to Austrian tourists, hence the name and the Viennese decor.

__Gremium Café__, Gorkého 11. The atmosphere here is quite pleasant, making it a good place to linger over a coffee and newspaper.

MÁRIA TERÉZIA, *Palisády 50. Tel. 07/325 590. 1,500-2,000 Sk. Credit cards: AE, MC, V.*

If you're in the mood to splurge, then you just might want to do it at this restaurant where you can have a dining experience almost as regal as the restaurant's name. Hungry? How about a whole roasted goat served at your table. Maybe something lighter, something nouvelle like the grilled salmon or brisket of lamb might suit you a little better. Burgundy-red carpets, harp music, and expert service all contribute to the refined ambience of this memorable restaurant.

THE DUBLINER, *Sedlárska 6. No tel. 150-300. No credit cards.*

As expat-central, this Irish pub is a nice place to meet other English speakers, especially on a cold day when there's a fire crackling in the fireplace. Bar pours the obligatory Guinness, while the kitchen serves a nice helping of Irish stew and vegetarian lasagna.

CHEZ DAVID, *Zámocká 13. Tel. 07/531 3824. 100-200 Sk. Credit cards: AE, DC, MC, V.*

This kosher restaurant and its menu of light dishes comes as a welcome surprise in a town that loves its rich and hearty sauces. Using only the freshest of ingredients, Chez David serves traditional Jewish fare such as *cholent, chrimsel,* and *barkhes,* but also offers some not-so-Jewish cuisine such as a tasty humus and an excellent roasted salmon in asparagus sauce. The prices here are very reasonable and the service is attentive, but the décor is somewhat lacking in creativity. Keep in mind that the restaurant is closed on the Sabbath (Friday evening and all of Saturday). Reservations are a good idea.

MODRÁ HVIEZDA, *Beblavého 14. Tel. 07/533 2747. 100-300 Sk. No credit cards.*

Sitting on a quiet lane leading up to the castle, this tiny restaurant dishes up some Hungarian-accented Slovak dishes in an intriguing vaulted cellar. The meats are tender here, and the sauces are sumptuously rich. Some outstanding choices are the veal with dried plums in a creamy red wine sauce, chicken ragout in a creamy paprika sauce, or the goulash filet with green pepper in a wine and cognac sauce. This is another good place to sample local wine.

RYBÁRSKY CECH, *Žižková 1. Tel. 07/531 3049. 350-450 Sk. Credit cards: AE, DC, MC. V.*

Carved out of an attractive Rococo villa at the foot of the castle, this restaurant specializes in fish, mainly saltwater. Dover sole, salmon, shark, and an excellent octopus in a creamy curry sauce grace the menu. Be sure to go for the spicy Hungarian fish soup that's laced with paprika.

CASABLANCA, *Jeséniova 53. Tel. 07/371 767, 400-800 Sk. Credit cards: AE, MC, V.*

Despite the ridiculous pseudo-Moroccan decor, this restaurant is one of Bratislava's best, offering a sensational lineup of traditional French meals, such as a creamy onion tart or beef medallions in a red wine sauce. The preparation of their fresh seafood, however, does hint more of Morocco than France. Located at the top of Koliba Hill, Casablanca is almost impossible to get to by public transportation, so you'll need to catch a cab if you don't have your own wheels.

SEEING THE SIGHTS
Staré Mesto
This cluster of Baroque lanes, alleys, and passages that make up the historic center of town is Bratislava at its most intriguing. It's also Bratislava at its liveliest, chock-full of students going in and out of shops, pubs, cafés, and restaurants. The best way to tackle Staré Mesto (Old Town) is at your leisure, giving yourself ample time to pop into a café now and again.

We'll start just outside the northern edge of Staré Mesto at the oblong **námestie SNP**, the city's main square and the focus of Velvet Revolution demonstrations and later Velvet Divorce celebrations. It's a pleasantly leafy space, centered around the **Monument to the Slovak National Uprising**, commemorating the ill-fated rebellion against Nazi fascism. Feminists may have a hard time stomaching the monument, with its bronze soldier standing heroically in front of two meek women, their hair covered and their heads bowed.

From námestie SNP head up to **Hurbanovo námestie** (square), overlooked by the most beautiful Baroque church in the city – **Trinity Church** (Kostel Trinitárov). The sooty exterior does little to prepare you for the misty single-nave interior, with its trompe l'oeil frescoes giving the impression of cornices forming a perimeter around a false cupola.

Across the square is an old footbridge which was at one time the first of two gates you had to pass through in order to enter the old town of Bratislava. The bridge spans across the old moat, now a lush garden that serves as the city library's "summer reading room." Just after you cross the moat, look to your left for a little Baroque house called U červeného raka (At the Red Crayfish), one of the oldest pharmacies in town now housing the **Pharmaceutical Museum** (Expozícia farmácie). Though it seems based on the barest of pretexts, this museum is actually pretty interesting.

Just inside the front door is the original 18th-century pharmacy, and beyond are displays taking you through the history of pharmaceutical science in Bratislava, beginning when it was an offshoot of alchemy. In addition to all the pharmaceutical stuff, there's a nice collection of Renaissance and Baroque furniture culled from the oldest pharmacies around Bratislava. *The museum is open Tuesday through Sunday from 10 a.m. to 5 p.m.*

Down the lane is Bratislava's last remaining watchtower gate – **St. Michael's Tower** (Michalská veža), providing an alluring entrance into Staré Mesto. This Baroque tower with its needle thin spire was built on top of a base dating back to the 14th century. Climb the tower for a pretty view of Staré Mesto's red roofs, and for a look at the **Exposition of Arms and Municipal Fortifications** housed inside the tower. *It's open daily except Tuesday from 10 a.m. to 5 p.m.*

Cutting through the middle of Staré Mesto, Michalská and its extension of Ventúrska form one enchanting lane lined with some of Bratislava's finest Baroque palaces and houses. The main university library is *at Michalská 1*, notable because it held the Hungarian Diet (Parliament) in the 18th and 19th centuries. Head through the passage here for a look at the **St. Clare Church** (Kostol sv. Klara) and its richly adorned Gothic spire – the best of its kind in Bratislava. The church, founded by the Cistercians in the 14th century, is usually closed, except for the occasional concert (see *Nightlife & Entertainment* below).

Back on Michalská, walk a short ways down to *Venturská 10*, where you'll find the **Mozart House** (Mozartov dom), one of several Baroque palaces built by the Pálffy family in the 18th century. It's named as such because a six-year-old Mozart performed here in 1762. Today, it houses the Austrian Embassy. Opposite is the **Academia Istropolitana**, the first Hungarian (and Slovak) university. Founded in 1465 and closed a quick 25 years later, it now houses the city's Academy of Fine Arts.

At the end of Ventúrska and to your left *at Panská 19* is another **Pálffy Palace**, this one housing a branch of the **Bratislava City Gallery**. Here you'll want to bypass the mediocre collection of European paintings from the 16th to the 19th centuries and head for the collection of 20th-century Slovak art, featuring notable artists such as Martin Benka and Janko Alexy. *It's open Tuesday through Sunday from 10 a.m. to 5 p.m.*

Towards the castle at the end of Panská, the **Bibiana**, *Tel. 07/331 314,* is a fine museum of art for children, inviting kids of all nationalities to its informal art classes (call for times.) *It's open daily except Monday from 10 a.m. to 6 p.m.*

Now you'll be confronted with what has to be the harshest bit of modern development to desecrate the city – a veritable highway ripping through Staré Mesto on its way to the SNP Bridge. Try to ignore the cars zooming by as you walk around the corner to the **St. Martin Cathedral** (Dóm sv. Martina), where 11 Hungarian Hapsburg kings and eight queens were crowned between the years of 1563 and 1830. Indicative of its royal past is the crown that tops (in place of what should be a cross) its rather lame steeple. Consecrated in 1452, the Gothic church doesn't inspire much gawking, and holds little of interest inside other than a couple of statues by George Raphael Donner, one of Vienna's best known sculptors during the 18th century. But it is a nice respite away from the traffic zooming by on the Staromestká thoroughfare, the vibrations from which are sadly wreaking havoc on the foundations of the cathedral.

Retracing your steps down from the cathedral, pass by Panská street and head around the corner into **Hviezdoslavovo námestie**, a narrow, green strip of a square named after the most famous Slovak poet of all time – Pavol Orságh Hviezdoslav, whose larger-than-life statue is plunked down in the middle of the square.

Crowning the square at the opposite end is the cream-colored **Slovak National Theater** (Slovenské národné divadlo), topped with a shimmering silver dome and fronted by a graceful fountain statue of the mythological Ganymede. Though it was the Hungarians and Germans who built the Viennese-style opera house in 1886, the Slovaks took it over for their own purposes, now presenting quality operas and ballets here. Just off the square on Mostová is another theater, the Art Nouveau **Reduta**, built in 1914 as a dance hall and casino and now home to the Slovak Philharmonic Orchestra. (See *Nightlife & Entertainment* below.)

From Hviezdoslavovo námestie head a few blocks north on Rybárska brána street to **Hlavné námestie** (Main Square), at one time Bratislava's main marketplace, but now a pleasant grassy space centered around a Roland statue fountain (replete with peeing cherubs).

Opposite the café is the **Old Town Hall** (Stará radnica), first erected in the 14th century but later added on to, employing a hodgepodge of styles. The hybrid building – with its Gothic core, arcaded Renaissance courtyard, handsome Baroque clock tower, and neo-Gothic annex – might well be Bratislava's finest piece of architecture. The town hall now houses the **Municipal Museum** (Mestské múzeum), devoted to different aspects of Bratislava's history. It's well worth your time to peruse this museum if only for its nicely restored rooms and its grisly exhibit on feudal justice, a euphemism for the different methods of torture used during the Middle Ages.

Here you can see all sorts of terrible instruments used to elicit pain in as many ways as possible. Unfortunately, there are no English captions, but it's not to hard to get the picture of how these instruments worked. Located on the other side of the courtyard is a **winemaking exhibit**, which attests to Bratislava's thriving winemaking industry. There's nothing much of interest here, especially since there's no English text to help you along. But you may want to buy a ticket anyway so as to check out the neat Gothic rooms the museum is housed in. *The Municipal Museum is open daily except Monday from 10 a.m. to 5 p.m.*

Just beyond the Old Town Hall is another architectural gem – the **Primate's Palace** (Primaciálny palác), occupying the strangely silent, utterly austere Primaciálné námestie (square). The neo-Classical palace was built in 1781 for the bishops of Esztergom, the Hungarian primates, which explains the 300-pound cast-iron bishop's hat set on top of a single gable in the middle of a line of statuary.

The palace takes its claim to fame from the Treaty of Pressburg, signed by Napoleon and Emperor Franz I in its Hall of Mirrors following Napoleon's victory at the Battle of Austerlitz in 1805. Recently renovated, the Hall of Mirrors now houses six rare English tapestries, made in the 1730s by the Royal Weaving Works in Mortlake, England. Also on exhibit are some sanguine Dutch and Flemish paintings from the 17th and 18th centuries. *The exhibit is open daily except Monday from 10 a.m. to 5 p.m.*

Just off Primaciálné námestie *at Kloubouč nícka 2* is the **Hummel Museum** (Múzeum Hummela), devoted to the 19th-century composer and concert pianist Johann Nepomuk Hummel. Not exactly internationally acclaimed, Hummel is the most famous Slovak composer. The small museum, housed in his birthplace, exhibits a number of his personal effects, but doesn't really cut the mustard unless you have a deep interest in the composer. Summer concerts occasionally take place in the courtyard. *It's open daily except Monday from 1 p.m. to 5 p.m.*

From here, retrace your steps back to Hlavné námestie and swing right into Františkánské námestie, fronted on the east side by the **Church of the Holy Savior** (Kostol Najsvätejšieho Spasiteľa). Built by German Protestants in 1638, this three-naved church was later confiscated by the Jesuits during the Counter Reformation, who then gave it a thoroughly Baroque facelift. Further along is the 600-year-old Franciscan **Church of the Annunciation** (Kostol Zvästovania Františkánský), one of Bratislava's oldest churches. But there's little left of the original church since receiving a bombastic Baroque reconstruction in the 17th century. An interesting tidbit of history about this church: it was here that the Hungarian nobility (the Estates) elected Hapsburg Ferdinand I as the king of Hungary in 1526, sealing the fate of Hapsburg rule in Hungary for the next 400 years.

At the northern end of Františkánské námestie, the **Mirbach Palace** (Mirbachov palác) counts as the most beautiful Rococo piece of architecture in Bratislava. The palace, with its single-gabled facade punctuated by a gilded coat of arms, houses another branch of the **Bratislava City Gallery**, this one displaying Central European paintings from the Baroque period. The highlight here is the collection of 300 miniature paintings set within wainscot panels. *It's open Tuesday through Sunday from 10 a.m. to 5 p.m.*

Bratislava Castle & Below

It isn't the most awe-inspiring castle in the world. In fact, it's rather generic. Often referred to as the "inverted bedstead," the castle is a boxy structure with four turrets rising from each corner. But it does command an impressive position 330 feet above the Danube.

The castle acquired its present shape in the 15th century, when Emperor Sigismund had it beefed up in fear of Hussite attack. During Bratislava's stint as capitol of the Hungarian Empire, the castle flourished as the seat of kings and queens. But once Buda reclaimed capital status, the castle turned into a barracks, its soldiers accidentally burning the place down in 1811. The castle sat as ruins until 1953, when the Communists finally decided to reconstruct it and turn it into prime ministerial offices. But the reason for hiking up to the top of the castle is not to admire its architecture, but to check out the fine museums it now houses and the view it affords.

First, the view. Though not necessarily beautiful, the view takes in not only the red roofs and steeples of Old Town, but also the mammoth SNP Bridge and the legions of Petržalka's concrete highrises, which seemingly span across the curvature of the earth. There are few displays of the historic and the modern that hit home quite like this one.

Now the museums. Entered through on the left side of the castle gate, the Slovak National Museum's **Treasury** exhibits a fine collection of Celtic, Germanic, and Slavic artifacts unearthed from around Slovakia. It's a fairly good exhibit, mainly because of the dozens of intriguing Celtic coins on view. But if you're short on time I'd skip it and head into the **Historical Museum**, occupying most of the castle proper.

The Historical Museum kicks off on the first floor with a look at the folk costumes from several regions around Slovakia. Meticulously stitched and colorfully embroidered, these costumes are really a joy to look at. All of the costumes, of course, correspond with particular folk dances, which you can see here on video.

On the second floor are exhibits on traditional Slovak crafts and Viennese silverware. But these exhibits don't hold a candle to the rest of the museum, which is mainly devoted to decorative arts through the ages. Renaissance chests, Baroque wardrobes, and Rococo escritoires lead up to an entire wing devoted to Historicist and Art Nouveau furniture. Instead of showing you a chair here and a table there, this wing features entire bedroom, dining room, and living room sets that are simply astounding. When you're finished gawking at the furniture, you can climb to the top of one of the castle turrets and take in an even more startling view of the city. (You'll want to snap some photos here, so be sure to bring your camera with you through the museum.) The finishing touch to the museum is its superb collection of Baroque, neo-Baroque, and Art Nouveau clocks.

Going back out the castle gate, follow the path around the east side of the castle to the wonderful **Music Museum**, set in the castle's Luginsland Bastion. The museum displays more than just instruments, but just about anything that serves a purpose for the sound it makes. Taken as a whole, this is a museum fascinating for its view of Slovak folk life, which seems to revolve around the making of music.

One floor is devoted to the instruments of the shepherds living in the mountain regions of Slovakia. Included in this exhibit are several enormous bugles, which were used by mountain shepherds to signal other shepherds on nearby mountain sides. (How they could carry these bugles, let alone play them, is beyond me.) But the real attraction is the upstairs collection of *fujaras* – huge wooden wind instruments indigenous to Slovakia. Meticulously carved with figures of animals, people, and landscapes, these fujaras are simply wonderful pieces of folk art.

All the museums at the castle are open daily except Monday from 10 a.m. to 6 p.m. May through September, and from 9 a.m. to 5 p.m. the rest of the year. The castle grounds are open daily from 9 a.m. to 10 p.m. April through September, and until 6 p.m. the rest of the year.

Around the base of the castle hill are several more museums worth checking out, not least the **Clock Museum** (Múzeum hodín), housed in a corner Rococo house *at Židovská 1*. Clocks throughout the ages, from Gothic on up to Empire, fill three narrow stories in this old Burgher's house called "At the Good Shepherd" (U dobrého pastiera). *It's open daily except Tuesday from 10 a.m. to 5 p.m.*

A little further up Židovská (Jewish) street *at number 17* is the **Museum of Jewish Culture** (Múzeum židovskej kultúry), occupying the late Renaissance Zsigray Mansion. This little museum testifies to the large Jewish community that has lived in Bratislava since the 13th century. At the dawn of World War II, Jews made up as much as ten percent of Bratislava's population. As many as 19 synagogues and prayer rooms huddled around the foot of the castle, which was Bratislava's Jewish quarter. What the Nazis didn't demolish of the Jewish quarter, the Communists did in order to construct the SNP Bridge.

In addition to numerous textiles, menorahs, Torah scrolls, and other religious paraphernalia, the museum features two 18th-century faience jugs found in the nearby town of Senec. Also on display are the writings of Rabbi Hatam Sofer, who in 1806 founded the Pressburger Yeshivah, the most illustrious center of Orthodox study in Europe until World War II, after which it was relocated from Bratislava to its present site in Jerusalem.

Just off the river embankment at the bottom of the castle hill is the **Archaeological Museum** (Archeologické múzeum), housed in the Kamper Mansion *at Žižkova 12*. In addition to the statuettes, lamps, glassware, and jewels from ancient Egypt and ancient Greece, there are some interesting grave units dating back to the Roman period, as well as numerous artifacts dating from the Bronze Age through the Middle Ages. But unless you have a particular interest in archaeology, I would skip this rather exhaustive exhibit. *It's open daily except Monday from 9 a.m. to 5 p.m.*

Outside the Historic Center

We'll start at the **Slovak National Gallery** (Slovenská národná galéria), on the river embankment *at Rázusovo nábrežie 2* (a few blocks east of the Danube Hotel). The venue for the gallery is a U-shaped Baroque palace, joined at its ends by an atrocious red skyway-like structure thrown up in the 1970s. This is Slovakia's largest museum of art, mainly concerned with the works of 20th-century Slovak artists.

The striking thing about modern Slovak art is its eccentric character. It bears little resemblance to Czech, let alone Western European, art. At times it can be frustratingly obtuse, other times wonderfully fresh. Some shining lights of Slovak art to look out for at the gallery include Ľudovit Fulla (whose work tends toward busy abstracts), Martin Benka (whose Expressionist portrayals of peasant life are quite poetic), and Janko Alexy, perhaps the most well known Slovak artist of the 20th century. *The National Gallery is open Tuesday through Sunday from 10 a.m. to 5 p.m.*

Further eastward along the embankment *at Vajanského nábrežie 2* is a branch of the **Slovak National Museum** (Slovenské národné múzeum), this one devoted to natural history. But I wouldn't waste my time here among the endless displays of stuffed animals and rocks. *It's open daily except Monday from 9 a.m. to 5 p.m.*

From here it's a 10 minute walk east along Vajanského nábrežie and Dostojevského rad streets and north on Bezručova street to what is perhaps Bratislava's most unique sight – the Art Nouveau **Little Blue Church** (Modrý kostolík). Designed by Hungarian Ödön Lechner, this sky-blue church with its undulating walls and rounded corners defies the notion that houses of worship be austere. In fact, the entire ensemble is so cute (for lack of a better word) that it appears straight out of some animated film. Inside, the church maintains that light-heartedness with its pastel colors that makes you want to taste the walls. Definitely do not miss this one-of-a-kind sight.

Slavín Hill

There are few opportunities these days in the Czech and Slovak republics to see one of the mammoth Soviet monuments that once littered the two republics, so you just might want to make the effort to visit the top of Slavín Hill, bulging up just north of the castle hill. Here you'll find the **Slavín Monument**, a spiky obelisk commemorating the 6,000 Soviet soldiers who lost their lives liberating West Slovakia from Nazi occupation. The soaring monument, topped by a soldier waving the victory flag, doesn't hold a candle in size to the liberation statue in Budapest, but it is visible from just about every street corner in Bratislava. To get there, take trolley bus #214 from Hodžovo námestie to the end of the line and then follow Timravina and Mišíkova streets up the hill.

But if you have no interest in seeing the monument, you still may want to go for the unbeatable views of Bratislava and to check out the well-to-do villas covering the hillside. One of those villas, *at Mišíkova 46*, was the home of the late Alexander Dubček, whose democratic reforms as president of Czechoslovakia provoked the Soviet invasion of 1968. Stripped of his presidency, Dubček underwent 20 years of surveillance at his job with the local forestry department and at his villa here on Slavín Hill. But he was a hero during the Velvet Revolution, after which he served as speaker of the National Assembly until his death (from a car accident) in 1992.

NIGHTLIFE & ENTERTAINMENT

To find out what's on in Bratislava, your best source is the English-language biweekly, *The Slovak Spectator*, presenting day-by-day listings of performances and films. Pick up a copy at most hotels and at newsstands around Staré Mesto.

The **Slovak National Theater**, *at Hviezdoslavovo 1, Tel. 07/533 0069*, is a beautiful Vienna-style opera house presenting world-class operas and ballets all year except in July and August. Pick up tickets at the venue box office or call the number above. Your best bet for classical music is wherever the **Slovak Philharmonic Orchestra** is performing, which can be at one of two places: the Art Nouveau **Reduta**, *Palackého 2*, or **Moyzes Hall** (Moyzesova sieň), *Vajanského nábrežie 12*. For performances at either venue, go to the orchestra ticket office *at Medená 3, Tel. 07/333 3513*.

More informal are the small chamber concerts happening at the **St. Clare Church** and the **Primates' Palace** (see *Seeing the Sights* above), both of which sell tickets outside their doors. Entertaining for children and adults alike is the **State Puppet Theater**, *Dunajská 36, Tel. 07/323 668*. Every October the **Bratislava Music Festival**, the city's biggest festival, draws classical performers and orchestras from around Europe. It's not as illustrious as the Prague Spring International Music Festival, but it's easier to get tickets to. A bit smaller but a lot more diverse is the **Cultural Summer Festival** each July and August. Chamber, jazz, and folk concerts take place in churches, courtyards, and even towers around Staré Mesto. Contact the Bratislava Information Service (see below under *Practical Information*) for ticket and schedule information for both these festivals.

For something less high-brow, check out the gigs happening at the **Rock-Pop-Jazz Club** *at Jakubovo námestie 12*. **Stará Sladovňa**, also known as Mamut, has live jazz on Thursdays and country (yes, country) on Fridays. Serving up smooth-as-silk Budvar, Mamut claims to be the biggest beer hall in Europe, drawing a lot of tourists and a lot of crazy locals, too. It's near the bus station *at Cintorinska 32*.

Other good beer-swilling joints around town include the expatriate-favored **Danglar**, *Hviezdoslavovo námestie 17*. (Forget going to this place if you hate cigarette smoke and loud music.) **Smíchovsky Dvor**, *Mariánska 6* and the nearby **U Čierneho Orla**, *Obchodná 17* are two other good watering holes.

The liveliest night spot in Bratislava has to be the **Charlie Centrum** (named after Charlie Chaplin) *at Špitálska 4*, featuring a four-screen cinema and a pub-cum-disco in its basement. Other places to see films around town are **Kino Hviezda**, *námestie 1. mája 11*, and **Kino Obzor**, *Wilsonova 1*. A good art house cinema is **Film Club Nostalgia**, *Starohorská 2*. Again, consult *The Slovak Spectator* for showings.

SPORTS & RECREATION

Soccer buffs might want to check out Bratislava's best *fotbal* team, **Slovan Bratislava**, which plays at the huge sports complex of **Tehelné Pole** *on Odbojárov street* (take tram #2 or #14 from Staré Mesto). You should have no problem getting tickets at the stadium just before kick off. There's also an Olympic-size outdoor pool here if you feel like taking a dip.

Less recommended for swimming is the lake, **Zlaté Piesky** (literally "Golden Sands"), located on the northern edge of town (take tram #2 or #4 to the end of the line). It's not the Bahamas, but Bratislavans come here by the tram-load anyway to swim in the tepid waters, despite the stench coming from the nearby chemical plant. If you don't like feel like jeopardizing your health in the water, you can rent a paddle boat or play tennis on one of the many courts here.

SHOPPING

The thing to buy in Bratislava are the colorfully-embroidered Slovak folk costumes for sale at several shops around town. These include **Ostredie**, *Michalská 4* and **Úluv**, *Dobrovičova 13* (near the Little Blue Church). Both shops also sell some practical items that you wouldn't be embarrassed wearing, such as some wonderful wool sweaters and vests. **Secession**, *Palackého 8*, offers a great selection of Art Nouveau antiques, mostly furniture. A great place to browse, even if you're not interested in carrying home a desk or chair. If you're in need of a book, newspaper, or magazine in English, check out the **Big Ben Bookshop**, *Michalská 1, Tel. 07/533 3632*.

Located on Kamenné náměstí on the northern edge of Staré Mesto, **Tesco** is the biggest department store in the city, complete with a good supermarket.

EXCURSIONS& DAY TRIPS

Devín

Impressively perched atop a rocky crag at the confluence of the Danube and Morava rivers, the ruins of Devín Castle are an impressive sight above the one-horse village of Devín. The castle dates back to the 5th century, but claims its fame from the 9th century, when the Great Moravian Empire fought (and won) battles here against the Germans. When the Hungarians took over the Slovak lands in the 10th century, Devín became their major Western bulwark instead of Bratislava Castle. It's hard to imagine now, but a palace once stood within the castle walls. However, Napoleon reduced it all to rubble when he stormed through the area in 1809.

Nineteenth-century Slovak nationalists, especially Ľudovít Štúr, waxed poetic about the castle's importance as a symbol of Slovak identity, and had the place turned into a national cultural monument. *The castle is open April through October, from 10 a.m. to 5:30 p.m. daily except Monday.*

There's not a whole lot happening at Devín these days, but you can walk around the ruins and inspect some ancient artifacts unearthed here. The view up the Morava and down the Danube is quiet good. And if you're a bird watcher, then you may spot some interesting species fluttering around the not-so-healthy riverbank as you walk along the road at the foot of the castle. This road marks the very edge of Slovakia (Austria is a stone's throw away on the other side of the Danube). You can imagine the tight border control here during Cold War times, when a wall of jagged barbed wire was strung along the riverbank and armed guards kept close surveillance from several tall watchtowers.

It's easy as pie getting to Devín, located five miles or so northwest of Bratislava. Just hop on city bus #29 at the station beneath SNP Bridge and get off about 15 minutes later at any stop in sight of the castle. Or, if you feel like hiking, take the red-marked trail, beginning at the end of tram line #4 or #9 in the suburb of Karlova Ves. It should take you no more than two hours to get there by foot.

Rusovce

This is another easy half-day trip from Bratislava. A little village 12 or so miles southeast, Rusovce features a three-story Tudor chateau embellished with an array of battlements and spires. There's nothing particularly historic about the Rusovce chateau, but it does front a huge park that makes for pleasant picnicking. There's also a nice lake here, which looks fairly safe for swimming.

Rusovce is also the locale of the third-century Roman camp, **Gerulata**, now a small museum devoted to the excavation work done on it. On exhibit are the remains of the camp's walls and some inscribed Roman tombstones. *It's open May through October daily expect Monday, from 10 a.m. to 5 p.m.* To get to Rusovce, take city bus #116 from the station under the SNP Bridge.

Modra & Červený Kameň

Some of Slovakia's best red and white wines are to be had in the small village of **Modra**, 27 kilometers (14 miles) north of Bratislava. The village is chock-full of wine bars (*vináreň*), from which you can sample the local *víno*. Modra also makes a good destination if you're in the market for folk pottery and ceramics. By car, head north on highway 502. Buses leave several times every hour from Bratislava's regional station on Bajkalská street (take tram #4, #6, or #10 there). It takes about 25 minutes to get there and costs about 30 Sk.

The castle of **Červený Kameň**, 10 or so miles northwest of Modra, strikes a handsome pose in the Lower Carpathian hills. The castle was built in the 13th century, when it served as an Hungarian border post. But its present appearance comes from the aristocratic Pálffy family, who kept it in perpetual restoration from the time they acquired it in the 16th century until they left Czechoslovakia in 1945. It's an imposing castle, thanks to its beefy bastions, which were supposedly designed by the Renaissance painter Albrecht Dürer. Today it houses a good **museum** of Empire and Biedermeier furniture and features a medieval torture chamber. *Hours are from 9 a.m. to 4 p.m. daily except Monday.*

To get here from Modra, take one of the regularly running buses to the village of Častá and then hike the one kilometer along the green-marked trail. From Bratislava, catch a bus from the main station to Častá, taking roughly 45 minutes and costing 50 Sk.

Trnava

Trnava's claim to fame is that it was the first town in Slovakia to get a royal charter (in 1238 from King Béla). Seat of an Hungarian archbishopric since 1541 and the locale of a Jesuit university since 1635, Trnava certainly has a lot of history going for it, but its ridiculous nickname of "Slovak Rome" shouldn't fool you into thinking that it's worth putting on your itinerary, even if its town walls are still standing. The old town hasn't seen a bit of restoration in years, and has irrevocably been transformed by insensitive redevelopment. On the weekends it's especially depressing, as the whole town seems abandoned.

If you still insist on going, catch one of the several trains departing daily from Bratislava's main train station. The 30 minute ride costs 50 Sk. By car, head 45 kilometers (28 miles) north on the E75 motorway.

PRACTICAL INFORMATION

Embassies
• **American**, *Hviezdoslavovo námestie 4. Tel. 07/533 3338*
• **British**, *Grösslingová 35. Tel. 07/364 420.*
• **Canadian**, *Kolárska 4. Tel. 07/361 277.*
• **Czech**, *29. augusta 5. Tel. 07/536 1204.*

Exchange Offices
• **K-mart**, *Kamenné námestie 35.*
• **Slovenská sporiteľňa**, *Štúrova 11.*
• **Všeobecná úverova banka**, *námestie SNP 19.*

Medical Attention
In case of an emergency, *call 444 44.* Otherwise go to the out-patient clinic at *Mýtna 5, Tel. 07/496 580.*

Post Office
The **main post office** (Hlavná pošta), *námestie SNP 35*, is where you can make international calls or send a telegram.

Tourist Office
Your best source for information about the city is **Bratislava Information Service** (Bratislavská informačná služba, or BIS), *Klobučnícka 2, next door to the Primates's Palace. Tel. 02/533 3715.* BIS can help you with accommodations and arrange tours of Bratislava. You can also buy a good map of Bratislava here.

Nitra

The agricultural center of Slovakia, **Nitra** and its friendly, slow-moving center give little indication of its 220,000-strong population that makes it the third-largest city in the country after Bratislava and Košice. In addition to being the oldest recorded settlement in Slovakia, Nitra was the site of the first Christian church in both the Czech and Slovak republics, founded by Prince Pribina in 833, after which it was swallowed up in the Great Moravian Empire and later in the Hungarian Kingdom.

Commanding an impressively high position in the middle of town, the **Nitra Castle** won't raise anyone's hairs, but the castle **cathedral** just might. There's also a peaceful Staré Mesto (Old Town) here, with several pretty churches to check out. Nitra works as a good day trip from Bratislava, but there is an excellent hotel (see Zlaty Kľúčik under *Where to Stay*) that makes it worth spending the night.

ORIENTATION

Sprawled out along the banks of the **Nitra River** in the Danubian plain, Nitra lies roughly 100 kilometers (62 miles) east of Bratislava. All of Nitra's worthwhile sights are found in the historic center, which consists of Staré Mesto and the castle, both of which occupy a bend in the river. Štefánikova and Farska are the two main streets in Staré Mesto, each leading up to the base of the castle. It's not hard at all to find your way around.

ARRIVALS & DEPARTURES

By Bus

If you don't have your own car, take one of the several buses departing every half-hour from Bratislava's main station. The hour-long trip costs 50 Sk. The Nitra bus station is a ten minute walk south of the center via Štefánikova.

By Car

Head northeast out of Bratislava on motorway E75 and then exit onto E571 all the way to Nitra. Parking should be no problem around the center. Just remember to put some money in the meter if you park on the street.

By Train

The Nitra train station is next to the bus station. Avoid going by train if you're coming from Bratislava. It takes much longer than the bus and involves multiple transfers.

GETTING AROUND TOWN

On foot is the best and only way of getting around Staré Mesto and up to the castle. Otherwise, bus is your only option. Tickets are available from the driver for 7 Sk.

WHERE TO STAY/WHERE TO EAT

HOTEL ZLATÝ KĽÚČIK, *Svätourbanská 27, 949 01 Nitra. Tel. 087/550 289, Fax 087/550 293. Rates for double only: 2,000-2,900. Credit cards: AE, MC, V. 35 rooms. Restaurant.*

This is the one and only good reason to spend the night in Nitra, which has a terrible shortage of hotels. Occupying two new houses high and above Nitra on Zobor Hill, Zlaty Kľúčik has an unbeatable view of the city that comes with every one of its cheerful rooms. Decked out with wood floors, tasteful art, satellite television, and direct-dial telephones, the rooms are some of the classiest I've seen in Slovakia.

Equally classy is the hotel restaurant, with its smartly decorated dining room and its patio providing the same sensational view of the city. Sit in plush, brasserie-style booths and enjoy the perfectly charred steaks, tender pork chops topped with a mushroom sauce, or anything from its list of Slovak specialties. Service is ultra-professional, to the point of being humorously snooty. The long, wood-studded bar is a great place to swirl a snifter of cognac, or just belly up for a beer. Prices range from 150 to 300 Sk. More discreet, but equal tasteful is the basement lounge.

Zlaty Kľúčik is a bit of a haul from the city center, at least 15 minutes by bus (take #10 from the Prior department store or from the bus station). But it's well worth the effort.

HOTEL ZOBOR, *Štefánikova 5, 949 01 Nitra. Tel. 087/525 381, Fax 087/525 060. Rates for single/double: 390-700/880-2,100 Sk. Credit cards: AE, MC, V. 110 rooms. Restaurant.*

This isn't a bad alternative to the more expensive hotel up the hill. Placed at the foot of the castle in Staré Mesto, it has a good, central location. Rooms are somewhat threadbare, but pleasant enough for the price. The hotel has a decent restaurant serving mainly Slovak standards at an affordable 80 to 150 Sk.

RADLINSKÁ KAVIAREN, *Radlinského 17. 50-150 Sk. No credit cards.*

This nice café with plush booths serves up basic Central European fare and good fish for a price that's right.

IZBA STAREJ MATERE, *Radlinského 8. 70-200 Sk. No credit cards.*

Traditional Slovak food, such as chicken and pork smothered in cream-based paprika sauces, grace the menu at this restaurant popular with the locals.

SEEING THE SIGHTS

If you're coming from the bus or train stations via Štefánikova street, you'll cross the big thoroughfare of Štúrova, forming the southern boarder of the sedate **Staré Mesto** (Old Town) and its handful of historic streets and buildings. At the intersection of Štúrova and Štefánikova, you'll find the city's big outdoor market, selling the local abundance of produce.

From the market, continue down Štefánikova and then veer up to Farská, just above which you can't help but notice the biggest of Nitra's churches – the **Piarist Church** (Kostol piaristov), effectively dominating the city center from its perched position. Built in 1748, the church recently underwent a noble restoration that has done wonders for its agrarian-themed ceiling murals and for the larger-than-life painting of Jesus behind the altar.

Down below on Farská is the **Church of St. Vincent de Paul** (Kostol sv. Vincenta Pavlánskeho), a neo-Romanesque church that's seemingly higher than it is wide. Around the corner on Pri synagogue street is the newly restored Byzantine **synagogue**, a testament to the large Jewish community that existed here before World War II. It's now a concert hall. Opposite is a lively garden pub, good for a glass of beer on a warm day.

Continue to the end of Farská street, where you'll run into the fine Art Nouveau **District Hall** (Župný dom), a handsome four-winged structure today housing the Nitra State Gallery. The 19th- and 20th-century Slovak art, especially that of the impressionist painter M. Schurmann, is well worth checking out. *The museum is open daily except Monday from 10 a.m. to 6 p.m.*

To the right of the District Hall, follow the winding lane up the hill to the sloping **Pribinovo námestie**, a haggard square centered around a modern **statue of Prince Pribina**. Not exactly the true believer he made himself out to be, this 9th-century prince brought Christianity to Slovakia so as to ease relations with his converted German neighbors. From here it's a steep climb to the **castle**, past some scarred statues and a particularly grand plague column. Before entering through the castle gate, veer off to the right for a fine view of the opposing Zabor Hill, the last in the Tribeč range.

Sadly, there's not a whole lot happening at the castle. A pivotal fortress under the Great Moravian Empire and later a retreat for various Hungarian kings and queens, the castle received a thorough bashing at the hands of the Turks in the 17th century, and seemingly hasn't recovered yet, despite half-baked attempts to have the whole thing restored. About all that's of interest here is the beguiling ensemble of three churches that make up the **St. Emeram Cathedral** (Katedrálny Biskupský

Chram sv. Emerama).

The first of the churches, to your right as you enter the cathedral through its antechamber, is a Romanesque rotunda, erected in the 11th century and later incorporated into the cathedral proper. Up the stairs is the Lower Church, built in 1642. Be sure to feast your eyes here on the extraordinary marble relief of Christ's limp body being taken down from the cross. Higher up is the crowning achievement to the cathedral – the Upper Church. Though erected in 1355, the Upper Church was transformed into a Baroque pearl. Awashed with frescoes, adorned with gilt figures, and decked out with red marble, the church has an other-worldly quality about it that could make the most ardent atheist a believer. Not so impressive is the Baroque **Bishop's Palace**, adjoining the cathedral. A bishop does indeed reside there, so it's closed to the public.

Back down in Staré Mesto, at the end of Štefánikova street, is a brand new municipal theater. Opposite is the not-too-shabby neo-Renaissance **Town Hall** (radnica), now the venue for the **Nitra Museum**. The museum's collection of stuffed animals is rather exasperating, but the ancient silver and gold work is worth a peek. You may just want to head for the nice café in the courtyard instead. *The museum is open daily except Monday from 10 a.m. to 6 p.m.*

NIGHTLIFE & ENTERTAINMENT

In the summer, the synagogue and churches become the venue for small chamber concerts. Check out the *Leto Nitra* brochure, found at any hotel, for a schedule of concerts, films, and other happenings.

A good place to go for a beer or something light to eat is the **Thurzo piváreň** *at the corner of Štefánikova and Pri synagog streets*. But if the weather is good, head for the beer garden at **Záhradná reštaurácia** *on Farská street*.

PRACTICAL INFORMATION

- **NISYS,** *Štefánikova 46. Tel. 087/410 906.* Offers help with accommodations and information on the town.
- **Všeobecná úverová banka,** *Štefánikova 44.* The place to change money.
- **Main post office,** *Svätoplukovo námestie.* Next to the Town Hall at the end of Štefánikova.

Piešťany

The largest and best-known spa town in Slovakia, **Piešťany** doesn't hold a candle to the lavish resorts of West Bohemia. But its sedate, riverside location amidst green hills is an attractive one, drawing a lot of unhealthy, wealthy Germans and Austrians to take the thermal springs and sulfuric mud that's said to cure rheumatism. If you haven't come to take the cure, then Piešťany offers little, except for some pretty parks and a few promenades that make for good lounging.

Piešťany works as a good base for seeing the nearby castle of Čachtice, where a crazy Hungarian countess tortured and murdered more than 600 peasant girls. Otherwise, I'd be hard pressed to recommend Piešťany as anything other than a stopover on your way somewhere else or as a long day trip from Bratislava. There are, however, two very nice hotels if you choose to spend the night.

But if you've got an ailment and are interested in taking the waters, experiencing the mud packs, and otherwise going the whole nine yards, you'll need to contact the main spa office ahead of time. Write or call: **Slovthermae**, *Winterova 29, 921 01 Piešťany. Tel. 0838/243 33, Fax 038/252 91.*

ORIENTATION

Piešťany sits on both sides of the **Váh River** at the southern tip of the **Považský Inovec mountain range**, 80 kilometers (50 miles) northeast of Bratislava. The main promenade in town is **Winterova**, on which you'll find a concentration of the town's hotels, restaurants, and shops.

ARRIVALS & DEPARTURES

By Bus

Several buses depart daily from Bratislava's main station. Tickets cost about 40 Sk for the hour-long ride. The bus station is a 20 minute walk south of Winterova along Šturova and A. Hlinku streets. Hop on bus #3, #9, or #12 if you don't feel like walking, or take a cab, which you should have no problem getting at the station.

By Car

From Bratislava head northwest on the E75 motorway. It's an easy 45 minute drive. Be sure to park in designated parking spots around the center, as police need little incentive here to slap a boot on your tire.

By Train

Piešťany is in the middle of the Bratislava-Žilina line. Fast trains depart the main station in Bratislava about every hour. The hour-long ride (longer if it's a slow train) costs about 60 Sk. The train station is behind the bus station.

GETTING AROUND TOWN

Except for going to and from the bus and train stations, you'll have no need for taking public transportation in this small town. All hotels, restaurants, and sights are within easy walking distance of each other.

WHERE TO STAY/WHERE TO EAT

Most of the hotels in town are for spa patients only. Here are some for regular tourists:

HOTEL EDEN, *Winterova 60, 921 01 Piešťany. Tel. 0838/723 369, Fax 0838/221 23. Rates for single/double without private bath: 420/720 Sk. Rates for doubles with private bath: 1,740 Sk. Credit cards: AE, MC, V. 50 rooms. Restaurant.*

From the outside this Functionalist, white hotel with its balcony flower boxes looks almost Mediterranean. Though the dark wood paneling inside the lobby and restaurant spoil that illusion a bit, the sunny rooms bring the Mediterranean feel back. Comfortable, new furniture enhances each of the pleasant rooms that come with satellite television and telephone. On the roof is an open-air fitness center. The terrace wine restaurant, serving moderately priced Slovak meals, is a great place to dine on warm summer evenings.

CITY HOTEL, *Winterova 35, 921 01 Piešťany. Tel. 0838/725 451, Fax 0838/724 662. Rates for single/double: 1,300/1,400-2,000 Sk. Credit cards: MC, V. 12 rooms. Restaurant.*

This small villa hotel opposite Hotel Eden is the best choice of accommodations in Piešťany. Very friendly, English-speaking service enhances your stay in one of the colorful, smartly-decorated rooms, outfitted with comfortable furniture, satellite television, and direct-dial telephones. If you feel like splurging, go for the spacious corner apartment (2,000 Sk), with a nice view up and down Winterova street.

The somewhat pricey restaurant maintains the same high standard of style, serving good steaks, as well as a hodgepodge of Slovak basics and vegetarian dishes. Definitely head for the restaurant terrace when the weather is good.

HOTEL MAGNÓLIA, *Nálepkova 1, 921 01 Piešťany. Tel. 0838/726 132, Fax 0838/721 149. Rates for single/double: 1,200/1,760 Sk. Credit cards: AE, MC, V. 120 rooms. Restaurant.*

This unattractive highrise hotel is frankly a blight on the town's skyline. Rates are overpriced for the small rooms that come with run-down furniture and a particularly ugly brownish paint. But you do get a telephone, television, and a balcony with a good view of Bath Island. In the restaurant is an atrocious mural that makes the food served here even more unpleasant than it already is.

PENZION BENÁTKY, *Topoľčianska 1, 921 01 **Piešťany**. Tel. 0838/721 189, Fax 0838/284 28. Rates for double only: 1,650 Sk. No credit cards. 5 apartments. Restaurant.*

This big house on the banks of the Váh looks like a cozy place to stay. But once you see the drab rooms and tacky furniture, you can't help but have a change of heart. The pension's wine restaurant, on the other hand, offers some fine Slovak meals (140-200 Sk) and a pleasant river view.

RESTAURANT CENTRAL, *Winterova 51. Tel. 0838/231 57. 100-200 Sk. No credit cards.*

If you don't feel like eating at one of the hotels, then try this fairly decent restaurant with a good variety of steaks.

SEEING THE SIGHTS

The main promenade through the center of town is called Winterova, lined with a rather dull array of turn-of-the-century Secession houses budding with souvenir shops and terrace cafés. More delightful is the nearby **Mestský Park**, a leafy expanse featuring a concert pavilion where classical recitals take place throughout the summer.

Most of the spa activity is happening on the other side of the river on **Bath Island** (Kúpeľny ostrov), accessed via the shop-stuffed **Colonnade Bridge**, and past the statue of Piešťany's mascot – **Barlolama** (or, the Crutch-breaker). Commanding the island is the Art Nouveau **Thermia Palace**, the town's best piece of architecture reminiscent of Piešťany's bygone days when it was the playground for Central European nobility.

Statues and spring-fed pools dot the island park, which makes it a nice place for a romantic saunter. Lining the east edge of the island is a string of huge, ultra-modern Balneal spas, where patients go in for mud packs and other like treatments.

SPORTS & RECREATION

If you're in the mood for a dip, try the **Kúpalisko Eva** (Eva swimming pool), located in the middle of Bath Island. The warm, spring-fed waters here are open to the public for 15 Sk a head.

PRACTICAL INFORMATION

• **Aices,** *inside the Hotel Eden at Winterova 60, 921 01 Piešťany. Tel. 0838/276 89.* A helpful office offering information on accommodations, transportation, and events happening around town.

• **Satur,** *Winterova 38. Tel. 0838/215 06.* This travel agency sells tickets to cultural events, can help with accommodations, and offers sightseeing tours of the area. You can also change money here.

• **Main Post Office,** *Poštovna 1.*

Čachtice Castle

Those of you who are purveyors of vampire stories will no doubt recognize the name of one **Countess Elizabeth Báthori**, more sensationally known as the Blood Countess of Čachtice or simply as the "White

Lady." The popular legend surrounding this woman is that she bathed in the blood of virgins so as to preserve here youth. So much for legend. The truth, however, is no less startling. Born in the early 17th century, Countess Báthori was the daughter of a Transylvanian duke. After receiving an education in Paris, she married at age 15 to Ferenc Nádasdy, who spent the following 10 years abroad fighting the Turks, earning his title of the "Dark Knight."
With the count away, the countess grew bored, to say the least. At her castle residences of Čachtice and nearby Beckov, she found a way to alleviate that boredom by letting her sadistic nature run wild. She went on what could well have been the biggest individual blood binge of all time, taking the lives of some 600 peasant girls and women, but not before subjecting them to all means of torture, which included biting off bits of flesh from their breasts and necks.

Her days as a serial murderer came to end when she began singling out aristocratic girls as her victims, girls whose deaths were not so easily hushed up. When her misdeeds were found out, the local villagers demanded a lynching, but a distant relative of the countess saved her from the gallows by having her locked up in her own castle of Čachtice instead.

So with that bit of history in the back of your mind, a visit to Čachtice may or may not be in order. Besides some teetering walls and crumbling towers, there is very little left of the castle since it was burned down in 1708. But those with a penchant for gore should have a bone-chilling good time climbing up to the castle ruins, perched upon a lonely, wind-swept hill affording great views of the Váh River valley.

Getting here is not an easy matter if you don't have your own car. It's possible as an exhausting day trip from Bratislava, or as an easy excursion from either Piešťany or Trenčín. Wherever you're coming from, take the train to the grim as grim industrial town of Nové Mesto nad Váhom, located on the Bratislava-Žilina line half-way between Piešťany and Trenčín. From there hop on another train for the scenic 15 minute ride to Višňové (instead of Čachtice stop). From the Višňové station it's a twenty minute steep hike up the green-marked trail to the castle ruins. By car, take the E75 motorway, exit at Nové Mesto nad Váhom, and then follow signs southwestward to Višňové.

Trenčín

There is one very good reasons to stay the night in this surprisingly pleasant town cradled in the Váh River valley: the **Trenčín Castle**. The castle is one of Slovakia's most impressive, its hulking bastions and soaring tower sitting at an imposing height above the town. Erected in the 11th century to ensure the safe passage of goods passed along the Považie trade corridor, the castle fell into the hands of one **Matúš Čák**, a renegade feudal warlord who went down in history books for swiping much of present-day Slovakia from the Hungarian Kingdom. The Trenčín Castle served as the capital of Čák's short-lived fief, which died out with Čák in 1321.

The castle, along with much of the town, burned down in 1790. Its reconstruction has been coming along slowly since the 1950s, and is sure to be covered in scaffolding by the time you go. Still, the castle is a spectacular sight, especially as seen from the small, lively town at its base.

ORIENTATION

Trenčín is laid out along the **Váh River** 124 kilometers (70 miles) northeast of Bratislava. There's no problem finding your way around the small historic center, especially with a landmark as arresting as the castle.

ARRIVALS & DEPARTURES

By Bus

Buses depart Bratislava roughly every 90 minutes for Trenčín. Tickets for the two hour ride cost about 90 Sk. There are also two daily buses from Prague (stopping in Brno along the way), which cost about 230 Kč for the six-hour ride. The bus station in Trenčín, located in front of the train station, is a five minute walk east of the historic center on the other side of Štefánika Park.

By Car

From Bratislava, head northeast all the way on the E75 motorway. The drive should take you about 90 minutes, as should the drive along E50 from Brno. Parking is no problem on the streets. Just be sure to put some money in the meter.

By Train

Fast trains run about every hour from Bratislava's main train station. The ride takes roughly two hours and costs about 80 Sk. To get from the train station to the historic center, just walk through the park towards the castle.

GETTING AROUND TOWN

There's no problem getting around Trenčín by foot, which is the only way you can get around the historic center and up to the castle. Should you need a cab, *call 0831/353 66.*

WHERE TO STAY

HOTEL TATRA, *M.R. Štefánika 2, 911 00 Trenčín. Tel. 0831/506 111, Fax 0831/506 213. Rates for single/double: 2,200/3,200 Sk. Credit cards: AE, DC, V. 70 rooms. Restaurant.*

Located at the foot of the castle, the Hotel Tatra is a neo-Baroque confection looking all the more splendid after a recent restoration that took two years to complete. Slovakia's earliest written history happens to be inscribed just behind the hotel on a cliff face. It's a Latin inscription paying homage to Marcus Aurelius' victory over Germanic tribes in 179 AD, the year in which a Roman camp known as Laugaritio was stationed at this very site.

This is one of best hotels you could choose in the Slovak Republic. As you'll see, the Tatra is more than just a hotel, but a center of culture and food as well. The hotel strikes a unique introductory note in the lobby, where you'll find avant-garde paintings depicting the four humors. Off to the right of the lobby is the hotel's sunny Café Sissi, a favorite of the locals serving a bevy of cocktails and a variety of breakfast items such as scrambled and soft-boiled eggs and pastries. Off to the left is the Restaurant Tatra, the town's best restaurant decked out in pleasant earth tones and featuring a great menu of Slovak and international courses, including a tasty stuffed turkey breast drenched in a luscious gravy. The restaurant also has a salad bar that is sure to please North American travelers with a hankering for fresh vegetables. Prices at the restaurant run between 150 and 300 Sk.

In the basement of the hotel, the Victoria Wine Cellar is the place to go for a casual meal. The cellar features a different menu and a different style of cuisine every month or so. Some recent menus have featured French, American, and even Mexican specialties. During the evening, your meal is accompanied by a folk quintet playing heart-bleeding Romany songs. Prices at the wine cellar run between 50 and 150 Sk.

And don't forget the terrace in the back of the hotel, where you can sit in the company of the Roman inscription hanging on the cliff face.

As for the accommodations, you can expect smartly decorated rooms outfitted with writing desks, tasteful art work, big comfortable beds, satellite television, mini-bar, and direct-dial telephones. The service, from the reception desk to the restaurants, is tip-top. In fact, the whole place seemingly operates in a service-oriented fashion, which is rare in the two republics. None too surprising, the hotel is run by a joint Slovak-Canadian hotel management company.

ŠPORTHOTEL ZAMAROVCE, *Ostrov, 911 01 Trenčín. Tel. 0831/531 940, no fax. Rates for single/double: 500/1,000 Sk. No credit cards. No restaurant.*

If you're not in the mood to splurge at the Hotel Tatra, then this hotel provides a good alternative. It's located on an island in the Váh River –

about a five minute walk north of the Hotel Tatra. Rooms are threadbare, but suitably comfortable. The hotel offers tennis, and the chance to go up in a hot-air balloon.

PENZIÓN SVORAD, *Palackého 4, 911 01 Trenčín. Tel. 0831/530 322, no fax. Rates for single/double: 400/600 Sk. No credit cards. No restaurant.*

This pension, carved out of a wing of an old grammar school, is a place to fall back on if you can't find accommodations elsewhere. Rooms are very spartan, but do come with private baths. You'll find the pension just down the street from the Hotel Tatra.

WHERE TO EAT

HOTEL TATRA, *M.R. Štefánika 2. Tel. 0831/506 111* – see the restaurants reviewed above.

REŠTAURÁCIA INN 33 CLUB, *Palackého 33. Tel. 0831/534 728. 100-200 Sk. No credit cards.*

This is certainly a favorite with the locals. Decorated with Salvador Dalí prints, the restaurant serves up excellent cuts of meat including a tasty steak sprinkled with herbs. The onion soup is also a big winner. The menu here is in English, thanks to an American teacher who was in town volunteering for the Peace Corps. The restaurant's long bar and outdoor patio are good places to sip down a beer at night.

PIZZERIA VENEZÍA, *Hviezdoslavova 4. Tel. 0831/532 491. 70-150 Sk. No credit cards.*

The locals swear up and down by this place, but I found the pizzas baked here rather dull, mainly because there was a bare minimum amount of tomato sauce on them. But the terrace seating does make it a worthwhile place for lunch.

SEEING THE SIGHTS

As you come into town, your first instinct is to head straight up to the castle, but hold off and first have a look around the bustling main square, **Mierové námestie**, outlined with a fine array of fanciful Renaissance houses. At the east end of the square is the **Hotel Tatra**, where you'll definitely want to duck in for a coffee and inspect the Latin inscription in the hotel courtyard. Next to the hotel is the **Trenčín Museum** (Trenčíanské múzeum), whose natural history exhibits are not worth spending your time on. *The museum is open daily except Monday from 9 a.m. to 4 p.m.*

The west end of the square is punctuated by the town's one remaining gate tower, with a legend attached to it saying you'll never be married if you speak at the moment of walking through it. Next to the tower, nip into the **Piarist Church** (Piaristický kostol) for a look at its excessive Baroque flourishes.

Attached to the church is the old Piarist monastery, which is now the venue for the **M.A. Bazovský Gallery**, named after the 20th-century painter and sculptor who spent the later years of his life in Trenčín. The gallery, mainly filled with Bazovský's renderings of peasant life, is worth a perusal, if only for the stucco work in the gallery rooms and the appealing collection of regional art. *The gallery is open daily except Monday from 9 a.m. to 4 p.m.*

Down the narrow lane that runs next to the Piarist Church is Trenčín's **former synagogue**, which is now an exhibition hall. Step inside for a look at the synagogue's sky-blue dome and interior arcades.

Just south of the gate tower on Mierové námestie, a covered wooden staircase built in the 16th century leads up the hill to the blazing yellow **Parish Church**, a 14th-century construction which is sadly closed every day but Sunday, when it's jam-packed with the town faithful. From the church it's a short but steep hike up to the **Trenčín Castle** gate, which is where you buy your 50 Sk ticket for the museum, housed in the castle palace at the top of the hill.

Considering its sprawling network of fortifications and its imposingly high position, you can't help but gape at the sight of this fortress that seemingly weighs down on the town. The height of the castle certainly hits home when you have to climb to the top of it. But the exhausting hike is rewarded by a great view of the town and valley.

Still under extensive renovation, the castle palace houses a museum with various exhibits. In one section of the palace you'll find a rather uninspiring collection of portrait paintings of the Hungarian royalty and nobility who once owned the castle. You'll also see some gruesome, eyewitness scenes of medieval battles that took place in the region. From there, the guide takes you into the former palace jail, now housing a scant collection of medieval artifacts discovered at the castle. Then you're led to the Matúš Tower, which is where the warlord Matúš Čák lived during his reign as self-appointed "King of the Váh and the Tatras." Disappointingly, there are no exhibits or information of any kind that tells you about this character, Čák. Instead, you get a disparate collection of weapons from the 12th to the 19th century. If you have the energy after huffing up to the palace, then climb the several stories to the top of the tower for a look straight down on the web of fortifications and the town below.

As you're coming down from the palace, peer into the castle dungeon, which has a sign at its entrance saying there is no evidence that tortures ever took place here. In spite of that, the dungeon has a number of instruments of torture on display. Farther down, just behind the makeshift amphitheater, is a chapel and bastion, now rented out as commercial space. *The castle is open daily except Monday from 9 a.m. to 4 p.m.*

NIGHTLIFE & ENTERTAINMENT

Staropramen beer is served in a neat cellar at the classy **Steps Pub**, *located on Hviezdoslavova street just beyond the gate tower*. Another good place for a late night drink is **Reštaurácia Inn 33 Club** (see *Where to Eat* above). There's a **cinema** *on the main square* should you feel like taking in a flick. You may also want to see what's up at **Hotel Tatra**, which hosts the occasional cultural event.

SPORTS & RECREATION

There are lots of activities to get involved in at Trenčín, including horseback riding, hot-air ballooning, fishing, and plane rides. Contact the Cultural and Information Center (see *Practical Information* below), and they will set up whichever of these activities you prefer.

PRACTICAL INFORMATION

• **Aices**, *Štúrovo námestie 10. Tel. 0831/533 505.* The English-speaking staff here can help you find accommodations, get you on a tour of the town and region, give you the train and bus schedules, and arrange various sports and recreational activities.
• **Všeobecná úverová banka**, *Mierové námestie 37.* You can change money at this bank.
• **Post Office**, *Mierové námestie 21.*

21. CENTRAL SLOVAKIA

When it comes to landscape, no region in the Czech and Slovak republics can match **Central Slovakia**. Divided by beautiful lush valleys carved out by the **Hron** and **Váh** rivers, legions of mountain ranges span across this portion of the earth, providing all sorts of opportunities for outdoor recreation – from skiing to hiking to paragliding. Nowhere is this truer than in the **High Tatra Mountains**, where sublime, sawtooth peaks rise to monumental heights. These mountains are perhaps your greatest incentive for coming to Slovakia, and shouldn't be missed if you've come to pursue some great skiing or hiking.

Within a few hours' travel of the High Tatras are the **Low Tatras**, in particular the sweeping valley of **Demänovská dolina**, offering some of the best skiing in either republic. Farther to the north are the **Malá Fatra Mountains**, a less developed range where you'll find one of Slovakia's most gorgeous valley's – **Vrátna dolina**.

As for Central Slovak towns, there's not so much to get excited about. But there are a couple of places worth checking out, such as the regional capital of **Banská Bystrica**, featuring one of Slovakia's most beautiful squares. Nearby Banská Bystrica is the intriguing old mining town of **Banská Štiavnica**, once the second biggest town in the Hungarian Empire and now an impressive mirror of medieval times.

Banská Bystrica

The administrative capital of Central Slovakia, Banská Bystrica is by far the region's most attractive town, sporting a handsome main square that was recently renovated and made into a pedestrian plaza. The main square and the rest of the historic center attest to the fact that this was once a wealthy silver and copper mining town (*banská* means "mining"), founded by German colonists in the 13th century. The mines and refineries kept the town thriving until the 18th century, when the veins dried up and the town left to stagnate until industrialism gave it a new lease on life after World War II.

CENTRAL SLOVAKIA FINDS & FAVORITES

Hotel Arcade (see "Where to Stay" in Banská Bystrica)
Reštaurácia U komediantov (see "Where to Eat" in Banská Bystrica)
Námestie SNP (see "Seeing the Sights" in Banská Bystrica)
Banská Štiavnica
Hotel Salamander (see "Where to Stay" in Banská Štiavnica)
The valley of Vrátna dolina
Chata Mikulášska (see "Where to Stay" in Demänovská dolina)
Hotel Tatry (see "Where to Stay" in the High Tatras)
The gondola ride to the top of Lomnický štít (see "Hiking the High Tatras in the section on the High Tatras)

But the town is most forcefully remembered in Slovakia as the nerve center of the **Slovak National Uprising** (Slovenské Národné Povstanie or SNP), in which a military of Slovak Army deserters and foreign partisans rose up against the fascist Slovak government led by Jozef Tiso. Though the SNP was successful in toppling the Nazi puppet state, the uprising proved to be ill-fated, as German forces moved in two months later to crush the revolt and send more than 900 men, women, and children to their graves. You can learn all there is to know about the uprising at Banská Bystrica's **SNP Museum**, housed in one of the more bizarre pieces of architecture to come out of the Communist era.

ORIENTATION

Banská Bystrica lies right in the heart of Slovakia, 208 kilometers (129 miles) east of Bratislava and 214 kilometers (133 miles) west of Košice. The town sprawls across the lush **Hron River** valley in an area where several mountain ranges – **the Low Tatras, Veľká Fatra**, and **Slovenské rudohorie** – congregate.

Once you locate the town's main square of **námestie SNP** (which you can't help but running into), it's simple to find your way around the small center of town.

ARRIVALS & DEPARTURES

By Bus

Bus is probably your best option if you're traveling from Bratislava. Buses depart Bratislava about every 90 minutes. The journey takes roughly three hours and costs around 120 Sk. There are two daily buses to and from Prague, taking about nine hours and costing 400 Sk (330 Kč). The bus station in Banská Bystrica is on Nábrežie Duklianskych hrdinov street, about a 20 minute walk east of the center of town.

If you don't feel like huffing it, walk over to the adjacent train station and catch any of the trolley buses numbered one through seven.

By Car
From Bratislava, head east on the E571 highway through Nitra to Zvolen and then go north on E77. The trip should take about two-and-a-half hours. From Brno, take E50, exit onto E572 after you cross the border, and then head north on E77 at Zvolen. Parking in the center of Banská Bystrica is limited to a couple of parking lots around the historic core. Just keep an eye out for the blue "P" sign.

By Train
From Bratislava to Banská Bystrica requires a change in Zvolen. Count on about five hours to complete the journey and 160 Sk to pay for the ticket. There are two trains from Prague to Banská Bystrica each day. The trip takes about nine hours (roughly the same as the bus) and costs around 350 Kč. If you're traveling to Košice, definitely take the one direct train that goes there daily from Banská Bystrica. Perhaps the most scenic train ride you could take in Slovakia, the train follows the Hron River, clinging to precipitous hillsides and flashing incredible views of the Low Tatra Mountains.

The main train station is next to the bus station on Nábrežie Duklianskych hrdinov street, about a 20 minute walk east of the center of town. Any one of the trolley buses numbered one through seven will take you into the center. There's also a smaller train station, called Mesto, just down from the main square servicing towns in the immediate region.

GETTING AROUND TOWN
The public transportation system in Banská Bystrica is composed of buses and trolley buses. When you get on the bus, buy a 6 Sk ticket from the driver and validate it by sticking it into the gadget attached to the driver's door and pulling back on the handle.

If you're in need of taxi, *call 746 566* or just hail one from the street.

WHERE TO STAY
HOTEL ARCADE, *námestie SNP 5, 974 00 Banská Bystrica. Tel. 088/702 111, Fax 088/723 126. Rates for single/double: 1,970/2,170 Sk. Credit cards: AE, DC, MC, V. 14 rooms. Restaurant.*

Carved out of a Renaissance house on the main square, this brand new hotel is the plushest in town, offering large, gorgeous rooms furnished with two bathroom sinks and a great deal of sophistication. In the rooms and throughout the hotel is a series of vaguely erotic paintings that are somewhat out a synch with the refined air of the place. But the place is a dandy, reflected in its high rates.

HOTEL LUX, *námestie Slobody 2, 974 00 Banská Bystrica. Tel. 088/744 141, Fax 088/743 853. Rates for single/double: 1,058-1,652/1,586-2,406 Sk. Credit cards: MC, V. 150 rooms. Restaurant.*

Located just down from the SNP Museum, this giant 14-story hotel is frankly a blight on the skyline. Though the lobby and the restaurant look to be caught in the Communist era, the newly renovated rooms are extremely comfortable and smartly furnished. Definitely ask for a west-facing room on one of the top floors, so you can have a great view over town.

HOTEL NÁRODNÝ DOM, *Národná 11, 974 01 Banská Bystrica. Tel. 088/723 737, Fax 088/725 014. Rates for single/double without private toilet only: 500/720 Sk. No credit cards. No restaurant.*

Located a block down from the main square, this hotel isn't so seedy as it appears from the outside. It's not that nice on the inside either, but it is clean. The threadbare rooms are in serious need of renovation, but they are fairly cheap and do come with private showers.

HOTEL PASSAGE URPÍN, *Cikkerova 5, 974 00 Banská Byslrica. Tel. 088/724 556, Fax 088/723 831. Rates for single/double without private shower: 420/600 Sk. Rates for single/double with private shower: 460/680 Sk. Credit cards: AE, V. Restaurant.*

This is actually not a bad choice for budget accommodations. The rooms are totally out of date, but they are functional, clean, and suitably comfortable for their rates. The hotel has a good location a block down from the main square.

HOTEL TURIST, *Tajovského 9, 974 01 Banská Bystrica. Tel. 088/330 12, no fax. Rates for single/double: 440/650 Sk. No credit cards. Restaurant.*

This is a place to fall back on if you can't find accommodations elsewhere. It's located outside the center (about a 20 minute walk), just off the highway leading north to Donovaly. Rooms are very basic but worth their reasonable prices.

WHERE TO EAT

REŠTAURÁCIA ZLATÝ BAŽANT, *námestie SNP 11. Tel. 088/724 500. 125-250 Sk. Credit cards: AE, MC, V.*

No doubt that this flashy restaurant on the main square will catch your eye. But resist it, because the food doesn't live up to the restaurant's fine decor. The cold cucumber soup proved to be nothing more than sour yogurt with bits of cucumber thrown in. And the turkey breast stuffed with cheese and ham was disappointingly dry. The restaurant does, however, have a great cellar pub, which is a zoo compared to the lifeless restaurant.

REŠTAURÁCIA U KOMEDIANTOV, *Horná Strieborná 13. Tel. 088/ 525 54. 125-200 Sk. No credit cards.*
Located a block or two north of the main square, "At the Comedian" hunkers down in an intimate cellar painted in festive colors. No live Gypsy music or other gimmicks here, just straight-ahead Slovak specialties prepared in a colorful manner. Try the pork roast doused in a tangy tomato sauce (they call it ketchup, but it's not) or any one of the tender steaks prepared to perfection. Great service and a lively clientele contribute to making this a top pick in town.

AZIJSKA POD VEŽOU, *Kapitulská 9. Tel. 088/723 728. 150-250 Sk. No credit cards.*
This restaurant just down from the main square serves passable Chinese food, as well as some specialties from other Asian countries. A good place to go if you've had your fill of Slovak food.

REŠTAURÁCIA U TIGRA, *Dolná 36. Tel. 088/724 919. 120-200 Sk. No credit cards.*
This is a swanky-looking place offering a sizeable menu. The stuffed meats come in generous portions and the service is top-notch.

ZEMIANSKA REŠTAURÁCIA, *Dolná 35. Tel. 088/723 967. 50-120 Sk. No credit cards.*
This tiny restaurant serves up good Slovak standards such as the very filling *bryndzové halušky* (gnocchi topped with sharp cheese). This is probably a better choice for lunch than dinner, especially when it's a nice day and you can sit out on the patio.

SEEING THE SIGHTS

In the heart of town, Banská Bystrica's sloping **námestie SNP** is perhaps Slovakia's finest square, its Renaissance and Baroque burghers' houses accentuated by bright new paint jobs that have really livened the place up. Take a seat at one of the outdoor cafés and soak it all in over a coffee.

In the middle of the square, two fountains spout water over mossy boulders, their gleefulness dulled somewhat by a severe black marble obelisk commemorating the Soviet liberation. The phallic-like memorial certainly looks out of place these days right in the middle of a square that is obviously doing just fine by capitalism.

The square's architectural showpiece is the **Benického dom**, *Dolná 16,* a graceful edifice adorned with frescoes and an arcaded loggia. It houses a branch of the **State Gallery** (Štátna galéria), presenting temporary exhibits of 20th century Slovak art. *It's open Tuesday through Friday from 9 a.m. to 5 p.m. and on weekends from 10 a.m. to 4 p.m.*

On the south side of the square is the **Thurzo Palace**, *number 4*, its facade featuring four cute oval windows and a fanciful patchwork of sgraffito. The palace houses the **Central Slovakia Museum** (Stredoslovenské múzeum), worth a quick walk-through for its collection of folk clothing and crafts. *It's open Monday through Friday from 8 a.m. to noon and from 1 to 4 p.m., and on Sunday from 9 a.m. to 4 p.m. (until 5 p.m. in the summer).*

Presiding over námestie SNP at its top end is a mammoth, 16th-century **clock tower** that was undergoing major restoration as of mid-1996. Beyond the tower and a little ways up the hill is **námestie Štefana Moyzesa** – the locale for an ensemble of administrative and ecclesiastical buildings that make up what's left of the town's old castle. The lowest of the buildings is the old barbican (a tower-like fortification), set next to a fanciful Baroque gate tower. Footsteps uphill is the former town hall, now another branch of the State Gallery (see above), presenting changing exhibits of modern Slovak art. It's open the same hours as the gallery in the Benického dom.

But the real gem at námestie Štefana Moyzesa is the rouge-colored **Church of Our Lady** (Kostol Panny Marie Nanebevzatej), erected in the 13th century in a Romanesque style but later given a Gothic and then Baroque restoration. In the first side chapel to your left, dedicated to St. Barbara (the patron saint of miners), is the town's single greatest piece of art – a Gothic altar hand carved by Master Pavol of Levoča, who was perhaps the best Central European sculptor of the 15th century.

From námestie SNP head down Kapitulská street and take your first left to the **SNP Museum** (Múzeum Slovenského Národného Povstanie), a bizarre structure looking something like a huge flying saucer cracked in half. Despite its unfortunate design, the museum offers a gripping portrayal of the Slovak National Uprising. Captions are in Slovak only, so you'll need to buy a English booklet at the ticket office.

Though the museum was conceived as just another pompous monument to Communism's triumph over fascism, it now deals with the uprising and the war in a much more sober manner, offering a vast number of telling photographs of Tiso's meetings with Hitler, of Jewish deportations, of the men and women who served the cause of the uprising, and so on. In addition, the museum displays the uniforms and weapons of the SNP soldiers, coupled with a day by day account of the battles and events leading up to and following the military coup that began on August 29, 1944.

The museum also presents documentary films and slide shows in English, but are unfortunately shown only when a big group arrives. Outside the museum, set among the town's two remaining medieval bastions, is a collection of tanks and guns used in the uprising. *The museum is open daily except Monday from 8 a.m. to 6 p.m. (from 9 a.m. to 4 p.m. October through April). Tickets cost 10 Sk.*

NIGHTLIFE & ENTERTAINMENT

The center of haute-culture in Banská Bystrica is the **Divadlo J.G. Tajakovského,** a fine turn-of-the-century opera house located just off the main square *at Národná 11.* Young and old alike can have a fine time at the town's puppet theater, **Bábkové divadlo,** *Kollárova 18.* For schedule and ticket information to either of these theaters, go to the Culture and Information Office (see *Practical Information* below). There are three cinemas in the center of town: **Kino Urpín,***Cikkerova 5*, **Kino Hviezda,** *Skuteckého 3,* and **Kino Klub** *námestie Slobody 3, opposite the Hotel Lux.*

In the cellar of the **Zlatý Bažant** restaurant (see *Where to Eat* above) is the liveliest pub in town, pouring the fine Czech beer called, fairly enough, Zlatý Bažant. A good place for a late night drink is **Pub 21,** *down from the main square on Dolná,* playing loud rocks tunes and serving a number of beers, including Budvar and the Slovak Mních. You may also want to try the **Royal Pub** *on Horná Strieborná street,* which has a Caribbean theme that's worth a few laughs.

SPORTS & RECREATION

About fine minutes northwest of the main square is a big park that has several clay **tennis** courts, *Tel. 352 37.* Ask your hotel receptionist to book you a court or call them yourself.

SHOPPING

The place to buy local folk handicrafts and costumes is the **Uľuv** shop, *námestie SNP 7.*

EXCURSIONS & DAY TRIPS

Zvolen

There's only one good reason to drop into the big town of **Zvolen,** located 20 kilometers (12 miles) south of Banská Bystrica: to see the rectangular **Zvolen Castle,** set on a rocky pedestal right in the center of town. It's a bulky pile, erected in the 14th century as a chateau for the Hungarian King, **Louis I.** In the following century, it came into the possession of the exiled Czech Hussite leader, **Jiskra of Brandýs,** who ruled over much of present-day Slovakia for nearly 20 years. Much later, the Hungarian Esterházy family took it over. Fearful of Turkish attack, they transformed it into the hulking fortress you see today.

These days the castle is the venue for a branch of the **Slovak National Gallery** (Slovenská národná galéria), displaying a formidable collection of works by European masters from the 16th to 18th centuries. This is perhaps Slovakia's greatest treasure of international art, with works by the likes of Breughel, Caravaggio, and Veronese. But the real attraction here is the section dedicated to Master Pavol of Levoča, a wood sculptor who was perhaps the finest, if not the most original, Central European artist of the 15th century. In addition, the gallery features a lapidarium filled with Gothic artifacts discovered at the castle. *The gallery is open Tuesday through Friday from 10 a.m. to 5 p.m., on Saturday from 9 a.m. to 5 p.m., and on Sunday from 10 a.m. to 4 p.m. Tickets cost 30 Sk.*

Trains depart Banská Bystrica about every hour for Zvolen. Try to catch a fast train, which should take about 15 minutes to reach Zvolen.

PRACTICAL INFORMATION

• **Agrobanka**, *Dolná 17*. A bank which changes money.
• **Culture and Information Office** (Kulturné a Informačné Stredisko), *námestie SNP 1. Tel. 088/543 69*. This is a very helpful tourist information office run by English speakers. They can give you any information you need on the town, arrange guided tours, and sell you maps and tickets to cultural events. They can also tell you when certain trains and buses are departing.
• **Investičná a rozvojová banka**, *námestie SNP 15*. Another bank where you can change money.
• **Main Post Office**, *Horná 1, at the top of námestie SNP.*

Banská Štiavnica

Cradled in a narrow valley in the heavily wooded **Štiavnica Highlands**, the town of **Banská Štiavnica** couldn't ask for a grander, or steeper, location. As one of the major gold and silver mining towns in Europe, Banská Štiavnica was a glittering, fully-fledged town by the 13th century. By the 18th century, it had become the second largest town in the Hungarian Empire after Budapest, at which time Empress Maria Theresa founded here the world's first mining university.

But, as things went with virtually every mining town in Europe, Banská Štiavnica went bust once the gold and silver veins dried up. Thanks to its isolated location in the hills, which prevented the railroad from accessing the town until the 1950s, Banská Štiavnica missed out on the industrial boom, which probably did more than anything to preserve the town's medieval appearance.

After decades of neglect, Banská Štiavnica is making a comeback, but a very slow one. In 1993 the town was added to UNESCO's World Heritage List, which sparked restoration on the numerous Gothic and Renaissance houses and on the town's two castles. But the town still has a long way to go, as most of its buildings are still in a state of utter dilapidation.

For now, it's like one big open-air museum, but a very lifeless one at that, drawing a scant number of tourists and only a handful of locals. You can easily come to Banská Štiavnica on a day trip from Banská Bystrica. But I do recommend staying the night, because there are a couple of really good places to stay.

ORIENTATION

Located 45 kilometers (28 miles) southwest of Banská Bystrica, Banská Štiavnica has an idyllic location in the hills of the **Štiavnica Highlands** (Štiavnické vrchy). The small town is set on a number of hillsides, which can make getting around town extremely exhausting.

ARRIVALS & DEPARTURES

By Bus

At the time of writing, buses departed Banská Bystrica at 9 and 11 a.m. and returned at 12:45 and 1:45 p.m. only (check before you head out, because these times are subject to change.) Tickets cost 40 Sk and the beautiful journey takes under an hour. The bus station is two kilometers down from the old part of town. Just walk up and you'll eventually get there.

By Car

From Banská Bystrica, head south on E77 to Zvolen. From there go a short ways west on E571 until you see signs pointing you southward to Banská Štiavnica. Checkpoints around the old town charge you 20 Sk for a permit to park.

By Train

The train ride from Banská Bystrica is spectacular, but only recommended if you're staying the night in Banská Štiavnica. It requires two changes, in Zvolen and Hronská Dubrava. Depending on your luck with connections, it should take you two to three hours each way, compared to one hour by bus.

GETTING AROUND TOWN

Sorry, there is no public transportation in this small town to help you get up and down the hills. There are no signs of taxis either, but I wouldn't be surprised if one shows up now and again at the train station.

WHERE TO STAY

HOTEL SALAMANDER, *Palárikova 1, 969 01 Banská Štiavnica. Tel. 0859/239 92, no fax. Rates for single/double: 1,050/1,500 Sk. Credit cards: AE, DC, V. 18 rooms. Restaurant.*

Carved out of Renaissance house in the center of the old town, this hotel is fantastic, offering huge rooms with shiny wood floors, new leather furniture, refrigerators, direct-dial telephones, and satellite television. In addition to its good restaurant, the hotel has a café and a wine bar. This place makes it worth staying the night in town.

PENZIÓN MATEJ, *Akademická 4, 969 00 Banská Štiavnica. Tel. & Fax 0859/239 60. Rates for double without private bath: 500 Sk. Rates for double with private bath: 900 Sk. (No single-priced rooms available). Credit cards: MC. 4 rooms. Restaurant.*

This places resembles an American-style bed and breakfast, providing comfortable, homey rooms – two with private baths and two without. In the commons' room is a cozy fireplace and a video machine. The woman who runs the place is extremely nice, but speaks little English. Certainly, you can't complain about the prices she sets. The restaurant here is quite good also (see *Where to Eat* below).

PENZIÓN POD KLOPAČKOU, *Novozámocká 16, 969 01 Banská Štiavnica. Tel. 0859/219 45. Rates for single/double: 300/600 Sk. No credit cards. 7 rooms. No restaurant.*

This pension is a decent place to fall back on if the places mentioned above are booked up. Rooms are clean and comfortable, some of which come with private baths.

WHERE TO EAT

REŠTAURÁCIA HUBERT, *Strieborná 9. Tel. 0859/235 22. 100-200 Sk. No credit cards.*

The specialty here is game, and lots of it. Venison, wild boar, and pheasant (among other catches) are prepared with creamy, delectable sauces. Trophy heads hang on the walls, providing the appropriate setting.

REŠTAURÁCIA MATEJ, *Akademická 4. Tel. & Fax 0859/239 60. 100-200 Sk. Credit cards: MC.*

This cozy restaurant serves up a number of regional specialties with titles such as "The Drunken Bell Ringer," "The Hangman's Dainty," and "A Little Fire in the Gunpowder." The dishes are prepared with a creative flair, and served by a friendly staff.

PIZZERIA SORAGNA, *Akademická. Tel. 0859/221 01. 50-120 Sk. No credit cards.*

The tasty, thin-crust pizzas baked here are a good choice for lunch, or for dinner if you've had your fill of Slovak food.

SEEING THE SIGHTS

Note: All the museums and exhibits in Banská Štiavnica are open daily except Monday from 8 a.m. to 4 p.m. May through September, and from 8 a.m. to 3 p.m. October through April.

If you arrive by bus or train, you're in for a mile-long hike up to the historic center. Once you get past the ugly, modern apartment blocks, the town gives way to its medieval character, in which narrow alleys break off from the main thoroughfare and curve their way up the hillsides. If you keep on going straight, you'll eventually wind up at the **town hall** (radnica), notable for its clock which tells the time backwards. Perched next to it, the bright yellow **Church of St. Catherine** (Kostol sv. Katerína) is invariably closed except for services. If it happens to be open, check out its Gothic murals and statues and its lavish Baroque furnishings.

Opposite the town hall, the **Evangelical Church** (Evanjelický kostol) was built by the Lutherans in the 18th century, shortly after the Edict of Religious Tolerance was passed. For a Protestant church, it's extremely ornate, sporting two gilded urns atop an intricate tympanum.

Behind the old town hall and up the hill is the heart of the historic center – **Holy Trinity Square** (námestie sv. Trojice). The square's landmark is a grandiose sandstone plague column, posing dramatically above the town hall. When I visited, the square looked like a war zone, with construction crews working loud and furiously on restoring its stately burgher palaces and houses. However hard the crews work, it's doubtful that the square will ever be returned to its former glory. Gutted and graffiti-ridden, most of the houses on the square look like they're well past the point of being saved.

But there are some things to see on this square, such as the old **Hellenbach Palace**, *number 6,* which served as the Hungarian Mining Court from the 15th century onwards. It now houses hundreds of mineral and ore deposits culled from around Slovakia and abroad, which might be of interest only to geology buffs.

A few doors up *at number 12* is another handsome palace, its facade adorned with a rich layer of sgraffito. This is the venue for the good **Galéria Jozefa Kollára,** a formidable art museum with a small collection of Gothic statues and a large collection of works by Jozef Kollár and Edmund Gwerk – two early 20th-century painters who lived in Banská Štiavnica creating impressionist paintings of the town and the surrounding hills.

Looming above Trinity Square is the town's **Old Castle** (Starý zámok), a pillbox-like structure heavily fortified in the 16th century, a time when paranoia of Turkish attack was at fever pitch. Unfortunately, the deteriorated castle will be closed for restoration for a long time to come. To get up to the castle, take the staircase that runs behind the town hall.

Apparently, town officials believed that one castle was not enough to safeguard the town against a Turkish attack (which never came), so they built the **New Castle** (Nový zamok) five years after the Old Castle was completed. The tiny whitewashed fortress, anchored by bastions at each of its four corners, has a commanding position above town, but it lacks the ominous appearance you would expect from a castle. Inside, you'll find a not very enthralling museum entitled "History of the Turkish on the Territory of Slovakia." The museum details the Slovak-Hungarian struggle against the Ottoman Empire, showing you just how far north the Turks forged their way into the Hungarian Kingdom. You can also see some Turkish weaponry here, as well as some life-sized statues of Turkish soldiers.

But the best part of the museum may just be the spectacular view of town from the castle lookout tower. To get to the New Castle from the town hall, take Sládkovičova street up the hill past the **klopačka** house, which used to wake the miners at 5 a.m. with its big clappers. The wooden house, quaint as could be, houses a small collection of miners' tools.

From klopačka, the road continues up to **Piargska brána**, one of the town's old gateways fashioned in a lavish Baroque style that's indicative of the town's former importance in the Hungarian Empire. About a mile further down the road to Levice is perhaps the town's most interesting attraction – the open-air **Mining Museum** (Banské múzeum v prírode), featuring a number of machines that give you an idea of how mining technology has progressed through the ages. In addition, there's a handsome, three-level wooden church, and an opportunity to go down in a medieval mine (that is, if there is a group of 15 or more people on hand). The tour, through a series of narrow subterranean tunnels, is not recommended for claustrophobes.

If you've got the time or energy after all this, you might want to try and take in a few more sights. But I warn you, it means walking up some more hills. Go first to the **Academy of Mining and Forestry**; from the town hall, go down Andrejá Kmeťa street and turn left on Academická street. The congregation of stately 19th century buildings isn't so interesting as the academy's fine arboretum, apparently one of the biggest and best in Central Europe.

From the academy, go down a little ways on Hollého street, take your first left up A. Gwerkovej street, and then head up the green-marked trail to a series of chapels that make up the **Calvary** (Kalvária). Built in the 18th century, the chapels are lined up on the hillside, climaxing at the very top with a red-and-white church that's visible throughout the valley. The reward for this steep mile-long hike is a stupendous view of Banská Štiavnica.

NIGHTLIFE & ENTERTAINMENT

There's not much happening in Banská Štiavnica. You might want to check out the nightclub, **U červeného kohúta**, *námestie sv. Trojice 3*. Or catch a film at **Kino Akademík** next door.

PRACTICAL INFORMATION

• **Tourist Information Bureau** (Mestská Informačná Turistická Kancelaria), *Radničná 1. Tel. 0859/218 59*. Sells books and brochures in English and can give you the bus and train schedules.
• **Všeobecná úverová banka**, *Novozámocká 1*. A bank where you can change money.

Žilina

Situated at a river ford along several important trade routes, **Žilina** developed into a place of some importance early in its history, gaining status as a tax-exempt town from Hungarian King Karol Róbert in 1321. The Hussites sacked Žilina in 1429 and kept it until 1434, after which the town was pummeled by Hapsburg forces in the Thirty Years' War. The town really didn't come back to life until the 19th century, when the railroad made it an important industrial town.

This sizeable city of 85,000 is short on sights, so you certainly won't want to make it a major destination. But Žilina does have a certain amount of color and liveliness that make it worth a look, at least. Žilina also serves as a good base (or good point of transport connection) for exploring the **Malá Fatra Mountains** and for making the excursion to the adorable wooden village of **Čičmany**.

ORIENTATION

Žilina straddles both sides of the **Váh River**. It's located 202 kilometers (125 miles) northeast of Bratislava and 123 kilometers (76 miles) north of Banská Bystrica. The historic center is fairly compact, and easy enough to negotiate on foot.

ARRIVALS & DEPARTURES

By Bus

There are five or six buses departing Bratislava daily for Žilina. The trip takes about four hours and tickets cost 180 Sk. There are also two buses traveling each day from Prague (with a stop in Brno), taking about seven hours and costing 300 Kč (280 Sk). The bus station in Žilina is at the corner of 1. maja and Hviezdoslavova streets – a two minute walk east of the train station.

By Car

From Bratislava, take the E75 highway all the way here. The trip should take you about three hours. If you're coming from Olomouc, take E442 via Rožnov.

By Train

Žilina is a major railroad hub in Slovakia, with direct services to and from Bratislava, Prague, Poprad, and Košice. Fast trains depart Bratislava about every two hours, taking about two-and-a-half hours and cost 150 Sk. The eight or nine trains that depart Prague's Hlavní nádraží each day takes about six hours and costs around 350 Kč. As you walk out the train station, go through the underpass and walk straight down Národná street into the center of town.

GETTING AROUND TOWN

Buy your 5 Sk tickets for the bus or trolley from the bus or trolley driver. Unless you plan on visiting Žilina's Budátin Castle, you will probably have no need for using public transport, as everything in town is pretty manageable on foot. There's a taxi stand between the train and bus station.

WHERE TO STAY

HOTEL ASTORIA, *Národná 1, 010 01 Žilina. Tel. 089/624 711, Fax 089/623 173. Rates for single/double: 1,100/2,100 Sk. Credit cards: AE, DC, MC, V. 23 rooms. Restaurant.*

This newly restored hotel is your best choice of lodgings in Žilina. The clean, spacious rooms come with big bathrooms, satellite television, and a nice view of a square. The hotel has a comfortable café and a decent restaurant.

HOTEL SLOVAKIA, *námestie Štúra 2, 010 01 Žilina. Tel. 089/645 672, Fax 089/479 75. Rates for single/double: 1,270/1,860 Sk. Credit cards: AE, MC, V. 80 rooms. Restaurant.*

This big hotel just south of the city center offers plush rooms with all the expected amenities of a three-star hotel. The hotel has a snack bar, café, nightclub, sauna, and a swimming pool. It's a bit too big and impersonal for my taste, but there's no question you'll be comfortable staying here.

HOTEL POLOM, *Hviezdoslavova 22, 010 01 Žilina. Tel. 089/621 151, Fax 089/621 743. Rates for single/double with shower and toilet: 800/1,300 Sk. Credit cards: AE35 rooms. Restaurant.*

This isn't a bad choice if you're looking for someplace cheap to spend the night. Located opposite the train station, the hotel can get a bit noisy, but the rooms are clean and suitably comfortable for their rates.

WHERE TO EAT

HOTEL ASTORIA, *Národná 1. Tel. 089/624 711. Credit Cards: AE, DC, MC, V.*

The tiny restaurant at this hotel is fairly good, offering tender steaks, tangy chicken stir fries, and a decent stuffed turkey breast. You can also get a number of Slovak specialties, including *halušky* (gnocchi with cheese and bits of bacon). The hotel also has a comfortable café where you can sit in big plush sofas and enjoy a cocktail.

GMK CENTRUM, *Mariánské námestie 3. Tel. 089/622 136. 100-200 Sk. No credit cards.*

The first-floor restaurant serves tasty Slovak fare while the cellar pub offers light snacks and pours a good beer.

ZLATÝ DUKÁT, *Hodžova 201. Tel. 089/624 105. 80-150 Sk. No credit cards.*

This is a lively place that's popular with the locals. The good Slovak fare comes piled high for prices that are extremely reasonable.

SEEING THE SIGHTS

Around the Old Town

For such a big town as Žilina, there's just not a whole lot to keep you occupied. But the historic center does have a certain amount of attractiveness that makes it worth a stroll if you have time to kill waiting for a bus or train connection or if you decide to bed down here for the night.

The plaza of the town's main square, **Mariánské námestie**, has recently undergone renovation, enabling you to appreciate better the arcaded Gothic and Renaissance houses lining the square. The new fountain and lofty trees make the square an extremely pleasant location to have a coffee or beer at one of the outside cafés.

While in the square, pop your head into **St. Paul's Church** (Kostol sv. Pavla), its sooty facade sticking out on the east side of the square. Built by the Jesuits in 1743, the church has all the obligatory Baroque flourishes, such as stucco decorations, balconies, and vivid frescoes. Connected to the church is the old monastery, which now serves as space for the **Považská Galéria**, with contemporary Slovak art exhibits that won't knock your socks off, but may be worth a perusal anyhow. *It's open daily except Monday from 10 a.m. to 5 p.m.*

Just down the lane from Mariánské námestie is the town's most impressive structure, the pink **Church of the Holy Trinity** (Kostol Najsvätejšie Trojice). Built in 1400 as a Gothic parish church, Holy Trinity got a major Renaissance overhaul in 1540. Inside the church, you'll find an exquisite fresco of the Holy Trinity by J.B. Klemens.

Coupled with the Renaissance belfry standing next to it, called the **Burian Tower**, the church and its bulky tower make an impressive sight from **Hlinkovo námestie**, an austere square spread out at the foot of Holy Trinity's giant stone steps. The square is named after Andrej Hlinka, a Catholic priest who fought for Slovak independence, first against the Hungarians and then against the Czechs. Hlinka's statue sits off to one side of the square, and is inscribed with the words, "Andrej Hlinka, father of the nation."

ANDREJ HLINKA'S CONTROVERSIAL LEGACY

*There was probably no man who worked harder for Slovak independence than **Andrej Hlinka** (1864-1948), a Catholic priest from the Central Slovak town of Ružomberok. In 1906, he became famous among the Slovaks when he was sentenced to four years in prison for his fiery speeches against Hungarian rule in Slovakia. Nothing short of complete Slovak independence would suffice for Hlinka. Consequently, he was vehemently against the formation of Czechoslovakia and the centralization of power in Prague.*

*As the leader of the **Slovak People's Party** (Ľudová strana), the biggest political party in Slovakia between the wars, Hlinka organized a coalition that met in Žilina in 1938 to sign a formal demand for Slovak autonomy. Later that year, Hlinka died, but his successor in the People's Party, **Jozef Tiso**, secured Slovak independence through negotiations with Hitler. Tiso, the president of this new Nazi puppet state, kept Hlinka's name alive in the Hlinka's Guards, the Slovak equivalent of the SS.*

Though never a self-proclaimed fascist, Hlinka did lead a nationalist crusade that was only one step away from Nazi-style fascism, which makes his heroic stature in Slovakia rather dubious, to say the least.

Budatín Castle

Dating back to the 13th century, when its central Romanesque tower was built, the white-washed **Budatín Castle** (Budatínsky hrad) has had a number of reconstructions over the centuries, the last one turning it into

a Renaissance chateau. Though it's not the most majestic castle in the world, it does make for an interesting time nonetheless, thanks to the unique museum housed in the castle – the **Považské múzeum**. On exhibit here is the world's largest collection of works made by tinkers (people who create or fix things with wire and metal). Apparently, two-thirds of all men who lived in Žilina and surrounding villages at the beginning of the 19th century worked as tinkers, and their craft is now celebrated at this museum in the castle, where you can see wire dragons, wire airplanes, wire blimps, wire animals, and even wire people. It's a lot of fun, and may be the ticket if you brought the kids along. *The museum is open Tuesday through Sunday from 8 a.m. to 4 p.m.*
  To get here, take bus #24 from the bus station to the opposite side of the Váh River, or take the twenty minute walk.

NIGHTLIFE & ENTERTAINMENT
  Not a lot shaking in Žilina, I'm afraid. For a good glass of Slovak beer, head to the pub at **GMK Centrum** (see *Where to Eat* above). Or if you just want to catch a flick, go to **Dom odborov** *at Štúrovo námestie.*

EXCURSIONS & DAY TRIPS
Čičmany
  Located 38 kilometers (24 miles) south of Žilina, **Čičmany** is probably the most renowned village in Slovakia, due to its age-old tradition of painting the outside of its wooden cottages in white decorative patterns of flowers, snowflakes, and other shapes. What makes these houses so special is that the patterns, based on those used in lace, are particular only to this isolated region of Čičmany. The storybook cottages themselves, haphazardly huddled together along the banks of the Rajčanka River, are something to swoon over as well. The whole place, in fact, looks as though the last century has passed it by.
  One of the cottages houses a museum with old furnishings, costumes, and traditional embroidery. Should you be so enticed, you can buy some of the local handiwork at the museum giftshop. Opposite the museum is a cottage in which you can wander around and take a close inspection of the interior furnishings, which gives you a nice glimpse into the lives of the people who lived in it. *Both the museum and the cottage are open daily except Monday from 8 a.m. to 4 p.m.*
  From Žilina, three buses go to Čičmany daily on the weekdays, two on Saturday, and one on Sunday. There are no trains to Čičmany. If you're driving, head 33 kilometers south in the direction of Prievidza and then follow signs southwest to Čičmany.

PRACTICAL INFORMATION

Note: At press time, Žilina had no tourist information office, which should change in the near future.

• **Tatratour,** *Mariánské námestie 21. Tel. 089/620 071.* A travel agency that can help with accommodations in the region.

• **Všeobecná úverová banka,** *Na bráne 1.* A bank where you can change money.

• **Post Office,** *Hviezdoslavova street.*

Vrátna dolina in the Malá Fatra Mountains

Wedged in the center of the eastern flank of the **Malá Fatra Mountains, Vrátna dolina** (valley) is one of Slovakia's most popular valleys for outdoor enthusiasts, and certainly one of its most beautiful. The portal to the valley – a narrow slot through a fanged, limestone wall called **Tiesňavy** – sets the stage for bald peaks, pine-blanketed mountainsides, and lush ravines.

Here you can hike along an extensive trail system or go skiing down a number of challenging slopes. Vrátna dolina makes for a good day-trip from Žilina, but you may feel like shacking up in the valley instead.

ORIENTATION

The gateway to Vrátna dolina is the unappealing village of **Terchová,** which is 25 kilometers (16 miles) east of Žilina on the northern slope of the Malá Fatra Mountains. From Terchová, the road snakes its way up the valley through the rock walls of Tiesňavy, just beyond which the road forks. The left-hand fork goest to the tiny village of **Štefánova** (about five kilometers from Terchová), while the right-hand fork goes to the head of the valley, where you'll find a mountain chalet and chairlift (also five kilometers from Terchová).

ARRIVALS & DEPARTURES

By Bus

Buses depart Žilina about every hour for the 45 minute trip to Vrátna dolina. The bus stops in Terchová, Štefánova, and at Chata Vrátna. Tickets cost 30 Sk.

By Car

From the center of Žilina, cross over to the north side of the Váh River and then follow signs eastward to Terchová.

By Train

Sorry, Vrátna dolina is not accessible by train.

WHERE TO STAY/WHERE TO EAT

Note: There are plenty of comfortable private accommodations in Terchová and up in the valley. Just keep an eye out for the *zimmer frei* signs. Otherwise, try one of the following places. Also, the postal listing for all these hotels and pensions is Terchová, though they all aren't actually in Terchová. With this in mind, of the accommodations listed below, only the Penzión Covera is actually in the village of Terchová, and has the only restaurant in the village itself.

HOTEL BOBOTY, *Vrátna Dolina, 013 06 Terchová. Tel. 089/695 227, Fax 089/695 229. Rates for single/double: 900/1,300 Sk. No credit cards. Restaurant.*

This is the only hotel in the valley, located just off the road to Štefánova. Rooms are clean and comfortable, and come with private showers, but not private toilets. The hotel and its balconies have a great view of the rocky peak of Veľký Rozsutec. The hotel also has a sauna, swimming pool, and restaurant featuring live cymbal music and traditional Slovak cooking.

PENZIÓN POD LAMPÁŠOM, *Štefánova, 013 06 Terchová. Tel. 089/ 695 392, no fax. Rates for double only: 500 Sk. No credit cards. 10 rooms. Restaurant.*

Located in the hamlet of Štefánova, just below the majestic peak of Veľký Rozsutec, this pension is a quaint place to shack up for the night. Rooms come with private showers and toilets. The pension has a decent restaurant serving Slovak standards.

PENZIÓN CHATA VO VYHNANEJ, *Štefánova, 013 06 Terchová. Tel. & Fax 089/695 263. Rates for double only: 300-400 Sk. No credit cards. Restaurant.*

Rooms at this pension in Štefánova do not come with private baths or toilets, but they should suffice if you're just concerned with putting a roof over your head.

CHATA VRÁTNA, *Vrátna dolina, 013 06 Terchová. Tel. & Fax 089/695 223, no fax. Rates per bed in dorm room: 140 Sk. Rates for double: 590 Sk. No credit cards. Restaurant.*

At the head of the valley, this rustic mountain chalet is a bit worndown, but does suffice if you can't find nicer accommodations. Rooms are expectedly threadbare, none of which come with private baths, unfortunately.

PENZIÓN COVERA, *č.p. 285, 013 06 Terchová. Tel. 089/695 263, no fax. Rates for single/double: 300/500 Sk. No credit cards. Restaurant.*

Located in the village of Terchová near the turnoff for Vrátna dolina, this pension has comfortable rooms that come with private showers and toilets and satellite television. The pension also has the only restaurant in town, and it tends to fill up nightly.

SPORTS & RECREATION

Hiking & Skiing Around Vrátna Dolina

There are dozens of trails leading out of the valley and ascending the surrounding peaks of the west flank of the Malá Fatra Mountains, (this western range is called the **Krivánska Fatra Mountains**). If you're short on time but want a good a look at the mountains, then catch the year-round chairlift from Chata Vrátna (located at the head of the valley) to a saddle between the two peaks of Veľký Kriváň (1,709 meters) and Chleb (1,647 meters). From the top of the chairlift it's a half-hour climb to either of the summits, both affording a spectacular view across the range. It's only about an hour walk back down the hill to Chata Vrátna, if you're so inclined.

If you're based in Žilina and want to spend the day **hiking**, one possible way down from the top of the chairlift would be to descend the south face of Chleb along the blue-marked trail. The trail leads past a precipitous waterfall to the town of Šútovo, where you can catch a train back to Žilina.

The prettiest but most demanding hike out of Vrátna dolina starts at the village of Štefánova (two kilometers from the valley fork) and ascends the jagged summit of Veľký Rozsutec (1,610 meters). Take the yellow-marked trail from Štefánova to Podžiar. There, transfer onto the blue-marked trail, which takes you up Horné Diery, a steep cascading ravine negotiated using ladders and chain steps. The ravine ends at Medzirozsutec, from where you can retrace your steps down or take the red-marked then green-marked trails back to Štefánova. Either way, the hike should take about six hours round-trip.

Whatever hike you choose, make sure you have the proper footwear, plenty of water, and some food.

As for **skiing**, there are two chairlifts in the valley. One is on the road to Štefánova – nearby the valley fork. The other, mentioned above, is at the head of the valley at Chata Vrátna. With only two chairlifts in the valley, expect long lines and crowded runs.

PRACTICAL INFORMATION

Mountain Rescue Service (Horská služba), *one kilometer up the road to Štefánova, Tel. 089/695 232,* is the best place to go for trail information and weather conditions.

THE SLOVAK ROBIN HOOD

Born in the town of Terchová at the mouth of Vrátna dolina, Juraj Jánošík (1688-1713) is by far the most revered figure from Slovak history. His exploits as the "Slovak Robin Hood" have been recounted in hundreds of plays, poems, and novels, and his baggy garb has been reproduced in countless folk costumes that regularly appear at folk festivals throughout Slovakia.

So what made this young man such a heroic figure?

Like many men from the region, Jánošík took part in the uprising against Hapsburg rule in 1703, led by the Hungarian Ferencz Rákóczi. When the rebellion was crushed at Trenčín in 1711, Jánošík joined the monastery at Kežmarok, but left as soon as word came to him that his mother had died and that his father had been lashed to death by his landlord for taking time off from work to build his dead wife a coffin.

So Jánošík went back to Terchová and joined up with an archetypical band of merry men who went around stealing from the rich and distributing to the poor. But the story of Jánošík doesn't have the happy ending that the story of Robin Hood has. (Indeed, it seems as though no Slovak stories have happy endings.) After committing 12 robberies, Jánošík was caught by the authorities and sentenced to death. At age 25, he was hung by his rib cage in the town square of Liptovský Mikuláš.

Terchová, certainly not the bucolic village it was in Jánošík's day, has a small museum dedicated to life of Jánošík, featuring his brass-studded belt. It's open daily except Monday from 8 a.m. to 4 p.m. You'll find it just west of the village bus stand. Also, keep an eye out for the immense aluminum statue of Jánošík presiding over the village.

Liptovský Mikuláš

Besides being the place where Juraj Jánošík was hung (see sidebar above), **Liptovský Mikuláš** is an important town to Slovaks because it was the site of some pivotal events in the Slovak National Awakening. In the 1840s, the first Slovak literary society, called **Tatrín**, was founded here. And in 1848 the society wrote and published here the *Demands of the Slovak Nation*, the first document in which Slovaks outlined their demands for cultural freedom, for which the writers were forced to flee the country.

The town itself doesn't really cut the mustard as a worthwhile destination. But there are a few interesting museums (including one occupying a fortified house where Jánošík was held and tortured before his death), as well as a beautiful wooden church located in the suburb of

Palúdzka. Liptovský Mikuláš is also a convenient place to bed down for the night if you can't find accommodations in **Demänovská dolina**, the most beautiful valley of the Low Tatra Mountains located 15 minutes away by car or bus.

ORIENTATION

Located 73 kilometers (45 miles) north of Banská Bystrica and 90 kilometers (72 miles) east of Žilina, Liptovský Mikuláš has an ideal setting along the **Váh River** between the **Low Tatra Mountains** and the western flank of the **High Tatras**. To the west of town is the eastern shore of **Liptovská Mara** (Liptov Sea) – a vast reservoir that makes for good swimming or sunbathing.

ARRIVALS & DEPARTURES

By Bus

Don't bother taking the bus to Liptovský Mikuláš if you're coming from or going to Žilina, Poprad, Bratislava, or Prague, because the train is faster and runs more frequently. But if you're going to Demänovská dolina, bus is your only option, with departures about every 45 minutes.

Also, if you're coming from Banská Bystrica, bus is probably easiest, with two or three buses making the journey daily and taking about an hour. The bus station is adjacent to the train station – about a ten minute walk northwest of the town center.

By Car

From Žilina, head due east on the E50 motorway. The drive should take you about an hour. From Banská Bystrica, you can either head north on E77 and east on E50 or take the more scenic but slower route over the Low Tatras through Nemecká and Mýto.

By Train

Liptovský Mikuláš is on the Prague-Košice and Bratislava-Košice lines. Fast trains depart Bratislava about every two hours, taking three hours and 30 minutes and costing about 300 Sk. Trains leave for Poprad about every hour or two, taking less than an hour and costing about 60 Sk. The train station is on Hurbanova street, about a ten minute walk north of the town center.

GETTING AROUND TOWN

You'll have no problem getting around the center on foot. But if you plan on seeing a couple of the sights mentioned below, you may want to use the lousy bus system here. Buy your 5 Sk ticket from the driver. There's a taxi stand outside the train station.

WHERE TO STAY

HOTEL JÁNOŠÍK, *Jánošíkovo nábrežie 1, 031 01 Liptovský Mikuláš . Tel. 0849/522 721, Fax 0849/224 12. Rates for single/double: 700/1.026 Sk. Credit cards: MC. 70 rooms. Restaurant.*

This multi-story hotel is in need of renovation, but does offer decent rooms that come complete with satellite television and direct-dial telephones.

HOTEL EL GRECO, *Štúrova 2, 031 01 Liptovský Mikuláš . Tel. 0849/ 852 2713, no fax. Rates for single/double: 740/800 Sk. Credit cards: AE, MC, V. 20 rooms. Restaurant.*

The rooms at this centrally located, Art Nouveau hotel are sufficiently comfortable, and come with satellite television, telephones, and private baths. There's also a sauna in the hotel.

HOTEL KRIVÁN, *Štúrova 5, 031 01 Liptovský Mikuláš . Tel. 0849/852 2414, Fax 0849/242 43. Rates for single/double without private bath: 180/350 Sk. Rates for single/double with private bath: 220/410 Sk. Credit cards: MC. 25 rooms. Restaurant.*

Located in the middle of town, this is a good budget alternative. Rooms are pretty threadbare, but are clean enough. The hotel has a decent restaurant/café that's popular with the locals.

WHERE TO EAT

LIPTOVSKÁ IZBA, *Námestie osloboditeľov 21. Tel. 0849/514 853. 100-200 Sk. No credit cards.*

This restaurant, decked out completely in wood, has a wonderfully homey feel to it. And with appetizing smells wafting into the dining room from the kitchen, you can't help but feel hungry when you sit down. The restaurant specializes in regional cuisine, serving up a big bowl of *halušky* and a delicious turkey breast drenched in a mushroom sauce. In keeping with the folksy atmosphere, the restaurant serves beer in big ceramic mugs. A wonderful place that's worth going out of your way for.

HOTEL KRIVÁN, *Štúrova 5 . Tel. 0849/522 414. 100-200 Sk. No credit cards.*

The basic Slovak food served at this hotel is actually not too bad, but you may want to give it a pass if you disdain the smell of cigarette smoke when you're eating.

SEEING THE SIGHTS

A good introduction to Slovakia's literary establishment at the beginning of the 19th century can be had at the **Janko Kráľ Literary History Museum**, located on the **main square** (Námestie osloboditeľov) in the same Baroque house where Juraj Jánošík was sentenced to death. A lawyer by trade, Kráľ was one of Slovakia's foremost romantic poets, and an ardent nationalist to boot. The museum houses a number of his original manuscripts and personal effects, as well as those of other famous writers who were active in the Tatrín literary society. But if you have no interest in Slovak literature, then don't feel bad about giving the museum a miss. *It's open daily except Monday from 8 a.m. to 4 p.m.*

But if the Kráľ Museum has made you want to learn more about the literary movement of the Slovak National Awakening, then you may also want to check out the **exhibition on the Tatrín literary society**, housed in an 18th century Evangelical parish house where Michal Miloslav Hodža (the leader of Tatrín) worked as a minister and where the society wrote "Demands of the Slovak Nation." *The exhibit is located at Tranovského 8 and is open Tuesday through Friday from 8 a.m. to noon and from 12:30 to 4 p.m.*

Close by, *at Tranovského 3*, is the **Petr Michal Bohúň Gallery** (Oblastná galérie P.M. Bohúňa), devoted mainly to 20th-century Slovak art, with works dating right up to recent years. The gallery also houses a decent collection of Gothic altars and 19th century Slovak Romanticist paintings. *It's open daily except Monday from 9 a.m. to 5 p.m.*

About a mile west of the center in the suburb of Palúdzka is the so-called **Jánošík Dungeon** (Jánošíkovo Väzenie), a fortified manor house where the folk hero Juraj Jánošík (see the sidebar, above) was incarcerated and tortured before he was hung to death by his rib cage. Despite this sordid bit of history connected with the house, the museum here manages to be upbeat, presenting a lot of folksy artifacts from around the region. The museum also shows you how Jánošík's exploits have been represented in folk literature. To get here, jump on bus #2 or #11 from the center or walk down Štúrova street from námestie Mieru, cross the bridge, continue down Palúdžanská, and hang a right on Palučanská. *The museum is open Tuesday through Friday from 8 a.m. to 3:30 p.m. and on Saturday and Sunday from 10 a.m. to 4 p.m.*

One of the largest **wooden churches** in Slovakia used to stand near Jánošík's Dungeon, but was relocated in 1979 to the hamlet of **Svätý Kríž**, eight kilometers (five miles) southwest of Liptovsky Mikuláš, to spare it from being drowned by the encroaching waters of Liptovská Mara. It's a huge barn-like structure, built by the Lutherans in the 17th century and capable of seating some 2,000 worshippers. It's definitely worth seeing if you've got your own wheels. But you may want to think twice about it if you need to take the bus, which runs back and from the bus station to Svätý Kríž about five times a day.

NIGHTLIFE & ENTERTAINMENT

The occasional recital, performed on an 18th-century organ, is held at the Jánošík Dungeon during the summer. Check with the Informačné Centrum (see below) for exact times. A good place to go for a beer is at an outdoor terrace on the corner of Hodžova and námestie Mieru. If you feel like partying, you could venture into **Discoland** *on Šturova, next to the Hotel Kriváň*, which is a favorite with the local youth.

PRACTICAL INFORMATION

•**Informačné Centrum**, *námestie Mieru 1. Tel. 0849/514 449.* This office is a good place to go for information on the town and region. The English-speaking staff can set up all sorts of activities in the Low and High Tatras, including mountaineering, hiking tours, and even paragliding. They can also help you find accommodations in mountain chalets or in private homes in the area. There are a number of good mountain touring maps for sale here as well.

•**Všeobecná úverová banka**, *námestie Mieru.* You can change money at this bank.

•**Post Office**, *just off námestie Mieru on Hodžova street.*

Demänovská dolina in the Low Tatras

Though they don't have the High Tatras' sublime sawtooth peaks or their impressive verticality, the **Low Tatras** are a beautiful range of mountains nonetheless. The mountain summits have been swept bald by snow and wind, providing a gorgeous backdrop to the valleys. In the valleys, lakes sit like specks of crystal in forests of old-growth pines. The most accessible of these valleys is **Demänovská dolina**, its mouth no more than four miles south of Liptovský Mikuláš. At the top of the valley, you'll find one of the largest and best ski resorts in the country – **Jasná**.

When the snow melts, the valley is still an attractive destination, affording a lot of great hikes along the crest of the mountains or through the valley forests. But you don't need to be the rugged type to enjoy yourself here. You could happily spend a leisurely day touring two limestone caves at the lower end of the valley or taking an effortless ride on a chairlift to the top of **Chopok** peak, providing a splendid view of the mountain range.

ORIENTATION

The mouth of Demänovská dolina is just six kilometers (four miles) south of Liptovský Mikuláš. A narrow road twists and turns its way nine kilometers (six miles) to the top of the valley, where a diffuse collection of hotels, chalets, and pensions make up the ski resort of **Jasná**. Looming above Jasná is the rounded peak of **Chopok**, its summit accessed by a chairlift.

ARRIVALS & DEPARTURES

By Bus

Buses run about every hour from the Liptovský Mikuláš bus station up Demänovská dolina to Jásna, stopping at various points in the valley along the way.

By Car

From Liptovský Mikuláš and the E50 motorway, just follow signs southward up the valley. There's parking around the Hotel Grand Jasná or at the particular hotel or pension you're staying at.

By Train

Sorry, no trains go up the valley.

WHERE TO STAY/WHERE TO EAT

Note: Rates at hotels in the valley vary with the season. Generally, rates are highest during the ski season. If you do plan on skiing at Jasná, be sure to book a room well in advance, because walk-in possibilities are not good at all during the ski season. But you should have no problem in the summer. All of the places listed below are in Jásna, and are well sign-posted.

HOTEL GRAND JASNÁ, *032 51 Demänovská dolina. Tel. 0849/914 41, Fax 0849/914 54. Rates for single/double: 1,740-2,320/2,400-3,200 Sk. Credit cards: AE, MC, V. 122 rooms. Restaurant.*

This is a brand new American-style hotel built at the center of the resort. Outfitted with satellite television, direct-dial telephones, and built-in hair dryers, the rooms are definitely comfortable, but don't have that rustic, cozy feel you may desire when staying in the mountains. Be sure to ask for a room with a balcony, because not all rooms come with them. The hotel has a wide range of services, including a swimming pool, sauna, massage, fitness center, and ski rental.

There are two dining rooms. The better of the two is decorated in a Slovak folk style and feature a number of excellent Slovak dishes.

HOTEL JUNIOR, *032 51 Demänovská dolina. Tel. 0849/915 71, Fax 0849/915 75. Rates for single/double: 780-1,100/1,500-2,000 Sk. Credit cards: MC. Restaurant.*

If skiing is your main concern, then you might want to look into this hotel, which has a ski lift right next to it. Rooms are nothing fancy, but the hotel does have two restaurants, a bar, fitness center, swimming pool, sauna, massage, and ski rental.

HOTEL SKI ZÁHRADKY, *032 51 Demänovská dolina. Tel. 0849/916 02, Fax 0849/916 07. Rates for single/double: 800-1,000/1,200-1,600 Sk. Credit cards: AE, MC, V. 40 rooms. Restaurant.*

This rather ugly hotel is also next to a ski lift. Rooms are definitely in need of updating, but are suitably comfortable and clean. The hotel does have a sauna and can rent you skis.

MIKULÁŠSKA CHATA, *032 51 Demänovská dolina. Tel. 0849/916 76, Fax 0849/916 72. Rates for single/double: 340-500/700-1,000 Sk. Rates for apartment: 540-700/900-1,200 Sk. No credit cards. 12 rooms and 5 apartments. Restaurant.*

Now, this is more like it. This venerable old chalet has recently been renovated into the coziest place in the valley. The wood-studded rooms afford that snug feeling that makes staying in the mountains something special. Thankfully, there are no televisions and no telephones in the rooms; just peace and tranquility. The chalet is located footsteps away from a placid lake, with several trails looping around it and leading off into the forest.

The restaurant here is good, offering specialties from Slovakia, Hungary, and Italy. If you're staying here or not, don't miss the chalet's Vináreň Peklo, a rustic lodge sitting next to the chalet where you can sit by the fire and enjoy a glass of Slovak wine or Czech beer. All in all, a very fine place, with affordable rates to boot.

HOTEL LIPTOV, *032 51 Demänovská dolina. Tel. 0849/915 06, Fax 0849/915 81. Rates for single/double: 600-900/1,000-1,500. Credit cards: AE, MC, V. 72 rooms. Restaurant.*

This place is need of some modernization, but the rooms are decent enough. The hotel has a sauna, a small fitness room, and a couple of billiards tables. Take note that the hotel is closed from the end of the ski season to June 1.

HOTEL J. ŠVERMA, *032 51 Demänovská dolina. Tel. 0849/916 41, Fax 0849/915 58. Rates for single/double: 500-700/800-1,000 Sk. No credit cards. 100 rooms. Restaurant.*

The nicest thing going for the otherwise boring rooms at this tacky hotel are the balconies, which look out into the surrounding beauty. Just behind the hotel is a log cabin *koliba*, where you can get chicken roasted over an open fire.

SEEING THE SIGHTS

Of course, seeing the sights in Demänovská dolina means enjoying the great outdoors, or the great indoors – by which I mean two limestone caves in the lower section of the valley. Just as you enter into the valley from Liptovský Mikuláš, you'll see a sign pointing to **Demänova Ice Cave** (Demänovská ľadová jaskyňa), *open from May 1 to early September*. The thirty-minute tour of this cave takes in a huge cavern dripping with stalagmites and stalactites and covered in 18th-century graffiti. The tour then moves into the ice chamber, its walls and rock formations completely frozen. No matter what time of year it is, the temperature inside the cave is at around freezing. Message: dress warm.

A few kilometers further on is the valley's second cave, called **Demänova Freedom Cave** (Demänovská jaskyňa Slobody). Open year-round, this cave is more impressive than the Ice Cave (and every bit as cold), featuring a greater number of intriguing rock formations. Partisans during World War II used the cave for storage, hence the name.

If you're more inclined to stay above ground, then consider taking the year-round chairlift from Jasná to the summit of **Chopok** (2,024 meters). The 20 minute lift ride takes you 790 meters (2,591 feet) up, with a change half way up at Luková. After walking along the ridgeline and soaking in the grand view, you can return on the chairlift or hike back down to Jasná along the blue-marked trail. Another option is to take a chairlift (or hike 90 minutes along the yellow-marked trail) down the other side of the mountains into **Bystrá dolina**, a less-developed valley where you'll find a couple of hotels and the occasional bus to Banská Bystrica.

For more on the plethora of trails in Demänovská dolina and through the Low Tatras, pick up Slovenská kartografia's *Nízke Tatry* map at any bookstore or gift shop in the area.

SPORTS & RECREATION

Jasná is one of the more popular ski resorts for Slovaks, and for good reason. They have seven chairlifts, several rope tows, and a gondola accessing some 15 different runs that range in difficulty from easy to extreme. Price of lift tickets vary with the week. But you can count on higher priced tickets during the week of any holiday. Generally, a one-day lift ticket will run you between 200 and 300 Sk.

Most hotels, such as Hotel Grand Jasná and Hotel Junior, rent good ski equipment if you haven't brought your own. Rental of skis, boots, and poles costs between 200 and 400 Sk a day, depending on the quality of the gear and the number of days you rent.

There are countless opportunities for cross-country skiing around Jasná as well. In fact, you can probably ski out of whichever hotel you're staying in. Hotel Grand Jasná rents cross-country equipment for about 200 Sk a day. The people working at the rental office can give you the low-down on good tours in the valley.

Fun doesn't end in the valley when the snow melts. There are several summer activities you can get involved in as well. **Crystal Ski**, a recreation outfitter based out of the Hotel Grand Jasná, gives you the opportunity to go paragliding, river rafting, rock climbing, and horseback riding. Instruction and equipment are all part of the package. They can also arrange for you to go on a balloon flight, a sightseeing flight, or a mountain biking or hiking tour of the Low Tatras. Contact them at: **Hotel Grand Jasná**, *032 51 Demänovská dolina. Tel. 0849/914 60.*

PRACTICAL INFORMATION

•**Slovakotour**, *just past the turn-off for Pavčina Lehota at the mouth of Demänovská dolina. Tel. 0849/234 14.* Here, you can change money, buy maps, and get help with accommodations in the valley.

Poprad

With the snowy, sawtooth peaks of the High Tatras rising up in the north, **Poprad** couldn't ask for a grander location. Unfortunately, the town doesn't live up to its surroundings, offering a scant number of attractions – architectural or otherwise – that would make you want to consider it as a destination.

But Poprad is the transportational hub for the High Tatra resorts, which means you will most likely pass through here on your way to the mountains. Poprad can come in handy if you are not able to find any vacancies at the resorts.

Poprad also makes a viable base for visiting not only the High Tatras, but also the Spiš region of East Slovakia (see **Kežmarok, Levoča,** and **Spiš Castle** in the next chapter).

ORIENTATION

Poprad lies about ten miles away from the base of the High Tatras, 124 kilometers (77 miles) northeast of Banská Bystrica and 328 kilometers (203 miles) east of Bratislava. The **Poprad River** runs through the middle of town.

ARRIVALS & DEPARTURES
By Bus

Bus is easier and faster from Banská Bystrica if you don't have your own car. Buses run about every two hours. The two hour ride cost around 80 Sk. Bus is also the fastest way to go if you're going to the High Tatra resorts from Poprad (see *Getting Around the High Tatras,* below). The Poprad bus station, a block west of the train station, is a five minute walk from the center of town.

By Car
From Banská Bystrica head due east via Brezno and Telgárt. The drive, through the Hron River valley and over the Low Tatras, is spectacular. From Žilina or Košice, take the E50 motorway all the way there.

By Train
Poprad is on the Prague-Košice and Bratislava-Košice railway lines. There are six or seven trains departing Prague daily, including an overnight sleeper. The trip takes about nine hours and costs around 650 Kč. Trains depart Bratislava about every two hours. The journey takes about four-and-a-half hours and costs around 250 Sk. The train station in Poprad is about a five minute walk north of the center of town.

An old, rickety electric train – called the **Tatranská elektrická železnica** or **TEŽ** – connects Poprad with the High Tatra resorts. It departs about every hour from the upper story of the Poprad train station. Buy your ticket from the regular ticket window at the train station. For more on the "Tatra Train," see *Getting Around the High Tatras*, below.

GETTING AROUND TOWN

The only reason you'd want to get on the bus in Poprad is if you feel like seeing the village (now Poprad suburb) of Spišská Sobota. In that case, pay the driver 5 Sk for the ticket. Otherwise, you'll get around just fine on foot.

WHERE TO STAY

HOTEL POPRAD, *Partizánska 677/18, 058 01 Poprad. Tel. 092/721 521, Fax 092/721 284. Rates for single/double: 1,150/1,930 Sk. Credit cards: AE, MC, V. 120 rooms. Restaurant.*

In Poprad, you can't beat this brand new hotel, offering a lot of amenities including an indoor tennis court and swimming pool, sauna, fitness center, and satellite television. Excellent service can arrange just about anything you'd like to do in the region.

HOTEL SATEL, *Mnoheľova 826/5, 058 01 Poprad. Tel. 092/471 111, Fax 092/721 120. Rates for single/double: 1,135-1,235/1,770-1,920 Sk. Credit cards: AE, DC, MC, V. 122 rooms. Restaurant.*

Just walk through the park from the train station and you'll find this high-rise hotel glaring at you. It's an ugly place on the outside, but inside you'll find it's a fairly swanky hotel. Room are decked out in black and white fixtures, and are certainly comfortable. The hotel has an indoor tennis court, an indoor squash court, billiards rooms, fitness center, and sauna.

HOTEL GERLACH, *Hviezdoslavova 2, 058 01 Poprad. Tel. 092/721 945, Fax 092/636 63. Rates for single/double: 500/850 Sk. Credit cards: AE, MC. 75 rooms. Restaurant.* The prices are certainly right at this hotel next to the Hotel Satel. Rooms are clean and suitably comfortable. Definitely ask for a room on the north side, so you can wake up in the morning to the sight of the High Tatras in the distance.

WHERE TO EAT

EGIDIUS, *Mnoheľova. Tel. 092/722 898. 100-200 Sk. Credit cards: AE, MC.* Right across the lane from the Hotel Satel, this multi-story restaurant will charm your socks off. Everything, from the salt and pepper shakers to the clocks, is carved in wood, representing the regional folk style of decoration. Just as folksy as the decor is the food, including tasty potato dumplings as well as a hearty bowl of *halušky* (gnocchi smothered in cheese and tossed with bits of bacon). If it's a warm day, take a seat on the attractive balcony.

SLOVENSKÁ REŠTAURÁCIA, *1. mája 9. Tel. 092/722 870. 60-150 Sk. No credit cards.* This restaurant with the generic name of "Slovak Restaurant" is a lot like Egidius, but not as successful in its folksy, woody decor. The interior is decorated to look something like a Slovak village, with water running across the roof beams and a well planted in the middle of the floor.

SEEING THE SIGHTS

There's just not much to see in Poprad. But if the weather is too crummy for a hike in the Tatras or if you're bedding down here for the night, then you might want to take a walk around the elongated **main square** (námestie Svätého Egídia), through which runs a line of churches that are not all that interesting. The square is a nice place to be in the early evening, when everybody in town comes here for a stroll. Just off the east end of the square is **Podtatranské múzeum,** its natural history and archaeological exhibits worth a perusal only if you have time to kill. *The museum is open daily except Sunday from 9 a.m. to 5 p.m.*

A bit more pleasant than the center of Poprad is **Špišská Sobota,** a village-cum-suburb on the northern outskirts of town. Around the main square is a series of wooden burgher houses with stone facades and wide gables that jut out over the sidewalk. But the real reason for coming out here is to see **St. George's Church,** a late-Gothic construction with intricate vaulting and a beautiful main altar by the renowned Master Pavol of Levoča. Next to the church is a museum with a decent collection of church art and some boring archaeological exhibits. *It's open daily except Sunday from 9 a.m. to 5 p.m.*

To get to Spišská Sobota from the center of Poprad, walk northeast along the river on Štefánikova street and then take a left on Kežmarská street all the way to Spišská Sobota. Or just jump on bus #2 or #4.

PRACTICAL INFORMATION

- **Popradská Informačná Agentura** (Poprad Information Agency), *námestie sv. Egídia 2950. Tel. 092/721 700.* This is an excellent source of information about the High Tatras. The office organizes sightseeing tours of the region, can find you accommodations in the Tatras, and can arrange for you to go paragliding, rafting down the Dunajec River, horseback riding, hunting, and fishing. The office also rents skis, cars, and mountain bikes.
- **Mestské Informačné Centrum** (Town Information Center), *Hlavná 9. Tel. 092/186.* Sells maps, changes money, and can find you accommodations in town.
- **Nova**, *námestie sv. Egídia 95. Tel. 092/234 90.* This travel agency offers tours around the region in their Volkswagen mini-buses.
- **Všeobecná úverova banka**, *Mnoheľova 9.* A bank with an exchange office.
- **Post Office**, *corner of Mnoheľova and Štefánikova.*

The High Tatras

Jutting out of a flat expanse on the northern edge of Slovakia, the sublime peaks of the **High Tatra Mountains** are what draws most tourists to the Slovak Republic. Once you feast your eyes at the sublime outline of these mountains, cutting across the landscape like a row of fanged teeth, it's easy to understand the hype.

What most tourists come here to do is ski, and for good reason. The soaring elevations of the High Tatras ensure a thick base of snow throughout the ski season. And the exposed, glacial-carved valleys and peaks provide scenery that is nothing short of majestic. It should come as no surprise then that conglomeration of Tatra resorts made a serious bid for the 2002 Winter Olympics, and wasn't eliminated from the contention until the possible sites had been narrowed down to four.

Of course, you don't need to be a skier or even a winter enthusiast to soak in all this beauty. A user-friendly network of hiking trails and several year-round chairlifts and gondolas make it easy to get above the timberline and onto the sublime summits in no time. One of these gondolas, located about the resort of **Tatranská Lomnica**, takes you 2,890 hair-raising feet up to the top of **Lomnický štít**, the second highest mountain in the range.

Spanning only about 25 kilometers (16 miles) from east to west, the High Tatras are an extremely compact range of mountains, made easy to get around by an electric train servicing the string of resorts and sanatoria centers lined up at the base of the mountains. It's this compactness that has facilitated the overdevelopment of these mountains. The resorts and sanatoria centers, which started out as secluded retreats at the turn of the century, are these days so sprawling that it's hard to distinguish where one resort ends and the next one begins.

But the overdevelopment in the High Tatras pales in comparison to what's been done in the American Rockies (i.e. the resort towns of Vail, Park City, Deer Valley). Plus, the High Tatra resorts are thankfully still pretty affordable, and are not just the playgrounds for the wealthy and elite that the resorts in the Rockies and Alps are.

Whatever you do, don't expect to have the place to yourself. The crowds can get horrendous during the peak weeks of skiing and during the summer months. To avoid these crowds, plan on coming in April for the last bit of skiing or in May, September, or October. There's also a window of time between January 7 and January 27 when the ski crowds and prices are down to a bare minimum.

The High Tatras are managed by the **Tatra National Park**, Czechoslovakia's first national park, founded in 1949. The park asks you to adhere to some regulations. First, don't pick the wild flowers (they're beautiful, but resist the temptation). Stay on established trails. Pack out what you pack in. And don't build open fires.

ORIENTATION

The High Tatras run along an east-west axis on the northern edge of Slovakia, forming the natural border with Poland. There are several resort towns and sanatoria centers strung along the base of the High Tatras, all connected by bus or the electric train. The most central of the resorts is the resort complex of **Smokovce**, located roughly 12 kilometers (seven miles) north of Poprad. Smokovce is the collective name for a cluster of resorts, including **Starý Smokovec, Nový Smokovec, Horný Smokovec**, and **Dolný Smokovec** – all of which are in easy walking distance of another by paved trails.

About 13 kilometers (eight miles) west of Smokovce, at the western end of the electric train line, is **Štrbské Pleso**, the biggest and highest ski resort in the Tatras. About six kilometers east of Smokovce, at the east end of the electric train line, is **Tatranská Lomnice**, the most peaceful of all the resorts, situated in the shadow of the Tatras' second highest peak of **Lomnický štít**.

ARRIVALS & DEPARTURES

The transportation hub for the High Tatras is Poprad, so refer to *Arrivals & Departures* in the section on Poprad above.

GETTING AROUND THE HIGH TATRAS

By Bus

Though it isn't as quaint as the electric train (see below), the bus is a lot faster, and runs more often. From Poprad, buses leave about every thirty minutes for Starý Smokovec, from there veering either west to Štrbské Pleso or east to Tatranská Lomnica. The bus stations in Starý Smokovec, Štrbské Pleso, and Tatranská Lomnica show the times of departure on a big board. Find your destination on the board (listed in alphabetical order) and after it a list of departure times. Just tell the driver where you're going and he'll hand you a ticket with the price printed on it. But I warn you, the buses tend to get crowded and you may end up standing, consequently missing all the great sights.

By Car

With such good public transportation, there's really no need to use the car in the High Tatras. Public parking lots can be hard to find, and can also get kind of expensive. Plus, you'll feel better about yourself if you are not contributing to the fouling of the mountain air. Who needs a car anyway when you'll be spending all your time skiing or hiking?

By Taxi

At 200 to 300 Sk, the taxi from Poprad to one of the resorts is a rip-off. Prices between the resorts are a bit more reasonable, but not much. Have your hotel receptionist order you a cab or *call 2525*.

By Train

An electric train or "Tatra Train," which is actually a long-distance tram system (looking much like the one in Prague), was built here around the time of World War I. Called the **Tatranská električká železnica (TEŽ)**, the tram is a quaint, eco-friendly way to go, offering great views of the range at a leisurely, albeit slow pace. It runs from the Poprad train station up the hill to Smokovce and then either veers west to Štrbské Pleso or east to Tatranská Lomnica, servicing the string of resorts and sanatoria centers lined up along the base of the High Tatras. (If you're going to Tatranská Lomnica, you could also take a regular train.) Buy your tickets from the ticket window at the stations or from one of the conductors. The fare is dirt-cheap (in the ballpark of 10 Sk) and depends on how far you want to go.

WHERE TO STAY

I've arranged hotels here by resort. Rates vary with the season, so count on paying more during the ski season and the peak summer months and much less during late spring and early fall. Most of the hotels here date back to 1969, when there was a furious spurt of development in anticipation for the 1970 World Nordic Championships, which took place at Štrbské Pleso. Consequently, many of these hotels have a funky style of architecture that was thankfully left behind in the seventies.

Štrbské Pleso

The highest of the Tatra resorts, Štrbské Pleso also has the most dramatic alpine setting. It's the most commercial of the resorts as well, with a lot of high-rise hotels that somewhat mar the surroundings. A beautiful feature of the resort is its clear glacial lake (or *pleso*, from which the resorts get its name), set against the backdrop of a 1,000-foot granite wall. This is one of the better areas for skiing and hiking in the High Tatras, with trails and runs suitable for just about any level of hiker or skier. There's also a good cross-country ski trail here called Cesta Slobody (Path of Freedom).

HOTEL PATRIA, *059 85 Štrbské Pleso. Tel. 0969492 591, Fax 0969/492 590. Rates for single/double: 1,138-1,764/1,606-2,441 Sk. Credit cards: AE, MC, V. 150 rooms. Restaurant.*

Top of the line in Štrbské Pleso, this hotels offers comfortable, newly renovated rooms that come with either a great view of the mountains or of the big mountain lake down the hill. Either way, ask for a room on one of the upper floors so as to have a more commanding view of the area. The hotel features an indoor swimming pool, sauna, fitness center, massage, and a couple of good restaurants. In the hotel you'll find the Turist Centrum recreation outfitter, which rents mountain bikes and can arrange for you to go horseback riding, paragliding, and rafting. In the winter they rent skis and offers ski instruction.

HOTEL FIS, *059 85 Štrbské Pleso. Tel. 0969/492 357, Fax 0969/492 422. Rates for single/double: 700-1,100/1,200-1,620 Sk. Credit cards: AE, MC, V. 50 rooms. Restaurant.*

If you've come to ski, this hotel at the top of the resort is a good choice, because the ski lift is footsteps away. Rooms are cozy enough, and the hotel has a good range of services, including a sauna, fitness room, indoor swimming pool, and massage. The hotel rents skis and has English-speaking instructors for hire.

HOTEL PANORÁMA, *059 85 Štrbské Pleso. Tel. 0969/492 111, Fax 0969/492 810. Rates for single/double: 1,000-1,500/1,700-2,700 Sk. Credit cards: AE, DC, MC, V. 96 rooms. Restaurant.*

This high-rise hotel epitomizes the funky style of building that went on here in 1969. It's really quite an eye-sore. Like the rest of the hotel, the decor of the rooms are stuck in the late sixties, and are not worth their exorbitant rates.

HOTEL BANÍK, *059 85 Štrbské Pleso. Tel. 0969/492 541, Fax 0969/492 124. Rates for single/double: 550-750/850-1,300 Sk. Credit cards: V. 102 rooms. Restaurant.*

This is another ugly hotel, located below the train station on the banks of a mountain lake. Though they could use some updating, the rooms are decent enough, and worth their very reasonable rates. The hotel has a sauna, fitness center, and a tennis court.

Smokovce

This cluster of resorts – including **Starý Smokovec, Nový Smokovec, Horný Smokovec**, and **Dolný Smokovec** – are where most of the tourist services are. All of these resorts are based below the ski area called **Hrebienok**, which has pretty mild skiing compared to other areas in the Tatras. But the nice thing about Smokovce is that it's centrally located, with Štrbské Pleso and Tatranská Lomnica minutes away.

HOTEL GRAND, *062 01 Starý Smokovec. Tel. 0969/422 154, Fax 0969/ 422 157. Rates for single/double: 1,100-1,900/2,010-2,441 Sk. Credit cards: AE, MC, V. 75 rooms. Restaurant.*

Though it looks a bit forbidding from the outside, this turn-of-the-century hotel has a certain amount of coziness and charm that make it an inviting place for a ski vacation. The place is decked out in wood paneling and Oriental rugs. At the hotel you can go for a swim, sit in a sauna, play pool, or just sit and read in the library stocked with books in German, Russian, and English.

The hotel is also the best place in town to go for dinner, not because of the food, but because of the grand performances of the maitre d'hôtel (see *Where to Eat*, below).

HOTEL PANDA, *062 01 Horný Smokovec. Tel. 0969/422 614, Fax 0969/ 423 418. Rates for single/double: 1,100-1,600/1,700-2,400 Sk. Credit cards: MC, V. 45 rooms. Restaurant.*

This new hotel is not a bad choice. Rooms are nicely decorated, and are soothing places to be after a day in the mountains. The hotel gives you the opportunity to go horseback riding or play tennis.

HOTEL PARK, *062 01 Nový Smokovec. Tel. 0969/422 342, Fax 0969/422 304. Rates for single/double: 1,200-1,600/1,800-2,700 Sk. Credit cards: AE, DC, MC, V. 45 rooms. Restaurant.*

This is another one of those weird-looking hotels built in 1969. The rooms are in serious need of updating, which makes their rates way overpriced. Service here is extremely slack. You're better off avoiding this place.

VILLA DR. SZONTAGH, *062 01 Nový Smokovec. Tel. 0969/422 061, Fax. 0969/422 062. Rates for single/double: 700-900/1,300-1,600 Sk. Credit cards: MC, V. 20 rooms. Restaurant.*

Named after the physician who founded Nový Smokovec at the turn of the century, this turreted villa has a faded, 1920s elegance that is somewhat humorous today. But it's a nice place, and the receptionists are wonderfully accommodating. Though it has one of the tackiest dining rooms I've seen, the restaurant serves a lot of good international and Slovak meals. The hotel also rents cars if you're in need of one.

BILIKOVA CHATA, *Hrebienok, 062 01 Starý Smokovec. Tel. 0969/422 439, Fax 0969/422 267. Rates for single/double: 500-900/900-1,200 Sk. Credit cards: V. 12 rooms. Restaurant.*

You can't beat the views from the mountain chalet located above Starý Smokovec at the Hrebienok ski area. From the chalet you look up at the craggy Lomnický štít peak or out to the flat plains towards Poprad. Outfitted with private showers and toilets, the rooms are pretty basic. But with such an amazing location as this, who cares if the decor isn't top notch? To get here, you need to take the funicular up the mountain from a station located a couple of blocks behind the Hotel Grand.

Tatranská Lomnica

On the eastern edge of the range, **Tatranská Lomnica** is definitely the most peaceful of the resorts in the High Tatras. Much of the resort is overtaken by parks, strewn with pines and aspens. Tatranská Lomnica boasts some of the best skiing on the range, and offers one of the most thrilling rides you could ever take – up the gondola to the summit of the 2,632-meter **Lomnický štít**, the second highest peak in the range.

GRANDHOTEL PRAHA, *059 60 Tatranská Lomnica. Tel. 0969/467 941, Fax 0969/467 891. Rates for single/double: 1,300-2,500/2,300-3,400 Sk. Credit cards: AE, DC, MC, V. 91 rooms. Restaurant.*

Set on a ledge above the resort, this enormous, venerable hotel goes back to 1905, when it was a magnet for sojourning Hungarian aristocracy. Like all grand hotels in the former Czechoslovakia, the Communist directors gave it a half-baked restoration in the 1970s, a period most of the rooms now reflect. But the hotel is making a comeback, and is slowly but surely restoring the rooms and the rest of the hotel (so ask for a room that's been renovated). The hotel has a fitness center and sauna, and can arrange for you to go on a guided hike in the mountains.

HOTEL SLOVAKIA, *059 60 Tatranská Lomnica. Tel. 0969/467 961, Fax 0969/467 975. Rates for single/double: 1,430-1,640/2,125-2,525 Sk. Credit cards: AE, DC, MC, V. 40 rooms. Restaurant.*

This Slovak hotel looks like an American motel, but with all the amenities that make it a three-star establishment. Rooms are clean and functional, though a bit outdated. There's a swimming pool, fitness center, and sauna, as well as a fairly decent restaurant that's done up in a folk style.

HOTEL WILI, *059 60 Tatranská Lomnica. Tel. 0969/467 761, Fax 0969/ 467 763. Rates for single/double: 700-900/1,000-1,200 Sk. Credit cards: AE, DC, MC, V. Restaurant.*

Rooms here are very plain, but functional enough. The hotel can rent skis and mountain bikes. It also has a *koliba*-style restaurant where chicken is roasted over an open fire.

HOTEL TATRY, *059 60 Tatranská Lomnica. Tel. & Fax 0969/467 614, Fax 0969/467 724. Rates for single/double: 600/1,000 Sk (same year-round). No credit cards. 11 rooms. Restaurant.*

Located smack dab in the center of the resort, this small hotel is carved out of a quaint turn-of-the-century villa with a wrap-around porch. The rates here are too good to be true. And the cozier than cozy, wood-studded rooms – outfitted with lofts, satellite television, direct-dial telephones, contemporary furniture, and soft beds – are some of the nicest I've seen in the High Tatras. Add to that great service and friendly receptionists and what you come up with is an all-around great hotel.

The only drawback is that the hotel doesn't take credit cards (something, I imagine, that will change in the near future). It's a small hotel, and fills up quickly – so be sure to book well in advance for this gem.

WHERE TO EAT

If you're going to the High Tatras expecting to eat like a king, you're bound to be disappointed. So you're better off lowering your expectations. Restaurants stick mainly to the meat-potatoes-cabbage theme that you've probably come to know so well now through your travels in the Czech and Slovak republics. Your choice of restaurants is pretty much limited to hotels, as they've obviously got the monopoly on space in the High Tatra resorts.

Štrbské Pleso

SLOVENKA, *in the Hotel Patria, 059 85 Štrbské Pleso. Tel. 0969/925 91. 100-200 Sk. Credit cards: AE, MC, V.*

Meaning "Slovak girl," this restaurant and its folksy atmosphere seem a little forced. The stuffed cuts of meats and other Slovak specialties are quite good, though. There's a folk band to liven things up.

REŠTAURÁCIA PLESNIVEC, *on the east side of the bus station. Tel. 0969/492 366. 100-200 Sk. No credit cards.*

Live cymbal music accompanies your meal at this decent restaurant in the middle of the resort. The kitchen uses fresh ingredients for their typical Slovak meals that include a lot of grilled meats.

Smokovce
HOTEL GRAND, *062 01 Starý Smokovec. Tel. 0969/422 154. 200-300 Sk. Credit cards: AE, MC, V.*

It's not so much the typical Central European food here that's the attraction as it is the maitre d'hôtel's nightly performance of spinning crystal goblets on serving tables and turning a flambé preparation into a kind of circus act. The guy is a hoot, and, with his tuxedo and twirled mustache, looks like he came with the dining room's Art Nouveau decor.

The hotel's other restaurant, the **Taverna**, is a good choice for lunch, serving up a lot of Slovak standards such as fried cheese and roast pork. And on a warm day, the terrace is a nice place to relax.

VILLA DR. SZONTAGH, *062 01 Nový Smokovec. Tel. 0969/422 061. 200-300 Sk. Credit cards: MC, V.*

Talk about bad taste. How about chandeliers made out of deer antlers. Lime green curtains coupled with wood panelling. Ah well, it could be worse. Thankfully then, the choice of meats, including the steak topped with artichoke hearts, is pretty good, and the service is quite deft. Just come with a sense of humor and you should have an enjoyable meal.

TATRANSKÁ KÚRIA, *next to the bus station in Starý Smokove. No Tel. 75-125 Sk. No credit cards.*

This a good cheap place dishing out spicy chicken dishes and a wonderful goulash soup.

BILIKOVA CHATA, *Hrebienok, 062 01 Starý Smokovec. Tel. 0969/422 439. 75-100 Sk. No credit cards.*

If you're hiking or skiing at the Hrebienok area, stop here for lunch. The typical Slovak fare is nothing special, but the views from the sunny dining room are awesome.

Tatranská Lomnica
GRANDHOTEL PRAHA, *059 60 Tatranská Lomnica. Tel. 0969/467 941. 150-300 Sk. Credit cards: AE, MC, V.*

The chandelier-strewn dining room of this once-haughty hotel has a faded elegance that makes you feel as if you've stepped back to another era. The Slovak and international courses here are smartly presented, and are as close to haute-cuisine as you'll get in the High Tatras.

RESTAURANT JULIA, *just down from the train station (signs point the way). Tel. 0969/467 947. 100-200 Sk. No credit cards.*

With a thatched ceiling and all sorts of folksy knick-knacks, this restaurant provides the right atmosphere for enjoying any number of authentic dishes from the Spíš region of East Slovakia. Chicken stuffed with mushrooms and ham, tasty *halušky* (gnocchi with cheese and bits of bacon), and tangy paprika stew are just some of the items that grace the excellent menu. Members of the Imriščák family are your very congenial hosts.

HOTEL TATRY, *059 60 Tatranská Lomnica. Tel. & Fax 0969/467 614. 75-150 Sk. No credit cards.*

This is another good restaurant in which to sample some typical Slovak dishes, such as *halušky*, stuffed turkey, and potato dumplings. The folksy decor augments the dining experience, as does the good Slovak wine poured straight from the casket.

SPORTS & RECREATION
Hiking the Tatras

It's time to lace up your hiking boots, grab hold of your sense of adventure, and head for the mountains, for they are beckoning. You don't need to be a first-class mountaineer to conquer them – far from it. Chairlifts, gondolas, and a user-friendly network of trails have made it easier to come to terms with the majestic peaks, placid lakes, and drop-dead views of the **High Tatras National Park**. Whichever resort you're staying at, you can walk right out of your hotel and begin your trek.

I've suggested a number of hikes below that you might want to consider going on. But there are an infinite number of routes to choose from, so you may want to pick up a good map and plan your own. A good touring map to have is Slovenská kartografia's 1:50,000 *Vysoké Tatry*. Another helpful publication is the *Everyman's Guide to the High Tatras*, loaded with information on sights, hikes, and history. If you're interested in the flora and fauna of the High Tatras, pick up *The Tatra National Park – the Guide by Nature*. You can pick up any of these publications at any of the tourist information offices listed below (see *Practical Information*) or at one of the high-end hotels.

TAKE PRECAUTIONS WHEN HIKING THE HIGH TATRAS

Hiking in the High Tatras requires that you take some precautions. First and foremost, dress warm. It can get downright freezing in the higher elevations, even in the dead of summer. Rain, with the possibility of snow, is always a threat (especially during the summer), so bring your rain gear even if it's a clear and sunny day when you set out. If there are clouds hovering over the peaks, that means the weather is nasty in the higher elevations. In that case, go on a low-elevation hike or take a day trip to one of the nearby towns, such as Ždiar or Kežmarok.

Hiking Around Štrbské Pleso

The hike that most people opt for in Štrbské Pleso is the one heading up the trail called the **magistrála**, accessing **Popradské pleso** (lake) in about an hour. It's a gorgeous spot, but one you'll have to share with a lot of other hikers. If you're in excellent shape, then continue up the brutal blue-marked trail to sedlo pod Ostrvou, affording a sensational view of the lake below. Another option from Popradské pleso is to ascend the summit of **Rysy** peak via the mountain chalet called Chata pod Rysmi. The reward for this hard, seven-hour round-trip journey is a mind-bending view, one that brought Lenin himself here once. Don't be surprised if you hear a lot of Polish speakers at the summit, because the border runs right across the mountain.

If all that sounds too strenuous, then take a ride up the year-round chairlift to Solisko, from where it takes an hour to ascend the 2,093-meter summit of **Predné Solisko**. You'll find the chairlift near the Hotel Fis.

Hiking Around Smokovce

To make things a little easier, hop on the funicular that runs behind the Hotel Grand to the ski area of Hrebienok, which is a good starting point for a number of excellent hikes. A beautiful day hike from the funicular would be to head west on the magistrála to the Sliezsky dom mountain hotel, and back down to Smokovce via the orange-marked trail.

For something a bit more breathtaking, take the green path a kilometer past the Bilichova chata (chalet) to the cascading waterfalls of **Studenovodské vodopády**. A little past the waterfalls the trail forks. The left-hand fork takes you up to **Zamruznuté pleso** (lake), set thirty minutes away from the summit of **Vychodná Vysoká** – affording the best view you're going to get of Slovakia's highest mountain, **Gerlachovský štít** (2,655 meters). Count on nine hours to complete this hike.

Another option from the waterfalls is to take the right-hand fork up the valley of Malá studená to the Zbojnická chata (chalet). This trail is definitely not recommended for the faint of heart; it requires climbing 90 feet up a rock face on a chain. From Zbojnická chata, return to Hrebienok through the Veľká studená valley for a round-trip of about eight hours.

Hiking Around Tatranská Lomnica

Tatranská Lomnica offers less in the way of hiking, but it does feature what has to be one of the most hair-raising rides you could ever take – up the gondola to the 2,632-summit of **Lomnický štít**. First, you need to take the gondola from a station next to the Grandhotel Praha to the lake of Skalnaté pleso, sitting at 1,751 meters. There, brace yourself for the second, mind-blowing ride going 2,890 feet straight to the top of Lomnický

Štít. Needless to say, the view is nothing less than stupendous, affording a look across the range and over much of northern Slovakia and southern Poland.

Getting to the top of this part of the world doesn't come cheap, however. The ride to Skalnaté pleso costs 70 Sk each way, and the ride to Lomnický štít is another 300 Sk each way. But you won't regret spending it. Oh, remember to bring warm clothing, because it's burr-cold on the summit, even in the dead of summer. Whatever time of day you plan on going, be sure to buy your tickets early in the morning, because they tend to sell out, especially during the peak summer months. *The gondola runs year-round from 7 a.m. to 8 p.m. in June, July, and August and until 6:30 p.m. the rest of the year.*

After coming down from Lomnický štít, you may feel like taking a hike. In that case, consider taking the red-marked magistrála trail from Skalnaté pleso to Hrebienok, where you can catch the funicular down to Starý Smokovec and the electric train (or bus) back to Tatranská Lomnica. It's a hike with a lot of great views, taking most of the day to complete.

If the weather is too crummy to hike, then you may want to peruse the **Tatra National Park Museum** (Múzcum Tatranského Národného Park), located around the corner from the bus station in Tatranská Lomnica. The museum introduces you to the plants and wildlife of the High Tatras, and gives you the low-down on the history of the region. *It's open Monday through Friday from 8 a.m. to noon and from 1 to 5 p.m., and on Saturday and Sunday from 9 a.m. to noon.*

Skiing the High Tatras

In the winter, skiers from all over Central and East Europe gravitate to the High Tatra runs. It's no wonder; the skiing is some of the most breathtaking you'll find in this part of Europe and the snow is always plentiful in the winter.

Skiing begins as early as November and keeps going until mid-April (or whenever the snow melts). Though the snow is as good as you'll find anywhere in Europe, the facilities in the High Tatras are definitely not on par with the resorts in the Alps or Rocky Mountains. It's not that the lifts and gondolas are bad; they're just old. Also, lift lines can get pretty horrendous, especially during the holidays.

On the flip side of the coin, prices are much more reasonable than American or West European resorts. You can expect to pay anywhere from 200 to 500 Sk for a day of skiing, depending on the particular week. Two, three, four, five, and six-day passes are available, and are cheaper than paying day by day. A good thing to know is that you can use a six-day pass at any area in the High Tatras. It's also good to know that children under the age of six ski free and that children between the ages of seven and twelve can ski for nearly half the price of adults.

Don't worry if you haven't brought your own equipment, because there are plenty of shops that rent skis, boots, and poles. Count on paying anywhere from 200 to 300 Sk a day for the package, depending on the quality and age of the equipment.

Skiing Štrbské Pleso

Dominating the area here is an enormous ski jump, built for the 1970 Nordic World Ski Championships and the key to Slovakia's bid for the 2002 Olympics. No, skiers are not invited to try their luck on the jump, but they can ski down from the top of one of the area's four lifts. Two of those lifts are for beginners, while the other two are for intermediates.

You can rent skis or hire an English-speaking instructor from **Crystal Ski**, *across the way from the Hotel Fis,* or from the **Turist Centrum** shop *in the Hotel Patria.*

Skiing Smokovce

Skiing at Smokovce happens mostly at an area called **Hrebienok**, which is accessed by a funicular that runs up the hill from behind the Hotel Grand in Starý Smokovec. Hrebienok has four lifts, and several long runs that probably won't satisfy expert skiers. You can rent skis in Starý Smokovec at **Tatrasport Adam**, *located across the main road from Hotel Grand.*

Skiing Tatranská Lomnica

With seven lifts and two gondolas, this is the largest of the ski areas in the High Tatras, and is the most challenging. One of these gondolas, mentioned above in the hiking section, takes you to the top of the 2,828-meter Lomnický štít. You can rent skis in Tatranská Lomnica at **Tatrasport Adam**, *located at the train station.*

Biking & Other Activities

There's more to do than just ski and hike in the High Tatras. There's also some good mountain biking to be done. You can rent bikes from either of the two **Tatrasport Adams**, *located across the street from Hotel Grand in Starý Smokovec and at the train station in Tatranská Lomnica.* In Štrbské Pleso, go to the **Turist Centrum**, *located in the Hotel Patria.* Bike rentals go for about 225 Sk a day. The people working at these shops can give you advice on the best mountain biking trails in the area, and can provide you with a map of these trails.

In addition to renting bikes, **Turist Centrum**, *Tel. 0969/492 582,* can arrange a number of different activities for you to engage in, such as horseback riding, paragliding, sightseeing flights, and rafting. **Crystal Ski**, *Tel. 0969/492 824, located across the lane from Hotel FIS in Štrbské Pleso,* can arrange the same activities, plus rock climbing and guided mountain trekking.

NIGHTLIFE & ENTERTAINMENT

Besides whatever is going on at the discos, nightclubs, and bars at the hotels, there's really not much happening at the High Tatra resorts. There is one cinema called **Kino Tatry**, *located next to the Tatra National Park Museum in Tatranská Lomnica.*

EXCURSIONS & DAY TRIPS
Ždiar

Located on the eastern slopes of the High Tatras, the village of **Ždiar** is worth an excursion for its collection of half-timbered cottages, houses, and other buildings ornamented with colorful designs. Steeped in folk traditions, the village is certainly quaint, and is as authentically Slovak as you can get. But the forces of tourism from the nearby resort towns are encroaching, which may make Ždiar not so idyllic in coming years.

While in Ždiar, drop into the **Cottage Museum** (Ždiarská izba múzeum), housed appropriately enough in one of the traditional cottages. The museum introduces you to the folk customs of the village, such as making costumes as colorful as their houses. *It's open weekdays from 9 a.m. to 4 p.m. and on weekends until noon.* To get to Ždiar, jump on a bus at any one of the resorts. They run about every hour and take less than 20 minutes to reach Ždiar. Tickets cost around 20 Sk.

Other possible day-trip destinations from the High Tatra resorts include the very delightful towns of **Kežmarok** and **Levoča** and the awesome **Spiš Castle**, the biggest in all of the Slovak Republic. All of these destinations are dealt with separately in the next and final chapter, *East Slovakia.*

PRACTICAL INFORMATION

• **Slovenská sporiteľna** (Tatranská Lomnice), *behind the train station in the Hotel Mier.* This is a bank where you can change money.
• **Tatranská Informačná Kancelária** (Starý Smokovec), *just behind the train station. Tel. 0969/423 440.* This is the most helpful tourist information office in the Tatras. English-speaking staff provides all sorts of maps and publications on the High Tatras and can help you find accommodations. In front of the office are some telephones with direct lines to the hotels.

• **Turist Centrum** (Štrbské Pleso), *across the street from the train station. Tel. 0969/492 690.* Books, maps, and general information available here.

• **Všeobecná úverová banka** (Starý Smokovec), *across the street and up the hill from the bus station.* Another bank where you can change money.

• **Post Office** (Starý Smokovec), *next to the train station.*

• **Post Office** (Tatranská Lomnice), *two minute walk southeast of the train station.*

518

22. EAST SLOVAKIA

In more ways than one, **East Slovakia** intrigues. It's an area with some of Slovakia's best preserved medieval towns, set amidst the bucolic, low-lying hills that line up across most of this part of Slovakia. It's also a region with a startling mixture of peoples, including Hungarians, Gypsies, Ukrainians, Poles, Ruthenians, and even some Romanians. But for all its ethnic diversity, you have to hand it to the German settlers for building the region's most beautiful towns.

This is especially true when it comes to the **Spiš** region, situated just east of the High Tatras and stretching from the **Hornád River** north to the Polish border. From the 12th to the 14th century, Saxon settlers drifted into Spiš (called Zips in German), enticed here by the area's rich ore deposits and by royal offerings of tax-free living. The Germans turned this region into one of the richest areas in what is today Slovakia, eventually creating an economic and defensive federation of 24 towns that enjoyed profitable trading privileges handed down by the Hungarian kings.

Though the Germans were expelled at the end of World War II, their once-rich medieval towns remain, the two best-preserved of which are **Kežmarok** and **Levoča**. Of these two, the walled town of Levoča is the must-see, not least because it's located near **Spiš Castle**, the biggest and most impressive castle in the Slovak Republic.

As the eastern-most region in the former Czechoslovakia, East Slovakia receives nary an American or Canadian tourist, with the exception of the many emigrés who come to dig up their East Slovak roots. In my recent travels through East Slovakia, I ran into no Canadians and only four Americans (plus one Slovak who used to live in America). But that isn't to say that East Slovakia feels like the end of the earth. Granted, there are villages that look as though the 20th century has passed them by, but there are also some towns and cities with an unexpected amount of sophistication here as well.

EAST SLOVAKIA FINDS & FAVORITES
The walled, medieval town of **Levoča**
Hotel Satel *in Levoča*
Spiš Castle
The **Cathedral of St. Elizabeth** *in Košice*
The walled, medieval town of **Bardejov**
The **Andy Warhol Family Museum** *in Medzilaborce*

Case in point is the East Slovak capital and the country's second biggest city of **Košice**, which offers a welcome bit of urbane relief after traveling through this sleepy region. Another city with an unexpected cosmopolitan air is **Prešov**, which makes a good stopover on your way to the perfectly preserved medieval town of **Bardejov**. But the biggest surprise awaits in the remote, northeastern town of **Medzilaborce**, where you'll find a museum dedicated to perhaps the most famous Slovak-American of all time – **Andy Warhol**.

Kežmarok

Like other towns in the Spiš region, **Kežmarok** was founded by German settlers in the 13th century. By the end of the 14th century, it had been granted status as a free royal town, emerging as the second most important town in the Spiš region after Levoča. But, whereas Levoča remained loyal to the Hapsburg crown, Kežmarok and its large Hungarian population rose up in rebellion during the 17th and 18th centuries. In fact, there was no greater threat to Hapsburg rule in East Slovakia than a native of Kežmarok, **Count Imre Thököly**, who eventually sided with the Turks against the Hapsburgs and ended up conquering for himself a good deal of East Slovakia.

With its big German population, Kežmarok was also a hotbed of Protestantism, evident in the two unforgettable churches, the **New Evangelical** and the **Wooden Articulated**, which stand side by side just outside the old center.

Kežmarok, still much a village in its appearance and size, makes for a rewarding day trip from the High Tatra resorts. With its **Renaissance castle** and numerous quaint wooden houses, the town may even intrigue you enough to want to bed down here for the night.

ORIENTATION

Located just 15 kilometers (nine miles) northeast of Poprad, Kežmarok is an easy day trip from the High Tatra resorts. You'll have no problem finding your way around this small town.

ARRIVALS & DEPARTURES

By Bus

Buses depart Poprad and Starý Smokovec about every hour for the 25 minute ride to Kežmarok. Tickets cost about 15 Sk. From the bus station in Kežmarok, just walk five minutes southeast along Toporcerova street to the New Evangelical Church (one of the must-see sights), from where it's another two minutes north into the center of town.

By Car

From Poprad just follow signs north. The trip should take no more than 20 minutes. If you're coming from the High Tatra resorts, easiest would be to take the road south from Tatranská Lomnice to Veľká Lomnice and then head north. There's a parking lot next to the New Evangelical Church. You can't miss the church as you come into town from Poprad.

By Train

A two-car slow train chugs its way to Kežmarok about every hour from Poprad. The ride takes about twenty minutes, taking you past some startlingly poor villages along the way. The ticket is about 12 Sk.

GETTING AROUND TOWN

You'll have no problem conquering the small, flat town on foot. Taxis seem to be all but nonexistent here anyway.

WHERE TO STAY/WHERE TO EAT

Note: There are only two hotels in Kežmarok, and only one (Hotel Club) is located in the center. So book ahead before committing yourself to Kežmarok for the night.

HOTEL CLUB, *MUDr. Alexandra 24, 060 01 Kežmarok. Tel. 0968/524 051, Fax 0968/524 052. Rates for single/double: 900-1,160/1,060-1,660 Sk. 20 rooms. Restaurant.*

This is a friendly, small hotel that has recently been renovated. Rooms are generously large and come with smart wood furniture, satellite television, direct-dial telephones, and, in some rooms, a private terrace. The restaurant here is probably the best in town, offering a large selection of game and pork dishes prepared in a Spiš fashion. Meals cost between 150 and 300 Sk.

HOTEL ŠTART, *Pod lesom 24, 060 01 Kežmarok. Tel.0968/522 915, Fax 0968/522 916. Rates for single/double: 400/650 Sk. No credit cards. Restaurant.*

This venerable chalet-like hotel in the woods outside town has decent rooms for decent rates. Unfortunately, it's a fifteen minute walk from the center of town. Go to the rear of the castle and head straight on Pod lesom street, and you'll come across it.

SEEING THE SIGHTS

The most indelible sight in town, located just north of the center on Jakuba street, is the New Evangelical Church (Nový Evangelický Kostol). Festooned with stripes of green and red, the late 19th-century church has a unique Moorish dome, which seems a bit mismatched with the neo-Renaissance campanile and the bare, neo-Classical interior. Inside the church on the right-hand side, draped in the colors of the Hungarian flag, is the tomb and mausoleum of Count Imre Thököly, a Hungarian rebel and Kežmarok native who took sides with the Turks in fighting the Hapsburgs. In the 1670s, he briefly ruled over what is today East Slovakia before being defeated and exiled to Turkey, where he died in 1705.

In the shadow of the New Evangelical Church is something of a completely different nature – the Wooden Articulated Church (Drevený artikulárny kostol), which has recently undergone a complete restoration. Built in 1717 apparently without a single nail, the squat church is a fine testament to Spiš carpentry and artistry, its interior adorned with carved fixtures and colorful paint jobs. *Both churches are open daily from 8 a.m. to noon and from 1 to 5 p.m.*

From the New Evangelical Church it's a short stroll north into the center of town, its skyline dominated by the Church of the Holy Cross (Kostol sv. Krížu). The Gothic church, built in the 15th century, has been closed for restoration for years now. But if it happens to be open while you're there, take a look inside at the side altars, which were apparently crafted by apprentices of Master Pavol of Levoča. The church has a rather uninspiring tower that's topped by four miniature gables. Much more interesting is the nearby Renaissance belfry, its uppermost section smothered in lively sgraffito work.

From Kežmarok's main square (Hlavné námestie), it's a straight shot along Hradné námestie to the Kežmarok Castle, surrounded by some alluring Renaissance fortifications. Erected in the 15th century, the whitewashed castle belonged to the aforementioned Imre Thököly, but was confiscated by the Hapsburgs after exiling the count to Turkey. These days the castle houses the Kežmarok Museum, with displays of historical artifacts and period furniture.

Only if you have time to kill would I recommend joining the mandatory tour of the castle and museum, neither of which are interesting enough to justify the hour it takes. *The museum is open daily except Monday from 9 a.m. to 4 p.m. June through September, and Tuesday through Friday from 8 a.m. to 3 p.m. the rest of the year.* Tickets cost 30 Sk.

After taking a walk around the castle, head back to the center along Starý trh street, lined with wooden houses that are characteristic of the folk architecture in the Spiš region. Topped by fanciful gables and overhanging eaves, the houses are quaint as can be.

PRACTICAL INFORMATION

•**Kežmarok Information Center** (Kežmarské Informačné Centrum), *Hlavné námestie 46. Tel. 0968/4047.* The English-speaking staff can help you find private accommodations, supply you with maps and brochures in English, and change your money.

Levoča

There aren't many towns in Slovakia that strike such a strong medieval impression as does the walled town of **Levoča**. One of the first towns in the region to be founded and developed by Saxon artisans in the early 13th century, Levoča was the administrative capital of the Spiš region and one of the richest towns in Slovakia for more than four centuries. Not to be discouraged by the Tatar attack that wiped out the town soon after being settled, Levoča boomed into a major center of trade in gold and wood carving, which helped it gain status as a free royal town in the 14th century.

A fire that nearly burnt Levoča to the ground in the 16th century was perhaps a blessing in disguise. A furious spurt of development ensued, in which the town was endowed with scores of fantastic Renaissance structures. But soon after experiencing its golden age, Levoča slipped into decline, as uprisings in the region cut the town off from its royal benefactors. This caused a sort of architectural freeze, which means the historic walled town of Levoča you see today is pretty much the Levoča you would have seen in the 16th century.

Levoča has only recently sprung back to life after being seriously neglected during the Communist era, although most of the restoration work has occurred in the upper section of the old town. In the lower section, ancient houses formerly occupied by wealthy burghers have, in recent decades, become the decrepit dwelling space for destitute Romanies and Slovaks.

But this isn't to say that you should bypass Levoča. In fact, you should make it a priority destination on your travels through Slovakia. In addition to having the highest wooden altar in the world, Levoča has a couple of excellent museums, one of which is dedicated to the creator of that altar, **Master Pavol of Levoča**. The town also makes the perfect base for visiting the incredibly dramatic **Spiš Castle** (the biggest castle in Slovakia) and the ecclesiastical town of **Spišská Kapitula**.

ORIENTATION

Levoča lies 30 kilometers (19 miles) east of Poprad and roughly 60 kilometers (37 miles) northwest of Košice in a lush valley in the **Levoča Hills** (Levočské vrchy). The sloping old town, which is almost entirely walled, is laid out on a grid plan, making it easy to find your way around. Most of the attractions lie at the top of the hill around the main square of **námestie Majstra Pavla.**

ARRIVALS & DEPARTURES

By Bus

From Poprad, there's a bus to Levoča about every hour. The ride takes no more than 30 minutes and costs around 25 Sk. Coming from or going to Košice and Prešov is easiest by bus, both of which are about an hour away from Levoča. The bus station is a kilometer down the hill from the walled town center.

By Car

From Poprad or Prešov, take E50 all the way to Levoča. From Košice, follow signs northwest to Spišské Podhradie and then go west on E50. Parking is available at all hotels (if you're a guest there) and on side streets around the main square.

By Train

Levoča is at the end of a spur line. So if you're coming from Poprad or Košice, you need to change trains at Spišská Nová Ves (on the main Prague-Košice line). From there, a slow train chugs its way through the hills to Levoča about every hour, taking no longer than 25 minutes and costing 12 Sk. From the train station, walk a kilometer up the hill to reach the walled center.

GETTING AROUND TOWN

There is no other way to go than on foot in this small town where all the sights and hotels are all within easy walking distance of one another.

WHERE TO STAY

HOTEL SATEL, *námestie Majstra Pavla 55, 054 01 Levoča. Tel. 0966/ 512 943, Fax 0966/514 486. Rates for single/double:1,250/1,900 Sk. Credit cards: AE, DC, MC, V. 21 rooms. Restaurant.*

Not many hotels in Slovakia are as beautiful as this one. The building itself is a gem, featuring a pastel Baroque facade and intriguing vaulted ceilings. But the hotel's star attraction is its stunningly beautiful Renaissance courtyard, replete with delicate arcades, ornate ironwork, and a small fountain. Here you can have your breakfast, lunch, or dinner, or just sit back and soak it all in over a cocktail from the bar's huge drink menu.

The spacious, sunny rooms are nothing short of gorgeous, outfitted with polished wood floors, dark wood furniture, tasteful impressionist paintings, satellite television, and direct-dial telephones. It's hard to decide whether to take a room in the front of the hotel, offering a view of the main square, or in the rear, offering a view of the hotel's awesome courtyard. But you should be more than pleased wherever you end up. The hotel also has an excellent restaurant (see *Where to Eat*) and a wine cellar hunkering down under a vaulted ceiling. All in all, a most memorable place to stay.

HOTEL ARKADA, *námestie Majstra Pavla 26, 054 01 Levoča. Tel. 0966/ 512 255, Fax 0966/512 372. Rates for single/double: 660-730/960-1,050 Sk. Credit cards: AE, DC, MC, V. 24 rooms. Restaurant.*

If you can't get a room at the Hotel Satel, then you won't be disappointed having to stay at this great hotel across the square. It's carved out of another historic building, this one an old printing house where Jan Amos Komensky (John Comenius) had his *Orbis Pictus* published in four different languages. The regal, vaulted rooms are furnished with oriental rugs, tasteful furniture, satellite television, and a lot of other nice amenities. There are two restaurants, one in the vaulted cellar and the other upstairs, set under the building's original wooden beams. The nice, English-speaking receptionists make staying here all the more worthwhile.

HOTEL BARBAKAN, *Košická 15, 054 01 Levoča. Tel. 0966/514 310, Fax 0966/513 609. Rates for single/double: 620-920/990-1,390 Sk. Credit cards: AE, DC, MC, V. 15 rooms. Restaurant.*

Compared to the other two hotels in the center of town, the Barbakan just doesn't cut the mustard. The building itself is pretty enough, but the old leather furniture and the tasteless green wallpaper (found in some, but not all the rooms) mar the hotel. However, this isn't a bad place to stay. The rooms are certainly comfortable enough, and come with satellite television and direct-dial phones. The receptionists are top-notch, and the restaurant is fairly good (see *Where to Eat*).

HOTEL FAIX, *Probstnerova cesta 22, 054 01 Levoča. Tel. 0966/512 335, Fax 0966/513 554. Rates for single/double without private bath: 400/600 Sk. Rates for single/double with private bath: 600/850 Sk. No credit cards. Restaurant.*

Located just outside the walled center, this is a place you can fall back on if you are not able to get a room at the other hotels. Rooms are extremely threadbare, but at least they're clean.

WHERE TO EAT

HOTEL SATEL, *námestie Majstra Pavla 55. Tel. 0966/512 943. 150-250 Sk.*

The restaurant at this hotel features a well-rounded menu of regional specialties such as venison steak topped with a red wine sauce or leg of pork smothered in a delectable cream sauce. If you're in the mood for something more formal, have a seat in the dining room, a regal setting with parquet floors, carved stone columns, and the town crest stamped on the ceiling. Or if you feel like coming to dinner in shorts and a T-shirt, take a seat in the courtyard and dine by the fountain.

HOTEL BARBAKAN, *Košická 15. Tel. 0966/514 310. 150-200 Sk.*

If you ever get around to reading the huge menu, then you should have a fine meal, served in the cozy dining room or out in the plant-strewn atrium. The restaurant features a lot of game dishes, including venison ragout and pheasant drenched in a red wine sauce, as well as such tasty items as steak topped with a roquefort sauce or veal cutlets with a side of asparagus. The service is ultra-formal, to the point of being uncomfortably stiff.

REŠTAURÁCIA U TRI APOŠTOLOV, *námestie Majstra Pavla 11. Tel. 0966/512 302. 100-200 Sk. Credit cards: AE, MC, V.*

This restaurant has an attractive location above the square, but its menu is fairly generic, featuring a lot of typical Slovak dishes. Probably a better choice for lunch than dinner.

SEEING THE SIGHTS

Almost all of the must-see sights in Levoča are located, conveniently enough, in and around the main square, **námestie Majstra Pavla**. Plunked down in the middle of the square is a trio of exceptional buildings – a Catholic church, Protestant church, and the town hall. But we'll start with an unassuming building in the north side of the square by the park. Though it's not much to look at, the former **Municipal Weights House** (now a police office) is where Levoča earned a good deal of its wealth. Merchants passing through town were forced, by a 1321 decree of King Charles Róbert, to stay on in Levoča for at least 15 days and pay taxes on storage of their goods to the weights house. Just look around at the wealth of Gothic and Renaissance buildings and you'll have some idea of how this decree benefitted the town.

One structure the decree financed was the **Church of St. James** (Kostol sv. Jakuba), Slovakia's second biggest Gothic church topped by a syringe-like steeple and chock-full of priceless medieval art. Here you'll find Levoča's claim to fame – an extraordinary **wooden altarpiece** by Master Pavol of Levoča. At 19 meters high and six meters wide, it's the largest of its kind in the world. It took Master Pavol from 1507 to 1517 to complete the shrine, its branching pinnacles and spires nearly touching the choir ceiling. The focus is on the central panel, where the life-sized statues of the Madonna, St. James, and St. John the Baptist preside. Apparently having used local merchants as models, Master Pavol imbued the saints in the predella's Last Supper with a startling amount of expression and personality. They are all captured in some animated pose, such as eating, drinking, cutting bread, or, in the case of Saint John, snoozing on Christ's lap. Unfortunately, you can't get close enough to the altar to fully appreciate the predella. But you can see photographs and a model of it at the Master Pavol Exhibition (see below). *The church is open daily except Monday from 8 a.m. to noon and from 1 to 5 p.m. (on Sunday from 1:30 to 5 p.m.).*

By far the most impressive building in Levoča is the **town hall**, set right next to St. James'. Originally erected in a Gothic style, the town hall got a striking Renaissance facelift in the 16th century, in which the delicate arcades and the dizzying array of jagged gables were added. The upper stories of the town hall houses the decent **Spiš Museum**, with quaint exhibits on town history, local crafts, and fashion throughout the ages. The museum is well worth seeing, if only for a look at the beautiful ribbed vaults, which have recently been restored. Captions are in Slovak only, but cassette guides in English are available for 30 Sk at the ticket window. *The museum is open Tuesday through Sunday from 9 a.m. to 5 p.m. Admission is 10 Sk.*

As you're looking around the exterior of the town hall, take note of the **Cage of Shame** on the south side, an interesting wrought-iron contraption in which criminals and women of ill-repute were publicly humiliated. The third building in the middle of the square, the **Evangelical Church** (Evangelický kostol), was built in the early 19th century, its plain neo-Classical style nothing to get excited about.

Now have a look around at the Renaissance buildings lining the square. One you'll want to pay particular attention to is the L-shaped **Thurzov dom**, *number 7*, an outrageous edifice topped with a row of miniature gables, each of which has its own swirling shape. Further down on the east side of the square is the **Master Pavol Exhibition** (Expozícia Majstra Pavla), *number 20*, housed in the building where the man himself lived and worked.

The building itself isn't all that notable, but the small museum dedicated to the wood sculptor is definitely worth the 10 Sk admission. Though it exhibits few of the master's original works, the museum does have a number of photographs, copies, and casts that allow you a close inspection of the works' details. The museum also has an interesting section on the invaluable restoration work done on the master's sculptures. *The museum is open daily except Monday from 10 a.m. to 5 p.m.*

One more museum you might want to peruse on the square is the **Levoča Spiš Museum** (Spišské múzeum v Levoči), *number 41*. It contains a formidable collection of local art work dating from Gothic times on up to the 19th century. Thankfully, not all of the art on display is high-brow. Some of it is folk, and a lot more interesting for it. *The museum is open daily except Monday from 9 a.m. to 5 p.m.*

After seeing all there is to see around námestie Majstra Pavla, you could spend an enjoyable hour or two wondering through the old town, most of which is fairly run-down, but intriguing nonetheless.

THE MARIAN PILGRIMAGE

*Levoča is a sleepy little town, but you would think the opposite if you happened to arrive during the first weekend in July, when some 250,000 Catholics invade Levoča for the **Marian Pilgrimage**, the largest of its kind in Slovakia. The pilgrimage takes place in and around the neo-Gothic church on Marian's Hill, two kilometers north of Levoča's walled center. Mass is held every hour, beginning at 6 p.m. on Saturday evening. But the Mass everyone attends is at 10 a.m. on Sunday morning. The pilgrimage is no solemn occasion.*

In fact, it's one big party, with singing, dancing, and drinking going on throughout the night. Obviously, you can expect every spare room in Levoča to be occupied during this weekend. So it may, or may not, be a good time to come.

NIGHTLIFE & ENTERTAINMENT

There's really not much entertainment or nightlife to speak of in Levoča. The one **cinema** in town is located at *námestie Majstra Pavla 58*. There's a decent **pub** with outdoor seating at the Košice gate, in the northeast corner of the old town.

EXCURSIONS & DAY TRIPS
Spiš Castle

Located 15 kilometers (nine miles) east of Levoča is one of Slovakia's most gripping attractions – the **Spiš Castle** (Spišský Hrad). By far the biggest castle in Slovakia, Spiš recently joined UNESCO's World Heritage list. Its chalk-white ruins sprawl across the top of a tree-less hill, utterly dominating a broad sweep in the countryside. It's an incredibly photogenic sight, understandably given pride of place in virtually every Slovak tourist brochure.

As excavations of the castle site have shown, humans have been drawn to the castle hill ever since the early Neolithic period. The castle itself dates back to the early 12th century, when the Hungarian royalty had it built as their regional bulwark. A secession of subsequent owners endowed the fortress with palaces, churches, chapels, and courtyards. One of those owners was the exiled Czech Hussite leader, Jan Jiskra of Brandýs, who for 20 years ruled over what is today Slovakia. A century later, it became the property of the noble Hungarian family, the Csákys. When a fire laid the castle to ruins in 1780, the Csákys abandoned it, though it remained in their possession until 1945.

If you don't have your own car, be prepared for the rigorous two-kilometer hike up the hill from the rundown village of Spišské Podhradie (which is the closest you'll get to the castle by bus). You may be tempted to leave the castle as just a sight viewed from the distance. But resist the temptation, because the castle's vast fortifications, its few remaining windows and arcades, and its intriguing series of rooms all deserve a closer inspection. There's also a small exhibit of artifacts in the reconstructed tower that's worth a look, too. If that doesn't grip you, then the superb panoramic view, taken in as you walk along the top of the fortifications, should. *Spiš Castle is open May through October, daily except Monday from 9 a.m. to 6 p.m.* Admission is 40 Sk.

To get there from Levoča, take the bus that leaves about every hour for Spišské Podhradie, stopping at Spišská Kapitula along the way. Get off at the last stop and then follow the signs to *"hrad."* If you're driving from Levoča, take the E50 highway towards Prešov. A road branches off the highway a little ways past Spišské Podhradie and climbs up to the castle entrance. You'll need to pay a small fee to park there. If the parking lot is full, then you'll have to drive back to Spišské Podhradie, park in the lot at the foot of the castle hill, and then hike up.

Spišská Kapitula

You could do worse than begin your approach to Spiš Castle from **Spišská Kapitula**, a one-lane town located atop a hill a few miles west of the castle. Spišská Kapitula was founded in the 17th century as the bishopric and ecclesiastical capital of the Spiš region. Only clergy lived here until 1948, the year Communists went on a religious rampage and had the town cleared out. With the re-establishment of a seminary here, the town is coming back to life, but for the most part appears abandoned.

The only specific sight here is the **Cathedral of St. Martin** (Katedrála sv. Martina), completed in 1273. Its twin towers pierce through the town's low-level skyline, leaving an indelible impression in the foreground of the Spiš Castle. Inside the cathedral, you'll find a vivid series of early 14th-century frescoes depicting the coronation of King Karol Róbert.

To get here from Levoča, catch the bus bound for Spišské Podhradie and get off at the stop opposite the cathedral. By car, take E50 towards Prešov and turn right about eight miles east of Levoča. Signs point the way.

PRACTICAL INFORMATION

• **Culture and Information Center** (Kultúrno-informačné centrum), *námestie Majstra Pavla 58. Tel. 0966/513 763.* This office can arrange guided tours of the town and its surroundings, give you bus and train schedules, and help you find accommodations.

• **Všeobecná úverová banka**, *námestie Majstra Pavla 28.* You can change money at this bank.

• **Post Office**, *námestie Majstra Pavla 46.*

Košice

Starting out as a Slav settlement, **Košice** evolved into a full-fledged town in the 13th century with the help of German settlers, who came here to take advantage of the town's position on the Kraków-Buda (of the modern-day Budapest) salt trade route. When the Turks sacked Buda in the 16th century and the trade route was pushed westward to the temporary capital of Bratislava, Košice fell into decline, as most of the residents fled the town fearing that Košice was next on the Turks' list. But it wasn't the Turks who ended up sacking Košice; it fell to a Hungarian count from Kežmarok by the name of **Imre Thököly**, who took sides with the Turks against the Hapsburgs and proclaimed himself king of northern Hungary.

With its close proximity to a number of iron ore mines, Košice boomed in the 19th century, becoming the most industrialized town in what is today Slovakia. During World War II, Košice was occupied by pro-Nazi Hungarian forces until the Russians were able to liberate it in early 1945. Still waiting for Prague's liberation, Czechoslovak President Edvard Beneš set up a temporary seat of government in Košice, outlining the political program Czechoslovakia would take in the aftermath of the war (a program that ensured Communists would hold at least four major ministries).

The administrative capital of East Slovakia and the second biggest city in the Slovak Republic, Košice comes as a revelation to those who venture this far east. If East Slovakia were backwards, you would hardly know it by this vibrant, surprisingly cosmopolitan city inhabited by a large community of Hungarians and Romanies. The big attractions here are a handful of good museums and a sizeable historic center, replete with the country's most beautiful cathedral, **St. Elizabeth's**, and an enormous main street-cum-main square dotted with fountains.

ORIENTATION

Košice lies in the southern portion of Central Slovakia, just 20 kilometers (12 miles) north of the Hungarian border and roughly 364 kilometers (226 miles) east of Bratislava. The **Hornád River** runs through the eastern section of town.

It's fairly easy to come terms with the checkerboard layout of the historic center, which itself is centered around the broad **Hlavná ulice** (Main Street).

ARRIVALS & DEPARTURES

By Air

ČSA, *Tel. 02/201 043 10 in Prague and Tel. 095/622 6871 in Košice*, has daily, direct flights from Prague. **Tatra Air**, *Tel. 07/366 758 in Bratislava and 095/760 506 in Košice*, has daily flights from Bratislava. Count on paying about 3,000 Sk from either city. You'll have no problem catching a cab at the airport, which is about your only option for getting into town.

By Bus

There are two or three daily buses departing Banská Bystrica for Košice, taking roughly three-and-a-half hours and costing around 200 Sk. Train is easier and faster if you're traveling from Bratislava, Prague, or Poprad.

The bus station in Košice is adjacent to the train station, about a five minute walk west into the center of town.

By Car

From Bratislava take E571 highway all the way there. The trip should take between four and five hours. From Brno, take E50 all the way there.

By Train

Košice is a major European railroad hub, servicing Bratislava, Prague, Budapest, Kraków, and Moscow. Trains bound for Košice depart about every other hour from Bratislava, taking a good six or seven hours and costing around 300 Sk. There are four or five trains that come daily from Prague, taking about 11 hours and costing around 450 Sk (100 Kč).

The train station is five minutes from the center. Just walk straight out the station and through the park.

GETTING AROUND TOWN

Public transportation in Košice consists of trams and buses, both of which take the same 6 Sk ticket you can buy from tabaks or newsstands. Validate the ticket on board by sticking it in the little gizmo mounted to the handrail and pulling back on it.

Taxis are easy to hail from the street. There are also taxi stands at the airport, bus station, and train station. If you want to order one, call **Classic Taxi**, *Tel. 622 2244.*

WHERE TO STAY

In the Center

HOTEL CENTRUM, *Južna trieda 2/A, 043 23 Košice. Tel. 095/763 101, Fax 095/764 380. Rates for single/double: 1,850/2,000 Sk. Credit cards: AE, MC, V. 50 rooms. Restaurant.*

This high-rise hotel is pretty ugly from the outside, but they do have some of the nicer rooms you'll find in the center of town. The generous-sized rooms come with satellite television, direct-dial telephones, and bathrooms that definitely need to be renovated. The hotel has two restaurants to choose from: a folksy Slovak one and a high-class dining room. Both are quite respectable. The hotel also has a fitness center and a sauna.

HOTEL SLOVAN, *Hlavná 1, 040 01 Košice. Tel. 095/623 2716, Fax 095/622 8413. Rates for single/double: 1,620/2,510 Sk. Credit cards: AE, DC, MC, V. 211 rooms. Restaurant.*

This is another ugly high-rise hotel, just down the street from the Hotel Centrum. Though it's supposed to be a high-class hotel, there's usually a lot of shady-looking characters hanging out in the lobby bar. If riding in elevators makes you nervous, then either forget staying here or ask for a room on one of the lower floors (so you can use the stairs). The elevators here are minuscule and appear to be ancient.

PENZIÓN PRI RADNICI, *Bačíkova 18, 043 66 Košice. Tel. 095/622 8601, Fax 095/622 7824. Rates for apartments only: 3,500-5,100 Sk. Credit cards: AE, DC, MC, V. Restaurant.*

The apartments at this small pension are perhaps the nicest accommodations you'll find in Košice. They come complete with shiny wood floors, tasteful decorations, cable television, direct-dial telephones, and minibars. The pension has a nice summer terrace and good restaurant specializing in venison.

HOTEL EUROPA, *Protifašistických bojovníkov 1, 040 01 Košice. Tel. 095/622 3897, Fax 095/633 7780. Rates for single/double: 330/570 Sk. No credit cards. Restaurant.*

If you're looking for cheap accommodations, you have certainly come to the right place. But don't expect anything fancy. Rooms are very basic, but clean at least. And they don't come with private showers or toilets. The location, three minutes to the train station or the main square, is a good one.

Outside the Center
HOTEL COBRA, *Jiskrova 3, 040 01 Košice. Tel. 095/622 5903, Fax 095/ 622 5918. Rates for single/double: 1,650/3,100 Sk. Credit cards: AE, DC, MC, V. 12 rooms. Restaurant.*
This is Košice's top hotel. Unfortunately, it's located in a less-than-desirable neighborhood that's about a ten minute walk northeast of the historic center. Outfitted with satellite television, fax connections, and direct-dial telephones, the rooms are comfortable, but a little bit on the drab side. The hotel has a nice summer terrace in its courtyard and thankfully does have a private garage.
HOTEL HUTNÍK, *Tyršovo nábrežie 1, 040 01 Košice. Tel. 095/633 7511, Fax 095/633 7780. Rates for single/double: 780/1,260 Sk. No credit cards. 20 rooms. Restaurant.*
Another Communist-era hotel with rooms that are in serious need of cosmetic work. It's located about five minutes northeast of the center.

WHERE TO EAT
REŠTAURÁCIA U VODNÁRA, *Hrnčiarska 25. Tel. 095/622 8991. 150-300 Sk. Credit cards: AE, MC.*
This is a classy place with pretty arched window sills and a pleasant floral decor. The menu features a long list of steak and chicken dishes, which are prepared in a stylish manner and served by ultra-formal waiters. The restaurant also has patio seating in its courtyard.
REŠTAURÁCIA GRAND, *Kováčska 45. Tel. 095/622 7964. 100-200 Sk. No credit cards.*
A favorite with the locals, this restaurant has an art-oriented decor that compliments its creatively prepared dishes such as the grilled chicken breast topped with a spicy paprika sauce. Deft service and a lively clientele make eating here all the more enjoyable.
SEDLIACKÝ DVOR, *Biela 3. Tel. 095/622 0402. 100-200 Sk. No credit cards.*
This is the place to come for some authentic Slovak food, such as stuffed turkey breast and a big bowl of *halušky* (gnocchi with cheese and bacon).
PIZZERIA VENEZIA, *Mlynská 20. Tel. 095/622 4761. 100-150 Sk. No credit cards.*
This Italian restaurant bakes 15 tasty pizzas and provides seating out on the sidewalk or in its art-strewn café. A nice place to do some people watching.

AJVEGA, *Orlia 10. Tel. 095/622 3600. 60-120 Sk. No credit cards.*
Had your fill of meat? Then try this vegetarian restaurant occupying a three-story house in the heart of the historic center. Lot of fresh vegetables, soy burgers, freshly squeezed juices, and some incredible borscht grace the menu.
CAFÉ SLAVIA, *Hlavná 50. 50-150 Sk. No credit cards.*
This newly remodeled Art Nouveau café/restaurant is the place to come for a sophisticated espresso and a piece of cake. But I would head somewhere else for anything more substantial.

SEEING THE SIGHTS
Hlavné Námestie & Around
There's no better place to start than right in the middle of Košice's historic center along **Hlavná ulice** (Main Street), which is wide and long enough to contain two shady squares called Hlavné námestie and námestie Slobody. Fountains abound, chortling water under the shade of giant pines trees. One of these fountains dances to recorded music throughout the day, which is bit hokey, but manages to please the crowds.

The city recently lifted the tram rails and turned Hlavná into one giant, pedestrian-only promenade. Townsfolk now flood into Hlavná to meet with friends, relax around the fountains, or sit in the sidewalk cafés. Indeed, there's a Parisian sort of appeal to Hlavná that comes as a wonderful surprise this far east.

Plunked down in the middle of Hlavná is the town's gem, the **Cathedral of St. Elizabeth** (Dom sv. Alžbety). Completed in the late Gothic style of the 15th century, the sandstone-colored cathedral features two bristling towers and a beautiful painted roof reminiscent of the cathedrals in Budapest and Vienna. Take note of the busy relief work above the north and west doors, depicting scenes from the New Testament. The interior is furnished with a lot of impressive Gothic stone carvings that make up for a rather bare nave. The highlight of the interior is the pulpit, with no less than 48 gilt panels depicting the life of St. Elizabeth. Also be sure to have a look at the carved stone staircase by Master Štefan of Košice, located on the north side of the presbytery.

On the south side of the cathedral is the Gothic **St. Michael's Chapel** (Kaplinka sv. Michala), which looks a tiny version of the cathedral. It was used as an ammunition and weapons storehouse during the Turkish occupation of lower Hungary. Across the street, *at námestie Slobody 27,* is the Baroque **Župný dom** (Administrator's House), where the plan for Czechoslovakia's postwar government was presented by President Edvard Beneš on April 4, 1945. The Communists regarded this plan, which gave four ministerial positions to Communists, as the beginning of their revolution. The building subsequently became known as the House of the Košice Government Program, in which a museum of the working class was installed (big surprise).

These days the building houses the main branch of the **Július Jakoby Gallery**, with a fine permanent collection of 19th- and 20th-century Slovak art and changing contemporary exhibits. The gallery also shows art films during certain days of the week (see schedule posted outside). In the basement is a cozy café, which is a nice place to hang out after viewing the art. Another branch of the gallery, which is mostly dedicated to master engravers, is located nearby *at Alžbetina 22. Both branches are open Tuesday through Saturday from 10 a.m. to 6 p.m. and on Sunday from 9 a.m. to 1 p.m.*

On the north side of the cathedral is the arcaded **Urban's Tower** (Urbanova veža), with a small exhibit of metal works and tombstones that were discovered under the tower during a renovation in the 19th century. Beyond the tower, you can see the dancing fountain do its things to all kinds of recorded music (including American country music). It's a bit silly, but it is a cool place to relax on a hot summer day. A lot of the students are watching it all from the steps of the **State Theater** (Štátné divadlo), a pretty turn-of-the-century confection that recently underwent an all-out restoration.

Past the theater, at the corner of Hlavná and Univerzitná, is the **Premonstratensian Church**, built by the Jesuits in the 17th century to look like Rome's Il Gesu (the Premonstratensians were a Catholic order established by St. Norbet in France, who called for a greater devotion to the message of the Gospels; in Prague, you can see a much earlier version of their religious building by visiting Strahov Monastery – see Chapter 13, *Prague*). Though you probably won't be able to get inside, peek your head through the gate for a look at the excessive Baroque-clad interior.

A short detour down Univerzitná street brings you to the **Mikluš Prison** (Miklušova väznica), where you can descend into the former cells for a look at some grizzly instruments of torture (just so you know how these instruments work, instructional photographs are provided). To add to the effect, the curators have left piles of animal bones in the cells. Buy your ticket for the Mikluš Prison across the street at the geology and zoology museum, housed in the **Hangman's Bastion** (Katova bašta). This museum has a big exhibit of rocks and stuffed animals, as well as a replica of the house and some genuine items that belonged to Ferenc Rákóczi, a Transylvanian-Hungarian rebel who fought against the Hapsburgs until he was defeated in 1717 and forced to go into exile in Turkey. In 1906, his body was brought back from Turkey and interned in

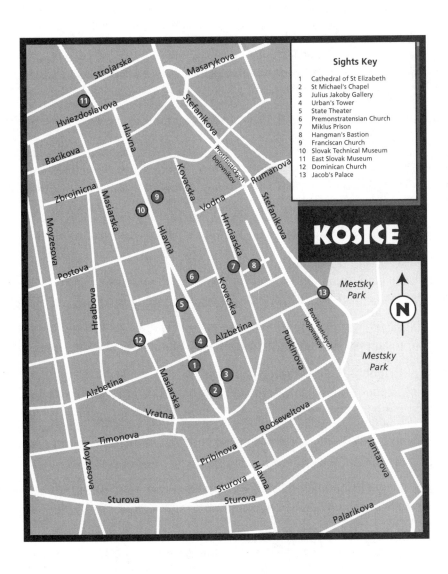

Sights Key

1 Cathedral of St Elizabeth
2 St Michael's Chapel
3 Julius Jakoby Gallery
4 Urban's Tower
5 State Theater
6 Premonstratensian Church
7 Miklus Prison
8 Hangman's Bastion
9 Franciscan Church
10 Slovak Technical Museum
11 East Slovak Museum
12 Dominican Church
13 Jacob's Palace

KOSICE

St. Elizabeth's crypt. *Both museums are open daily except Monday from 9 a.m. to 5 p.m. Admission is 20 Sk for each museum.*

Back on Hlavná, continue northward a few blocks to the **Franciscan Church** (Kostol františkánov) *at the corner of Františkánska.* The church goes back to the 14th century, but little of its Gothic character was spared in the heavily Baroque restoration given it in 1724. Opposite the church, the **Slovak Technical Museum** (Slovenské technické múzeum) is stuffed with an eclectic collection of old machines and fancy gizmos. The museum is worth a perusal for its wealth of ornamental wrought ironwork, for which this region is renowned. Everything from lampposts to bells to gates are on display. *The museum is open Tuesday through Friday from 8 a.m. to 5 p.m. and on Sunday from noon to 5 p.m. Admission is 20 Sk.*

At the north end of Hlavná, *at Hviezdoslavova 3,* is a branch of the **East Slovak Museum** (Východoslovenské múzeum), to which there are two parts: the ground-floor natural history section (with live snakes and other reptiles) and the fine arts section (housed in the upper floors). The fine arts sections has a number of uninspiring portrait paintings of Košice luminaries, as well as a mock-up of a 19th century pharmacy and some sets of period furniture.

If you're short on time, skip this museum altogether and go across the street to the main branch of the East Slovak Museum, *at námestie Maratonu 2.* Housed in a sprawling neo-Renaissance pile, the museum features some fairly interesting exhibits on the town history. But the real reason to come here is to view the glittering **Košice Gold Treasure** (Košický zlatý poklad). The treasure amounts to 2,920 gold coins, which were stashed away by Hapsburg loyalists when rebel Imre Thököly captured Košice in the 1670s. In 1935, workers doing renovation on the Spiš Chamber at Hlavná 74 accidentally discovered the coins in one of the walls. *Both branches of the East Slovak Museum are open Tuesday through Saturday from 9 a.m. to 5 p.m. and on Sunday until 1 p.m. Tickets cost 10 Sk.* Just behind the museum, don't miss the wooden **Uniate Church**, relocated here from Slovak Ruthenia.

Other Sights

The oldest ecclesiastical building in Košice is the **Dominican Church** (Kostol Dominikánov), located a block west of Hlavná *on Dominikánské námestie.* Dating back to the end of the 13th century, the church has a series of graceful Gothic arches set within in its single nave.

Two blocks west of the cathedral, *at the east end of Mlynská,* it's hard not to miss the neo-Gothic **Jacob's Palace** (Jakabov palác), outfitted with a frenzy of spikes and turrets. The place looks like a tiny fortress, which is maybe why President Beneš took residence here in early 1945 while hashing out the new government plan for Czechoslovakia.

NIGHTLIFE & ENTERTAINMENT

Smack dab in the middle of Hlavná street, the gorgeous neo-Baroque **State Theater** (Štátne divadlo) is the venue for opera, musicals, and ballet. A five-year-long restoration of the theater was recently completed. Now the theater is in tip-top shape, making it superb place to catch a performance. For classical music, see when the **Košice Philharmonic Orchestra** is performing next at the Dom umenia (House of Art), *Moyzesova 66*. The orchestra, or some small chamber ensemble, play now and again at the cathedral.

If you have any knowledge of Hungarian, then you might want to see what's on at the **Thália Hungarian Theater** *on Mojmirova street*.

For ticket and schedule information for any of these venues, contact the Town Information Center (see *Practical Information* below).

You catch a film at **Kino Tatra**, *located through a passage at Hlavná 8*, **Kino Úsmev**, *located through a passage at the north end of Hlavná*, or at **Kino Kapitol** *at the corner of Masarykova and Tyršovo nábrežie streets*.

For some live jazz try the **Jazz Klub**, *Kovačska 39*. But go early if it's a weekend night, because the place fills up fast. The place to go for a glass of the local **Smädny Mních** beer is a pub of the same name *at Hlavná 80*. Best to go when the weather is nice, so you can sit out on the big patio. Another place you could try is the friendly neighborhood pub, **U Dominikánov**, *Mäsiarska 15*.

PRACTICAL INFORMATION

- **Hospital** (Fakultná nemocnica), *Ratislavova 43. Tel. 095/622 5251.*
- **Pharmacy**, *Toryská 1.* Open 24 hours.
- **Police Station**, *Hlavná 105. Tel. 095/622 0237.*
- **Slovenská štátna sporiteľňa**, *Hlavná 98.* A bank where you can change money.
- **Town Information Center** (Mestské Informačné Centrum), *Hlavná 8. Tel. 095/186.* English-speaking staff can provide you with maps and brochures, give you the train and bus schedules, and sell you tickets to cultural events.
- **Všeobecná úverová banka**, *Hlavná 112.* Another bank where you can change money.
- **Main Post Office**, *Poštová 18.* You can make international calls here.

Prešov

Like Košice, **Prešov** is an undeniably vibrant city that gets overlooked on most tourist itineraries. Granted, there's not a whole to see around the city's historic center, but it is worth your while to make the day trip up from Košice or stop off on your way to Bardejov (see below) if you have the time.

Founded by Slavs, colonized by Hungarians, developed by Germans, and inhabited by Ruthenians and Slovaks, Prešov has been a cultural and religious melting pot from time immemorial. Protestantism caught on fast in Prešov, especially with its German community, which is perhaps why Imre Thököly found steadfast support in Prešov for his anti-Hapsburg revolt in the 17th century. As a result of this support, the Counter Reformation came to Prešov with a vengeance, as 24 Protestants were beheaded on the main square in 1687.

SLOVAK RUTHENIA & THE RUTHENIANS

Since World War I and the dissolution of the Austro-Hungarian Empire, Ruthenia has been tossed around like a political football. Czechoslovakia acquired the region in 1918, but lost it to pro-Nazi Hungary in 1938. And at the end of World War II, Czechoslovakia gave up most of Ruthenia as war booty to Russia. These days, most of Ruthenia lies in Ukraine, but a good chunk of it makes up what is now the eastern corner of Slovakia, loosely taking in the areas of Prešov, Bardejov, Svídnik, and Humenné.

A Slavic community spawning from the Lower Beskydy Mountains, the Ruthenians are some of Europe's most enigmatic peoples. They've never been self-governing. But after centuries of isolation under the Lithuanian, Polish, and Hungarian crowns, the Ruthenians developed their own distinct culture, their own Ukrainian dialect, and their own brand of Christianity called the Uniate Church.

The Ruthenians were originally Russian Orthodox. But in the 16th century, the Ruthenian priests broke from the Orthodox church after a series of theological and political clashes, and consequently sought out union with the Catholic Church. This resulted in the Treaty of Brest-Litovsk of 1596, which established the Uniate Church.

The Uniate Church practices Orthodox rites and uses the Slavonic liturgy, while still honoring the authority of the papacy. Because of the church's ties to Rome, the Communists banned the Uniate Church in the 1950s. Hundreds of priests were thrown in prison, and 123 of them ended up dying there. But since 1989, the church has made a strong comeback. It has reacquired a number of its churches and received a new bishop, appointed by Pope John Paul II. However, the number of Slovaks who consider themselves Ruthenian has dwindled greatly. In the 1990 census, 40,000 Slovaks declared themselves as Ruthenian. But no one can be sure of the true number; estimates are put at around 130,000.

But Prešov is by no means a strictly Protestant town. It happens to be the Slovak capital of the **Uniate Church** (see the sidebar on Ruthenia, below), which has made a strong comeback after its 40-year ban in Czechoslovakia. In fact, it would seem that the Uniate Church now has just as much authority in Prešov as the municipal government. Here, you can't get away from the church's influence. Bibles are conspicuously placed on hotel nightstands. and pictures of the pope, taken during his 1995 visit to Prešov, hang in shops, hotel lobbies, and restaurants.

ORIENTATION

Prešov lies in the Šariš region of East Slovakia, 36 kilometers (22 miles) north of Košice and 50 kilometers (31 miles) east of Levoča. The city is quite big, but the sights and hotels are concentrated in the small historic center, which is basically one wide avenue called **Hlavná**.

ARRIVALS & DEPARTURES

By Bus

Bus is easiest from Levoča, with departures about every hour. Tickets cost around 40 Sk and the ride takes about 90 minutes. Buses depart Košice about as often for the 30 minute ride to Prešov, which costs 25 Sk.

The bus station in Prešov is located opposite the train station. Any one of the buses or trolley buses that stop outside the station will take you the two kilometers into the center of town.

By Car

From Levoča, head due east on E50. The drive should take no more than 45 minutes. From Košice, go north on E50/D1. Parking is available on side streets around Hlavná. Just look for the blue "P" sign.

By Train

Trains run back and forth between Košice and Prešov about every hour. It's a scenic, 30 minute ride that costs 20 Sk. Any bus or trolley bus heading north will take you from the train station into the center of town.

GETTING AROUND TOWN

Buses and trolley buses take the same 6 Sk ticket you can get from the orange dispenser posted at most stops. Validate the ticket on board. To order a taxi, *call 315 15.*

WHERE TO STAY

HOTEL DUKLA, *námestie Legionárov 2, 080 01 Prešov. Tel. 091/722 741, Fax 091/732 134. Rates for single/double without private shower: 867/ 1,396 Sk. Rates for single/double with private shower: 1,011/1,579 Sk. Credit cards: AE, DC, MC, V. 62 rooms. Restaurant.*

This is the nicer of the two hotels in the center of town, which isn't saying much. Rooms are very lackluster, but they come with satellite television and telephones. The hotel is at the south end of Hlavná street.

HOTEL ŠARIŠ, *Sabinovská 1, 080 01 Prešov. Tel. 091/716 351, Fax 091/ 716 551. Rates for single/double: 960/1,890 Sk. Credit cards: MC, V. 100 rooms. Restaurant.*

This is an ugly, Communist-era hotel that is in serious need of modernization. Rooms are expectedly ugly, and not very comfortable. You'll find the hotel at the north end of Hlavná street.

PENZIÓN LINEAS, *Budovateľská 14, 080 01 Prešov. Tel. 091/723 325, Fax. 091/723 206. Rates for single/double: 320/640 Sk. No credit cards. No restaurant.*

Located about ten minutes north of the train station, this is a place to fall back on if you can't find accommodations elsewhere. Rooms are very basic, but do come with private bath.

WHERE TO EAT

REŠTAURÁCIA MELÓDIA, *Hlavná 61. Tel. 091/732 162. 120-200 Sk. Credit cards: MC.*

This is a classy joint with tasty regional specialties, deft service, and good cocktails.

REŠTAURÁCIA ADRIA, *Hlavná 2927. Tel. 091/329 313. 60-120 Sk. No credit cards.*

Here you can get a nicely prepared steak grilled in red wine or a decent cut of roast beef served with broccoli. The service is good, and the prices are definitely reasonable.

REŠTAURÁCIA FLORIÁNKA, *Baštová 32. Tel. 091/340 83. 60-120 Sk. No credit cards.*

Students from the adjacent restaurant and hotel academy train here to be servers and cooks. The basic Slovak fare isn't bad, especially when it's served on the nice outdoor terrace. But it's a more suitable place for lunch than dinner.

SEEING THE SIGHTS

Almost everything worth seeing in Prešov is located in or around **Hlavná ulice** (Main Street), which is a lot like Košice's counterpart in that it's more like an elongated square than a street. Lining both sides of

Hlavná are rows of Renaissance and Baroque buildings, all looking quite smart after recent restorations.

At the south end of Hlavná is the **Uniate Cathedral of St. John the Baptist** (Gréckokatolícky Chrám sv. Janá Krstiteľa), a pretty yellow Rococo edifice harboring a lot of Orthodox regalia, including a spectacular iconostasis. Next door to the church is the **Uniate Bishop's Palace**, which has only recently regained its original purpose after a 40-year ban on the Uniate religion in Czechoslovakia.

Further up Hlavná is the **Šariš Gallery**, *number 51*, housed in two burgher houses originally built in the Gothic style. The gallery has an interesting collection of Uniate icons, which is a nice divergence from its respectable collection of 20th-century East Slovak art. *It's open Tuesday through Friday from 9 a.m. to 5 p.m.*

One of the more eye-catching of the buildings on Hlavná is the **Rákócziho dom**, *Hlavná 86*, a flamboyant Renaissance palace topped with a row of painted gables. It houses the very good **Homeland Museum** (Vlastivedné múzeum), with a neat exhibit on firefighting. Old two-wheel and four-wheel fire engines are on display, as well as some captivating photographs of firemen in action. The museum also has a decent collection of regional folk crafts and paintings. *The museum is open Tuesday through Friday from 10 a.m. to 5 p.m. and on Saturday and Sunday from 11 a.m. to 3 p.m.*

Opposite the museum is the **Church of St. Nicholas** (Kostol sv. Mikuláše), its spiky Gothic tower dominating the main square. Take a look inside at the dazzling stained glass and the immense gilt altar. Just north of St. Nicholas is the **Evangelical Church** (Evanjelický Kostol), an austere structure bravely built in the mid-17th century at a time when the Counter Reformation was in full swing in Hungary.

If you're at all curious how cities looked in the former Soviet Union, take a short stroll to the north end of Hlavná and you should have some idea. On your right you'll find a concrete square (called **námestie Mieru**) dominated by the **Regional Building**, a Stalinist monstrosity erected in the heady days of the 1950s. The square's fountain, which dances to recorded music played over a circa-1945 loudspeaker, does nothing to ease the severity of this place. Not surprisingly, you don't see many people sitting around the fountain and relaxing. Who could unwind in a square so oppressive as this?

NIGHTLIFE & ENTERTAINMENT

For drama, operas, and ballet, see what's on at the **Divadlo Jonáša Záborského**, a modern theater *on námestie Legionárov*. If you by chance understand Ukrainian, then catch a play at the **Ukrainian Alexander Duchnoviča Theater**, *Jarková 77*. For tickets and schedules to both these venues, contact the City Information Service (see *Practical Information* below). Films can be seen at **Kino Panorama** *on námestie Mieru*.

PRACTICAL INFORMATION

•**City Information Service** (Mestský Informačný Servis), *Hlavná 67. Tel. 091/731 113.* This office can help you find accommodations, give you train and bus schedules, or sell you a ticket to one of the cultural events happening in town.
•**Slovenská Sporiteľna**, *Hlavná 74.* This is a bank where you can change money.
•**Post Office**, *Masarykova 2.*

Bardejov

If there is one town in East Slovakia worth going out of your way for, it would have to be **Bardejov**, a perfectly preserved walled medieval town not far at all from the Polish border. In fact, a group of Polish Cistercian monks were the first to set up residence here in the late 12th century, before German settlers came to town and colonized it into a major center of weaving and trade. Like Levoča and Kežmarok, Bardejov benefited richly as a free royal town, erecting scores of wonderful Gothic and Renaissance buildings that are looking great after a major restoration to the town that lasted from 1970 to 1990.

Most tourists who to come to Bardejov stop in for a of couple hours and then head elsewhere. It makes sense because there is a terrible dearth of accommodations and good restaurants in town. But there are a couple of decent hotels in **Bardejovské Kúpele** (see *Day Trips & Excursions* below), a lush spa town six kilometers north of Bardejov.

Bardejov is an easy day trip from Prešov. It can also be done as a long day trip from Košice. But you might want to stay for a night or two so you can visit the several Ruthenian wooden churches in the area (see the sidebar below).

ORIENTATION

Bardejov lies in the foothills of the **Lower Beskydy Mountains**, 76 kilometers north of Košice and 40 kilometers north of Prešov. Finding your way around the tiny historic town, which has only five or six streets and one big main square, is no problem whatsoever.

ARRIVALS & DEPARTURES

By Bus

Bus is much easier from Prešov, with departures about every hour. The ride takes about 45 minutes and costs 40 Sk. There are only four or five buses a day from Košice. If you're not able to catch a direct bus to Bardejov from Košice, then take the train or bus to Prešov and then make a bus connection from there. The bus station, which is adjacent to the train station, is a five minute walk northeast of the historic center.

By Car

From Prešov, head a short ways northeast on the E371 highway and then follow signs north to Bardejov. Just outside Prešov you'll see an airbase, past which you'll travel on an unusually wide, four-lane highway that was used as a spare runway during the Cold War days.

By Train

You might want to think twice about coming from Prešov by train. It takes at least 90 minutes, as compared to the 45 minute bus ride. But it is a scenic ride, costing about 30 Sk. The train station in Bardejov is a five minute walk northeast of the historic center.

GETTING AROUND TOWN

All the sights in Bardejov are within very easy walking distance of each other, so you'll have no problem getting around on foot. If you need a cab, there's usually one hanging around the train station or at the Hotel Republika.

WHERE TO STAY

BAAL ŠPORT HOTEL, *Kutuzovova 16, 085 01 Bardejov. Tel. 0935/724 949, no fax. Rates for single/double: 350/700 Sk. No credit cards. 15 rooms. Restaurant.*

It's not great, but it is your best option in town. Rooms are clean and somewhat comfortable and come with private baths. The hotel is about a ten minute walk north of the center across the Topľa River.

HOTEL REPUBLIKA, *Radničné námestie 50, 085 01 Bardejov. Tel. 0935/722 721, no fax. Rates for single/double: 400/800 Sk. No credit cards. 30 rooms. Restaurant.*

This place is a dump, charging way too much for rooms that do not come with private baths. It's a damn shame that it's the only hotel in the historic center.

HOTEL MIER, *086 31 Bardejovské Kúpele. Tel. 0935/724 524, no fax. Rates for single/double: 500/900 Sk. No credit cards. 45 rooms. Restaurant.*

This is decent hotel set back in the woods above the spa town of Bardejovské Kúpele (see *Day Trips & Excursions*), six kilometers north of Bardejov. But you'll probably want to stay here only if you have a car, because it's terribly inconvenient otherwise. Follow signs from Bardejovské Kúpele up to the hotel.

HOTEL MINÉRAL, *086 31 Bardejovské Kúpele. Tel. 0935/724 122, Fax 0935/724 124. Rates for single/double: 450/810 Sk. No credit cards. 75 rooms. Restaurant.*

This is a big, ugly hotel right at the center of the spa in Bardejovské Kúpele. Rooms are extremely threadbare, but are comfortable enough. Buses run about every hour here from the train station in Bardejov.

HOTEL TOPĽA, *Fučíkova 25, 085 01 Bardejov. Tel. 0935/724 041, Fax. 0935/722 636. Rates for single/double: 330/440 Sk. No credit cards. 40 rooms. Restaurant.*

This hotel is not a bad option, considering it's a short walk to the historic center. It looks a bit dubious from the outside, but inside you'll find decent rooms with private baths and satellite television.

WHERE TO EAT

U ZLATEJ KORUNY, *Radničné námestie 41. Tel. 0935/5310. 100-150 Sk. No credit cards.*

The typical Slovak food at this upstairs restaurant is probably the best you can get in town, which isn't saying much. Try the curry chicken or the spicy goulash.

REŠTAURÁCIA NA BRÁNA, *Hviezdoslavova. Tel. 0935/722 348. 70-135 Sk. No credit cards.*

This is a popular lunchtime spot in town, dishing up Slovak food with little fuss or imagination.

SEEING THE SIGHTS

Perhaps the most intriguing way of entering Bardejov's historic center is through **Dolná brána**, one of the town's several remaining gate towers located in the northeast corner. From there, it's a straight shot into **Radničné námestie**, a pleasing square lined with gabled, storybook houses and centered around a Renaissance town hall.

Appearing strangely isolated in the center of the square, the **old town hall** is an alluring edifice, sporting two perfectly triangular gables and a steeply slanted roof. It houses a branch of the **Šariš Museum** (Šarišské múzeum), with a good exhibit on printing, weaponry, and weaving during the town's Golden Age in the 14th and 15th centuries. It also contains some interesting church art, including a statue by Master Pavol of Levoča. *The museum is open Tuesday through Sunday from 9 a.m. to 6 p.m. (until 4:30 p.m. October through April).*

More impressive is the **Šariš Museum's icon exhibit**, located at the top of the square on Rhodyho street. Inside you'll find Slovakia's largest collection of icons, dating from the 16th to the 19th centuries, as well as some neat models of the region's wooden Uniate churches (see the sidebar below). This exhibit is open same hours as the one at the town hall.

At the bottom of the square is the **Church of St. Egrid** (Kostol sv. Egídia), featuring a lavish Gothic interior chock-full of beautiful paintings and wood-carved altars. A brochure in English, available at the church entrance, points out all the details of the church, including a fine altar carved by Master Pavol of Levoča.

Finally, you might want to do a circuit of the town gates. Besides the aforementioned Dolná brána (gate), there are two excellent gates at the south entrance to the town, called Prašna and Horná.

WOODEN CHURCHES AROUND BARDEJOV

In several villages around Bardejov and further east along the Polish and Ukrainian borders are a number of fascinating wooden churches, most of which date back to the 18th century. Topped by onion domes (sometimes as many as three on one church) and covered with shingled roofs, the churches are unique to this region known as Slovak Ruthenia. Most of the churches are of course Uniate (Greek-Catholic). But there are some Russian Orthodox churches here as well.

*What they all have in common are interiors cordoned off into three sections: an entrance porch (narthex), main nave, and sanctuary (naos). Between the nave and sanctuary is the obligatory **iconostasis**, on which are the usual icons of St. Nicholas, Madonna and Child, the Last Judgment, the Last Supper, and whomever the church is dedicated to.*

*If you don't have your own car, getting to these churches can be a hassle. In that case, you may be better off just visiting the skansen at Bardejovské Kúpele, or the one at the nearby town of **Svidník**, 35 kilometers or 22 miles east of Bardejov. (Buses to Svidník depart about every hour from Bardejov.)*

Otherwise, here are some churches in villages located close to Bardejov that are fairly easy to get to:

*•**Lukov** (14 kilometers west of Bardejov) boasts the Orthodox **Church of Saint Cosmas and Saint Damian**, built in the early 18th century. The brilliant iconostasis features a vividly brutal depiction of the Last Judgment. Buses to Lubotín stop here.*

*•**Jedlinka** (14 kilometers north of Bardejov) has a tiny Uniate church erected in 1763 and adorned with a beautiful Rococo iconostasis. Buses stop here on the way to Svidník.*

*•**Tročany** (12 kilometers south of Bardejov) features a simple Uniate church with another hard-hitting icon of the Last Judgment. Buses to Prešov stop here.*

NIGHTLIFE & ENTERTAINMENT

There's not much of either to speak of in this sleepy little town. But there is a good cocktail **bar** with an outdoor patio *on Rhodyho street next to the town gate.* For a glass of Šariš beer, try **U Zlatej Koruny**, *Radničné námestie 41. Tel. 0935/5310* (see *Where to Eat* above).

EXCURSIONS & DAY TRIPS

Bardejovské Kúpele

This spa town six kilometers north of Bardejov is actually a bit livelier than Bardejov, but in no way as interesting, thanks to a fire in 1912 that devastated the town's ornate wooden structures. But it is a pleasant spot nonetheless, and does feature a **skansen** of traditional half-timbered houses, thatched cottages, and a couple of wooden Uniate churches relocated here from surrounding villages.

The skansen feels like a quaint little village itself, and may be your best chance for seeing folk architecture from the region. During the summer, folk singing and dance performances are held here, and local folk craftsman come to demonstrate their skills. *The skansen is open daily except Monday from 9 a.m. to 6 p.m. (until 3:30 p.m. October through April).*

PRACTICAL INFORMATION

• **Tourist Information Center** (Turisticko-Informačné Centrum), *Radničné námestie 21. Tel. 0935/186.* The English-speaking staff here can help with accommodations, give you train and bus schedules, and set you up on a tour of the town.
• **Post Office**, *Dlhy rad street (opposite the Hotel Republika).*

Medzilaborce

There is only one single reason to come to this boring town in the remote northeast corner of Slovakia, and that's to see the **Andy Warhol Family Museum** (Múzea Moderného umenia rodiny Warholovcov), *Andyho Warhola street, Tel. 0939/210 59*, perhaps the most bizarre attraction you could imagine in this part of the world. How a museum dedicated to the New York Pop artist found its way into this backwater region has to do with Warhol's roots.

Though he was born in Pittsburgh as Andrej Varchola, his parents hailed from the Ruthenian village of Miková, eight kilometers northwest of Medzilaborce. His parents emigrated to America early this century, and brought Andy up speaking both English and Ruthenian (a dialect of Ukrainian). But Warhol never acknowledged his Slovak roots, deferring rather to his famous line, "I came from nowhere."

Through efforts by Andy's brother John, the museum was founded in 1987 shortly after Warhol's death. In 1991, the town built the bold modern white building to house the museum, which is fronted by two giant Campbell's soup cans. Inside you'll find 18 Warhol originals, including *Campbell Soup II, Ingrid Bergman*, and (appropriately enough) *Hammer & Sickle*. The museum also exhibits original paintings by Andy's brother Paul and his nephew James, in addition to a lot of family memorabilia. *Hours are 10 a.m. to 5 p.m., daily except Monday. Entrance is a very reasonable 20 Sk.* The museum does have friendly, English-speaking guides who will lead you through the museum.

ARRIVALS & DEPARTURES
By Bus
There are three or four departures daily from Košice and Prešov. The ride from either city takes roughly two-and-a-half hours and costs 70 Sk.

By Car
From Košice, head east on E50 to Michalovce and then north through Humenné. From Prešov, head east to Stražske and then north to Medzilaborce.

By Train
From Košice, you'll need to change trains in Michalovce. From Prešov, you'll need to change trains in Stražske. If you're lucky with connections, the trip from either city should take about two-and-a-half hours and cost around 60 Sk. You're probably better off taking the bus.

WHERE TO STAY/WHERE TO EAT
HOTEL LABOREC, *Andyho Warhola 195/30, 068 01 Medzilaborce. Tel. & Fax 0939/213 07. Rates for single/double: 300/600 Sk. No credit cards. 50 rooms. Restaurant.*

This is the only hotel in town, offering decent rooms for a price that is certainly right. The restaurant dishes out tasty Slovak fare that's about as good as you'll get in this town.

INDEX

Air travel, 67-68
Andy Warhol Family Museum, 546-547
Astronomical Clock, 177-178

Banská Bystrica, 473-480
Banská Štiavnica, 480-485
Bardejov, 542-546
Bardejovské Kúpele, 546
Battle of White Mountain, 47
Bechyně, 261
Beer, 103-107
Beneš, Edvard, 49-51
Bethlehem Chapel, 189-190
Beverage glossary, 102-103
Bicycling, 68, 84
Bílek, František, 163-164
Bílkova Villa, 163-164
Bouzov Castle, 431
Bratislava:
  Arrivals & departures, 440-441
  Embassies, 459
  Exchange offices, 459
  Excursions & day trips, 457-459
  Getting around, 442
  Health service, 459
  Hotels, 442-445
  Nightlife & entertainment, 455-456
  Orientation, 440
  Post office, 459
  Restaurants, 445-447
  Shopping, 457
  Sights, 447-455
  Sports & recreation, 456
  Tourist office, 459
Břevnov Monastery, 222
Brno:
  Arrivals & departures, 372
  Excursions & day trips, 384-387
  Getting around, 372
  Hotels, 373-375
  Nightlife & entertainment, 383-384
  Orientation, 371
  Practical information, 387

  Restaurants, 375-376
  Sights, 376-383
  Sports & recreation, 384
Business hours, 73
Bus travel, 69-70

Čachtice Castle, 466-467
Čák, Matúš, 57, 471
Car Rentals, 70
Caving, 84
České Budějovice, 261-269
České Švýcarsko, 333-337
Český Krumlov, 273-281
Český ráj, 356-363
Český Šternberk, 243
Charles Bridge, 172-174
Charles IV, 44
Charter 77, 53
Cheb, 312-316
Church of Our Lady Before Týn, 179-180
Church of St. Nicholas (Malá Strana), 165-166
Church of St. Nicholas (Staré Město), 178
Čičmany, 489
Civic Forum, 53-54
Convent of St. Agnes, 191-192
Counter Reformation, 47-48
Customs, 66
Cyril & Methodius, 42
Czech history, 41-57
Czech Greenways, 92-93
Czech National Revival, 48-49
Czech people, 30-36

Děčín, 329-333
Defenestrations, 45, 47
Demänovská dolina, 497-501
Devín, 457-458
Dobrovský, Josef, 48
Dubček, Alexander, 52, 54
Dzurinda, Mikuláš, 62

Fishing, 84
Food, 94-102
Food glossary, 100-102
Františkový Lázně, 316-317

George (Jiří) of Poděbrady, 46
Golfing, 85
Gottwald, Klement, 50-51

Havel, Václav, 53-54
Health services, 76-77
Heydrich, Reinhard, 50
High Tatra Mountains:
    Arrivals & departures, 506
    Excursions & day trips, 516
    Getting around, 506
    Hotels, 507-510
    Orientation, 505
    Practical information, 516-517
    Restaurants, 510-512
    Sports & recreation, 512-516
Hiking, 85-86
Hlinka, Andrej, 59, 488
Hluboká Castle, 268
Hockey, 86
Hradec Králové, 345-352
Hřensko, 333-336
Hrubá Skála, 361
Hunting, 86-87
Husák, Gustav, 52
Hussites, 45-46
Hus, Jan, 45

Itineraries, 23-28

Jaroměřice nad Rokytnou, 395-396
Jičín, 357-360
Jihlava, 387-391
John of Luxembourg, 44
Joseph II, 48

Jungmann, Josef, 48

Kampa Island, 168-170
Karlovy Vary, 302-311
Karlštejn, 244-245
Kežmarok, 519-522
Klaus, Václav, 56

Konopiště, 243-244
Košice, 529-537
Křivoklát, 246
Krkonoše, 363-368
Kroměříž, 418-422
Kutná Hora, 246-252

Land, 29-30
Language learning programs, 65
Lednice, 406-412
Levoča, 522-527
Liberec, 337-343
Liptovský Mikuláš, 493-497
Litoměřice, 323-329
Loket nad Ohří, 311
Loreta, 162
Low Tatra Mountains, 497-501

Malá Fatra Mountains, 490-493
Mariánské Lázně, 293-301
Marie Theresa, 48, 58
Masaryk, Tomáš Garrigue, 49
Matica slovenská, 59
Mečiar, Vladimír, 55, 60-62
Medzilaborce, 546-547
Mezná, 333-336
Mezní Louka, 333-336
Mikulov, 401-406
Modra, 458
Moravian Karst, 385-386
Moravský Krumlov, 386-387
Mozart, Wolfgang Amadeus, 223
Munich Agreement, 49-50
Museum of Decorative Arts, 185-186

National holidays, 74
National Museum (Prague), 200
National Technical Museum
    (Prague), 219-220
National Theater (Prague), 204
Nerudova ulice, 166-167
Nitra, 460-463

Olomouc, 424-432

Palach, Jan, 52
Palacký, František, 47, 185
Pardubice, 352-356

Passports, 65
Pernštejn, 386
Petřín Hill, 171-172
Piešťany, 463-466
Plzeň, 283-293
Poprad, 501-504
Prachovské skály, 360-361
Prague Castle, 149-159
Prague City Museum, 198
Prague hotels:
    Adria, 134
    Ametyst, 136
    Belvedere, 129
    Betlem Club, 133-134
    Casa Marcello, 131
    City, 137
    Dům U Krále Jiřího, 134
    Evropa, 135
    Hoffmeister, 124-125
    Inter-continental, 132
    Interhotel Ambassador Zlatá Husa, 135
    Maximilian, 131-132
    Olea, 136
    Orion, 136
    Paříž, 130-131
    Parkhotel Praha, 128
    Pod věží, 125-126
    President, 132
    Savoy, 124
    Sax, 126
    Schweigerov Gardens, 129
    U klenotníka, 133
    U Krále Karla, 125
    U křžíe, 128
    U páva, 126
    U raka, 124
    U tří pštrosů, 126
    U zlatého stromu, 133
    Větrník, 129-130
Prague restaurants:
    Adonis, 146
    Ambiente, 147
    Bar Bar, 141
    Circle Line Brasserie, 139
    David, 140
    Flambée, 142
    Globe, The, 142
Hanavský pavilón, 139
Hotel Paříž, 143
Hotel Savoy, 138-139
Kampa Park, 140
Konírna U vladaře, 141
La Perle de Prague, 144
La Provence, 144
Lobkovická vinárna, 140
Myslivna, 146
Na zvonařce, 147
Nebozízek, 141
Opera Grill, 144
Parnas, 143
Pizzeria Rugantino, 146
Praha Tamura, 143
Quido, 147
Radost Café FX, 147
Taj Mahal, 146
U čínského labužníka, 144
U maltézskych rytířů, 140-141
U zlaté hrušky, 139
Victoria Saloon, 146
Vinárna nad přístavem, 144
Zlatý býk, 141-142
Prague Spring, 52
Prague:
    Bicycles, 121-122
    Boat tours, 119-120
    Bus stations, 69
    Bus tours, 119
    Cafés, 145
    Car rentals, 121
    Changing money, 252
    Day trips & excursions, 241-252
    Embassies, 253
    Hotels, 122-137
    Laundromats, 253
    Libraries, 253
    Medical Services, 253-254
    Metro system, 118
    Nightlife & entertainment, 224-236
    Orientation, 115-116
    Places of worship, 254
    Post office, 254
    Pubs, 224-227
    Restaurants, 137-147
    Shopping, 239-241
    Sights, 147-224

Sports & recreation, 236-239
Taxi, 120
Tickets, 228
Tourist information offices, 254
Train stations, 71-72
Tram system, 118-119
Walking tours, 117
Přemysl Otakar II, 43
Prešov, 537-542

Old Jewish Cemetery, 196
Old Town Square, 175-180

Royal Way, 180-184
Rožmberk nad Vltavou, 280
Rožnov pod Radhoštěm, 432-436
Rudolfinum, 184-185
Rudolf II, 47
Rusovce, 458

Sázava Monastery, 242-243
Skiing, 87
Slavkov U Brna, 384-385
Slavonice, 395
Slovak History, 57-62
Slovak National Revival, 58-59
Slovak National Uprising, 60
Slovak people, 36-40
Soccer, 87-88
Spas, 88
Špindlerův Mlýn, 366-368
Špiš Castle, 527-528
Špišská Kapitula, 528-529
Star Summer Palace, 222-223
State Jewish Museum, 194-197
Sternberg Palace, 160-161
Šternberk, 430-431
Strahov Monastery, 162-163
Study tours, 65
Štúr, Ľudovít, 58-59
St. Vitus Cathedral, 152-155
Sudeten German Party, 49

Tábor, 256-261
Taborites, 46

Telč, 391-395
Telephones, 81-82
Tennis, 89
Terezín, 319-322
Tiso, Jozef, 59-60
Tosovky, Josef, 56
Trade Fair Palace, 218-219
Train travel, 71-72
Třeboň, 269-273
Trenčín, 467-472
Trnava, 459
Troja Chateau, 221
Trosky Castle, 361
Turnov, 362

Utraquists, 46

Valdštejn Castle, 361-362
Valtice, 406-412
Velvet Revolution, 53-54
Villa Amerika, 209
Villa Bertramka, 223
Visas, 65
Vranov nad Dyjí, 400-401
Vrátna dolina, 490-492
Vrchlabí, 364-368
Vyšehrad, 210-213
Vyšší Brod, 280-281
Výstaviště (Prague), 217-218

Wallenstein Palace, 167-168
Wenceslas (Václav) I, 43
Wenceslas Square, 198-201
Wine, 107-108

Zbraslav Monastery, 223-224
Žďár nad Sázavou, 390
Ždiar, 516
Želivský, Jan, 45
Zeman, Milo , 56
Žilina, 485-490
Žižka, Jan, 46
Zlatá Koruna, 279-280
Zlín, 412-418
Znojmo, 396-401
Zvolen, 479-480